Competent Communication

Competent

St. Martin's Press   New York

Communication

Dan O'Hair
University of Oklahoma

Gustav W. Friedrich
University of Oklahoma

John M. Wiemann
University of California
at Santa Barbara

Mary O. Wiemann
Santa Barbara City College

Editor: Suzanne Phelps Weir
Development editor: Sylvia L. Weber
Managing editor: Patricia Mansfield Phelan
Project editor: Talvi Laev
Production supervisor: Joe Ford
Art director: Sheree Goodman
Text design: Heidi Haeuser
Graphics: Fine Line Inc.
Photo research: Suzanne Skloot
Cover art: Jacob Lawrence, "Pacific Northwest Arts and Crafts Fair" poster design, 1981. Photolithograph.

For information, write to:
St. Martin's Press, Inc.
175 Fifth Avenue
New York, NY 10010

ISBN: 0-312-04057-1

ILLUSTRATION CREDITS

P*reface*

Successful communication requires more than just common sense. Many students recognize the value of a communication course for building their skills in public speaking, but they may also need to realize that even informal conversations with close friends and family can be made more productive by the study of communication. Competency-based instruction in communication goes beyond common sense to provide both the theory and the application that will help promote communication success.

In *Competent Communication*, we address two related pairs of concepts: *knowledge acquisition* and *skill building* to achieve *effective* and *appropriate* communication. Our approach is based on a model of communicative competence that applies to a variety of relationships, from interpersonal communication to small-group and organizational communication to public speaking and mass communication. This model, introduced in Chapter 1, serves an integrating function as well as a pedagogical purpose throughout the text. Once students have mastered the model, they can plan their communications and analyze their efforts. They can understand when certain skills are appropriate and effective, and they can evaluate and improve their skills.

Today, two aspects of competent communication are receiving increasing attention from communication scholars, both in the classroom and in research. These two areas of study, *ethics* and *intercultural communication*, are essential to our model and are addressed in every chapter of this text.

Our treatment of intercultural communication includes not only relationships involving people of different nationalities or ethnic backgrounds but also cultural differences between women and men and among various racial, age-based, economic, regional, and occupational co-cultures.

Among the ethical issues addressed throughout the text are stereotyping, management of conflict to achieve mutually acceptable goals, and balancing persuasion and image with accuracy.

Organization of the Text

The text is divided into four parts. Part 1, "Basic Communication Processes, " introduces the general principles that apply to all communication situations. The three remaining parts cover, respectively, interpersonal communication, small-group and organizational communication, and public speaking, including mass communication. The model of communicative competence is presented as a foundation in Chapter 1. Chapter 2 discusses how people process the information they receive through communication and how they use this information to form impressions or schemata about their communication partners. In Chapter 3, the role of the self in communication is considered; intrapersonal communication and presentation of the self are included. Chapters 4 and 5 describe verbal and nonverbal communication, respectively. Chapter 6 discusses listening as an essential skill in creating a competent relationship.

In Part 2, "Interpersonal Communication," both social and more formal interpersonal relationships are considered. Chapter 7 reviews the life cycle of a relationship from development through maintenance or dissolution. Managing conflict, with the goal of producing mutually satisfying and constructive results, is the topic of Chapter 8. Chapter 9 focuses on a particular interpersonal situation, the interview; this chapter has special practical value in preparing students for job interviews.

Part 3, "Group and Organizational Communication," can be applied in both classroom and work situations. Chapter 10 discusses communication in small groups, and Chapter 11 focuses on the role of the group leader, especially in decision making.

"Public Communication" is the subject of Part 4. Chapters 12–14 may be used as a resource for the public speaking component of the course as well as a guide for making presentations beyond the classroom. General advice for preparing and delivering presentations is given in Chapter 12. Chapters 13 and 14 consider informative and persuasive presentations, respectively. Chapter 15 approaches mass communication and other forms of mediated communication primarily from a consumer's perspective. Thus, from start to finish, the text takes the reader through the gamut of communication interactions, from the deepest, most intimate and enduring relationships to the broad world of nonpersonal communication.

Pedagogical Devices

A competency-based approach demands a systematic teaching methodology built on techniques that have proved effective in promoting knowledge acquisition and skill development. To help achieve these goals, each chapter begins with objectives and an outline of the chapter's contents. Thus the reader can preview the chapter and anticipate its practical application.

Throughout the book, new technical terms are introduced in **boldface type** and terms are defined where they are introduced. Each definition is repeated in the margin for easy reference and at the end of the text in a comprehensive glossary.

Photographs and line drawings reinforce the concepts presented verbally. In the model of communicative competence and other diagrams, color is used for pedagogical purposes. Photographs demonstrate the multicultural nature of competent communication.

Each chapter concludes with a review to reinforce the objectives and summarize the main points. Suggested readings are provided for students who want to study the subject matter in greater depth.

Two types of exercises are presented in boxes, interspersed throughout each chapter. *Reality Checks* are thought-provoking discussion questions designed to test the students' understanding of new concepts and to encourage them to analyze their attitudes and opinions. *Self-Checks* are self-evaluation instruments focused on building competencies. Boxed exercises that address the subjects of intercultural communication and ethical issues are identified by special symbols.

Each part concludes with an epilogue that summarizes the major topics and relates the discussion to the model of communicative competence. A case study presents a realistic scenario to give readers practice in identifying and applying communicative competencies.

Recent research and classical studies and theories are cited throughout the text. Notes are placed at the end of the book so as to avoid disrupting the continuity of the text and yet provide references for those who wish to consult the original sources.

Ancillaries

Competent Communication is supported by a full complement of ancillaries designed to enhance competency-based learning. The *Instructor's Resource Manual*, prepared by Joan Aitken of the University of Missouri–Kansas City, includes a guide designed especially for teaching assistants and other new communication educators. Practical advice is also provided for course directors and other experienced instructors. In addition to a full discussion of the philosophy of competency-based communication education and model calendars for semester and quarter courses, this unique guide includes reports from current and recent teaching assistants, focusing on practical problems that they have encountered and giving the benefit of their experience. Chapter-by-chapter teaching notes and a broad selection of supplemental exercises and other teaching suggestions for each chapter serve as a foundation for classroom and outside activities.

A test-item file in the *Instructor's Resource Manual* includes short-answer and essay questions for each chapter along with an answer key. A computerized version of the test-item file, including Micrograde, is available for both Macintosh and IBM-compatible systems.

A set of 25 professionally prepared color transparencies, including diagrams from the text and additional visual presentations of important concepts, is an enhancement to classroom lectures.

Videotapes specifically designed to correlate with the text are also available. One tape examines the stages of interpersonal relationships; another covers communication in groups; and a third provides models of public speaking. The accompanying video guides suggest ways to integrate the tapes into classroom lectures and include additional exercises and activities.

Acknowledgments

Competent Communication benefited from the advice and assistance of many colleagues. We particularly want to acknowledge the help of Joan Aitken, who read and field-tested the manuscript and prepared the *Instructor's Resource Manual*. Cheri Simonds of the University of Central Oklahoma generously shared her expertise in the use of media to review the scripts for the videotapes and help prepare the accompanying video guides. We thank the following people for their assistance in researching and preparing portions of chapters in this book: David Williams (Chapter 2), Leeza Bearden (Chapter 5), Melissa Stone and David Worth (Chapter 7), Karl Krayer (Chapters 8, 10, and 11), and Carol Cawyer (who, with the assistance of Mike Chanslor and Mark Hovind, largely wrote Chapter 15).

For their insightful reviews of the manuscript, we thank Ruth Aurelius, Des Moines Area Community College; Phil Backlund, Central Washington University; Melissa Beall, University of Northern Iowa; Michael Bruner, University of North Texas; Marcia Dixson, Indiana University–Purdue at Fort Wayne; Rich Edwards, Baylor University; Laura Fleet, Howard University; Colan T. Hanson, Moorhead State University; Fred Jandt, California State University–San Bernardino; John Nussbaum, University of Oklahoma; Sharon A. Ratliffe, Golden West College; R. Jeffrey Ringer, St. Cloud State University; Renee Stahle, Aquinas College; Gail Sorensen, California State University at Fresno; and Jo Young Switzer, Manchester College.

We are indebted to our editors at St. Martin's Press for their patience, encouragement, and professional advice. Suzanne Phelps Weir, our acquiring editor, Sylvia L. Weber, our development editor, and Talvi Laev, our project editor, turned the manuscript into a book. We are delighted with the attractive and pedagogically enriching design created by our designer, Heidi Haeuser, and we thank our production supervisor, Joe Ford, for overseeing the schedule and quality of the composition and printing.

Dan O'Hair
Gustav W. Friedrich
John M. Wiemann
Mary O. Wiemann

About the Authors

DAN O'HAIR

is Professor and Chair of the Department of Communication at the University of Oklahoma. He has also taught at Texas Christian University, New Mexico State University, and Texas Tech University. He is co-author or co-editor of six communication texts and scholarly volumes and has published more than 40 research articles and chapters in dozens of communication, psychology, and health journals and books. He is a frequent presenter at national and international communication conferences, is on the editorial boards of various communication journals, and has served on numerous committees and task forces for regional and national communication associations.

GUSTAV W. FRIEDRICH

is Professor in the Department of Communication and Faculty Administrative Fellow in the Office of the Senior Vice President and Provost at the University of Oklahoma. He previously taught at Purdue University and the University of Nebraska. He has published widely in the professional communication journals and is editor or co-author of seven books. He has served on a variety of committees for regional, national, and international professional communication organizations and as president of the Central States Communication Association and the Speech Communication Association.

JOHN M. WIEMANN

is Professor of Communication and Asian American Studies at the University of California, Santa Barbara. He co-edits the Sage Annual Reviews of Communication Research series and has recently co-edited special issues of *Communication Research* and *American Behavioral Scientist*. He is author or co-author of seven books and has published more than 50 research papers and book chapters about communication, psychology, speech and hearing, and education. He is a recipient of the Speech Communication Association's Woolbert Research Award (1991) for his communication competence research and has been a W. K. Kellogg Foundation National Fellow and a Fulbright-Hays Senior Research Scholar at the University of Bristol, England.

MARY O. WIEMANN

is Assistant Professor and Chairperson of the Department of Communication at Santa Barbara City College. A longtime educator of beginning college students, she contributes a strong teaching perspective to this book. She has written communication manuals for student use at many levels as well as instructor's manuals in the areas of nonverbal communication and interpersonal communication. A recipient of awards for outstanding teaching, she has developed a communication laboratory with audiovisual and computer support and has directed classroom research projects in the community college setting.

Contents in Brief

Contents in Detail

Part One

Basic Communication Processes

1

Chapter 1

Communicating
Competently

O*bjectives*

After reading this chapter you should be able to

1. Differentiate your social environment from your physical environment.

2. Describe the six characteristics of communication.

3. Describe the functional perspective of communication.

4. Apply the three general functions of communication to the relationships in which you are involved.

CHAPTER CONTENTS

L ET'S BE CLEAR about one thing from the very beginning: *The quality of your life depends directly on your ability to communicate!* The better you understand the communication process, the more likely you will be to use your communication skills appropriately and effectively. The more appropriate and effective you are, the more likely you will be to create satisfying, productive, meaningful (that is, competent) relationships in your personal, social, business, and public lives. We wrote this book to help you improve both your understanding of the process and your communication skills that put your understanding into action. Both skills and understanding are necessary for competent communication; neither is sufficient without the other.

You communicate in order to accomplish social tasks and to coordinate physical ones. In the process, you create relationships; you define them; you modify and dissolve your relationships. And you do these things through both the content and style of your communication.

Indeed, when we communicate with each other, we all create ourselves and our social environment in important ways.

The Nature of Communication

Given the centrality of communication in our lives, we spend surprisingly little time trying to understand this important process in any systematic way. To be sure, parents devote a great deal of effort to teaching their children the technical aspects of communication; that is, they help their children learn the language and social norms, or the general rules of politeness that guide communication decisions. But we acquire most of what we know about both the technical and social aspects of communication without explicit instruction. For the most part we muddle through, learning effective and appropriate communication behavior on a trial and error basis.

The purpose of this course is to help you develop and apply a systematic, analytic understanding of communication processes. This understanding will take some of the trial and error out of your learning experiences. With some effort you should become more scientific in your predictions about how your communication choices will affect others—and why their communication choices affect you as they do. Ultimately, then, we believe that your ability to influence your environment, especially your social environment, will improve as your understanding of communication increases.

Throughout this book, we will be asking you to take advantage of what you know about communication—your personal theories of communication (sometimes called naive theories because they are not based on scientific research). Your experience as a communicator is important to our goal of helping you become a more skilled communicator.

We will also ask you to question your theories of communication and to examine them in terms of what works and what doesn't, given your goals. We will ask you to test your theories against those of communication scholars (sometimes referred to as sophisticated theories because of the way they were developed). By juxtaposing personal and scholarly theories, you will derive insight into human communication, both your own and that of others in your social environment. It will allow you to consider how meaning is created and changed and how relationship goals are realized. In the process, we hope you will develop an understanding of scholarly theories of communication and how to apply them to everyday life.

A first step to improving your own communicative competence is to gain an understanding of the communication process, and for this purpose we need to examine the characteristics of communication basic to this process.

The Six Characteristics of Communication

Communication has proved to be a rather slippery term. Since the time of Aristotle, scholars have offered definitions of the term, each of these more or less appropriate for a specific purpose or situation. All, however, have been incomplete because all have failed to capture the richness and complexity of the communication experience. In 1976, Dance and Larson listed over 100 definitions of communication published in the previous 20 years.[1] If we attempted such a list today, we would likely double that number.

Rather than attempt a new definition of communication or rework an old one for the purposes of this book, we believe it is more useful to discuss the characteristics of communication. This approach will help you to learn to evaluate various stimuli (messages) in your environment in terms of their communicative value. Some "messages" are more obviously meant to be communicative than others. For example, the behavior of 6-year-old Ellie sticking her tongue out at Jake is very purposeful; that of 21-year-old Sara making one-second eye contact with Alan across the room is less clear. The more ambiguous the stimuli, the more difficult it is to be certain that the message received is close to the message intended—or even whether a message was intended at all.

Communication is defined by six characteristics: (1) the extent to which the code of the message is symbolic, (2) the extent to which the code is shared, (3) the intentionality of the sender, (4) the presence of a medium, (5) the extent to which the process of encoding and decoding messages is transactional, and (6) the degree to which the message is culturally bound.[2] Each characteristic can be thought of as a continuum, anchored on one side by "always" or "definitely" and on the other by "never" or "definitely not." Behavior that clearly possesses all of these characteristics is communication and can be analyzed as such. In practical terms, we can and do hold people responsible for their communication. Much of our behavior, however, is not so clearly at the "definitely communicative" end of each of these continua.

Throughout this book, we use these characteristics of communication as tools for analyzing utterances and interactions. The "more or less" nature of each characteristic naturally leads to misunderstanding and sometimes dissatisfaction in communication episodes. This does not imply that the more an utterance is symbolic, intentional, and so on, the "better" or "more effective" it is;[3] rather, it means that we can use these characteristics in analyzing how and why some utterances are effective and others are not. Because competent communication frequently depends on interpreting messages appropriately, we need to be sensitive to the characteristics that make messages easy or difficult to interpret.

Symbolic Behavior

Behavior is symbolic when it has an arbitrary relationship to some "object"—the thing it symbolizes. *Object* refers here to *any* person or thing in your physical or social world, including your internal states (moods, feelings), relationships, and other intangibles that are nonetheless real for you.

The archetypal **symbolic behavior** is language. Each language is a code that allows those who know it to transform sounds produced by the human vocal system (speech) into meaningful utterances or messages. The key here is the arbitrary nature of the relationship between the symbol and the object it represents. There is no particular reason why the speech-sound (phonemic) combination "T-R-E-E" (again, an arbitrary transcription of the vocalization of these speech sounds, or phonemes) should represent a very large variety of plant life forms. But in our code, American English, it does.

SYMBOLIC BEHAVIOR
*Behavior that uses
a shared symbol
system.*

Behavior can also relate to objects in nonsymbolic ways. In this connection, symbols can be contrasted with *signs,* which are most usefully thought of as "natural and intrinsic representations"[4] of the objects to which they refer, rather than being arbitrarily connected to those objects. Cave paintings depicting a hunt, for example, are signs referencing the people and animals of ancient cultures. Rapid hand and arm movement during conversation may be a sign that the person displaying this behavior is excited about the topic or is very involved in the conversation. Much nonverbal behavior is composed of signs because it is intrinsically linked to its referents, though not always so.

Although language is the primary form of symbolic behavior in our culture, nonverbal behavior can also be symbolic. Hand gestures, in particular, may have symbolic properties. For example, joining the thumb and forefinger in a circle while extending the other three fingers means "Okay" in middle-class U.S. culture. Gestures of this sort, "autonomous gestures,"[5] operate in much the same way as language. That is to say, we do not need words to know what they mean. Facial expressions (e.g., smiles) and some graphic representations (e.g., a circle with a diagonal line through it, the international sign for "NO") also have symbolic qualities.

Interestingly, behavior is typically regarded as either symbolic or nonsymbolic; there are no shades of gray! But consider that not all utterances are clearly symbolic. Onomatopoetic words (those that imitate the sound they signify, such as *buzz* and *cuckoo*) do not cleanly fit the definition of symbols. Furthermore, some nonverbal behavior can hold a very ambiguous relationship to a particular "object," especially a person's internal states. For example, how would you interpret the "meaning" of the crossed arms of a man you observe standing on a street corner? Is that man responding to cold weather, or showing he is lonely or angry, or what? Similarly, expressions that denote internal states (e.g., smiles) are intrinsically linked to that internal state—but a smile can be forced or faked, thus moving this sort of behavior closer to the symbolic end of the sign–symbol continuum. In addition, symbols can have a more or less strong connection to the referent object. The stronger the tie, the more confident we can be that the meaning of the symbol will be similar for two speakers. For example, *Eiffel Tower* has a very strong connection to a structure in Paris, to which this combination of symbols refers. *House,* on the other hand, has quite a large number of referents, and we would need more information before we could be confident that we understood the speaker.

We will have more to say on this subject when we discuss language and nonverbal behavior (in Chapters 4 and 5, respectively). For the moment, suffice it to say that symbols are arbitrary constructions and that they are more or less strongly related to their referents. The stronger the connection between symbol and referent, the clearer the intended meaning should be. Competent communicators take this relative ambiguity into consideration when they construct messages for others and interpret the messages they receive.

▨ A Shared Code

CODE
The symbols, signals, or signs used to construct messages.

In order for communication to take place, the participants must share the **code** (the set of symbol–meaning relationships—for example, a language) used to construct the messages. The greater the overlap, the greater the probability that one person's meanings will be similar to another's. Speaking a common language is the most obvious example of sharing a communication code, but it is not the only one. Each culture (and each co-culture within larger cultures) also shares *specific* meanings for gestures, graphics, and facial expressions.

Some aspects of these codes cross cultural boundaries, making them especially powerful communication vehicles. Facial expressions of surprise, fear, disgust, anger, happiness, and sadness seem to have universal meaning.[6] Thus they allow people from different cultures to understand each other's most basic feelings, even though they cannot speak the same language.

CULTURE
The shared beliefs, values, and practices of a group of people.

We use the term **culture** to refer to the shared beliefs, values, and practices of a group of people. A group's culture includes the language or languages used by group members as well as norms and rules about how behavior can appropriately be displayed and how it should be understood. Language is probably the most important group behavior because it both embodies the beliefs and values of the culture and transmits the culture.

SUBCULTURE
A group that is part of a larger culture but distinguished from it by various characteristics.

When we refer to people as being in the same culture, we emphasize their similarities rather than their differences. But sometimes the differences are worth noting. Thus, the term **subculture** is used to refer to groups within a larger culture distinguished from the rest of the population by various characteristics. For example, white Protestant males and African-American Catholic females constitute two *subcultures* in the United States. They are **co-cultures** of each other.

CO-CULTURE
One of two or more subcultures within a culture.

This characteristic of communication is so obvious that people are frequently blind to its importance. The tendency is to assume that because they share a code (e.g., a language), they must necessarily also have com-

Symbolic Codes and Group Identity

How do people express approval of a thing or person? List as many words as you can. Some examples are: *cool, groovy, totally awesome, sassy, radical,* and *rad.* Rank the words by how widely they are used in U.S. society and across generations. Are there words on the list that you and your peers don't use but that your parents, grandparents, younger siblings, or children do? What purposes—other than actually expressing approval—do these different terms serve?

mon meanings for the symbols they use. This is clearly not the case; communication is much more problematic. For example, American travelers to and from England are frequently surprised (and amused) that the same words have different referents in the two versions of the English language. A British person in a U.S. drugstore asking for a "rubber" would be sent to the pharmaceutical counter for a condom rather than to the stationery aisle for an eraser. As was noted earlier, people create and negotiate meanings in the course of their interaction. A symbol can take on new meaning if at least two people agree that it will have that meaning for them. Social groups use this technique to establish their uniqueness and to create boundaries between themselves and the "outside" world. A pertinent example is the slang that different generations develop to mark themselves as different from their parents. The point we want to make here is that what appears to be a shared code is not always that.

Intentionality

Does a behavior have to be **intentional** to be communicative? This is a question that communication investigators (scientists and nonscientists alike) frequently debate. The popular form of the argument is more interesting than its scientific versions. It goes something like this: If you see me do something or hear me say something I did not intend for you to see or hear, did I communicate with you? In other words, am I responsible to you for what I did or said in the same way as if I had intentionally formulated a message and transmitted it to you? For example, I tell a mutual friend that I did not like a play you were in, but I thought you didn't hear me and I didn't want you to hear me. Was I communicating with you?

INTENTIONALITY
The level of consciousness or purposefulness of a communicator in the encoding of messages.

Some scholars would answer no to that question. They would say that communication takes place only when a message is intentionally constructed and transmitted.[7] But this position leaves some vexing situations unexplained. As we have mentioned, emotional displays are easily read across cultures,[8] but are not symbolic (i.e., they are not arbitrarily linked to their referent) and are frequently not intentional. (Can you stop yourself from blushing when you don't want to blush?) Yet they are communicative in everyday usage because there is consensus about their "meaning." (Again, consider the unintended blush. When you see one, you know what it "means.") Some scholars have begun to talk about two communication systems. One is characterized by behavior that is *primarily* (if not totally) symbolic and intentional and has a cognitive basis. The second system, based on emotional and physiological considerations, is characterized by a widely shared code that has few, if any, cultural boundaries (see the section "Cultural Boundaries" later in this chapter) and is spontaneous.[9]

The distinction between the two systems can be seen as one of *giving information* versus one of *giving off information.*[10] The practical importance of the distinction is that we tend to see a person as more accountable when he or she consciously or purposefully gives information to someone else than when the recipient gleans information from observation or overhearing.

This is not to say that information given off is unimportant. In fact, that information may be evaluated as more honest because the other person did not have the opportunity to censor or package it. It is useful to note, however, that although some messages transmitted through the emotional communication system are highly reliable and easily interpreted (e.g., emotional displays like grief and anger), most are ambiguous and open to a variety of interpretations (what does a flushed face mean?). Most of this sort of information can be interpreted only in the light of contextual cues, and even then the validity of judgments is frequently open to question.

Competent communication requires a sensitivity to the fact that both your intended and unintended messages have an impact on the people around you. These people will interpret your behavior in an attempt to make sense out of it. Keep in mind that the intended meaning (if there was one) of your behavior is not always as clearly expressed or accurately received as you would like. The more obvious it is that behavior is intentional, the more likely it is that the behavior is truly communicative.

The Medium of the Message

Communication requires a medium of some sort—a vehicle to transport or carry the symbols. In face-to-face interaction, the vehicle is the air, through which the sound and light waves travel. As we move away from face-to-face contact and technology intervenes between us and our "audi-ence," the characteristics and the social impact of our messages change, sometimes in very subtle ways. Face-to-face communication is the proto-type to which other kinds of communication are usually compared. With new communication technologies becoming more accessible, distinctions between face-to-face and other methods of communication are beginning to break down.[11] Nonetheless, some medium is a prerequisite for communica-tion to take place. While we don't want to downplay the importance of thinking about, planning, and rehearsing what one wants to say or do (called by some *intra*personal communication), this characteristic of com-munication removes from our consideration telepathic thought transfer, extrasensory perception (ESP), Vulcan mind melds, and the like.

Competent relationships can be maintained through a variety of media. Long-distance relationships are becoming ever more common. With the ad-vent of the "information superhighway," which will merge television ca-ble, telephone, and online computer services in the home, we are likely to see an increase in several types of long-distance relationships. These rela-tionships include not only those between parents and children, siblings, and close friends, but also commuter marriages and even "telecommut-ing"—arrangements in which the employee is connected to the workplace by computer and audio/video media and so can go to work without leaving home. As the number and complexity of available media multiply, it will become increasingly important that you give much thought to your selec-tion of the appropriate media to convey certain types of messages, to the timing of your contacts with your partner, and the like. If you are or ever have been in a long-distance relationship, consider when you chose to write a letter rather than use the phone (or vice versa). Were some types of mes-sages best delivered when an immediate response was impossible (via let-ter) in your relationship? Did you ever send a videotape or audiotape "let-ter" to your partner?

▨ *A Transactional Process*

Communication is transactional; that is, two or more people must be in-volved for symbolic exchange to occur. From our perspective, it doesn't make much sense to talk about one person communicating with him- or herself. This is not to say that intrapersonal communication isn't impor-tant,[12] but what makes symbolic behavior communicative is that it is the medium of exchange between and among people. When you engage others in communication, you are attempting to influence them in some way (a point that we make in various contexts throughout this book). Equally im-portant, but perhaps not so obvious, is the fact that you are opening yourself to influence by others. We are all involved in the **transactional process** of

TRANSACTIONAL PROCESS
A process in which two or more people exchange speaker and listener roles, and in which the behavior of each person is depen-dent on and influ-enced by the behavior of the other.

FIGURE 1.2

*How is the responsi-
bility for communica-
tion shared in your
classes? Does it differ
from class to class?*

communication—not in a static exchange of symbols but in a dynamic, ever-changing adjustment of symbols based on the communication behavior of our partner(s). Thus, all parties to an interaction are responsible for its outcome and have a hand in whether or not individual and relational goals are met. This, after all, is the point of the transactional characteristic of communication. Whether you are talking with your "significant other," a parent, a work group in a class, or the audience for a public speech, you share responsibility for the outcome of the interaction because by engaging in communication, you enter into a situation in which you become mutually dependent (interdependent) on the others in the interaction. The burden of responsibility will be more or less equally distributed, depending on the communication situation. In public speaking situations, the speaker tends to assume most of the responsibility and is seen as the person attempting to influence the audience. But even in this apparently lopsided situation, the audience still retains a good deal of influence over both the speaker and its constituent members. The audience's power is most obvious when applause or catcalls interrupt a speech.

In informal social relationships, responsibility and influence are more or less evenly distributed—and we expect as much. Betty, for example, comes home from work tired and irritable. So does Fred. They begin to argue. Betty puts her knowledge of the transactional nature of communication into practice when she says, "Fred, we're both tired from a hard day. Let's stop picking at each other and start the evening over again." (Fred, being a nineties kind of guy, gives her a kiss and says, "Okay. How bad was your day?") Betty could have said, "Why are you being so mean? Leave me alone!" This statement would have implied that the quarreling was exclusively Fred's fault and she had no responsibility for it. We'll leave to you to imagine Fred's response. Competent communication is marked by the people involved sharing responsibility for the way the interaction is progressing.

Cultural Boundaries

If you've ever traveled to a foreign country or even through different neighborhoods of a city, you have first-hand knowledge that communication is difficult to separate from culture. The most obvious way in which the two are related is language. People from different cultures usually speak different languages, which are (usually but not always) unintelligible to "strangers." But the communication–culture relationship goes well beyond obvious language differences. For example, cultural experience and aspects of everyday life strongly influence what in the environment is important enough to name, how fine our linguistic distinctions are, and how language influences our interpretation of the world around us.[13] For example, interior decorators, artists, and people with similar occupations and interests use language to make fine distinctions among colors and shades of colors. A decorator may find it useful, or even necessary, to distinguish among lavender, mauve, burgundy, violet, plum, lilac, magenta, amethyst, and heliotrope. For many of us, however, these fine distinctions are unimportant; purple is purple!

Similarly, our nonverbal behavior is wrapped up in culture. Different cultures use and interpret time and space differently.[14] In Mediterranean cultures, for instance, men tend to stand very close together, frequently touching each other during conversation. In North Atlantic cultures, generally the appropriate conversational distance is about 3 feet—and, in case you hadn't noticed, men seldom touch each other during social conversation except when they shake hands in greeting. Punctuality is also said to have more importance (that is to say, more meaning) in some cultures (e.g., North Atlantic ones) than in others (e.g., some South American ones). We'll have more to say about these influences in the next two chapters.

Even within a single country, culture and communication are equally intertwined, though perhaps more subtly so. People often assume that since they "speak the same language" they will have little trouble "really" communicating. Of course, this is not the case. Subcultural, co-cultural, and ethnic differences can lead to implicit differences in the way people use and interpret language and nonverbal behavior. An utterance that counts as an insult in one subculture can be seen as a compliment in another. Talking with an adversary in order to resolve a dispute is not considered as appropriate in all subcultures as it is in middle-class U.S. culture; fistfighting might be the preferred form of resolution for some kinds of disputes.[15]

Recently, Buck has argued that some "messages"—notably, expressions of emotions—are, in fact, not culturally bound but are universally understandable.[16] Both the encoding (display) and decoding (understanding) of several expressions of emotion seem to be universal.[17] (We will have more to say about emotional displays in Chapter 5.) Interestingly, even one of the most obvious characteristics of communication—its embeddedness in culture—cannot be asserted without qualification. We do seem to have the capacity to be transactionally linked with each other even across great cultural divides.

Let us now turn our attention to the primary reason for constructing these messages in the first place: achieving satisfying relationships in which we can accomplish our personal and interpersonal goals. Thus we now take up the topic of communication competence.

Communication Competence

Communication can be studied in a variety of ways, including structural, rhetorical, historical, and critical approaches. Each approach has its own strengths and limitations. In order to help you develop communication skills as well as knowledge about these skills, in this book we take a **functional perspective**, focusing on *what kinds of communication behaviors work* for people, and why they work, in various situations.

FUNCTIONAL PERSPECTIVE

A focus on what kinds of communication behaviors work for people, and why they work, in various situations.

The Functional Perspective

A functional or pragmatic perspective allows us to see that, as communicators, we make decisions and then act (speak, listen, gesture, etc.) based on these decisions.[18] This perspective presupposes that our communication is goal-directed—that is, that we do things with some conscious or unconscious purpose in mind (see the earlier discussion of intentionality). To behave with a goal in mind is to attempt to exercise control (or influence; we use these terms interchangeably) over our environment—most importantly, the people in the social environment. Our primary goal, then, is to have an optimal amount of control over the people and events in our lives, or what some observers call our social environment. Communicators always exercise at least some influence on their social environment, usually more than they think. (We return to this idea time and again throughout the book.)

Achieving Communication Goals

Consider an important relationship in which you are currently involved. What goals do you have in that relationship? In what ways do you think you might communicate to achieve each of those goals? How do you know when you are successful? Are some of your goals in conflict with others? How do you plan to achieve them?

When you decide what person you want to influence, how and when to attempt to do so, and what you want to get from the target of your attempts, you are setting communication goals and selecting communication strategies and tactics. Your implicit concern is a functional, pragmatic one: "What can I do communicationally to get what I want? What will work for me in this situation with these particular people?" Knowledgeable functionalists know that the same goal can be achieved in a variety of ways. Similarly, the same strategies and tactics can be used to achieve a variety of goals at different times.[19]

It is useful to distinguish between general and specific strategies and goals. General strategies and goals are abstract and not limited to specific situations or even necessarily specific relationships. These strategies and goals are typically related to the communication process rather than the outcome and to conceptions of the self. For example, one general goal you might have is for each partner to maintain an optimal, usually approximately equal, amount of control in informal social relationships. Various strategies and tactics might work to help you achieve this goal.

Specific strategies and goals, as you might have guessed, are related to particular situations or relationships and tend to be outcome oriented. To continue our control example, although your general goal is to maintain approximately equal control in social relationships, you may feel that it is important for you to win *this* argument with your friend *now* so that he or she knows you can't be pushed around.

The relationship between general and specific strategies and goals is somewhat fluid. Attainment of today's goal may be seen as one part of a long-term strategy in the service of higher-order goals. For example, Bill's immediate *goal* is to get an assistant manager's job in a fast-food restaurant so that he can pay his school fees, and it also may be a *strategy* for starting a career in the food service industry. Although specific goals help us understand why a person is behaving in a particular way now, general goals are more relevant to understanding how communication works in relationships for a variety of people with a variety of specific goals. This is because general goals relate directly to the communication functions of control, affiliation, and goal achievement, to which we now turn.

The General Functions of Communication

A long line of research conducted in a variety of contexts, including task groups, decision-making groups, families, and social relationships, has found that communication behavior falls along three dimensions.[20] The first of these dimensions is almost always labeled "control." The second has typically been termed "affiliation," "empathy," or "liking." The third dimension has been given various names, all of which directly relate to achieving a goal or completing a task.

Control, affiliation, and goal achievement may be described as *primary* (one might say *ubiquitous*) functions because every message contains some information about how control is distributed among the interactants, how much each likes the other, and what progress they are making toward defining and achieving some goal. This information is conveyed at what is called the *relational level* or *meta-level*[21] of the message as contrasted with the content level. The content level of a message is what the interactants are saying, whereas the relational level is information about how the content is to be taken, whether seriously, or sarcastically, or as a joke. The two levels can reinforce or contradict each other. When they are contradictory, the content is given a different meaning than a literal reading of it would indicate. For example, Jack knows that when his wife says, "Isn't this just a fun party?" with a forced smile on her face, she means, "I'm having a terrible time; let's get out of here." Or when Enrique scolds his son for misbehaving, but touches him gently while doing so, he is communicating at the relational level that the negative content of the message does not mean that he has stopped loving his son.

At a more holistic level, our general manner and choice of words tell our partner how we see the relationship. If we are equals, one of us can't get away with ordering the other around in most circumstances. Giving orders would communicate at the relational level that I have more control in the relationship than you—and you can't do anything about it. Other influence strategies would be more appropriate for our equal status. Elena, for example, may want Brian to go shopping to get party supplies (orientation to achieving a specific goal), but she doesn't order him to do it (which would be a direct, high-control tactic inappropriate for a marriage in which both partners share responsibility for accomplishing household tasks). Rather, she smiles and hugs him (positive affiliation) while mentioning how he could help out by doing the shopping now (a low-control tactic appropriate for their relationship). Note that the hug accompanying the request emphasizes that positive affiliation is an important part of this relationship and that the request should be interpreted in light of that positive feeling.

The primary functions of communication are conveyed more by how a message is structured and presented than by the content of the message. Structure and presentation can be varied meaningfully at several levels. For example, at a microscopic level, the type of statement (command, question, and so on) carries information about how to understand the content.[22] At a macroscopic level, the arrangement of the environment might inform those who use it about control distribution. The amount of space in a room allocated to specific people or categories of people not only conveys information about their relative status in this particular environment, it also structures who can easily talk to whom.

As an example of this sort of "message structure," consider the arrangement of your classroom. Who has the largest desk? Who controls the most space? Who has the best visual access—and thus communicative access—to the most people? How does rearranging the furniture from the traditional rows of student desks facing the instructor's desk into a circle change the communication dynamics of the class? The arrangement of the room tells people how control is distributed without anyone ever having to bring up such a touchy subject. (If the instructor has to say, "Let's not forget who's in charge here," he or she is already in trouble!) On an even larger scale, institutional structures—of the television industry, for example—provide functional information both to members of those institutions and to people who must interact with the institutions.

At the microscopic level, presentation includes changes in tone of voice or facial expression. At more macro levels, presentation includes choice of timing and place for delivering a message (e.g., the president of the United States deciding to address a joint session of Congress, rather than the American Legion Convention, about a particular topic).

These functions cannot be edited out of messages; even supposedly "neutral" statements say something about how you feel about the other person. For example, Paul may be telling Randy that he doesn't want to go to the movies with him simply because he just wants to stay home. Because of Paul's facial expression or his tone of voice, Randy may think Paul's not being honest with him, that Paul actually has other plans.

This notion may be easier to understand if you consider that all messages are sent in the context of a relationship. The ever-popular and adaptable handshake greeting may not be warmly received by your long-term romantic partner. Indeed, when a handshake replaces an expected kiss, you are saying something about (and doing something to) your relationship— and your partner will likely notice.

There are, of course, exceptions but they can all be explained by reference to the context. Specifically, the context of most of your messages is the relationship you have with the target of your message. In some cases, however, formal contexts (e.g., a courtroom or a classroom) override relational contexts, and, predictably, your message will be modified accordingly without damage to your relationship. Relationships extend beyond social dyads. Public figures like politicians have relationships with their constituents, as do performers with their audiences. Professors have relationships with their students and students with their classmates, both as members of a class and, possibly, as individuals.

Control

Of the three primary functions of communication, control is probably the most important. It could be argued, in fact, that it *is* the most important because it seems to permeate both affiliation and goal orientation functions. By **control** we mean the ability of one person to influence both another person or persons and the manner in which their relationship is conducted. Let us quickly note that we are not equating control with dominance, although one person may be dominant. Nor are we using the term *control* in a negative way. Control (the influence of each partner on the other or others) is a necessary part of every relationship, including marital, boss–worker, parent–child, doctor–patient, lecturer–audience, and even friend–friend. In fact, control is a defining characteristic of every relationship.

Recall that we described the communication function as being the *negotiation* of the distribution of control. Distribution is important to our concept of this function because relational control is a zero-sum game. That is to say, the more control one person has, the less the other(s) have; hence, my 60 percent control leaves you with only 40 percent. In social relationships, people expect control to be distributed approximately evenly. The exact distribution of control in interpersonal relationships is worked out communicatively—by the way people talk with each other, how they structure their conversations (including their timing), as well as the content of the conversations. This negotiation takes place in all relationships, from the most informal and unstructured to the most formal and structured. It would be a serious error to assume that one person imposes control over another even in the most apparently one-sided of relationships.

Consider, for example, the parent–infant relationship. The infant exercises considerable control over the parents, even to the extent of determining the parents' sleeping schedule. Parents, for their part, try to influence their infant to behave in a way that is acceptable to them. (As you know, parents persist in these attempts well beyond their child's infancy.)

The more obvious kind of negotiation is that in which superiors (managers, teachers, and the like) and their subordinates (employees, students) participate to see how much each will be able to influence the other and in

CONTROL
The function of communication that is concerned with the ability of one person to influence another person or persons and the manner in which their relationship is conducted; one of the three primary functions of communication.

what facets of their work relationship. You might consider how you attempt to influence your professors, as well as how they attempt to influence you.

Happiness and relational satisfaction do not depend on equally distributed control; to the contrary, they depend on the appropriate distribution and exercise of control. In many relationships, you expect, if not demand, that your partner(s) have a larger or smaller share of control than you do. Along with the control goes responsibility for the relationship and various tasks relevant to the relationship. For example, as a new employee at a bank, Manny looks to his manager, Sally, for direction and advice about how to do his job well. He expects to be told what to do and how to do it. The lopsided control distribution is appropriate for this type of relationship and meets both Manny's and Sally's expectations of their job responsibilities. Thus, it should lead to satisfaction for both of them—with regard to this aspect of their relationship, at least. Note that their expectations for their relationship are congruent: Both expect Sally to exercise more control than Manny.

As situations become more formal and more structured, and as the number of people involved increases, there is less opportunity to negotiate control. In a public speaking situation, for example, individual members of a large audience cannot easily shift the distribution of control from the designated speaker to themselves. Heckling the speaker can be seen as an attempt to accomplish such a shift. Television viewers try to exercise control over stations and networks by participating in viewer surveys, writing letters, and watching or not watching particular shows. Viewers can organize into groups in an effort to influence television programming. Later in the book we will have more to say about how negotiation is accomplished.

SELF-CHECK

Control in the Student–Teacher Relationship

Consider your relationship with a specific professor. How do you approach that professor when a paper is late, or you want to take an exam early, or you disagree in class? Are certain areas of your relationship "off limits" to influence attempts by one or the other or both? Are there control strategies that you think are more appropriate? less appropriate? How will a failed influence (control) attempt affect your relationship? Are there times when failure to attempt to influence has a negative impact on your relationship?

Affiliation

AFFILIATION
The function of communication that is concerned with how feelings for another, ranging from love (high positive affiliation) to hate (high negative affiliation), are communicated; one of the three primary functions of communication.

By **affiliation**, the second primary function, we mean the affect, or feelings, one has for another or others along a love–hate continuum. Unlike control, affiliation is not distributed in a zero-sum fashion; all parties to a relationship can have a high level of affiliation (in everyday, lay terms, they love each other). In other words, in our social relationships we expect our partners to feel about the same amount of affiliation for us as we do for them. The more intimate and personal the relationship, the more we expect this to be the case. But, of course, not all partners have the same feelings, whether positive or negative, about each other all the time. Thus we specify that it is the *expression* of affiliation that must be negotiated. At times you might want to hide your feelings for another person, or you might find it desirable or strategic to do so. For example, you might not want to show your feelings about a potential dating partner until you find out whether that person is interested in you. Or you might be dating someone who defines your relationship as that of "just friends"; any attempt you make to communicate the higher level of affiliation you feel may threaten the partner and thus the relationship. Hence, you do not express the affect you feel—at least for now!

Two quick caveats about affiliation are in order. First, affiliation can range from highly positive (love) to highly negative (hate). In our usage, low affiliation is the equivalent of feeling neutral about another person. Second, affiliation is not synonymous with intimacy. Intimacy is knowledge about another. You can have high positive affiliation and low intimacy. (For example, you may experience "love at first sight.") Similarly, you can have high negative affiliation and high intimacy. (For example, you may know a lot about your spouse and want to get a divorce.)

In thinking about this function of communication, you might ask yourself how you let people with whom you are in various relationships know

---

SELF-CHECK

Communicating Feelings

Call to mind two different types of relationships in which you have been involved that have undergone change (for example, with a parent and with a romantic partner). As each relationship changed, how did your way of expressing affiliation change? Did you use different strategies or tactics for expressing affect in the different relationships? Are there some relationships in which you could not (or cannot) communicate your feelings about the other person? Why?

---

how you feel about them. Again, we will have more to say about affiliation later.

Goal Achievement

Our third primary function of communication, **goal achievement**, also called *task orientation*, refers to the focus of attention on the task at hand in order to achieve one's goal. Communication that is highly goal or task oriented focuses on getting the job done. In unstructured social relationships, it is useful to think of maintenance of the relationship as the goal toward which both parties should be oriented. In more formal situations, the goal may include completing an interview or participating in a public speaking event as either the speaker or an audience member.

Like the previous two functions, the task or goal to which communication partners are to be oriented can be negotiated. The task agreed upon during a meeting or get-together can shift during the course of the meeting. For example, a department meeting called by the manager to discuss the production schedule can become a forum for employees to voice their complaints about having to work overtime. Furthermore, groups can have competing tasks, and they will have to deal with the allocation of time and attention to each of them. For example, students who are assigned to do a group project for a course often have to allocate their time between "being friends" and "getting the project completed/getting a good grade." If you have had this experience, you know what we're talking about, and you know that sometimes it is very difficult to accomplish both tasks in a satisfactory manner.

These three primary functions—control, affiliation, and goal achievement—can be seen as general goals of communication. From a competence perspective, when you evaluate your success at attaining your communication goals, especially your relational goals, you are monitoring yourself according to (1) how well you function in terms of the amount of control you have over others and they over you, (2) the manner and degree to which you express affect appropriately, and (3) the degree to which you communicate to others about your focus on specific tasks and what you hope to accomplish. You also evaluate how well your partners are accomplishing these goals. How well your communication in terms of these functions matches with that of your partners determines how competent your relationship is.

GOAL ACHIEVEMENT
The function of communication that is concerned with the focusing of attention on the task at hand in order to achieve a goal; one of the three primary functions of communication. Also called task orientation.

Secondary Functions

Communication also serves functions in a relationship that are not part and parcel of *every* message. We refer to these functions as secondary. If your messages fail to serve these functions when your audience or the situation demands, relational difficulties can—and probably will—arise. Here

FIGURE 1.3

The functions of communication can be depicted as a three-dimensional space onto which messages can be plotted. For example, a message that is highly controlling, moderately positive affiliatively, and very goal-directed would be in the front upper right-hand area of the cube. Think about the messages you exchange with a specific relational partner. Where would you plot them? What does the plot tell you about the relationship?

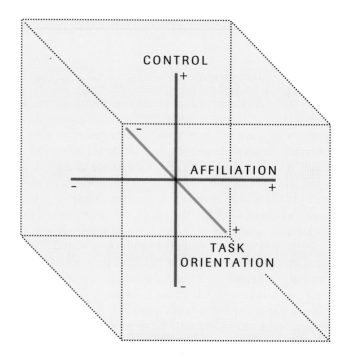

we concentrate on three functions that seem to be particularly important in a variety of contexts. A competent relationship might also be characterized by communication that (1) is empathic and supportive, (2) minimizes the display of apprehension,[23] and (3) demonstrates the involvement of relational partners.[24]

Empathic communication consists of messages that indicate to your partner, "I know how you feel." In technical terms, when you take the role of the other—that is, when you see and experience the world as he or she does—you are said to be *empathic*.[25] When the messages you construct for that other person indicate that you have taken his or her role, you are communicating empathically. Although you might not agree with what your partner is doing or saying, you are in essence communicating to your partner that you understand his or her position or point of view. Empathic messages are almost always seen as supportive, but some supportive messages are not empathic in the technical sense. Hence, we make a slight distinction between these types of messages. For example, "I think it's fine for a person who has been treated the way you have to be angry" does not indicate that the speaker shares his or her partner's feelings or experience.

Much has been written about communication apprehension[26] and the negative effects an apprehensive person has on his or her audience. Competent relationships provide a "safe" environment for communication, thus usually reducing the apprehension participants in the relationship may feel.

When communication in a relationship begins to show consistent evidence of apprehension on the part of one or more partners, this could be a sign that the relationship is in the midst of or soon to undergo some sort of change.

Competent relationships are involving for their participants. That is, when people find a relationship satisfying, they will communicate that satisfaction in a way that shows their involvement by being responsive to their partners. This is the case even if the relationship is short-term or defined by a specific task. For example, in a job interview, both interviewer and interviewee indicate their involvement with each other and the conversation (i.e., their relationship) in the way they ask and answer questions, in their nonverbal responses to each other, and the like.

A discussion of functions leads us necessarily to questions of evaluating communication behavior. How do we determine whether we are successful communicators? How do we know whether we are meeting our goals and what we should do if we think we are not? In an attempt to provide answers to questions of this sort, we next turn our attention to characteristics of relationships and communicative competence.

Communication Relationships

We can approach the study of communication from the vantage points of (1) the individual—focusing on either the sender or the receiver, (2) the relationship in which people communicate—with each person alternately sending and receiving messages, (3) the social group(s) of which individuals are members, (4) the institutional or organizational context in which people live and work, and (5) the cultures in which they were raised.[27]

At each of these levels of analysis, we can ask about how people use media and what effects mediated messages have. All of these foci are important for fully understanding communication.

Analyzing communication in relationships, however, provides an optimal starting point for understanding how communication works at all levels of analysis. In fact, with the exception of purely intrapersonal aspects of communication (e.g., planning what you are going to say at some time in the future or rehearsing specific messages), the relationship is a pivotal component in the communication process.

What Is a Communication Relationship?

A **relationship** is the interconnection or interdependence of two (or more) people in order to achieve some goal. A *communication relationship* is one in which the interdependence is based on symbolic exchange. If this

RELATIONSHIP
The interdependence of two or more people.

definition leads you to think that you begin and end several communication relationships each day, you are correct. Technically, each exchange with a new person opens a new relationship. For example, under this definition, you had a "relationship" with the person you stopped on campus to ask the time. In your attempt to achieve a goal, a symbolic interchange took place. But such "minimal" relationships are usually not very interesting, so we will confine our remarks to relationships that are meaningful for the participants over a period of time, including informal social relationships, such as close friendships, as well as more formal, more structured ones, such as employer–employee, parent–child, and professor–student. Some relationships (e.g., parent–child, husband–wife) have both formal and informal aspects.

DYAD

A pair of individuals maintaining a relationship.

Although the remainder of this chapter focuses primarily on informal relationships between pairs of people, or **dyads**, the discussion applies equally well to a variety of relationships, many of which are discussed in subsequent chapters—for example, speaker–audience and interviewer-interviewee.

We also want to point out that social and task groups and cultures have relationships with each other. That is, when someone communicates as a member of a specific social group rather than as an individual, when speaking with nongroup ("outgroup") members, we can say that the two groups have a relationship. During labor negotiations, representatives from management and a union speak to each other as members of their respective groups, not as individuals who might even know each other personally. This line of thinking leads to concepts such as "race relations" or relationships between national governments. It is interesting that *individual* members of groups can have good relationships with one another while their groups may not. In Northern Ireland, for example, Eileen and Moiré may be personal friends, but the Catholic religious community to which Eileen belongs is at extreme odds with Moiré's Protestant community. The same kinds of variables that characterize interpersonal relationships can be extrapolated to describe social and cultural group relationships. For the moment, let's turn our attention to informal interpersonal relationships composed of two people.

▧ *The Individual in the Relationship*

By adopting the relationship as our unit of analysis, we are not discounting the important characteristics of the people who make up the relationship. Obviously, individuals embark on relationships with their self-concepts, personal experiences, preferred styles of communicating and thinking (cognitive processing), individual goals, and the like. All of these characteristics profoundly influence how they will communicate in any given conversation or relationship.

Although individuals are not lost in relationships, the influence of their partners usually leads to changes in the participants. The more important the relationship, the more influence the individuals will have on their partners and, thus, the more susceptible each is to change. This is especially the case if the participants in the relationship like each other or if one has a lot of status or desirable qualities in the eyes of the other(s). As romantic partners become more involved and committed, for example, they usually adapt to one another, taking on similar habits, mannerisms, and attitudes. This adaptation is a consequence of the influence or control the partners have over each other. A manager may have a similar effect on employees, with the employees coming to see the business world—and talk about it—in much the same way as the boss does. In hostile relationships, the partners may change in ways that make them more distinct from each other.

Self and Other as Audience

When you see the term *audience,* you probably tend to think of a public situation: a speaker on a platform talking *to* (rather than *with*) a large group passively listening, more or less silently, to what the speaker has to say. The speaker has a plan for what he or she wants to say and has prepared remarks. In other words, the speaker has a strategy and is employing specific tactics in order to accomplish a goal. The people in the audience, on the other hand, do not necessarily prepare for their role as audience members, and their individual goals are neither necessarily clear nor congruent with each other's or with those of the speaker. In other words, we tend to attribute a high degree of intentionality and control to speakers, and less to audiences. (This is not always true, of course. Consider, for example, the relationship of a jury to a defendant who is giving testimony. We are here asking you to think in terms of generic public forum presentations and related small-group situations.)

We introduce the term **audience** here to make the point that in a variety of relationships, participants in the relationship act much the same as do the prototypical speaker (message sender) and audience (message receiver) described above. In fact, the speaker is his or her own audience, even while speaking. Of course, in many situations, the roles of speaker and audience change frequently. The same principles that guide you in communicating with your parents, employer, or a loved one apply as the "audience" gets larger—from one, to a small group, to a large group. Later in this book we

AUDIENCE
One or more people who are listening to what a person is saying and/or watching what that person is doing.

FIGURE 1.4
The principles of competent communication apply no matter how many partners are in the relationship or how long the relationship lasts.

discuss specific skills for different types of communication events (interviewing, group discussion, and public speaking) with different-sized audiences. It is especially important for you to remember that when you communicate with others—develop symbolic interdependence for even a short time—the size of the audience does not alter the fact that you are in a communication relationship. The principles that are relevant to competent communication apply across the board.

Successful Communication

Our references to goals, strategies, influence, control, and the like indicate concern about the "success" of our attempts at communication. The issue of success in communicating is so difficult and complex that we spend the rest of this book discussing it. But it is important to remember that success is typically a subjective experience and can be evaluated only against some sort of criteria applied in a particular context.

Generally, one of two approaches is taken to assess successful communication. The first approach, which is more prominent in the communication research literature and in our everyday experiences, emphasizes *outcomes*. More recently, communication scholars have begun to consider a second approach, which emphasizes the manner in which communication is conducted—the *process*—as the key component of success. In everyday life, both are important.

Success as Outcome

Outcomes have to do with the product of an interchange. In an argument, the outcome is "who won"; in a negotiation (an important type of communication context, given our emphasis on communication functions), "who got the other to give up what" is the outcome. In many contexts, outcome analysis tends to focus on winning and losing and shows little concern about how the outcome was achieved.

Consider a real-world, if somewhat simplified, example: a salesperson trying to sell a car. If success is measured in terms of achieving the desired outcome, the salesperson is successful if the customer buys the car. That's it. It does not matter what tactics the salesperson used, how honest he or she was, or even whether the customer returns sometime in the future to buy another car. The outcome, a sale, is the measure of success. Other outcomes might also be desirable, of course—for example, customer satisfaction or a large commission for the salesperson.

OUTCOME
The product or end state of a communication encounter or series of encounters.

Success as Process

PROCESS

The manner in which a communication encounter is conducted.

Process measures of success have to do with how an episode is accomplished. What is said and how it is said take on greater significance, although outcomes still play a role in a process analysis. Process measures would focus the preceding car sale example on how the sale was achieved. Was there an open discussion of the car's qualities or were high-pressure tactics used, for example? Success would be measured in terms of the satisfaction with the way the sale was conducted from the point of view of both parties.

From the process perspective, it is better to optimize outcomes for both partners than to maximize outcomes for one. This way of thinking has led pop psychologists to write books about resolving conflict by "fighting fair."[28] More to our point, a process orientation to success gives serious consideration to communication variables such as strategies, general skills, and specific messages. The negotiations involving distribution of control, level of expressed affiliation, and task accomplishment place greater emphasis on accomplishing your goals in light of your relationship with your partner and your partner's goals than on winning as much as you can.

We prefer the process to the outcomes approach when we are trying to understand communication "success." One of the best ways to assess success from this perspective is to look at mutual satisfaction. That is to say, are both parties satisfied with the outcome of an episode? (Even for process-oriented types like us, there is no way to avoid outcomes.) Sometimes winning isn't the most important thing—especially when long-term relationships are involved! Geoff may win most of the arguments he has with Betsy, but she increasingly sees him as stubborn and uncaring—a view that may eventually lead her to leave him.

Behavior is both *appropriate* and *effective* when it serves to optimize outcomes for both partners, rather than maximize outcomes for one partner at the expense of the other, while generally leading to mutual satisfaction.[29]

Appropriate Behavior

Behavior is appropriate when it meets the expectations of (1) one's specific communication partner, (2) other people in one's immediate presence, and (3) the demands of the situation. In almost all situations, cultural norms and rules set the standards for expectations. The more intimate you are with your partner, the more likely some idiosyncratic expectations will influence what you judge to be appropriate or inappropriate, but cultural norms are always in the background. The expectations generated by these different people and situations can, of course, be in conflict with each other.

Which set of expectations you choose to honor and which you decide to ignore can say a great deal about your relationship.

Even in informal, unstructured social situations, such as when you are walking in a park or at a party given by a close friend, general cultural norms (e.g., "Be thoughtful of those around you") are supplemented by norms specific to that situation ("Don't talk about your grades at parties"). Nonetheless, these still provide a great deal of communicative latitude. In other words, a wide variety of communication behaviors will be considered appropriate. In such situations, the expectations of your partner and others will be of primary importance.

As the situation becomes more formal and more structured, what counts as appropriate gets more specific. Consider the minimal communication latitude one has in a courtroom or a church.

REALITY CHECK

The Discovery of Communication Norms

The purpose of this exercise is to help you better understand (1) the nature of communication rules and norms and (2) the problems that "strangers" to a culture encounter.

Many rules and norms are peculiar to one or a few cultures. They are observed unselfconsciously by members of the culture, and are not thought about until they are ignored or broken. That is, you take the rules and norms of your culture for granted, you typically follow them, and you expect your partners to follow them. But when you move from one culture (or from one sub- or co-culture) to another, rules that were taken for granted and behaviors that were automatic may become the source of interpersonal difficulties.

Observation of communication patterns: Spend 15 to 30 minutes in a familiar environment (preferably your home or dorm) observing the communication behaviors and patterns of those around you from the perspective of a visitor from a different culture. Do not take anything for granted. For now, do not act out the assumption that you are a stranger. Do not indicate to your subjects that you are observing their behavior.

Record the results of your observation, with special attention to how you understood what was appropriate behavior. What rules and norms can you list? How did you identify these rules and norms? Do they apply to more than one "culture" (that is, are they peculiar to the context you observed or can they be generalized to other, similar contexts)?

Intervention: Spend 15 to 30 minutes in the environment that you previously observed, acting out the assumption that you are a visitor

continued on next page

from another culture. Conduct yourself in a circumspect and polite fashion. Avoid "getting personal," use only formal address, and speak only when spoken to. Do not take *anything* for granted (for example, that you may use the bathroom without the permission of the host). Do not indicate that you are role-playing.

At the end of the intervention, tell the people around you why you were behaving the way you were. Don't be surprised if they don't let you finish your planned intervention. Ask them how they felt about what you were doing and about your relationship with them. Record their answers along with the behaviors in which you engaged and their reactions to you. How did you feel during this exercise? Were you able to complete your intervention? If not, why not? Would you modify the list of norms and rules you made earlier?

How does your experience compare with those of your classmates? Were conflicting or different norms "discovered" by different people from either the same or different "cultures"? How could a person from one culture best discover a rule in another culture? How can (or should) a person from one culture adhere to another culture's rule when that rule violates a rule from his or her own culture?

Ethical considerations: Conduct your observations and intervention with respect for the people you are observing. The intervention should be done with care so that norm violations are minor and can be easily repaired. Do not conduct the intervention in contexts where you might harm your relationship with the person(s) being observed (for example, at work, with your boss as the target).

Knowing what is appropriate and what is not with a wide variety of audiences and in a wide variety of situations is necessary if you are to be a successful communicator.

Effective Behavior

Communication is considered *effective* if it helps you meet your goals. This might sound obvious and straightforward, but in practice it is not always easy to know what messages will serve us in pursuit of our goals. Decisions about how to "design" your messages so that they might be most effective for a given situation or audience are further complicated by the fact that in many situations you have multiple goals.[30] For example, even though Travis might be in a conflict with Jan and wants to have the conflict resolved in his favor, he will still want Jan to continue to like him. (This is also an example of the distinction between process thinking and outcome thinking when communicating with others.)

Some knowledge of your audience's expectations and the normative demands of the situation helps you decide which messages will be relatively more effective than others. In addition, knowing that you have multiple goals and prioritizing them—a task that is not always easy—also helps you construct effective messages.

Successful messages are usually, but not always, both appropriate and effective. Given your goals, the audience, and the situation, you might have to choose between messages that are primarily effective but inappropriate, and messages that are appropriate but not particularly effective. Once again, process versus outcome considerations come into play.

Sue, for example, is about to leave for an important business meeting and is very concerned about being on time. She is wearing a new dress that her husband, Bill, has not seen before. Bill thinks the dress is not conservative enough for the meeting and that it doesn't look good on Sue in any case. An *appropriate* thing for him to do (based on their relationship history) is to indirectly suggest to Sue that she might consider wearing some-

---

SELF-CHECK

A Balancing Act

How would you handle the following situation? What, if anything, would you ask your boss?

You want to take four days off so you can go to a wedding out of state. *But* you don't have any vacation time left for this year and don't want to take the time off without pay. *And* you want to maintain your boss's belief that you are a reliable, motivated employee. The job is important to you; so is attending the wedding.

Role-play what you might say to your boss (1) if attending the wedding were your primary goal and (2) if maintaining your boss's high regard of you were your primary goal. Have your partner role-play your boss and vary his or her characteristics or those of the relationship or of the situation—for example, the boss in a good mood versus the boss in a bad mood; a new boss versus one for whom you've worked for a year; other employees who might or might not want special consideration; and so forth. How did your messages change as characteristics of the relationship and the situation changed? What aspects of your messages made them more or less effective? Do you and your partner agree on which messages were effective and what made them so?

thing else. This kind of suggestion would open up a discussion about what's "right" to wear to this sort of meeting, what options Sue feels she has available, and the like. But all that takes time and Sue is in a hurry. The *effective* move in this case would be to make a direct statement to Sue that she should change—and run the risk of hurting her feelings. Bill's dilemma is not uncommon. We can't know the "right" thing for him to do without knowing more about the relationship, but we can be fairly certain that in this instance it will be difficult for him to be both effective and appropriate.

Competent Communication

Communicative (relational) **competence** is the ability of two or more people jointly to create and maintain a mutually satisfying relationship by constructing appropriate and effective messages. Communication is competent when it (1) produces optimal distribution of control, expressed affiliation, and orientation to the goal and task at hand, (2) is process oriented, and (3) is generally appropriate and effective for a given relationship.

As we have mentioned, we adopt the relationship, rather than the individual, as the unit of analysis. For us, competence is in relationships; messages must be interpreted in the context of relationships. Individuals, on the other hand, can be characterized by the number of skills they bring to the relationship, their knowledge of how and when to use those skills, and their motivation to do so.[31] In everyday conversation we frequently describe a highly skilled person as competent. We make the distinction between competent relationships and skilled individuals because a person does not have to possess a great many communication skills to enjoy a successful relationship. **Communication skills** are behavioral routines based on social understandings and used by communicators to achieve their goals. You may know people who have few communication skills and do not use them in a very sophisticated manner, but who nonetheless are in mutually satisfying, long-term relationships. Conversely, even the most highly skilled person will occasionally get involved in an unsatisfying relationship. Thus, we want to keep the communication skills and other competencies of an individual conceptually distinct from the quality of relationships. (**Communication competencies** are skills and understandings that enable communication partners to exchange messages appropriately and effectively.)

The primary dimensions along which we evaluate communicative competence are the primary functions of communication: control, affiliation, and goal achievement. Competent relationships, be they interpersonal, in a small group, speaker–audience, or mass media–audience, are marked by messages that (1) communicate an appropriate (mutually satisfying or mutually agreed upon) distribution of control, (2) express a level of affiliation

COMMUNICATION
SKILLS
Behavioral routines based on social understandings and used by communicators to achieve their goals.

COMMUNICATION
COMPETENCIES
Skills and understandings that enable communication partners to exchange messages appropriately

that is comfortable for all participants, and (3) are consistent with both the goals of each participant and their jointly constructed relational goals.

In informal social relationships, an approximately even distribution of control is usually seen to be appropriate. In contrast, in business relationships, an uneven distribution of control favoring members higher in the hierarchy is expected. Distribution of control in relationships can be adjusted as people in the relationship change. For example, the distribution of control in families tends to change as children grow older, with children assuming more control and responsibility. Such shifts in distribution can be difficult to accomplish, and the negotiations are not always smooth (or competent). Similarly, the amount of control a leader has within a work group can change—for example, as membership changes or the expertise of different group members is demanded by problems the group has to solve.

The appropriate display of affiliation, of course, varies from situation to situation. In new, developing relationships what counts as appropriate affiliation display can change rapidly. Couples can very quickly go from a "just friends" relationship, which typically does not involve physical contact, to a "dating" relationship, which might be marked by hand-holding and kissing in public. The sort of behavior that "marks" the relationship also defines it. That is, if you are holding hands with your partner, you are communicating to your partner and to those around you what you think the definition of the relationship is or should be.

A speaker addressing an audience must also be careful to display an appropriate level of affiliation, depending on the established relationship between speaker and audience. If the two know each other well and are friendly, a high degree of expressed affiliation may be appropriate. For example, the speaker might tell "in" jokes during the speech or refer to members of the audience by name. Such a strategy would not be appropriate or effective if speaker and audience were not well known to each other or were openly at odds. For example, when President Clinton speaks to veterans' groups—which are very critical of his avoidance of the draft during the Vietnam War—he can express only moderate affiliation. He can't implicitly say, "We are close friends" or "I'm like you."

Although a wide variety of goals can characterize a relationship, maintaining the relationship is typically a very important general relational goal. Individual goals vary widely, of course, but might include support of one's self-concept, happiness, and security.

The three dimensions of communicative competence allow us to describe communication in relationships in abstract terms (e.g., controlling, affiliative, goal-directed) that relate to specific message choices people make. These message choices are influenced by both audience and situation. Because this process is a complex one, to help you (and us!) put these concepts together, we have developed a model of communicative competence, to which we now turn.

A Model of Communicative Competence

The model presented in Figure 1.5 is a graphic representation of the primary aspects of communication discussed in this chapter. In this sense it is an abstraction, which omits many details for simplicity's sake but which you can fill in when you are considering specific interactions or relationships. Even in its simplicity, the model is complex. First, we dissect the model into its component parts, and then, in the remainder of the book, we put it back together in various ways.

Context

The context in which you communicate is important. As mentioned earlier, the context seriously constrains which messages are seen as appropriate and effective. Your social environment is the context of both your communication and your relationships. This environment is composed primarily of the people with whom you associate, but it is also made up of aspects of the physical environment, including where you live and work, your house furnishings, your pets, and the like. In your social environment, you create meanings for the objects (e.g., people, places, wall hangings, furniture, time, and temperature) that are distinguished from mere physical or biological description. People, for example, populate our physical environment, but friends, co-workers, classmates, and the like populate our social environment. The distinction between physical and social environment is important because we mutually create the meanings for the physical objects by communicating with each other.[32] This creation of meaning produces a shared social reality and can be seen as a negotiation process in which we engage. The point is that we help create and maintain the social environment in which we live by the way we communicate with each other. The social environment we help create can be friendly or hostile depending on how the people in it communicate with each other. It can also be seen as a place to work or play, for example, again depending on the communication that takes place within it. We participate in the creation of the meaning of our social environment against the backdrop of our culture.

Three types of context are especially important in communication: (1) the cultural context, (2) the immediate physical context, and (3) the relational context.

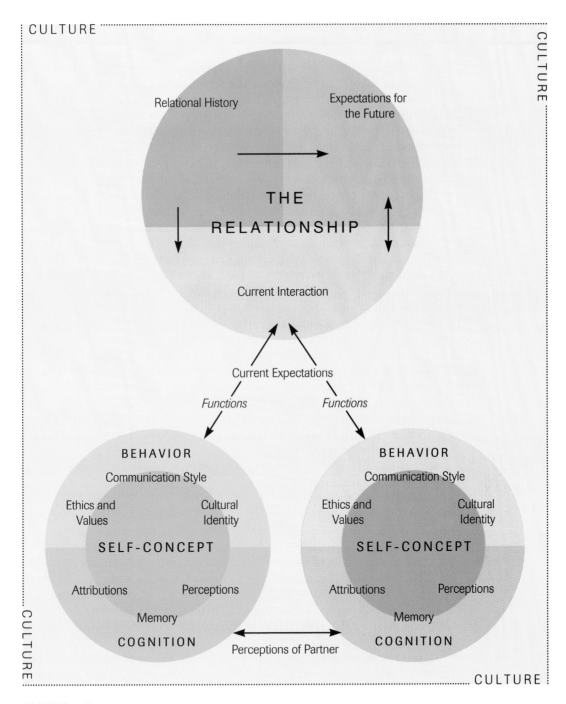

FIGURE 1.5

A model of communicative competence.

Source: J. M. Wiemann & M. O. Wiemann (1992), *Interpersonal communicative competence: Listening and perceiving,*
unpublished manuscript, University of California at Santa Barbara.

The Cultural Context

We discover much of the richness of our social environment as we are growing up. Culture carries these rich meanings; to be socialized into one's culture is to learn how to interpret the social environment in a way that is consistent with other people in the culture. For example, Juan learns to show respect for his elders by not questioning their authority; his friends are raised that way, and their behaviors mutually reinforce respect and unquestioned control from adults. Another sign of respect for older generations is passing down objects that have been in the family for years from generation to generation. Lana, by contrast, is raised in a social environment that gives her many choices and encourages her to talk to and question her elders. Her friends, raised in similar fashion, mutually reinforce a different type of respect for elders, which includes frequently questioning the exercise of control. Lana treasures few old objects; her society throws out the old and buys new things. Both Juan and Lana view their own behaviors as natural, but if each were to look at the other's behavior, it would seem very "different," and perhaps even odd or unnatural—and probably not respectful at all.

The assumed naturalness that attaches to the meaning of objects and relationships in our environment is both a blessing and a curse. On the positive side, the world is more predictable and more understandable than it otherwise would be. We generally *know* what to do and how to act because we learn what is "right" from our parents and peers. On the negative side, the communication difficulties and blind spots experienced by those who socialized us are reinvented in us. We lose sight of the complexity of communication because it seems so natural—*it is so natural.* The dotted border of the model illustrates that all communication is influenced by its cultural context. The culture of the interactants has a pervasive effect on every aspect of their communication.

Interestingly, we are almost completely unaware of this effect—probably much as the proverbial fish is unaware of water. Not only does our culture provide us with a language (including a regional, subcultural, or co-cultural dialect or dialects), it also contains information about how to interpret the symbols of our language. For example, the concept of politeness is universal, but each culture identifies for its members the kinds of utterances that count as "polite" and indicates when these utterances are optional and when they are mandatory. Although this information is usually provided implicitly, members of the culture must know it if they are to be seen as skilled communicators.

The culture also provides guidance about the appropriate sanctions for those who disregard the culture's norms; for example, it reveals how to reprimand someone who is acting in an "impolite" manner. The importance of culture is probably best understood when an attempt is made to interact with someone from another culture, and things are not going as expected.[33]

The Physical Context

The physical context is more obvious than the cultural context. Physical spaces can either encourage or discourage interaction or limit what is thought to be appropriate interaction to specific topics. Part of the physical context is made up of people who are not members of your immediate interaction. How close these other people are (their proximity) to you and your partner, whether or not they can overhear you, and the like, all influence what you might appropriately and effectively say to your partner. Consider, for example, two friends riding in an elevator. While they are alone, their conversation can be intimate. But when someone else enters the elevator, their intimate conversation ceases and they may even fall silent. The influence of physical context is taken for granted in the model and is not graphically illustrated.

The Relational Context

A third type of context, the relational context, is the most important contextual influence of all. The relational context has pervasive influence, allowing us to talk about generic types of relationships (e.g., between parent and child, boyfriend and girlfriend, lovers, roommates, best friends, spouses, employer and employee, work-group members, professor and class) and to generalize about communication across these types. Every aspect of our communication is evaluated in terms of the relationship we have with the person(s) with whom we are interacting.

Our messages are given meaning by our relationships. A kiss has a different meaning when bestowed on your mother than it does when shared with your lover or your child. In one relational context, saying "Let's be friends" (e.g., when said to a new acquaintance) is an invitation to explore relational possibilities. The same phrase, when said to someone whom you've been dating for the last year, can have an entirely different meaning (as in "Let's *just* be friends," which some say is the coldest sentence in the English language!).

Similarly, a seemingly intimate self-disclosure has a different meaning when uttered to a close friend or said as part of a public speech or a television commercial. Consider the "meaning" of saying "I'm an alcoholic" to your best friend, to your boss or co-worker, to a large group assembled for an Alcoholics Anonymous meeting, or as part of a television commercial. An important part of the meaning of the statement is the impact it may have on your relationship with your audience.

▨ *The Individual in the Relationship*

The lower half of the model of communicative competence depicts two "individuals" as circles. It is easier for us to talk about two individual persons, but it is very important to keep in mind that these "individuals" (circles) can represent small or large groups, classes of people who share an occupation or co-culture, and so forth. The model is designed to explain a variety of types of relationships, including two persons going out together, a professor lecturing to a class, a reporter interviewing a news source in private, a reporter interviewing a news source on television, two enemies fighting with each other, representatives of management and labor negotiating a contract, lovers chatting with each other, and many, many more interactions and relationships. For ease of explanation, we will discuss the model in terms of two people in an informal social relationship.

Each individual comes to a new relationship as a person with a self-concept, a past, and expectations for the future—all the characteristics, in fact, that make the individual a person. Rather than getting lost in the relationship, the individual retains and maintains some sense of uniqueness even as the relationship exerts its influence and causes changes in the person. Most important here is the *self-concept*. As a person's own definition of his or her being, it is at the core of each of us.

You interpret the messages of others in light of your self-concept. That is, you actively seek out people who will confirm or support aspects of your self. You like people who like you, for example, because they tell you in many ways that they agree with you about who you are; they support you by acknowledging and supporting your self-concept.[34]

Similarly, your own messages let others know who you think you are or who you would like to be. Aspects of your self-concept are "ideal" until others support them, when these aspects become "real" for both yourself and your audience.[35] Your communication is geared toward presenting a positive self that can be supported by your relational partners. When you fail at this task—that is, present a self that others cannot support—they respond negatively. When people make claims about themselves that others do not believe are true, the audience frequently evaluates these speakers

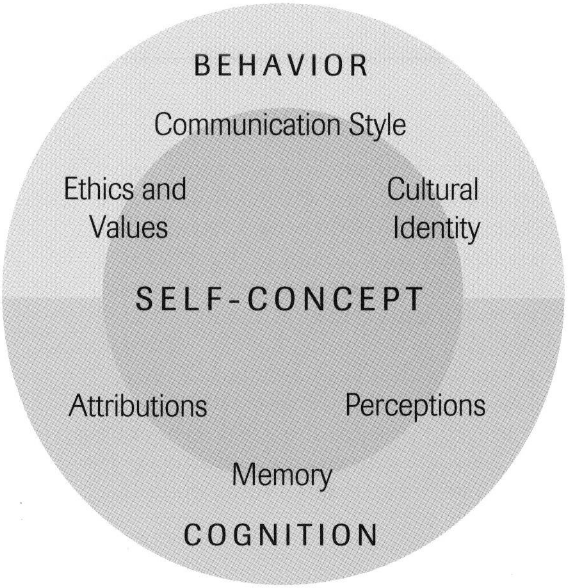

FIGURE 1.6
*Each partner, as rep-
resented at the bot-
tom of the model,
may be an individual
or a group.*

BEHAVIOR

Communication Style

Ethics and
Values

Cultural
Identity

SELF-CONCEPT

Attributions

Perceptions

Memory

COGNITION

negatively and lets them know how they feel. In fact, our culture has a term for one sort of such behavior: bragging. In this sense, your self-concept is the product of your communication with others. But since you base the construction of your messages on who you are, self-concept is also the trig-gering mechanism for your communication.

As you become more intimate and involved with others, your relation-ship with them becomes entwined in your self-concept. You take the rela-tionship on as a critical part of who you are; self and relationship can be-come difficult to distinguish. It is in this way that the relationship experience changes the individual. Even when a relationship is over, its ef-fects on the people involved can be long lasting. The more important the re-lationship, the more true this seems to be. Grieving for years after the death of a loved one is a common example of how a past relationship can continue to affect a person, as is the generalized hostility displayed by a person who has gone through a difficult divorce after several years of marriage.

An important part of many people's self-concept is their *cultural iden-tity*, their view of themselves as a member of a specific culture. This identity influences the communication choices they make and how they interpret messages they receive from others. For example, an African American stu-dent of ours points out that for people of color, race is frequently a salient aspect of their interactions, whereas this is not necessarily true for Cau-

Ethical Standards

What ethical considerations do you think are important for competent communication? Make a list of your ethical standards (values). Are some standards more important than others? Are there some standards that apply in only one type of relationship, or that apply differently in different types of relationships? Do the three types of context influence your standards? If so, how? Do your standards change as the size of the audience changes? That is, do you have different standards for yourself as a public speaker than as a student in a class or as a friend?

Compare your standards with those of your classmates and discuss the similarities and differences you think are important. What might account for the differences? Can you detect cultural differences? How might these differences affect your ability to enter into a competent relationship?

casians. A member of a cultural or ethnic minority may sometimes have trouble interpreting criticism because that person does not know whether the criticism is based on the merits of his or her behavior or on his or her membership in a minority culture. Cultural identity as part of the self-concept is reinforced by the messages people receive from those around them (including members of their own cultural or ethnic group as well as members of other groups). Like other aspects of the self-concept, cultural identity is bound to affect how one communicates and the types of relationships one establishes.

Closely related to your self-concept are the ethics or *ethical standards* you hold. These standards are the values you hold about what is moral and just. Your ethics influence your evaluation of both your messages and those of others in terms of appropriateness. Communication is a powerful tool that can be used to help or hurt others; thus your ethics about the use of this tool are important for those in your social environment. As important as these standards are for people's general well-being as individuals and as a society, there is agreement on only the most basic issues of communication ethics. There are several approaches to ethical communication, each of which leads toward different conclusions about how to behave responsibly.[36] And even people with a comprehensive, well-articulated set of standards (which few of us have) may find that contextual or situational

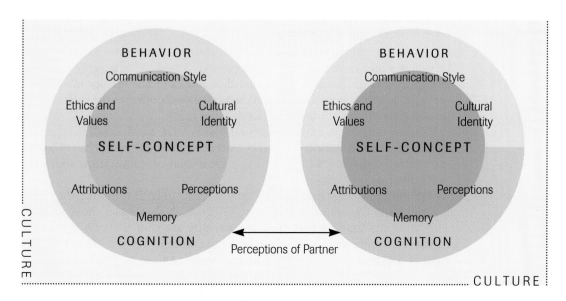

FIGURE 1.7

Each partner in a relationship has perceptions of the other, both as a partner and beyond the relationship.

features make it difficult to decide how to act most appropriately. For example, you might have an ethical standard that says that honesty is a crucial feature of competent communication. But there might be times when complete honesty would be hurtful to your partner. You are faced with an ethical dilemma: Do you give your honest opinion and report of the facts, or do you protect your partner's feelings (and possibly your relationship)?

General cognitive processing skills are also part of what people bring into relationships. **Cognitive skills** are mental capacities—one's ability to think, reason, remember, and make sense of one's world. People view their relationships in more or less complex ways.[37]

Some people process information *linearly*; that is, they understand the world around them in terms of a sequence of events stretched out in time. Others understand events in their general context, without necessarily seeing any causal or temporal connections; these people process information holistically.

People bring to their relationships other cognitive processes that are potentially important to the way they communicate. These processes include memory and perceptual and attributional biases. *Perceptual biases* govern how one sees the world. Optimists, for example, have a perceptual bias to

COGNITIVE SKILLS
Mental capacities including the ability to think, reason, remember, and make sense of one's world.

evaluate their experiences in positive terms. *Attributional biases* are the intentions of others and the causes of events one assigns to the perceived world. Relational partners also have perceptions of each other that seem to be independent of the current conversation. These are relatively enduring perceptions of the partner as an individual (for example, the optimist might perceive Leah as a generous person), as well as a member of the relationship (as when the optimist observes, "Leah loves me").

These attributional and perceptual biases have an especially important bearing on how a person evaluates potential partners and behaves at the start of relationships, before having a great deal of information about the new partners.

On the behavioral side, people vary in terms of both the skills they have mastered and the communication style in which they enact those skills.[38] The behaviors that are part of your repertoire are your tools for communicating. The more tools (skills) you have, the more likely you are to have the appropriate tool for specific relational work. As we pointed out earlier, however, the total number of skills does not determine the success of a relationship. Furthermore, the manner in which you use your skills (your style) has a potentially great influence on the effect of your behavior. Note the difference between a smooth exchange of speaking turn (i.e., when one person stops talking in a conversation and the other starts) and one in which an abrupt interruption is responsible for the exchange of the speaking turn. The outcome in both exchanges may be that a different person is speaking, but the process results in different evaluations of the conversation and one's partner. Depending on the smoothness of the exchange of turns, a partner may be considered either friendly or rude.

▨ *Interactional Goals*

Both individual goals and relational goals come into play in any interaction. Our model calls attention to the "current interaction" because we believe that any interaction is a microcosm of the relationship of the people interacting. This is especially clear in the case of conversation. We can learn something about a relationship by analyzing a conversation of the people involved in the relationship. The more conversations we have to analyze, the more confident we can be that we truly understand the relationship. In fact, it is through conversation or other forms of interaction, such as conducting an interview or public speaking, that relationships are defined. For example, you know you are a "student" to your professor because he or she communicates to you as you would expect a professor to commu-

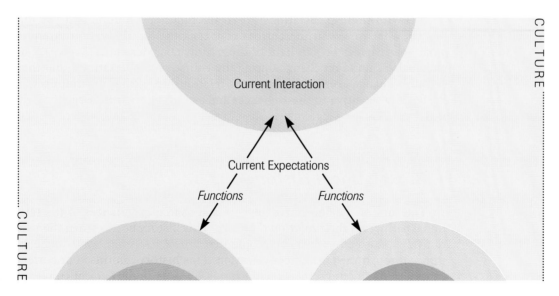

FIGURE 1.8

Relationships are defined through current interactions.

nicate to a student. (Note that self-concept comes into play here.) Thus we have the current interaction in the model as part of "the relationship."

Recall that communication defines the relationship along three dimensions: control, affiliation, and goal achievement. The functional level of communication is important in our model because it is the congruence of the partners' communication goals in terms of the three functions that are at the heart of communicative competence. If you and your partner are not communicating the same distribution of control, for example, your relationship will be in a state of stress. If your goals for control distribution do not match over time (i.e., if a lack of congruence persists), we would evaluate your relationship as incompetent and would predict that you and your partner are both dissatisfied and will probably end the relationship. Lack of congruence in communication about control occurs when both partners try to be dominant or, conversely, when neither is willing to take any responsibility for the relationship.

Your expectations for the current conversation, of course, influence the goals you set. These expectations are informed by what you know of your partner and his or her goals and expectations, the constraints the situation places on your communication options, the nature of your relationship, and so on.

It is with these expectations, goals, and functions in mind that you formulate what to say in the current conversation. Similarly, you interpret what your partner says in light of these same considerations. Expectations and goals can and do change during the course of conversations, and they certainly change over the life span of a relationship. Skilled communicators are usually sensitive to these changes and can adjust their messages accordingly.

Relational History

The sum of the "objective" events and shared experiences of the relational partners is their *relational history*. This history begins when the relationship is formed—when the people first interact in some way—and continues through the current conversation. This history informs your current expectations and interpretation of what is going on in the current conversation. For example, if you and a friend went camping together and had a terrible time because of the weather, you both might develop an understanding by which any of your future references to camping would have a negative connotation. ("Do you want to go to the opera with me?" "I'd rather go camping!") This idiosyncratic meaning for camping is implicitly negotiated in the way we discussed earlier. The reference to your relational history indicates to you, to your partner, and to others that there is something special about this particular relationship and that it has some substance beyond the current interaction.

History is conceptually different from individual memory, even though history is obviously stored in each individual's memory. The reason for this conceptual distinction is that some things are brought into the relationship (memory) and others are created by the partners together (history). Reference to this common history can be an important defining characteristic of a relationship, both for the participants and for the participants' associates. An interesting example of common history came up in the 1992 presidential campaign. Longtime associates of soon-to-be-president Bill Clinton were referred to as FOBs (Friends of Bill) by Democratic party officials who were newcomers to his campaign after he received his party's nomination. Apparently, this designation was originally meant to be disparaging of Clinton's old associates, but they soon began to use the term to refer to themselves! Why? It was a way of referencing their history with the president and marking their relationship as special, distinguishing it qualitatively from the relationships of newcomers.

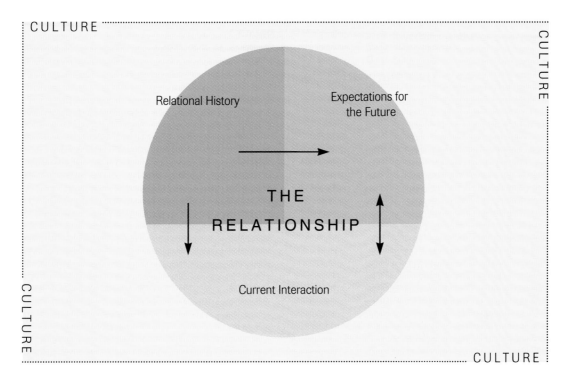

FIGURE 1.9
Each partner's understanding of the relational history and expectations for the future influence that partner's communicative behavior in the current conversation. The way these individual behaviors fit together, in turn, shapes the relationship.

Expectations for the Future

Expectations for the future include long-term goals, both individual and relational. Expectations seem to be more closely tied to what you think your partner will do (or "outside forces" will cause to happen) than they are to what you plan for the relationship. You may want a relationship to continue (a goal), but at the same time, you may think that it won't (expectation). Again, as in the case of relational history, your understanding of the current conversation is influenced by these expectations. If you plan to marry your partner, you are likely to behave very differently in a conflict than you would if you expected to break up in the near future. Sometimes

Communicative Competence

This questionnaire is used by researchers to assess a person's communicative competence. The questionnaire can be used to assess your perceptions of a partner's competence or to assess your self-perceptions. Self- and partners' perceptions do not always match. Complete the scale twice—once for a partner you think is a competent or skilled communicator and once for a partner you think is not particularly competent or skilled. Be sure to keep the relationship type consistent (for example, evaluate a competent and an incompetent friend or boss or classmate) so that comparison of the evaluations will be consistent. If you'd like a real challenge, complete the scale a third time to assess your self-perceptions, replacing "My partner" with "I" and making other necessary changes.

Scoring: Indicate how you evaluate your partners (and yourself) on each statement using the following scale: 5 = strongly agree; 4 = agree; 3 = neutral or undecided; 2 = disagree; and 1 = strongly disagree.

Competent Partner	Incompetent Partner	Self	
			1. My partner finds it easy to get along with others.
			2. My partner can adapt to changing situations.
			3. My partner treats people as individuals.
			4. My partner interrupts me too much.
			5. My partner is rewarding to talk to.
			6. My partner can deal with others effectively.
			7. My partner is a good listener.

Competent Partner	Incompetent Partner	Self	
			8. My partner's personal relationships are cold and distant.
			9. My partner is easy to talk to.
			10. My partner won't argue with someone just to prove he or she is right.
			11. My partner's conversation behavior is not "smooth."
			12. My partner ignores other people's feelings.
			13. My partner generally knows how others feel.
			14. My partner lets others know he or she understands them.
			15. My partner understands other people.
			16. My partner is relaxed and comfortable when speaking.
			17. My partner listens to what people say to him or her.
			18. My partner likes to be "close and personal" with people.

continued on next page

Competent Partner	Incompetent Partner	Self	
			19. My partner generally knows what type of behavior is appropriate in any given situation.
			20. My partner usually does not make unusual demands on his or her friends.
			21. My partner is an effective conversationalist.
			22. My partner is supportive of others.
			23. My partner does not mind meeting strangers.
			24. My partner can easily put himself or herself in another person's shoes.
			25. My partner pays attention to the conversation.
			26. My partner is generally relaxed when conversing with a new acquaintance.
			27. My partner is interested in what I have to say.
			28. My partner doesn't follow the conversation very well.
			29. My partner enjoys social gatherings where he or she can meet new people.

Competent Partner	Incompetent Partner	Self	
			30. My partner is a likable person.
			31. My partner is flexible.
			32. My partner is not afraid to speak with people in authority.
			33. People can go to my partner with their problems.
			34. My partner generally says the right thing at the right time.
			35. My partner likes to use his or her voice and body expressively.
			36. My partner is sensitive to others' needs of the moment.

Add up your scores on items 1–3, 5–7, 9–10, 13–27, and 29–36. Now reverse the scoring on items 4, 8, 11, 12, and 28 (5 = 1, 4 = 2, 2 = 4, 1 = 5). Finally, add these scores to the sum you calculated from the previous items.

Now that you've completed the ratings, think about how you feel about each of these partners. What sort of specific messages do they characteristically send to you that lead to your overall evaluation? How do you respond to each of them? How do you think each of them would evaluate you? How competent a *relationship* do you think you have with each of them?

Source: Adapted from J. M. Wiemann (1977), Explication and test of a model of communicative competence, *Human Communication Research*, 3, 195–213.

these expectations can become self-fulfilling. Denise would like to stay with her boyfriend, Ramón, but she expects him to break up their relationship, so she communicates in a way that distances her from him. He interprets Denise's communication (correctly, as it turns out) as pushing him away, and he decides to leave. Her expectations are fulfilled, but her goal is not achieved.

The Reflexivity of the Process

Relationships are reflexive processes. We think about them; we talk about them; we evaluate our own and our partner's behavior. It is important that we can and frequently do make adjustments in our behavior to accommodate our partner or the situation. As previously mentioned, we can adjust our goals in an attempt to align them with our partner's goals (or try to get our partner to pay attention to our goals) if we want the relationship to continue. This sort of responsiveness to our partner is an important characteristic of competent communication. It is also the point of studying communication.

The Complexity of the Process

The complexity of the communication process is staggering. Yet, you manage to communicate more or less successfully, day in and day out. Your experience with different types of communication situations helps you to decide how to communicate when you enter a novel one. That is, you generalize from one experience to another. For example, you learned how to respond to people with relatively high status and power early in life during your interactions with your parents and other family members. Your ability to generalize this knowledge to your interactions with teachers made your transition to school easier than it might have been. During your first few years of school, you might have seen each new teacher or class situation as somewhat problematic ("How should I act in *second* grade?"). By now, you "know" various strategies for communicating with your teachers, even though each one presents you with a new style, a new set of expectations, and other changes.

We can use the way you learned to simplify the complex communication challenges with which you were faced to help you understand a variety of communication episodes and a variety of audiences. Basic communication principles apply across the spectrum of situations and people. The model of communicative competence directs your attention to aspects of the process that are important and that operate in similar ways cross-situationally. You don't have to learn an entirely new set of concepts and skills when you move from one type of episode or audience to another (e.g., from job interview to group leader). The basic concepts and functions that are relevant at the dyadic level are equally relevant as the audience grows larger.

Three important dimensions along which communication episodes vary are (1) informal to formal, (2) small audiences to large audiences, and (3) familiar (known) situations to unfamiliar (unknown) situations. Because changes along these dimensions are systematic and make predictable demands on your communication abilities, we use them in this book to ease you along in your study of communication.

You spend most of your time in informal, familiar situations with small audiences. In Part 1, we start with these types of situations and examine how competent communication relationships are developed and maintained in them. As situations become more formal, your communication options become more restricted—for example, in interviews and work groups.

Depending on your skills and experience and the importance of the interaction, you may need to devote more planning to prepare for larger audiences simply because it is more difficult to monitor and adapt to larger audiences than it is to one or a few partners. As a result, specific skills, together with practice using them, become important, although the development of "special" skills and practice is not unique to large audiences. Our point here is that over time people accumulate a good deal of experience rehearsing what they're going to say for particular audiences. For example, the first time a teenager calls someone to ask for a date, generally he or she will carefully plan and rehearse the call. After making several of these calls, rehearsal isn't necessary—until the teenager meets someone he or she thinks is really special, when saying just the right thing might become especially important again. In fact, people encounter the need to rehearse at various points in their social and work lives. The way you introduce yourself to a new employer is probably well thought out. If you are your new employer's first employee, he or she may also have done some rehearsing. Everybody likes to make a good first impression.

The same learning process occurs when one moves to new situations with different kinds and sizes of audiences. It is useful to remember that the same communication principles and processes that apply to informal, familiar situations apply across the board. In this book we begin with the familiar and move to the unfamiliar; as we do, formality increases and usually so does the size of the audience.

Our approach, the communicative competence approach, will help you synthesize what you learn about one kind of episode and apply it to less familiar ones.

REVIEW

The goal of this text is to help you improve your understanding of your everyday communication experiences, your communication skills, and your effectiveness in relationships through the systematic study of communication processes.

In this chapter we discussed the characteristics of communication and the functions communication serves, especially control distribution, level of expressed affiliation, and orientation to goals and tasks. We then presented a model of communicative competence that relates individual communicators to functional relational concepts. From the perspective presented here, communication must be analyzed in the context of specific relationships, whether they be interpersonal or public or mediated. The concepts developed in this chapter set the stage for the analyses of specific skills that are presented in the following chapters.

The conception of communication-in-relationships is central to our approach because the relational context of an interaction forms the basis for understanding the meaning of any message. Thus studying only the individual's behaviors, removed from the relational context, fails to provide an accurate understanding of communication. This is the case whether the relationship is that of two people, several people in a group, a person (leader) and a group, or a speaker and a large audience. (The audience may be present in the same place as the speaker, or the communication may be mediated by some technology.)

The relationship is the product of the communication of the people in the relationship. This is why the communication behavior of relationship participants toward each other is our unit of analysis. That is, the "fit" of one partner's behavior to the other's (or others') as well as the "fit" of their goals, expectations, styles, and the like are important for successful communication relationships. The better the fit, the more competent the relationship. The more competencies you develop, the better able you will be to create a good fit with your relational partners.

SUGGESTED READINGS

Coupland, N., Giles, H., & Wiemann, J. M. (Eds.). (1991). *"Miscommunication" and problematic talk.* Newbury Park, CA: Sage.

Grove, T. G. (1991). *Dyadic interaction.* Dubuque, IA: Brown.

Hecht, M., Collier, M. J., & Ribean, S. A. (1993). *African American communication.* Thousand Oaks, CA: Sage.

Knapp, M. L., & Vangelisti, A. L. (1992). *Interpersonal communication and human relationships* (2nd ed.). Boston: Allyn & Bacon.

Wiemann, J. M. (1977). Explication and test of a model of communicative competence. *Human Communication Research, 3,* 195–213.

Wiemann, J. M., & Giles, H. (1988). Interpersonal communication. In M. Hewstone, W. Stroebe, G. Stephenson, & J. Codol (Eds.), *Introduction to social psychology: A European perspective* (pp. 199–221). Oxford: Basil Blackwell.

Williams, F. (1992). *The new communications* (3rd ed.). Belmont, CA: Wadsworth.

2

Processing
Communication

Objectives

After reading this chapter you should be able to

1. Recognize how different factors affect your ability to process communication.

2. Recognize how memory affects communication and be able to improve your short- and long-term memory.

3. Describe the importance of attributions and the influence they have on communication processing.

4. Evaluate your reasons for using certain communication channels.

5. Recognize the importance of cultural diversity as a factor in communication.

CHAPTER CONTENTS

THINK BACK TO WHEN you first decided to enroll in this or any other communication class. What were you anticipating? What subject areas did you think the course and text content would address? You may have assumed that the course would examine how to improve your oral and written communication and how and why others communicate in particular ways in certain situations. You might even have anticipated that the material would address the topic of how you come to understand others. This chapter focuses on how you come to understand others by looking specifically at the ways you process the communication you receive.

Your ability to process communication goes way beyond seeing, hearing, or reading information. Actually, that is just the beginning of the process. **Communication processing** is the means by which you gather, organize, and make judgments about the information you receive. A number of questions surround communication processing, including: What information do you see, hear, or in any way receive, and why does other information get filtered out or forgotten? How do you assign meaning to the information you receive? How much information can you process? What affects your processing abilities?

In this chapter, we address these questions, and others, by focusing on the factors that most directly affect your ability to process communication: *perception, expectations, attributions, memory, cognitive complexity, cognitive load, channel capacity, culture,* and *goals.* Taken together, these elements of communication processing act much like a computer does in monitoring, coordinating, and directing the operation of an automobile engine. If every part of the computer operates according to factory specifications, a car's engine should run smoothly, provided that the parts of the engine are in working order. But if one part of the computer breaks down, the entire engine is put in jeopardy. Similarly, if one of your communication processing elements or factors breaks down, you will have little chance for competent communication.

COMMUNICATION PROCESSING
The means by which one gathers, organizes, and evaluates received information.

Perception

Have you ever met someone for the first time and immediately thought that you did or did not like that person? Your perception of others can create very strong feelings that develop with amazing speed. Whenever you engage in a conversation, whether it is with a longtime friend or a recent acquaintance, you will encounter numerous, specific bits of information that may influence your perception. For instance, in a leisurely walk across campus, you will likely come across at least one person to whom you say hello. Even in the briefest encounter you will receive input, including the exact words of the message, the person's tone of voice, the facial expression, and the presence or lack of eye contact. When considering the amount of information you receive in even a brief interaction, you might question how it is possible to make accurate perceptions. If you think of perception as the process of making sense of your world, you can understand the importance of perception for communication competence.

Schema Theory

Your ability to make sense out of the endless variety of inputs you receive when forming perceptions of people or events can be explained by schema theory. Cohen explains that **schemata** (plural of *schema*) are mental structures that put together individual but related bits of information.[1] These chunks of information then work together to create meaning and understanding at a more complex level. In essence, you develop a schema that helps you understand how things work or anticipate how they should proceed. As you go through life, you develop a multitude of different schemata. You continually discover new bits of information that combine with related information to help you structure and understand different situations.

SCHEMATA
Mental structures that assemble chunks of remembered information, which in turn work together to create meaning and understanding.

For example, assume that during the leisurely walk across campus, you come across an acquaintance from class. You have a schema that explains to you how you should handle a brief conversation with a classroom acquaintance. When your classmate approaches and says, "Hi, how's it going?" you will recognize this as part of the chunk of information that tells you that you will both exchange hellos and then, after a brief discussion of mostly nonpersonal concerns, go your separate ways. This schema, along with the multitude of other schemata you possess, assists your perception process. When you recognize one component of the schema, the entire schema is activated and you know what should follow.

Researchers Taylor and Crocker have provided more insight into the impact of schemata on your perception process.[2] They show that you develop schemata for people, roles, and events. *People schemata* allow you to recognize a few signs to make a general assumption about an individual. You pick up a few personal characteristics or notice a few specific actions of a person, and you use those bits of information to make a more general overall conclusion about his or her personality. For example, suppose that you enter a classroom on the first day of school and observe a young woman with braided black hair wearing a brightly colored outfit. She is adorned in 24-karat-gold jewelry, and she is sitting in the center of the classroom. In the middle of her forehead is a red dot. You may assume that your new classmate is from India because you have a schema that describes the brightly colored attire as an Indian sari. The dot (*bottu*) on her forehead, along with her attire and appearance, forms your schema, although you can't be sure that identifies her as Indian.

Role schemata allow you to develop a perception based on another's role in a group, position in a hierarchy, or occupation. If you have a job, you probably have some expectations about your boss's behavior. These expectations come from your role schemata for an "employer." Furthermore, you have schemata that define for you how a mother, father, leader, and follower should act. When someone is presented to you as a leader, for instance, you will have some expectations about how that person should behave and what that person should do. To the extent that the leader's actions and communication conform to your schemata, you believe that person is fulfilling a leadership role.

Event schemata allow you to expect that a particular event or occurrence will proceed in a particular way. For example, a job interview will consist of a few predictable events such as questions about your background, qualifications, and interest in the position. Before you go into the interview, you are able to envision what is likely to happen because of the schemata. Once in the interview, as soon as the interviewer starts to ask questions, your schema is brought to focus and you understand the interviewing process. Imagine the confusion that would arise if you went into an interview and the interviewer ignored you. Such behavior would not fit into your schema, and you might question your existing schema.

Your use of schemata plays an important role in the perception cycle. Neisser explains that perception involves a constructive process that allows you to anticipate and more readily receive information.[3] The **perception cycle** is a continual process of receiving information, enacting a schema, and exploring for more information based on the schema. The cycle is initiated when an object or other form of information is observed. Based on that information, a particular schema will be enacted to interpret the object and begin anticipation of what will happen next. With the schema directing the perception, the person will then explore for the new anticipated information. The new information will in turn refine and modify the original schema, and the perception cycle will continue. Let's look at this process in a little more detail. Figure 2.1 demonstrates how the schema process works.

The process of enacting an existing schema could occur at any time with a stimulus entering your awareness. *Stimulus* in this case refers to anything that your senses pick up from your world. It could simply be an idea that you have. Your perceptual system will take the stimulus and match it with an existing schema that best fits the information. In many cases, the existing schema will *explore* the environment (your world) for support and confirmation. If you discover this type of information, or what is called *pro-*

PERCEPTION CYCLE
A continual process of receiving information, enacting a schema, and exploring for more information based on the schema.

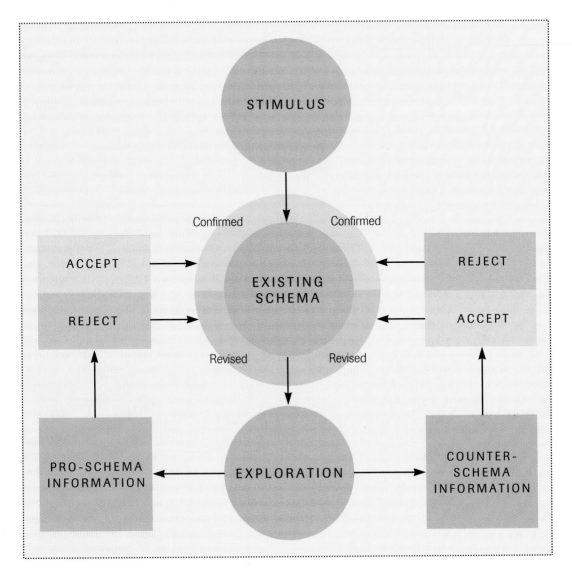

FIGURE 2.1
The schema process.

schema information, you will usually make one of two decisions. You can either accept the supporting information and confirm your existing schema or reject this pro-schema information and question whether your schema is actually valid. Why would you question and reject pro-schema information? There are lots of reasons, but the most obvious one is that you do not believe the pro-schema information as it is presented to you.

You will also encounter information from your exploration attempts that do not support your existing schema, or what is referred to as *counter-schema information*. Again, you can make one of two decisions. You can accept the counter-schema information, causing you to revise your existing schema, or you can reject this information, leaving your schema intact. In many cases, when you receive counter-schema messages (those that contradict your schema), you tend to reject them in favor of pro-schema messages. Receiving counter-schema messages forces criticism of the existing schema, and research has shown that people will cling strongly to existing beliefs even in the face of strong evidence to the contrary.[4] If pro-schema messages are available, you generally find it much easier to attend to those messages and discount the others.

Consider the following example as an illustration of the schema process. Assume that you notice that a close friend of yours, Naomi, is acting very distant, cold, and noncommunicative (stimulus). You enact an existing schema that best fits this stimulus. You have seen Naomi act this way before, and you assume that her behavior is a result of her volatile relationship with her father (existing schema). You decide to ask her some questions (explore) to confirm your schema, and she tells you that in fact she just had a fight with her father (pro-schema information). Just as you are about to accept this information and confirm your existing schema about Naomi, her father, and her moodiness, you remember that Naomi's father has been away on a business trip and has not called home for two weeks, which means that she couldn't have just had a fight with him (counter-schema information). You suspect that Naomi is lying to you, and yet you have to reject this counter-schema information because it makes you question your existing schema.

As you explore for more information to confirm or rebuild your schema that Naomi's moodiness results from her relationship with her father, you talk to a mutual friend and learn that Naomi has been diagnosed with diabetes (counter-schema information). At first, you reject this information so that it confirms your original schema, but when you confront Naomi about the diagnosis, she admits she is depressed and embarrassed about her medical condition. You can now accept the counter-schema information (diabetes vs. father) and revise your old schema that Naomi can *also* act cold and distant because of her feelings about her diabetes.

The schema/perceptual process is a critical part of communication competency. In order to send and receive messages that are effective and appropriate, you must be able to process information in a way that makes sense to you and at the same time reassures you that your assumptions are correct. Competent communicators possess strong, highly developed, and accurate schemata that facilitate their communication with other people. Competence requires that we search for, objectively evaluate, and learn from information.

Changing a Schema

How many of your existing schemata could hamper your perceptual accuracy? Are you willing to accept new information that could strengthen your schemata? When was the last time one of your schemata was significantly altered? In writing, describe a recent situation that made you stop and wonder how you could have been so wrong in your understanding of another person. You may want to select a situation that involved a first date, an interaction with a person from a culture different from your own, or a conversation with a professor outside the classroom. In your description, detail how your existing schema may have caused selective perception such that you were unable to process communication from that person.

Mindlessness

The process of focusing one's mind on the task at hand is referred to as **mindfulness**. The use of schemata may make you a less critical processor of information by producing a state of **mindlessness**. When a schema is enacted, you might automatically process its content instead of doing an in-depth analysis of the available information. Mindless processing of information might even cause you to ignore some of what you see or hear and to attend only to information previously stored in the schema.

Roloff describes three signs of mindlessness: reduced cognitive activity, inaccurate recall, and uncritical evaluation. First, mindlessness will result in *reduced cognitive activity* (less critical thinking) when the schema takes effect. In essence, when mindless processing occurs, you will simply have fewer thoughts. A second sign of mindlessness is *inaccurate recall* of information. When asked about the situation in question, uncritical processors will recall fewer specifics than their mindful counterparts. The third sign is the *uncritical evaluation* of what is processed. The mindless processor will not question the information that is being received and will passively react to the situation.[5] In the previous example, you might have just dismissed Naomi's behavior as moodiness and missed an opportunity to be a competent communicator and good friend.

Consider another example. You might observe someone giving signs of being shy (avoiding eye contact, not attempting to talk with others), and you might assume that this person is an introvert. The shallow processor of

MINDFULNESS
The process of focusing one's mind on the task at hand.

MINDLESSNESS
The process of performing behaviors or actions without being conscious of what one is doing.

How Mindful Is Your Mind?

How often do you find yourself daydreaming while someone is talking to you? Have you ever walked across campus or driven from one town to the next and afterward had no memory of the event? Do you find yourself unable to recall specific details of a circumstance that should stand out vividly in your mind? Have you ever agreed to something that you later regretted because you were mindless when making the commitment? Answering "yes" to these questions demonstrates that mindlessness can affect your communication processing and your ability to act competently.

this information might not question why that person is avoiding eye contact. There would probably not be any thought as to whether those cues might be evidence of something other than being an introvert, such as that person's being angry or embarrassed. The mindless observer would react only to the few cues received and not consider the situation further.

Selective Perception

The perception cycle is not a neutral, unbiased process. If a group of five people watched a televised debate between two candidates, they would likely have five different interpretations of what took place and what was important. Based on their existing schemata, one person might focus on the issue of budget deficits, another might be most concerned with foreign affairs, while a third might be intrigued only with the candidate's physical appearance. This biased nature of perception is referred to as **selective perception.**

SELECTIVE PERCEPTION
Biased or filtered processing of information based on strongly held attitudes, timing, or other phenomena.

You can easily identify selective perception at work in everyday life. Simply gather a few people who have watched a late-night talk show. Ask people individually to comment on what they liked about the show, what they thought was funny, and what they thought was worthless. Write down each person's response and then share with them your results. You will likely have a few different accounts of what the speaker really said during the interview or conversation.

Selective perception can be explained by the presence or absence of schemata. If the schema for a particular input is present in the receiver, he or she is more likely to attend to that information than is someone who does not possess the schema. Someone who does not have an understanding of or interest in economic matters may not attend to something the speaker said about balancing the budget or reducing the foreign trade deficit.

Selective perception can also occur when a person has the schemata to understand two competing messages but attends to one instead of the other. In these cases it is possible that the person's mind will filter the competing messages, or inputs, and attend to a particular one because it is expressed in a preferred style of language or has some preferred physical feature. Furthermore, once the mind has focused attention on a particular input, the amount of attention that can be devoted to a secondary message will be limited.

For example, during the Persian Gulf crisis in 1990–91, then-President George Bush addressed the nation concerning the situation in the Persian Gulf and the domestic economy. Many people have schemata to comprehend both of those issues. At the time, however, many listeners did not attend to the president's discussion of the economy because the Persian Gulf

 REALITY CHECK

Focus on Ethics

Selective perception can be deliberate. This sometimes translates into communicators' using their selective perception in ways that are less than innocent. You can see the ethical implications of selective perception at work in many professions. Journalists who work for liberal or conservative newspapers or television stations may focus their perceptual attention on those statements and actions by political candidates that best suit the needs of their story or the political convictions of their employer. Arts and entertainment reviewers almost always have biases about certain acting, directing, or production styles and techniques. When they see theatrical productions that violate their preferences, they may selectively perceive and then report aspects of the performance that conform to their preconceived attitudes. Are these journalists and entertainment reviewers ethical in their selective perceptions? What if you are expected to attend a speech given by someone you do not like? If you focus your perception on those aspects of the speech that will strengthen your case against this person and choose to ignore information that would weaken arguments you could make later, are you being an ethical communication processor? How often are you faced with situations in which your selective perception may be unethical?

situation was their primary focus. In addition, the president's remarks on the Gulf War utilized language and a vocal style that were more dramatic and attention grabbing than his coverage of the economy.

Improvement of Perception

A few guidelines can help you improve your perception abilities, leading to greater communication competency. First, you should always try to verify your perceptions. If you should notice a classmate sitting near the back of the room who is looking from side to side during a test, your initial perception might be that this person is cheating. However, further observation may reveal that the person is simply rubbing the back of his or her neck or stretching the shoulders back, indicating merely an effort to work out a stiff neck. Sometimes verification of a perception may involve gathering information beyond your own observations.

Second, you should resist your natural tendency to fall back on the most obvious influence or explanation for what you observe. For example, occasionally scuffles break out among players in college and professional basketball games. Your tendency is to assume that the person who shoved first, or who threw the first punch, initiated the incident. Frequently, however, a scuffle starts when someone else says or does something that the fans do not easily perceive. In these situations, you need to ask yourself whether some information or action might have preceded what you observed. You also need to question whether you may be unaware of the reason that someone did or said something. Adopting this approach to verifying perceptions is difficult at first, for it is much easier to make immediate perceptions and not worry about the work it takes to check their validity.

A third way to improve the accuracy of perceptions is to resist the tendency to rely completely on your very first impressions. Often these perceptions can lead to inaccurate conclusions. Consider this example: Todd has a tendency to stutter and to slur his words when excited. When people initially meet Todd, they assume he has a learning disability, so they talk slowly and loudly to him. Todd actually has a speech impediment, but he is of average intelligence and is not hearing impaired. Whenever possible, it is wise to delay reaction or judgment on a matter until further perceptions are made.

By now you will have concluded that the perception process is somewhat complicated. Schemata are constantly being evaluated for their accuracy. As a competent communicator, you have to remain on the lookout for information that ensures that you are perceiving people, events, issues, and information accurately. Selective perception and mindlessness are only two

Perceptual Matters

Answer the following questions as they pertain to your perceptual attitudes and abilities. Think about how various areas of perception could be enhanced and improved in your own communication behavior. Place an A in the blank if the statement is always true about you, an S if it is sometimes true, and an N if it is never true.

_____ Do you find yourself making snap judgments when it comes to personal issues?

_____ Are you too impatient to listen to all of the evidence before drawing conclusions?

_____ Do you have a tendency to weigh some types of information more heavily than others?

_____ Do you allow your personal biases to affect the conclusions you draw about people you do not understand?

_____ Are you more influenced by who a person is than by what he or she says?

_____ Do you have a tendency to ignore information that does not suit your preestablished opinion?

_____ Have you been told that your perceptions are different from those of others?

_____ Do you fail to verify your perceptions with other people?

_____ Do you attend to the most obvious influence or explanation you observe?

_____ Do you tend to rely completely on initial perceptions?

How well did you score? Did you have very many A's? If so, you may want to take stock and redirect your energies toward better perceptual awareness. If you scored mostly N's and S's, you rated yourself as an above-average perceiver. One class average was three A's, four S's, and three N's. How does your score compare? What score do you think a competent communicator should have?

of the factors affecting perceptual accuracy. In the next section, you will discover how your expectations affect your competence.

Expectations

Rarely, if ever, do you enter a communication situation with no thoughts or feelings as to what will or should happen. You will generally have an intuitive thought or conscious desire in regard to your upcoming encounter. You might even have a strategic purpose or goal such as a desire to change another's mind or to gain compliance with a request. Frequently, these thoughts or desires are expressed as **expectations**, and each can affect how the communication will take place. Therefore, you need to be aware of why you develop expectations and the effect they can have on how you process communication.

Social psychologists Hilton and Darley explain that when you enter a situation with an expectation of how the encounter should progress or what the outcome should be, that expectation can affect how you process communication.[6] These expectations can lead to self-fulfilling prophecies. Sometimes when you enter a situation with a preconceived notion about the outcome, you will attend only to the information that supports your predisposition. Think back to our discussion of schemata. Existing schemata direct your exploration for information that confirms how you think and perceive. These schemata generate expectations, and the information that is obtained is compared against what you currently believe. Most of the expectations we generate about people are based on the known social norms of the groups they belong to and their current situation. Expectations from schema can also be generated from the unique or idiosyncratic behaviors of that particular person.[7] Our schema for that person will produce expectations for our anticipated interaction with him or her.

You can, however, reasonably assume that if people anticipate future interaction, they will increase their communication processing efforts. The expectation of a future interaction places increased importance on the present encounter. Therefore, people will want to make certain that the present encounter has an outcome that is positive or in their favor. In addition, when people anticipate future interaction with others, they tend to focus more on what their partner is saying, causing better recall of the information that is exchanged.[8] When future interaction with a person is anticipated, there is a natural reaction to learn as much as possible about that person. All of these concerns will lead to more detailed communication processing.

EXPECTATION
An intuitive thought or conscious desire in regard to an upcoming encounter.

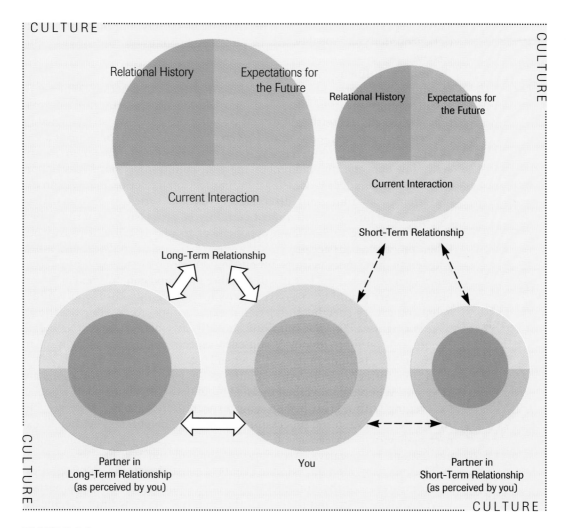

FIGURE 2.2

If you perceive a particular relationship as a short-term interaction, your processing will be different from the processing that will occur if you perceive the relationship to be long-term. A long-term relationship plays a larger role in your life, and creates stronger connections, than does a short-term relationship.

Imagine yourself on the first day of a new job. You certainly expect to have future interactions with your employer and others in the workplace, and so you think about the effort you will put into being a good employee and courteous co-worker. On the first day these concerns will make you very attentive to what is going on around you and how things are explained.

Three weeks later you may not listen quite as closely, but during that initial encounter you probably will be processing communication at peak efficiency.

Another influence of expectations comes into play when we consider the differences between processing for assessment and action. When processing communication for assessment, you are simply gathering information about a person with whom you do not expect to have an extended or important encounter, for example, when briefly talking to someone at a bus stop or when ordering lunch at a restaurant. In these situations there is generally low expectation, and processing your communication is less important and less detailed. Processing communication for action involves an expectation of an important discussion, event, or series of events with a person. Therefore, you will almost certainly be processing for action when you are preparing to debate an opponent or to play a game of basketball. When processing for action, you pay greater attention to detail and allow yourself to draw more definite conclusions. Your processing will not necessarily be more accurate, but it will be more vivid and conclusive. For example, if you are planning to ask your boss for an overdue raise, you will develop some very specific and detailed expectations about your boss (e.g., "She is a tightwad"), what you think she will say when you ask ("Oh, I wish I could get you more money"), and even aspects of the setting ("I want to make sure she is alone in her office when I ask").

A final influence from expectations occurs when those expectations are violated.[9] When the proverbial dreaded blind date turns out to be a wonderful evening with a great person, your expectations have not been met. In such a case, information processing will become heightened. Although expectation violations can result in positive or negative evaluations, most evaluations are negative. According to Burgoon and Walther, expectation "violations" are often undesirable events because they lead you to question the competence of the violator. Why would someone act in inappropriate ways that disconfirm our schema of that person? Are they immoral, inconsiderate, or just plain incompetent? With your expectations disconfirmed, you will put more effort into processing information in an attempt to reevaluate what has happened to your existing schema. If a normally supportive friend of yours criticizes you in front of others, your expectations of this friend are violated. These violations may cause you to question the loyalty of your friend and the strength of your relationship, and perhaps even to question yourself.

On the other hand, some expectation violations are viewed positively. You could be pleasantly surprised by the unusually friendly behavior of an attractive acquaintance. According to Burgoon's work, positive violations depend on how you interpret the violation in light of social norms ("Well, I guess since we're at a party, it's okay for her to act that way"), and whether you see the unusual behavior as a reward ("Boy, he sure smelled nice when he got close"). Perceiving this type of behavior as rewarding is often based on personal characteristics such as status, attractiveness, and reputation.

Attributions

When processing communication, frequently you may try to determine why someone said something or what caused that person to act in a certain way. In other words, this person's behavior does not exactly fit your existing schema. When you look for personal characteristics to explain other peoples' behavior, you are seeking **attributions**.[10] The keys to understanding why you make attributions are causality and control. On one hand, as a communicator you make attributions to understand causes of behaviors. But with understanding comes control, and the more you make causal attributions for another's behavior, the greater control of the situation you possess.

ATTRIBUTION
A generalization that uses personal characteristics to explain communication behavior.

When someone makes an unflattering comment, the person insulted will have a strong desire to ask or try to determine *why*.

EMMA   Oh, you cut your hair so short! It makes your face rounder.

NANCY   (Why did Emma have to say that?) I think it looks more professional, and I like it.

Nancy may consider Emma jealous, envious, irate, or inconsiderate. It is important to figure out why the comment was made, for people feel a certain uneasiness about not being able to explain behavior. But if the behavior can be attributed to something (e.g., the comment was made because that person is inconsiderate), then you are put at ease now that you understand the situation more fully and are in greater control.

Try to recognize how many times during a day you try to explain (understand) someone else's behavior by making attributions. You might also want to check how often you make negative and positive attributions about others. Do you tend to look for positive reasons for other people's behavior? Do you give them the benefit of the doubt, or are you more cynical?

The greatest attribution pitfall you can fall into is to overemphasize the internal and underestimate the external causes of behaviors you observe. That is, when you see someone doing something wrong, you are likely to believe that person has a character flaw, and you may be less likely to attribute that person's behavior to circumstances beyond his or her control. Attribution errors of this type can be detrimental to your communication processing effectiveness.

You can prevent future problems by paying closer attention to your own attribution tendencies. When you make an attribution about someone's behavior, that attribution can affect your future encounters with that person. For example, suppose that during the first or second day of classes you observe that a classmate seems inattentive and uninterested in the lecture. Based solely on that observation, you may conclude that he or she is unmotivated and irresponsible. The person might actually be a very good student who was feeling the effects of a 24-hour flu that day. Now suppose that during the next class period you and this student are assigned to the same group for a major course project. You will initially have concerns about this person because of your one unverified attribution. When you recognize how easily this problem could arise, you can imagine how much confusion your inaccurate attributions may cause in your social and personal relationships.

You can further improve your attribution abilities by becoming more patient. If you find yourself making an attribution about someone in one instance, wait for another opportunity to observe this person before committing yourself to a firm attribution. First impressions, unexplained actions,

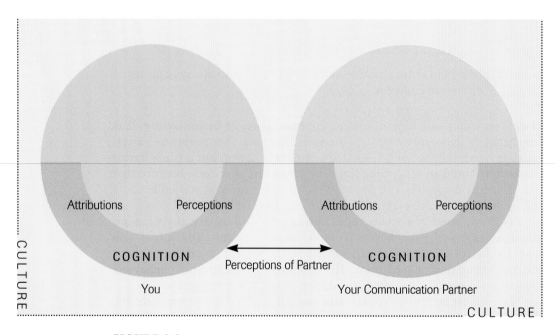

FIGURE 2.3

As the model of communicative competence demonstrates, attributions play an important role in determining your perceptions of your communication partner. They combine with your perceptions to affect your impression of your partner and your own communicative behavior. These aspects of the model in turn affect the current conversation as well as your longer-term impressions of your communication partner.

and strange behavior are not always the best evidence for making decisions about people or their communication.

Memory

Memory is a necessary component in communication processing. Competent communicators are able to retrieve schemata and utilize them to understand the present situation. However, it is the rare person who remembers past occurrences precisely as they happened. Actually, you tend to recall past occurrences in general and adapt them to fit the present situation. Your ability to adapt information from your memory, which makes it easier to understand what others say or do, will greatly enhance communication.

The Memory Process

As researcher Loftus explains, the memory process involves three stages: sensory register, short-term memory, and long-term memory.[11] Information enters your awareness through any of the senses (as when Javier tells you a very funny joke). The information is lost (forgotten) within a couple of seconds if it is not transferred to short-term memory. Short-term memory is an "immediate" memory that suspends information long enough for it to be used, or to permit repetition of the information and the association of related or similar items together. For example, without an organizing system it would be difficult to remember the names of seven people. However, it would be easier to remember their names if you thought of them in groups of males and females, by their majors, or by hair color.

You can also improve your short-term memory when you pay attention to the way a message is organized. Trying to remember a speech in which someone explains a brief history of the United States could be impossible if you concentrated only on dates. Remembering its content could be made easier, however, if you allowed the natural chronological organization of the events to guide your processing of the information. Here's an example of a U.S. history review: The 13 original British colonies declared their independence from England and started the Revolutionary War in 1776. President Lincoln issued the Emancipation Proclamation in 1863 in order to free all slaves in the territories. Women's suffrage, the right of women to vote in governmental elections, was enacted in 1920. Prohibition by federal law of the manufacture, transportation, and sale of alcoholic beverages was lifted in 1933. By finding or creating an organizational scheme or plan for remembering information that you hear, you enhance your ability to process communication.

Improvement of Long-Term Memory

Long-term memory can be improved with the use of imagery and information storage. Imagery aids memory because it allows you to associate a mental image with the information. Suppose you need to remember that your instructor has explained that during initial encounters between strangers, people will generally speak in short sentences, maintain appropriate distances, and not disclose personal information. Instead of trying to remember only these three elements, you should picture yourself in the situation your professor has discussed. Thus, imagine yourself in a familiar place, meeting an unfamiliar person. Think about what might be said and how you would appear to a third person watching the interaction.

You can also improve your long-term memory through various information storage techniques. Perhaps the most frequently used of these techniques involves associating each letter of a word with a word in a sentence. For instance, many people remember how to spell the word "arithmetic" by recalling the sentence "A rat in the house may eat the ice cream"; or learn the treble clef lines on a musical staff (EGBDF) as "Every Good Boy Does Fine" and the spaces between the lines (notes F-A-C-E) as "FACE." You can also remember information by placing bits of information into categories or related clusters and by associating the information with other things. This technique may help if you have trouble remembering people's names. When you meet someone, you can associate the person with the place where you met or the new person's job or major. Upon meeting the person a second time, you will have a greater context of information to help recall his or her name.

The ancient Greeks employed a memory system that can still be used today. The system of *loci* ("places") works by associating parts of what you are remembering with parts of something that is very familiar to you. You can remember a speech you have to give by associating your main points with different parts of your dorm room, apartment, or home. You can, for example, associate the introduction of your speech with walking through your front door and then proceed to associate different points of the speech with different parts of your home as you would come across them. In this way, when you give your speech, you can remember the content by visualizing yourself walking through your home. This concept shows why using analogies is an effective communication skill.

Finally, you can improve your memory by simply exaggerating the qualities of whatever it is you are trying not to forget. For example, if you have to remember to buy cheese, spaghetti, and a loaf of bread at the store, you can create a memorable little story by giving these items qualities of movement. Picture yourself making a bow and arrow out of spaghetti and then shooting a wedge of cheese through a loaf of bread which breaks into several pieces. This is a silly story, and no doubt you can come up with an even more outlandish scenario. However, the fact that it is exaggerated (funny or vivid) will make it memorable. You can visualize the story of the bow and arrow and easily remember to buy the spaghetti, cheese, and bread.

Cognitive Complexity

Cognitive complexity is crucial to your ability to process communication. As you grow and learn, you develop personal constructs. **Constructs** are mental structures that give you the ability to make judgments such as good-bad, honest-dishonest, dominant-submissive. You develop and organize these constructs to assist in interpreting and understanding situations you encounter.

Cognitive complexity refers to the amount of differentiation a person can make in a given construct. Someone with a low level of cognitive complexity might refer to an argument as either good or bad. A person with a higher level of cognitive complexity would recognize that the argument may not be totally good or bad but somewhere in between and would be able to explain the issues involved. The various colors that are used in merchandising schemes can serve as an analogy. Years ago, lipstick was available only in basic colors: red, pink, and orange. Now, you can buy lipstick in dozens of colors, including many differing shades of red, pink, orange, violet, and bronze. The differentiation of color has become more complex to meet the consumer's desire for greater variety and choice in merchandise colors.

The level of cognitive complexity is different on given issues. One person might have a low level of cognitive complexity for understanding the rules and norms of interpersonal interaction. The same person, however, might be able to discuss at length the various and different components of personal computers. As you develop more constructs, you will become more cognitively complex.

Integrative capacity is an aspect of cognitive complexity that refers to the ability to make connections between different concepts. The concern is not only with determining how good or bad something is but with how good or bad it is in comparison to a related issue or concept. For example, if you grow a healthy rose, you might look at it and conclude that on the attractiveness scale, your flower is quite beautiful. In this way, you have displayed some cognitive complexity regarding the rose. If you are also able to demonstrate how attractive the rose is compared to other similar roses or,

CONSTRUCTS
Mental structures that enable a person to make differentiations in judgments.

COGNITIVE COMPLEXITY
The degree to which one can perceive information in more complicated and intricate ways.

INTEGRATIVE CAPACITY
The ability to make connections between different concepts; an aspect of cognitive complexity.

better yet, to a different type of flower, then you have demonstrated integrative capacity.

Schroder, Driver, and Steufert, in their book *Human Information Processing: Individuals and Groups Functioning in Complex Social Situations*, provide characteristics of low, moderate, and high integrative capacity.[12] They state that low integrative capacity is characterized by

- Categorical, black-and-white thinking
- Minimization of conflict
- Placement of behavior in external conditions
- Abrupt shifts in categorizations

When operating at the first level, you would see only a particular rose that was either very attractive or very ugly. You would not be concerned with determining how beautiful the flower was and you would not really be aware of the specifics of what makes for a flawed or flawless rose. Also, if someone told you that the rose was flawed, you might change your mind dramatically from thinking you had a beautiful flower to thinking the flower was terrible.

Schroder, Driver, and Steufert also observe that moderate integrative capacity is characterized by

- More flexible thinking
- Suggestion of reasons or causes for conditions
- Ambivalence and lack of consistency in decision making
- "Pushing against" present or alternative schemata

At the moderate level of integrative capacity, you will stop seeing the rose as beautiful or ugly and will start to make distinctions between the two extremes. You will also be able to explain why the rose is at a certain level of attractiveness. For example, you might indicate that the color is too light or the flower is too small, and these imperfections cause you to see the rose as being less attractive. You probably will also take more time in determining the rose's level of attractiveness. The moderate level of complexity would allow some questioning of your existing schema about roses.

Finally, the high level of integrative capacity is characterized by

- Greater openmindedness
- The simultaneous perception of the situation from two points of view
- Greater use of internal thinking processes in generating possibilities

At this level, you can now make your own distinctions about the beauty of a rose without having to rely on general rules or principles for what makes a beautiful flower. You can also view the rose from the perspective of both an expert and a novice. This means that you would be able to look at the rose, evaluate it on the basis of its attractiveness, and then explain your decision in an understandable way to someone who knows nothing about flowers.

The level of cognitive complexity therefore plays an important role in communication processing. You can increase your ability to use information from your environment if you make broader, more detailed, and more objective assessments produced by cognitive complexity. In this way, your schema will be richer, and your attribution processes can be based on better and more meaningful information.

How can you increase your cognitive complexity? Work on making more detailed and multidimensional judgments about people and issues. In other words, develop a schema about the person that includes many of his or her attributes (friendly, intelligent, silly, quick-tempered, and loyal). To get you started, the next time you get into an argument with someone or find yourself questioning the person's character, ask yourself the following questions:

- Is this how I always think of this person? Am I in a rut?
- Is there any other possible explanation for this person's behavior?
- What are three possible reasons for my feelings?
- What is this person thinking about me at this moment?
- Am I jumping to conclusions for some reason (selfishness, jealousy)?
- How would this person feel about the way I am thinking?

Coming up with answers to these questions will help you broaden your perspective and develop a more differentiated construct of the other person. You will be able to make attributions in a more competent way.

Cognitive Load

In addition to cognitive complexity and integrative capacity, cognitive (or information) load can also affect your ability to process communication. **Cognitive load** refers to the amount of information an individual is asked to process at one time. According to communication researchers Farace, Monge, and Russell, "Load is based on the rate and complexity of the communication inputs to an individual."[13] Since individuals have different levels of cognitive complexity, they also differ in the amount of information they can handle simultaneously. When you are faced with an excess of information, the accuracy of your processing will decrease. Cognitive load is generally affected by environment, the individual's processing capacity, and the desire for information. If you are not really interested in a wildlife video being shown in your science course, and more interesting things are going

COGNITIVE LOAD
The amount of information a person has to process at one time.

on around you, you will probably not be able to absorb much of the information that appears on the monitor. A member of the ecology club who has no surrounding distractions and has equal processing capacity will probably be able to attend to more of the details on the video.

CORRESPONDENCE
BIAS
The belief, excluding other possible factors, that another individual is the sole cause of an action or actions.

Correspondence bias represents one general error people tend to make when experiencing cognitive overload. **Correspondence bias** occurs when a person believes that one or a variety of actions were caused solely by another individual and disregards the possibility that other factors in the situation caused them. When you reach cognitive overload, you naturally tend to attribute too many things to a single individual or group. For example, in any given workplace a subordinate may become swamped with a variety of tasks and decisions. When cognitive overload is reached, the subordinate may tend to blame the manager for the workload. In so doing, the subordinate might overlook other factors such as an increase in the amount of work coming into the organization, an unorganized work system, or the inefficiency of other co-workers. The level of cognitive complexity at this point is probably pretty low.

Even when you are able to manage the information load that is presented to you, you may still tend to remember the first and last things you observe. Research into the *primacy-recency* phenomenon reveals that when you enter a situation and begin processing communication, you will pay closer attention to the initial inputs you receive because your attention will be primed as you enter a new situation. You are also likely to remember the last thing you see or are told. Therefore, whatever communication occurs in the middle of an overload encounter is the most likely to be forgotten.

Political speech writers take advantage of this tendency. Whenever a candidate has to talk about something that is going to be less popular than other issues, you can bet the writer will bury it in the middle of the speech.

SELF-CHECK

How Heavy Is Your Cognitive Load?

Take a sheet of paper or a notepad and your telephone into the room where your television is located. Call up a friend or relative while you are watching a favorite television program. If possible, get your roommate or a family member to engage you in conversation as you talk to your phone partner. As you watch television, talk on the phone, and converse, note what gets your attention the most. What do you remember the most about your cognitive ordeal? How did the person on the phone feel about your exercise?

Whenever possible, candidates will try to start and end with popular comments or issues in the hopes that the necessary but unwelcome information in the middle of the speech will be forgotten.

When you feel you are experiencing communication overload, it is time to stop and reassess the situation. It is better to take the time to plan your strategy than to become overwhelmed with information. Prioritize your communication needs and concentrate on the people and communication that are most critical to achieve your goals.

Channels

How do you send and receive communication? Your initial answer to this question is probably "I talk and I listen." After a few more seconds you might add, "Oh, I also write and read written communication." You are beginning to identify communication channels. **Channels** are simply the vehicles or mechanisms that transmit a message from sender to receiver. The channels that come to mind first would include sound waves (oral communication) and light waves (nonverbal communication). However, you could quickly compile a list of many other frequently used communication channels. Consider, for example, the possible channels used for written communication (memos, letters), electronic communication (radio, television), and computer-transmitted communication (BITnet, Ethernet).

CHANNEL
A vehicle or mechanism that transmits a message from sender to receiver.

A variety of communication channels are capable of relaying messages, but quite often not all the choices are available to you or those that are available may not be practical. For example, large stockbrokerage companies will sometimes attempt to attract new clients by offering a satellite or teleconferencing session. During these sessions, the potential clients will assemble in several locations to hear from a financial expert who is somewhere else in the country. The stockbrokers and their prospective clients might have preferred a face-to-face meeting with the expert, but, for financial and other reasons, they are limited to using satellite signals or phone wires as a communication channel.

Part of your effort in processing communication will involve making decisions about channels. If you love to talk on the telephone, your processing skills are likely to be directed toward that channel. You also have to process information about *why* people use certain channels. Aren't you curious about why some people show up unexpectedly on your doorstep without calling first? Do they insist on face-to-face communication? Do you wonder why people act differently in a group of people compared to when they are only talking with you? Are you one of those people who refuses to leave a message on a phone answering machine?

Channel Preferences

CHANNEL
PREFERENCE
*The preference of a
communicator for
one type of communi-
cation channel over
others.*

Your **channel preference** will be affected by (1) the communicative situation, and (2) the media richness.

Different channels are more conducive to certain communication situations. Communication traveling via light and sound waves will permit quicker transmission and feedback as well as bring people physically closer to each other. Other communication channels, such as public speaking, may tend to be less interpersonal, less receiver specific, or less concerned with the receiver's immediate response. If your personality lends itself to frequent personal contact, you will likely have a channel preference for face-to-face communication. Those who are not as strongly drawn to interpersonal communication may prefer a more detached channel such as written communication.

Media Richness

Another way of deciding on a communication channel is through *media richness,* which refers to the ability of a channel or medium to carry information to a receiver. Some messages are best communicated through rich media, whereas other messages are more appropriately communicated with less rich media. The following criteria can help you decide whether your message requires a rich media channel.[14]

Will the media increase the chance of immediate feedback from the receiver? Immediate feedback is an important component of media richness. In instances when you need to gauge your receiver's level of understanding, rich media will be required.

Can the media be tailored or designed to specific targets? Tailoring or specifying a message for a particular receiver is a key element of media richness. Gossip or confidential information usually requires media that can fine-tune and tailor a message.

Can the media communicate multiple messages (visual, auditory, nonverbal)? The richest media convey meaning through numerous messages. Telephones allow you to hear a person's voice but restrict much of the nonverbal system. Letters or memos are very limited in conveying multiple communication cues. Sometimes you must be able to use as many communication signals as possible, especially when the message is sensitive or complex.

Will the media allow a diverse range of word choice? The richest media allow messages to be conveyed with a variety of words or terminology. Vulgarity and profanity are highly inappropriate in public set-

FIGURE 2.4
Rich media are effective for communicating complex messages.

tings. By the same token, intimate words and phrases between two people in love are best conveyed with rich media. Sensitive language usually requires a rich channel.

According to these criteria, the richest types of media would include face-to-face speaking and telephones, which permit quick feedback, specific targets, and a wide range of word choice. The media lowest in richness are general memos, statistical reporting, and public speaking, which have slow feedback, few cues, and no specific targets.

How do you know which media to use? Rich media are most effective when messages are vague or complex. Media low in richness work best with simple messages. Approaching complex problems with less rich media will oversimplify the situation because too few cues and too little feedback will hamper your efforts. Using rich media for simple problems complicates the situation by presenting too many cues and too much noise and misinterpretation.[15] Most importantly, messages are best sent through multiple media.[16] The best way to conclude an important telephone conversation with a colleague is to follow up with a short note.

Limits of Channel Capacity

Have you ever heard the warning about "too much of a good thing"? The same warning could apply to communication. Most people would agree that communication is beneficial, yet you need to be aware that, along with

Channeling Your Communication

Communication channels are conduits for exchanging meaning with other people. Some people are prone to using particular types of channels. You may not be aware that you have a channel preference. By answering the following questions, you will be able to learn about your own channel priority system. In each of the following situations, put in the blank the letter that best represents the channel you prefer.

A = Face to face   D = Post-it note

B = Telephone   E = Electronic mail

C = Letter   F = Third party

_____ 1. Telling a friend that you got an A on a term paper.

_____ 2. Telling your family that you want to change your major or drop a course.

_____ 3. Telling your mate that you want to break off the relationship.

_____ 4. Telling your boss that you are quitting.

_____ 5. Chatting with an acquaintance about your career goals.

_____ 6. Objecting to some new policy at school or at work.

_____ 7. Confiding a secret.

_____ 8. Congratulating a friend on being selected for the swimming team.

_____ 9. Complaining to management about poor service at a restaurant or store.

_____ 10. Meeting a new person.

_____ 11. Informing a loved one of bad news.

_____ 12. Thanking a friend for a gift.

Look at your scores. Do you seem to prefer one channel to the others? Why? Go back to each of the questions and see whether your answers change if you ask yourself, "Which channel do I prefer when I am the receiver in these situations?" Do your answers change? Why or why not?

cognitive or information overload (discussed earlier in this chapter), there are limits to channel capacity. **Channel capacity** refers to the rate and amount of information that you can receive without experiencing processing errors. When you are receiving information from a single channel at a reasonable rate, you will generally be able to process the information while making adequate judgments and discriminations about the content. When you begin to receive information from two or multiple channels, your ability to process the content will initially increase until you reach a breaking point and your processing falters.

Farace, Monge, and Russell explain that certain roles will have more communication flow than others. As they report, a manager in charge of 30 individuals who require a great deal of attention will receive more information than a manager who deals with 10 employees on a less frequent basis. You can informally examine the situations you encounter on a daily basis (home, school, work) and attempt to determine how many channels are operating and how much of a processing burden each presents. Your processing capacity will be determined by how well you employ memory, attributions, and other issues raised in this chapter. However, there is some evidence to suggest that improving your organizational and time management skills will increase your individual capacity. Finally, the desire to process communication will have some effect on how much channel capacity you might have. If you are motivated and believe the incoming information is of value, your channel capacity will increase.

CHANNEL CAPACITY
The ability to process information competently via a particular communication channel or channels (e.g., face to face or over the telephone).

Culture

Recall the discussion of culture in Chapter 1. With the world becoming more culturally diverse each day, it is very important that you understand the role of culture in communication processing. Previously, you learned that people attempt to explain human behavior through attribution; that is, when they observe a particular behavior, they usually seek a personal characteristic that they can say causes the behavior. The attribution process can play an important role when two people from different cultural backgrounds try to communicate. Obviously, people of different cultures will display behavioral and communication differences. These **cultural factors** make it necessary for individuals from both cultural backgrounds to work harder to achieve competent communication.

Once again, the biggest attribution trap is the tendency to overemphasize internal responsibility for the behavior. In the case of intercultural interactions, people tend to attribute behavior to the culture and to disregard individual situational factors. Consider the following hypothetical

CULTURAL FACTORS
Ways in which different cultural backgrounds can affect communication processing.

FIGURE 2.5

The model of communicative competence shows that all aspects of the communication process are contained within cultural constraints. The challenge of competent cross-cultural communication is to be willing to modify your behavior to accommodate the different expectations generated by your partner's culture and your own. At the same time, you must be careful not to make attributions based exclusively on your perceptions of your partner's culture.

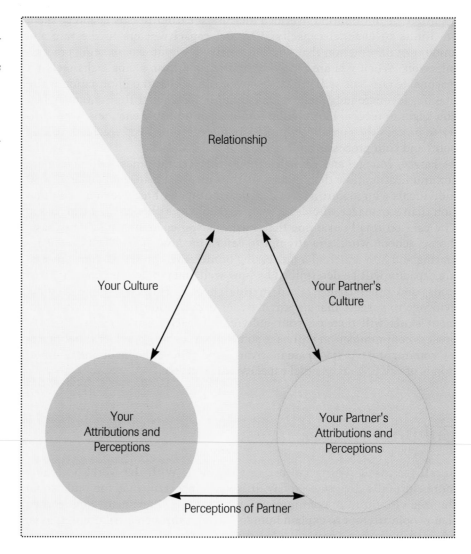

Relationship

Your Culture

Your Partner's Culture

Your Attributions and Perceptions

Your Partner's Attributions and Perceptions

Perceptions of Partner

situation: At a college in the Northeast, Spanish 101 students are asked to stand up at the beginning of each semester and state in Spanish their names, hometown, and major. Those students with Hispanic surnames who stumble or mispronounce the information are routinely ridiculed by the Spanish instructor. This instructor assumes that all Hispanics can speak Spanish. However, the teacher is attributing characteristics to the students based on her perception of the culture and not on students' individual circumstances.

When you observe a behavioral characteristic among people from a different culture, you may fall into the trap of making the easiest assessment and determining that the behavior is culturally derived. In these situations, you have to catch yourself and remember the importance of asking if a separate factor might be responsible for the behavior. As we noted earlier in this chapter, some self-monitoring and retraining of your attribution-making tendencies might be in order.

Responsibilities of the Host Culture

Members of the host culture need to be as wary of overlooking cultural explanations for an outsider's behavior as they are of making negative attributions falsely based on cultural causes. For example, Frank recalls being in a small seminar with Akemi, a student from Japan. After several weeks, Akemi had rarely spoken and chose to sit back quietly while other members of the class became actively involved in class discussions. A few of her classmates attributed her quiet behavior to a lack of interest in the class. Eventually, Akemi explained that in Japan, students answer only direct questions from professors and otherwise rarely speak in class. Thus, rather than being uninterested in the class, actually, she was just having trouble getting used to the host culture's openness in the classroom.

The *Bulletin of the Association for Business Communication*[17] reported a survey that asked 183 international students from 61 countries about their impressions of U.S. culture. Respondents reported their positive and negative impressions of the United States (see Table 2.1 on p. 84).

Responsibilities of the Foreign Culture

The individual from a foreign culture is responsible for learning how people communicate in the host culture. If you are a native of the United States and plan to travel outside the country, you should try to learn as much as possible about the communication practices of the cultures you will visit. For example, Janet recently traveled to Pakistan to visit a close friend. In preparation for her trip, she read about the Muslim culture and her friend, who is a native of Pakistan, thoroughly explained its customs to her. But even with Janet's extensive advanced preparation, she found it difficult to adjust to and communicate with the Pakistanis.

TABLE 2.1 PERCEPTIONS OF U.S. CULTURE

POSITIVE IMPRESSIONS	NEGATIVE IMPRESSIONS
Educational opportunities	Rudeness
Friendly people	Weak family structure
Freedoms	Money consciousness
Career opportunities	Ethnocentricity—arrogant, snobbish people
Living conditions	Prejudice against international people
Organized and clean society	Drugs and alcohol
Lack of government red tape	Crime

Source: M. Cassady (1992), An international perspective of the United States, *Bulletin of the Association for Business Communication, 55.*

Kim's *Communication and Cross-Cultural Adaptation* (1988) details how to become a competent communicator in a host culture.[18] She explains that competent cross-cultural communication will depend on (1) knowledge of the host communication system, (2) cognitive complexity in responding to the host environment, (3) effective co-orientation with the host culture, and (4) behavioral understanding of how people interact in the host culture. When members of the host culture remember to limit unwarranted attributions, and when those who enter the host culture work to adapt, cross-cultural communication competence can be achieved.

Initially, those seeking knowledge of a host culture's communication system should have modest expectations. When encountering a host culture for the first time, you may make oversimplifications and false generalizations. These inaccuracies can lead to miscommunication in later situations. Aside from the obvious concerns associated with learning the host culture's language, newcomers must also study the nonverbal behaviors and various communication rules. This is where the visitor to Pakistan had difficulty. Janet had not fully prepared herself for the Pakistani attitudes toward women, which limit women's opportunity to discuss important issues with men, and she had not anticipated a cultural belief that frowns on women openly disagreeing with men.

Oversimplifications and mistaken generalizations can be a sign or result of the newcomer's cognitive complexity. Although the initial generalizations can be expected, a competent communicator in a new culture must be able to make the distinctions and judgments about host culture behavior that are reflective of a cognitively complex individual.

Along with the necessary cognitive complexity, newcomers must be able to co-orient themselves with the host culture. To facilitate communication with those in another culture, the newcomer must be willing to accept and affirm that culture. The ultimate sign of accepting a new culture is to gain an appreciation for that culture's aesthetic and emotional drives and distinctions.

Much of this development is reflected in the newcomer's behavioral competence. Eventually, a competent communicator will learn how to blend the various verbal, nonverbal, and behavioral skills and tendencies into his or her own communicative behavior. This will be the ultimate goal of a competent cross-cultural communicator.

Cultural Diversity

Culture and communication are inextricably linked. Cultural background plays a large role when communicating with people from other countries and when exchanging messages with culturally diverse colleagues who live and work in the United States. The basic rules of intercultural communication apply regardless of where a person resides.

But what is cultural diversity? According to Loden and Rosener, cultural diversity reflects differences in age, ethnic heritage, race, physical abilities or qualities, gender, and sexual orientation. A culture that fosters diversity is "an institutional environment built on the values of fairness, diversity, mutual respect, understanding, and cooperation; where shared goals, rewards, performance standards, operating norms, and a common vision of the future guide the efforts of every employee and manager."[19]

So why is an appreciation of cultural diversity important to your communicative competence? With the face of the nation changing, the culture of the Founding Fathers—white, male, Christian, and English-speaking—is less widely accepted as the standard of normality than it was in the past. Members of this co-culture are already a minority, and although many as-

REALITY CHECK

Cultural Awareness

Have you ever visited a foreign country? What were some of the most unexpected things that happened to you? Besides the language barrier, what cross-cultural communication barriers did you experience? Was the host culture receptive to your needs?

pects of their culture remain dominant, members of other co-cultures are asserting the equal worth of their cultural characteristics. Females, people of color, homosexuals, the elderly, people who have physical and mental challenges, non-Christians, and other groups that have long been oppressed are refusing to accept second-class status. To communicate effectively, everyone must recognize the heterogeneity of our society; members of both sexes and all ethnic, racial, and religious groups, people of all ages and abilities, must view each other without prejudice and with respect for the value of cultures other than their own.

Barriers to Competent Intercultural Communication

In the following sections we discuss in turn the major types of barriers that exist to competent intercultural communication. In each case, we then consider a variety of ways that you can face these barriers and work to overcome them.

Cultural Myopia

"The belief that one's particular culture is appropriate in all situations and relevant to all others" is cultural myopia.[20] If you are a member of a particular cultural group and are very proud of its origin, heritage, and status, you are susceptible to cultural myopia. Problems occur when you view your cultural group as superior to other groups. You become "myopic" in your views of values, tastes, attitudes, and even communication practices. Cultural myopia is especially dangerous when members of a dominant group are unaware of, or are insensitive toward, the needs and values of members of different cultures.

Ethnocentrism

Ethnocentrism is the process of valuing your own ethnic culture so much that you are comfortable only with people similar to yourself.[21] *Why aren't those people more like us? If they would only act like me, they would get the respect they want!* These are the types of comments usually made by ethnocentric individuals. Ethnocentrism is a major roadblock toward competent communication because it prevents you from understanding the expectations and goals of culturally different people. Your inability to appreciate their culture hampers the processing ability that leads to competent communication. The more often you have an ethnocentric attitude when you approach a person who is culturally different from you, the less likely you are to process information about that person in a competent way.

Stereotyping

Stereotyping is the process of organizing information about groups of people into categories so that you can generalize about their attitudes, behaviors, skills, morals, and habits. Stereotypes may be positive, negative, or neutral; they may be about a group to which you belong or one that is different from your own. In essence, you form biased schemata about particular cultural groups. As you can imagine by now, stereotypes have a powerful influence on your perceptions of other people. Stereotyping is the act of fitting individuals into an existing cultural schema.

Stereotyping is done all the time in mass communication by marketers who focus their commercials and advertisements on what are believed to be the shared values of their audience. Think of the commercials for cereal and toys that accompany the Saturday morning cartoons, for example, or the beer commercials during sports telecasts. The advertisers are assuming certain stereotypes about their audiences.

When communicating within small groups or speaking in public, you too may be compelled to assume that the group members share some characteristics and stereotype them accordingly. But like smart advertisers, you need to realize that you cannot rely totally on stereotypes. Have you noticed how beer commercials have changed in recent years to encourage moderation in drinking and to appeal to drinkers of light beer? If the advertisers had been content to accept a static, limited stereotype of their customers, the brewers would not be aware of their market's changing values and attitudes.

REALITY CHECK

You've Seen One, You've Seen 'Em All—or Have You?

How many of your existing schemata are cultural stereotypes? Think about your views of the groups listed below. How strong are your stereotypes for these groups? What are the sources of your stereotypes? What evidence do you have that every member of a group acts according to your stereotype?

Mexican Americans	African Americans
Men	Women
Arabs	Redheads
Athletes	Police officers
Japanese	Jews

The effects of stereotyping may be even more profound in interpersonal communication. Recall the last time you thought to yourself that someone was acting just as you expected a member of that individual's cultural group to act. You may have concluded that this was an efficient way of understanding this person, when in fact you limited your ability to gain information about the individual's unique qualities. You lost your chance for meaningful and competent communication.

It might help to remember that stereotyping is a lack of cognitive complexity and reflects a rigid, inflexible perspective. In contrast, competent communicators make judgments about people and groups that are varied, flexible, and multidimensional.

Prejudice

Prejudice is a deep-seated feeling of unkindness and ill will toward particular groups based on negative stereotypes. These stereotypes (schemata) categorize thoughts and feelings about cultural groups, leading to prejudicial attitudes. These attitudes make it easy to protect your own cultural group's attitudes and behaviors, while maliciously abusing those of other people. Sadly, prejudices often result from the insecurities and fears you have about the legitimacy or value of your cultural group. Forming prejudices is a defense mechanism against groups that threaten your (perceived) superiority. Prejudice becomes most noticeable when cultural groups assert their values and rights. It is difficult to understand why some cultural groups resent other groups' having the same rights as they themselves do. Raise this issue in class to see how other people feel.

Discrimination

Discrimination is the process of acting on your prejudices. Discrimination comes in many forms: speaking ill of a cultural group, refusing their members access to your own group, or denying them their basic rights and privileges. The intensity of discrimination depends on the degree of prejudice and desire for social approval. Some people are very prejudiced and do not hesitate to demonstrate their feelings. Merton calls these people "active bigots," or those who are most obvious in their discriminatory practices.[22] "All-weather liberals" are just the opposite and will actively uphold the rights of other cultural groups. Most of us fall somewhere in between these two extreme positions. You may be a "timid bigot"—that is, have prejudices but not want to demonstrate discrimination because of social and legal constraints. Or maybe you're a "fair-weather liberal"—in other words, you don't have very many prejudicial attitudes toward other cultures, but at the same time you want to go along with the crowd and therefore don't always stand up for what you really believe. Some people discriminate against everyone who is not just like them, whereas others may discriminate only against one particular group. What about your discriminatory practices? What can you do about them? You can start by changing your stereotypes.

Changing Stereotypes

You can change your schemata that categorize cultural groups; it is not easy to do, but it is worth the extra effort. By working to make the necessary changes, you can become a more culturally sensitive, and therefore more competent, communicator. Stereotypes can be changed in three ways.[23] One approach is to change and modify the assumptions underlying your attitudes. A second, and one of the simplest ways to transform stereotypes, is to concentrate on the positive qualities you attribute to members of a cultural group. For example, you might notice that African Americans are very serious students, grandparents are polite to other people, and Arabs are very friendly. Making these qualities a part of your schema about these cultural groups will erode your negative stereotypes and build more positive ones. Positive stereotypes of individuals within a particular culture will likely help you communicate with them more pleasantly, but your stereotypes will not necessarily be more accurate in describing an individual than negative stereotypes would be.

FIGURE 2.6
Throughout history and around the world, discrimination based on ethnic and racial stereotypes has been a source of social unrest and even war. A contemporary example is the institution of apartheid (segregation of races), which until recently was officially sanctioned in South Africa.

Third, a more effective approach might be to *dismantle* broad stereotypes by recognizing the various co-cultures that exist within a cultural group. Being a member of a cultural group does not tie you to every characteristic of that group. Does being a male necessarily make Fred a chauvinistic pig? Of course not. Instead, it is more realistic to believe that he is a chauvinist if he views females as inferior and treats them as subordinate to males. Can we assume that because Carmen is Puerto Rican, she likes rice and beans, brightly colored clothes, and music with a Latin beat? She may have all, some, or none of these personal tastes. Reducing stereotypes to smaller, more specific schemata allows you to become more accurate in characterizing people. During the process, you are becoming more cognitively complex. You can also *disintegrate* stereotypes by perceiving culturally different people as "individuals" instead of categorizing them as elements of a stereotype. By doing so, you begin to disassemble the stereotype, which no longer fits neatly into your perceptual process. Individuals are difficult to categorize. Think about close friends of yours. When other people ask what your friends are like, you can talk about their qualities and characteristics, but you would seldom say that they are stereotypical of some group. You see your friends as individuals, and that is the best way to perceive them. The key to disintegrating stereotypes is to emphasize the unique qualities of each person (personality, intelligence, skills), regardless of their cultural background.

Embracing Differences

Every cultural group possesses admirable qualities. For example, different Latin American, African, Asian, and European cultures are each noteworthy in various respects. Understanding the different qualities of cultural

SELF-CHECK

Your Favorite Cultural Groups

Draw a line down the middle of a sheet of paper. Write at the top of the left column, "My favorite cultural groups," and label the right column "My least favorite cultural groups." List your favorite and least favorite cultural groups in the appropriate columns with a brief explanation for your choices. Consider including your own cultural group in one of the columns. Look again at your lists. Do you really have solid reasons for liking some groups more than others? Is your dislike for some groups a result of ignorance or of bad experiences with members of these groups?

groups is a fascinating process that leads to personal growth. Competent communicators view cultural diversity as an opportunity, not a handicap. Diversity gives them the chance to question old ways of thinking and to eliminate bad habits. Embracing diversity is an opportunity to enrich communication processing beyond previous levels.

Goals

Communication goals also affect the success or failure of an exchange between people. Your communication goals directly determine your openness to new information and also help you to process new information more competently. When an instructor announces that the upcoming lecture will be covered on the exam, students will be at their peak ability for receiving and processing the new information. Their attention becomes focused because they can visualize a goal for the information they are about to receive. A similar result is achieved when you can foresee a direct application of what is being taught. In a cardiopulmonary resuscitation (CPR) class, students are usually very attentive because they see a specific goal or use for the valuable information. This attention to the information will make the listeners want to rehearse the information as they hear and see it and to practice the techniques they learn. Therefore, communication goals enhance information processing.

COMMUNICATION GOAL
A desired outcome that can affect how communication takes place.

Processing goals also affect how you organize information. If you listen to a friend explaining why his or her grades have dropped, your processing goal will affect how you organize the information. If you simply want to empathize with your friend, you might organize the information according to the reasons he or she provides (e.g., classes too difficult, too many exams at once, lack of interest). However, if your goal is to provide advice, you might organize the information in such a way as to help your friend (e.g., study tips, exam strategy, relating classes to personal interests).

Finally, communication goals affect your ability to remember new information. In general, when you have a goal for information, you tend to remember it better. Furthermore, the type of goal affects the type of information remembered. For example, suppose you listen to someone giving a speech and you wish to form an overall general impression of his or her personality. You would be more likely then to remember statements that reflect the speaker's personality. If you were listening with no specific goal, you would instead remember specifics of the content not related to the speaker's personality.

Berger and Jordan indicate that memory also plays a role in how you try to achieve goals.[24] These researchers state that when people establish a goal, they search their long-term memory for insight into how that goal can be achieved. They go back to their long-term memory in the hopes of recalling the strategies they previously used to reach the same or a similar goal. Thus they do not need to develop a new approach for each goal. According to Berger and Jordan, the use of previous plans results in cognitive efficiency and is much easier than constantly developing new plans for each goal.

REVIEW

This chapter focused on how you process communication. Communication processing is influenced by the particular communication channel selected for any one interaction. Because communication processing is primarily a cognitive act, a number of theories related to cognition were discussed. Perception refers to how you make sense of the world around you. Schema theory is a useful mechanism for understanding perception. Schemata are categories of information you store in your memory that are used to assimilate new information. The perception cycle uses existing schemata to verify information that you know about or to direct additional exploration to explain new information. Schemata are formed for people, roles, events, and issues. Selective perception is attention to certain types of information to the exclusion of others. Having expectations about people and communication events is a natural process. Problems occur when expectations restrict the communicator from processing information in an objective way. Expectations can also be violated, which causes communicators to question the motives or qualities of the violator and to search the environment for information to help explain the violation.

Attributions were also discussed as part of the communication process.

Attributions are inferences or explanations of personal characteristics that you make based on what you observe, feel, or sense. When you observe someone communicating, you naturally tend to attribute some quality to that person. The problem with attributions is that they can often fail you. If you make generalizations about someone too hastily, you may perpetuate misperceptions when you communicate with that person.

Memory is also part of communication processing. Memory guides how you select words and serves as a benchmark for selecting the appropriate communication strategy. There are several different types of memory, such as short-term and long-term memory. Committing information from short-term to long-term memory takes some effort on the part of the communicator.

Cognitive complexity is the ability to process communication more abstractly and with more intricacy. Cognitive load refers to the quantity of information a communicator is required to process at any one time.

Channel preference differs according to the person and the situation involved; some people generally prefer face-to-face communication, but others like to talk on the phone. When channels are cluttered with noise or competing information, that channel's capacity may be stretched beyond its limits, and processing errors can occur.

Cultural factors can have a significant impact on communication processing. When people from different cultural backgrounds communicate, there can be a tendency to attribute information to the culture rather than to focus on the individual. Overgeneralizing in this way could create problems in processing accurately the information being exchanged. As a communicator, you must remain aware of cultural factors that affect message exchange but at the same time avoid inferences that could damage your ability to process information as it is sent.

Communication goals affect the success or failure of an exchange between people. Your communication goals will directly affect how open you are to new information. Communication goals help you process new information more competently. When listeners have a goal for what they are about to hear and see, they are usually more open to the information-message exchange but at the same time avoid inferences that could damage your ability to process information as it is sent.

Communication goals affect the success or failure of an exchange between people. Your communication goals will directly affect how open you are to new information. Communication goals help you process new information more competently. When listeners have a goal for what they are about to hear and see, they are usually more open to the information.

SUGGESTED READINGS

Carroll, J. S., & Payne, J. W. (Eds.). (1976). *Cognition and social behavior.* Hillsdale, NJ: Lawrence Erlbaum.

Cody, M. J., & McLaughlin, M. L. (1990). *Psychology of tactical communication.* London: Multilingual Matters.

Donohew, L., Sypher, H., & Higgins, E. T. (Eds.). (1988). *Communication, social cognition, and affect.* Hillsdale, NJ: Lawrence Erlbaum.

Goss, B. (1991). *Processing communication.* Prospect Heights, IL: Waveland.

Kim, Y. Y. (1988). *Communication and cross-cultural adaptation.* Philadelphia: Multilingual Matters Ltd.

Roberts, C. V., & Watson, K. W. (1989). *Intrapersonal communication processes.* New Orleans: Spectra.

3

The Self and Communication

O*bjectives*

After reading this chapter you should be able to

1. Describe the importance of self-concept and self-esteem to human communication.

2. Explain how feedback and self-certainty affect communication processes.

3. Demonstrate how self-efficacy leads to communication success.

4. Recognize how self-presentational processes affect communication competence.

5. Identify various responses to communication competence assessment and how they affect the self.

CHAPTER CONTENTS

U NQUESTIONABLY, THE SELF is an extremely important part of communication competence. Chapter 1 suggested that your self-concept plays a large role in helping you to use your skills as a competent communicator. Acquiring the ability to understand who you are is not easy, however. Your view of "self" is often so biased that you misinterpret or ignore information that you need in order to communicate effectively. Furthermore, your ability to express who you are is limited by your knowledge of other people and how well you know yourself. It is perhaps even more difficult to modify your view about self based on feedback received from your communication performances. People who have a very strong, or even rigid, self that is resistant to change will experience more difficulty in developing new communication skills. Other people have a view of self that is easily influenced by information from people, the environment, and themselves—perhaps too easily influenced. A third group of people have a stable view of self that is sensitive to feedback from their communication performances. You can become a more competent communicator by (1) developing knowledge about self, (2) learning to communicate about who you are, (3) assessing your ability to communicate self to others, and (4) responding to feedback about your level of competence. This chapter explores how the self, your very being, is related to communication competence.

The Self and Communication Competence

Few concepts in the humanities and sciences are more complicated than that of the self. To simplify our discussion of this concept and communication competency, we will describe a process that is illustrated in Figure 3.1. Examine it for a moment.

At the core of this process is the self. At the center of the self are the self-concept (knowing and understanding the self), self-esteem (evaluating the self), and self-efficacy (predicting success). Self-efficacy influences communication performance, and the performance is then assessed for competence, ranging from positive to negative. A reaction or response to the competence assessment could range from satisfaction to dissatisfaction. The reaction or response provides feedback to the self, affecting the self-concept, self-esteem, and self-efficacy in various ways. The remaining sections of this chapter provide a more concrete discussion of how this process works.

Self-Concept

Think for a moment about who you are. Although you may be able to describe yourself by identifying your status as a college student, son or daughter, spouse, or friend to others, there is much more to the self than just name, rank, and serial number. Numerous definitions of self-concept have been proposed, but we are partial to the views of Snyder, who suggests that you learn to understand the attitudes you hold, your personal traits, and your behaviors by observing what you do, witnessing your reactions, watch-

FIGURE 3.1
The self and communication competence.

Thinking about Yourself

How often do you reflect on your self-concept? What kinds of questions do you ask that reveal your understanding of your actions, abilities, goals, and other self-related matters? When does this happen? When you are going to sleep at night? While you are driving alone in your car? Do you often wish you knew more about yourself?

ing others' reactions to you, and being aware of how situations can influence your behavior and feelings about life.[1]

Some writers argue that self-concept comprises many selves, each with its own framework of values, perceptions, and thoughts.[2] According to this view, you could have a separate self as student, as automobile operator, as pianist, as conversationalist, and so forth. In Chapter 1 we defined self-concept as a person's own definition of his or her being. Now we can expand that definition. **Self-concept** is your awareness and understanding of who you are as interpreted and influenced by your thoughts, actions, abilities, values, goals, and ideals, and those of other people.

SELF-CONCEPT
Awareness and understanding of who one is as interpreted and influenced by one's thoughts, actions, abilities, values, goals, and ideals.

The Importance of Self-Concept to Competent Communication

How does knowing about yourself affect your communication with others? From the start, you have certain views of who you are as a communicator (for any situation that involves speaking, interviewing, or just talking with others), and how you view yourself in other respects could also affect your communication. For example, if you feel strongly about the issue of the homeless, you are more likely to communicate in ways that support your viewpoint. You may think of yourself as an effective communicator when it comes to that topic. Moreover, self-concept can be a powerful influence on your communication processes; specifically, it can affect how apprehensive you get in certain communication situations,[3] whether or not you are willing to interact with others,[4] or how you approach someone with a request (e.g., whether you are meek and timid or strong and confident). The self has a strong influence on your attitude toward communication. Think about people you know who take great pride in their communication ability. Do you find these people placing themselves in situations where they are able to use those skills? Do you know some people who have a less favorable concept of their communication skills and who prefer to stand back while others communicate?

The self influences communication processes in other ways. In the last chapter you learned how important cognitive processes are to communication. The self influences many of the mental operations that eventually affect your communication with others. Specifically, your perception of others is the product of how you view yourself.[5] If you believe that certain attributes about self, such as honesty or wit, are important to you, you will also see them as important traits for other people. If you feel that using profanity makes you appear cheap and vulgar, you are likely to think the same of others when they use such language. As you make decisions about your communication with others, your self-concept influences how you perceive the communication of others.

Self-concept can also affect the processing of memory and recall. Simply put, you can retrieve information that is stored in memory more easily if it is related to the self. Several research studies conclude that if you are able to relate incoming information to something about the self, such as a personality trait or comparable past experience, you can remember and act on it much more quickly.[6] Moreover, you are likely to resist information that is contrary to your self-conception (e.g., you will ignore information that contradicts your view of self). For example, you may dismiss the fact that an important person ignored you at a social gathering.

Finally, although self-concept strongly influences communication, the reverse is also true. When you interact with other people you get impressions from them that reveal their evaluation of you as a person and as a communicator. If someone you value daydreams as you tell him or her about your plans for the future, you are likely to think that the person is not interested in you or that he or she finds your conversational skills lacking. Many researchers and writers in the area of self-concept identify social interaction as a key to developing one's self-concept.[7] Communicating with others provides both direct and indirect information that you can use for developing, confirming, or disconfirming your self-identity. Direct evidence comes in the form of compliments, insults, support, or derogation. If someone important to you such as a professor tells you that you have great potential as a manager because you possess excellent interviewing skills, you make this information part of your self-concept. Indirect evidence that influences your self-concept might be manifested through innuendo, gossip, subtle nonverbal cues, or even no communication at all. If you ask someone to evaluate your promise as a public speaker and he or she changes the subject or looks a bit pained, you will probably get the impression that a lot of work lies ahead of you before you can assume public speaking competence as part of your self-concept.

Who You Are

Take out a sheet of paper and entitle it "This Is Who I Am!" Write a brief autobiography of yourself. Avoid demographic characteristics and instead concentrate on your attitudes, behaviors, life-style, values, and beliefs. Once you have finished, ask three people who know you very well to comment on your autobiography. Ask them to judge its accuracy, honesty, clarity, and comprehensiveness. They should be encouraged to provide any important detail that you left out. Comment in writing on your reactions to these people's observations. Bring this assignment to class for discussion.

Ways of Viewing the Self

You can use several methods for knowing and understanding the self. These methods do not necessarily compete with one another, nor is any one of them better than the others. You may find all of them worthy of attention and consider adopting each and every one. If you find one way particularly relevant for your approach to knowing who you are, you should embrace it enthusiastically.

Self-Schemata

SELF-SCHEMA

A structure or framework, composed of the various pieces of information that a person attributes to self, that helps that person develop a sense of self, guides the person's actions, and facilitates the acquisition and storage of new information as it pertains to self.

One approach to viewing the self is the self-schema theory, as popularized by Markus. The **self-schema** theory states that the various pieces of information that you attribute to self are organized into separate structures or frameworks that help you get a sense of who you are, guide your actions, and facilitate the acquisition and storage of new information as it pertains to self. According to Markus, *self-schemata* are "cognitive generalizations about the self, derived from past experience, that organize and guide the processing of self-related information contained in the individual's social experience."[8]

Because schema theory was discussed in the last chapter, we do not need to pursue a full-blown discussion of it here. Rather, the focus is on how self-schemata and communication are related. You may begin by imagining the various self-schemata as boxes of information that you absorb from your social world. Included in these boxes are facts, data, examples, experiences, and even feelings associated with a particular schema. For example, you

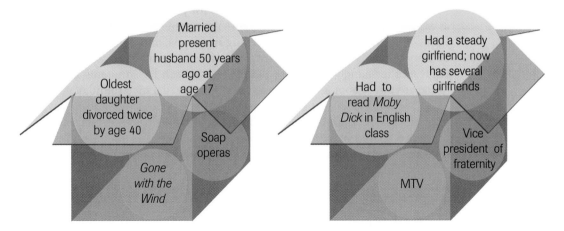

FIGURE 3.2

Self-schemata are affected by communication. Here are two individuals' self-schemata for romantic love, represented as boxes containing pieces of information from various sources in their respective social worlds. For simplicity, only a few examples of the bits of information influencing each of them are shown; using these representations, one could describe these two individuals and their self-schemata for romantic love.

probably have a schema (or box of information) that contains information about your views of self in terms of romantic love. This box will be much larger and more varied for some people than for others. It may contain perceptions about romance that you acquired through books, movies, or stories from other people. Your own romantic experiences may shape this schema in ways that are different from those of other people. In addition, you may compare your romantic love schema with other people's schema, causing you to adjust your own. However, the stronger your schema for this topic, the less likely you are to allow its modification by new information. This last point is important. As Berger points out, the more entrenched or specifically defined the self-schema, the more likely it is that you will (1) collect information that is consistent with your reestablished views, (2) process and recall relevant information more quickly, and (3) perform communication behavior that is consistent with your self-schema.[9] To extend our example a bit further, if someone has a generally negative self-schema of romantic love (perhaps owing to past experiences or no experiences at all), he or she is more likely to resist information that portrays this type of love as blissful and will be less likely to capture this information in a way that becomes part of his or her own schema. Such a person may even deny claims that romantic love is a wonderful idea.

Some topics hold very little relevance for people and would not qualify as strong or clearly defined schemata. Your schema for such communication contexts as interviewing, working in groups, and public speaking may be only partially developed as a result of your knowledge and experience. On the other hand, if you gave a campaign speech for someone running for office at your school a few years back and received a nice round of applause, and your candidate won the election, your self-schema for public speaking may be only partially developed, but it is likely to be positive. You would therefore be receptive to new information about this topic. In fact, you might even seek out college courses such as this one in order to further develop your existing self-schema on public speaking. The information you receive may confirm or disconfirm your existing self-schema, and you may seek additional information in order to expand your self-knowledge. You can therefore view self-schemata as a frame of reference whereby you communicate according to organized knowledge you have in this area at this particular time.[10] Each of the self-schemata you hold in your consciousness provides you with a road map, recipe book, or checklist for communicating with other people about specific topics.

The following two examples illustrate how communication and self-schemata are linked.[11] The first example is in the form of nonverbal communication. According to self-schemata theory, people whose self-schema is consistent with the demands of the situation are more likely to exhibit

---

REALITY CHECK

Telling Jokes

Do you like to tell jokes? Do you admire people who can tell one good joke after another? Have you ever wondered why you can't remember jokes you've been told? Do tone of voice, pauses, facial expressions, and gestures affect the success of a joke? Some people have highly organized self-schemata about joke telling. They receive positive reactions to their jokes and therefore possess a certain organizational framework for hearing and telling them. These people probably view communication as an opportunity to make people laugh or get a desired reaction. People who do not tell jokes very often, or whose jokes fall flat, would hold a very different schema about joke telling. Not that they don't like to hear jokes, but they have resigned themselves to the fact that they can't tell jokes. You have heard many people make this claim! Describe your self-schema for joke telling. In class, compare your self-schema to your classmates' evaluation of your joke telling.

competent nonverbal behavior. In other words, when your view of self corresponds to what is expected of you as a communicator in a particular situation, you are more likely to avoid speech errors, hesitation pauses, and nonfluencies. Take the example of someone who maintains a self-schema of being good at deceiving others and doesn't feel much guilt about lying. When put into a situation requiring either truth or deception, such a person may choose lying (if it seems justified) and pull it off more skillfully than someone whose self-schema is focused on "truthfulness always."

The second example linking self-schema and communication is that of persuasion. Research demonstrates that persuasive messages containing viewpoints, information, or tactics compatible with a receiver's self-schema will be more persuasive than messages inconsistent with the schema.[12] A person with a strong religious self-schema will be more susceptible to persuasive messages that contain some appeal to spiritual values. People with a strong altruistic self-schema will be more easily persuaded to give a higher percentage of their income to charity than someone without such an altruistic schema.

Possible Selves

A different but compatible perspective views self-concept as composed of different possible selves, each with its own values, viewpoints, knowledge base, feelings, and so on. Markus espouses this perspective. In essence, possible selves represent your aspirations, motives, goals, and threats and reveal to you what you hope to accomplish or become in life. They also represent what you hope to avoid or what you fear in yourself.

> These are the selves we could become or would like to become. They are also the selves we are afraid of becoming. Possible selves reflect the dynamic and future-anchored properties of the self. They include the selves that are hoped for (rich, happy, competent, loved) and the selves that are feared or dreaded (alone, depressed, afraid, incompetent).[13]

In a sense, you can think of the self-schema as a concept of self in the here and now—its present form, if you will. On the other hand, **possible selves** can be regarded as what the self might be like, given particular circumstances, or its future form. This idea of future self gives rise to an exploration of how self-concept influences potential communication behavior. If you formulate thoughts about how you can become a competent negotiator in order to be a successful salesperson, you will develop a possible self in the area of negotiation. Your subsequent thinking in this area will likely lead you to search for methods, tactics, and skills that make your possible self a self-schema.[14] You may take courses in bargaining and nego-

POSSIBLE SELVES
A view of self-concept as composed of different possible selves, each with its own values, viewpoints, knowledge base, feelings, and the like.

tiating skills, talk to successful negotiators, or even practice negotiating strategies in the sanctity of your bedroom. The point is that having a possible self leads to actions that can transform a mere possibility into a reality. In this sense, possible selves serve as the impulse and driving force toward maximizing your potential. Of course, they may also help you avoid developing negative selves (drug addict, thief).

Possible selves can also provide a backdrop by which you evaluate your current successes and failures.[15] If one of your possible selves can skillfully manage conflict with a diverse set of people, you are likely to have a much more positive view of your ability to settle a long-standing argument with an adversary than does someone with no such aspirations. On the other hand, if Roberto reluctantly possesses the possible self of being an unsuccessful marriage partner, he will view getting into an argument with his fiancée much more negatively than will someone who exhibits a more favorable possible self as marriage partner.

Because possible selves are transitory or changeable and susceptible to variation based on situational variables, they often serve as buffers against permanent or fundamental changes based on startling or unexpected information directed toward self. We can explain this idea best by examining the case of the student in a communication class who knew that her ambitions as a public relations specialist depended on good interpersonal communication skills. Even though Cassandra was a bit shy, she hoped (possible self) that she would develop the necessary techniques to excel in a public relations firm. One day, through the grapevine at her part-time job, Cassandra learned that she was perceived as sensitive and caring because of her laidback but empathetic style. Cassandra knew that meant people saw her as socially reserved, but this knowledge did not disturb her because she knew the positive aspects of the rumors. On another occasion, Cassandra learned that some people at her place of business thought she was ineffective because she had no spunk. Again, Cassandra allowed her possible self as an effective PR agent to cushion the attack; she realized that she would have other opportunities to demonstrate her skills in the area of interpersonal relations.

REALITY CHECK

Self-Schemata and Possible Selves

How would you connect theories of self-schemata and possible selves? Is it possible that one or more of your schemata include the category of "possible selves"? Does each schema possess possible selves?

Self-Esteem

Self-esteem usually refers to how someone thinks of himself or herself. It is essentially a set of attitudes that people hold about their feelings, thoughts, abilities, skills, behavior, and beliefs. Although self-concept and self-esteem are often equated, generally self-concept is thought to refer to *knowledge* about self whereas self-esteem is defined as how people *feel* about what they know. Of course, the key to the last-named condition is that self-esteem depends on self-concept. If people do not know themselves, it is difficult to have an attitude about self. Therefore, many people believe that the self-concept is formed first, after which attitudes develop.

SELF-ESTEEM
A set of attitudes that one holds about one's feelings, thoughts, abilities, skills, behavior, and beliefs.

Attitudes toward Self

How do you feel about yourself? What is your opinion of *you?* Your attitudes toward yourself are what make up self-esteem. Your attitudes should be based on accurate information that comes from your self-concept. Campbell believes that some people have low self-esteem, or a poor view of self, because of their lack of knowledge or because of their mistrust of the knowledge they do possess.[16] For example, you may feel that you are an effective listener, but you can't be sure of that attribution because you feel anxiety in some listening situations. Similarly, low self-esteem may result from an inconsistent view of self.[17] You may know of people who experience good days and bad days in persuading and influencing others. These same people have low self-esteem when it comes to persuasive communication because of the inconsistency they experience in this area. On the other hand, some people who think they possess shortcomings or negative traits may prefer to ignore these issues so that these traits will ultimately not affect their more enduring self-esteem. We do not recommend that you use this self-delusionary tactic, but you should recognize the reasons for it.

You have probably noticed that people with high self-esteem enjoy confidence in what they do, how they think, and how they perform. These individuals, realizing that they are responsible for their own destiny, are better able to incorporate successful ventures and performances into their self-concept. Low-self-esteem people are particularly sensitive to how others view them.[18] Because they have less confidence in their abilities and skills, they are more likely to maximize weaknesses instead of focusing on strong points; to believe negative information about self; to attempt to lower other people's expectations about their potential performance; and to communicate less confidence about future performances.[19] In many instances, low self-esteem is part of a vicious cycle. A negative attitude about ability can

Self-Esteem Inventory

The following items should be useful in helping you determine your level of self-esteem. Answer each of the questions as sincerely and honestly as you can. Use a five-point scale for your answers: 5 = strongly agree; 4 = agree; 3 = neutral; 2 = disagree; and 1 = strongly disagree.

_____ 1. I am a very happy person.

_____ 2. I am smarter than the average person.

_____ 3. I enjoy being sensitive to other people.

_____ 4. I am a very honest person.

_____ 5. I wish I were better looking than I am.

_____ 6. I am proud of my accomplishments.

_____ 7. I can be trusted with sensitive information.

_____ 8. I communicate better than most people.

_____ 9. I am a great listener.

_____10. I am seldom shy in social gatherings.

_____11. I am mature for my age.

_____12. I wish I weren't so lazy.

_____13. I wish my friends and family trusted me more.

_____14. I really like myself.

_____15. Most people hold me in high regard.

Add up your scores on items 1–4, 6–11, and 14–15. Now reverse the scoring on items 5, 12, and 13 (5 = 1, 4 = 2, 2 = 4, 1 = 5). Finally, add these scores to the sum you calculated from the previous items.

If you scored 15–34, your self-esteem is pretty low for a college student. If you scored 35–55, you have average self-esteem. If you scored 56–75, you have high self-esteem. How do you feel about the scores you received? What can you do about it?

Source: Scale partially adapted from J. S. Fleming & D. J. Whalen (1990), The personal and academic self-concept inventory: Factor structure and gender differences in high school and college samples, _Educational and Psychological Measurement, 50,_ 957–967.

lead to poor performance, which can then strengthen negative attitudes about ability. Like a dog chasing its tail, low self-esteem is an unproductive enterprise.

Self-Certainty

Earlier we mentioned that low self-esteem might result from an uncertain self-concept. Baumgardner proposes an idea that speaks to the concept of uncertainty or ambiguity about self. **Self-certainty** refers to a strong sense of identity.[20] Self-certainty is composed of strong self-attributes or ideas about self that are unaffected by adverse or competing information. It can be seen as a measure of self-confidence that you have in your view of the self. People with high degrees of self-certainty will be more likely to understand themselves and their abilities in various communication situations.

Self-certainty could lead to successful outcomes for three reasons.[21] First, if you are certain that you can perform a task well—say, leading and conducting group meetings—you will have more confidence going into those situations and so will more likely give a good performance. Second, when you are certain about your skills, you are more likely to seek out those situations that are conducive to bringing out your competence. In this example, you may search for opportunities that allow you to emerge as a group leader. Third, self-certainty is not necessarily tied to high self-esteem. It pertains to negative self-esteem as well; that is, you may feel certain that you are a poor conversationalist. In this case, you can avoid those situations where you would perform poorly and therefore would not have to endure confirmation of negative attributes. According to Baumgardner, you can gain control of self by using self-certainty to control situations to your advantage. Problems emerge for communicators who have not developed certainty about their abilities. Low-certainty communicators are less likely to take risks when communicating in uncertain situations.

Self-certainty gives you control over your life by helping you to search for appropriate situations and to avoid inappropriate ones. In addition, it helps improve your positive feeling for self. Even if you are not competent in some areas of your personal and professional life, the fact that you are certain of your strengths and weaknesses allows you that control that was discussed earlier. When you know you have control, you are more likely to possess a positive opinion of self than if you feel out of control—even though you may be successful at many things. In other words, you do not have to have supreme competence in all areas of your persona; you need only possess good knowledge of your attributes and be certain of your opinions in these areas. Therefore, self-certainty leads to control, which leads to positive self-feelings, or esteem.[22]

SELF-CERTAINTY
A strong sense of identity; composed of strong self-attributes or ideas about self that are unaffected by adverse or competing information.

Are You Certain?

The following inquiries are designed to raise the certainty level of your communication skills. Although you may feel that you know your ability levels and that you have an opinion about those abilities, you may not be confident or certain about those feelings. When you are more certain, you can exert more control in communication situations, which in turn makes you a more successful communicator.

1. Do you know how to avoid situations that will make you feel uncomfortable?
2. Do you have concrete evidence about your ability as a listener? public speaker? group member? conversationalist? leader?
3. How can you prove that you are not successful in some communication situations?
4. What courses of action could you use to gain more certainty in some areas of your communication competence?
5. In what types of communication situations do you feel especially confident?
6. How do you describe yourself as a communicator?

How can you become more certain about your knowledge, skills, and abilities in communication situations? One way is by reading this book, doing the exercises presented, and following the lectures and class discussion during the semester. Another method is by conducting self-diagnostic inquiries periodically in order to get a sense of how certain you are about what you know and how you feel about self. Many self-diagnostic tests exist. We provide one in the Self-Check "Are You Certain?"

Self-Efficacy

SELF-EFFICACY
The ability to predict actual success from one's self-certainty; viewing oneself and predicting how competent one can be in anticipated situations.

This section explores the idea of self-efficacy as proposed by the famous psychologist Albert Bandura. **Self-efficacy** is that part of your mental and behavioral system "concerned with judgments of how well you can execute courses of action required to deal with prospective situations."[23] Whereas self-certainty is the confidence you feel about your self-concept and self-esteem, self-efficacy is the ability to predict actual success from your self-certainty. From a communication perspective, self-efficacy can predict your actual competence at communicating by making use of your self-certainty regarding your knowledge and skills. Of course, the other side of this coin is that people can possess a low sense of self-efficacy because they have an uncertain self or a negative view of self about communication skills. Two issues of self-efficacy that are particularly important are *effort* and *coping* skills.

▨ Self-Efficacy and Effort

Your perceptions of self-efficacy guide your ultimate choice of communication situations. You are much more likely to avoid situations where you perceive low self-efficacy. Moreover, you make less rigorous efforts in those situations where you cannot avoid low-efficacy situations than in situations where you perceive high efficacy. For example, Rebecca is seven years old and extremely bright. She has been placed in advanced classes of reading, composition, grammar, and spelling. However, Rebecca perceives a low level of self-efficacy in math. Because of her negative attitude about her math competency, she avoids practice and generally has a negative attitude about math and self. She will not even try to learn it. On the other hand, as a second grader she reads at the sixth-grade level and gives maximum effort to reading class and practice. In fact, Rebecca never turns down a challenge. (She has been reading restaurant menus since she was four.)

You may know many people who avoid public speaking opportunities because of their low self-efficacy in this area. Even when they are forced to perform a speaking role, they will often put in only a minimum effort because they are resigned to the perception that they will not perform competently under any circumstances. In other words, they feel that even a supreme effort would not convert them into competent speakers. Experienced public speaking instructors demonstrate that this perception could not be farther from the truth. Instruction added to effort can produce positive results, helping to break this cycle of low self-efficacy in communication. Before concluding the discussion on self-efficacy and effort, we should point out that those with high efficacy may want to be careful about overconfidence. Bandura has also learned that those with very high levels of self-efficacy may withhold effort because of supreme confidence in their abilities. How many times have you seen athletes lose games or matches because their confidence was greater than their effort level? Bandura recommends that people maintain a high level of self-efficacy with just enough uncertainty to cause them to anticipate the situation accurately and prepare according to the demands of the situation. Your effort must rise to the occasion no matter how confident you feel.

■ *Self-Efficacy and Coping*

Self-efficacy also has an effect on your ability to cope with failure and stress. Simply put, feelings of low efficacy may cause you to dwell more on your shortcomings and failures than will perceptions of high self-efficacy. A snowball effect occurs such that when you possess feelings of inadequacy and then fail at some event, it takes its toll on your self-esteem, causing you to experience stress and negative emotional reactions. These feelings then contribute to a lower self-esteem, which then lowers your self-efficacy level even further. High-self-efficacy individuals are less emotionally affected by failure because they usually chalk up their shortcoming to a "bad day." Their feelings of positive self-efficacy can counteract the experience of a temporary failure. Short-term setbacks may make high-self-efficacy people even more determined to succeed the next time. The bottom line for low-self-efficacy people is to (1) avoid situations that may cause them stress until they have begun a program of improvement in those particular areas, (2) recognize that nearly all of their skills, abilities, and knowledge can be improved with instruction and practice, especially communication skills, and (3) recognize that there is always "another day." Few people in this world fail at every attempt. Effort will lead to at least occasional successes, and these experiences must be made a part of one's self-efficacy level.

Self-efficacy is that part of the self that organizes how the self-concept and self-esteem affect communication performance. Self-efficacy is the intermediary between how you think of yourself and how well you communicate with other people, that is, your *communication performance.* The following two sections describe how the self is communicated to others. An indirect approach to communicating self through communication performance is self-presentation; a more direct strategy for communicating self is self-disclosure.

Self-Presentation

As you will discover from reading this book, communication serves many functions. Certainly, one function is to let others know about your "self," and a primary method for making the self known to others is self-presentation. **Self-presentation** is an intentional communication tactic designed to unveil elements of self for strategic purposes. You may need to create an impression in others that you are competent in group communication, so you may tell stories of previous instances of successful group work. Not all of your attempts at communication involve self-presentation. When you decide to self-present, it is usually based on criteria identified by

SELF-PRESENTATION
An intentional communication tactic intended to unveil elements of self for strategic purposes.

Canary and Cody: Self-presentational goals are relevant anytime your social identity is subject to evaluation by others.[24] Sometimes you know in advance that others will be evaluating elements of self (e.g., conducting a group meeting); in other instances you may not anticipate evaluation of self but may find that it happens unexpectedly (e.g., you go to a party only to find an ex-mate there).

Much of your self-presentation becomes so routine and automatic that you are not aware of your efforts. You do not have to pay attention to your self-presentational activities because you feel comfortable with this automaticity under normal conditions. Langer calls this *latent mindfulness*.[25] You can place self-presentational goals and associated behaviors in the back part of your consciousness in order to attend to other things that require your concentration. However, when a situation requires it, you can call upon that knowledge and those skills to appear in your "consciousness" in order to attend to the needs of the situation. Langer calls this *expressed mindfulness*.

Just as self-presentation is affected by self-esteem, self-presentation, in turn, influences self-esteem. Self-presentation serves the same function that feedback from others serves in shaping your self-esteem. When performing, you have the opportunity to observe your own success as evaluated by you and by others. Research generally concludes that those with high self-esteem usually find their own performance positive, while those with negative self-esteem are more critical of their own behavior.[26] Schlenker and his colleagues suggest that low-self-esteem people take the safe path to performance, one of self-protection rather than one of self-presentation, in order to minimize losses.[27] High-self-esteem people are more likely to go for the gold. On the other hand, if you have low self-esteem in a particular area, say romantic relationships, and you perform quite nicely (and unexpectedly so) in your communication skills, you may elevate your self-concept to a higher level. According to Canary and Cody, self-presentation has the most impact on areas of your communication performance about which you vacillate. In such situations, self-certainty is not an effective trait. Improvement of behavior depends on the communicator's willingness to perform competently in spite of past beliefs. Self-certainty would block the ability to believe that communication could be enhanced.

A unique way of viewing self-presentation is through the self-monitoring activities of individuals. Snyder developed and popularized the concept of **self-monitoring** to account for the tendency of some people to watch their environment and the people in it for cues as to how to act in particular situations. According to Snyder:

> The prototypic *high-self-monitoring individual* is one who, out of a concern for the situational and interpersonal appropriateness of his or her social behavior, is particularly sensitive to the expression and self-

SELF-MONITORING
The process of viewing communication as portraying "the right person in the right place at the right time."

FIGURE 3.3
Being in a new environment or situation may promote high self-monitoring.

presentation of relevant others in social situations and uses these cues as guidelines for monitoring (that is, regulating and controlling) his or her own verbal and nonverbal self-presentation. By contrast the *low-self-monitoring individual* is not so vigilant to social information about situationally appropriate self-presentation. Neither does he or she have such well-developed repertoires of self-presentational skills.[28]

High-self-monitoring individuals view their role in interpersonal communication as portraying "the right person at the right place at the right time." These people watch others for hints of how to be successful in social situations and attempt to emulate those verbal and nonverbal cues that seem most appropriate. You may know a person who is a high-self-monitoring communicator. During office meetings, this person always sits in a certain strategic position, raises his or her voice when others do so, gestures in a similar manner to others, and, when it is time to let others talk, is very strategic with silence. Snyder[29] terms such people "sufficiently skilled actors" who are able to implement situationally appropriate communication behaviors.[29] They consider themselves alert and flexible, ready to tackle a number of communication situations with ease. Are you one of these sufficiently skilled communicators? Is it important to you to "fit in" in each communication situation?

Self-Monitoring Test

To test your own perceived level of self-monitoring, complete the following items, being careful to answer them as accurately and truthfully as possible. Use a five-point scale for your answers: 5 = strongly agree; 4 = agree; 3 = neutral; 2 = disagree; and 1 = strongly disagree.

_____ 1. I am concerned about acting appropriately in social situations.

_____ 2. I find it hard to imitate the behavior of others.

_____ 3. I have good self-control of my behavior. I can play many roles.

_____ 4. I am not very good at learning what is socially appropriate in new situations.

_____ 5. I often appear to lack deep emotions.

_____ 6. In a group of people I am rarely the center of attention.

_____ 7. I may deceive people by being friendly when I really dislike them.

_____ 8. Even if I am not enjoying myself, I often pretend to be having a good time.

_____ 9. I have good self-control of my emotional expression. I can use it to create the impression I want.

_____ 10. I can argue only for ideas that I already believe in.

_____ 11. I openly express my true feelings, attitudes, and beliefs.

_____ 12. I'm not always the person I appear to be.

Add up your scores on items 1, 3, 5, 7, 8, 9, and 12. Now reverse the scoring on items 2, 4, 6, 10, and 11 (5 = 1, 4 = 2, 2 = 4, 1 = 5). Finally, add these scores to the sum you calculated from the previous items. If you scored 43–60, you are a high self-monitor; if you scored 30–42, you are an average self-monitor; and if your score was 12–29, you are a low self-monitor.

Source: Adapted from M. Snyder (1974), Self-monitoring and expressive behavior, _Journal of Personality and Social Psychology, 30,_ 526–537.

Low-self-monitoring individuals do not see themselves and communication situations in the same way as high self-monitors do. Low self-monitors are not nearly so sensitive to situational cues that prescribe communication behavior. Rather, they communicate in accordance with what they feel are their deep-seated values or beliefs. They do not feel the need to "adapt" to the situation or people; rather, they feel that people and the situation must take them the way they are, at face value. Low self-monitors have a strong sense of self and prefer to exhibit this self when they find it appropriate. This accounts for their unwillingness to modify their behavior for the situation. If low self-monitors anticipate a communication situation that is different from their own self-presentation style, they will either avoid the situation or accept the fact that they may not be able to please all the parties involved. Tamara is a low-self-monitoring person and has a pleasant, friendly demeanor. At the same time, she is very consistent in her handling of small talk and conversation. No matter whether Tamara is talking with her boss, her mother, her best friend, or a group of strangers, she always limits her conversational time to just a few moments. While at the office, Tamara values her time and prefers to keep conversations short.

It would be a mistake to conclude that low self-monitors have stronger self-concepts than high self-monitors. High self-monitors may view themselves as flexible, adaptable, strategic, and situationally adept at communication. Low self-monitors may have lower self-esteem regarding some communication situations such as public speaking. The fact of the matter is that both high and low self-monitors probably exhibit strong self-concepts because both demonstrate strength in how they deal with communication.

Self-Disclosure

SELF-DISCLOSURE
Revealing parts of the self to others.

One way in which you reveal your self-concept and self-esteem to others is through the process of self-disclosure. Simply put, **self-disclosure** is the act of revealing information about the self to other people. Some writers argue that self-disclosure must be intentional. However, in some instances you probably reveal information about the self without your awareness or intention. In numerous instances in your life, you may say something to others, only to learn that you have unwittingly provided information that exposes part of your inner being. Several factors influence your patterns of self-disclosure. How much you trust someone affects your level of self-disclosure. Other factors include your opinion of the target, your relationship with the target, the setting, the consequences resulting from what you disclose, the topic, and, of course, how and what you think of yourself. We discuss these issues in later sections of this chapter; for now it is important simply to understand that self-disclosure is a complex form of human communication.

Your ability to self-disclose competently is determined largely by what Wheeless and Grotz term the six *dimensions* of self-disclosure: amount, accuracy, honesty, depth, valence, and intentional/unintentional.[30] With regard to the first of those dimensions—*amount* of self-disclosure—how much you say to another person about yourself can greatly influence future interactions. If you self-disclose too much or too little, depending on the target, you may be seen as too open or too closed. Some people have difficulty with those who want to tell others a lot about themselves. Others, on the other hand, may feel cheated when their relational partners will not self-disclose enough.

A second dimension involves *accuracy* of self-disclosure, or the ability to represent precisely how you feel. Sometimes it may be difficult to explain exactly how you feel about yourself, and if you disclose information, you are risking inaccurate self-disclosure. The same holds true for a poorly developed self-concept. How can you make disclosure about yourself if it is unknown even to you? Accurate self-disclosure involves knowing yourself,

---

REALITY CHECK

Self-Disclosure

In class, find a partner whom you do not know very well. Look over the questions below and be prepared to give an honest response to your partner about each question. You can choose three questions that you do not have to answer. Select these questions carefully because you must answer the remaining questions.

- How do you feel about where you live?
- How do you prefer to spend your summers?
- Are you sexually active?
- How much money do you have to spend each month?
- What do you honestly think of your spouse/boyfriend/girlfriend?
- How do you spend your weekends?
- What things really annoy you?
- If you were going to brag about your best quality, what would it be?
- Do your parents really love you? How can you tell?
- How would you describe your personality?
- Do you consider yourself an attractive person? If so, why? If not, why not?

finding the words to express what you know, and relating the information to another person.

Third, the *honesty* of self-disclosure can be a very important issue. It is sometimes tempting to portray yourself in a better light than you actually believe. You may know that you cannot sketch and construct a designer outfit the way a professional designer can; or attentively juggle a career, parenthood, and a loving partnership effectively; or compare your skills at any sport with those of a professional star. However, when pressed by other people who are positively disclosing their talents, you may stretch information about yourself to create a better impression.

Information about the self can be shallow or trivial, such as telling someone the name of your hair stylist, or it may contain *depth*, providing the target with private information that is buried well below the surface. "I know how you feel. I had a miscarriage before our son was born. Please call me when you are discharged from the hospital so we can talk." In the case of public speaking, a speaker is expected to be accurate and honest, but disclosing in-depth information about the self would be deemed inappropriate in most public contexts.

Valence refers to whether the information that you disclose about yourself is positive or negative. You probably know people who mostly reveal negative information about themselves ("I have a cyst on my bladder that will have to be removed"). Others may disclose primarily positive information ("I won $200 in the lottery last year"). Most of us disclose both positive and negative information, depending on the target of the self-disclosure. Positive information is usually reserved for people we like and for people we are trying to impress. Negative information about the self is usually reserved for people we trust. Negative information in the wrong hands can hurt one's pride or reputation.

Finally, self-disclosure can be viewed according to whether or not it was *intentional.* You may know many people who tend to get caught up in the emotions of a communication exchange and then will say things they really do not intend ("Oh, I love you too"). Conversely, other people may feel strong emotions and want others to know their feelings—that is, may intend to self-disclose—but may then end up not saying anything ("I just couldn't get it out").

Trust

Trust is one of the most important factors affecting the decision to self-disclose. Wheeless has studied the relationship between self-disclosure and trust and generally concludes that trust is a necessary but not sufficient condition for self-disclosing to another person.[31] Based on the several dimensions of self-disclosure we have mentioned, you know that trust is not the only factor influencing your self-revelations. You have to understand, however, that some measure of trust in the target of the self-disclosure is usually present. What kinds of factors influence your trust in another person, especially someone you do not know very well? Figure 3.4 shows a trust scale used in self-disclosure. Think about how important each of these items is to you in deciding to self-disclose (1) to a close friend, (2) when giving a speech, (3) when talking in a work group, and (4) when conversing with a stranger in a department store.

Are some of these items more appropriate for disclosing to some people and less appropriate for disclosing to others? Which of these items are especially useful for deciding to self-disclose to acquaintances? friends? family members? Of course, you may not disclose some information even to the most trusted individual. Take, for example, something you have done in your life that you are most ashamed of. Even if you believe that a trusted person would never reveal your dark secret, you may want to conceal this information to prevent the person from thinking badly of you.

Sometimes in your relationships you will have no basis for knowing the trustworthiness of another person. People will often self-disclose to someone else in order to determine whether they can keep a confidence. In this way, the self-disclosure and trust connection works in reverse—you reveal information about the self in order to establish trust. In this instance, much of what you reveal is not likely to be very risky, so that you can build the trust you feel is needed in order to move to more private and concealed information. It should be safe to assume that the link between trust and self-disclosure is very strong, and when one of these components breaks down, the relationship can suffer.

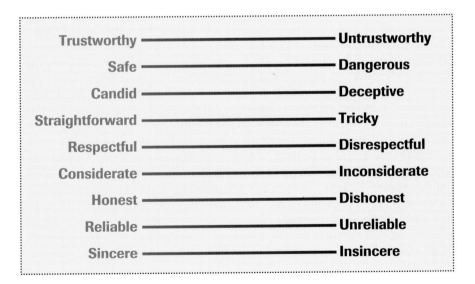

FIGURE 3.4
Individualized trust scale.

Where Does Trust Fit In?

Has someone ever told you some very private things about himself or herself that you wanted to tell others? It is tempting to repeat to others confidential self-disclosures that we were trusted with. Have you ever betrayed the self-discloser's trust by repeating private and confidential information? Did the person find out? Has someone ever betrayed the confidence you put in him or her when you self-disclosed? How did it make you feel about him or her? About your relationship? Keeping confidences is an ethical prerogative that requires a great deal of strength and trust. How easy do you find it to trust others? How well do you think others can trust you? How high do you place the value of trust in your life?

Targeting Self-Disclosure

In the previous section we established the idea that a measure of trust is a necessary ingredient in self-disclosing to others. This section explores further those people who are likely targets for disclosures. There is a tendency to self-disclose to people who disclose first. In what is often referred to as reciprocity, or the *dyadic effect*,[32] people tend to exchange self-disclosure once someone gets the ball rolling. The reasons for reciprocity could include an obligation factor so that you feel indebted to those who reveal themselves to you. Another reason may be that you see someone's self-disclosing as an opportunity to develop a relationship with the discloser. You may also reciprocate in order to ensure that the other person does not get the upper hand or feel superior to you by revealing his or her personal thoughts ("I want this person to know I think well of myself too!").

You may also target self-disclosure to those people you like.[33] Self-disclosure is an opportunity to create a certain impression in others. The more you like someone, the more you want him or her to like you back. One way of accomplishing this effect is by providing the person with information that is useful in building a favorable impression of you. In early relationships, it is best to disclose positive information, thereby putting yourself in a favorable light. Later in the relationship, you can increase another person's liking by showing that person that you trust him or her with negative information about yourself. You may self-disclose more often to people who appear to be similar to you. Research demonstrates that you are more likely to self-disclose to people in your own age group, people who have the same status and power as you, and those who appear to share similar personality traits.[34]

The length of the relationship also influences to whom you target your self-disclosure. Interestingly, there appears to be a U-shaped curve reflecting the association between length or closeness of the relationship and self-disclosure.[35] It is quite easy to understand that you would self-disclose to your best friends and confidants, but why might you also self-disclose to total strangers? The reason is that strangers pose no risk to you if you decide to confide to them your thoughts and feelings. This is sometimes referred to as the "bus rider" syndrome: You know that strangers cannot use anything you say against you because it is unlikely you'll ever see them again. In this sense, you can actually trust them with the information. Have you ever gotten on a bus, train, or plane and found yourself listening to the life story of someone who has temporarily trusted you with this information? Have you ever confided in a stranger because you wanted to get something off your chest and knew that person couldn't use the information against you?

Earlier we mentioned that age is a factor in disclosing to others. When growing up, adolescents will often shift their focus of self-disclosure from parents and family toward friends. In your early years, the family provides a source of confirmation and support for your self-revelations. It is easy to

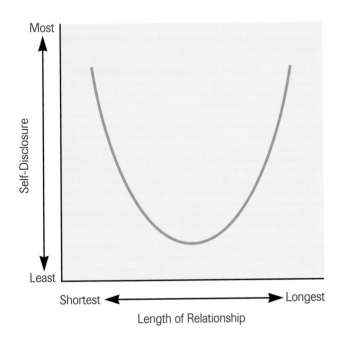

FIGURE 3.5
The U-shaped curve indicates that people are likely to self-disclose most to strangers and to close friends and least to people with whom their relationship is between these two extremes.

Where Can You Let It All Out?

Do you feel particularly competent self-disclosing to certain people? Which ones? Do you rely on your brother or sister for self-disclosure? What type of friend is a ready target for self-disclosure? Are you someone whom people seek out to reveal themselves to?

confide in a mother, father, or sibling since they can understand your point of view relatively easily. With the onset of puberty, however, it is more difficult to find similar others at home, and self-disclosure becomes more difficult. Experiencing this difficulty, referred to as "emotional distancing," adolescents redirect their self-disclosures to those who share the same problems, concerns, and difficulties.[36] Emotional sharing is more likely with other adolescents. This does not mean that adolescents clam up in front of their parents, but it does indicate that this age group is looking for kindred spirits with whom to exchange and confirm information about the self.[37] According to Papini and her colleagues, emotional self-disclosure to friends is a healthy sign that adolescents have an identity in a peer group and have established enough self-esteem to exchange private information with people outside the family.[38] This type of self-disclosure facilitates an adolescent's social development. When adolescents do self-disclose to the family, they are more likely to do so in those families where the parents are seen as warm and affectionate, providing a supportive atmosphere. In addition, mothers are the most likely target when a family member is selected for emotional self-disclosure.[39]

Reasons for Self-Disclosure

In the discussion so far, we have hinted at the reasons why you self-disclose to other people. Now let's look more closely at your possible motives or reasons; you may be surprised at some of them.

Relationship Development

Perhaps the most frequent reason for self-disclosing is to develop relationships. Have you ever tried to get to know someone better, even to establish a more permanent relationship, without exchanging self-disclosures? It must have been a pretty difficult process! The act of revealing yourself to others creates a special atmosphere in the relationship conducive to liking and sometimes intimacy. The special relationship between trust and self-disclosure discussed earlier deserves brief mention here. With additional self-disclosure comes trust in the person. You are saying to this individual, "You are special" because something as risky as self-revelation is reserved for exceptional relationships. Wheeless[40] has conducted research in this area and has determined that as two people increase their self-disclosures and trust builds, the relationship enjoys a bonding termed *interpersonal solidarity*. Relationships built on solidarity are warmer, more sensitive, and more fulfilling than more loosely connected relationships.

As noted earlier, many of us search for similar others to share confidences. However, some people enjoy establishing many new friendships because the variety excites them. *Sensation seekers* are people who seek out unique, offbeat, and unusual sensations and experiences.[41] This search almost always includes pursuit of friends or acquaintances who can help provide these experiences. One approach to rapidly establishing such relationships is through self-disclosure. Sensation seekers are more open and less inhibited people and encourage others to open up as well.[42]

Reassurance

Have you ever talked with friends who, during a conversation, "beat themselves up" to a point where you were arguing with the negative things they were saying about themselves? Self-disclosure is often used as a tactic to obtain *reassurance* or comfort from a trusted friend.[43] Some people may have relatively healthy self-concepts and positive self-esteem, but they may maintain some doubt about particular areas of their self. One way to acquire information about these doubts, in hopes of disconfirming your suspicions, is to self-disclose negative information. Some people are always worried about their personal appearance and will self-degrade to elicit reactions from their significant others.

MATT   My hair looks terrible. [Grooming in the mirror.]

DEBBIE What's the matter with it?

MATT   It's thinning, and what's left is turning gray!

DEBBIE I think the silver specks around your temples make you look more distinguished.

MATT   Do you really think so?

Self-disclosure is a powerful tool sometimes used to confirm self-esteem.

Impression Formation

Self-disclosure is also used to make *positive impressions* on other people. When you are unfamiliar with people who appeal to you, you want to give them as good an impression of yourself as possible. Sometimes you do not or cannot wait for them to realize your talents, skills, abilities, intelligence, and other good qualities through your acts or behavior. You may have to tell them. As observed earlier, self-presentation is a communication strategy used for promoting the self to others. Frequently, then, you will find it necessary to promote yourself. For example, job interviews require that you demonstrate how your knowledge and skills are superior to those of other job candidates. Oral presentations, sales and marketing strategies, and public relations tactics all require that you demonstrate personal competence.

Where do you draw the line between promoting your best features and *boasting* about your positive values? Bragging and boasting serve their purposes as long as the target accepts and accommodates the self-promoter's goals, but many people are turned off by a braggart style of communication. As you know from research, however, positive self-disclosure is more favorably evaluated than negative self-revelations.[44] Miller and her colleagues have studied the differences between positive disclosures and boasting.[45] Boasting is used for purposes of emphasizing power, status, wealth, and other qualities of self that can be exaggerated or emphasized. Boasts are also used to emphasize how your personal qualities are better than those of other people. Miller and colleagues feel that boasting is a competitive tactic and can be associated with masculine qualities.

Positive disclosures differ from boasts in that these tactics give more credit to others for accomplishments; they are less exaggerated and more tentative; and they are perceived as more interesting, likable, honest, and attractive forms of communication. Because they are viewed as sensitive forms of communication, they are likely to be associated with feminine qualities. How does one decide which self-disclosure tactic to use? Bragging may be useful when the situation calls for competition and when the communicator must appear competent and successful. Positive disclosures are preferable when the communicator wants to appear socially sensitive and is concerned about an overall positive evaluation rather than about competence in a particular area of self.

Manipulation

There is another reason for using self-disclosure—manipulation.[46] In this context, you can think of *manipulation* as any attempt to control another person's behavior by revealing portions of the self. At first glance, using self-disclosure for manipulative purposes may seem selfish and counter-productive. In many cases, that is probably so, although sometimes self-disclosure as manipulation can serve altruistic needs. Self-disclosure is used as manipulation in five ways: sympathy, influence, defiance, shock value, and deception.

First, you may self-disclose negative information to others to gain their *sympathy*. Shannon confides to Michael that her parents use her as a scapegoat (blame her for all their problems) in the family. Shannon's intent is to get Michael to understand why she is so defensive at times. She wants Michael to understand her protective nature and to sympathize with her background. Here's another example: When Phyllis discloses to Veronica that she got a 63 on the last chemistry exam, Veronica decides to give Phyllis some study tips. Because Veronica scored a 90 on the same exam, she feels sympathetic and wants to help her friend.

Second, in some instances you may want to persuade or *influence* others indirectly by revealing parts of yourself. You may tell others something about you that leads them to perform some task, change their mind, or otherwise modify their behavior. When Jacquelyn tells Derek that sexist and racist jokes offend her, he knows not to make his crude comments in her company. Jacquelyn persuaded Derek to alter his behavior when in her presence. Similarly, Gabe is graduating in six weeks. He's gained weight over the last two semesters, and he wants to lose the weight by commencement. Gabe has asked his best friend and roommate, Ralph, to help encourage and support his weight-loss plan. Gabe knows that Ralph really wants to lose a few pounds too, so Gabe has achieved control of the situation by exerting an influence over Ralph. Whether you are attempting to obtain or resist compliance, you can use self-disclosure to influence others.

Third, self-disclosure can be used as a method of *defiance*. Josh has had a romantic relationship with Angela. He may tell Angela, "I'm interested in dating other women," in order to defy Angela's attempt to dominate their relationship. Similarly, a teenage boy reveals to his parents that he is gay (when he is not) in order to defy his parents' demand that he drop out of a certain social group that supports gays in the military. The primary purpose behind defiance as a self-disclosing strategy is to rebel, revolt, or rebuke someone or some authority by revealing parts of the self that would otherwise remain hidden. A point to consider is whether the defiant self-disclosure is completely honest. You may be tempted to mislead someone about your true self in order to elicit a reaction to the defiance you are seeking. Whether deception qualifies as actual self-disclosure is an issue addressed later in this section.

Related to defiance is a manipulative strategy that uses *shock value* as its purpose. With this fourth strategy, the self-discloser reveals something so unexpected, outlandish, or unusual that the information shocks the recipient. Several motives may be behind using shock treatment as a manipulative strategy. Sara tells Jeff, whom she is dating, that she detests his parents in order to make him more sensitive to her needs. In order to become the center of attention in a small group of people making conversation, Mike reveals that he was once in a street gang. Or Fernando may disclose that he once was an undercover security agent at a fashionable department store. One might also want to shock people just for the fun of it. You may know people who will tell acquaintances that they are sterile (infertile) just to see the target's reaction.

Shock treatment can be used as a relationship check. To determine how the other person really feels about the relationship, one relational partner tells the other that he or she has had several other sexual partners in the past. Using shock treatment carries some risk. You may get a different kind of reaction than you were hoping for (a dirty look, indifference, rejection, reciprocation, etc.).

Finally, *deception* is sometimes used as a manipulation device. Some people might argue that deception cannot qualify as self-disclosure because it involves something that is not true about the self. Yet, it is a strategy used from time to time, and it is information that you may portray as part of yourself. Deception is used to create a false impression in the minds of others in order to accomplish certain goals or satisfy particular needs. Gregg has falsified educational credentials as a computer programmer to get a job at a large firm. Chantel lies about her age in order to purchase alcoholic beverages. Tammy drives an expensive, preppy automobile, wears designer clothes, and always has manicured nails and a trendy hair style; however, she's exhausted her credit cards and bill collectors are having trouble locating her. Deception is yet another manipulation strategy with risky consequences. If the deception is discovered, a great deal of harm can come to the relationship or situation. Obviously, honesty, one of the qualities self-disclosure is often meant to convey, is not achieved when deception is used.

Emotional Expression

The feelings you experience in response to the thoughts and behaviors of self and others are called *emotions*. Everyone experiences emotions, though to varying degrees. How these emotions are disclosed to others also varies greatly depending on the people and circumstances involved. You are familiar with people who are highly emotional and do not hesitate to reveal their emotions to you. Other people you know are much more reserved and restrictive with their emotional disclosures. Why do people differ in these respects, and what motives do they have for disclosing their emotions to others? Research reveals that emotional self-disclosure is a mechanism for enhancing the psychosocial development of early adolescents.[47] Exploring emotions with friends and family at an early age allows you to understand yourself as well as to recognize how these emotional expressions affect others' reactions to you. Your self-identity can be formed in a particular manner based on your emotional expressions. For example, gender roles are determined to some extent by the reactions you get as you express your emotions to others. Males are not expected to disclose their emotions with the same frequency and intensity or in the same manner as females. In fact, in more traditional settings, there are sanctions against males' disclosing their emotions:

JIM   Mom, I'm afraid of my teacher!

MOTHER   Jim, be a man! I don't want to hear you talk about your fears.

Less traditional settings are less restrictive of a male's emotional expression.

Emotional self-disclosure can be viewed according to two important dimensions: valence and intensity.[48] Emotional *valence* refers to whether emotional disclosure is positive or negative. Societal norms seem to dictate that positive emotional self-disclosure is more socially appropriate than negative self-disclosure. Most people frown on negative emotional disclosure.[49] Negative emotions are best reserved for those people with whom you are most familiar and trusted. *Intensity* of emotional disclosure refers to the depth and strength of the emotion being expressed. Emotional intensity can be demonstrated both verbally and nonverbally. Adjectives and adverbs facilitate one's ability to increase the intensity of emotional disclosure. "I really, really hate being wrong." "I am extremely happy with the direction of my new career." In addition, how much you elaborate on the emotional expression and how sincere you are can reflect intensity. Nonverbally, you can signal emotional intensity by raising your voice, using different vocal tones, gesturing flamboyantly, and using highly demonstrative facial expressions. Howell and Conway conducted a study of emotional valence and intensity and found that negative disclosures, whether intense or not, were rated as more intimate than positive disclosures.[50] Apparently, when you hear negative emotions expressed, you sense that the person is allowing you to see a deeper part of himself or herself than with positive emotions. Most people also rate highly intense positive emotional expression as intimate. Expressing jubilation or triumph in demonstrable ways reveals a deeper, more intimate side that is usually reserved for certain people. Generally, with regard to emotional self-disclosure, you must be willing to disclose how you feel to others, but at the same time you should carefully consider the target of your emotional expression.

Norms for Self-Disclosure

Why do men and women self-disclose differently? Are these differences based on genetics or hormones? Probably not. More likely, self-disclosure differences are based on the cultural norms that guide the behavior of men and women. Think of specific rules or suggestions that you have heard or been given that regulate how men and women should self-disclose as part of your culture. Do the rules change regarding self-disclosure to members of the opposite sex? to close family members versus strangers? to persons older or younger than you? to social versus business communication partners? Be ready to discuss these issues in class.

Cultural and Gender Differences

Before leaving the topic of self-disclosure, we will briefly touch on cultural and gender differences in self-disclosure patterns. Not all cultural groups self-disclose in the same manner. People in the United States, for example, tend to express their thoughts and feelings more openly than people in other cultures. In Japan, for example, self-disclosure is not seen as a primary means of developing relationships. In addition, the Japanese maintain relative privacy in their personal affairs. People living in Eastern European countries are also less likely to self-disclose than their Western European counterparts or people living in the United States. The Eastern European cultures tend to conceal their thoughts, feelings, and emotions in order to maintain harmonious relationships with those around them. Even within the United States, some co-cultures may be less willing to self-disclose than others.

Although much of the research on gender differences and self-disclosure suggests that women are more likely to self-disclose than men,[51] this assumption is an overgeneralization of actual communication patterns. Some studies have revealed no gender differences for self-disclosure,[52] while others have found that the two sexes have different reasons for disclosing. For example, women disclose more on the basis of liking the target, whereas men disclose on the basis of trusting the target.[53] Men are more likely to avoid self-disclosure in order to control the relationship ("Sure, I like you"), whereas women avoid self-disclosure in order to prevent hurt feelings ("Well, I didn't want to say anything").[54] The topics that are self-disclosed also vary between men and women. Women are more likely to discuss their feelings about women friends and spouses or lovers than men are.[55] Women are also likely to make disclosures about different topics than men.[56]

Competence Assessment

As a communicator, you are constantly assessing your competence level for signs of strengths and weaknesses. Competence assessment is especially conducted just after a communication performance, and particularly when the self has been exposed to other people. After instances of self-presentation and self-disclosure, you are likely to make four assessments of your level of communication competency. These competence levels range from very positive to very negative evaluations of how you communicated about the self. Four general assessments are self-actualization, self-adequacy, self-doubt, and self-denigration.

Self-Actualization

The most positive evaluation you can make about your competence level is referred to as **self-actualization**—the feeling and thoughts you get when you know that you have communicated perfectly, or almost perfectly. Assessments of communication competence at this level can provide you with a sense of fulfillment, allowing you to know that you have "come into your own." Obviously, self-actualization is a desirable condition, and communicators should consider it the ultimate achievement

SELF-ACTUALIZATION *The most positive evaluation one can make about one's competence level.*

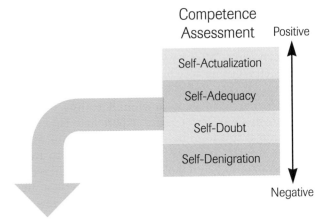

Competence Assessment

Positive

Self-Actualization

Self-Adequacy

Self-Doubt

Self-Denigration

Negative

FIGURE 3.6
In the model of the self and communication competence, assessment usually occurs immediately after performance. The assessment ranges from positive to negative.

level. We are not saying that a communicator actually communicates perfectly, but only that the communicator believes this to be so. As you recall from Chapter 2, perceptual accuracy depends on a number of factors, not the least of which is self-bias. Furthermore, as a communicator you may feel a sense of self-actualization even when you recognize that you haven't communicated perfectly. You may understand that this is the best job you could possibly do, and that may be enough for you to enjoy a feeling of fulfillment.

One of the potential pitfalls facing communicators who assess their competence at the self-actualization level is a false sense of security. Most communication performances are not perfect, and assuming such a level could lead to overconfidence or even arrogance, when in fact additional practice or effort would enhance communication competence. There is a second potential problem: You may allow an average performance to be elevated to self-actualization simply because you are unwilling to accept the fact that you could perform less than perfectly. You must strive toward self-actualization when you communicate while pursuing accuracy and honesty as you assess your performance after the fact.

Self-Adequacy

At times you may feel that your communication performance was good enough to get you through the situation. You may feel that you got your point across and made a pretty good impression on your communication partners. Although your assessments are still positive, they are less so than when you are self-actualized. When you assess your communication competence as sufficient or acceptable, you are feeling a sense of **self-adequacy.** Feelings of self-adequacy can lead you in two directions. First, you may feel that your ability to present the self needs to be extremely effective and that you need to improve your communication skills further. In this case, self-adequacy is your self-perception that you want to reach a higher level (self-actualization). Second, you may think that self-adequacy may not be all that bad. In fact, if you have been working very hard to improve your public speaking abilities and you realize that you performed competently, you may feel very proud and satisfied with your newfound feeling of self-adequacy. In this case, self-adequacy is a wonderful experience. However, you probably do not want to stop at this level because most communication skills require continuous fine-tuning, and you may be surprised to learn that with a little more effort, practice, and patience, you can achieve at even higher levels of competence. In other words, self-adequacy is a nice feeling, but more rewarding experiences may be ahead with a higher level of competence.

SELF-ADEQUACY
Assessment of one's communication competence as sufficient or acceptable.

Self-Doubt

In some instances you will feel uncertain about how you performed in a communication situation. The skepticism you feel about your communication performance could be based on the feedback you received from your listeners (raised eyebrows, ignoring you, arguing with you, etc.), or on lack of any feedback at all. **Self-doubt** is a feeling that your communication performance was probably below average, yet you are unsure how to assess your overall skill level. Self-doubt is not a positive assessment of your communication performance and could lead you to question your communication abilities, at least in that type of situation. It is uncomfortable to find yourself in a self-doubt situation, for it yields few tangible cues from which you can improve your skill level.

The best way to handle feelings of self-doubt is to objectively and systematically sort out those elements of your performance that you can safely assess as either positive or negative, and to put those that you are unsure of in a third group. You cannot always use other people as your sole source of feedback. You also have to rely on your ability to assess your own skills from your own perspective. When you separate what you know was good and bad about your performance, you can go to work to maintain and improve these elements, just as you would with an assessment of self-adequacy. Then you work on getting information about the questionable features of your performance. Ask yourself, "Why am I uncertain about these aspects of my performance?" "Is there someone who can shed some light on my competence level in these areas?" There is also the issue of time. An instantaneous assessment of your communication performance may not always serve your purposes best. Instead, by reflecting on your performance an hour later, or a day or a week later, you may discover things that were hidden from you just after the communication event. The key to reducing self-doubt is to get information that will remove your uncertainty so that you can work on improving your competence.

SELF-DOUBT
A feeling that one's communication performance was probably below average, coupled with uncertainty about assessing one's overall skill level.

Self-Denigration

The most negative assessment you can make about a communication performance is **self-denigration.** The word *denigration* refers to criticizing or attacking someone or something. When you really get down on yourself for a poor communication performance, you are pursuing a course of self-denigration. Why do people blame themselves for poor behavior or performance? Self-denigration is most likely to occur when communicators place undue importance on the weaknesses or shortcomings of a performance. Sometimes self-denigration is the final step in a self-fulfilling prophecy ("I

SELF-DENIGRATION
The most negative assessment one can make about one's communication performance.

The Case of Claire

Claire was recently promoted to manager of the student health center on a large university campus. In spite of her outstanding qualifications, she harbored deep negative feelings about leading staff meetings. She was a great one-on-one communicator but had no confidence in herself when she needed to face a group of her peers and subordinates. Each meeting seemed to her to be a disaster because people would ask tough questions that she was unable to answer. After each meeting (performance), she would spend the rest of the day reproaching herself for her poor communication. Claire's self-denigrating tendencies led to anxiety, and she began to question her ability to lead the student health center.

What should Claire have done about her self-denigrating attitude? Was she being realistic about her abilities? Why do some communicators focus on the dark aspects of performance instead of considering all the features involved? What are some ways that a person like Claire could work toward establishing a more positive pattern—toward "defeating" her self-denigration?

knew I would mess up that speech, I was just awful"). In other cases, communicators will misread the feedback in a communication situation and perceive an average or acceptable performance as poor. Because communication is an activity that is easily evaluated, the tendency is to look for things that can be perceived negatively. In almost every instance, however, self-denigration is unnecessary and unwarranted, and prevents real improvement in communication competence. One exception should be noted. Some cultures encourage its members to use self-denigration as one of its norms. Self-put-downs are seen as a means of respecting others and indicating that other people, God, and the environment are more important than the self. Self-denigration, therefore, is seen as part of the cultural fabric rather than as an incompetent communication skill.

How does self-denigration act as a major roadblock to communication competency? By attacking yourself for a poor communication performance, you will divert your attention and focus away from your needs as a communicator and toward self-defeating feelings of helplessness. Blaming yourself for poor performance can lead to self-pity, which will often feed on itself. Instead of focusing on how certain aspects of a communication performance can be improved, self-denigrating communicators choose to concentrate on the past by emphasizing the dark features of a performance.

You can move past self-denigration as a competence assessment by becoming more objective about the self and the communication situation. The following steps can be very helpful in *objectifying your assessment* of communication competence.

Remember that things are seldom as bad as you think they are. Self-denigration is a self-defeating condition that emphasizes the negative. Rarely is the situation as negative as it seems. Thoughts like "People think I'm no good because I made a lot of mistakes in my speech" are unrealistic and irrational. Instead, most people are probably thinking, "That speech was pretty good, except it could have been better organized." There is a big difference between these two perceptions.

Give yourself the benefit of the doubt. You might be surprised how many people are willing to give others the benefit of doubt. Think about how often you are willing to cut someone some slack because you want to help them. Most people are like you. If you are in a situation where you feel a great deal of pressure to communicate well (making acquaintances, leading a group, delivering a speech), you can expect a lot of support from people who sympathize. Most people are supportive communicators, and you should make the most of it.

Depersonalize the assessment. Self-denigration can be weakened when you move your perspective of self from the first to the third person. Taking a third-person perspective involves making your assessment of a communication performance as if someone else were conducting the evaluation. Third-person observers usually compare the skills of one person to those of another, and they do so objectively. You can be more objective by comparing your actual performance to the performance of people similar to you. Identify someone in your communication class as a source of comparison for the next assignment.

Give yourself feedback. Feedback from others is also helpful for making these comparisons. Although it is a bit more complicated, you can also become a third person by listening to yourself on audiotape or viewing your performance on videotape. You will be amazed how much objective information this technique yields. Even though many self-denigrators may fear such a review of their performance, over time they learn that a more first-person perspective is less honest and more self-defeating than the third-person, objective approach.

Claire, whose experience is described in the Reality Check "The Case of Claire," took a course in communication confidence at her university and learned to give herself more credit for her group leadership skills. She realized that most people were supportive of her efforts and that her performance was much better than she thought. She even videotaped a meeting and actually saw that she was motivating and organizing people to do their task better at the health center. Her major improvement was to become more objective in her self-competence assessment. In her words, "As I learned to see myself as others saw me, I was able to improve my skills at a very rapid rate."

Reacting to Competence Assessments

Once you make an assessment of your communication competency, you will almost always have a *reaction* or *response.* This response will lead to feedback that influences *the self* (see Figure 3.7). Your response to a competence assessment can range from *satisfaction* to *dissatisfaction.* At the extreme end of satisfaction is self-contentment, or a feeling of fulfillment based on a gratifying communication performance. A less satisfied response is self-improvement, which is a desire to do even better the next time. Self-protection is a dissatisfied response to competence assessment, reflecting a need to rationalize or explain away a less than perfect communication assessment. At the extreme end of dissatisfaction lies self-concealment, or the desire to hide the self from others as a result of a negative communication assessment.

Self-Contentment

SELF-CONTENTMENT

A person's reaction to knowing that he or she is very competent at something.

Have you ever been really satisfied with the way you felt about your communication performance? **Self-contentment** is the reaction you have when you know you are very competent at something. It is a pleasurable feeling because you can reflect positively back on your assessment of competence. Self-contentment is communicated to the self via feedback (see Figures 3.1 [on page 97] and 3.7) and can boost your self-esteem because of the gratifying communication performance that you assessed. In essence, a reaction of self-contentment sends strong signals to your self that you can be a very competent communicator in that particular situation. Erika went to see her friend José, to comfort him on the death of his father. Although nervous at first about saying the right thing, afterward, while driving home from José's house, she felt very good about the experience. In fact, she was quite content that she had been very supportive and comforting to José. This type of feedback about her performance added information to that part of her self-concept that holds information about comforting communication. In turn, this information led to a higher level of self-esteem, and for future instances when she needs to be comforting, her self-efficacy will be stronger.

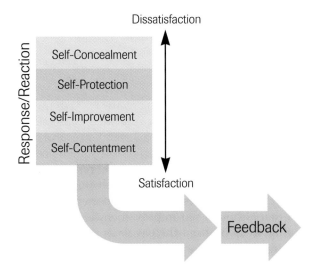

There is a flip side to self-contentment that you should be cautious about. Carried too far, self-contentment can cause you to be smug about your communication competence and become complacent about further improvement. John gave a presentation in his political science class and was very pleased with the results. His self-contentment led to a feeling of self-efficacy, a sense that "he could do no wrong." When he was faced with another presentation for his history class, he thought that he didn't need to prepare because he knew he was a great speaker. Unfortunately, he learned from the instructor that his poor preparation had resulted in a lackluster performance, and he was embarrassed with the results. John learned a valuable lesson. Self-contentment is a great reaction to competent communication as long as it is used to improve self-esteem and enhance self-efficacy, eventually leading to even more competent communication performances. Complacency is the wrong signal to send to the self.

Self-Improvement

When you recognize from your competence assessment that you could communicate even better the next time around, **self-improvement** is a typical reaction. Although self-improvement is placed near the satisfied end of the reaction/response continuum, self-improvement may be activated because you are very dissatisfied with your competence assessment. Self-improvement is a signal that you send to the self that you desire to be even more competent in your communication, regardless of current levels. You

SELF-IMPROVEMENT
Recognition, based on one's assessment of one's communicative competence in a particular situation, that one could communicate even better the next time around.

FIGURE 3.8

Self-evaluation of your communication competence must be honest and accurate if it is to help you improve. You may not start out exactly in the middle of the scale, but you should progress as you study.

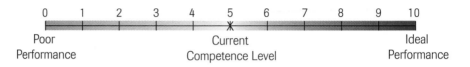

0 1 2 3 4 5 6 7 8 9 10

Poor Performance

Current Competence Level

Ideal Performance

probably know some very competent people who are always striving for perfection. In spite of their excellent skills, they react to a competence assessment with self-improvement ("How can I be even better the next time?"). Self-improvement is a constructive reaction to competence assessment, and we encourage you to consider it as the ideal response.

As a constructive source of feedback for the self, self-improvement must focus on a realistic method of progress toward greater competence. First, you need to realize that although self-improvement is not an easy process, it is very gratifying. Keep in mind the payoff as you tackle the job of enhancing your competence. Second, you need to plot or chart your current competence level relative to where you would like to be. For example, positioning your competence level on a 1 to 10 scale could be helpful in plotting a self-improvement path. This method allows you to see where you are now (somewhere around 5, an average communicator), where you would like to be (8 or 9, an ideal performance), and where you will never be (1, very poor performance). Your self-improvement response can now focus on moving your competence level toward the ideal performance end of the scale. You can use any method for this process, but make sure that you are accurate and honest.

The next step toward a self-improvement response is identifying your strengths and weaknesses. Although you may enjoy several communication strengths (strong speaking voice, effective gestures), you have to ensure that these are maintained. Don't let your strengths fade while you are working on your shortcomings. When examining your weaknesses, identify very specific and tangible aspects of your communication performance that can be refined. Avoid the trap of assuming that a general shortcoming can be improved. It is much easier to work on little things than it is to correct major problems. By way of illustration, as a small-group member it would be much easier for you to improve your negative attitude about one member of the group by focusing only on the task and leaving personalities out of the discussion, rather than to attempt self-improvement by trying to be a more productive group member. Find *specific* aspects of your communication that you can focus on and then work toward progressive improvement in these particulars.

Throughout this process you are sending feedback to the self that indicates your willingness to become more competent. In turn, this will affect your self-esteem and self-efficacy, giving you a better chance for real improvement in your communication.

Self-Protection

The self will on occasion come under attack or feel vulnerable owing to outside forces or your own failures. For many people, **self-protection** refers to the self's use of communication as a device to ward off the harmful effects of negative evaluation (by both self and others) owing to failure. Self-protective strategies can also be used to preempt or prevent potential instances of negative evaluation (by both self and others) based on predicted failure. In this section we will discuss ways in which self-protection techniques work.

SELF-PROTECTION
The self's use of communication as a device for warding off the harmful effects of negative evaluation (by both self and others) owing to failure.

Once you form a self-concept with its evaluative component, self-esteem, it is in your best interest to preserve your self-esteem as best you can. Research demonstrates that many high-self-esteem people view failure and success differently according to this principle.[57] They see failure as a result of external factors ("circumstances beyond my control") but view success as something they are responsible for ("I feel proud of my accomplishments"). Lower-self-esteem individuals are more likely to attribute failure to self. Self-protection also occurs when you attribute failure or potential failure to the difficulty of the task or problem and credit luck with the misfortune.[58] Using task difficulty ("It was a difficult topic to speak on") as a self-protection device shifts the focus of failure onto external causes that are beyond the person's control. Luck or misfortune can be seen in the same way ("I sounded nervous because I had to speak first").

Researcher Jones has presented a related concept to account for the way people will associate success and failure with their self-esteem. It is termed the *discounting principle* and it refers to how people exaggerate task difficulty while deemphasizing their effort during a performance.[59] According to Jones, people in society place a great deal of value on natural ability. If you fail at some communication task, such as interviewing for a promotion, you can protect self-esteem by emphasizing how difficult it is for someone with your limited experience to get such a position (task difficulty) and by indicating that you really didn't try very hard (effort). In this way, your abilities (and esteem) do not come under as much scrutiny as if you simply said, "I'm not good enough for the position." This type of self-protection is targeted for others by protecting your self-presentational image with them, and it is also targeted for your own view of self.

Should none of these strategies work, there is always a fallback position defined as intentionality. When failure occurs, you can always claim that you did not intend for things to happen the way they did.[60] Your intentions were good, but circumstances prevented you from being able to perform your communication responsibilities competently. "Oh, I didn't intend for it to sound that way," "That's not what I meant," and "I didn't plan it to turn out that way" are all messages used to avoid negative evaluation of communication. You protect your self by suggesting that you may have communicated inappropriately but you didn't mean to. Self-protection is not a very constructive response to a negative competence assessment; self-improvement is a much better strategy when you realize that your presentation of self was inadequate.

▓ *Self-Concealment*

The most negative response you could make to a competence assessment would be to decide to conceal future information about the self. When you feel the need to withhold from others information that is distressing or negative, you are involved in **self-concealment.** Put another way, "self-concealment involves the conscious concealment of personal information (thoughts, feelings, actions, or events) that is highly intimate and negative in valence."[61] Although research shows that any given person will self-conceal more or less than others, the primary reason behind self-concealment is an effort to obscure from others the most traumatic and painful experiences of one's life. Some of these experiences may result from the aggressiveness of others (child abuse, rape, humiliation) and others may be a result of the person's own shortcomings (embarrassment, failure, fears). Or an individual may conceal serious medical conditions, dark personal secrets, or betrayal by others.

In many instances, self-concealment may be appropriate to the situation or to the person or people with whom you are communicating. For example, in a job interview, you would not want to disclose embarrassing information that was irrelevant to your qualifications for the position. In more personal relationships, you might postpone negative revelations until you felt confident that your relational partner could be trusted with the information. There is legitimate reason to be concerned that you might be characterized by negative self-disclosures to the exclusion of other aspects of your personality ("She's the unwed mother who gave her baby up for adoption"; "He used to do drugs").

To have no one in whom you can confide, however, can be painful and harmful. The physical, emotional, and psychological problems associated with self-concealment are numerous. According to most psychological theories, expressing traumatic and negative information is therapeutic in that the discloser does not have to harbor these dark feelings alone. The act of confiding dark information to another improves self-esteem and mental health. As Pennebaker suggests, "The act of not discussing or confiding the event with another may be more damaging than having experienced the event per se."[62] Psychological symptoms such as depression and anxiety can result from self-concealment, as can physical symptoms such as reduced immune system functioning.[63] In essence, self-concealment hinders a coping process that could result from discussing these dark secrets with others.

How can you learn to overcome self-concealment tendencies? First, you need to recognize that everyone has failed or has experienced traumatic events in life. Other people are harboring dark secrets as well. Second, you need to realize that sharing negative information is not an incompetent communication act. When the circumstances are right, commiserating with others about distressing information is a valuable experience for everyone concerned. You may learn that numerous people share your same secret. Third, you should search for a trusted confidant and reveal, little by little, your traumatic information. The confidant you choose may actually be flattered to be trusted with such intimate information. Fourth, if you cannot find someone to confide in on a personal level, you can seek out support groups that focus on your problems (substance abuse, incest, etc.). These groups provide moral and emotional support when you reveal your confidential information; again, you may also find that many other people harbor the same secrets. Finally, you can enlist the help of a professional who can help you work through the reasons for your self-concealment. The key is getting this information out in the open so that you can deal with it more objectively. This is especially important when self-concealment is painful or inhibits your ability to function well in your environment.

Feedback

Information you receive about self is termed **feedback.** It comes in many forms. Some types of feedback are positive, some are ambiguous, and still others are negative. The response you make to your competence assessment is a very important source of feedback. From Figures 3.1 and 3.7 you can observe how feedback, in the form of reactions to competence assessments, flows back to the self. Ideally, the self is permeable (as demonstrated by the dotted line in Figure 3.1 on p. 97) so that it can learn from the feedback. The solid line on the inside of the self reflects a degree of stability.

How you incorporate feedback into the self depends on several factors. One of the most important factors is your *sensitivity level* to feedback. Research demonstrates that some individuals are highly sensitive to feedback, whereas others are largely unaffected by such information.[64] Presumably, people who are more sensitive to feedback are susceptible and receptive to information about their abilities, knowledge, talents, and the rest. Low-sensitive people would be less responsive to information about their self. For example, when Joan ignores suggestions that she bathe more frequently, she is being insensitive to feedback about her personal hygiene.

FEEDBACK
Information learned about the self that is used by the self to learn and mature.

Feedback is a more complicated picture than what was just painted. First, the type and source of feedback can make a big difference in how high and low sensitives view this information. Edwards believes that low sensitives may be susceptible to feedback from particular sources they find worthy, such as teachers, other authority figures, parents, and best friends.[65] They have a low sensitivity to feedback because they rely on just a few sources of feedback. High sensitives, on the other hand, probably rely on many different sources. They look for feedback from parents, friends, neighbors, salesclerks, and even college professors. Furthermore, it is assumed that high sensitives have a more fully developed self-schema than low sensitives.[66] People who receive and interpret more feedback will assimilate more information about the self. The number of self-schemata will increase, resulting in a self-concept that is more vast (and probably more accurate) than that of low sensitives. Therefore, sensitivity to feedback has a positive effect on self-concept because people gain knowledge about self through this process.

What about feedback sensitivity and self-esteem? At first glance, it might be convenient to assume that high sensitives possess a stronger and more positive self-esteem than low sensitives. Such an assumption overgeneralizes the nature of feedback sensitivity. Simply because high sensitives search for, and are receptive to, information about self does not guarantee an enhanced self-esteem. Negative information can be incorporated into an already negative self-schema ("I knew I couldn't make small talk with strangers!"). Furthermore, being a low sensitive and someone who is less susceptible to feedback does not ensure low self-esteem. Low sensitives may be less interested in external feedback simply because they already

---

SELF-CHECK

Are You a High Sensitive or a Low Sensitive?

Stop for a moment and reflect on your sensitivity to feedback. Would you characterize yourself as a high sensitive or a low sensitive? Answer the following questions to get a better idea of your sensitivity to feedback.

1. Do you ignore what other people say when they comment on your abilities, skills, physical appearance, success level, or intelligence?
2. Do you seek out feedback from people concerning these areas of self?
3. Are you interested in learning what other people have to say about you?
4. Do you often wonder whether people really mean what they say about you?

possess high self-esteem and really do not need any more information for making judgments about themselves. Low sensitives simply may not care ("I don't have time to worry about comments from someone subordinate to me at work").

A larger issue than feedback sensitivity exists. Assuming that even low-sensitive people receive some feedback about their self, how do high- and low-self-esteem people react to feedback, regardless of their sensitivity level? There are two possibilities. The first possibility is termed *self-enhancing theory* and refers to the notion that low-self-esteem people have a need to improve their view of self and seek information or feedback that is positive and favorable.[67] They will react more favorably to positive then to less positive information. Accordingly, low-self-esteem people are more likely to "enhance" their self by attributing positive information to self ("We won the game; I guess I *am* a great softball player") and attribute negative information to other sources ("We lost; I wish the team hadn't let me down"). As a communicator, you may use self-enhancing theory to search for information that will build your self-esteem in the social skills area. How often do you seek out friends who bring out your best in communicating?

The second possibility is termed *self-consistency theory.*[68] According to this notion, people will be sensitive to information that is consistent with their existing self-esteem and resistant to information that contradicts their self-view. From this perspective, high-self-esteem persons will react favorably to information that supports their positive view of self and ignore or disbelieve information that is inconsistent with their self-esteem. On the other hand, low-self-esteem persons will maintain consistency by accepting information that confirms their poor view of self—that is, negative information—and will react unfavorably to positive information that might contradict their low-self-esteem perspective ("I don't believe him when he says I am attractive; he just wants something from me").

Regardless of which theory is correct, Shrauger suggests six different ways of looking at the reactions or responses that people can have to feedback.[69] As you read the following list, ask yourself what reaction you usually have when hearing positive and negative feedback about yourself.

- Your initial reaction when hearing the information. Are you always optimistic? *"I can count on my leadership skills."* Pessimistic? *"I knew it wouldn't work to my advantage."*

- Your assessment of the dependability and legitimacy of the person providing the feedback. *"Does this person's opinion count?"* *"I can count on this person."*

- Whether you accept responsibility for the action or performance or attribute it to something or to others. *"Did I do this?"* *"I'm glad I'm a positive person."*

- Whether you feel satisfied with the feedback. *"Finally my hard work paid off." "If only I had finished two weeks earlier."*
- Whether you change your behavior after hearing the feedback. *"This didn't work; let's try another plan." "I don't believe it; this must be a mistake."*
- Whether you change your self-evaluation and expectations for yourself as a result of feedback. *"Well, this minor setback is simply an annoyance." "Oh, well, I'm a klutz." "Thank goodness I found this out in time; now I can really develop a plan."*

The next time you receive feedback, try to use this list to determine whether you are making the best use of the information for the self. The bottom line is making feedback work for you and your self.

REVIEW

This chapter discussed one of the more important aspects of competent communication. How you view yourself affects the way you communicate with others. Similarly, communicating with others can shape how you conceive of yourself. Self-concept was defined as the awareness and understanding of who you are as interpreted and influenced by your thoughts, actions, abilities, values, goals, and ideals. Self-concept affects a number of factors influencing communication, such as memory and recall, perception, and self-evaluation.

Self-schema theory was discussed as a way of understanding the self; it involves organizing your thoughts about self into frameworks (self-schemata) that facilitate social interaction. Another way of viewing self-concept is through a consideration of possible selves which refers to aspirations, motives, goals, and fears you have about yourself. They are predictions of what could happen to you.

Self-esteem is an evaluation of the self-concept or how you feel about self. Self-esteem influences communication in many ways. The stronger your self-esteem, the more likely you will view communication situations as positive. The feedback you receive about your self-esteem allows you to constantly review your feelings for self, as long as you are sensitive to such information. Self-certainty refers to how strong your sense of self-identity is for a particular area. The more certain you are about areas of your self, the more likely you are to feel positive self-esteem.

Self-efficacy was discussed as the process of predicting, on the basis of your self-concept, how successful you can be in communication situations. More positive predictions of self-efficacy should lead to more successful communication performances. Self-presentation was discussed as a method of conveying yourself to others. You reveal your positive traits through this process. Self-monitoring—how people communicate in ways that are socially appropriate—was reviewed. It is related to self-concept in that viewing yourself as sensitive to situational contexts allows you to communicate according to the requirements of the situation. Self-disclosure, discussed as providing information about the self that you make known to others, depends on several factors, including trust, liking, length of the relationship, and gender.

After a communication performance that reveals the self to others, you will make a competence assessment. Four general assessments are possible, ranging from positive to negative: self-actualization, self-adequacy, self-doubt, and self-denigration. As a communicator, you will want to find ways to use the more positive competence assessments as methods to improve communication performance.

As a method of providing feedback to the self about your communication skills, you will react or respond to the competence assessment. Self-contentment is a feeling of gratification, an awareness that you did an excellent job of communicating. Self-improvement is a reaction that indicates that you want to enhance your communication competency even further. Self-protection is a method of attributing failure to external causes so that your self-esteem is protected. Finally, there are some things in your past that you may not wish to disclose to others, and self-concealment involves the conscious sheltering of that information. Self-concealment can have injurious effects on your physical and mental well-being. Feedback allows the self-concept to learn and grow. Self-esteem takes its cue from this information by forming opinions about assessments of communication competence that lead the self-efficacy process to new levels. This constantly evolving process should improve both your view of the self and your communication.

SUGGESTED READINGS

Jourard, S. M. (1971). *Self-disclosure: An experimental analysis of the transparent self.* New York: Wiley-Interscience.

Ross, L., & Nisbett, R. E. (1991). *The person and the situation: Perspectives of social psychology.* Philadelphia: Temple University Press.

4

Language and Communication

Objectives

After reading this chapter you should be able to

1. Describe how language operates with other behaviors to generate meaning.

2. Explain how language is acquired and developed.

3. Distinguish acquiring language from acquiring communication.

4. Apply the five functional communication competencies to communication behavior.

5. Recognize the thinking process and language skills necessary for understanding media.

6. Use the triangle of meaning to explain the relationship among symbols, thoughts, and their referents.

7. Apply the abstraction ladder to the use of specific versus general language.

8. Recognize how culture and language interact.

9. Recognize the applications of context to language.

10. Describe how language communicates information about relationships, control, and affiliation.

CHAPTER CONTENTS

Sticks and stones may break my bones,
but names will never hurt me.

THIS FAMILIAR RESPONSE to some childhood taunt was meant to deny the power of language, to say that words don't count, that they can't possibly affect a person the way physical attacks can. You probably didn't believe that playground response when you were compelled to use it, but you used that language in an attempt to stand up for yourself, to counter a perceived insult. Language served a function for you—that of maintaining your image in the face of adversity.

Even if you didn't believe your own words at that time in your childhood, you already knew that words are powerful weapons. They can hurt, manipulate, deceive, or lead a person astray.

But you also know that words are powerful tools. They can protect, express feeling, gain influence, restore peace, provide comfort or a compliment. Talking with someone can ease your burdens, cheer you up, or calm you down.

The childhood saying is actually quite accurate; words can't hurt you. The meaning, however, that you get from those words can hurt you deeply. If friends were teasing you, you might respond with a laugh, but if one of your known enemies taunted you, you would likely become defensive and interpret the taunt in a very negative way. Then your "sticks and stones" response would be your form of protection.

LANGUAGE
A symbol system used to think about and communicate experiences and feelings.

Language is a symbol system used to think about and communicate experiences and feelings. It is the meaning people attach to language that gives it its power, not the words themselves. The communication adage is, "Meanings are in people, not in the words themselves."

This chapter on language and communication examines how you acquire language, how culture influences your thoughts and your language, and how you use language in your relationships to influence others and express affection.

Of course, language is not spoken by itself. That is, a number of nonverbal behaviors accompany language—pauses, stutters, tone and volume of the voice, the speed at which someone speaks, the accents he or she employs, the gestures made while speaking, and the many other messages sent through body movements that tell us how much meaning can be conveyed in just a few words. Those forms of nonverbal communication are studied in depth in Chapter 5. As you read Chapter 4, it is important that you understand that language does not occur in isolation—that nonverbal behaviors, especially those associated with the voice, always accompany speech. Our goal in this chapter is to examine the way we extract meaning from language. Here we set the foundation for understanding the interplay of both verbal and nonverbal communication by focusing on language itself.

Language Acquisition

The first word you spoke as a child was probably greeted with much celebration by parents and family. No doubt, many phone calls were made to announce your accomplishment to anyone who would listen, and it was duly recorded in your "baby book." You were simply amazing, and you were encouraged to produce more words.

Many researchers, as well as laypeople, have long been acutely interested in the way children acquire language. From the early work of the psychologist Piaget,[1] who studied his own two children in great detail, to the more recent and comprehensive summaries of research by Wood,[2] people have been fascinated with a child's acquisition of language and have debated how it occurs.

For many years, a great controversy has raged over whether animals can use language. Despite many individual claims that a chimpanzee can "sign," solid research concludes that the animals do not really use language to communicate on a level comparable to human language expression. Research also shows that children isolated from human language communities do not develop language on their own.[3] So, how do people acquire language?

Here are some basic questions: Do you have to be able to think about something before you name it? Do you have to engage in nonverbal behaviors (such as pointing) before you produce a word? Or does language come before thought or nonverbal behaviors? How do children learn to respond? Perhaps they don't, and the response is just innate, preprogrammed. There are five basic views.

Nature

Some people argue that the infant's response is built in, that language is *species-specific.*[4] That is, according to the **nature approach**, children are equipped with specific clues to the structures of language because of their genetic makeup. They point out that all children acquire language at about the same age, just as they acquire certain physical skills.

Scholars who argue that language is innate point out that language acquisition parallels the development of coordination in young children (see Table 4.1 on p. 146). The beginning coos and chuckles of the infant of 4 months give way to the continuous babble of the 6- to 9-month-old ("babababab"). The child of 12 to 18 months, standing and walking alone, uses a few words ("dink" for drink or "bada" for bottle) and sometimes follows simple commands ("Stop" or "Come here"). The child of 18 to 21 months can understand simple questions ("Where is the ball?") and put two

NATURE APPROACH
An approach to language acquisition which holds that language acquisition is an innate human developmental process and does not depend on environmental factors.

TABLE 4.1 LANGUAGE DEVELOPMENT

AGE	LANGUAGE BEHAVIOR
4 months	Children coo and chuckle when people play with them.
6–9 months	Children babble ("gagagaga," "mamamama").
12–18 months	Children use a few words and follow simple commands; they know what "no" means.
18–21 months	Children form two- or three-word sentences and understand simple questions.
24–27 months	Children use their 300- to 400-word vocabularies to form short sentences.
30–33 months	Children sound more adultlike as they form three- and four-word sentences from their increased vocabularies.
36–39 months	Children talk in well-developed sentences, applying rules of grammar; others can usually understand them.

Source: Adapted from B. S. Wood (1981), *Children and communication: Verbal and nonverbal language development* (2nd ed.) (Englewood Cliffs, NJ: Prentice-Hall), pp. 27–29.

or three words together in sentences ("Me up."). A child of 2 years (24–27 months) can use short sentences from a 300- to 400-word vocabulary ("Baby play ball outside"). By 30–33 months, as the size of their vocabulary increases, children create three- and four-word sentences easily, beginning to sound more adultlike. And by the age of 3 (36–39 months) children can usually talk in well-formed sentences, applying elementary grammar to their utterances and understanding their own communication.

Because most children acquire language similarly within these age categories, the nature theorists argue that language must be built into our genetic code.

▨ *Nurture*

NURTURE APPROACH
An approach to language acquisition which holds that language is acquired because of the language environment surrounding a person.

Other researchers believe that children learn language through *imitation and reinforcement*. The **nurture approach** views environmental factors as the most important determinants of language acquisition.[5] As children are stimulated by their parents, siblings, and other care givers, they respond by imitating what they have seen and heard. The responses that others make to them reinforce their communication, and thus they continue to learn.

From this perspective, children strive to produce early sounds that are like the adult speech they hear. They listen to older children talking and try to mimic them. From the positive responses they get from family and peers (reinforcement) they receive the motivation to continue their efforts at imitation.

▨ Cognition

Another argument is that thinking must precede language. These *cognitive* models emphasize that certain thinking abilities, such as causality and intentionality, are precursors to language development. Thus a child must develop certain thinking patterns before producing language.

Piaget studied children's thinking patterns. In particular, he infers from their behavior (including their language) what their thinking patterns are (see Table 4.2 on p. 148). His stages of thinking are important because they link thought and language, and because they deal with the older child as well as the younger.

Stage 1, from birth to 2 years of age, is a time of identifying the main features of the child's environment—air, water, and food, for example. Children at this stage (Acquisition of Perceptual Invariants) learn that a toy hidden behind the sofa still exists even though it is not visible. (Piaget called this object-permanence.) This process of thinking about objects as permanent should, according to Piaget, precede naming them. Once acquired, the "name" of an object can be applied in multiple situations. A child at Stage 1 will produce "water" for the liquid in the cup, on the floor, in the tub, or down the drain.

Stage 2, Preoperational Intuitive Thinking, occurring from about the ages of 2 through 7, is a time of processing the elementary concepts of time, space, and causality. Thus children would think about time passing before talking about being late or early, would conceptualize distance before talking about inches or miles, and would grapple with cause and effect before producing language that accepted responsibility for having broken the living-room lamp.

Stage 3, Concrete Operational Thinking, ages 7 to 11, is the stage of understanding complex relationships, such as the conservation of volume and weight. Observations of liquids and solids could produce language about them. Observations about human relationships could also produce explanations of "why" so-and-so likes or hates someone else.

Not until age 11 or beyond, says Piaget, do children develop the ability to make complex inferences, go through logical propositions, and make hypotheses. This Formal Propositional Thinking, Stage 4, would enable complex language arguments and logical statements. The child could make a case for being allowed to stay up longer, or to buy that video game or CD *now*, instead of waiting until later, when it might be sold out or more expensive.

TABLE 4.2 DEVELOPMENT OF COMMUNICATION SKILLS

AGE	COMMUNICATION BEHAVIOR
birth–15 months	*Interpersonal Communication*
	Uses primarily one-to-one communication
	Uses primarily nonverbal communication (sounds, facial expression, touch)
	Learns times for interaction/withdrawal
	Engages in game playing and cooperative activities
4 months–3 years	*Communication Effects*
	Participates in interactive routines (turn taking)
	Alters messages to accomplish goals
	Acquires linguistic communication (from single words to complex sentences)
3–5 years	*Communication Strategies*
	Uses wide range of communication behaviors to adapt to different situations (e.g., uses politeness conventions, asks questions)
	Initiates and sustains conversations
5 years and up	*Communication Monitoring*
	Checks for message accuracy and adequacy
	Comments about conversations ("talk about talk")

Source: Adapted from B. Haslett & A. Alexander (1988), Developing communication skills. In R. P. Hawkins, J. M. Wiemann, & S. Pingree (Eds.), *Advancing communication science: Merging mass and interpersonal processes* (Newbury Park, CA: Sage), p. 229.

Interaction

Another group of language acquisition researchers supports the interactionist model of language acquisition. Interactionists emphasize the social aspects of language acquisition. They believe that the richness and quality of interaction are the primary determinants of the quality and rapidity of communication acquisition. They point out that if you grow up in a communication-rich environment, you acquire language quickly; you develop skills that you can practice.

Observe a mother or father interacting with an infant. The mother and father use language to talk to the infant and, in speaking, also pattern the intonations and rhythms of the language they speak. They speak to the child and then stop expectantly, smiling and waiting for some response. Slowly, infants learn it is their turn to communicate, and they smile or cry or babble something back.

The more the various types of communication interactions are repeated, and the greater varieties of language used, the more developed the child becomes in language use. Perhaps you have even known parents who, in addition to vocalizing all the time to create a language-rich environment, write labels for all the objects in the house to hasten their child's development of language skills.

There is some value in each of these four approaches. Obviously, those who believe language is innate or inborn are at the complete opposite end of the scale from those who believe that language is solely the result of environment. But each of these approaches contains some truth, and some value is to be gained from considering all of them together.

FIGURE 4.1
Reading to a child regularly from the time the child is an infant is one way to provide a language-rich environment.

Homology

HOMOLOGY MODEL
A model of language acquisition which holds that thinking, coordination, and language capabilities develop simultaneously.

Bates has proposed what is called a **homology model** of language acquisition.[6] The term *homology*, when applied to behaviors, means that behaviors have a shared structural base. Thus language, thought, and social interaction all contribute to the acquisition of language and the further development of thought and more social interaction.

Language is seen to develop on a parallel course with some cognitive capacities, to follow certain others, and to constitute the building blocks of future thought. Social interaction may be the necessary environment in which language develops; at the same time, social interaction may be seen as the *result* of language acquisition.

In Bates's terms, "there is a Great Borrowing going on,"[7] in which language, thought, and social interaction enable the production of one another, often simultaneously.

Bates points out that certain precursors to the production of language are known to exist and that language development is related to the development of gestures in young children. She maintains that communicative pointing is the best predictor of the beginnings of language production.[8] For example, many toddlers begin to give names to objects shortly after they develop the behavior of pointing to indicate what they want. Thus a child would move an arm or hand toward an object before naming it, would point at his or her father before producing "Dada," and would at least gesture toward the cookie jar before attempting "cookie." And later in language development, a child would gesture toward him- or herself before producing, "Me want cookie." Bates argues that this latter accomplishment is significant in that it distances the person from the object (i.e., the child from the cookie), illustrating more complex thought and language.

REALITY CHECK

Reflections on Language Acquisition

What were your first spoken words? At what ages were they spoken? Can you or others recall the events or people that prompted these words? How big a role did environment play in your language acquisition? Which of the approaches to language acquisition do you think makes the most sense? How would you encourage language acquisition in children around you? Answers to these questions can help demonstrate the complexity of language acquisition.

It is the complexity of thought and language structures that makes human children different from chimpanzees, who are able to learn certain symbols only under certain conditions. Human children produce more language, and their language and cognitive skills enable them to produce new configurations of language, to adapt what they already know to novel situations.

Thus, the child goes from stretching arms upward, to vocalizing sounds ("uh, uh") while stretching arms upward, to saying "up" while stretching arms upward, to saying, "Daddy, up!" to saying "Daddy, please pick me up." Many years later, the child says, "Daddy, pick me up around the corner from the movie theater so my friends won't see you."

Understanding language acquisition is important for a number of reasons. As parents, teachers, and relatives of young children, we need to help them develop language; we need to be patient as their learning goes on and to realize the frustrations they may encounter; we need to encourage both the simple and complex forms of language; we need to help children learn in a fun, creative, and positive way. The acquisition of language is crucial to communication skills. Finally, we need to help children use language in positive ways because they will encounter it in negative ways in other contexts. The "sticks and stones" quote at the beginning of this chapter illustrates the result of negative language.

Communication Acquisition

Competent communicators need to acquire not only language but also communication.

When you learn language, you are learning isolated words and grammar, but when you acquire communication, you are learning how to use the entire symbol systems of a culture appropriately, how to construct meaningful messages. Communication is competent when meaningful messages are created that are appropriate and effective. Thus the real emphasis in language acquisition is communication acquisition.

Communication acquisition, then, requires not only that people learn language, but also that they decide how to use that language to accomplish goals. Chapter 1 pointed out that communication is functional when it accomplishes goals for the participants. As you acquire communication skills, you are learning how language and other behaviors *function*, how they work for you.

Wood cites five basic functional *communication competencies* that children acquire as they move toward adulthood. They develop these functional competencies concurrently; that is, they acquire aspects of one at the same time as they acquire aspects of others. These competencies develop as children interact with family and peers, and as they process the media, especially television, which give them a broader picture of the social world. The five functional competencies are controlling, feeling, informing, imagining, and ritualizing.

Controlling

A child learns to use language to control self, others, and the environment. The appropriate use of language can make children appear "cute" or "smart," giving them influence. At age 2, some children attempt to control their parents; "no" seems to be their favorite word. Or a child may scream, "I *won't* do it!" in front of an audience to intimidate parents. Although these sound like negative examples, control is actually a neutral term; it may be positive or negative. Learning how to control (influence) others is a crucial social skill.

A child of 3 or 4 can boss other children around, give orders, or gain compliance through quiet words and smiles. A 4-year-old can request action from peers or adults.

Older children bargain ("I'll eat my peas if I can have ice cream") or manipulate ("You're the best, Mom—can I stay up just a little longer to finish watching this movie?"). And by the time children reach age 16, most learn how to get the car from their parents, push their friends to see the movie they want to see, or convince a romantic interest to go out with them.

Feeling

As with many of these functional competencies, effectively expressing emotions is not easy. We cry or laugh in the early stages. Children as young as 3 or 4 can say, "I'm sad." Children have to learn how to express liking, love, respect, empathy, hostility, pride—a complex set of emotions.

Children sometimes express feeling by comforting someone else ("I'll be quiet while you rest your headache, Aunt June"). And Wood points out that third and fourth graders routinely use threats, bribes, insults, and praise as ways of trying to express their feelings.[9]

Teens spend hours talking about who likes whom and how much, about how they resent or care for their parents, or about how they "love" or "hate" school or some other person.

As an adult, you are sometimes chided for not having acquired the ability to express your feelings appropriately. "You never tell me how you really *feel*," a loved one may say. What you may have learned is that expressing feelings is not always a good idea, so you don't express a feeling, judging it to be inappropriate, or at least risky, for a given situation.

In a small-group setting, you might have to express your feelings of frustration to other group members or express your feelings of relief and happiness once your group project is completed. In business, you might save your company a lot of money by effectively explaining your fears and hesitancy about a proposal to your vice president.

Informing

Giving people information that they can understand is an important skill to acquire. And understanding the messages of others is an equally important skill.

Anyone who has ever tried to get a young child to "Tell me where it hurts" realizes the difficulty he or she may have in informing you in an understandable way. If "everywhere" is the answer you get, you have difficulty pinpointing the problem. Of course you try to use your adult skills, questioning more effectively to get at the source of the problem.

Questioning and describing are important functional competencies in this category. Parents and teachers may ask children of 6 or 7 to repeat directions to their school or their home. They are encouraged to produce questions they would ask if they were lost ("May I use the telephone?" "In which direction is State Street?"). Older children develop complex vocabularies for describing action; they can give details about how each Super

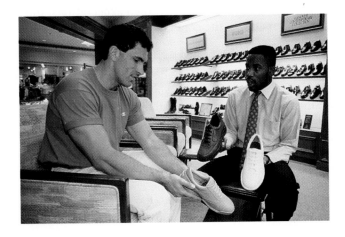

FIGURE 4.2
Without language, informing others and obtaining information from them would be very difficult.

Nintendo character moves, or they can describe the behaviors of all their classmates at the school dance.

At the adult level, this functional competency exhibits itself in very important ways. If you miss a class lecture, you seek out someone who can give you the lecture notes and then use clear language that helps you with the details and examples the professor used to explain the notes. You, in turn, ask sufficient questions to clarify the material you don't understand, so that your questioning skills often enhance your classmate's descriptive skills.

Effective informing skills are vital when you give a speech; you must choose powerful language to get your points across, but you must be careful not to use language that might offend anyone in your audience. The functional competency of informing remains a crucial one even to adults.

▨ Imagining

Probably the most complex functional competency is imagining. It is the ability to think, to play, to be creative in communication. Children pretend to do something or to be someone (a superhero, a cartoon character, a person from a movie). They also role-play ("You be the bad guy, and I'll be the good guy"). They use images, creating glorious sets in their minds for the dramas they enact. They are spaceship captains or graceful and famous dancers.

"What do you want to be when you grow up?" You may even have asked that question jokingly of a friend of yours recently. But when you were a young child, you could imagine great things and tell wondrous tales of what you would do. Some people become embarrassed by the question as they grow older. Afraid that they may not live up to their own expectations, they use language that limits or shuts down the conversation ("When I grow up, I'll be a bum").

Imagining in the adult world is the source of new theories, complex solutions, crazy jokes, and pleasurable plans. On the job, it is the ability to use language to convey to your co-workers your vision for the company. In public speaking, imagining may create hypothetical examples to draw in an audience. In a debate, imagining skills enable you to think ahead of your opponent, to put words to each side of an argument, and to use language in ways that are logical and convincing.

An architect must use language, as well as blueprints and models, to explain the images the building will evoke. The comic chooses language that calls up vivid funny images in the mind of the audience.

Plan a trip or party with your friends, and you'll realize the language competency needed to communicate your image to them.

Ritualizing

The fifth basic functional competency involves learning the rules for managing conversations and relationships. Learning to say "hi" or "bye-bye" or "please" means internalizing early politeness conventions.

You usually get immediate rewards managing conversations well, and thus you feel involved with others. Early peek-a-boo games may teach the beginnings of turn-taking in conversations, followed by how to introduce others and yourself. Teasing, joke telling, and even gossiping may become early lessons in how to manage relationships.

REALITY CHECK

Observing Functional Competencies

Observe the five basic functional competencies in those around you. From memories of your own childhood or by observing children, note the language behaviors that are used to control, feel, inform, imagine, and ritualize. Then note the parallel adult examples of the functional competencies.

FUNCTIONAL COMPETENCY	CHILD BEHAVIOR	ADULT BEHAVIOR
Controlling		
Feeling		
Informing		
Imagining		
Ritualizing		

Note the similarities and differences between children and adults.

In adulthood, ritualizing effectively means you say and do the "right" thing at weddings, funerals, dinners, dates, athletic events, and other social gatherings. Rituals may be as formal as the highly prescribed Japanese tea ceremony (where every nonverbal movement and nuance is also important) or as informal as the party organized with your friends to watch the Super Bowl.

The five functional competencies of controlling, informing, feeling, imagining, and ritualizing are thus important aspects of communication development. Learning how to make language and other behaviors work together for you helps you function effectively.

Acquisition of Media Skills

Acquiring functional competencies is complicated by the many contexts in which you must observe and use language. Media present other challenges for communication acquisition. In addition to the interpersonal skills you develop (which carry over to understanding media, especially television), you have to develop media-specific skills. Children today process not only newspapers, magazines, comic books, radio, and television, they also make extensive use of cassette tapes, compact disks, music videos, movies, computers, and video games.

Acquiring communication also means acquiring skills for understanding media (see Table 4.3). Being able to talk *about* the media we use, being able to use language appropriate *to* that media (e.g., using codes and "shorthand" in electronic mail), and being able to understand the language of the media being used—all are important to competent communication. Communication in our society today is increasingly being mediated; television, movies, video games, radio, telephones (and car phones), computers (and electronic mail and computer games), and fax machines provide new challenges for understanding language and behavior.

Effective communication acquisition in today's society must involve acquiring some skills for understanding media. Table 4.3 indicates that parents, peers, and siblings play social roles in helping children interact with media. Children gradually develop skills in five main areas: distinguishing main content, understanding the formal features of production, making sense of order and sequence, testing reality and accuracy, and retaining elements of the story line.

Main Content

Between the ages of 2 and 5, children learn to separate the main story from what else is going on around it. Young children will not differenti-

TABLE 4.3 COGNITIVE DEVELOPMENT AND MEDIA COMMUNICATION SKILLS

PIAGETIAN DEVELOPMENTAL STAGES	MEDIA COMMUNICATION SKILLS
Sensorimotor (0–2 years)	Visual and auditory attention to media begins
	Sounds (loud, sudden) cause shifts in visual attention
Preoperational (2–5 years)	More attention to media
	Little sense of order and sequence
	Some use of media characters in play
	Peer influence on attention patterns
	Coviewing with parent increases comprehension and learning
Concrete operational (6–11 years)	Gradually increases understanding of order and sequence
	Gradually increases understanding of motives and consequences
	Gradually separates main content from peripheral
	Talks about media with peers and siblings
	Parental influence on perception of importance, relevance, and truthfulness of media segments
Formal operational (12 years and up)	Adultlike comprehension of media
	Makes media inferences consistent with level of social knowledge and experience

Source: Adapted from B. Haslett & A. Alexander (1988), Developing communication skills. In R. P. Hawkins, J. M. Wiemann, & S. Pingree (Eds.), *Advancing communication science: Merging mass and interpersonal processes* (Newbury Park, CA: Sage), pp. 232–233.

ate the commercials from the rest of the show, for example. A half-hour-long show of *Mighty Morphin Power Rangers* will be exactly that—the children won't leave at commercial time to get a drink or use the bathroom! It is one long story to them. The persuasive messages of commercials are not seen as attempts to influence.

Some people therefore reason that young children should be kept from watching television unsupervised, or advertising should be regulated so that clear language distinguishes the story from the commercial and so that the "stars" of the show are not also the stars of the commercials.

Others argue that it is the adults' responsibility to teach children how to distinguish main content. Adults can watch shows with children, using language to educate them. Pointing out to children the language of persuasion is part of educating them.

Children who talk to their grandparents on the telephone often have trouble telling their parents about their conversation. It is hard for them to pick out the main content. They also have to rely only on language (and the tone of voice) to get ideas. Young children often do not realize that their grandparents cannot see them and their surroundings—ask where "mommy" is, and they are likely to say, "Over there."

Even some adults who use the media have difficulty distinguishing main content. If you have ever listened to a five-minute message left on your answering machine, you might have wished that the caller knew how to summarize the main point in a shorter period of time. People using electronic mail or voice mail often face the same set of challenges.

Production

It is not until about the age of 4 that children begin to understand the production conventions that are used to show that time has passed or that the scene has shifted. The formal features of production, such as cuts and pans, are lost on them.

Cutting from one scene to another probably results in a loss of comprehension. Panning out the window to indicate thinking probably results in loss of train of thought for the young child.

Seldom is any language used to help explain these formal features of production. Occasionally, a place/date line will come on the screen to enable you to know that the first scene, for example, was in Chicago in 1952 and the next in New York in 1945. Because young children can't read, this is also lost on them. The explanations of features of production fall to the adults or older children using the media with the young child—when they bother to explain.

Computer games often require older children and adults to understand the formal features of game construction to pass levels of the game. Knowing how to make the scepter appear or how a particular keystroke can phase you into another section of the game is often crucial to success.

Order and Sequence

Understanding the order in which things happen is a complex and gradual process. Between the ages of 6 and 11, children's concepts of order and sequence mature so that they can distinguish a "flashback" as something that came before the part of the story they are watching. They realize that the segment showing Sara, the main character, as a child portrays the same person as the part about Sara in the present day. Language helps with this skill through the use of dates and past, present, and future tenses.

It is hard to know how closely language is tied to this media skill, however. Even 3-year-olds can recite a sequence of events for things that are important to them, such as eating and shopping.[10] It is highly possible that parents' or peers' explanations of media events help even young children to understand order and sequence better.

As an adult, you still have challenges with order and sequence. One of the authors of your text created a Hypercard stack on the computer to teach students about types of support for their speeches. It was designed so that students could study seven different types of support and cycle back to the beginning at any time. Some students complained that they didn't know when they were finished with the program because they could keep repeating segments. They couldn't see the beginning and end of the lesson the way they could in a book. Putting in an outline and using language to indicate "I am finished" solved the problem.

Reality and Accuracy

It is not until about the age of 6 that children begin to understand that not everything is "real life." They learn that the news reporter's words describe a real situation but that the drama they witness in a movie is made up.

You can see the problem when the child of 4 jumps out the window with the Superman cape on, thinking he or she can fly. Or when the face of your niece falls when she sees that the toy demonstrated in the Saturday morning commercial is only a little piece of plastic and doesn't really move by itself. This, of course, brings up some ethical questions about children and advertising products.

As children mature, the distinctions between what is real and not real must continue. A young teen may recognize that the violence in the video game "Mortal Kombat" is not real, but there are many parents who argue that their young teens are not immune to the effects of that violence. Parents who comment on the inappropriateness of violence in society may have a mediating effect.

▨ Retention

Children gradually develop the ability to retain the details of a story line. Between the ages of 6 and 11, children develop abilities to remember the complete story line; eventually, they can link later episodes of the same story. A young child will watch *Young Riders* and remember Teaspoon because he has a "funny" eye and watch the action of horses and guns. By about the age of 6, a child will begin to understand how the scene at the beginning leads to Teaspoon's behavior toward the end of the story. Older children will understand how the behavior of Teaspoon this week is tied to a previous episode; they will be more likely to notice motivation and result.

From soap operas to television miniseries, there are many examples of the importance of retention in adult communication. For many, missing an episode of a favorite show absolutely requires finding someone who can effectively communicate what happened to them.

▨ Adultlike Comprehension

By about age 12, children have acquired enough language and media skills to understand media in much the same way as adults. If you have younger brothers or sisters, you may remember actually enjoying watching a movie with them and appreciating their "maturity." You could talk about the humor of *Saturday Night Live* with them; you could argue about whether this week's episode of *In Living Color* was better than last week's; you could talk with them about the accuracy or inaccuracy of the hamburger commercial.

By the age of 12, most children have acquired at least one language. They are functioning in their relationships at least somewhat competently,

---

REALITY CHECK

Awareness of Media Language Skills

Watch or listen to three different types of media segments. What skills are necessary to understand them? Could a child of 2 understand them? How about a child of 7? A young teen? Would you allow your own children to watch or listen to these media segments? How might you help them understand the media better?

---

and they understand the major aspects of how to use media. They can appreciate the process of acquiring language and the role that it plays in achieving communication competency in relationships.

One challenge inherent in communicating appropriately lies in your ability to use language appropriately for the person and the situation. This involves understanding the roles of *thought* and *culture* in effective communication.

Language and Thought

A family is sitting in church on Easter Sunday; their particularly angelic-looking 18-month-old is toddling among the chairs. When he becomes noisy and knocks over a chair, his mother picks him up. He yells, "F—you!" loudly enough for about 50 people to hear him over the sounds of service. An embarrassed father carries him out.

This child has certainly acquired language. It is doubtful that he knows the true meaning of his words, and he certainly has not developed the ability to adapt language use to situation. He may have known what he was doing (using language to express anger or frustration), but for this toddler the words have no meaning in and of themselves. He is oblivious to the church communication norm that cursing is not appropriate.

Semantics refers to the meaning that words have for people, either because of their definitions or because of their use in a sentence's structure (its *syntax*). Semantics involves the relationship between symbols and objects, people and concepts. The toddler in the preceding example understood the relationship between the words he used and the concept of being unhappy; he was unhappy being pulled away from making lots of fun noise, so he uttered the same words he had probably heard family members use when they were unhappy with someone or something. He may have also observed strong response from others to that word.

What the toddler had not learned was **pragmatics**, the ability to use the symbol systems of a culture appropriately. He may have gotten a few laughs by saying his words in front of his family at home, but he didn't realize that the "culture" of church made his words inappropriate. (Some would argue that they are inappropriate in many other, if not all, circumstances.)

When you acquire language, you are learning semantics, but when you learn how to use those verbal symbols of the culture appropriately, you are learning pragmatics. People communicate competently when they adapt the use of their verbal tools—symbols—to the situation and the attendant people. This is not always an easy thing to do.

SEMANTICS
The meaning created between communicators by language and thought.

PRAGMATICS
The appropriate use of language in context; requires mastery of communication rules, not merely language rules.

Words have both *connotative* and *denotative* meanings. The denotative meaning of a word is its dictionary definition; words like "church" or "computer" have clear descriptions listed in the dictionary for all to see. What is not so easy to see about words is their connotative meaning—the emotional or attitudinal response people have for words.

The word "church" in the dictionary may be "a building for public worship" (denotative), but people may have very different connotative meanings for it. Some may have positive responses to the word because they associate it with spirituality and rituals that bring them great personal joy. Others may feel negatively toward the word "church," regarding it as a silly and meaningless place.

Everyone can agree that a computer is "an electronic machine that performs high-speed calculations" (denotative meaning). Some respond to the word "computer" with dread (connotative), imagining all the complex things they would have to know to make it work; others respond to the word with excitement (connotative) because they enjoy the many functions it can perform for them.

Obviously, choosing words carefully is important. You not only have to share the denotative meanings of words (using a six-syllable word that no one understands will not create meaning very effectively), but you also have to be aware of the many connotative meanings possible for a word you use.

Thinking about how to use language appropriately—developing the ability to choose effective words or to censor oneself at times—is part of competent communication.

The Triangle of Meaning

SYMBOL
A sign (usually a word) used to describe a person, idea, or thing (a referent).

It is our *thoughts* that link **symbols** to an actual person, object, or concept. The "triangle of meaning," a classic representation of this process, explains how we know what a particular word or sentence means.[11] Figure 4.3 shows how symbols, thoughts, and their referents are related. An example will make this easier to understand.

A mother says to her son, a college student, "I want you to meet a lovely young woman who is the daughter of your dad's business partner." He thinks, "Warning bells—awkward moments, pressure to behave appropriately, probably boring."

The person, the woman he is supposed to meet, is the referent. The **referent** is the real thing—the actual presentation of a person, object, or event—as seen in the lower right corner of the triangle.

REFERENT
The actual person or thing that a symbol or symbols represent.

The lower left corner is the *symbol*—the idea, the words we use for the referent, the operational definition of the referent. The mother's words, "a

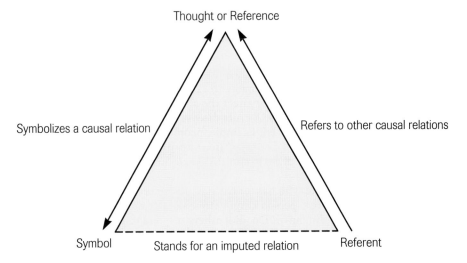

FIGURE 4.3
The triangle of meaning.

lovely young woman who is the daughter of your dad's business partner,"
supply the symbols.

The upper corner of the triangle is the report of cognition, the *thought* or
reference. The son's musings to himself, his imaginings of what the woman
would look like, and his projected behavior constitute the thought or reference.

The dotted line between symbol and referent shows that there is no direct connection between the words and the objects they represent. The
mother cannot cause the young woman to appear by using her words. And
the young woman, even by her presence, does not automatically call up the
same symbols the mother used to describe her. If the son's roommate said,
"You've gotta meet this dynamite babe who's my lab partner," how would
the son know his roommate was talking about the same woman his mother
wanted him to meet? The symbols (and the person who uses them) call up
very different images.

The two-way arrow between symbol and thought illustrates that the use
of symbols can cause thoughts or that thoughts can result in symbols being
used. The mother's words caused particular thoughts about the woman, and
those thoughts might create other symbols—"Mom, you know I hate to
meet people that way."

The one-way arrow between referent and thought illustrates that the object, person, or concept—the referent—*can* cause thoughts. Actually seeing

REFERENCE
*The thoughts that
occur in a person
when symbols are
used or referents en-
countered.*

Restricted Language

Some people suffer from being unable to express their thoughts fully through language. A stroke may affect the ability to speak without interfering with thought processes. A cruel disease may likewise affect the ability to produce language. For example, people with amyotrophic lateral sclerosis (Lou Gehrig's disease) think like others, but they slowly lose their ability to control their muscles, including those that create speech.

Talk with someone who has (or has had) restricted speech. What strategies does (did) this person employ to make the most of the language use he or she does (did) have? Do (did) others respond to this person differently—for example, by acting as if the person's thoughts were restricted, too?

Special computers offer a promise of some help for people with language restrictions. Research advances have been made in this area.

the woman may confirm the young man's original thoughts of "boring" or it may cause a reassessment: "This won't be so bad, after all—what *was* I thinking?" However, the one-way arrow also illustrates that thoughts cannot make the referent appear. How many times, in your longing for a special person or thing, have you wished that your thought could make the reality appear before you? No such luck.

Finally, the two solid lines and one broken line of the triangle illustrate the important connections of the *symbol–thought–referent* triangle. Meaning is in the head of the person using or hearing the symbols. Thoughts are at the top of the triangle, which helps explain the ways thought and language interact.

The triangle of meaning shows that language determines thought. You can stimulate different thought processes by the words you use. Calling someone a "sweetie" and calling them a "slug" cause different thought processes in both yourself and your listeners. Calling a boss "unreasonable" as opposed to "strict" determines the thought responses.

Language can also cause misinterpretation. Saying someone lives in the "big house" may mean to one listener that the person lives in a mansion; to another, in the big apartment house—or to another perhaps the halfway house! If you are involved in an argument with someone, you can bet that you are using language that conjures up very different images for you and your opponent. "Pro-choice" means killing babies to some and personal freedom to others.

▨ *The Abstraction Ladder*

Language operates at many levels of abstraction. You can speak about virtually anyone or anything in a very specific way or a very general way. You can talk so broadly that no one knows what you are talking about ("Life is so complex; you never know if you can trust people"), or you can speak so specifically that people think you are keeping notes for a court case against them ("I saw you at 10:32 P.M. on Friday, January 29, at the right-hand corner table of Harry's Bar with a 6-foot, brown-haired man wearing black jeans, boots, and a powder-blue T-shirt").

Hayakawa has illustrated the way words can be used to describe the specific versus the general in what is termed the **abstraction ladder**[12] (see Figure 4.4 on p. 166). The top rungs of the ladder are high-level abstractions; the lower down the ladder you go, the more specific the language becomes. High-level abstractions may also be evaluative ("You jerk"), whereas low-level abstractions are usually more descriptive ("I didn't like it when you told my father I'd run out of gas"). Low-level abstractions may also involve counting things ("You've been *five* minutes late to work *three* times this week"), or dating ("Last *Saturday* you told me you'd pay me $50 by *October 5.*"). High-level abstractions may have multiple meanings ("Don't treat me like *that*") while low-level abstractions limit the possible interpretations ("I'd prefer to order my own dinner").

A woman tells her husband she wants to talk about their relationship (high abstraction); it could be their romantic, sexual, business, or family relationship. If she lowers the level of abstraction to, say, their financial relationship, this might involve who makes the money, who spends the money, how the money is divided, how it is allocated, how much of it is saved, and so on.

Lowering the level of abstraction still further, the wife says, "Let's talk about how we allocate our money." Now, does she mean that her husband spends too much on clothes or that she wants more money for entertainment—or is it that she is having trouble just getting the money allocated to cover the rent, utilities, and food?

"Let's talk about how we spend our entertainment money," she says, lowering the abstraction still further. Does that include eating out, renting movies, driving to visit family and friends, or buying a new VCR?

"Let's talk about how much money we spend on restaurant meals every month" lowers the abstraction again. At some point, the abstraction becomes too specific for the conversation. "I want to talk about the $78.52 we spent on dinner last Saturday" may sound picky and threatening. But some-

ABSTRACTION LADDER
An illustration of how words can be used to describe topics ranging from the specific to the general.

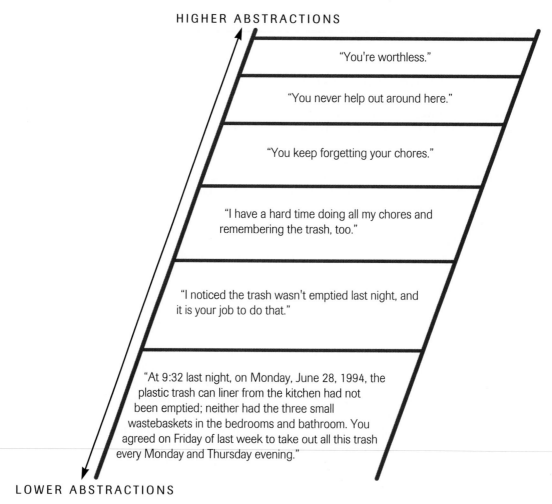

HIGHER ABSTRACTIONS

"You're worthless."

"You never help out around here."

"You keep forgetting your chores."

"I have a hard time doing all my chores and remembering the trash, too."

"I noticed the trash wasn't emptied last night, and it is your job to do that."

"At 9:32 last night, on Monday, June 28, 1994, the plastic trash can liner from the kitchen had not been emptied; neither had the three small wastebaskets in the bedrooms and bathroom. You agreed on Friday of last week to take out all this trash every Monday and Thursday evening."

LOWER ABSTRACTIONS

FIGURE 4.4
An abstraction ladder.

times that level of abstraction may be necessary to get the attention of another or to hold a person to a commitment.

In competent communication, the parties try to choose the appropriate level of abstraction. It should be higher in some circumstances and lower in others. Determining the appropriate level of abstraction involves considering yourself, your audience, and the situation.

When considering your own goals for the situation, you decide whether you want to use high abstractions to group people or concepts together ("my classmates"), to avoid confrontation or evaluation ("I was out"), or to provide a generality that you think someone can identify with ("I've been there").

When you consider the person(s) you are talking to in determining appropriate levels of abstraction, you ask yourself whether they are likely to be offended by specifics ("You put two cloves too many in the sauce"), whether past encounters have led you to believe that they will listen better to high or to low abstractions, and whether they are feeling defensive (in which case you may want to avoid words that would make them more so).

You also consider the situation or context. In giving a speech, you may often use high abstractions to get people to identify with your position ("Everyone here loves freedom"), but you might have to give low abstractions in the form of statistics to justify a major point ("Handguns kill 65,000 people in this country every year"). If you are talking with defensive employees, you may have to use high abstractions to compliment them and show them how much they are valued ("You are such a great worker") but use low abstractions to give them specific instructions about how to correct the errors they have made ("This report will be much better if you go back and put in the subtitles I've asked for and run it through the spellchecker"). Skilled communicators know how and when to move up and down the abstraction ladder.

People often use high-level abstractions to avoid the pain of specifics. "I'm sorry for your loss" (high) may be more sensitive than "I'm sorry your little brown cocker spaniel was run over by the blue Nissan Pulsar" (low). The politician says, "We should guarantee the personal freedoms of every citizen" (high) to avoid offending some (and losing their votes) by saying, "I think you should be able to carry a handgun if you want" (low).

Lower-level abstractions are usually clearer; they help you understand more precisely what people mean. While "Get something interesting at the video store" (high) allows a wide range of choices, saying, "I'd like to watch a mystery movie tonight" (lower) is more likely to get you something you'll appreciate. Asking for a specific movie (lower still) will ensure your satisfaction with the choice.

Saying, "Do this report over right this time" (high) may get you the same report back reprinted more clearly, but saying, "Put in subtitles to indicate the divisions called for in the prospectus and run it through the spellchecker by tomorrow at noon" (low) may get you what you want—and save your receiver a lot of time and frustration, too.

Some situations call for the use of both high- and low-level abstractions. Others demand a medium level of language abstraction. At still other times, your ethical sense will tell you what type of language is appropriate. The other person, the situation, and your own goals for the interaction will determine the most effective level of abstraction.

Determining Appropriate Levels of Abstraction

Reword the following high- and low-level abstractions to achieve what you think is the appropriate level of abstraction.

Situation	**Rewording to appropriate level**
You tell your employee, "Do a good job this time."	
You invite friends to "bring something" and "come over."	
You tell your roommate, "I told you eight times in October and seven times in November to take out the trash."	
You tell the new office worker, "Take a 20-gallon black plastic bag from the second left shelf in storeroom 5, place a wire tie from the shelf in your pocket, and empty the trash cans in offices 101 through 127 into the plastic bag. Twist it at the top and twist the wire tie from your pocket around it. Put the bag in the third blue trash can at the bottom of the northeast stairwell."	

Language and Culture

The culture you are raised in influences your thoughts and your language. How you talk and what you think about are determined by the culture and its language. It is difficult to say whether culture shapes language or language shapes culture. Perhaps a parallel of the homology language acquisition model might apply here. Perhaps there is another "great borrowing" going on, in which you simultaneously learn your culture through language, reshape your culture by the language choices you make (and create), and simply reflect your culture by the language you use.

The Sapir/Whorf Hypothesis

The Sapir/Whorf hypothesis claims that language determines thought.[13] If a culture does not speak about something, has no words for something, according to this hypothesis, that culture will have few thoughts about that thing or concept. Cultures without a future tense would thus harbor individuals with little concept of working for something that they could acquire next year. A person from a culture with 50 different words for "snow" would clearly attend to many more details about the "white fluffy stuff" than a person from the desert. The Quechua Indians of Peru have more words for potatoes than Eskimos have for snow; they certainly have different thought processes because of this extensive language about one food item.

High- and Low-Context Cultures

Culture can influence language use in another important way. Gudykunst points out that some cultures use language that is very *indirect;* they are sensitive to situational factors, preferring to observe those factors rather than comment on each one.[14] Japan is a high-context culture; if a Japanese person disagrees with someone, he or she usually says nothing, and the person disagreed with must look for cues for disagreement in the context. Thus a **high-context culture** is also more likely to attribute your behavior to factors related to the situation, rather than to your personality. In other words, people in a high-context culture would not assume you were rude because you said nothing; they would be more likely to think that you didn't respond because the situation called for restraint and politeness.

A **low-context culture**, on the other hand, uses very *direct* language. A low-context disagreement would be expressed directly and clearly to the person: "I don't think you are right about the health care plan, Jane." They tend to find explanations for behavior in the person ("She's so uninformed"). The United States and Canada are such low-context cultures. In these countries, it would seem normal for someone to say, "Alex, I need a list of 20 items for the Allan project from you by 5 P.M. today." Someone from a high-context culture would more likely say, "We are starting the

HIGH-CONTEXT CULTURE
A culture that avoids the use of direct language, relying more on context to convey meaning.

LOW-CONTEXT CULTURE
A culture that relies more on the use of direct language than on the nuances of context to impart meaning.

Language and Your Culture

To what extent does your language use reflect your culture? Do you come from a high-context or a low-context culture? To what degree do you use language to reduce uncertainty? Do you adapt your language use when you find yourself with people from different cultural backgrounds? Is it necessary to adapt language use in the multicultural society in which we live? Answers to these questions will help you be aware of the effect culture can have on language use.

project," and would assume that you would have the needed list ready in time because you understand the situation as the speaker does.

If you did not get the list completed on time, the low-context culture would blame it on your laziness or incompetence, whereas the high-context culture would blame it on situational constraints, such as there being too many things going on for you to finish.

The way these culture types reduce *uncertainty* may also cause problems interculturally. Whenever you meet someone new, you try various uses of language to reduce the uncertainty of the situation—to know more about the other person so you will know how to act.

People from low-context cultures will normally try to reduce uncertainty by asking about the other's attitudes, feelings, and beliefs, whereas people from high-context cultures will ask questions about the other's status and background. This high-context strategy for reducing uncertainty is very practical, especially in high-context cultures that have different ways of speaking to people who are seen as superior, equal, or inferior. Uncertainty reduction involves knowing how to talk to others according to their status.

But if you are from a low-context culture and someone starts asking you about your position, your age, and whom you work for (in an effort to know "how" to address you), you will probably think the person rude. Similarly, low-context requests for a high-context person's feelings are seen as equally rude.

Whatever the culture you are raised in, context is important to understanding what language to use. And in a multicultural society (as the United States is becoming more and more), it is important to realize that language that is "straightforward" to some is probably "invasive" to others.

Cross-Cultural Language Use

Interview someone from another culture about his or her language use. Be particularly aware of comparisons and contrasts in language use, but also find similarities. People usually notice differences, but they often fail to notice how much they have in common. Note your findings about direct and indirect language, uncertainty reduction, and use of high versus low language. Report your findings to your classmates and engage them in a discussion of language use from culture to culture.

Language and Context

Language is sometimes referred to as something that occurs on its own; in fact, it seems to take on a life of its own in the study of grammar and sentence construction. But the study of the production of language from the perspective of producing sentences from grammatical rules is not really a communicative approach; it takes social context as a given and studies language apart from its social uses. Without the consideration of context, communication is no longer the real subject; to ignore context is to omit the social world in which you live.

Sometimes people act as if language could communicate without context. They might say whatever comes to mind without thought as to who is around, where they are, or the effect their words may produce. But competent language does not operate that way. There are three main ways in which language and context are related; language reflects, builds on, and determines context.

Language Reflects Context

The situation in which language is spoken determines that language. Thus you will choose certain types of language for different situations or different people.

Most people change their language at least a little when they talk to their grandparents. You talk differently to a person who is interviewing you for a job than you do to the people you go out with on Friday night. Depending on the situation you are in and the people you are with, you can select from among various categories of language behaviors, called *speech repertoires.*

SPEECH REPERTOIRES
The possibilities communicators have for language use in any given situation, based on their experiences, cognitions, and acquired skills.

Speech repertoires are the "files" of your language possibilities; they are the types of language you can choose from to meet the demands of the situation. The authors of your text talk differently with their children than they do with their students; they have different speech repertoires for talking with their parents than they do for talking with their colleagues.

High and Low Language

HIGH LANGUAGE
The language used in the more formal contexts of a person's life, such as work.

In addition to whether you belong to a high-context or low-context culture, you probably also have both high and low language use within that culture. **High language**—the more formal, polite, or "mainstream" language—is used for business, in public, and even in the classroom. **Low language** is reserved for home and everyday activities. In bilingual communities this is especially apparent, as people actually switch the language they use to reflect the context. For example, in the United States many people speak English at work and another language (e.g., Spanish, Italian, Mandarin) at home.

LOW LANGUAGE
The relaxed language usually used in the home or with close friends.

Euphemisms

Some communication contexts reflect a preference for *euphemisms,* words that substitute an inoffensive term for one considered offensive. The medical context is one with many euphemisms. A surgeon makes an "incision" rather than "cuts you open." You go to the "procedure center" to have an "injection" rather than to the "shot office" to let the doctor stick a needle into you. The funeral business is also a rich source of euphemisms with terms like "slumber room."

Male and Female Speech

Some speech repertoires divide along gender lines, particularly in same-sex contexts. Females talking together use more language about relationships (e.g., family, close friends, health), whereas males use more language about doing things (e.g., sports, music, business).[15] So, we can sometimes determine the gender of the participants from the content of a conversation. Within the context of a same-sex conversation, there are few language problems. But when men and women engage in conversation with each other,

FIGURE 4.5

Women's and men's speech differ in a number of ways, including the topics of conversation.

each gender sometimes complains about the other. Women criticize men for talking about business or the news while ignoring relational issues (feelings, how people are getting along); women report enjoying, even *needing*, the sharing of feelings. Men criticize women for talking about "trivial" topics such as who attended the meeting and "how" each person talked to the others (relational issues) while paying too little attention to getting things done; men report enjoying the ease and fast pace of all-male conversations.

Decades of research into the language of women and men reveal both differences and similarities.[16] Although women have traditionally been thought to use less powerful language than men (see the discussion of control later in this chapter), studies have found that women adapt their language use to the situation. In other words, a woman lawyer would use as powerful language as other lawyers (male or female) when in the role of lawyer, and a male nursery school teacher would talk at the same "power" level as other nursery school teachers (male or female) when doing his job. In another area, male speakers were thought to interrupt more than female speakers, but the situation and the status of the speakers are probably better predictors of interruptions than their gender.[17]

In general, the language you use reflects the context you are in. Men and women adapt their language use in same-sex and mixed-sex situations. Both genders adapt language use somewhat to reflect their occupations and their roles in society. But references to "girl talk" and "guy talk" are more than casual labels; the ability to fit into a gender group often depends on your ability to adjust your language to meet the demands of the group.

In-Group/Out-Group Distinctions

The ability to "talk like us" often determines whether one is accepted into a group. Speech repertoires are important in the secret passwords of childhood play and the "cool" language of teen groups. As adults, being able to speak the language of a job marks one as an in-group member. One who knows about computers ("You need more RAM in order to run Microsoft Word and PageMaker at the same time") and can understand the acronyms ("At the CSA meeting we'll discuss ICC") used in the workplace is on the way to being an in-group member.

The language used for in-group members versus out-group members differs at times. Some interesting findings indicate that members of a gender in-group will use more abstract language about a gender out-group.[18] Thus, if females are talking with other females about males, they will be more likely to use generalizations about them than about members of their own gender. This is perhaps the source of stereotyping statements like "Women are so emotional" or "Men are so insensitive."

The young and the elderly are often the target of language aimed at making in-group and out-group distinctions. "Those silly, reckless kids" and "Those terrible old-people drivers" are attempts to stereotype the young and the elderly and to exclude them from the in-group. Patronizing language (talking down to members of a particular group) is sometimes aimed at these groups, but it also comes from them ("You're a bunch of party animals" or "When you grow up, you'll understand"). Patronizing language is valued negatively by the recipients of the patronizing, no matter what their age group.[19]

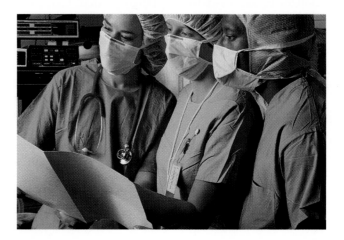

FIGURE 4.6

The technical language of a profession enables its practitioners to communicate with each other effectively. What social function does such specialized language serve?

The Ethics of In-Group Language Use

What is your attitude concerning the ethics of using language to prevent outsiders from participating in a communication interaction? For example, consider parents who spell words when conversing within earshot of their preschool-age children or immigrants who speak a particular language when they want to discuss a private matter in the presence of others (for example, their children) who don't speak the language. Or think of tourists in a foreign country who use their native language to make comments critical of their host country. Have you ever been involved in a situation in which language was used this way? Were you included in or excluded from the conversation? Is such behavior ethical? Does your answer depend on the situation? Does it depend on whether you are included or excluded? Considering this issue will help you clarify your values and understand how your values affect your communicative competence.

Speech repertoires reflect the context of your family, your neighborhood, your religion, your education, and your employment. You learn which ones to use by observing the language patterns of others, asking others questions, and exchanging information about yourself (self-disclosure).

Language Builds on Context

People share an array of assumptions on which language choice is based. When you get to know a little about another person, you discover which speech repertoires are appropriate. As you become acquainted, however, fewer questions are needed. You each develop an array of assumptions about the other. There is a shared knowledge of the social context and thus much less need to ask, "What do you mean?"

Social context also influences how people like to be addressed ("Don't call me Johnny in front of people outside of the family" or "I prefer to be referred to as 'black' rather than 'African American' "). From the earliest stages of your language development, you become aware of words that others will find offensive ("Don't say 'it sucks' in front of Grandma"). And you learn what words please others ("I really liked your calling me the manager in the meeting today").

Your development of social context also contributes to your self-confidence and reduces your feelings of uncertainty. You develop internalized assumptions about appropriate communication and times to speak or not. When you sense that if you speak up, trouble will occur, you don't say anything. This awareness helps you both in group situations and among your close associates. When you sense that others will disapprove if you say something, you don't say anything.

At other times, deception may be your motivation not to speak. You might let your partner be happy with an assumption about where you were, whom you were with, or what you were doing. You may employ the "let it pass" rule purposefully to let your partner "misunderstand."

Mostly the "let it pass" rule indicates that you know someone quite well, that you are taking more for granted in conversation. One of your friends says, "Let's get tickets for the concert." You don't say, "You mean *us* go *together?*" You assume he or she doesn't mean you'll go separately and sit on opposite sides. When the "let it pass" rule is suspended, it is an indication of a "problem" in the relationship. If you say, "What do you mean, us go on a *date?*" the context needs some clarification.

As language builds upon context, context becomes a resource for constructing meaning.

▨ *Language Determines Context*

We may create a context by the language we use.

Language is rarely neutral. Sexist language is an example. Use of the word "chick" for a woman implies far more than her gender. Many women today object to being called "girl" for reasons similar to those that black men have for objecting to being called "boy." Attempts to rid the language of sexist terms (*chairman, foreman*) point out that language determines context.

Some campuses have "fighting words" that are recognized as causing problems between genders or ethnic groups; using those words in certain ways can leave a person open to legal action.

Use of "high" language mentioned earlier may define you as fitting into the workplace and thus determine your context. Using language that is more formal language and that is grammatically correct identifies you as a member of the group and sets expectations for the rest of the interaction.

Using formal address often determines context. If one of the authors tells her students, "Call me Mary," one context is created. If she says, "I'm Professor Wiemann," they have a different set of expectations about how the context will be managed and, thus, how they should behave and speak.

Using "baby talk" with children defines them as inferiors not capable of creating accurate representations of sounds.

"Political correctness" is an important concept today. Referring to persons as "physically challenged" instead of "disabled" determines the way we approach them and the way they feel about themselves, so that a context of greater equality is established. Many people need to be made aware of the terms they use that are offensive or demeaning to others. One segment of the television comedy *Seinfeld* illustrates how using terms like "Indian giver" can be very offensive to an American Indian, but it also points out that the sensitivity can be carried too far when, instead of telling his date that he has made a "reservation" for them for dinner, Seinfeld tells her he has made an "appointment" for them.

You can often determine context by the kind of language used. How you feel about an interaction is also language-linked. In interpersonal relationships, there is a whole set of language considerations associated with initiating, maintaining, and terminating relationships.

The Language of Relationships

The role of language in interpersonal relationships includes defining the relationship, expressing the level of commitment, and achieving influence or control over one's relational partner.

Relationship Definition

Language helps define relationships. The English language is better at defining some relationships than others. For example, it is fairly easy to label your mother, father, sister, brother, aunt, uncle, grandfather, grandmother, son, daughter—your closest blood relations—as you introduce any of these people to others.

"I'd like you to meet my *boss*, Mr. Ramiro Sanchez" describes the status and professional relationship that you have. The introduction sets out how people are to be treated and what further communication might go on.

Introducing someone as a "stepbrother," however, can require more explanation than a person wants to give. So it may be preferable to introduce him as a "brother," without bothering to produce the complex relational definitions. You might introduce a co-worker who has a slightly higher or lower status than you by saying, "Rosalinda and I work together," to avoid implications of superiority or inferiority.

Just as the English language presents few options for defining work relationships, it also lacks a very developed language system for defining the complex relationships involving friends and romantic partners. Besides the terms "husband" and "wife" and "friend" and "best friend," we have very few terms available to describe the various levels of intimacy that we have with friends and romantic partners.[20]

A first romantic interest may occur around the age of 10 or 12. At some point such relationships evolve from "this girl I know" to "Amber and I are going out." Preteens may not really be "going out." More likely they walk around school together, hold hands, or sneak kisses. Maybe they meet after school secretly, but what they mostly do is talk on the telephone. English is lacking in terms that can really describe this relationship clearly.

And in high school, were you "going out" with someone or "seeing each other"? Maybe you actually *did* "go out." At least you felt more comfortable introducing someone as your boyfriend or girlfriend. By age 30, however, referring to the person you have been living with for two years as "my girlfriend" or "my boyfriend" somehow doesn't adequately describe the relationship.

One practical function of the lack of defining terms for relationships is that this permits keeping the level of commitment unsaid. Some commitment negotiation goes on when you move from "going out" to "living together" or becoming "engaged." Language becomes more specific as to what is expected and how the future is to be.

In some circles invitations to parties indicate that you and your "significant other" are invited. Others include your "spouse-like other." There is obvious strain in trying to define relationships.

The language of "disengagement" is not much clearer. English uses the terms "ex-wife" and "ex-boyfriend," but there are many levels to those relationships, too. Some involve a lot of hostility, some involve redefinition

---

SELF-CHECK

Romantic Labels

How do you label your romantic partner? Do you have no words or many to describe "where you stand" with each other? Do you label your partner differently to different people (family, friends, co-workers)? Do you have pet names for each other? How does your labeling of each other affect your understanding of the relationship? Answers to these questions can help you understand both the influence and the limitations of language in relational definition.

as friends, and some involve amicable arrangements for certain behaviors such as shared custody of children.

■ The Language of Intimacy and Distance

In spite of language's limited ability to define relationships, you can observe language *in* relationships for clues to the levels of commitment. Knapp observes that language use helps people understand what is going on at various stages of relationships.[21]

Levels of Self-Disclosure

In the early stages of your relationships, language is very general. You usually do not verbally disagree with others, and you spend most of your time trying to find out things you and your partner have in common ("You like basketball? I *love* to watch the Lakers"). You may share a lot of biographical information, and you usually stick to "safe" topics, engaging in the "small talk" of not-so-intimate relationships.

Telling people about yourself and finding out about them occurs at all levels of building relationships. The more intimate the level of your relationship, the more intimate are the revelations that usually occur. Speaking about intense feelings or opinions does not normally occur in beginning relationships. Your thoughts and feelings—more intimate disclosures about self—are reserved for relationships that have built a base of trust.

If you are unsure of the other, or if you are trying to put more distance in your relationship, you will generally disclose less. Basically, the language of experimentation, of finding out about the other and revealing yourself, is shut down. You revert to the more general language of beginning relationships.

Inclusion and Exclusion

As relationships become more intimate, the language of inclusion begins. "We like Chinese food" indicates that one person feels free to speak for another. This language of inclusion makes extensive use of "we" and "us" language. Talking about the other and self increases ("Leticia and I always rent videos on Friday night"). The use of pet names ("honey," "snookums") usually occurs, as well as sarcasm or teasing. This language of *affiliation* defines the relationship to those within it, as well as to those outside of it. (You may at times feel embarrassed or repelled by hearing some of the intimate terms people call one another.)

Relational Language Detective

Become a "relational language detective" for a few hours. While pretending to study, take notes, or watch television, write down the terms that your family members or roommates use to talk to one another. Note terms of affection, powerful/powerless language use, and amounts of self-disclosure. Also note any "in" language—language use that is unique to your family or group of friends and that outsiders might not understand. Note the ways people tease one another or complain about one another. Note the forms of address. Prepare a summary of your notes for class discussion.

When you establish a relationship, you know enough about the other so that your language use is less restricted. The language of intimate relationships may "sound bad" to outsiders. Partners who have developed habits of teasing each other or who give "friendly digs" at the other may have their own language of inclusion. Calling your brother "Snake" may sound degrading to those outside the family, when inside the family it is a name of affection recalling a shared experience.

Relationships that are becoming less intimate reverse the "we" talk of past involvements. The language of differentiation relies more heavily on the use of "I" and "you" ("I like sushi, but you never want to eat it" or "He always wants to watch TV, but I like to go out dancing"). Partners cease using pet names or telling inside jokes. Exclusionary talk becomes the norm.

Future Talk

More intimate relationships use language that implies future commitment ("Where shall we spend the holiday next year?"). Planning goes on, and decisions are made jointly. "Maybe in a few years we can afford a bigger house" makes use of "we" language as well as future planning.

Mutual understandings guide language use—"Let's get the families together for a big barbeque" is possible because the parties assume they will be together in the future and that they have some claim on each other's future.

If people in a relationship are disengaging, they will often talk around important topics—like the status of their own relationship. They maintain a stony silence, or they fill the silences with "empty talk" or "safe talk" about topics that don't involve the discussion of the relationship.

▨ The Language of Control

Competent relationships involve mutual influence. As is indicated in Chapters 1 and 7, relationships work out many different ways of balancing control or influence.

Asking another for favors indicates a more intimate relationship, but it is also a control move: You are trying to get the other to do something for you. Interrupting another or changing the subject of a conversation is also a control attempt. In such instances, the role of control is obvious.

The use of control is not always so obvious. Refusing to talk about something the other wants to talk about can appear to be trivial but is actually a very influential move. Cajoling, or "sweet talk," may persuade the other to do what you want even though it doesn't seem very forceful on the surface.

Language that sounds hesitant is usually perceived as lacking in power. Sometimes people use *disclaimers* in their conversation (*"This probably doesn't mean anything, but . . ."* or *"I'm not really sure of this, but . . ."*). Or they make use of *tag questions* ("She seemed really angry, *didn't she?*" is less powerful than "She seemed really angry"). Others speak less powerfully by using *hedges* ("I *guess* it would be okay" or "I'm *sort of* upset by all this"). "It's okay" and "I'm upset" are more powerful.

In competent relationships, language that seems less powerful may actually contribute to the competence of the relationship. Using hesitant language with your partner may be a way of *accommodating.*

Using disclaimers and tag questions in a business meeting would probably not be very effective, but *not* using them in an intimate exchange of feelings and opinions with your best friend may be equally ineffective. Sometimes you can encourage your partner's sharing of ideas by using language that doesn't sound so definitive.

Relationships make use of a wide variety of language strategies to define themselves, to create intimacy and distance, and to negotiate levels of control. The language being used can give clues to the intimacy of the relationship and to where the partners "stand" with one another. The language can express liking, love, and respect—or dislike, hate, and disrespect. The language can say, "Let's be best friends," or "Let's give it a rest for a while." The language can define us as friends, business partners, family, enemies, past lovers, or former neighbors. Not only are the labels you use for your partner language clues to your relationship, but also the topics you discuss or don't, the degree of depth of your conversations, and the things you don't say all help define your relationship.

REVIEW

Language is acquired through a complex process of thinking and developing your biological potential. Although all children acquire language at about the same time (according to the nature theory that language use is innate), there are many variations in language use and complexity. A language-rich environment probably contributes to language development.

In practice, language is probably acquired as you develop thinking, coordination, and your social relationships simultaneously. The homology model of language acquisition takes all of these aspects into account.

As you acquire language, you also learn how to use it appropriately. You develop the basic functional communication competencies of controlling, feeling, informing, imagining, and ritualizing.

Language use and media use are also intertwined. You must learn to recognize the main content of media events, how media are produced, how order and sequence are portrayed, how real or accurate the media representation is, and how you can retain information from one segment to apply to another.

Semantics illustrates how language and thought are related. The use of language by one person does not necessarily call up the original image in another. Highly abstract language creates many opportunities for misinterpretation between communicators. Lower abstractions, more specific language, leaves less room for misinterpretation. Finding the appropriate level of abstraction in language use is important to competent communication.

Culture is an important influence on the use of language. The ways in which cultures talk or don't talk about certain things create many words for those things—or very few. The directness or indirectness of language is culturally linked, as is the way in which cultures reduce uncertainty through language use.

Context is an important aspect of understanding language. Language reflects the context in which it is used, builds on that context, and in many instances, determines the context of the relationship.

You can understand relationships better by looking at the language that defines and builds them. You name your relationships as friends or lovers, as co-workers or enemies. And within those relationships, you send messages of liking or hating, influence or powerlessness, and inclusion or exclusion.

Communicating competently requires that you understand the many uses of language and how to adapt them appropriately to your various communication situations.

SUGGESTED READINGS

Bates, E. (1979). *The emergence of symbols: Cognition and communication in infancy.* New York: Academic Press.

Giles, H., & Robinson, W. P. (1990). *Handbook of language and social psychology.* Chichester, England: John Wiley and Sons.

Tannen, D. (1986). *That's not what I meant! How conversational style makes or breaks your relations with others.* New York: Morrow.

Tannen, D. (1990). *You just don't understand: Women and men in conversation.* New York: Morrow.

Wood, B. (1982). *Children and communication: Verbal and nonverbal language development* (2nd ed.). Englewood Cliffs, NJ: Prentice-Hall.

5

Chapter 5

Nonverbal
Communication

Objectives

After reading this chapter you should be able to

1. Describe the importance of nonverbal communication in your personal and professional life.

2. Distinguish among the various nonverbal codes (kinesics, haptics, proxemics, etc.).

3. Identify the effects of culture, context, and situation on nonverbal communication competence.

4. Describe the functions of nonverbal communication.

Chapter Contents

The Impact of Nonverbal Communication

Origins

Codes
  Appearance and Artifacts
  Kinesics
  Facial Expressions
  Oculesics
  Paralanguage
  Haptics
  Proxemics
  Chronemics
  Olfactics

The Relationship between Nonverbal and Verbal Communication

Competence Factors
  Culture
  Context and Situation

Functions
  Relationship Management
  Interaction Management
  Social Influence
  Deception
  Self-Promotion

Competent Nonverbal Communication

SUPPOSE THAT AS you pass one of your professors, Dr. Lewis, in the hall, he smiles and pats you on the shoulder. Or suppose that on a visit to your parents' home, you pull up in your car to see your mother waiting in the front doorway with hands on her hips and a strained smile on her face. Or suppose one of your classmates, with clenched teeth, glares at you from across the room. These people have all communicated with you without saying a word. Although these examples are obvious ones, they illustrate the significance of nonverbal communication.

You probably have an idea of what constitutes nonverbal communication, but it is hard to define. Even among communication experts, any consensus that does exist boils down to two convictions: (1) that nonverbal communication involves behavior rather than the content of spoken words, and (2) that behavior is attributed meaning. Therefore, **nonverbal communication** is the process of signaling meaning through behavior that does not involve the content of spoken words. Nonverbal communication is messages (intentional or unintentional) that are encoded and decoded with meaning and that serve specific functions. Because virtually every behavior can be interpreted as having meaning, you are continually communicating. A sigh, a nod, and a tapping foot can all convey meaning.

The Impact of Nonverbal Communication

Nonverbal communication affects every facet of your life—relationships, social interactions, and careers. Nonverbal behaviors are often better indicators of true thoughts and feelings than spoken language. This makes relationships especially vulnerable to nonverbal communication. For example, maintaining a well-timed silence or avoiding touch with another can signify the beginning of the end of a relationship. On the other hand, smiling and open arms can lead to intimacy.[1]

Socially, nonverbal communication can direct interaction and determine future encounters with others. For instance, interruptions during a conversation are perceived negatively, and the interrupters are viewed as less than competent.[2] If you are at a party and, either verbally or nonverbally (raising a finger), interrupt a small circle of people talking, you may be seen as self-centered and overbearing, and this may cause people to avoid you in the future. If, however, you enter the conversation at the signal of another, by eye contact or someone pointing at you, you will be perceived as interesting and friendly, and others will want to talk with you further.

Nonverbal behaviors also influence the success of your career. In one recent study of business organizations, 94 percent of the respondents rated nonverbal communication in the business world as either fairly or very important.[3] This suggests that nonverbal behaviors can either help or hinder your growth in the professional arena. If you show up at work dressed in extremely informal attire (blue jeans and a T-shirt), yawn during business meetings, and display stress-related behaviors (biting your nails), you will probably be passed over for that promotion!

Origins

How do people know that laughing is associated with pleasure, frowning with sadness, or wristwatch glancing and foot tapping with impatience? Why do some people shake hands upon introduction while others bow? Why do some people find stares so uncomfortable? Two primary perspectives can answer these questions: those who emphasize **phylogeny** posit that human behavior is innate and the result of evolution, whereas those who focus on **ontogeny** view behavior as shaped by social and cultural expectations.

One of the earliest supporters of phylogeny was Charles Darwin, who believed that facial expressions were survival mechanisms that evolved in much the same way as other physical characteristics. Later research conducted by Eibl-Eibesfeldt substantiated this hypothesis. After extensive observation of blind and deaf children, who could not be influenced by the facial expressions of others, Eibl-Eibesfeldt noted that a number of facial expressions were common among the children and concluded that primary emotions are expressed by inborn facial expressions.[4] These primary emotions are sadness, anger, disgust, fear, interest, surprise, and happiness. Fur-

PHYLOGENY
The evolutionary development of a species over time (as distinguished from the development of individual members of that species).

ONTOGENY
The course of development of an individual organism (as distinguished from the development of a species over time).

REALITY CHECK

Nature or Nurture? Expressing Emotions

The seven primary emotions are identified in this chapter. Make a list of other emotions and, for each one, indicate whether you were born with the ability to express the emotion or learned nonverbal behavior to express it. What does this list tell you about your ability to interpret nonverbal expressions of emotion by other people?

ther studies conducted by Ekman and his colleagues proved that these basic facial expressions may be considered universal.[5]

Proponents of the other perspective, ontogeny, assert that nonverbal behavior is learned and developed throughout childhood according to social and cultural norms. Research studies conducted by Michael and Willis,[6] and later by Kumin and Lazar,[7] trace how children interpreted gestures. The studies discovered an increased recognition ability in older children. Golomb found that physical attractiveness is perceived by children as young as age 3.[8] Lerner and Schroeder discovered that by kindergarten age, children have developed perceptions of stereotypical traits associated with body type.[9] Children realize the appropriate use of space around the third grade.[10] More recently, Fromme and co-workers concluded that the expression of emotions is related to the development of social skills.[11]

Both of these perspectives, phylogeny and ontogeny, supplement your understanding of nonverbal communication. You are probably born with some nonverbal behaviors, and you learn others through your social and cultural interactions. Although you can recognize primary emotions through facial expressions, other nonverbal behaviors are expressed through subtle cues that are socially or culturally learned.

Codes

Although nonverbal codes are not as sophisticated as those of *Star Trek* or as secretive as those in a James Bond movie, the codes of nonverbal communication, as with any other coding system, are the means by which messages are sent and received. Simply put, these are the types of behavior that produce potential messages. In order to better understand the meaning of a message, it is important to know the codes used in communicating messages. Nonverbal behavior can be classified into the following categories: appearance and artifacts, kinesics (gestures and body movement), facial expressions, oculesics (eye behavior), paralanguage (voice qualities), haptics (touching), proxemics (the use of space), chronemics (the use of time), and olfactics (scent and smell).

Appearance and Artifacts

People are judgmental creatures. Whether subconsciously or deliberately, they make judgments based on appearance. Most people are aware of the significance of attractiveness; it's why, collectively, billions of dollars are spent every year on designer clothes, haircuts, makeup, and even plastic surgery. Indeed, society accords attractive people certain advantages. For instance, attractive students receive more interaction from their teachers;[12] attractive defendants are more likely to be found innocent in a court of law;[13] "good-looking" people have a three to four times greater chance of being hired;[14] and attractiveness is the predominant factor in dating behavior.[15] Although some standards are set by cultural norms, the extent of attractiveness is influenced by individual tastes. Nonetheless, appearance affects not only perceptions of attractiveness, but also judgments about a person's background, character, personality, status, and future behavior.[16] These perceptions are inferred from body shape and size, facial features, skin color, and clothing.

Body shape has been categorized into three types: **endomorphic**, which is rounded (oval or pear-shaped and often heavy), **mesomorphic**, which is triangular (broad shoulders and slim waist), and **ectomorphic**, which is straight (thin and bony with little muscle tone). The culture determines the "ideal" body type. Some cultures are proner to endomorphic body types while others prefer mesomorphic or ectomorphic. If you were to look through fashion magazines from 30 or 40 years ago, you would notice that the models appearing in those publications were not as thin or as tall as today's models. Indeed, attitudes about attractiveness can change with the times, as Figure 5.1 (on p. 190) shows.

Generally, people attach certain personality traits to body types—for example, when they view rotund people as happy—but make character judgments based on facial features. For example, people tend to see dishonesty in small, close-set eyes, innocence in dimples, and maturity in gray hair.

In an ideal world, there would be no reason to include here perceptions based on skin color. Unfortunately, in the real world, biases and prejudices based on skin color are still prevalent. No doubt you are already quite familiar with the racial stereotypes in U.S. culture based solely on skin color. However, this kind of prejudice exists in most cultures, although the attributions given to a particular color can be radically different. Do you think skin color is important in South Africa? What about in France (or in Algeria), England (or in the Commonwealth nations), or Germany? Of course it is. Can you think of cultures where white or pale skin is perceived negatively? Competent communicators must be aware not only of their own biases that they bring to a particular interaction but also of others' prejudices.

We have thus far discussed those aspects of appearance that are largely innate and unchangeable: body build, facial features, and skin color. There is, however, one element of appearance that is under your control, clothing. Clothing deliberately communicates sociocultural messages from the

ENDOMORPH
A person with a rounded, oval, or pear-shaped and often heavy body.

MESOMORPH
A person with a triangular and athletic body.

ECTOMORPH
A person with a thin, angular body.

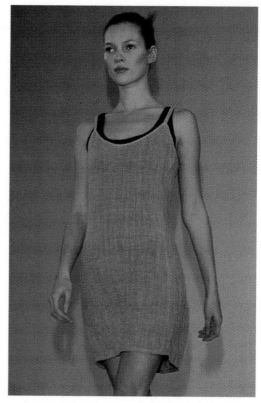

FIGURE 5.1

The "ideal" body type changes over time, as these celebrities, past and present, demonstrate. The voluptuous movie star Marilyn Monroe was an ideal type in the 1950s. Kate Moss, a fashion model of the 1990s, exemplifies a slender "waif" image.

sender about status, economic level, social background, goals, and satisfaction.[17] The image you promote through dress can affect the acquisition of a promising job or affect the advancement of your career. Many businesses expect their employees' dress to complement the image of the company.[18] Clothing also communicates social intent. Clothing that conforms to current styles and trends can increase your popularity.[19] Dress can also send messages of power and status. More formal attire and uniforms, for example, are perceived as status symbols.[20] Extensive research by Aiken,[21] and later by Rosenfeld and Plax,[22] was conducted to determine the link between clothing selections and personality traits. It was determined that choice of clothing, or **clothing orientation**, was linked to personality traits. Rosenfeld and Plax looked at four clothing orientations: clothing consciousness,

CLOTHING
ORIENTATION
Clothing preferences.

Self-Description Test

By completing the following two-part test, which has been used in a number of studies conducted on the relationship between personality characteristics and body types, you will discover whether your body type affects your perception of your own personality.

Fill in each blank with a word from the suggested list following each statement. For each blank, three in each statement, you may select any word from the list of adjectives that is directly below that statement. An exact word to fit the way you are may not be on the list, but select the adjectives that seem to describe you most closely.

1. Most of the time I feel _____ , _____ , and _____ .

calm	relaxed	complacent
anxious	confident	reserved
cheerful	tense	energetic
contented	impulsive	self-conscious

2. When I study or work, I seem to be _____ , _____ , and _____ .

efficient	sluggish	precise
enthusiastic	competitive	determined
reflective	leisurely	thoughtful
placid	meticulous	cooperative

3. Socially, I am _____ , _____ , and _____ .

outgoing	considerate	argumentative
friendly	awkward	shy
tolerant	affected	talkative
gentle-tempered	soft-tempered	hot-tempered

4. I am rather _____ , _____ , and _____ .

active	forgiving	sympathetic
warm	courageous	serious
domineering	suspicious	soft-hearted
introspective	cool	enterprising

continued on next page

5. Other people consider me rather _____ , _____ , and _____ .

generous	optimistic	sensitive
adventurous	affectionate	kind
withdrawn	reckless	cautious
dominant	detached	dependent

6. Underline one word out of three in each of the following lines that most closely describes you:

(a) assertive, relaxed, tense
(b) hot-tempered, cool, warm
(c) withdrawn, sociable, active
(d) confident, tactful, kind
(e) dependent, dominant, detached
(f) enterprising, affable, anxious

The table below has three columns containing the same adjectives. Place a check mark beside each adjective you chose earlier on the test. (If you chose an adjective twice, place two checks next to it.) After checking the adjectives, add the number of checks for each column and place the totals in the blanks underneath the columns. Your three totals should add up to 21.

Endomorphic	Mesomorphic	Ectomorphic
affable	active	anxious
affected	adventurous	awkward
affectionate	argumentative	cautious
calm	assertive	considerate
complacent	cheerful	cool
contented	competitive	detached
cooperative	confident	gentle-tempered
dependent	courageous	introspective
forgiving	determined	meticulous
friendly	dominant	precise
generous	domineering	reflective
kind	efficient	reserved
leisurely	energetic	reticent

Endomorphic	Mesomorphic	Ectomorphic
placid	enterprising	self-conscious
relaxed	enthusiastic	sensitive
sluggish	hot-tempered	serious
sociable	impetuous	shy
soft-hearted	impulsive	suspicious
soft-tempered	optimistic	tactful
sympathetic	outgoing	tense
tolerant	reckless	thoughtful
warm	talkative	withdrawn
Total:	Total:	Total:

From these three numbers, you can now determine your general temperament or psychological type. If you chose 4 adjectives from the endomorphic list, 12 from the mesomorphic list, and 5 from the ectomorphic list, your score would be 4/12/5. The highest of the three numbers indicates the body type most often associated with your psychological characteristics; in this case, you would have a mesomorphic body. Research suggests that your body shape corresponds with how you describe yourself psychologically. Did your choice of adjectives correlate with your body type? Is it a mistake to develop stereotypes based on how someone looks?

Source: Adapted from J. B. Cortes & F. M. Gatti (1965), Physique and self-description of temperament, *Journal of Consulting Psychology, 29,* 432–439. © by American Psychological Association.

exhibitionism, practicality, and designer (see Table 5.1 on p. 194). People with a high *clothing consciousness* orientation believed it was important for others always to notice what they wore. Those scoring high in the second orientation, *exhibitionism,* approved of themselves' and others' wearing "skimpy" clothing. People with a high *practicality* orientation were more concerned with the practicality of clothing than with beauty. Finally, scoring high in the fourth orientation, *designer,* were those people who would love to be clothes designers. This study established an association between the characteristics of individuals and their preferences for particular clothing. Personality characteristics were associated with both males and females who scored either high or low on the four clothing orientations.

TABLE 5.1 CLOTHING ORIENTATION AND PERSONALITY TRAITS

CLOTHING ORIENTATION	PERSONALITY TRAITS
Clothing Consciousness	*"People always notice what I wear."*
High females	Inhibited, anxious, kind, loyal to friends
Low females	Independent, dominant, logical
High males	Deliberate, guarded, deferential to authority
Low males	Aggressive, independent
Exhibitionism	**"I approve of skimpy bathing suits . . ."**
High females	Radical, having high opinion of self-worth
Low females	Timid, sincere, patient, having feelings of inferiority
High males	Confident, outgoing, moody, impulsive
Low males	Guarded about self, having low self-concept
Practicality	*"I'm interested in the practical, not beauty."*
High females	Outgoing, clever, confident, having no desire to lead
Low females	Detached, self-centered, independent
High males	Cautious, rebellious, inhibited, dissatisfied
Low males	Analytical, serious, forceful, mature
Designer	*"I would love to be a clothes designer."*
High females	Uncritical, expressive, quick, irrational
Low females	Resourceful, efficient, persistent

TABLE 5.1 CLOTHING ORIENTATION AND PERSONALITY TRAITS (CONT.)	
CLOTHING ORIENTATION	PERSONALITY TRAITS
Designer	*"I would love to be a clothes designer."*
High males	Cooperative, warm, helpful, demanding
Low males	Adventurous, anxious, egotistical

Source: Based on findings in L. B. Rosenfeld & T. G. Plax (1977), Clothing as communication, *Journal of Communication, 27,* 24–31.

Closely related to clothing is the use of **artifacts**, or accessories used for decoration or identification. Jewelry, glasses, hats, badges, tattoos, purses, and briefcases are all personal artifacts, and they can communicate your self-image, affiliation, and social attitudes.

Recently, Ruth went to the artists' sale at the community center. After admiring a painting for quite some time, she asked about the price of the painting. "Fourteen hundred," the artist answered. Ruth took out her checkbook. "Okay," she said, "I'll take it." While she was writing the check, the artist, in an attempt to make conversation, casually remarked, "You're not like most people who come through here; most of them try to 'Jew' me down, and I really hate that!" Ruth looked up, her face turning red, tore up her check, and snapped, "You, sir, have just lost a sale!" With storm in her eyes, she abruptly turned and vanished into the crowd. The artist had not noticed the communicative artifact: Around Ruth's neck, at the end of a long chain, was a star of David. Ruth was Jewish.

ARTIFACT
An accessory used for decoration or identification.

SELF-CHECK

You and Your Artifacts

What are your most cherished artifacts? What is your favorite jewelry, perfume, or cologne? What does your hairstyle convey to others? What do these artifacts convey about your personality? How do your choices of artifacts reflect who you think you are?

▨ *Kinesics*

KINESICS

The communicative ability of gestures and body movements.

The nonverbal behavior code with which you are probably the most familiar is kinesics. Sometimes called "body language," **kinesics** refers to the way gestures and body movement send messages. There are five categories of kinesic behavior: emblems, illustrators, regulators, adapters, and affect displays.[23] First, **emblems** are movements and gestures that have a direct verbal translation, and these movements are known to a specific group or culture. The sender intentionally displays emblems to replace words. Examples include the hitchhiker's thumb, two-finger victory sign, and wave of the hand to say hello. Examine the list of cultures in Table 5.2 for their distinctive methods of greeting others.

EMBLEM

A movement or gesture that has a direct verbal translation.

TABLE 5.2 GREETINGS FROM AROUND THE WORLD: CULTURAL DIFFERENCES IN SAYING "HELLO"

CULTURE	DESCRIPTION
Japan	The bow—bending forward and down at the waist.
India	*Namaste*—placing hands at the chest in a praying position and bowing slightly.
Thailand	*Wai*—same as *namaste* (India).
Middle East	*Salaam*, used primarily among the older generation. Right hand moves upward, touching first the heart, then the forehead, and then moving up into the air.
Maori tribespeople (New Zealand) and Eskimos	Rubbing noses.
East African tribes	Spitting at each other's feet.
Tibetan tribesmen	Sticking out their tongues at each other.
Bolivia	Handshake accompanied by a hearty clap on the back.
Russia	Friends begin with a handshake and move to a "bear hug."
Latin America	*Abrazo*—embracing with both arms.

Source: Data from R. E. Axtell (1991), *Gestures: The do's and taboos of body language around the world* (New York: Wiley).

The second type, **illustrators**, accompany verbal messages and illustrate what is being said. They are usually intentional by the sender and cannot normally be interpreted without the use of words. Holding your hands a foot apart while saying, "The fish was this big!" is an example of an illustrator.

Regulators, the third kind, are used to regulate conversations. Examples include raising your hand, lifting your head, and raising your eyebrows to gain the floor during a conversation. Leaning back and lowering your voice help to signal that you want to relinquish the conversation floor.

The fourth type, **adapters**, are behaviors exhibited to satisfy some physical or psychological need. Physical adapters include rubbing your eyes when tired and shifting positions in a chair after sitting for a long time. Psychological adapters are used for emotional release and include twisting your hair and biting your nails when you're nervous. Adapters are not conscious behaviors; they are used in response to heightened emotional arousal.[24]

Affect displays, the last category, are used to indicate emotional or affective state. They convey mood and reactions. These are usually unintentional movements that reflect the sender's true emotions. An example is slumping in a chair, indicating fatigue or boredom, or a sad face reflecting problems in your life.

Another aspect of kinesics is **posture**. The way you stand, sit, and walk is highly communicative, although factors such as gender and age also affect posture. The two primary dimensions of posture are immediacy and relaxation.[25] **Immediacy** is the degree of closeness you feel toward another. Body movements that reflect an attitude of immediacy are direct body orientation, symmetrical positioning, and leaning forward. You convey the second dimension, **relaxation**, by means of a relaxed posture, asymmetry of positioning, and leaning backward. By the use or nonuse of these two dimensions, you demonstrate your openness or willingness to communicate.

The postural stances between interactants can be grouped into three major classifications:[26] (1) inclusive or noninclusive, which are the positions of a group that either include or disregard other people, (2) face-to-face or parallel body orientation, which is the postural relationship between two people during a conversation, and (3) congruence and incongruence, which are the similarity and dissimilarity of posture between interactants. These postural stances provide information about status, affiliation, agreement, liking, and attitudes.[27] For example, parallel body orientation indicates a liking and an interest in each other, while face-to-face orientation indicates formal or professional interaction. A higher status individual will display a more relaxed posture, while the subordinate will display a rigid stance. If two people share a similar postural stance, it may be signaling equality and liking. Thus two friends talking are likely to display parallel body orientations or congruent postural stances to show a mutual affection for each other,

ILLUSTRATOR
A movement or gesture that accompanies and illustrates a verbal message.

REGULATOR
A movement or gesture that regulates conversation.

ADAPTER
A movement or gesture that satisfies some physical or psychological need.

AFFECT DISPLAY
An unintentional movement or expression that conveys a mood or emotional state.

POSTURE
The way one stands, sits, or walks.

IMMEDIACY
The dimension of nonverbal communication that reflects the degree of closeness felt toward another.

RELAXATION
The dimension of posture that, combined with immediacy, can reflect openness or willingness to communicate.

FIGURE 5.2

Paying respect, communicating greetings, and meeting people do not always begin with the firm handshake typical of Western cultures. Cultures from around the world use different kinesic (and sometimes touching) behavior as a greeting.

whereas a military general and a first lieutenant will display formal, rigid, and incongruent postural stances to signify the difference in their status.

Kinesics is influenced by individual communicator styles.[28] The *assertive* communicator is active in maintaining the attention and interest of others. Assertive communicators are commonly perceived as dominant and independent, and they use frequent and dynamic gestures and movements. The *responsive* communicator projects understanding, sympathy, warmth, and friendliness. This style demonstrates immediate and open body positions. The *versatile* communicator adapts to the behavior of the other. A person who uses this style is flexible in behavior and adapts body movements to complement the situation and the other interactant. This style increases adaptability.

Facial Expressions

Facial expressions, though the primary nonverbal codes used to display emotions, can be problematic because of the complexity they present. The human face is capable of producing over a thousand different expressions.[29] Nonetheless, different facial expressions are associated with different emotions, and these emotions are displayed by distinct areas of the face. Happiness is shown in the cheeks/mouth and eye/eyelid area of the face; sadness and fear are conveyed in the eye/eyelid area; surprise is portrayed in the cheek/mouth, eye/eyelid, and brow/forehead areas. Anger is not easily noticeable unless two or more areas of the face are used for its expression. Although anger is difficult to recognize from facial expressions, other emotional states are clearly apparent.[30]

One expression that has been given particular attention in the literature is the smile. Ekman and Friesen have classified smiles into three types: felt,

FIGURE 5.3
*What is your interpre-
tation of the emo-
tions of each of these
people?*

false, and miserable.[31] *Felt smiles* are automatic reflexes to positive emotions, such as happiness or delight.

False smiles are used to portray positive emotions that aren't actually felt. There are three kinds of false smiles: *phony smiles*, used when no emotion is felt; *masking smiles*, used to cover up negative emotions; and *dampened smiles*, used to conceal positive emotion.

Miserable smiles are responses to negative emotions, with no attempt made to conceal unhappiness. Felt and miserable smiles are true reflections of emotions, whereas false smiles are concealers of emotion.

False smiles are just one of the many ways that people control their facial behavior. When people manipulate their facial expressions, they are using facial management techniques. The four most commonly employed techniques are **intensification**, or exaggerating what you feel (e.g., when you exaggerate surprise about the birthday gift from your parents even though you found it hidden in the closet a week earlier); **deintensification**, or downplaying what is felt (e.g., withholding tears at a sad movie even though you want to cry); **neutralization**, or eliminating all expression of emotion (e.g., when a paramedic remains expressionless at the scene of a car accident so the injured will stay calm); and **masking**, or replacing an expression that shows true feeling with one that is deemed appropriate (e.g., congratulating a new bride with a smile even though you dislike her new husband intensely).[32] The primary emotions can be concealed by facial management techniques, and social norms help you determine which techniques are appropriate to which situations.

Consider the following scenario: Every Saturday night after the restaurant where he works closes, Anthony invites his co-workers over to his house for a quarter ante poker game. Each hand has a $5 limit, so Anthony feels comfortable (guilt-free) winning. Anthony's poker buddies have trouble reading his facial expressions because these rarely show any emotion (excitement, disappointment, etc.). Anthony is using facial management to *neutralize* his expression so that his companions will have trouble guessing whether he holds a strong or a weak hand of cards.

Some people utilize certain styles of expression regardless of circumstances.[33] A chronic set of behaviors tends to be associated with their facial expressions.

Withholders intentionally neutralize all emotion from display.

Revealers show their true feelings all the time and make no attempt to conceal emotions.

Unwitting expressors believe they are masking their emotions, but their true feelings are still evident.

Blanked expressors believe they are displaying the emotion they are feeling, but their faces are expressionless.

INTENSIFICATION
The facial management technique of exaggerating what is felt.

DEINTENSIFICATION
The facial management technique of downplaying what is felt.

NEUTRALIZATION
The facial management technique of eliminating all expression of emotion.

MASKING
The facial management technique of replacing an expression that shows true feeling with one that is deemed appropriate for a particular situation.

Substitute expressors unintentionally substitute one emotional expression for another.

Frozen-affect expressors show, at least in part, one particular emotion all the time.

Ever-ready expressors use the same initial expression as a response to any situation.

Flood-affect expressors expose their faces with one particular expression that will always be recognizable even when they display another emotion.

Oculesics

If you ever get bored with day-to-day life and need something to perk you up, try this experiment—provided you are in a familiar environment such as work or school.[34] Step onto a crowded elevator and instead of facing the door, face the people and keep your eyes on them. Don't speak; just look. To the people on the elevator, a 30-second ride will seem like an eternity! They will begin to squirm with uneasiness as they feel your eyes scrutinize them. Once you look down, their uncomfortableness will begin to subside. This is the power of oculesics. **Oculesics** refers to eye behavior and plays an important role in communication. Eye contact with another person commands involvement. Even when you pass strangers and make eye contact, you are connected to that person, albeit remotely. It can also stimulate arousal, either positive or negative. You can probably remember as a child receiving "looks" (eye contact) from your parents that communicated a specific meaning and emotion to you—eye contact that sent messages of "Be careful," "Surprise," "You're in trouble when we get home," and the widening eyes that meant "Didn't you understand that first look I sent you?" Even now, you communicate with friends in much the same way. Imagine meeting a classmate as you walk with your best friend. With eye contact, you could communicate to your friend such messages as "Can you believe that outfit?" and "Hurry, I don't want him to see me!"

The eye area is one of the least controllable regions of your face, and as a result, your eyes can expose your emotional state. There is a significant change in the eyes with surprise and fear, but only little change with happiness and disgust.[35] Interpersonal encounters usually begin with eye contact to signal interest, and in the Western culture, increased eye contact with a speaker indicates interest and attention. The type and amount of eye contact can indicate the nature of a relationship and can show status, type of relationship, and stage of relationship. If you think about it, the amount of eye contact you make with others is indicative of how much you like them.

From a general perspective, eye behavior can serve six important communicative functions.[36] The eyes can (1) influence attitude change and per-

OCULESICS
Eye behavior.

suasion, (2) indicate degrees of attentiveness, interest, and arousal, (3) express emotions, (4) regulate interaction, (5) indicate power and status, and (6) form impressions in others.

Think of eye behavior from the perspective of mutual gaze, gaze aversion, and gaze omission. *Mutual gaze* involves two people looking in the direction of each other; that is, they share mutual eye contact. Mutual gaze is used for a number of reasons, such as ensuring someone is listening, flirting, and establishing a connection with someone.

When only one person is attempting to make eye contact, gaze aversion has occurred. An intentional behavior to turn one's gaze away from another person, gaze aversion is often used to signal disinterest in a person or topic or to signal the end of a conversation.

Gaze omission is similar to gaze aversion in that one person does not make eye contact with another. The difference is that the avoidance of eye contact is unintentional. For some reason, the attempt by another to make contact has gone unnoticed. Of course, the factor of intentionality involved in these two behaviors makes it extremely difficult to interpret. As a result, it is easy to misunderstand someone's eye behavior. When was the last time you avoided eye contact with someone else? What was your motivation?

Staring is one aspect of eye behavior that has negative connotations; by most standards, it is considered rude and socially unacceptable. Staring is regarded as an invasion of privacy or a threat to the individual. At the onset of a relationship, it may indicate interest, but most of the time, it is perceived negatively and may not be completely effective in establishing meaningful relationships. How do you feel when you are being stared at? Flattered? Annoyed? Anxious? What do you do about it?

Paralanguage

Paralanguage refers to *how* something is said, not *what* is said. To further illustrate this point, try saying "great" to convey these messages: disappointment; excitement; congratulations; disgust. The word (what you said) didn't change, but the voice characteristics (how you said it) changed. People make judgments about personal characteristics (age, gender, status, etc.), emotional states, and attraction on the basis of vocal cues. Vocal cues also influence persuasion and aid comprehension.[37]

Trager, an early researcher in paralanguage, classified paralinguistic activity into several categories. Of these categories, one that is especially closely related to communication competence is voice qualities.[38] **Voice qualities** encompass pitch range (actual range of pitch), vocal lip control (the degree of hoarseness in a voice), glottis control (sharp or smooth transitions in pitch), articulation control (precise or slurred speech), rhythm con-

PARALANGUAGE
The communicative value of vocal behavior; the meaning of how something is said.

VOICE QUALITIES
The vocal cues of tempo, resonance, rhythm, articulation, pitch and glottis control, and pitch range.

VOCALIZATION
A vocal cue that does not have the structure of language.

VOCAL CHARACTERIZER
A sound that conveys the emotional or physical state of the speaker.

VOCAL QUALIFIER
A vocal cue that qualifies or regulates verbal messages.

VOCAL SEGREGATE
A sound with a connotative meaning.

trol (level of smoothness), resonance (thickness or thinness of tone), pitch control (ability to vary range of pitches), and tempo (rate of speech).[39]

Trager also mentions another type of paralanguage, **vocalizations**, or vocal cues outside language structure. There are three types of vocalizations: vocal characterizers, vocal qualifiers, and vocal segregates. **Vocal characterizers** include sounds such as laughing, crying, giggling, moaning, sighing, and yawning. Vocal characterizers give information about the speaker's emotional or physical state. **Vocal qualifiers** are cues that provide variety within a specific utterance. This category includes intensity (loudness or softness), pitch height (high or low), extent (duration of sound), and rate. Vocal qualifiers indicate emotional states and are used to add emphasis to meaning, as in the utterance "There *is* no Tooth Fairy." For example, an uneven rhythm (shakiness in the voice) and a fast tempo (rate) might indicate nervousness, and little resonance (thinness in voice) and slurred speech (articulation control) might signal fatigue. Vocalizations that are used in place of words and have connotative meaning are **vocal segregates**. These include "uh-huh" (yes), "shhh" (be quiet), and "uh-uh" (no). Filler sounds like "er" or "ah" are also considered segregates.

One interesting aspect of paralanguage is Giles's speech accommodation theory. Giles believes that people change their vocal patterns in respect to another's (i.e., *accommodate* them) in order to obtain a desired response from the other person. Changing vocal patterns can affect social inclusion, maintain group identity, or increase distance between interactants.[40] The cues used to achieve a desired response from another are accent, speech rate, utterance duration (how long people speak), and pause duration. The changes made in vocal cues to increase similarity in vocal patterns can add perceptions of liking and attraction; the changes made in vocal cues to become dissimilar with the other's vocal patterns can produce negative perceptions. Stop for a moment and think about a business acquaintance, such as a boss or co-worker, whose relationship is important to you. Have you ever noticed how you "accommodate" this person's vocal patterns? Are you aware of how the two of you may use accommodating vocal styles in order to seem similar and therefore more attractive to each other?

Haptics

Tactile communication, or **haptics**, refers to touching behavior. Touch is one of the most fundamental types of communication. It is the first communication experienced in life. As a newborn, you get your first information about yourself, others, and your environment from touching. Touch is powerful communication and provides meaning when words often fail. A father's loving touch soothes a crying baby; a handshake thanks a public speaker; a supportive pat on the back bolsters the confidence of the unsure. Although people have different perceptions of touch, it is a primary means of communication and a basic human need.

One classification system for touch is Heslin's intimacy continuum.[41] This continuum defines the uses of touch based on the relationship between the interactants. Heslin divides the uses of touch into five types: functional-professional, social-polite, friendship-warmth, love-intimacy, and sexual arousal. The first type of touch, *functional-professional,* refers to touching that is used to perform a job. This type of touch is incidental to the purpose of doing the job and is used without interpersonal involvement. Physicians, dentists, and hairstylists use this type of touch in the course of their work.

The next type of touch, *social-polite,* is used as a social function and is restricted by the social rules of the culture. Although it is more interpersonal than functional-professional, social-polite touch is used in a social role. A handshake between American men and a kiss between Arabic men are examples of this type of touching.

The third kind of touching, *friendship-warmth,* conveys liking and affection between people who know each other. Because it is used in interpersonal relationships, it is often difficult to interpret and frequently confused with intimacy. Back-patting and hugging are messages of affection and friendship, but not necessarily love.

The fourth category, *love-intimacy,* is used by lovers and spouses to communicate love and closeness. Kissing, embracing, and caressing the cheek are love-intimacy touches. Although this type of touch is intimate, it does not necessarily involve sexual activity. In fact, this type of haptic communication may be used by parents and children and other relatives.

Sexual-arousal touch is the fifth type of touching. Sexual touch is an intense form of touch and plays an important part in intimate relationships. However, sexual-arousal touch is also used in nonintimate relationships and should not be equated with intimacy. The whole notion of one-night stands serves as a reminder that sexually charged tactile communication does not have to involve relational intimacy.

Another classification system for touch distinguishes between the different kinds of body contact. Morris separates body contact into fourteen primary types.[42] Although Morris's system is different from Heslin's intimacy continuum, each of these body contact types can be associated with Heslin's continuum for the use of touch. Handshakes, body-guides, and pats usually serve social-polite functions. The arm-link, the shoulder embrace, the full embrace, the hand-in-hand, and the mock attack demonstrate friendship-warmth. Love-intimacy touches include the waist embrace, the head-to-head, and the caress. Table 5.3 (on p. 206) identifies Morris's primary types of body contact along Heslin's intimacy continuum.

TABLE 5.3 HOW PEOPLE TOUCH

TYPE OF CONTACT	PURPOSE	TYPE
Handshake	Relational ties can often be measured by the strength of the handshake.	Social-polite
Body-guide	Touching is a substitute for pointing.	Social-polite
Pat	Often used as a congratulatory gesture but sometimes meant as a condescending or sexual one.	Social-polite or sexual-arousal
Arm-link	Used for support or to indicate a close relationship.	Friendship-warmth
Shoulder embrace	Signifies friendship; can also signify romantic connectiveness.	
Full embrace	Often called a hug, this gesture shows emotional response or relational closeness.	Friendship-warmth
Hand-in-hand	With adults, the gesture suggests equality within the relationship.	Friendship-warmth
Waist embrace	Indicates intimacy.	Love-intimacy

Touching can communicate a variety of messages. Although not all people interpret touch in the same way, it allows people to communicate emotion—and the intensity of that emotion—more effectively. You are more likely to touch someone you like than someone you dislike. In fact, withholding touch can communicate negative emotions, while touch can increase interpersonal attraction and positive perceptions. An exception to this is the *touch avoider,* a person who generally finds touching annoying. This person finds touching discomfiting and will recoil from touch.

TABLE 5.3 HOW PEOPLE TOUCH (CONT.)

TYPE OF CONTACT	PURPOSE	TYPE
Kiss	The placement, length, and openness of a kiss signal the degree of closeness or of the desire for closeness.	Love-intimacy or sexual-arousal
Hand-to-head	Shows a trusting and often intimate relationship.	Love-intimacy
Head-to-head	Usually agreed upon by both people involved as a means to close themselves off from the rest of the world.	Love-intimacy
Caress	Normally used by romantic partners; signals intimacy.	Love-intimacy or sexual-arousal
Body support	Touching used as physical support.	Love-intimacy
Mock attack	Aggressive behaviors performed in a non-aggressive manner, such as arm punches or pinches meant to convey playful touches.	Friendship-warmth

Numerous studies indicate that the touch avoider was taught as a child to associate touching with "not nice" or "bad" behavior and has continued the "nontouching" into adulthood.[43] Studies designed to identify the personality characteristics of nontouchers have found that they report more anxiety and tension in their lives, less satisfaction with their bodies, and more suspicion of others. Nontouchers are less sociable and more rigid in their beliefs.[44] Touch communicates positive or negative affects, and it conditions your perceptions and the perceptions of others.

What Is Your Touch Index?

What type of touch "index" do you have? Are you repelled by touches from strangers? What about elderly people? Children? Members of the opposite sex? Does it depend on the situation? How so?

Preferences for touch can also depend on culture. Some cultures depend on touch as an important form of communication, whereas other cultures are less touch sensitive or even tend to avoid touch. For example, Latin American, Mediterranean, and Eastern European cultures rely on touch much more than do Scandanavian and some North American cultures. Can you think of co-cultures within the United States that are more dependent on touch as a form of communication than other co-cultures?

Proxemics

PROXEMICS
The communicative aspects of the use of space.

PERSONAL SPACE
The space around one's body to which one attaches owner-ship.

Proxemics refers to how you use and communicate with space. One area of proxemics is **personal space**, the space around your body to which you attach ownership. Cultural norms and personal feelings about space will affect your choices about the use of this space.

Hall devised a system of identification for the space used, or spatial zones, according to the type of interpersonal relationship.[45] Hall categorizes spatial zones as

Intimate (0–18 in.)
Personal (18 in.–4 ft)
Social (4–12 ft)
Public (12 ft and beyond)

The *intimate zone* is reserved for lovers, very close friends, and intimate family members; the *personal zone* for close friends and relatives; the *social zone* for professional interactions, such as business transactions or teacher–student conferences, and for casual talks; and the *public zone* to keep distance between the interactants, such as public speakers and concert performers with their audience.

Although you may have different personal space needs, how you feel about allowing another person to be in one of your spaces really depends on who that other person is. Some families are close and use intimate and personal zones exclusively; other families are uncomfortable with that much closeness. Different cultures around the world vary a great deal in their preferences for proxemic closeness. Arab cultures, for example, encourage very close proxemics so that sight, smell, and touch are heightened for communicators.

Although the use of personal space is individualized, some generalizations are possible. Harper and his colleagues found that some personality characteristics influence the use of space.[46] Extroverts require less space than introverts, and highly anxious persons and shy persons prefer greater distances. People with a high need for affiliation or for control will narrow the distance between themselves and others. After researching deviant populations (criminal, schizophrenic, disruptive, and violent individuals), Ma-

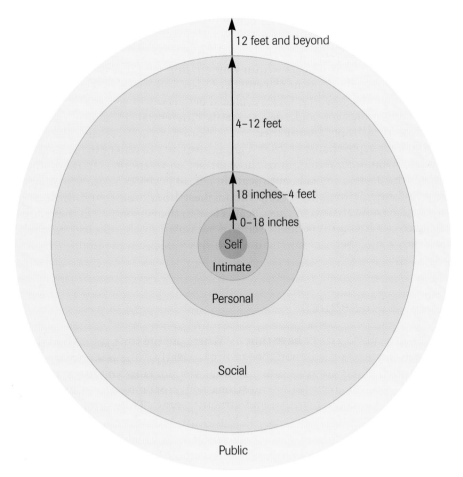

FIGURE 5.4

The four zones of personal space described by Hall indicate ranges that apply across cultures.

landro and Barker discovered that deviants require more space and that they depend on that space as a means of protection.[47] The space requirements for deviants are abnormally large for the social norms of the interaction. Spatial distance between communicators must be mutually determined. Concerns for privacy, intimacy, dominance, and status all govern how people position themselves during interactions.[48]

TERRITORIALITY
The claiming of an area, with or without a legal basis.

Territoriality is another concept of proxemics. **Territoriality** is the claiming of an area, with or without legal basis, and is most commonly established through continuous occupation of that area. Territories are claimed, staked, and defended by the individuals who occupy them. Some territories that easily come to mind are your home, your car, and your office. But territories also encompass implied ownership of space, such as a favorite livingroom chair, a seat in a classroom, a parking space, a "usual" table in a restaurant, or a frequented spot on the beach. When territoriality is encroached upon, it will be defended by its owner, and this defense will utilize nonverbal behavior. The behaviors used in defense are *withdrawal* (retreat from the invader), *insulation* (gestures and body movements to block the invader), and *turf defense* (fighting).

How you arrange objects within your *environment* also communicates a message. For example, your placement of your desk and chairs conveys your degree of approachability. Objects placed between you and another will inhibit communication and suggest status differential. In addition, seating arrangements imply dominance and subordinance. Riess and Rosenfeld found that people choose seats in a group situation to reflect their desires to lead, to avoid interaction, or to show attraction to another. In their study, those who desired to lead chose seats in a head position; those who wished to avoid interaction chose seats the furthest from others; and those who wanted to show attraction chose seats close to the person whom they found attractive.[49] If you think about some of your own seating choices, you will probably remember making them with a specific reason in mind.

▨ *Chronemics*

CHRONEMICS
The communicative ability of the use of time.

TIME ORIENTATION
Time preferences.

"Time's up!" "I don't have time." "Where did the time go?" All of these utterances express the importance of time. Clearly, time is a primary force in your life, and it controls much of what you do. How you use your time and how you feel about time send strong nonverbal messages. **Chronemics** refers to how people perceive and structure time. **Time orientations** fall into three categories: psychological, biological, and cultural.

Psychological time orientation is the way you perceive or feel about time. There are three principal applications of psychological time orientation: *past-oriented* people assign particular value to past events; *present-oriented* people live and work for the present; and *future-oriented* people live and work for the future.[50] A person's orientation will determine the importance that person ascribes to conversation content, the length of the interaction, the urgency of the interaction, and punctuality.[51]

Differences in psychological time orientation can create communication problems. A past-oriented person, for example, will not value punctuality as highly as people of the other orientations might. A present-oriented person will work toward shorter interactions. In each case, the result can be feelings of irritation and impatience that will hinder communication. For example, a past-oriented instructor who keeps a present-oriented student waiting for a scheduled appointment may hinder open or effective communication.

Biological time orientation is determined by biological cycles. This is your "biological clock." It determines when you are most active, both physically and mentally. People who are at their best in the morning are referred to as "sparrows"; those who are at their best in the late afternoon and evening are considered "owls."[52] Biological time affects how you perceive others and how they perceive you and can thus be a source of communication problems. A cheerful sparrow in the morning will perceive an owl's lack of attention negatively, whereas the owl will perceive a sparrow's tiredness in the afternoon in an unfavorable way.

Cultural time orientation is the way a culture uses time. Hall proposes that three time systems operate in any culture: technical (scientific measurement), formal (the culture's system of measuring time), and informal (casual time of a culture).[53] Formal time involves the way a culture measures, values, and uses time. The phrase "time is money," used extensively in Western cultures, indicates how people value time. Informal time involves punctuality and duration. For example, most Western cultures find it extremely rude to be late, but in most Latin cultures lateness is the norm. Hall further divides the informal use of time into two types—monochronic,

---

SELF-CHECK

What Time Do You Have?

Which type of psychological time orientation do you have? Do you live in the past, present, or future? Does your time orientation depend on the situation? How so? How does your orientation affect communication with others?

which means doing one thing at a time, and polychronic, which means doing several things at a time.[54] This, too, varies with culture. Which of these two types of informal time do you believe U.S. culture uses?

▓ *Olfactics*

The perception of scents and smells is referred to as **olfactics**. The word *scents* usually refers to odors and aromas associated with people or animals. *Smells* are usually associated both with people and inanimate objects or the environment (garbage, flowers). Although smell is one of the primary senses, it is one of the least researched codes of nonverbal communication. Nonetheless, scents and smells can produce strong reactions and can add intensity to positive or negative perceptions. Consider how bleach stings the eyes and forces people to retreat from the odor. Consider, too, how the aroma of fresh-baked bread brings a pleasant smile. In much the same way, personal scents and smells affect interactions. Offensive odors will increase distance between interactants and shorten the time of the interaction. Pleasant smells will increase communication with another.[55] Body scents and smells in the environment communicate things to us about others. Our judgments about other people may be influenced by the odors those people allow in their environment.

Attractiveness is associated with scent. Those who smell attractive and pleasing will receive more attention and touch.[56] Not all people prefer the same scents, however. The norms of the culture provide guidelines to distinguish between offensive and pleasant scents and smells. Western cultures consider body odor offensive, but many other cultures prefer the natural body scents to perfume. Extremely strong scents, such as those of heavy fragrances, copiously applied perfume, hair spray, and hair permanents, are offensive to most people and can shorten the interactions between people. Other offensive odors include the smell of smoke on clothes

---

REALITY CHECK

The Sweet Smell of Success

What smell(s) do you like most in members of the opposite sex? How about members of the same sex? Why do some real estate agents place cinnamon sticks in a preheated oven before potential clients arrive to view a house on the market?

---

and bad breath. Offensive scents are perceived negatively and will often determine whether an interaction is initiated, continued, or terminated.

The Relationship between Nonverbal and Verbal Communication

Nonverbal behavior uses codes to form messages. Even though the different types of nonverbal behavior can communicate meaning by themselves, they are rarely used alone. Rather, they work in conjunction with verbal behavior to form a complete message. In most cases, nonverbal communication interfaces with verbal communication to form a message system.

Nonverbal messages have specific operations within this message system. Ekman defines the functions of nonverbal messages when integrated with verbal communication as complementing, contradicting, repeating, regulating, substituting, and accenting.[57] **Complementing** behavior clarifies the meaning of the verbal message, such as giving a pat on the back while saying "Good job." **Contradicting** behavior indicates the opposite of the verbal message, such as saying "I'll miss you" while smiling and skipping off. **Repeating** behavior is nonverbal behavior that mirrors the verbal message, such as holding up three fingers while saying "Three." **Regulating** behavior is used to coordinate verbal interaction, as when one looks directly at another person to signal, "Don't give away the upcoming surprise party." **Substituting** is used to replace words, such as a traffic police officer's outstretched, open hand substituting for the word "Stop." **Accenting** emphasizes the verbal message; someone who pounds his or her fist on the table while saying "No" is engaged in accenting. These functions help to integrate nonverbal behavior and verbal utterances into a complete message system.

COMPLEMENTING
Nonverbal behavior that clarifies the meaning of a verbal message.

CONTRADICTING
Nonverbal behavior that conveys a meaning opposite to that of the sender's verbal message.

REPEATING
Nonverbal behavior that mirrors the accompanying verbal message.

REGULATING
Nonverbal behavior that is used to coordinate verbal interaction.

SUBSTITUTING
Nonverbal behavior that replaces the use of words.

ACCENTING
Nonverbal behavior that emphasizes the accompanying verbal message.

Competence Factors

Nonverbal communication constantly (and dramatically) undergoes change, reversal, and modification. The way you perceive and interpret nonverbal behavior is influenced by a number of factors, and as a competent communicator, you must be aware of what they are: culture, context, and situation.

■ Culture

The well-known story of a past president is the best demonstration of why culture is such an important factor to consider in nonverbal communication. In the late 1950s, then–Vice President Richard Nixon made a goodwill tour of Latin America, where there was already a feeling of hostility toward the United States. Of course, the press followed his tour. On one of his stops, Nixon stepped off his airplane and, smiling, gestured with the "A-OK" sign to the waiting crowd. The crowd booed. The next day, published photographs of Nixon and his gesture appeared on the front page of major newspapers. Nixon had made headline news—not for his accomplishments on the tour, but for his gesture. In that culture, Nixon's gesture had a completely different meaning; it meant "Screw you!" Days of delicate diplomacy were undone by two seconds of nonverbal behavior![58]

All nonverbal communication is influenced by culture. Social norms are established by cultures, and these norms greatly affect the perceptions of nonverbal behavior. Obviously, gestures have different meanings in different cultures. But the other nonverbal codes are also influenced by culture. Although the expression of primary emotions is universally recognized, how, when, and where these expressions can be displayed are under the social rules of the culture. For example, the Japanese are conditioned to mask emotion. Eye behavior also takes different forms; Americans and Canadians use eye contact as a form of acknowledgment or politeness in greeting, but

BY JOHN McPHERSON

"Apparently I have done something to upset you."

FIGURE 5.5

Placement of objects within the environment can communicate a strong nonverbal message about approachability.

Observing Nonverbal Behavior in the Classroom

How many different cultural groups are represented in your communication class? Which nonverbal behaviors can you identify as being associated with particular cultures? Why do you think it is important to understand the nonverbal cues of other cultures? How do kinesics, paralanguage, and touch affect intercultural relationships?

in other cultures, such as those of Nigeria and Puerto Rico, this is often considered disrespectful. Because attractiveness is determined by social norms, appearance preferences change from culture to culture. Anyone who does not fit the physical norm of the culture will have trouble communicating in that culture. Touch is a relevant form of communication in any culture, but, again, the social norms control where, when, and how touching should occur. The British culture is a noncontact culture, whereas the French culture is high contact. Proxemics also vary widely among cultures. Arabs and Italians require very close proximity when interacting; Americans place themselves farther apart. The value and use of time differs from culture to culture. Polychronic cultures (e.g., that of Latin America) may find the North American monochronic culture extremely irritating.[59]

Context and Situation

Think about your favorite professor and hold the image of that person in your mind. In the classroom, you have a certain rapport with this professor. Your communication with that person is defined by the classroom setting. Now imagine that you see this same professor at a local restaurant. Your communication would change because you see the professor in a different context. **Context** is the physical and psychological setting of an interaction.

The context determines the rules of behavior and the roles people must play. Two of the primary factors involved in context are the public–private dimension and the informal–formal dimension. The *public–private dimension* refers to the degree to which the context is public or private. The invasion of privacy (physically or psychologically) solicits reduced smiles and other adapters such as restless body movements, leaning backward, gaze aversion, and vocal tension. You will be perceived negatively if you interfere with the private context of another.

The *informal–formal dimension* refers to whether the setting is personal or impersonal. This dimension involves various rules of behavior; it

CONTEXT

The physical and psychological setting of an interaction.

TABLE 5.4 STATUS INDICATORS

POWER AND HIGH STATUS INDICATORS	POWERLESSNESS AND LOW STATUS INDICATORS
Relaxed posture and body position	Erect and rigid posture and body position
Less attentive to others	More attentive to others
More expansiveness	More restrictiveness
Seated position	Standing position
Dark, conservative suit	Light suit or strange clothing
Tall stature	Short stature
More access to space	Less access to space
Finger pointing	Receipt of finger pointing
Less direct body orientation	More direct orientation toward superiors
Closed arm position	Open body orientation
Giving less/receiving more eye gaze	Receiving less/giving more eye gaze
Sarcastic smiling/laughing	Respectful smiling/laughing
Touches others more/touched less by others	Touches others less/touched more by others
Makes others wait	Waits for others (superiors)
Determines meeting time and length	Told of meeting time and length
More flexible time schedule	Rigorous and strict time schedule
Expensive office furniture	Economical office furniture
Larger office in nicer and more private location	Office location dependent on job duties

Source: Adapted from D. O'Hair & G. W. Friedrich (1992), *Strategic communication in business and the professions* (Boston: Houghton Mifflin), p. 141.

tinual contact.[65] Greetings can be complicated. Kendon and Ferber describe six stages of greetings: (1) sighting, orientation, and initiation of approach (acknowledgment of the other's presence), (2) the distant salutation (a wave), (3) the head dip (lowered head), (4) approach (eye contact and open body position), (5) the final approach (less than 10 feet, mutual gaze, and smiling), and (6) close salutation (verbalizations, such as "Hi!").[66]

Greetings!

What is the strangest greeting you have ever received? Was touch involved? How did you react?

Greetings are normally initiated by a vertical or sideways motion of the head accompanied by eye contact and smiling. Smiling indicates a positive mood, and eye contact conveys the willingness to communicate. Body movement and gestures are also used extensively in greetings.

Greetings can then lead to conversation. Nonverbal cues are employed during conversation to ensure speaking turns. The components of **turn-taking behaviors** are turn yielding (giving up the floor), turn maintaining (maintaining control of the floor), turn requesting (requesting the floor), and turn denying (denying the obligation to take the floor). Nonverbal behaviors are used to display these intentions (see Table 5.5). The exchange of turns during a conversation is a mutual process between speaker and listener, and the nonverbal cues facilitate the turn-taking sequence. Nonverbal behaviors can also alter the conversational topic. The listener's restlessness, shown by shifting or looking away and fidgeting, will convey his or her boredom with the topic.[67]

TURN-TAKING BEHAVIORS
Cues used by a listener to signal to a speaker that the listener is attentive to the speaker, to encourage the speaker to continue to talk, or to indicate that the listener would like to speak; also, cues used by a speaker to signal to his or her partner that the speaker role is (or is not) available at that moment in the conversation.

TABLE 5.5 NONVERBAL COMMUNICATION AND MANAGEMENT OF TURN TAKING		
TURN-TAKING FUNCTION	DESCRIPTION	NONVERBAL BEHAVIORS
Turn yielding	Giving up the floor	Extended pauses and gazes
Turn maintaining	Maintaining control of the floor	Touching, filled pauses
Turn requesting	Requesting the floor	Rapid nods, vocalizations
Turn denying	Denying control of the floor	Silence, avoidance of eye contact

Deception Cues

What has your experience taught you to be reliable "cues" of deception? Do some people you know (friends, family) express consistent nonverbal cues when you think they are lying? What about you? What cues do you communicate when you have to tell a lie?

SOCIA
A proc
one pe
cause
anoth
and b

such as rubbing and scratching. When a deceiver falsifies information (lying about factual data), more head movements can occur.[78]

Deceivers will often be aware of the nonverbal behaviors associated with lying and may try to mask these behaviors. The cues thought to be indicative of lying are leg and foot movements, illustrators, adapters, and postural shifts. In an attempt to reduce these cues, the deceiver may become abnormally rigid or stiff. Therefore, sometimes the best evidence of deception is not an increase or decrease of nonverbal behaviors but a deviation from the deceiver's normal behavior.

Self-Promotion

You may have been told since childhood that inner beauty has higher value than physical beauty, that goodness is in the heart, and that it is what's inside that counts. But judgments and inferences are made at the beginning of a relationship or interaction, not after many detailed encounters. In fact, if you make a negative impression, more than likely you will not have the chance to reveal your inner beauty. Thus impressions play a significant role in how you relate to others, and nonverbal behavior is the predominant influence on the formation of impressions. The following principles control how you form impressions:[79]

- You develop evaluations of others based on limited external information. Lack of personal information about another and uncertainty of the situation cause you to form opinions.[80]
- Impressions are based partly on the stereotypes you hold. Common stereotypes include those based on skin color, hair, body shape and size, and age. Stereotypical traits are preconceived by the interactants.
- First impressions are often based on outward appearance. Physical appearance information is readily available.
- Initial impressions form a baseline of comparison for subsequent impressions and judgments and may affect future interactions.

Impressions consist of judgments you make on three levels: physical, sociocultural, and psychological. Physical judgments consist of evaluations about age, gender, and body shape and size. These judgments are readily noticeable, though not always completely accurate. This category does not include personality traits or character judgments, but rather demographic information (male or female, general age, etc.). Appearance and vocal cues are the most important influence on these judgments.

Sociocultural judgments are made about socioeconomic status, residence, occupation, education, and group membership. Clothing is a symbol of status, and perceptions of success and education are based on dress. A person dressed in a business suit will be perceived as having more status than someone in jeans. In addition, hairstyle is associated with success. Short hair is viewed as professional for both men and women and is associated with intelligence and corporate status.[81] Dress and artifacts, whether they be T-shirts or rosary beads, also designate group membership. Psychological judgments are judgments of personality, character, and mood. Physical features are exceptionally vulnerable to these inferences, and most stereotypes are derived from the psychological judgments of physical features. Character analyses based on skin color, body shape and size, hair color, and age are commonplace—thus the frequent stereotyping of redheads as hot-tempered, heavy people as lazy, and elderly people as slow-witted. Vocal qualities are also stereotyped: soft-spoken people may be viewed as passive, breathiness as sexy, and people with orotund voices as lively and gregarious. Even if they are inaccurate, such perceptions may affect interactions. For example, a business executive who has a small body frame may not be perceived as powerful in a meeting; an anchor who is soft-spoken on the evening news may not be perceived as credible; and an elderly public speaker may be perceived as boring.

Managing behavior so that others will have positive impressions is called impression management, or **self-promotion**. Several techniques can

SELF-PROMOTION
Presentation of the self in a way that will create a favorable impression in others.

SELF-CHECK

The Real You

What are the ethics involved in trying to create an impression that is not really "you"? How many of the behaviors just discussed do you use to get people to think positively of you? How successful have you been in creating positive impressions of yourself? Do you worry that giving a false impression will come back to haunt you later? Think of some examples in which other people have managed their nonverbal behaviors to create a false positive impression. What is your opinion of these people?

be employed to increase the formation of positive impressions. Cues used to produce feelings of attractiveness and likability will enhance positive impressions. The behaviors that create social positiveness are smiling, mutual gaze, increased gestures, relaxed body positions, leaning forward, head nods, variations in vocal pitch and range, close proximity, and increased touch.[82]

Competent Nonverbal Communication

Nonverbal communication affects every interaction, every relationship, and every dimension of your life. It can destroy careers (e.g., when a businessperson touches a colleague inappropriately), elevate relationships (e.g., when congratulations are expressed by a handshake or a pat on the back), or determine future interactions (e.g., when an appropriate greeting is used in a foreign culture). Its communicative power is endless. As a competent communicator, you must remain aware of how nonverbal communication manages relationships, controls interactions, persuades, deceives, and forms impressions. You should take into consideration all the variables that can modify the message: culture, context, situation, and relational dimension. Admittedly, this is an overwhelming task, but before you leave this chapter grumbling with frustration, remember the innate and socially learned skills you have already developed. You can recognize the primary emotions, and you know, at least in your own culture, the socially acceptable behavioral rules. You now have the knowledge you need to enhance the skills you already possess and be aware of the magnitude of their underlying implications.

One ingredient not mentioned previously is as much a part of nonverbal communication as any other factor—individuality. Nonverbal behavior is not always transmitted by the same channels, received with the intended message, or sent with explicit meaning. Individuals will differ in the codes they use, how they use them, and the messages they apply to them. The variety of messages and ways to communicate those messages are infinite. That is one of the fascinating aspects of nonverbal communication. Life would be boring and monotonous if people were all alike. Isn't it amazing that even with highly individualized behaviors, everyone can still communicate and understand that communication? Individual differences, preferences, and variations of behavior should be enjoyed. An appreciation of nonverbal behaviors that are culturally different from our own enriches our communication experience and enhances our competence. The competent communicator recognizes the importance of individual expression.

REVIEW

Nonverbal communication is a system of codes used to send messages. Two perspectives suggest that these messages are developed from innate and learned behaviors. The nonverbal codes used to send and receive messages include appearance and artifacts, kinesics, facial expressions and oculesics, paralanguage, haptics, proxemics, chronemics, and olfactics. Perceptions of personality traits are often linked to body type, clothing orientation, and artifacts. Kinesic behavior includes emblems, illustrators, regulators, adapters, affect displays, and posture. Facial expression and oculesics primarily convey emotional states. Paralanguage includes voice qualities and vocalizations. Haptic behavior is described by the types of touch, such as functional-professional, social-polite, friendship-warmth, love-intimacy, and sexual-arousal. Proxemics includes personal space and territoriality. Chronemics provides three categories for time orientation: psychological, biological, and cultural. Olfactics associates scent and smell with perceptions. These nonverbal cues are affected by and changed according to culture, context, and situation.

The functions, or outcomes, of nonverbal communication include relational management, interaction management, social influence, deception, and self-promotion. Nonverbal codes work in conjunction with each other to serve these functions. Relationship management illustrates messages regarding intimacy or status. Intimacy is expressed by less personal distance, direct eye contact, smiling, and touch. Status can be conveyed through clothing, open body position, access to space, and use of time. Interaction functions regulate greetings and turn taking in conversation. Cues that increase immediacy and liking, such as increased eye contact, gestures, and attractiveness, aid in social influence. Deception can be detected by a change in eye contact, a higher voice pitch, pupil dilation, and stress-related behaviors. Self-promotion includes first impressions and impression management. Impressions consist of judgments on physical, sociocultural, and psychological levels. Nonverbal cues affect how you will be perceived by others. However, individual preferences and diversity in nonverbal messages should be appreciated as an aspect of what makes each person unique.

SUGGESTED READINGS

Argyle, M. (1988). *Bodily communication* (2nd ed.). London: Methuen.

Feldman, R. S. (1992). *Applications of nonverbal behavioral theories and research.* Hillsdale, NJ: Lawrence Erlbaum.

Poyatos, F. (Ed.). (1988). *Cross-cultural perspectives in nonverbal communication.* Toronto: Hogrefe.

Woodall, K. (1993). *How to talk so men will listen.* Chicago: Contemporary Books.

6

Developing
Listening Skills

Objectives

After reading this chapter, you should be able to

1. Define the process of listening.

2. Describe three costs of ineffective listening and three rewards of competent listening.

3. List the components involved in managing listening skills.

4. Describe how listeners can adjust to speakers.

5. Describe the effects of context on listening competence.

6. List the steps involved in active listening.

7. Explain how interactive listening is critical to competent listening.

CHAPTER CONTENTS

Listening: The Least Developed Communication Skill

One of the big problems, I believe, we all have in our lives is to know who[m] to listen to, but in my experience as you grow older and have had a few bad experiences in listening it becomes even harder and more of a problem to listen at all. I have known some of the most powerful minds who found it difficult to influence their surroundings, to influence their companies, and to gain influence in proportion to their abilities because they could not listen. The fact is that over the years there have been people I remember who were such profound thinkers, such outstanding minds, whose influence could have been very, very great. . . . [T]he reason they couldn't influence the company to the extent they should have is that they . . . had this crazy defect: they couldn't listen.[1]

This quotation from Jack Goldman, senior vice president and chief scientist at Xerox, suggests a very common problem in the world. All too often, people with great ideas or wonderful minds are unable to influence others because they do not listen well. The tragedy of this problem is rooted in the perceptions and assumptions people possess about listening. Most people think that they are at least average listeners. The improvement of listening, therefore, becomes a low priority.

A Definition of Listening

Listening is such a broad term that it is difficult to define simply. The best way to define it is to describe its important features, to develop an understanding of the critical concepts it entails, and to associate some of the common descriptions given to it.

The Most Frequently Used Communication Process

One way to describe the listening process is to examine how frequently you engage in this communication act. Research studies report that high school and college students spend from 42 to 54 percent of their waking hours listening.[2] Research surveys of Fortune 500 company personnel reveal that listening is one of the most prevalent and important skills that a college graduate can possess. If you think about it, the time you spend listening to your professors, other students, family members, friends, radio, and television consumes a very large part of your conscious awareness. Listening could even be your most common activity.

Different Conceptions

Listening is different things to different people. Students have a different concept of listening than do construction workers, who think of it differently from parents, physicians, or airline pilots. With so many different ideas about listening, it is little wonder that listening abilities vary so widely. Some people you know view listening as a passive activity that simply "happens" to them. They remark, "Listening is easy, what's all the fuss?" Those are the same people who must have information and instructions repeated to them often. Other people with whom you are familiar conceive of listening as the most important thing they can do in their lives. They are conscious of the rewards associated with effective listening. They are among the most efficient and successful people you know. Often they are also the most enjoyable people to be around. This chapter focuses on describing the basic skills of effective listening and on presenting techniques that you can use to build more effective listening skills.

Descriptors

As a first step toward building a common definition of listening, we present some of the descriptors associated with listening. Descriptors are useful because they provide synonyms and referents for how listening is viewed. Brownell conducted a study among business managers who likened good listening to the following behaviors of the skilled listener:[3] He or she shows sensitivity to the emotional aspect of the message; understands and remembers information; remains objective and nonjudgmental; concentrates; and encourages information sharing. Each of these descriptions is positive and action oriented. Of course, not all descriptions of listeners are positive. Steil conducted a study in which participants were asked to think of the best and worst listeners they had ever known and to provide three words describing these people.[4] Table 6.1 (on p. 230) presents some of the more common descriptors reported by respondents for best and worst listeners.

This book approaches listening from a competency perspective. **Listening** is the process of recognizing, understanding, and accurately interpreting the messages communicated by others. Competent listening involves a complex process of *cognitive, behavioral,* and *affective skills* other than just hearing. Since a model of competent listening is developed in later sections, you will understand how important listening is to your well-being.

LISTENING
The process of recognizing, understanding, and accurately interpreting the messages communicated by others.

TABLE 6.1 DESCRIPTORS OF BEST AND WORST LISTENERS

BEST LISTENER	WORST LISTENER
Advising	Abrasive
Aggressive	Absent
Alert	Argumentative
Approachable	Arrogant
Challenging	Careless
Concerned	Closed
Confident	Deceptive
Friendly	Defensive
Judicious	Frustrated
Kind	Insecure
Mature	Lazy
Open-minded	Opinionated
Patient	Prejudiced
Perceptive	Reactionary
Precise	Self-centered
Reflective	Shallow
Relaxed	Shifty
Trusting	Stubborn

Source: Data from L. K. Steil, J. Summerfield, & G. de Mare (1983), *Listening: It can change your life* (New York: Wiley), p. 177.

Ineffective Listening

In 1957, Ralph Nichols, one of the pioneers of listening research, reported in *Nation's Business* that the average businessperson listened at only a 25 percent efficiency rate. Recent surveys of top companies in this country report that listening rates are still less than desirable. Most of these studies focused on informational listening, but the emotional aspect of the message is also often ignored. Stewart suggests that listeners are oblivious to almost 100 percent of the feelings communicated in messages and that they ignore or misunderstand 75 percent of the informational content.[5]

Your Own Best and Worst Listeners List

From the descriptions of listeners presented in Table 6.1, do you get a sense that people value good listeners? Do you hold similar values? What descriptors would you add to each of the two lists?

A Skill in Need of Development

When was the last time you received any instruction in listening improvement? Communication instructors are surprised and disheartened when they raise this issue with their students because they find that most students have had little or no training in listening skills. Listening is a skill that is taken for granted for two reasons. First, it is the first communication skill you learn and you have been at this process much longer than speaking, writing, and reading. Because of listening's long history, its importance has a tendency to be dismissed. Second, poor listening is not as immediately noticeable as its speaking, reading, and writing counterparts. Some people have become experts at getting away with poor listening in the short term.

These reasons do not excuse the need for a concentrated effort in listening improvement. Wolvin and Coakley in their book *Listening* report that dozens of businesses, nonprofit agencies, and government organizations demand formalized and systematic listening instruction in school systems, college and university campuses, and business settings.[6] Listening is recognized as one of the most important, yet underdeveloped, skills in this country.

Barriers to Listening

What do you consider to be the greatest barriers to competent listening? Barriers take various forms and differ from one person to the next. Jill often finds herself inattentive when she feels she already has enough information. Yoko, on the other hand, feels that her greatest barrier to competent listening is being distracted by thoughts of other conversations. Fernando's ego is so large that he perceives himself as a totally competent listener! According to a study conducted by Golen, college students reported that their most common **listening barriers** were *laziness, closed-mindedness, insin-*

LISTENING BARRIERS
Factors that interfere with competent listening (e.g., laziness, insincerity, boredom, and closed-mindedness).

FIGURE 6.1
*Closed-mindedness is
a common barrier to
competent listening.*

cerity, boredom, and *inattentiveness.* How do these compare with your own barriers to listening? This chapter presents strategies for overcoming the barriers to listening that you may face on a regular basis.

■ The Costs of Ineffective Listening

In this chapter, we can only begin to describe the great costs that result from ineffective listening. Teachers mention the loss of knowledge or learning that occurs when students fail to listen. Judges grieve about the injustice perpetrated on the judicial system when jurors or lawyers do not listen well. Businesspeople are outraged by the economic costs associated with listening errors. And patients are constantly complaining about the poor listening habits of physicians. Ineffective listening does exact costs of many types, and knowing the nature of these costs is helpful in creating motivation to develop more effective skills. **Listening costs** take many forms, but they have been categorized in four areas: economic, physical, emotional, and psychological.

LISTENING COSTS
*Direct and indirect
penalties associated
with poor listening;
can be economic,
physical, emotional,
or psychological.*

Economic Costs

Recall a recent situation when you answered the phone and a telemarketing salesperson was on the line attempting to persuade you to purchase a product. Did you listen carefully enough to accomplish your goals? You may know of an instance when an unsuspecting, poor listener agreed to purchase a condominium share on a payout plan of five years. This person had no intention of becoming involved with a profit-sharing investment, but made a commitment because of poor listening habits. This kind of business mistake can be very expensive. One source has estimated that businesses lose millions of dollars each year because of listening mistakes alone.[7] These costs take the form of repeated or duplicated tasks, missed opportunities, lost clients, botched orders, misunderstood directions or instructions, and missed appointments.

Physical Costs

The various costs incurred because of poor listening are not just economic. The physical costs associated with poor listening can create significant problems. For example, a mother was nervous that her daughter was very ill from influenza. When the physician prescribed a liquid antibiotic at a dosage of "one ounce to be taken four times a day," the mother thought she heard "four ounces once a day." When her daughter developed complications from the overdose, the mother realized that her listening error had created a physical cost. Finally, when tasks must be repeated or redone, fatigue can also take its toll on an ineffective listener.

REALITY CHECK

The Costs of Poor Listening

Have you ever lost something because of poor listening skills? Have you missed opportunities, been charged a fee, or gotten a bad grade because you missed important information? In some cases you may have lost more than you think. Perhaps you misunderstood something to such a degree that you were unable even to realize that you had an opportunity. These are the kinds of questions you must ask yourself in order to determine whether you need to improve your listening skills.

Psychological and Emotional Costs

Have you ever been frustrated with someone for not listening carefully to you? Frustrations are one of the most common emotional costs associated with incompetent listening. "Why do I waste my time if he is not going to listen?" "Why bother trying to explain myself if she ignores what I say?" In addition to frustration, poor listeners can annoy and anger those around them. A clerical worker was fired when he failed to respond to an order by an angry superior. One of the costliest results of poor listening is the effect it has on self-concept. If you find that you often make mistakes, cause errors, and create problems for yourself and other people, you may begin to question your value, without even knowing why. Whether or not you actually recognize it as your problem, the costs associated with ineffective listening will lower your self-image. You may even begin to expect problems in advance because of a self-fulfilling prophecy.

◼ *The Rewards of Competent Listening*

So far, a dreary picture has been painted of how ineffective listening can cause you a lot of grief. Just the opposite is true of effective, competent listening. The **listening rewards** that come to competent listeners are innumerable; we will briefly discuss three broad categories of benefits.

LISTENING REWARDS
Benefits of competent listening, such as time saving, enhanced relationships, and professional advancement.

Time Benefits

Competent listeners save a great deal of time by allowing themselves to be more productive in their lives. When you listen competently to someone giving you directions to a hotel to attend a meeting, you do not have to go early to make sure that you can find the place. Or, if someone tells you about a shortcut in getting advised and registered, you can save time enrolling in school. Businesspeople save themselves and their companies time when they are able to act quickly and accurately on information presented to them. Time is a nonrenewable resource, and good listening can allow you to make the most of it.

Relationship Benefits

One of the skills that people in healthy and committed relationships most often praise in their partners is understanding and sensitive listening. Strong interpersonal relationships are built on competent listening. For example, when one relational partner self-discloses to the other, competent listening facilitates an appropriate response. When one person in a relationship needs the other to listen empathically, competent listening supplies this important need. Competent listeners become trusted friends and enjoy a wide variety of relationships.

MIRIAM   I get nervous and tongue-tied every time I audition for a new part in front of an unfamiliar director.

NORA   You know, I've been a struggling actress for ten years, and there's no simple remedy.

MIRIAM   Are you telling me this feeling of anxiety never ceases?

NORA   Well, confidence and practice help. I'm free this evening, if you'd like to review your lines.

As you noticed from the interaction above, Nora not only listened as a friend, she also provided supportive or empathic statements to Miriam, a sure sign of effective listening.

Professional Benefits

We have discussed some of the economic and professional costs associated with poor listening. On the positive side of this process, competent listening is valued and rewarded professionally. Take another look at the positive descriptors associated with good listeners. These are the types of characteristics that are attributed to people who listen competently. Being seen as alert, confident, mature, and judicious is just a token of the professional rewards that will accrue to the competent listener. A successful businessman in the Southwest explained to one of the authors of this book why he repeatedly promotes a particular young manager ahead of her older, more experienced colleagues. "Denise makes me realize that she is absorbing everything I have to say. I never worry about her leaving my office with a misunderstanding." In a fiercely competitive economic and financial cli-

---

REALITY CHECK

A Listening Balance Sheet

Form a group in your communication class and brainstorm about personal examples in the last year when (1) poor listening caused costs, and (2) competent listening produced rewards. Record your answers in two columns on a sheet of paper. Discuss with your group how some of the skills involved in the competent listening examples could be used to improve the outcomes in the poor listening examples.

mate, one of the true advantages individuals and companies have for getting the edge is competent listening. Listening to clients, customers, suppliers, subordinates, co-workers, managers, and economic advisors is required of everyone.

Listening Competently: A Process

Improving listening competency is a process. It begins with a commitment to become a more effective listener and extends to developing the skills needed to achieve that goal.

Making a Commitment

Most people are average listeners. In order to become more competent, you must make a *commitment* to improve. If you are satisfied with your current listening abilities, it will be very difficult for you to improve. You will need to believe firmly that competent listening really helps you to rise above the crowd and allows you to develop your true potential as nothing else can. Making a commitment to listening improvement requires an adjustment in your attitudes toward your listening and a reminder of the rewards associated with competent listening (or the costs related to poor listening). You probably already realize that you have developed some strong attitudes about the role of listening in your life. These attitudes can fall into two areas, and they essentially affect how you view your own listening. The areas of **listening attitudes** are:

LISTENING
ATTITUDES
One's view of one's own listening competence and the listening abilities of others.

How you view your own listening competence. If you view yourself as a good listener, then making a commitment to become even better will be more difficult.

How you view the listening abilities of other people. If you compare your listening abilities unfavorably to those of other people, you may either become discouraged or you may view the better listeners as models and strive for their level of competency.

Another aspect of making a *commitment* is to remember the rewards associated with competent listening. Most people are not interested in a mediocre life. They want good friends, a loving family, and a rewarding career. All of these goals or rewards are within your reach when you make a commitment to improve your listening. Your potential can be realized if you are ready to develop competent listening skills. Make the commitment now!

Listening Attitudes

To clarify your attitudes toward your own listening skills and those of others, take this quick test. Circle the answer that reflects your natural reaction to each statement.

1. I am a better listener than most people I know.	Yes	Maybe	No
2. I wish other people listened to me better.	Yes	Maybe	No
3. I can tell when I am not listening well to other people.	Yes	Maybe	No
4. It irritates me to see other people listen poorly.	Yes	Maybe	No
5. I get frustrated when I make mistakes because of poor listening.	Yes	Maybe	No
6. If I could change anything about people, it would be their listening habits.	Yes	Maybe	No
7. I wish I were a better listener.	Yes	Maybe	No

Take a look at your responses. What are your attitudes about listening? Do you find that you can form an attitude about listening that will lead you to a commitment to improving your own listening? If you answered "yes" to most of the questions, you are a communicator who is concerned about competent listening. If you answered "maybe" or "no" to many of them, your attitude about listening is not very intense. Only through a committed attitude can you become a more competent listener.

Developing Skills

To carry out a commitment to improve your listening abilities, you must realize that listening is a communication skill, and communication skills are mastered by study, concentration, and practice. This chapter will provide you with a basis for starting that training.

It is also critical to understand that listening is more than just hearing. Hearing is an audiological sequence that involves mostly involuntary physiological processes, much like breathing or the senses of sight and smell. Your capacity for hearing is only part of your ability to listen. There are many audible sounds that you hear, but listening to them is a different story. Imagine this scenario of a friend telling you something. Your friend's vocalizations penetrate your outer and inner ears, yet you do not pay attention. You are able to hear the words but do not listen. The point is, you must have good hearing to listen properly, but hearing is only the first step toward competent listening.

FIGURE 6.2
A framework for listening competence.

The good news about the approach to listening improvement is that skills can be improved. Now that you have made the commitment to improve your listening, here is a framework that will enhance your competency. This framework involves a five-step process: (1) managing your skills, (2) adjusting to the speaker, (3) managing the context, (4) listening actively, and (5) listening interactively.

Managing Your Skills

Assessing Your Listening Self-Concept

LISTENING
SELF-CONCEPT
The image one has of oneself as a listener.

As you recall from the model of communicative competence, self-concept is an important aspect of communication. How you think of yourself affects your motivations, goals, attitudes, and even skills. Some people have a much clearer idea of their own listening skills than do others. There are people who don't give listening much thought at all. There are others who think of themselves as poor, average, or superior listeners. **Listening self-concept** varies depending on the person. Even those who think they listen poorly may actually

Listening Self-Assessment

This Self-Check is designed to help you assess your listening self-concept. In answering the questions, remember to trust your initial reactions because only by doing so can you evaluate yourself accurately.

For each statement, determine whether you strongly agree (SA), agree (A), don't know or have no opinion (?), disagree (D), or strongly disagree (SD), and check the appropriate box.

Question	SA	A	?	D	SD	Score
1. I interrupt others too frequently.						
2. I am not able to respond effectively to others' messages.						
3. I am effective at showing others that I understand what they are saying.						
4. I get apathetic when boring people talk to me.						
5. Sometimes I expect too much of myself when listening to others.						
6. My mind wanders when people talk to me.						
7. I am easily distracted by extraneous sounds when I listen to others.						
8. I am effective at asking questions when I feel I don't understand someone.						
9. I maintain good eye contact when I listen to others.						
10. Sometimes I have to have information repeated to me.						
11. I have been told that I am a good listener.						
12. I am comfortable listening to other people's problems.						
13. I can immediately grasp the main point or idea that a speaker is trying to make.						
14. I have good hearing.						
15. It is sometimes difficult for me to understand someone when other people are talking at the same time.						

continued on next page

Question	SA	A	?	D	SD	Score
16. I am often overconfident of my listening abilities.						
17. I have a good memory for what people have said.						
18. I consider myself to be an effective listener.						
19. I can tell when people are listening carefully to what I am saying.						
20. I am a much better listener in some situations than in others.						

Total Score:

Scoring: Place the score for each item in the right-hand box labeled "Score." For items 1, 2, 4, 5, 6, 7, 10, 15, and 16, use the following scale: SA = 1; A = 2; ? = 3; D = 4; and SD = 5. For items 3, 8, 9, 11, 12, 13, 14, 17, 18, 19, and 20, use the following scale: SA = 5; A = 4; ? = 3; D = 2; and SD = 1.

Add up all of the scores and write the total score in the box provided. The higher your score, the higher your listening self-concept. If you scored between 50 and 70, you have an average listening self-concept. If you scored above this (70–100), you have a favorable listening self-concept. If you scored below this (20–50), you have an unfavorable listening self-concept. You can improve a low listening self-concept through work and practice that focus on developing your potential as a listener. The rest of this chapter can help you achieve this goal.

have average listening skills. Those who believe they listen well may possess only moderate skills.

It should be pointed out that self-concept is only one piece of the puzzle toward **listening self-assessment**; that is, evaluating your overall listening competence. Your actual listening skills may exceed or not measure up to your evaluation of yourself as a listener.

LISTENING
SELF-ASSESSMENT
Evaluation of one's own listening abilities and skills.

▦ *Determining Expectations*

Forming expectations enables you to prepare for communication situations and thereby contributes to your communication competency. Some expectations are not fulfilled during the experience, whereas other expecta-

Expectations and Reality

Think about yourself as a communicator. How do your communication experiences compare to your expectations of how they will turn out? Are you usually right or wrong about the outcome? Why?

tions are. Regardless of how closely your expectations match outcome, forming them prior to your communication gives you an opportunity to plan your thinking and behavior so that you can communicate more competently. It is important to remember the following points when forming expectations about listening situations. First, ask yourself what you expect to get out of this situation. Will this be an enjoyable experience? Is it going to be difficult to listen to this person? Have you had difficulty listening effectively in situations like this before? How long will this listening situation last? Will there be any unusual circumstances surrounding this situation? Second, avoid overestimating your expectations for the event. Remain objective about what to expect from the person or situation. Previous experience comes in handy when forming realistic expectations.

Recognizing Your Listening Habits

People have **listening habits** that they would prefer to change or improve upon. Many people have poor listening habits that they do not even recognize. Habits become so routine that they often operate below their level of consciousness. When this happens, the best method of changing undesirable listening habits is to recognize them. This section discusses some of the more common listening difficulties that plague college students. Ask yourself if some of these are your own habits.

LISTENING HABITS
Routine listening behaviors such as neglect, apathy, over-confidence, and defensiveness.

Neglect and Apathy

In some situations you feel that listening is a waste of your time. It may be that you have underestimated your expectations or you simply do not feel that a particular listening situation is worth the effort. Neglect can also result from a preoccupation with other listening situations. When this happens, you are likely to listen only halfheartedly or to ignore the person altogether. How many times have you said to yourself, "Oh, I really don't want to listen to that man. He is so boring." How often have you remarked to yourself, "Uh, they are not going over that information again, are they?"

There are many times when you simply have no interest in the person or the topic. The problem with this attitude is that neglected listening situations may be the very ones that could provide excellent opportunities. When you find yourself becoming apathetic about a listening situation, think to yourself that you can always learn something from a situation and that the effort expended is not going to be overwhelming; rather it will be worthwhile.

Overconfidence

Sometimes your expectations can cause you to be overconfident about certain listening situations. Overconfidence comes in the forms of poor preparation and planning, expecting too little from speakers, ignoring important information, and exhibiting an arrogant attitude. Overconfidence can lead to some unexpected listening problems. Think about this incident: Randall walked into a business meeting certain that he knew everything that was going to be said. As he confidently sat through the meeting only half listening, several of his co-workers and his boss began asking him questions that he was unprepared to answer. Randall had to admit that he hadn't anticipated their questions, and he felt very foolish. Overconfidence can lead to surprises that could and should be avoided.

Apprehension

LISTENING
APPREHENSION
A state of uneasiness, anxiety, fear, or dread associated with a listening opportunity.

A third listening habit for many people, **listening apprehension** is a state of uneasiness, anxiety, fear, or dread associated with a listening opportunity. In many situations you may be apprehensive about listening. Going to a job interview, being called in for a reprimand, having to listen to someone else's problems, listening to highly detailed or statistical information, listening to people with heavy dialects—all are likely to trigger listening apprehension. You can probably think of other listening situations that are particularly stressful for you. The problem with listening apprehension is that it can affect your ability to concentrate on what is said or affect your memory of what was said. You can become so distracted by your apprehension that you lose out on what was said.

How do you feel about your apprehension score? If your score for the Self-Check "Receiver Apprehension" indicates that you have a low level of apprehension, you listen with confidence. If you have a moderate to high score, you are probably like a lot of people who experience some apprehension in a few listening situations. Try two things to reduce the effects of your apprehension when you feel it coming in a listening encounter. First, focus your mental concentration on the speaker's ideas. Minimize thoughts about your nervousness by using your energy to understand the message.

Receiver Apprehension

Wheeless has developed a test that identifies listening areas that make some people apprehensive. Some of these are listed below. Answer the following questions to get an idea of your listening apprehension level.

Score your answers to the following questions according to whether you strongly agree (1), agree (2), are undecided (3), disagree (4), or strongly disagree (5).

_____ 1. I am not afraid to listen as a member of an audience.

_____ 2. I feel relaxed when I am listening to new ideas.

_____ 3. I generally feel overexcited and rattled when others are speaking to me.

_____ 4. I often feel uncomfortable when I am listening to others.

_____ 5. I often have difficulty concentrating on what is being said.

_____ 6. I look for opportunities to listen to new ideas.

_____ 7. Receiving new information makes me nervous.

_____ 8. I have no difficulty concentrating on instructions given to me.

_____ 9. People who try to change my mind make me anxious.

_____10. I always feel relaxed when listening to others.

Scoring: Add up your scores for items 1, 2, 6, 8, and 10. Now add up your scores for items 3, 4, 5, 7, and 9. Subtract the total of the second set of answers from the first total to get a composite score. If your final score is positive, you have a tendency toward receiver apprehension; the higher the score, the more apprehension you report. If the score is negative, you have little or no apprehension.

Source: Adapted from L. R. Wheeless (1975), An investigation of receiver apprehension and social context dimensions of communication apprehension, *Speech Teacher, 24,* 261–268.

Second, if you experience physical tension, relieve your apprehension by taking a few slow, deep breaths and by tensing and relaxing muscle groups that feel tight. You will notice a refreshed sensation that can relax you during tense listening situations. You will find that becoming a more competent listener will bolster your confidence, leading to a calmer outlook on any listening situation.

Defensiveness

Defensiveness is a problem for most people because they resent being criticized by others or they dislike feeling threatened by other people. Becoming defensive affects your listening in two ways. First, you become preoccupied with determining the other person's motive for attacking you or your group personally. This is true whether or not there is an actual personal attack. Think about the last time you became defensive. Didn't you spend a large amount of time thinking about *why* the speaker would criticize or threaten you? You probably missed much of what the person was saying while you were preoccupied with these thoughts or with your counterattacks.

A second listening problem associated with defensiveness is becoming distracted with counterattacks. One of the first reactions to defensiveness is to immediately find ways to go on the offensive. If you are being attacked, that is a reasonable strategy. However, if you fail to listen to the entire argument or criticism, you may miss some valuable information that would be useful in your own arguments. You can stem your defensive tendencies by pursuing the following steps:

1. Wait for the speaker to finish before devising your own arguments. Hear the speaker out. You do not want to rush into an argument without knowing his or her position.

2. While listening to the speaker, focus on the person's motives for saying what is being said. You may have done something that the speaker is reacting to; you might be the cause.

3. Take a deep breath and smile slightly at the speaker. Your disarming behavior may be enough to force the speaker to speak more reasonably.

4. After the speaker finishes, paraphrase what you think was said and ask if you understood the message correctly. You will be surprised how often a speaker on the offensive will back away from his or her aggressive stance when confronted with an attempt at understanding.

▩ *Recognizing the Importance of Hearing*

Good hearing is, of course, essential to competent listening. Hearing is an audiological process that involves physiological and cognitive elements. You cannot simply assume on your own that you have good hearing. Numerous sounds can escape your attention without your awareness. In addition, slight hearing loss can prevent you from discerning spoken messages in a crowd of people or with audible distractions going on around you. That is why it is essential to have your hearing checked periodically to ensure that you have an effective hearing range. Most colleges and universities have testing centers that offer free hearing tests. It would be a good idea for you to take advantage of this opportunity.

Overcoming Distractions

A number of factors compete for your attention. From a listening perspective, these are considered **distractions**. They may be environmental, emotional, or psychological.

Environmental Distractions

External noise such as jackhammers, traffic, conversations outside your room or office, and doors slamming are examples of environmental distractions that can divert your attention from a listening task. Visual distractions are also possible. Poor lighting, people walking or running outside a window, lightning, and the like can cause you to refocus your listening attention. Even the comfort level of your environment can cause you to be distracted. Poorly ventilated and excessively warm or cold rooms can preoccupy you to the extent that you do not listen well. Environmental distractions must be avoided if you are to listen effectively. If at all possible, think of ways that you can prevent being distracted by environmental elements.

Emotional Distractions

When you become so emotionally aroused or upset that you don't listen well, you are being distracted. Anger, sadness, happiness, jubilation, depression, anxiety, and other emotions tend to preoccupy your attention. When this happens, you do not listen as effectively. You are likely to notice that it is difficult to control emotions so that they do not interfere with your listening. However, when you realize that your emotions are becoming intense, you should use this as a warning signal that your listening could be affected. At that time, you should redouble your efforts to concentrate on your listening abilities. Another method of overcoming these distractions is to deal with the problem or situation that is creating the emotional arousal. If you had an argument with your boss and it is preoccupying your thoughts, settle the issue before going into an important meeting with other people. Your mind will be more at ease, and you will be both more willing and better prepared to concentrate on the meeting at hand.

DISTRACTIONS
Various factors that compete for one's attention, such as environmental, emotional, and psychological circumstances.

Psychological Distractions

Psychological distractions are usually categorized as daydreaming. There are valid reasons to daydream. For example, psychological distractions can be useful to give your consciousness time to recoup. However, when you daydream during lectures, discussions, or conversations, you can miss out on a lot of useful information. One method for avoiding excessive daydreaming is to recognize that those dreams will be there for you after you have listened properly. Put these distractions off until an appropriate time and reward your good listening behavior with a wonderful daydream.

◼ *Understanding Listening Functions*

In a complex and turbulent world, people find that their listening needs vary. In some situations you need to listen for information; in others you must listen for ideas, understanding, emotions, or enjoyment. In other words, you don't listen the same way in every situation. Rather, you listen according to your needs. Four types of **listening functions** are the focus in this section.[8]

LISTENING FUNCTIONS
Different types of listening that satisfy different needs.

Comprehensive Listening

The type of listening used to understand or comprehend the message of another person is **comprehensive listening**. It is basic to your existence because you could not accomplish even fundamental goals without understanding information, ideas, and opinions communicated by other people. You use comprehensive listening a great deal in class when trying to understand what the instructor is presenting. A person giving you directions, someone providing instructions, or an individual recounting an experience all qualify for comprehensive listening. It is a basic listening skill and one of the most important.

COMPREHENSIVE LISTENING
Listening in order to understand the message of another person.

Empathic Listening

Listening to people with an open, sensitive, and caring ear constitutes **empathic listening**. Empathy refers to sharing the feelings of another person. If you listen with an empathic ear, you are attempting to know how the other person feels at that time. Sometimes called therapeutic, this type of listening can provide emotional support for someone in need, functioning as therapy. Sometimes a distressed person simply needs someone to listen. Empathic listening can also serve as a comforting strategy when disaster or disappointment has struck. People in love engage in empathic listening when they are exchanging deep thoughts about their relationship.

EMPATHIC LISTENING
Listening to people with an open, sensitive, and caring ear.

They want each other to understand the feelings involved. Empathic listening is a behavior that improves life satisfaction for many people.

Critical Listening

When you listen in order to evaluate or analyze information, evidence, ideas, or opinions, you are engaged in **critical listening**. Critical listening involves a great deal of judgment about the nature of the message. You may hear something on television that you find difficult to believe, or you may listen to a political speaker on the radio and suspect that the person is just trying to win votes. These are examples of critical listening. You may even find classroom material to be suspicious. If you listen with an evaluative posture, you are listening critically. This type of listening is very valuable when you cannot take the message at face value.

CRITICAL LISTENING *Listening in order to evaluate or analyze information, evidence, ideas, or opinions.*

Appreciative Listening

The fourth category of listening is suited for listening enjoyment. **Appreciative listening** is the type used when your goal is simply to appreciate the sounds that your listening mechanism receives. Listening to music, poetry, narrations, comedy routines, plays, movies, or television shows for the sheer enjoyment would qualify as appreciative listening situations. Some people find this type of listening so important that they actually schedule

APPRECIATIVE LISTENING *Listening in order to appreciate the sounds received by one's listening mechanism.*

FIGURE 6.3
Political speeches demand critical listening.

TABLE 6.2 FUNCTIONS OF LISTENING

TYPE	DESCRIPTION	STRATEGIES
Comprehensive	Listening to understand, learn, realize, or recognize.	Listen for main idea; listen for details; listen for organizational pattern; take speaker's perspective; use memory effectively.
Empathic	Listening to provide therapy, comfort, and sympathy.	Focus attention on speaker's perspective; give supportive and understanding feedback; show caring; demonstrate patience; avoid judgment; focus on speaker's goal.
Critical	Listening to judge, analyze, or evaluate.	Determine speaker's goal; evaluate source of message; question logic, reasoning, and evidence of message.
Appreciative	Listening for enjoyment of what is being presented.	Remove physical and time distractions; know more about source (e.g., artist, composer); explore new appreciative listening opportunities.

time when that is all they do. Appreciative listening can help to relieve stress, unclutter the mind, and refresh the senses. Some doctors feel that playing soft music while patients wait for appointments helps to relax them. Table 6.2 lists the four types of listening, accompanied by descriptions of each and of ways they can be best applied.

Setting Listening Goals

The previous section demonstrated how listening needs vary depending on the situation. Now that you are aware of listening functions, it will be easier to meet your listening needs through those functions by setting

Focus on Ethics

We all encounter situations in which one type of listening function turns into another during the course of a conversation. Assume the role of a woman whose friend is telling her about a problem that she has. You recognize that you will probably be listening at the empathic level, since you want to provide comfort and sympathy for your friend. Obviously, your friend is expecting you to listen empathically. However, as you listen to the friend talk about how her ex-husband has been telling stories about her love affairs to the judge who can adjust child support payments, you begin to shift your listening to a critical function. This shift results from your knowledge that your friend did indeed cheat on her husband while they were married. In fact, one of the people with whom she had an affair was someone you occasionally dated, and you have never forgotten this fact. You begin to realize that you have almost shifted into an appreciative listening mode, since your friend probably deserves her fate. Of course, your friend did not expect you to listen critically or appreciatively to her problem. Is it ethical to use one listening function when a speaker expects you to listen with an entirely different function?

goals. This section of the chapter is a chance for you to see the value of setting **listening goals**. You will not achieve the type of listening effectiveness that you desire without listening goals. Here are four steps you should follow when you are setting listening goals.

LISTENING GOAL
A specific plan or objective for listening.

Determine Needs

Do you ever think about your listening needs? Sometimes you may take the listening situation for granted and expect that you will listen effectively without anticipating your needs. That is when trouble can appear. One of the best methods of determining your needs is to assess what you *have* to get out of the situation, what you *expect* to get out of the situation, and what you *hope* to get out of the situation.

- Think about your obligations. What *must* you know, understand, feel, or react to in this situation? What are those issues, events, or people that require you to listen effectively? Make a list of goals ("I need to know her four-day flight schedule").

- List similar types of listening features that you anticipate or expect to get from the listening situation. These are the events or results that should happen, and with conscientious listening, you expect them to occur ("I think that I will understand why she wanted to go on this business trip").

- Write down items that reflect some results that you hope will happen in this situation ("I hope she tells me why she got mad at me yesterday"). Now that you know your needs, you are ready to continue your goal-setting.

Set Performance Standards to Meet Needs

With your needs identified, it is time to develop some benchmark for judging whether or not you are achieving your goals. You do this by setting performance standards that reflect the level at which your needs are met. Football teams, debate squads, orchestras, and even fund raisers set performance standards to use in assessing whether their goals are actually met. In a listening situation, you could list a specific set of qualities or factors that must be accomplished to satisfy your goal: *"I will know all of the main points presented by the guest speaker in class today."* Performance standards are a method of knowing if you are on track with your listening goals. Write down some standards.

State the Goal as an Action

The third step in this process is stating the goal in a way that encourages action. Look at the needs you identified and the standard you set, and develop an action statement incorporating those components into a goal. From the preceding business-trip example, you could make a goal statement that goes something like this: *"I will ask her to give me three reasons why this trip was more important than others."* This type of goal statement considers the need, sets a standard, and is action-oriented. Try one for yourself on the same sheet of paper you're working on.

Develop Steps for Assessing Goal Attainment

The last step in this process is developing a plan for assessing your listening performance. You do this by identifying methods that reveal whether the performance standard is being met. Assessing goal achievement must be accomplished during the listening situation and after it is over. Reflecting on the situation after it is over provides an excellent chance for you to see how well you listened. It is also crucial that you gain some idea of how well you are doing while you are listening so that you can take corrective action if you see you are not meeting your needs. Following is an example to demonstrate how all four steps work together in goal setting.

Need "I need to know her four-day flight schedule."

Performance Standard "I will determine her arrival and departure times for each city she's visiting on her trip."

Action Statement (Goal) "Before I call her, I will make a list of all the cities and establish 'arrival' and 'departure' columns for each city, so that when I talk to her I can simply fill in the blanks. I will take careful notes when she tells me about her itinerary."

Assessing Goal Achievement "Before we get off the phone, I will review my notes carefully to make sure I got all the information."

Managing your skills, the first step toward competent listening, serves as the foundation for supporting the next steps toward listening improvement. Assessing your listening self-concept gives you an idea of what you think of your current skills level. When you determine expectations, you can get a sense of the conditions involved in the listening situation, which is a big help in preparing for the listening event. Other skills to manage in this step involve recognizing your listening habits, becoming aware of your hearing skills, overcoming distractions, understanding the functions of listening, and setting listening goals. With these skills developed, it is time to turn to the second step of this process, adjusting to the speaker.

Adjusting to the Speaker

This section focuses on the person or persons who are speaking during the listening situation. In a later section, techniques that help the speaker adjust to you and to the listening situation are discussed. However, you should concentrate on adjusting to the speaker for now. After all, some speakers either can't or won't adjust. In those cases, you will have to adjust to the speaker in order to accomplish your goals. This section focuses mainly on understanding and tolerating the communication goals and behaviors of speakers.

Communication Style

Communication style is an overall characterization people make of a communicator. It includes nonverbal cues, such as vocal characteristics; word choice; and impression formation (sometimes referred to as communicator style).

COMMUNICATION STYLE
An overall characterization consisting of a communicator's nonverbal cues, word choice, and impression formation.

Nonverbal Cues

Recall from Chapter 5 that nonverbal cues are an important part of the communication process. Although all **nonverbal cues** are important during the listening process, this section touches on those that have the most impact. *Vocal characteristics* influence your listening in several ways. Voice qualities such as pitch and throaty, breathy, or nasal-sounding tones can carry their own meaning to the listener. Rod Stewart has voice qualities that are unique and characterize him as a throaty pop singer. Sharon Stone has a breathy voice that identifies her as an alluring actress. It is sometimes easy to stereotype people according to their voice qualities. However, people can be fooled by such stereotypes, which can lead them into listening trouble. Remain wary of labeling someone just because of the way his or her voice sounds. The same is true of *accent,* which refers to how people pronounce words. Accent is often associated with a particular region of a country. You are probably familiar with southern, New England, and midwestern accents. People for whom English is a second language may speak it with an identifiable Spanish, Eastern European, or Chinese accent. Sometimes people can get so preoccupied with an accent that they fail to listen to everything said.

Speech errors can also cause listeners to miss something that is said. Speech errors include silent pauses (gaps in talking), filled pauses ("Uh," "Um"), and mispronounced words. When you interact with someone who commits a number of speech errors, you must guard against judging the person's content too quickly. In between the errors is information that you may need. A final category of vocal characteristics is fill-ins. *Fill-ins* are superfluous, often irritating expressions that people use in their speech. A few classics are "you know," "like," and "well, uh." Consider the following example:

> Well, Wendy went to, like, Dallas, and saw the Cowboys play the, you know, Giants and couldn't get in the gate because, well, uh, like, she was carrying a cooler full of, you know, beer.

Fill-ins distract the listener because they break up the continuity of speech that is important to comprehension. As a listener, you have a responsibility to make sense of the broken language. You can do this by focusing on the thesis of the message (*Cowboys, Giants, couldn't get in gate because of beer*), and by asking questions if you are unsure of the meaning ("What happened to the beer?").

Gesturing is another type of nonverbal cue that can greatly influence your listening. As Chapter 5 points out, gesturing can aid the verbal message by providing cues about the meaning of a message. However, if people wave their arms widely when they speak, you can become distracted. If someone is talking with hands on hips or with arms crossed, you may get a sense that the person is annoyed or, perhaps, feels powerful at the time. Try to avoid becoming distracted by the gestures themselves. See them for what they are—emotional displays. Use that information to decipher what the person is really telling you. It is difficult to listen well if you ignore the nonverbal cues that another person provides.

Word Choice

The influence of word choice on listening is a rather broad subject. Obviously, some words are more easily comprehended than others, and some are more easily distracting than others. This section limits the discussion to words that may create special problems for listeners. Words that are perceived as *vulgar* or *profane* can distract listeners. Such words can turn off people who would otherwise be interested in what is said. What is your first reaction when you hear vulgarity and profanity? How do you cope with it if it really bothers you? Sometimes you may need to ignore the vulgarity because the person has information you must obtain. Your best bet is to ignore the words that offend you and concentrate on the rest of the message.

Each generation will produce words that are unique to its values and life-style. During the 1940s, teenagers used connotative words that were modern at the time (*23-skidoo, zoot suit, hooch*), and in the late 1960s they used jargon (*booze, boogie, cool, out-of-sight*) that may still be in use today. Think about the newer locutions being used by the current younger generation (*NOT!, you be right, for sure, duh, fake-n-bake*). Do the people you know understand all the new words being used today? Do you understand them all? What about jargon, or in-group language? Physicians (*stat, cauterize*), accountants (*zero-base budgeting*), carpenters (*sharp-shooter*), and even college professors (*walk, "I," dead-day*) use specialized language as part of their in-group communication system. As a listener, it is important that you correctly identify the meanings of the new words as they are used since their meanings are important to your communication success.

Pointed words or phrases are another type of word choice that can distract listeners. These are word choices that a speaker uses to command, instruct, intimidate, or criticize a listener. "Do it my way, or else." "You're not very good at that, are you?" "Gosh, you're getting gray-headed." When pointed words are directed your way, you may become defensive, or you may become preoccupied by the person's apparent rudeness. You may also miss other parts of the message because you are trying to figure out the speaker's motive in being so rude or blunt. Again, it is important to ignore those aspects of the message that have little real meaning and concentrate on the information you need.

The use of pointed words makes it hard for listeners to concentrate on the meaning of the message. Sexist, racist, and ageist language can be particularly troublesome. In some cases, a speaker who uses sexist language may be trying to convey a message of chauvinism. In other cases, a speaker may not intend sexism but may use sexist language out of habit or ignorance. Regardless of gender, it is not always easy to overlook the ill-advised or rude language of sexist speakers; however, as a listener your primary task is to understand the message. If the message is one of sexism and you understand this, you can act accordingly. If it is an unintended mistake, you are probably better off concentrating on the content of the message itself and saving your criticism of the person's language choices for an appropriate time.

Impression Formation

People form impressions about speakers constantly. You may find some speakers dull, others exciting, still others interesting, and so on. The general effect that a communicator has on a listener is called **impression for-**

IMPRESSION
FORMATION
*The general effect
that a communicator
has on a listener.*

SELF-CHECK

Listening to Speakers, Hearing Messages

Do you prefer to listen to some speaking styles rather than others? The following questions are intended to help you focus on how a speaker's style can affect your competence as a listener. There is no scale for scoring your answers to this Self-Check, but your responses should make you aware of factors that may interfere with the effectiveness of your listening.

- Are you more attentive to a speaker who is animated and dramatic or one who does not use gestures much?

- Do you find yourself being overly critical when someone uses fill-ins? incorrect grammar?

- Are you impressed—favorably or unfavorably—by a speaker who occasionally uses foreign words? Does your reaction depend on the language used?

- Are you impressed—favorably or unfavorably—by foreign or regional accents that are different from your own? What is your favorite accent? Your least favorite accent?

- What words or categories of words (for example, curse words, slang, or technical jargon) bother you? Are these words always offensive, or are they more acceptable when some speakers use them than when other speakers do? How can you maintain your own standards for choosing appropriate words and, at the same time, listen competently to speakers who violate your standards?

mation. You form a general impression based on each speaker's verbal and nonverbal styles. Norton identified a concept called communicator style which is composed of several different types of communication behavior.[9] Following are some of these behaviors.

- attentive
- contentious
- open

- dominant
- dramatic
- friendly

- relaxed
- animated
- precise

A communicator can leave an impression that includes several of these behaviors. Haven't you communicated with a person who was animated, attentive, and friendly? What type of impression did that person have on you? What about someone who was dramatic, dominant, and precise? What effect do these overall impressions have on your ability to listen? Some general communication styles are more likely to enhance listening than others. You need both to decide which impressions create the most difficulty for your listening competence and to develop techniques for overcoming any problems. Think about the most irritating mannerisms people have when they speak to you. Are irritating speakers too loud or too soft-spoken? Too laid-back or too intense? Do boisterous speakers make you nervous? From the preceding list, think about the styles that create the most problems for you as a listener and ask yourself why these affect your listening. Most likely you are being distracted by the way a person is communicating to you. The next time you encounter an irritating communication style, ignore everything about the speaker except the message. You will be surprised how much you can learn by focusing only on the content of the message. With practice, you will be able not only to listen competently to the verbal message but also to desensitize yourself to the irritations of an aggravating communication style.

Relational History

Recall from the competence model that relational history affects your communication choices. Relational history also affects how you listen to someone else. If you are listening to someone whom you remember as having once reneged on a promise similar to what he or she is promising now ("Oh, don't worry, I'll pay you back"), you may not have much faith in what the speaker is saying. You may even ignore the rest of the message. Many other issues can affect relational history. Hurt feelings, trust, intimacy, lying, affection, and loyalty are just some of the dynamics operating in relational history. To use relational history effectively as a listener, you need to follow through on four important steps. *First, objectively assess how the relational history with the other person affects your attitude toward him or her.* How has the past influenced your feelings toward this person? Do you consider this person a friend, enemy, acquaintance, colleague, or something else? *Second, determine whether there is relational agreement.* That is, do you and this person see the relationship in the same way? Is this person aware of how you feel? *Third, avoid positive and negative biases that may exist as a result of the relational history.* There is a tendency to skew information in the direction of how one feels about a person. If you like someone, you may tend to overlook that person's mistakes and to exaggerate his or her strengths. The opposite is the case for those people whom you dislike. These misdirected inference processes can create listening deficiencies. *Finally, don't take the relationship for granted.* You may not listen carefully because you think your friend will excuse your poor listening. Sometimes when you rely on a relationship for help and support, you may neglect to listen carefully because you know your partner will forgive you or overlook your mistakes. This is often a source of difficulty when someone feels taken for granted.

◼ Expectations

The importance of expectations for facilitating effective communication has been mentioned before. Listening is enhanced if you can determine what a speaker is expecting from you, the listener, and from the communication situation. Consider the following example to illustrate this point.

> The instructor in Math 1212 was conducting a review for the final exam on a Wednesday night. Stacy and her friends went to the review because they were not doing well in the class. Even though they brought their notebooks and textbooks, they didn't prepare for the review, nor did they have any real expectations about it. When they arrived, the instructor asked if they had any specific problems with the course. Some students did, and the instructor addressed those problems. When the instructor had answered all of the questions, she reminded everyone of the time and place of the exam and dismissed the class. Stacy left the review disappointed because she got nothing useful out of it. Had she anticipated that the instructor was expecting the students to be prepared for the review, Stacy could have brought up points that concerned her and could have benefited more from the review.

What are some ways in which you can determine a communicator's expectations? First, reflect on the nature of the situation itself. Does the situation require an active role on the part of the listener? Large audiences do not require such participation, but small groups do. What about the track record of the speaker? Is the speaker someone who usually does most of the talking and expects you to take in passively what is said? Or does the speaker usually ask for input so that you have to be ready to respond? What do you perceive the speaker will expect you to get out of the situation? Will you have to follow up on the information? You should also consider the other listeners in the communication situation. Will the speaker expect more of them than of you? Attempting to figure out the speaker's expectations is a necessary step toward priming your listening skills. Even if your expectations are wrong, you will be in a better position to respond than if you had no expectations at all.

Goals and Motivations

Besides anticipating what a speaker expects of you, it is also important to determine what the speaker expects to get from the situation. It is your job as a listener to ascertain the goals and motivations of the speaker. In this way, you will be in a better position to determine your role as a listener. For instance, if you determine that an individual will be attempting to get you to do something you do not want to do, then you can prepare yourself to listen with a more critical ear. If another individual wants your sympathetic ear for a sob story, then you can prepare yourself in a different way. A speaker may have any of several motives for communicating. Some of these have already been mentioned. Table 6.3 lists the most common

TABLE 6.3 GOALS AND MOTIVES OF COMMUNICATORS

SPEAKER'S GOAL	WHAT TO EXPECT	LISTENING FUNCTION
Inform	Information, facts, opinions, advice, data, news	Comprehensive, critical
Persuade	Compliance gaining, compliance resisting, influence on attitudes and opinions	Comprehensive, critical
Inquire	Questions, examination, interrogation, probing, scrutiny, analysis, request	Discriminative, comprehensive, critical
Entertain	Amusement, humor	Appreciative, therapeutic
Confront	Criticism, reprimand, setting straight	Comprehensive, critical
Seek support	Requests for sympathy, empathy, moral support, understanding	Therapeutic

goals or motives. Listeners should be aware of them and determine how they can be handled by using the appropriate listening function discussed in an earlier section.

If you have doubts about a speaker's motives or goals, simply ask what he or she is expecting to get out of the communication situation. You are better off being direct with the speaker than mistaking his or her motive.

Managing the Context

Those aspects of the encounter that affect your understanding of how communication can be possible, appropriate, and effective make up the *communication context.* From a listening perspective, context includes the setting, culture, and third parties.

Setting

Physical Setting

The place in which you listen probably has a greater impact on your ability to listen effectively than you realize. Your classrooms vary in their acoustics, a lunchroom can produce a great deal of ambient noise, and some theaters have poor audio systems. Consciously or unconsciously, you consider the physical setting when you anticipate a listening encounter. It is important that you take into consideration as many factors in this situation as possible. The most obvious concern is acoustics. How much difficulty will you have in actually hearing the speaker? What steps can you take to enhance your ability to hear sounds? Remember that hearing is only one part of the listening process. The physical setting will also offer visual cues that facilitate understanding the message. Gestures, facial expressions, visual aids, or other objects that help message comprehension must be seen in order for you to take full advantage of the entire message. The physical setting also includes factors that affect your ability to listen, such as the temperature of the room, the color scheme, the comfort offered by the seats, the proximity of others, and your familiarity with the setting. Managing these factors is an important step toward better listening. How can this be done? Preparing for the situation is one method. If you know the room will be cold, dress appropriately. If it will be a crowded auditorium and you are claustrophobic, go early and sit on the aisle. If you are going to a group meeting and you have trouble hearing when others are talking at the same time, sit next to the leader so that most of the messages will be directed toward or close to your position in the room. Take the time to anticipate the physical setting and prepare accordingly.

Emotional Atmosphere

When was the last time you were unable to listen effectively because of the emotional tension in the atmosphere? Much too often people are caught up in the emotionality of a situation or setting and become mentally distracted. People differ in their ability to handle emotions, especially when it comes to listening.

It is often difficult to avoid the distractions of emotionality when you listen. Emotions can preoccupy your mind with thoughts unrelated to the issues at hand. One way for you to fight such distractions is to allow the emotions to heighten your concentration level for listening to the content of the message. Athletes are proficient in channeling the excess energy created by emotional arousal into energy that can be used in their sport. Channel your energy into a more focused concentration on the speaker and message.

Time

Time is a dimension of your life that affects listening in an inescapable way. Time can be your listening ally or enemy. Ignoring the impact of time is one of the mistakes people make with their listening. If you get into a time bind, you are more likely to listen differently than if you have ample time to listen. Sometimes having too much time on your hands can also

---

SELF-CHECK

Listening and Emotions

For each of the emotions listed below, think of a recent listening situation in which the speaker or the situation aroused that emotion in you.

Happiness	Sadness	Fear
Surprise	Anger	Disgust

What effect did the emotional atmosphere have on your listening ability? Were the emotions you experienced created by the situation, the speaker, or both? Were you distracted by the emotionality of the context?

lead to ineffective listening. Time is a part of the setting that dictates the magnitude of communication opportunities. Your listening has to adjust to the temporal constraints for you to benefit fully from the situation. Some people are better listeners when time is short. Others function better when they enjoy ample time to digest the information slowly, carefully, and methodically. For example, given a choice, you may want to select Monday-Wednesday-Friday classes because they are shorter than Tuesday-Thursday classes, or you may want to avoid late afternoon classes because you have less energy at that time. You will have to decide whether you need more or less time to handle listening situations. Do you have difficulty assimilating information in a short period of time? Can you handle information presented in a rapid-fire manner? Do you hate to be rushed when you are in a listening mode? You need to assess your temporal listening profile. If you have difficulty when time is short, you should develop strategies that accomplish your goals while simultaneously accommodating the time that is available. Focus on the main issues when time is short. This strategy is elaborated in the next section.

Cultural Factors

How often have you noticed that your listening was compromised because the speaker "didn't speak your language"? Cultural factors include language barriers that embrace all variations of the English language. Many co-cultures in the United States communicate in ways that may be difficult for you to understand. Cultures are made up of people with similar values, life-styles, norms, and rituals that cause them to think of themselves as a unified body. When a culture develops its own language system, those outside of it have difficulty deciphering what is said. This is an obvious problem if English is your first language and you are speaking with someone for whom English is not the first language, or vice versa. Cultural problems are less obvious when people speak the same verbal language but differ in how they use this language. Slang, jargon, euphemisms, and connotative meanings can cause listening problems. For example, in certain businesses jargon is frequently used as an efficient system of communication for those who are familiar with it. Listening and understanding are difficult for those outside of this culture. The medical care community is a prime illustration of the cultural language barrier.

What do you usually do about communicating with people of different cultures? Here are some suggestions that can help you. *First, make an effort to learn or to recognize the cultural background of the communicator.* If the person has a different ethnic background from yours, take into account the speaker's heritage and use this information in understanding his or her perspective. If the person is a devout member of a particular religious organization, keep this in mind as you listen, recognizing that the speaker's beliefs can be a factor in his or her communication. *Second, reveal your cultural needs to the speaker.* Many speakers do not pay enough attention to the cultural needs of the listener. Remind the one you are talking with if you find that your cultural differences are preventing good communication ("Hey, I don't think we are in sync here—can you say that again, more slowly, please?"). *Third, adjust to differences.* Ask more questions if necessary, but make a special effort to recognize the difficulties associated with cross-cultural communication. Ask the speaker to work with you in making the cultural differences enjoyable. The following example illustrates how two people from different "cultures" adjusted to one another.

> Gloria and Charlie were assigned to work on a task force together at their office. Charlie, a feminist activist, is outwardly critical of traditional organizations that assign males more responsibility and authority than females. Gloria, raised in a traditional home in which everyone, including her mother, deferred to her father, expects Charlie to take a leading role on the task force. Charlie thinks that Gloria is shirking her responsibility. The cultures of feminism and traditional gender-based male authority collided in a very obvious way. At first, they argued bitterly over their respective roles, and finally they quit talking altogether. When their boss intervened and suggested that their jobs were on the line, they met to discuss how they could perform their responsibilities. Charlie revealed that his feminist background was part of him and that he could not divorce his deep-seated feelings from the way he worked. Gloria confessed that she was only interested in accomplishing their goal. Both agreed to respect each other's background and put aside their differences when they worked together. Even though Gloria and Charlie never converted to each other's way of thinking, each was able to listen effectively to the other once they agreed that their cultural differences did not have to prevent them from communicating.

Third Parties

Another factor to consider when managing the context is how other people influence either your listening or someone else's speaking. Recall the last time you were talking to another student and someone you both knew joined the conversation. Did you become distracted by this person's presence? For example, some listeners may feel that third parties are *intruding* on their time with the speaker and may become distracted with those thoughts. Others may feel more pressure when a third person or other people join the conversation, and this stress distracts them from listening effectively. Still others may feel that they have to impress the third party and begin preparing what to say instead of listening to the speaker. There are some instances, however, when a third party may enhance your listening. The added presence of such a person may actually help you to focus your attention on everything that is said. The best advice is for you to remain aware that third parties can influence your listening, and you need to use that influence as a listening enhancement rather than a listening distraction. For instance, you can watch the third person or the other people as they listen and react to the speaker, in order to determine how much they got out of the speaker's message. Other people may catch things that you miss, and you can use their reactions to improve your own listening accuracy.

Listening Actively

The fourth stage of competent listening involves active listening. *Active listening* refers to a series of steps that facilitate your ability to process the messages you receive from a speaker. Included in active listening are (1) adjusting your listening/speaking ratio to a proper level, (2) focusing your energy on listening, (3) decoding nonverbal cues accurately, (4) determining the speaker's main point, and (5) using your memory effectively. When you employ these tactics, you will be a much better listener.

Adjust Your Listening/Speaking Ratio

One of the oldest and most frequently recommended suggestions for listening improvement is to stop talking. You cannot listen when you are talking. Of course, this is easier said than done, especially when you have important things to say. It is recommended that you assess your listening-to-talking ratio to see if you talk excessively. You can make this assessment by completing a communication log that tracks the time you speak and listen. After completing the log, ask yourself the following questions: Were you surprised at your ratio? During what activities did you notice that you needed to listen more than you did? Why do you need to listen more during these activities? Why do you talk more than you want to? Do you see a pattern of talking during similar or consistent activities? Do you seem to talk more during certain parts of the day? Are there times when you are listening and you should be providing information or opinions? The log is an excellent tool for profiling when and where you do most of your talking and listening. It is a barometer of who you are as a communicator.

If you find that your speaking-to-listening ratio is too high on the speaking side, there are a couple of things you can do. First, stop talking! Just don't say as much as you normally would. You will be surprised how much you can learn by remaining silent. Second, maybe the time you spend talk-

Communication Log

For a 16-hour period, keep this log with you and write down the percentage of time you spoke, listened, or were silent.

Time	Activity	% Time Speaking	% Time Listening	% Time Silent
8:00 A.M.				
9:00				
10:00				
11:00				
12:00 noon				
1:00 P.M.				
2:00				
3:00				
4:00				
5:00				
6:00				
7:00				
8:00				
9:00				
10:00				
11:00				
12:00 midnight				

ing can be better used to facilitate the interaction. Asking questions, giving support, providing clarification, and other instances of speaker support can allow you a chance to interact, but in a way that increases your chances for listening.

▨ *Focus Your Efforts*

During those times when you are actively listening, it is necessary to focus your efforts on the task. You can focus your efforts in three ways: store up energy, concentrate, and avoid distractions.

The first step involves *storing up energy* for the job ahead. Competent listening takes a lot of energy and effort. Listening requires cognitive, physical, and emotional energy. With a limited supply, it is best to store your energy for those listening situations that are most important. One way to do this is by secluding yourself from others when you need a listening break. You could explain to someone who is about to require your attentive listening that you need some time to prepare because you want to listen effectively. Another method is to schedule slack times right before important listening tasks. This gives you a chance to catch your breath and collect your thoughts. You could also generate energy or at least store what is left by using muscle relaxation and deep breathing exercises. Here is what to do:

1. Sit or lie in a comfortable position. Close your eyes.
2. Allow your mind to wander to places that are far away but pleasant.
3. Identify some muscle group area (e.g., legs, shoulders, neck, feet) that feels tired or tense. Tense these muscles and hold the tension for three seconds.
4. Relax the muscle group and think about how good the relaxation feels.
5. During this time, take several long, slow, deep breaths to clear your system of stale oxygen.
6. After several of these muscle-relaxing and breathing repetitions, your body will feel replenished and you will have some new energy to listen with.

Concentration is the second key to focusing your efforts on the listening task. By now you are probably an expert in concentrating on a task when it really counts. Taking exams, giving a presentation, and keeping a calm and straight face while disciplining children all require concentration. Using concentration skills during listening is not very different.

Focusing your efforts is also made easier by *avoiding distractions.* Various distractions that plague the listener were discussed earlier. Now these distractions are placed into three major categories: psychological, emotional, and physical. Examine the table that follows. You will notice examples that fit into the three categories and suggestions for avoiding each type of distraction. What other distractions can you name that hinder your listening? What similar suggestions can you generate that can reduce the influence of these distractions on your listening?

Decode Nonverbal Cues Accurately

Listening with your ears is only part of the listening competency process. As we discussed in Chapter 5, much of the message is communicated in the nonverbal channel. A key to competent listening is to monitor carefully the nonverbal cues and to decode them accurately in order to support, amplify, illustrate, or contradict what the speaker is saying verbally.

TABLE 6.4 AVOIDING DISTRACTIONS

CATEGORY	EXAMPLES	REDUCING DISTRACTIONS
Psychological	Perception of a higher listening priority	Decide which is more important.
	Preoccupation with other thoughts	Make a note to yourself to focus on the preoccupation later.
Emotional	Hurt feelings	Save the self-pity and anger for another time.
	Emotional triggers	Delay judgment about something said in an emotional tone.
Physical	Fatigue	Redirect energy for listening or postpone listening until rejuvenated.
	Illness	Make speaker aware of special circumstances. Postpone listening.

Follow the Cues

On a sheet of paper, list five people whose nonverbal behaviors have been helpful in making you listen better. Beside each name, list the speaker's most noteworthy helpful behaviors. Do you demonstrate these skills when speaking? Your instructor may want to list these behaviors on the board to stimulate class discussion.

Remember the importance of expectations. Watching a speaker's nonverbal behavior can provide impressions of his or her mood which are helpful in anticipating the nature of the message. It is difficult to quantify the contribution that the observation of nonverbal behavior makes to your listening, but you know it is significant. From the preceding chapter, you are already more sensitive to the impact of nonverbal communication. This section provides some additional suggestions to help make your listening more nonverbally sensitive. *First, form an overall impression of the speaker from nonverbal mannerisms.* Do they suggest happiness, sadness, confusion, or anger? Consistently test your accuracy by confirming or disconfirming your original impression. *Second, watch for subtleties in the speaker's nonverbal behavior.* Even though many people may be sophisticated in masking or hiding their feelings, there is usually some cue that is "leaked" out, revealing the speaker's true feelings. Subtle cues could include less or more body orientation, less or more eye gaze, presence of adapters, or even abnormal vocal tones. *Third, inquire about inconsistencies when you observe them.* Tell the speaker that he or she is communicating one thing verbally and quite another thing nonverbally. Confronted with the inconsistency, the speaker may be willing to level with you.

Determine the Thesis or Main Point

MAIN POINT
The thesis of a speaker's message; a key to understanding and remembering the message.

One of the most widely suggested tips for effective listening is understanding the **main point** of the speaker's message. The proverbial question "What's the bottom line?" is appropriate here. What is the most important thing that the speaker wants you to get from the message? Determining the thesis of a message is not always easy, especially if the speaker is not a skilled communicator. Speakers can ramble, go off on tangents, lose a train of thought, become entwined, or have no clear thesis at all. Here are some strategies that can help you pull out the main point from a message. *First,*

What's the Main Point?

Often, determining the main point of a speaker's message is the most difficult thing to do when listening. Try practicing this in class. Instead of mindlessly taking notes, be alert to the unifying theme or structure of the lecture. As each point is made, try to determine how it fits into the lecture. Practice anticipating the direction the lecture will go in. This will improve your listening skills and your understanding of the lectures.

watch for verbal identifiers or phrases that clue you in on the main point. "What I am trying to say . . ." "The issue is . . ." "Look, I know that . . ." "Okay, here's the deal . . ." When you hear one of these identifiers, make a mental note that this is likely to preview the bottom line in the message. Pay careful attention at this point. *Second, watch for a more direct eye gaze.* Speakers are more likely to look at you when they are trying to make their point. *Third, develop a mental outline of the speaker's message.* Think about the points the speaker is making and prioritize the most important ones. *Finally, if you are in doubt about the main point, ask the speaker for clarification.* "Are you saying that . . . ?" "Am I to understand that . . . ?" "Could you give an example of what you mean?" Once the main point is established, it is easier to incorporate the rest of the information from a message.

Use Your Memory Effectively

Incorporating and making sense of a message are important steps to active listening. Remembering that message is just as important. Recall from Chapter 2 that when you process information from your environment, especially communicators, you store this information in short-term memory for a few seconds until long-term memory is ready to take over. Sometimes long-term memory is not engaged; that is when you forget something that you heard. Short-term memory can be used more effectively by double-checking your perceptual awareness. Are you hearing and seeing what you should? Do you have any immediate concerns or questions as the speaker communicates? Is the message important enough to transfer to long-term memory? After all, not everything that is heard is worth committing to memory banks. You must prioritize your listening alternatives.

Once you commit yourself to remembering what someone says, you use long-term memory efficiently. To do so, you sometimes need to employ an

FIGURE 6.4

The model of communicative competence points out the importance of memory. Recall that memory directly influences the process of cognition, combining with attributions and perceptions to form your cognitions.

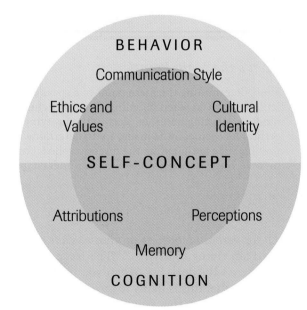

REHEARSAL

A temporary storage area that processes information directed from short-term memory to long-term memory.

intermediate memory system often called rehearsal. **Rehearsal** refers to a temporary storage area that processes information directed from short-term memory to long-term memory. People's names, phone numbers, and addresses, and even flight times are bits of information that often spend time in the rehearsal stage of memory.

Some researchers recommend that you use visual imagery as a way of remembering what is said.[10] Visual imagery involves producing vivid mental images that can be associated with verbal messages. For example, when your significant other or roommate asks you to pick up his or her laundry when you are running your own errands, you might envision what the cleaner's building looks like, including the sign out front, so that you will remember to include that stop in your errand trip. Some students may associate the face of a favorite musician with each of their major assignments in class. The association does not have to be direct; rather, it serves as a memory trigger for specific items.

Listening Interactively

Dominique is a friendly but quiet person who seldom reacts to things people say. Though an attentive listener, she fails to nod, shake her head, or exhibit any facial expressions when others talk. A classmate and acquaintance, Vicki, once told her, "You know, Dominique, when I talk to you I am never quite sure whether you understand what I'm saying. You never give me any feedback." Dominique seemed very surprised that Vicki felt it necessary to receive feedback. Vicki continued, "It seems that I have to explain a lot more to you since I don't know whether you're following me."

Dominique is an individual who does not respond to speakers with nonverbal cues. It doesn't mean that she is not listening. But it does mean that people she talks with may perceive her as incompetent, lazy, uncaring, or bored with them. Conversational rules dictate that people should give appropriate nonverbal or verbal cues to speakers to regulate their talk. Besides improving the speaker's confidence in a listener, interactive cues can save listeners time, since speakers won't have to repeat or embellish to get their points across. When you can make a speaker perform more efficiently, you will automatically become a more competent listener. That is why this stage is interactive. Listeners must play an important role in creating competent communication between the two interactants. There are three strategies that may help you become a more *interactive* listener: nonverbal cues, verbal reinforcers, and questioning techniques.

FIGURE 6.5
Interactive listening is an important technique in psychoanalysis. As a layperson, you can apply this competency by empathic listening.

⬛ *Nonverbal Cues*

Dominique was not being an interactive listener when she failed to provide nonverbal cues to Vicki. Eye gaze is an important nonverbal cue influencing the speaker–listener relationship because it is a very obvious indicator of interest. When you look at the other person, you gain valuable nonverbal information. If you look down or away, you can give the speaker the impression that you would rather be elsewhere. The speaker forms this impression whether or not it is your intention. You can lose valuable information if the person decides to cut off the conversation because of a perceived lack of interest on your part. Think about your own eye gaze patterns during listening. Do you normally look at people when they talk? When do you look elsewhere and why?

Facial expressions are another form of interactive cue that facilitates other people's speaking. Timely expressions greatly aid the speaker in reading the listener. For example, frowning is an effective way to signal confusion, disagreement, or fear; smiling is an expression used to indicate enjoyment and agreement; and a widening of the eyes can communicate surprise or disbelief. When you use these expressions strategically and judiciously, the speaker can become more accurate in reading your thoughts and communicate with you in a more competent manner.

When you want to signal interest in listening to a speaker carefully, how do you adjust your body orientation? You may give the speaker a full and direct body orientation. You may also lean forward, possibly putting your hand or elbows on your knees. Body orientation is one of the most pronounced interactive cues that a listener can use. If you are tired of listening to a speaker, what body orientation strategy is best? Turning the body laterally directs your nonverbal attention away from the speaker and gives an impression of disinterest. Even standing up may express your interest in changing topics or moving the conversation to a new location. All of these nonverbal cues are quite useful in facilitating speaker communication.

⬛ *Verbal Reinforcers*

VERBAL REINFORCERS
Short verbal cues used by listeners to coordinate speaker–listener communication.

Dominique was also guilty of neglecting to provide verbal reinforcers. **Verbal reinforcers** are short, quick words or sounds that express agreement, disagreement, confusion, surprise, or other listener's reactions. Think of verbal reinforcers such as "yeah," "uh huh," "umm," "uh uh," "ahhh," or even laughter. Verbal reinforcers are especially important when you are talking on the telephone because nonverbal cues are useless. Howard was negotiating a contract on the phone with a person who did not provide verbal reinforcers at any point during the negotiation process. Howard became suspicious that the other person either was being cagey and trying not to respond, as a strategy to keep him off balance, or was an incompetent listener. Howard chose the latter and began to ask the listener some questions. "Are you still there?" "Do you understand the terms?" "Are you able to provide these services?" "Will you agree to the time frame I discussed?" The listener answered all of the questions affirmatively. In this case, the listener's lack of verbal reinforcement created difficulties that Howard had to rectify.

◼ Questioning Techniques

Dominique could also have been a more interactive listener if she had used effective **questioning techniques**. Questions from the listener serve two functions.

First, questions signal that listening is occurring. If you are asking questions, the speaker knows that you are tuned in and interested, and this gives the speaker some needed confidence. *Second, questions can actually help the speaker become more effective by getting to the points that will do the listener the most good.* Consider the following example.

QUESTIONING TECHNIQUES
Inquiries that a listener can make to coordinate what the speaker is saying with what the listener is hearing.

MR. HENSLEY	I have your career assessment test results back.
LENA	Were there any job areas that I excelled in?
MR. HENSLEY	Yes, quite a few. You are definitely a "people person," and you scored high in the health care profession.
LENA	Well, that's nice, but I was considering attending a business college and earning a court reporter certificate. Did I show any promise in that field?
MR. HENSLEY	Listen, with your eagerness to learn and focused direction, you could one day be a judge!

In this case, Mr. Hensley gave Lena the encouragement she was seeking, and he also opened her eyes to aim even higher. As this example illustrates, questions can be used to encourage more information from the speaker, to verify points of view, or to clarify issues. Chapter 9 discusses a number of questioning techniques regarding interviewing. For now, Table 6.5 (on p. 272) outlines three types of questions that are particularly useful during listening.

As the final step to competent listening, interactive listening creates mutual participation between you and the speaker. Your listening behavior

TABLE 6.5 QUESTIONING TECHNIQUES

TYPE OF QUESTION	PURPOSE	EXAMPLE
Open	Encourage more information. Allow speaker full latitude of remarks.	"Tell me more about your work." "What else is important to you?"
Probing	Dig deeper into speaker's remarks. Clarify speaker's position.	"Why do you feel that way?" "Why?" "How can that be done?"
Reflective	Verify information from speaker.	"Let me get this straight— you want to move to Columbus?" "Are you saying that we are responsible for Chapter 6 on the exam?"

is no longer passive; it is dynamic and engaged. Do not hesitate to use nonverbal cues, verbal reinforcers, and questions to ensure a high level of interactive listening.

By now you have recognized that you and other communicators are co-creators in competent listening. Competent listening can be realized when communicators mutually depend on one another in creating the greatest possible shared meaning. As you recall from the competence model, communicators must recognize how their relationship is mutually dependent and strive toward a mutual understanding of the issues they communicate.

REALITY CHECK

Sound Bites

Tune your TV to a news or public television program that presents competing points of view. Make notes about how well the speakers listen to each other's arguments. What do they focus on? From what you have read in the chapter, how could their listening be improved?

REVIEW

This chapter presents a framework for becoming a better listener. The five steps that guide competent listening represent a plan you can enact anytime you face listening opportunities. Some listening situations are more important than others, and it will not always be possible for you to use all five steps every time you listen. However, when you begin applying these steps on a regular basis in most of your listening, you will find that they become automatic after a while. Since listening involves cognitive and behavioral skills, you have to work at them in order to increase your competence level.

The first step toward competent listening is managing your skills. First assess your listening self-concept to understand how you feel about yourself as a listener. Next, determine your actual listening efficiency with standardized listening tests. Listening tests give you an idea of your strengths and weaknesses. Once you have determined your self-concept and objectively measured your skills, it is time to determine your listening expectations. Are they too low or high? This leads to an assessment of listening habits. Are you apathetic, anxious, or defensive when some people speak? Managing distractions, understanding listening functions, and goal-setting round out Step 1 of this process.

Step 2 focuses on the speaker. Because many speakers are not competent and will not adjust to their listeners, it is your job as a listener to adjust to them as best you can. Understanding a speaker's communication style is the first step and involves accurately decoding nonverbal cues, remaining objective about a speaker's word choice, and understanding how a speaker's style can form particular impressions on you as a listener. Adjusting to the speaker also involves assessing your relationship with that person, understanding expectations, and determining goals and motivations.

Step 3 in this plan is managing the context. The listening context includes the setting, the culture, and third parties. The setting is a composite of the physical surroundings, the emotional atmosphere, and time. All of these factors have their own influence on the listening context. Cultural factors are important as well. Being sensitive to and respecting one another's cultural background are prerequisites for competent listening. In addition, when other people are introduced into a situation, speaker and listener changes may occur. Sometimes the influence of third parties is an advantage and you can directly benefit from their presence. In other instances, third-party influences may hinder your listening and you must take steps to avoid any distractions they create.

Listening actively is Step 4 in this framework, and it engages several dynamic processes that make you receive messages more effectively. To listen actively, first you must assess your listening/speaking ratio to see if you talk too much. Next, you must focus your energy on the listening task so that your efforts are mobilized for the job ahead. Because many communication encounters involve emotional issues, you must control your emotional reactions so that they don't become a distraction. Besides its importance in decoding the verbal message, active listening requires recognizing and understanding the speaker's nonverbal cues. In order to use the information communicated by the speaker, you must determine the main point of the message and use your memory effectively.

Step 5, interactive listening, is a process of facilitating the speaker's communication so that his or her messages are easier for you to maximize. One way to help speakers understand your level of listening competency is to provide appropriate nonverbal cues. Eye gaze, facial expressions, and body orientation contribute to speaker-listener coordination. Listeners can also provide verbal reinforcers to let the speaker know that they agree, understand, or are confused by the message. Listeners can use questions to keep the speaker on track or to ask for clarification or verification of information in the message. This framework is a plan for listening success. It is one way of making you a competent communicator.

SUGGESTED READINGS

Floyd, J. J. (1985). *Listening: A practical approach.* Glenview, IL: Scott Foresman.

Journal of the International Listening Association. See recent issues.

Steil, L. K., Barker, L. L., & Watson, K. W. (1983). *Effective listening: Key to success.* Reading, MA: Addison-Wesley.

Wolff, F. I., Marsnik, N. C., Tacey, W. S., & Nichols, R. G. (1983). *Perceptive listening.* New York: Holt, Rinehart, & Winston.

Wolvin, A., & Coakley, C. G. (1988). *Listening* (3rd ed.). Dubuque, IA: Wm. C. Brown.

Communication Competence as a Goal for Social Interaction

The purpose of this epilogue, and those at the end of subsequent parts, is to pull together concepts covered in each chapter within the part, relate them to one another, and show how each contributes to competent communication.

The systematic study of communication has a long history. Throughout that history there has been a common underlying rationale for trying to understand and improve people's ability to communicate: the enhancement of the general well-being of society. Aristotle taught rhetoric to the men of ancient Athens so that they might more effectively participate in the public debates about how the city-state was governed. The better the quality of the public discussion, the better the decisions about governing were. This concern with the public welfare and how people's ability to communicate affected society was one reason why public speaking was taught in early American universities. In a democracy, people need to be able to articulate their ideas clearly so that they can participate effectively in public decision making. A similar concern for the public's welfare was behind the addition of professional journalism courses to university curricula at the beginning of the twentieth century. The sensationalist excesses of the "penny press" led people to see the need for news people who were trained in both the technical aspects of reporting and the ethical responsibilities of journalists in a free society.

Organizational communication, as it is studied and practiced today, grew out of attempts to create optimal work conditions for the new workforce that filled the country's factories during World War II. This workforce was for the first time largely female because so many men were on the battlefront, and old-line managers were not sure how to motivate their new employees. Efforts to learn about how to manage and motivate turned into concerns for the quality of the work environment, the "human relations" approach to management. Again, social scientists were concerned about improving communication in organizations to address part of a national need.

The communication discipline continues to be concerned with promoting the common good. In this book we highlight personal values and ethical considerations that should go hand in hand with skilled, competent communication. Your personal values, as well as your culture's values, will provide guidance about the appropriate construction of your messages and how to critically analyze the messages directed toward you.

In Part 1, we present a model of communicative competence and discuss basic communication processes that operate in a variety of communication contexts. The concepts apply to the full range of types of communication: from two friends speaking informally, to communication in groups large and small, to formal presentations by one person to a large audience, to mass communication.

The processes discussed—cognitive, linguistic, nonverbal, listening, and the development of the self through communication—are best illustrated in an informal interpersonal context because such contexts are the simplest and most familiar. Fortunately, your understanding of these concepts in interpersonal contexts can be generalized to other, possibly less familiar, contexts like interviews, group projects, working with others in organizations, and giving speeches to large audiences.

Competent communication occurs when that communication is both *appropriate* to your communication partners and the situation, and *effective* in meeting your own goals while helping fellow communicators meet theirs. This places competence in relationships as much as in individuals, and we talk about relational competence as something that incorporates and transcends individuals. In referring to individuals in these chapters, we use the terms *skilled* and *competent* interchangeably. But it is important to remember that people with few communication skills—because of either social or physical difficulties—can and do communicate competently and have competent relationships. This is a crucial point in a multicultural environment, where what counts as an important skill in one culture or co-culture might be irrelevant or even rude in another. The way in which a professor is addressed in the classroom—or whether he or she is addressed at all—is a pertinent example. The manner in which one performs the simple act of addressing

another says much about the skill or competence of the individual and can have an important impact on the definition of the relationship. Let's look at each of these aspects of communicative competence—the individual and the individual-in-relationship.

Competent People

People are competent or skilled communicators to the extent that they can both process (receive and interpret) and create messages that are directed toward achieving their goals. As we pointed out in Chapter 2, message processing involves dynamic processes, such as perception and attribution, as well as more static aspects of cognition, such as memory, expectations, and complexity. Attribution and perception skills are dynamic because, in most instances, they involve active attention. You bring static features of cognition with you into an interaction. You have specific ideas and images in your memory when you enter a communication encounter. You bring with you certain expectations. You are more or less cognitively complex.

As we pointed out in the chapters, you can develop your memory, increase your cognitive complexity, and fine-tune your expectations. In fact, the more important a relationship is to you, the more likely you are to work at improving these relatively static aspects of yourself. As you develop these cognitive skills, you will be seen as a more desirable communication partner by a greater number of people. Furthermore, you will be more likely to enter into competent relationships with a larger number of people.

The static aspects of message processing are relevant to the dynamic ones. The better your memory of another person and the more complexity with which you view that person, the more realistic your expectations will be. Your perceptions will increase in accuracy, as will your attributions. Perceptual and attributional accuracy are important because your partners want to be understood and they want you to let them know that they are understood. Given the importance of messages that confirm the self-concept (as we discussed in Chapter 3), this is not surprising.

Communication with other people, especially those who are important to you, is crucial to the development and maintenance of your own and their self-concepts and self-esteem. From this view, you know yourself as an individual only because of the way you relate to others! You are more likely to experience competent communication in relationships when your communication skills allow you, among other things, to support the presented self of your partners without doing damage to your own self-concept. This support of another's presented self is accomplished by the language choices you make and the nonverbal behavior in which you engage, as well as the content of your messages.

Because your self-concept has many facets, not all facets are exposed or made public to all of your partners (or audiences). You probably have some attributes that you want to disclose to your partners in all your communication encounters—for example, honesty, helpfulness, or assertiveness. Some of your attributes will be part of only your social relationships, whereas others will be reserved for business and professional relationships. It may be important to you for your social partners, for ex-

ample, to see you as a wild party animal, whereas you might work very hard to conceal this part of yourself from your employees or your boss.

The message processing skills you bring into an interaction or a relationship (your perceptions of your various audiences, along with your expectations of them) provide guidance for you in deciding how to communicate (how to present yourself) in specific contexts and specific relationships. These cognitive skills are related to what might be called message design skills: your use of language, nonverbal behavior, and listening.

A competent communicator can "design" messages that take into account the self-concept needs both of the self and of the partners. The more you consider the needs and goals of your partners in both the content and style of your messages, the more likely you will be perceived as a competent communicator—and the more likely you are to have competent relationships. This means checking your perceptions and expectations for accuracy, attending to your audience's reactions to your messages, and adjusting your messages—if that is possible and desirable—in response to your audience. In our complex society, for example, some people argue that sexual harassment is a problem of message accuracy. Some individuals claim they are showing concern for and involvement with their employees when they pat them on the back or touch their shoulder or talk to them in "personal" ways. Others see this sort of behavior as demeaning or a sexual advance.

In face-to-face situations, such as social conversations or interviews, monitoring your partners is relatively easy. The larger the group—the greater the distance between you and them—the more difficult this observation of partners becomes. In some instances—for example, a prerecorded radio show—monitoring will be delayed and probably indirect. Similarly, adjustment of the message to suit the audience is not always possible or desirable. Human resources interviewers, for example, may have certain questions they must ask all applicants for a job, even though these questions are threatening to some people. "Have you ever been fired from a job?" is such a question. If you are giving a prepared public speech, you may be unwilling to make changes during your presentation, even if you see the audience is getting restless.

What's important here from a *theoretical* view is that individuals bring a self with them to their communication encounters and to their relationships. They communicate—design messages and process the messages of their partners—in a way that is congruent with their expectations of the encounter, their goals for the encounter, and what they believe to be the goals of their partners. In a competent relationship, the goals of both parties will more or less be met, at least over time. Unattainable goals will be revised. Expectations will be either confirmed or revised. From the encounter, a definition of the relationship will emerge in terms of distribution of control (how much influence each party can legitimately exert) and the level of affiliation (degrees of liking, love, or respect) that is appropriately expressed. The control and affiliation definitions of the relationship will be open to negotiation from time to time. That is to say, people redistribute control in their relationships as they negotiate the changes in their lives, and they de-

cide to display more or less affection depending on how they feel about each other. Cultural expectations regarding gender roles may influence what is considered appropriate. Some people think that public displays of affection are entirely inappropriate, whereas others consider the lack of public displays to be indicative of a problem in their relationship.

In *practical* terms, this means that you approach communication encounters with a preferred way of doing business—that is, thinking about and perceiving the world, making attributions, and the like. This "you" is fairly consistent across encounters, but you know you have to adjust how you act based on whom you're talking with and what you're trying to accomplish. Based on your audience and the situation, you use language, nonverbal behaviors, and possibly the social and physical context to construct messages that will make sense to your partners and that will make you look good to them. You monitor how they respond to your messages. If the encounter is going as you expect, you continue designing messages in the same way. If your expectations are not being met, you determine whether it is possible and/or desirable to redesign your messages so that they will have the intended effect on your partners. You are concerned at some level with how much they like you and with who is in control of the encounter and, ultimately, the relationship. From the standpoint of ethics, you are concerned about the effects of your communication on both yourself and your partners.

The theoretical view tells you how to behave in the practical situation. This view also links the individual to the relationship. The individual is defined in and through his or her relationships. Your competence is measured in your relationships.

Competent Relationships

Competent relationships are those marked by mutual satisfaction with the communication on the part of all parties to the relationship. This evaluation applies to relationships of all types, from intimate and personal, to corporate, to public.

The president of a large company has a relationship with the employees, even though he or she may know only a few by name. This relationship is a communication relationship in that the president sends messages to employees—some in meetings, spoken to a large audience, some passed orally down the hierarchy, most in writing—and the employees respond. Their responses can be direct, such as asking a question at the meeting, or indirect, such as working more slowly because they don't like what the president is saying. The president can respond to both of these types of messages—or not. The relationship is competent to the extent that all parties are satisfied with the appropriateness and effectiveness of the communication in terms of control distribution, affiliation, and goal achievement—the last of these probably being the most important in a boss–staff relationship.

Putting It Together

In this part of the book we have discussed the basic process of communication and its constituent parts—how people attend to and process messages, the effects that messages have on the way people think about themselves, language, nonverbal behavior, and listening. The better you understand this complex process, the more likely your relationships will go the way you want them to.

In the following case study, several people are at the beginning of their relationships with one another. As with all new relationships, these people have the opportunity to construct relationships that are satisfying and productive for them and their partners. The decisions each makes about what to say and how to say it are crucial. How well do the interactants succeed, in your opinion?

CASE STUDY 1

The Case of the Communication Class

During the first week of class, the professor of the Introduction to Communication course gave an in-class assignment. Students were to give impromptu speeches of approximately one to two minutes in which they were to (1) identify an issue of importance to many, and (2) link that issue to themselves personally. The professor indicated that this assignment would raise issues for the rest of the term and would let students get to know one another a little.

continued on next page

The five minutes the students were given to prepare these speeches seemed too short to most of them. Leah and Tom looked at each another, rolling their eyes; both said they were "blanked" on what to talk about. Corlynne and Travis were jotting down ideas and smiling as they wrote. Louis looked nervously around the room, imagining he was the only one who had nothing to say. Alicia looked over at her friend's paper, thinking she might "piggyback" off the friend's idea. Hallmein felt catatonic; he just knew he would not be able to speak well, especially in English, his second language. Leticia thought the assignment was dumb; what could you learn about anyone or anything in one or two minutes, anyway? she thought. At the end of five minutes, despite the protests and groaning, most of the students had a skeleton plan of what they would say.

Miguel went first, speaking about how immigration was an important issue that affected him personally because his parents were still trying to get the rest of their family from Nicaragua into this country. He said he resented the people who "have it all" and want to close the borders to those who have little.

Julie spoke next, about the influence of the media. She thought that people liked to blame the media for many problems, such as violence or children's low achievement. She said her father worked in the entertainment industry as a sound editor for a movie studio and that she didn't appreciate all the finger-pointing that was being done at the media because of society's ills.

Bashar spoke about the campaign to get people to use condoms. He said he thought it was "lame" because condoms hadn't even been successful at preventing his girlfriend of two years from getting pregnant; he was sure they were not any more successful at guarding against AIDS or other sexually transmitted diseases.

Cali spoke about animal rights activists. She said she was against terrible tests and inhumane conditions for animals but that the activists too often went overboard. She cited the time when her mother, wearing a 20-year-old fur coat her husband had given her for an anniversary, had had blood thrown on her by the activists.

Bud spoke about gun control. He said that there were a lot of problems with guns but that in his opinion criminals would get guns no matter what controls were established. He thought it was not right to restrict the right of responsible citizens to own guns. He said he and his brothers had grown up in Texas using guns to hunt or kill snakes or other animals that came close to the house. He cited the Constitution's reference to "the right to bear arms."

The professor asked for comments on the speeches that had been given so far. How were class members responding to the speeches, the topics, and the persons delivering them?

Naro said he was uncomfortable about the condom speech. In his native Japan, it was not appropriate to talk about such personal things in front of people. Other class members asked him whether condoms were advertised and sold in Japan. Yes, he responded, condoms were advertised; but many people looked away from those advertisements, thinking them rude or in poor taste. He would not talk about a condom ad with his mother, for example. He also said that, because condom use wasn't considered very "manly," they were not as popular in Japan as he believed they were in the United States. Leticia wanted to know whether Naro would consider using condoms, but the professor intervened before Naro could reply, indicating that it was time to share reactions to some of the other speeches.

Gretchen said that, while she didn't want to criticize Bashar, his use of the term "lame" offended her. She added that the label was common usage and not meant to hurt anyone, but that her older brother, who had lost his leg from the knee down, objected to being called lame. She thought that everyone needed to have more sensitivity to language.

Brad agreed. A number of the speakers, he said, addressed the class members as "guys" and "girls." Many of the women he knew objected to being called "girls" but wouldn't say anything because they were afraid of being labeled "strident feminists."

"I liked the fact that a few of our speakers today weren't afraid to take what's viewed as an unpopular stance," said Kate. She cited Cali's story about her mother's fur coat and Bud's feeling about guns. "I learned something about these people today," Kate added. "I can admire their willingness to take a position, even if I don't agree with them."

The professor agreed and pointed out that many of the topics brought up that day, such as immigration, could be discussed in greater depth in the weeks to come in the class. "Sounds like we've got an interesting group of people with some important things to say in this class—looks like a good term ahead."

DISCUSSION QUESTIONS

1. What elements of the model of communicative competence described in Chapter 1 were at work here? What factors helped communication be more effective? less effective?
2. What aspects of presentation of the self were at work? How did thinking about self affect the communication of the students in this class? How might the criticisms that some students directed at their classmates affect the self-concept of the speakers? the future self-presentations of the speakers?

continued on next page

3. What do you think about the use of "politically correct" language? Do your classmates agree with you? Were the people in this case study out of line in using the terms they used—or did some people overreact?

4. How might the nonverbal aspects of message presentation change the "meaning" of what was said?

5. Did the fact that this discussion was held in a classroom make a difference to what was said and how it was taken?

6. How would you rate the respondents to the impromptu speeches as listeners? Identify comments that showed competent or incompetent listening.

Part *Two*

Interpersonal Communication

7

Developing and Maintaining Relationships

Objectives

After reading this chapter, you should be able to

1. Identify four goals people have in developing relationships.

2. List three ways that people reduce uncertainty about their relational partners.

3. Illustrate the six stages of relational development.

4. Describe three types of relational rewards.

5. Describe three characteristics of friendship.

6. Identify three ways to improve family relationships.

Chapter Contents

A S YOU MAY RECALL from the model of communicative competence, relationships play a central role in determining the type of communication that is most effective and appropriate. In turn, competent communication permits more meaningful relational development. Each of you is involved in a number of relationships, some of which are more important than others. Although there is no guaranteed master plan for a perfect relationship, perhaps by understanding how relationships form and disengage and what components make up a relationship you may better understand your own relationships.

Relational Knowledge

Relational knowledge is the information you gain through your experiences in relationships. This knowledge greatly influences your behavior, communication style, perceptions, and self-concept. As you grow and develop along with your relationships, you begin to form theories about how others will act, feel, and think in response to your actions. These hypotheses are referred to as *schema*, and it is your schemata that guide your processing of information. As you recall from Chapter 2, **relational schemata** are the bits and pieces of information that you use to interpret messages that you receive in a relationship.[1] Jay has never had a serious girlfriend and considers himself unlucky in love. Whenever Jay has attempted a serious relationship, he has been told that he is immature, insensitive, and incapable of maintaining an adult relationship. Jay and Lesley have gone out a few times, but Jay will not pursue a serious relationship with Lesley because of his fear of rejection. Jay's previous experiences have formed a schema that causes him to hesitate to initiate any serious relationship.

Relational history plays an important role in relational knowledge as well. **Relational history** is the set of thoughts, perceptions, and impressions you have formed about previous relational partners. If you hold positive views about a former relational partner and later run into that person again, you will react differently than if your history were more negative. For example, Isabella has always focused on what she wants in life. She has worked in the county hospital since her volunteering days during high school and has become far more knowledgeable in her field. Louise, the head nurse in pediatrics, first met Isabella as a candy striper and has recently seen Isabella obtain an LVN (licensed vocational nurse) degree. Louise's relational history of Isabella helped Louise nominate Isabella for the RN (registered nurse) college scholarship. As this example shows, remembering things about a relational partner contributes to your overall impression of the relationship, adding to your relational schema about that person.

RELATIONAL
SCHEMATA
Information used to interpret messages received in a relationship.

RELATIONAL
HISTORY
The sum of the "objective" events in a relationship and the shared experiences of relational partners; also, a set of thoughts, perceptions, and impressions that one has formed about one's previous relational partners.

Goals and Motivations for Relationship Development

Why do you enter into relationships with certain individuals and not with others? Each individual and each relationship is unique; no two are exactly the same. The goals and motivations behind the initiation and development of relationships also vary. Expectations play a big role in why you enter into relationships, why you have relationships with certain people, and why certain relationships continue to develop while others do not. However, there are yet other influences that lead you to form relationships.

Interpersonal Attraction

What attracts you to certain individuals? their looks? their personality? their sense of humor? Why is it that two people who are very similar may not be attractive to each other? It is not always easy to explain why some people are attracted to others. Two people might be attracted to the same individual for completely different reasons. For instance, Jeremy and Chris both met Shellee at a community Fourth of July picnic. Both were attracted to her because of a "special quality" they saw in her. To Jeremy, Shellee was special because she had lived in Colón, Panama, where he had grown up. In contrast, the special quality that Chris admired in her was her satirical sense of humor.

Physical attractiveness presents a special case of interpersonal attraction. Western society places great emphasis on having a pleasant physical appearance. Of course, looks aren't everything, but they do play an important role in attracting others. In fact, keeping your body up through eating healthful foods, working out, and getting adequate sleep has become an obsession in the 1990s. What is more, television and fashion magazines keep you up to date on what is in style so that your clothing can always be "in." Plastic surgery and cosmetic dental work, once options chosen mainly by the wealthy, are now widely used to achieve the look people want.

Physical Proximity

Long-distance relationships are difficult to maintain simply because of lack of proximity. Although some would argue that "absence makes the heart grow fonder," it can also be said, "out of sight, out of mind." Julie and

Chad had a relationship that seemed very successful. They were attracted to one another and enjoyed each other's company. When Chad graduated and moved away, however, the relationship quickly lost its fire. At first the two would talk almost every day, but after only a few weeks they became involved in their own activities and their talks grew less frequent, until they spoke every once in a while but not on a regular basis. As so often happens, they decided to meet new people and enter into new relationships rather than continue their relationship apart from one another.

Julie and Chad's story is possible in all types of relationships, and not just in romantic relationships. The simple fact is that people who have frequent, regular contact are more likely to develop a relationship than individuals who see one another less regularly. As proof, think a moment about your current relationships. How many of these formed because of your frequent contact? No doubt, you will find that you formed your relationships with roommates, classmates, teammates, co-workers, and neighbors because of frequent interaction.

Similarity of Attitudes

People with similar beliefs, values, and morals are more likely to enter into a relationship than those with dissimilar attitudes. For example, only in unusual circumstances will a religious person become romantically involved with an atheist, or a liberal Democrat develop an intimate relationship with an extremely conservative Republican. Instead, people are attracted to others who tend to think much as they do. A familiar saying suggests that opposites attract, but more often than not this is not true. At first you may be attracted to your opposite because that person has some qualities or characteristics that you lack. As time goes by, however, these differences may become a source of disagreement, representing a major conflict in your respective values, beliefs, and ideas. Although differences can be a source of interest for some couples, by and large, it is similar attitudes that bond individuals together, creating opportunities for relational stability.

Alleviating Loneliness

Humans feel a natural need for companionship. Between 10 and 20 percent of the population is estimated to experience chronic loneliness, which can result in severe psychological problems.[2] Such problems as anxiety, stress, depression, alcoholism and drug abuse, and poor health have been tied to loneliness. Most people, however, are lonely only from time to time, and it is then that they seek out relationships with other people. A person who feels lonely naturally tends to see a relationship as a logical answer to the problem. Relationships act as a security blanket, helping to ward off the chill of loneliness. Do you know people who form friendships for no apparent reason other than to escape loneliness?

Stimulation

People have an innate need for stimulation, as is most readily seen in the popularity of entertainment sources such as television and movies. The interaction between two people provides a unique kind of stimulation that occurs on a personal level. This stimulation has an intellectual as well as an emotional and physical form.

At an *intellectual level*, stimulation has many guises. For example, it stems from conversations about topics of shared interest, especially current events, movies, books, and societal issues. Such conversations help people explore issues and formulate their opinions about them. On a different level, because people have *emotions*, they naturally feel a need for emotional stimulation. This need is unique in that it is best filled by a person who can mutually benefit from emotional gratification. The bond created between two people through a relationship, then, provides an opportunity to exercise their emotions.

Physical stimulation is yet another form. Humans love to touch and be touched. Some people love to hug, others are great kissers, and still others find the greatest pleasure in using their hands, lips, or tongues as sources of physical stimulation. You probably know people who touch while they talk or kiss and hug "hello" and "goodbye" after every encounter. Physical stim-

---

SELF-CHECK

What Stimulates You about Relationships?

How do you feel when someone you don't know well takes a special interest in you? Which sources of relational stimulation are most important to you? Do your priorities or goals change as your relationships develop and grow?

FIGURE 7.1
Relational partners can provide intellectual, emotional, and physical stimulation for each other.

ulation can be a pleasurable, healthy, and natural part of relationships—as long as it does not interfere with other relational goals.

Learning about Oneself

As you learned in Chapter 3, your self-concept is greatly influenced by how others perceive you. Relationships give you the opportunity to learn about yourself in unique ways. Often your actions or feelings about someone else help you think about yourself. On a more direct level, relationships give you direct feedback about your actions or feelings. A relationship creates a situation in which two people are close enough to be honest, sometimes even painfully honest. Thus, two people in a relationship are more likely to express honest evaluations of the other when asked or when needed. Relationships also allow people to develop their self-esteem. Feeling worthy of another's attention is important, and knowing that you are a significant part of another's life builds your self-worth.

Achieving Goals

Some people enter into relationships to achieve certain goals. For example, if you have dreamed all your life about doing public service work overseas, you might seek relationships with influential people in that field. Similarly, if you are looking to advance your career, you might try to develop relationships with your superiors and co-workers. Often your initial motivation for developing a relationship with a particular individual is to see what that person can do for you or how he or she can help you. Of course, the other person in the relationship will have his or her goals which may or may not be compatible with your own. Therefore, the negotiation of mutual or compatible goals is an important process in relationships.

SELF-CHECK

Goals and Motivations in Intercultural Relationships

Are your relationships with people from other cultures and co-cultures different from your intracultural relationships? Consider two important relationships—both business or both social relationships—for comparison, one with a partner from a culture other than yours and one with a partner from your own culture. For each relationship, answer the following questions; then compare your answers for the two relationships.

1. What were your goals and motivations in developing the relationship?
2. What did you believe to be the goals and motivations of your partner?
3. Did your goals and motivations seem compatible with your partner's? What factors led you to choose this partner?
4. Describe your relationship now. Has it developed as you expected? Did you encounter any obstacles? If so, how did you and your partner respond? Describe your progress toward achieving your goals. Describe how your goals and motivations have changed, if at all, as the relationship has developed.

From your answers to these questions, you can make some observations about the role of cultural differences in your relationships. Are cultural differences an important factor in relational development? Research shows that people do not view the relationship development process any differently simply because a person is from another culture.* Rather, the main issue in your relational development is how similar the other person seems to you. Intercultural relationships are as strongly grounded in perceived similarity as are intracultural relationships.

*W. B. Gudykunst (1985), An exploratory comparison of close intracultural and intercultural friendships, *Communication Quarterly, 33*, 270–283.

Expectations

Recall from Chapter 1 that the model of communicative competence gives expectations a central position in forming the proper messages. How much do your expectations affect your relationships? Whenever people enter into a relationship, they form ideas as to what they think will or should happen. As the relationship develops, these ideas will change and some new ideas may form. Expectations have a way of influencing how people act and feel toward others. You may form expectations not only about the individual with whom you have a relationship, but also about the relationship itself.

■ *Expectations about Relationships*

Many people have romantic ideas about marriage ("Once we're married, we'll have it made"). Unfortunately, Richard Gere (groom-elect) will not show up in a white limo and ride off into the sunset with Julia Roberts (bride-elect) as they did in the movie *Pretty Woman*. Some romantics develop expectations about relationships without having particular individuals in mind. They may think they have certain "requirements" for their future mate, but in reality they just know they want a marital relationship. It is possible to have expectations about a relationship without thinking of a particular person. Even before relationships begin, you form expectations about future partners. Friends, families, novels, and the media offer many models for you to choose from. Some people may prefer relationships that are hot and heavy but last only a short period of time, whereas others prefer

---

REALITY CHECK

What Are Your Expectations for Relationships?

Do you expect relationships to be long and meaningful? Do you tolerate the idea of short, relatively meaningless relationships? Have you started a relationship knowing that it would probably end in hurt feelings? How would you characterize the ideal relationship? How do your relational expectations influence your communication? Can you explain how relational expectations affect the communicative competence model?

---

relationships with people who are intellectually deep. Every person develops a strong individualistic view of relational expectations based on relational knowledge and personal tastes and preferences.

■ *Expectations about Relational Partners*

When you meet people for the first time, it does not take long before your initial impression has been set in stone, and only after a great deal of interaction will your initial opinion change. When people meet for the first time, they form expectations about each other as David and Marissa did.

DAVID   When I first met Marissa, I thought she seemed a little conservative and straitlaced. She acted as if going out and having a good time were against the law. She seemed to think that I was wild and out of control. Little did I know that we would start dating just a short time later.

MARISSA   I thought David was a real jerk the first time I met him. He seemed so full of himself and acted as if the only purpose in life were going out and getting drunk every night of the week. He treated me like some naive little girl. I never would have believed it if someone had told me that we would ever date.

Unrealistic expectations can create problems in a relationship. Unrealistic expectations may arise because of what society says is important in a relationship. Examples of these societal standards are: males should be taller than females, husbands should be better educated than their wives, women should bear children before age 35, and people should not marry outside their ethnic group or culture.

How realistic is this couple?

JOANNIE   Being in love means we'll never fight.

STEPHEN   I know, it's great. You know I'll never make you mad.

The greatest problem with unrealistic expectations is that they produce a great deal of unnecessary stress because the expectations are hardly ever met. As a result, people tend to dismiss relationships that might have ultimately been beneficial if only they had had more positive early experiences.

Realistic expectations can help prevent the development of potentially unsuccessful relationships. Yasar has a strong Muslim background and considers religion to be an important part of his life. Rachel is Jewish and has had very little exposure to the Muslim religion. The two are considering dating, but Yasar feels that their religious differences are too great to overcome. He feels that Rachel will never be able to meet his expectations concerning religion. Yasar's expectation has prevented him and Rachel from entering into a relationship that would be unlikely to succeed.

Violated Expectations

Roberto and Carol had been dating for two months, seeing each other every Friday and Saturday night and on Wednesday afternoons. Although they had occasionally discussed dating each other exclusively, they had never made a formal agreement to that effect. Roberto went out of town for several days and told Carol that he did not expect to return until after the weekend. But Roberto finished his trip early and arrived back in town on Friday night. On his way home, he decided to go by Carol's house to ask her out for Saturday night. He was stunned to learn that Carol was entertaining another man at her house. Roberto had formed certain expectations about his relationship with Carol, and now those expectations had, in essence, been violated. He was hurt and sad that Carol would "go out on him."

Was Carol wrong to violate Roberto's expectations? What happens when your expectations are not met? What do you do if things do not turn out as you had hoped they would? Why are some people willing to ignore some expectancy violations, whereas others deal with unmet expectations severely? The difference probably has to do with the kind of relationship and individuals involved. The more important the relationship or the individual is to you, the more you will allow violations. You may feel that maintaining a relationship with an individual is more important than having your expectations met, or perhaps you may alter your expectations in order for them to be met. Unrealistic expectations can be a problem in many relationships. Many people enter into relationships expecting a fairy-tale ending, but soon enough realize that life seldom follows a story line for very

---

REALITY CHECK

How Do You Handle Expectations?

When was the last time someone violated your relational expectations? Were you too optimistic in your predictions? Too pessimistic? How do you avoid making your expectations too high?

long. At times, then, you may have to revise your expectations. You may find situations in which you realize that the relationship or person is less important than your expectations.

Knowledge, Motivations, and Expectations

When you consider knowledge, motivations, and expectations together, it becomes clearer how relationships begin, develop, grow, and maybe even deteriorate. (See Figure 7.2.) You initiate a relationship because of your goals and motivations (loneliness, stimulation, etc.), and then you form expectations about the person and the relationship based on your level of relational knowledge. This knowledge changes as you interact with your relational partner and your interactions modify your expectations, which in turn affect your motivations for being in the relationship. Relationships are highly dynamic, requiring a continuous assessment of these three elements. As you study the process of relationship development, you will come to understand the dynamic and evolving nature of these aspects.

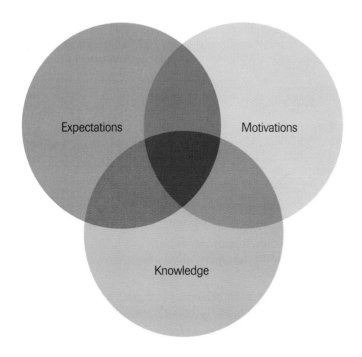

FIGURE 7.2
Knowledge, motivations, and expectations affect one another as a relationship develops.

Costs and Rewards

Every relationship produces advantages and disadvantages for the relational partners. In a widely cited book, *Social Penetration Theory*, Altman and Taylor suggest that relationships begin, develop, grow, and deteriorate based on the rewards and costs that come from the interaction of the two relational partners.[3] *Rewards* are those relational elements that you feel good about, whereas *costs* are those that annoy you. For example, negative expectancy violations are costs, and warm companionship is a reward. When people believe the rewards outweigh the costs, they will most likely find the relationship beneficial and will work to make sure it continues. A

SELF-CHECK

Determining Your Own List of Costs and Rewards

Consider the following list of traits and behaviors and decide which are most important to you as relational rewards and costs. Write "R1" in the blank for items that you consider primary (very important) rewards, "R2" for those you view as secondary rewards (nice to have), and "R3" for rewards that are relatively unimportant to you. Write "C1" before items that you consider primary (very important) costs, "C2" before those you view as secondary costs, and "C3" before costs that are relatively unimportant to you.

_____ Laughs at my jokes
_____ Is affectionate
_____ Is physically attractive
_____ Fits in with my friends
_____ Fits in with my family
_____ Tells inappropriate jokes
_____ Refuses to share emotions
_____ Ignores my feelings
_____ Is career oriented
_____ Wears clothes I dislike
_____ Has views about religion different from mine
_____ Has views about children similar to mine
_____ Has an exciting personality

Do you notice a pattern? Are traits or behaviors in certain areas (e.g., appearance, emotional expressiveness) particularly important to you?

person who feels that the costs are greater than the rewards will most likely not attempt to develop that particular relationship.

Three categories of rewards are available to relational partners. **Extrinsic rewards** are gained purely from association with another person. These types of rewards range from new opportunities, to "contacts" that may later be useful, to a perceived higher social status. A struggling actress trying to become a star may become involved with a director in show business who can help her career. **Instrumental rewards** are rewards that relational partners give to one another—for example, a basic exchange of goods for services. Two people may decide to live together because one can provide appliances and furniture and the other can provide a steady income to pay the rent. **Intrinsic rewards** are rewards that result from an exchange of intimacy.[4] People looking for these types of rewards are interested in each other for personal reasons. For example, two people who are working out at the local gym may become physically attracted to each other. They may meet later for drinks and end up having an intimate relationship.

EXTRINSIC REWARDS
Benefits gained from association with another person, including new opportunities and contacts.

INSTRUMENTAL REWARDS
Rewards that relational partners give to each other, including material benefits.

INTRINSIC REWARDS
Benefits that result from an exchange of intimacy.

Strategies for Reducing Uncertainty

According to the uncertainty reduction theory developed by Berger and Calabrese, when two people meet, their main focus is on decreasing the uncertainty that lies between them.[5] Early in a relationship, uncertainty acts as a double-edged sword, creating both excitement and frustration. The excitement comes from the mystery of a new relationship which pumps your heart a little harder, stirs the butterflies in your stomach, and moistens your palms. The frustrations stem from expectancy violations, hurt feelings, and insecurity. Three factors explain your motivation for reducing uncertainty. First, if you believe that developing a relationship with a particular person will benefit you in some way, you will be more motivated to secure a level of certainty with that person. Second, if you believe that you will have frequent contact with that person in the future, you will want to reduce any uncertainty that you may have. Finally, if the person acts in a manner that is unexpected or not considered "normal," you will want to reduce uncertainty to help you better understand and explain his or her behavior.

The best way to reduce uncertainty is to obtain information about a person that is unique to that individual. In this way, you will know that person at a more intimate level. Uncertainty reduction allows you to predict your relational partners with more accuracy, which in turn, makes you feel more comfortable in developing your relationships even further. Although you will never know everything about your partner, the more you understand, the more likely you will be able to make your relationship with that person richer and more fulfilling.

How do you reduce this uncertainty? As with many things in your life, when you are uncertain you seek information. Once you have sufficient information about your partner, you will be able to make educated predictions about that person. Predictions determine what the partner will say and how he or she will react or feel in a particular situation. In the beginning stages of a relationship, partners will make predictions about one another and the relationship. The less uncertainty between the two, the more often their predictions will be correct. Information-seeking behaviors can take three forms: monitoring, proactive, and direct.

Monitoring Strategies

When Rob wants to learn more about Deanne, he takes advantage of an opportunity to observe her as she talks with her friends in the hallway before class. He learns that she laughs frequently, that she likes to touch her friends on the shoulder when she is talking to them, and that her friends like her a lot. This type of information seeking, monitoring, is useful to Rob because it allows him to observe Deanne in her everyday settings and to obtain knowledge about her as a potential relational partner. Of course, talking to friends in a hallway gives him only a small picture of what a person is really like, so Rob may want to observe Deanne in different settings. If he knows that she attends the public relations club, for example, he may go to one of their meetings to see Deanne in action again. Monitoring strategies allow you to observe people as they communicate with others. Do they act normal? Do they seem like people you would want to be out with? Is their behavior like that of people you enjoy being with?

Sometimes just observing others as they go about their business does not give you the information you need. You may want to see people operate in situations that interest you. Rob, for instance, may want to know how Deanne would act around his friends, so he asks her out and they go to a party where his friends will be. In this way, he can monitor her actions in a situation that is important to him.

Proactive Strategies

Proactive strategies help to reduce uncertainty by letting you obtain information about a person more directly. Rob is acquainted with one of Deanne's friends, Shelly, and calls her up to ask some questions about

Deanne. Rob finds out that Deanne is not dating anyone exclusively right now, that she loves Mexican food, and that she goes to aerobics classes on Monday and Wednesday afternoons. Of course, Rob is aware that Shelly might tell Deanne that he called and asked about her, but he feels that it is worth the risk. Besides, he reasons, it wouldn't hurt for Deanne to learn of his interest in her from a third party.

An even more forthright method is direct questioning of the person you are interested in. Sometimes referred to as *interactive strategy*, this technique increases your chances of learning what you really want to know about a person and gives the person an impression of your interest. Both purposes increase your opportunities to reduce uncertainty.

ROB   [Talking with Deanne in the student union] Are you going to stay in Seattle after you graduate?

DEANNE   [Thinking, "Hmm, he must really be interested in me"] I really haven't decided yet. The job market looks pretty bleak. What about you?

ROB   [Thinking, "Good, she wants to know about me too"] Well, I'm hoping my uncle can use me at his firm. Have you thought about graduate school?

DEANNE   Yeah, but I'll have to retake the GRE to get into grad school here.

Obviously, direct questioning is helpful in uncertainty reduction, but it also entails risks. If you ask questions that are forward or inappropriate, you may do more harm than good.

ROB   Do you plan to have kids after you marry?

DEANNE   [Thinking, "Hey, slow down, Speedy"] I don't know. Hey, isn't that Richard over there? I need to talk to him. See you later.

An even riskier proactive strategy is self-disclosure. Recall from Chapter 3 that self-disclosure is revealing personal information that would otherwise remain hidden from others. How does self-disclosure function as information seeking? Quite often, recipients of self-disclosure counter with personal information of their own, either out of a sense of obligation or because they see this as an opportunity to exchange information. The risk comes when self-disclosure is not reciprocated. Disclosing things about yourself gives away some of the power you hold over other people in the form of information about yourself. If you self-disclose and they elect not to reciprocate, they have an information advantage over you. On the other hand, self-disclosure is an excellent method for two people to reduce uncertainty, for it is one of the most direct means of exchanging information.

ROB   I've always felt uncomfortable about long-term relationships.

DEANNE   Really? Me, too. Although I'm willing to give the right person a chance to change my mind.

▨ Indirect Strategies

When monitoring strategies cannot provide specific information and proactive strategies are too direct or risky, a third alternative is available: indirect strategies. These techniques are designed to help you obtain information from a relational partner without directly asking for it. They are used when issues are too sensitive to bring into the open or when the relationship may not be ready for a full-blown discussion of some topics. Two types of these roundabout methods for uncertainty reduction are discussed here: affinity-seeking strategies and secret tests.

Affinity-seeking strategies are used to learn how your partner feels about you or the relationship itself—not about general topics such as politics and world hunger. Douglas claims that relational partners can use seven affinity-seeking strategies.[6] **Networking** is learning about your partner by asking friends of your partner what they like and dislike about him or her and whether the partner is currently involved in a relationship with someone else. **Offering** is increasing opportunities for frequent interaction by setting up situations in which you will be able to interact with a specific individual. Walking or jogging in the same park, frequenting the same restaurants, and using the same mechanic are all situations in which the two might "accidentally" bump into each other. **Approaching** is using actions that imply the desire for increased intimacy. Touching, leaning in close to speak, long gazes into the other's eyes are all behaviors that would suggest increased intimacy. **Sustaining** is keeping the interaction going, continuing the conversation. **Hazing** is using negative actions to determine whether the partner feels that the relationship is worth the trouble. Planning a schedule so that the partner has to go out of his or her way to find time to spend with you, and picking fights over insignificant matters are strategies an individual might use to see how far the partner is willing to go to continue the relationship. **Confronting** is asking the partner direct questions about his or her feelings. Do you like me? Do you want to continue this relationship? The seventh strategy is **withdrawing**—using silence or distance in order to see how the partner will react. For example, you may

NETWORKING
Learning about a relational partner by asking questions of others who know that person.

OFFERING
Increasing opportunities for frequent interaction with someone by setting up situations that will promote interaction.

APPROACHING
The use of actions that imply a desire for greater intimacy.

SUSTAINING
Keeping an interaction going; continuing a conversation with a particular individual.

HAZING
The use of negative actions to discover whether one's partner feels the relationship is worthwhile.

CONFRONTING
The use of direct questions to a relational partner to ascertain the partner's feelings.

WITHDRAWING
The use of silence or distance in order to see how a relational partner will react.

not call or see the other for several days, or you may be quiet or not say much when in the company of the partner.

Secret tests, the second indirect strategy used in learning about your partner, involve searching for information in a more roundabout manner.[7] This approach is especially useful when you are trying to determine what a partner thinks about the relationship. Examples are *jealousy* tests (making a partner jealous to see his or her reaction), *self-putdowns* (making self-deprecating remarks in the hope that your partner will correct you), and *forced choice* (giving the partner an ultimatum to decide between you and someone else). Ellen and Scott have been dating for about three months and seem to be developing a good relationship. The two have not talked yet about the relationship or their feelings for each other. Ellen is beginning to wonder whether Scott truly has serious plans for their relationship or if he is just having fun but not taking the relationship as seriously as she is. When they go to a party one night, Ellen spends a great deal of time talking to Jack. She stands close to him and touches him several times as she speaks to him. While talking with Jack, Ellen is constantly observing Scott to see his reaction to her behavior. This is an example of a jealousy test, and it works to decrease the uncertainty the partners might have about one another. Once uncertainty is reduced, they can make educated guesses or predictions as to what the other will do, say, think, and feel.

Stages of a Relationship

How do relationships develop? Do they all develop at the same rate and with the same intensity? Although each relationship is unique, most relationships will go through certain stages. (These stages depend on the issues discussed in previous sections.) The stages are graphically presented in the model of relational development (see Figure 7.3 on p. 302). Expectations, motives, and relational knowledge constitute one part of the model. These elements affect the relational partners' perceptions of each other and the relationship. Changes in any of these can significantly affect how a relationship will develop. Rewards and costs always play a role in the process. If rewards exceed costs, you are more likely to move further in this process; if costs overwhelm rewards, relational decline can result. Uncertainty reduction is a key feature of this model because gaining information about the relational partner will affect expectations, motives, and knowledge as well as costs and rewards.

Examine Figure 7.3 carefully. As you will see, there are six possible stages of relational development. There is a wide range of stages because

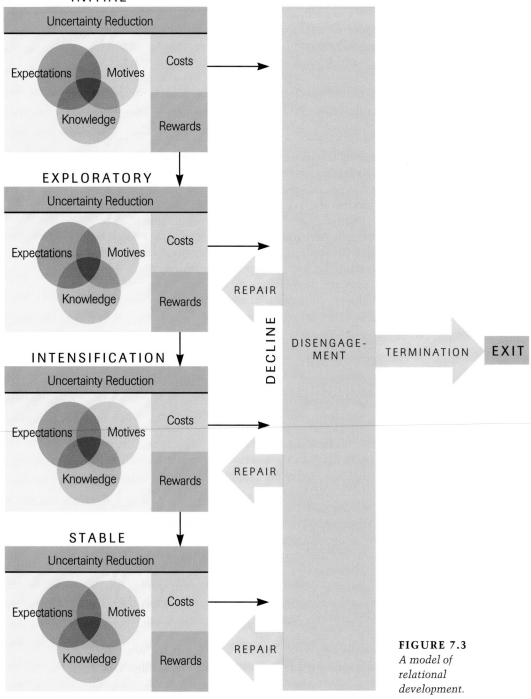

INITIAL

Uncertainty Reduction

Expectations Motives

Knowledge

Costs

Rewards

EXPLORATORY

Uncertainty Reduction

Expectations Motives

Knowledge

Costs

REPAIR

Rewards

INTENSIFICATION

Uncertainty Reduction

Expectations Motives

Knowledge

Costs

REPAIR

Rewards

STABLE

Uncertainty Reduction

Expectations Motives

Knowledge

Costs

REPAIR

Rewards

DECLINE

DISENGAGE-MENT

TERMINATION

EXIT

FIGURE 7.3
A model of relational development.

not all relationships experience each of these stages, particularly the last two, decline and exit. Assume that all relationships start with an initial stage. Many will proceed to an exploratory phase, some of these relationships will go on to intensification, and others will become stable. If at any point in the process costs exceed rewards, relational decline may result. If relational partners are willing to make the relationship work, repair strategies may be attempted, moving the relationship back into one of the previous stages. If relational decline has arrived at a "point of no return," termination strategies may be used to exit the relationship altogether.[8] We will now discuss the six stages in some detail.

The Initial Stage

When you begin a relationship, you are probably uncertain about the potential partner. Your expectations and knowledge are based on general information gained from the partner's appearance, demeanor, and behavior. After some contact with the person, you may begin to form impressions that confirm or modify your knowledge, expectations, and motives for being in the relationship. Positive impressions (assessments) translate into rewards, whereas negative impressions are perceived as costs. If costs seem to outweigh rewards, relational decline is likely to result. If enough rewards are present, the relationship moves to the next stage, the exploratory.

The Exploratory Stage

The exploratory stage, true to its name, involves a great deal of information seeking. It assumes that both relational partners want to reduce uncertainty. Monitoring, proactive, and indirect strategies are evidenced in this stage, so that enough relational knowledge is accumulated to make further assessments. In the exploratory stage, relational partners are still hesitant to delve into highly intimate topics, and testing of the relationship may be the norm. As information is exchanged, expectations, knowledge, and motives are reassessed, resulting in rewards/costs examination. If costs exceed rewards, relational decline is likely; if rewards are abundant, the next stage further intensifies the relationship.

The Intensification Stage

By the time relational partners reach this stage, they have made an investment in each other and can afford to intensify their relationship. This will be especially evident in the means they use to reduce uncertainty fur-

FIGURE 7.4

How can you recognize the exploratory stage of a relationship?

ther. Instead of seeking personal information about each other, the partners are more likely to focus on the relationship. This is especially true if the relationship is a romantic one. Intensification efforts reflect a desire to move the relationship to a new level. Both relational partners realize that their expectations, motives, and knowledge are different from those in the earliest stage, and so they assess rewards and costs along new areas. For example, two friends who are intensifying their relationship will know not to hold unrealistic expectations because their relational knowledge has grown. They may even develop new motives for being in the relationship. In the earliest stages, they may have valued companionship, but now they value the relational partner's trust more than anything else. Rewards and costs may change as well. It is in the intensification stage that relational intimacy or closeness may be felt for the first time.

The Stable Stage

By the time partners have reached the stable stage, their relationship is no longer volatile or temporary. Relational partners now have a great deal of knowledge about one another, their expectations are accurate and realistic, and they feel comfortable with their motives for being in the relationship. Uncertainty reduction is not a major issue in this phase unless events in the lives of the relational partners change. Perceptions of rewards and costs become more stable, providing a measure of predictability in the relationship. This is not to say that relationships don't continue to evolve, for in order for relationships to enjoy stability, they must continue to interest the partners.

Wilmot characterizes stable relationships in the following three ways: "(a) relationships stabilize because the participants reach some minimal agreement on what they want from the relationship, (b) relationships can stabilize at differing levels of intimacy, and (c) a stabilized relationship still has areas of change occurring in it."[9] The concept of intimacy is worth considering in more detail.

Intimacy

Intimacy is a special form of relational development that is found in the stable phase.[10] **Intimacy** is a deep understanding of another person and is one of the highest levels that a relationship can aspire to. One popular misconception of intimacy is that it is usually sexual. On the contrary, intimacy is not restricted to romantic relationships. As noted earlier, it can occur between parent and child, best friends, and colleagues; even adversaries can enjoy intimacy if they have a deep understanding of one another.

INTIMACY
A relationship in which the relational partners share a deep understanding of each other.

Contemporary society is traditional in the sense that it seems to dictate that all members be paired off. Some individuals feel that something is "wrong" with them if by their early thirties they are not married, engaged, or involved in a deeply intimate relationship that will most likely develop into marriage. The *cultural guidelines* of this society promote the ideal of intimate relationships, as is evident in all aspects of life, television, music, books, and magazines. Even advertisements attempt to persuade the general public that having that "special someone" is much better than being alone, no matter how unhappy that "special someone" makes one feel. Indeed, some individuals tend to be more in love with the idea of being in love than with any particular individual. Others seem to reach a point where a feeling of desperation kicks in and they start to believe that if they don't attach themselves to the next person who comes along they may not get another chance. Whatever the reasoning, people in this society have the idea that individuals are not truly individuals until they have a partner.

Once partners have achieved a satisfactory level of intimacy, they must continuously work to sustain that intimacy. Any number of strategies can be used to maintain intimacy, but this section suggests using one of the following.

> *Reciprocal self-disclosure and trust* If individuals feel that they can completely trust their partner and their partner has complete trust in them, then they are more likely to self-disclose private and personal matters and create a greater sense of intimacy. Marissa stated that she felt that David did not trust her because whenever she disclosed

FIGURE 7.5

The pressure on young adults to find a romantic partner remains a strong force in contemporary society.

something personal, he would not give a response and would seldom follow up with a self-disclosure of his own.

Supportive interchanges[11]   If you feel confident that your partner supports you 100 percent, you will most likely feel a greater closeness or intimacy. In order to give supportive interchanges, you should become more aware of your partner's successes and improvements, give frequent approval of his or her activities, and avoid expressing disapproval.

Commitment talk   Relationships sustain intimacy when the partners feel an involvement and use commitment talk to express commitment to the relationship. Many different forms of commitment are possible. Rejection of competing alternatives, a willingness to exert effort to resolve any problems in order to maintain the relationship, and acceptance of personal responsibility for the relationship are just some of the ways that you can exchange commitment talk.[12]

Enchantment   People can deliberately be enchanting in order to sustain intimacy. In the beginning, relationships are new and exciting, full of surprises. Later, this newness can wear off and leave the partners feeling as though every day were the same. To help maintain intimacy, partners can be playful, mysterious, or unpredictable. Intimacy is unique in each relationship, and how you and your partner sustain a satisfactory level of intimacy is also unique. No matter which strategy you use, you should remember that a relationship requires continuous maintenance.

A Definition of Love

Love expresses a wide range of feelings, from deep passion for another person to great fondness for a favorite dessert. Saying "I love you" seems to have lost its emphasis and does not appear to have the definite meaning it once did.

Love, unlike friendship, is an exclusive kind of relationship. The particular relationship of the parties who claim to be "in love" is supposed to be different from any relationship either might have with other people. To follow the storybook definition of love, love can be described as a permanent relationship with deep emotional ties and it is passionate and intense. However, that is the fairy-tale version. For this section, we define **love** as a deep affection for and attraction to another person.

According to Sternberg's triangular theory of love, love is made up of three components: *intimacy, passion,* and *commitment.*[13]

> *Intimacy* is the aspect of love that is the most emotional and involves the feelings of support, sharing, and respect. It is the connection that the two parties feel with one another. (This is the same type of intimacy we discussed earlier.)
>
> *Passion* is the physical attraction, the desire or sexual excitement.
>
> *Commitment* is the aspect that develops with the relationship, and it is the idea that the relationship could possibly be long term. It is made up of the decisions that each individual makes affecting whether or not the relationship will continue.

Sternberg claims that the presence or absence of any of these three components will greatly affect the relationship.

LOVE
A relationship that is more exclusive than friendship; a deep affection for and attraction to another person.

Types of Love

Have you ever thought that love can be different for different people? Do you experience different types of love depending on who the person is? The Canadian psychologist John Allen Lee conducted extensive research with the goal of placing different types of love into categories.[14] His research involving hundreds of people revealed six different types of love.

> *Eros—beauty and sexuality* Erotic love views sex as the most important aspect of love. This type of relationship is quite intense, both emotionally and physically. The focus is on beauty and attractiveness more than on qualities such as intelligence and sense of humor.
>
> *Ludus—entertainment and excitement Ludus* means *play* in Latin, and the ludic lover views love as a game. Ludic love does not require great commitment or feeling, for it lacks passion and intensity. It

lasts only as long as the partners find each other entertaining or fun. When things begin to dull, new partners are found. The casual dating of many different people is a prime example of ludus.

Storge—peacefulness and slowness   Storge is a type of love that lacks passion and excitement. It develops over an extended period of time and often begins in friendship. Storgic lovers may have difficulty pinpointing the precise moment when they knew they were in love. For them, falling in love was a gradual process that happened without their realizing it until much later. Storgic lovers often share common interests and activities, but rarely disclose any feelings about their relationship.

Pragma—practicality and tradition   In Greek, *pragma* means *life work.* Pragmatic lovers are extremely logical and practical in seeking a companion. They want a long-term relationship with an individual who shares their goals in life. If a person wants a relationship that does not require much time or effort, then he or she will search for a mate who is looking for the same things. Pragmatic relationships seem to last longer than any of the others, perhaps because both parties enter with realistic expectations—"with open eyes."

Mania—elation and depression   This is the love that is often referred to as "romantic love." It exhibits extreme feelings, ranging from high excitement and passion to deep depression. Manic lovers are often so concerned with the thought of losing their mate that they are unable to enjoy the relationship. Mania love is characteristically intense, obsessive, desperate, and painful. Manic relationships often appear out of control; the partners act impulsively and often get hurt. Mania love is full of excitement and intensity, but it reaches a peak and then quickly fades away.

Agape—compassion and selflessness   In this type of love, the individual gives willingly and expects nothing in return. This type of lover can care for others without close ties; a deep relationship is not necessary for agapic love to develop. The agapic lover always wants

---

REALITY CHECK

Thinking about Love

How many times have you experienced love that resembles the types outlined here? Can you add any new categories? Is love always different for every person, or can you list qualities that are common to many types of love? If so, what are some of these qualities?

the other to be happy, even if it results in his or her own pain or unhappiness.

No map of the road of love has ever been prepared; only trial and error, along with the passing of time and experience, will help you to find your one true love. Nonetheless, Goss and O'Hair give several helpful hints on how you may establish *effective love.*[15]

1. Develop insight into and empathy for a partner's concept of love.
2. Analyze your own and your partner's expectations of love.
3. Accept the fact that, even though two people have different concepts of love, neither owns the truth.
4. Be flexible. Adapt the way you show love to meet a partner's image of loving behavior.
5. Recall what you said or did to show loving feelings in the early stages of the relationship.
6. Notice what your partner does to make you feel loved.
7. Think of change not as giving something up but as a way of getting new rewards.

REALITY CHECK

Love on the Move

Joyce and Jim, who were introduced by common friends, have been dating for six months. Joyce has told Jim on several occasions that she loves him and wants them to be together forever. Jim is thrilled to hear this and always reciprocates Joyce's sentiments and feelings. The fact of the matter is that, although Joyce does love Jim, she knows full well that her career will cause her to move soon. Jim owns a thriving business in the community where they both live, and all of his family, including his ex-wife and three children, live near him. Joyce knows that Jim would never move with her. Even though she knows they will break up in a few months, Joyce continues to discuss their future, including marriage, with Jim. Joyce fears that Jim would look elsewhere for a relationship if he knew about her impending move, and she wants to maintain the relationship as long as she is in town.

Is Joyce using unethical communication to maintain her relationship with Jim? If so, does the fact that she really loves him make her behavior less unethical? Would it be unethical for Jim to find another relationship if he thought Joyce was moving? Should ethics always come before love?

Stable Relationships

Maintaining successful relationships requires a great deal of effort. Partners must gain an understanding of their individual relationship, work within its limits, and utilize its strengths. You can approach relationships with stability as the goal by adopting the following behaviors.

Be understanding. Try to understand how your partner views the world. Empathize with his or her fears, pain, and dreams. It is important to be supportive. Do not judge these concerns. Aim only to understand in order to communicate more effectively with your partner. Show that you care.

Reveal your feelings. Reveal yourself cautiously. It may be detrimental to self-disclose too much. Knowledge of past acts or certain feelings may harm the relationship if disclosed at the wrong time. Consider how the knowledge will affect your partner's actions and feelings, Use good judgment. Still, self-disclosure is an essential part of a relationship. It strengthens the bond between relational partners.

Be flexible. Recognize that people and relationships naturally change and that these changes must be handled. Often, conscious change is necessary on the part of one or both of the relational partners. Thus, an understanding that change is natural and essential is crucial.

Be accommodating. Conflict naturally occurs. Relational partners who accept this reality and proceed in conflict situations with the right intentions will benefit greatly. Proceed with the goal of reaching a compromise instead of winning the argument; otherwise, one or both partners may get hurt. Conflict can be healthy, but when approached incorrectly it can be very detrimental.

Don't demand too much. Be realistic in your expectations of your partner and of the relationship. Do not compare your relationship with other relationships that are perceived to be better than your own. Actually, most relationships experience the same kinds of trouble that your own does. Therefore, do not set your expectations too high.

▨ *Relationship Decline*

Relationship decline, the erosion that occurs over time to some relationships, has several causes. Although no two relationships are the same, the causes of relationship decline share some similarities. As you observe from the model shown in Figure 7.3, relational decline results when costs exceed rewards and relational partners put less effort into the relationship. Rewards/costs result from an assessment within all stages of the model. Four factors in the costs/rewards evaluation typically lead to relational decline: (1) uncertainty events, (2) unmet expectations, (3) change (self, relational partner, goals, motives), and (4) interference (family, work, timing, money, etc.).

Uncertainty Events

Uncertainty events are events or behavioral patterns that may cause uncertainty in a relationship, leaving one or both partners wondering about the cause of the events and their significance for the relationship. Planalp and Honeycutt studied these events and found several factors that cause uncertainty in a relationship:[16]

- Competing relationships, either dating relationships or platonic ones
- An unexplained loss of closeness
- Change in sexual behavior
- Deception or betrayal of confidence
- Unexplained change in personality or values

These events or changes may be sudden and very noticeable, or they may be subtle and escape immediate attention.

UNCERTAINTY EVENT
An event that causes uncertainty in a relationship (e.g., a competing relationship, unexplained loss of closeness, deception, or an unexplained change in the personality of one partner).

Unmet Expectations

The way two people interact is greatly influenced by their expectations for the relationship and their perception of each other's expectations. These expectations range from where the relationship is going in general to very specific expectations about how the other person will react to a certain situation.

Dissatisfaction with a relationship often begins when a gap forms between a person's expectations about a relationship and the actual course the relationship is taking. This is often a result of differences between the partners' respective expectations. Susannah and Craig dated for two years while they attended the same university. Upon graduation, Susannah ex-

---

REALITY CHECK

Causes of Unmet Expectations

Unmet expectations can result from any area of a relationship. Personality differences, uncompromising attitudes, differing levels of sexual attraction and enjoyment, and lost romance constitute only a few of the reasons why one partner may fail to meet the expectations of the other. Can you cite other reasons?

pected the two of them to begin making plans for marriage. However, Craig felt that they should go their own ways in order to find out whether their relationship was truly "meant to be." Susannah was shocked that Craig did not want to get married immediately. Craig did not necessarily want to terminate their relationship, but he was not ready for marriage. Susannah mistook Craig's hesitation to mean he no longer wanted to date her exclusively. When their relationship went in a direction opposite to Susannah's expectations, she decided to end the relationship.

Change

Inevitably, people change, and how relational partners handle the change affects the health of the relationship. Change may come in the form of *psychological change* in which partners develop differing attitudes, beliefs, values, or interests. This type of change is a mental change that interferes with the compatibility of the partnership.

Change may also come in the form of *behavioral change.* This kind of change deals with differences in the behavior of one or both of the partners. For example, someone who spends less and less time with the partner, becoming more involved in work or school, demonstrates a behavioral change.

Status change, another potential cause of relationship deterioration, refers to a change in the status of a person's life. For example, a person who enters a relationship while a student may see the relationship deteriorate after he or she graduates and enters the professional world. This may be the result of differences in goals between the partners, such as when one person is not ready to make a monogamous commitment, or it may stem from differences in the careers the partners have chosen.[17]

Regardless of the source of change, relational partners must allow change to become part of their relationship if they are going to avoid relational decline. You should keep in mind that change is a synonym for growth and that over time most people do mature.

Interference

Many obstacles may crop up in a relationship, interfering with its growth. Timing, third-party relationships, the family or friends of one partner, and problems with work or money can all contribute to the decline of a relationship.

Timing

The amount of involvement time a particular relationship endures usually determines the timing of the breakup. The great majority of relational breakups (71.1 percent) occur during the spring and summer months, from

April to September. Research has also found that the degree of involvement in the relationship plays a part in determining when to end it.[18] The relational partners who were more emotionally involved in the relationship broke up during the school year, while the less involved relational partners ended the relationship during vacation time.

Third-Party Relationships

Often a relationship fails to meet a person's needs, and when this happens, that person may seek fulfillment in a source outside of the relationship. A third party may not necessarily be a competing romantic interest; it may be a friend or family member. Whoever it is, however, that person fulfills needs that the relational partner cannot, making the presence of the partner unnecessary. When Natalie refused to go to the golf course with Carl while he played, Carl invited another friend, Katherine, to play. The two enjoyed playing together, and their golf games soon became a regular occurrence. Although Natalie herself was responsible for their playing together, she became extremely jealous of Carl and Katherine's relationship. When she told Carl that she did not think it was right for him to play golf with another woman instead of his girlfriend, Carl did not understand why Natalie was so upset. After all, his relationship with Katherine was strictly platonic and he had asked Natalie to play with him before he had ever contacted Katherine. Although the relationship between Carl and Katherine was a friendship based on a hobby both enjoyed, Natalie found this third-party relationship threatening.

Family or Network

Often problems develop within relationships because of differences between one member and the family or friends of the partner. These problems often result from personal differences or differences in value systems, leading to an implicit or explicit disapproval shown by the family or friends of the relational partner. This may cause problems as the partner "caught in the middle" tries to reconcile the competing views and decide what to do. When Rosa and Charles announced that they were getting married, their families were pleased. Rosa's Mexican heritage taught her that the groom's family was responsible for the bulk of the wedding expenses, whereas Charles's American culture led him to believe that the bride's family carried the load. As plans for the wedding began to take shape, each family had its own ideas of exactly how everything should be and who should bear most of the costs. Rosa's family also believed that the couple should be married in a large church wedding with all the trimmings, whereas Charles's family felt that was too elaborate and a waste of money. Both Rosa and Charles felt caught between the two families. When the disagreement between the families continued, Rosa and Charles decided to elope. That was the only way their relationship could survive the family interference.

Work-Related Problems

Problems associated with work occur on many levels. Two of the most common complaints made about relational partners involve spending too much time at work or "bringing the office home." At issue here is time spent on one's job in proportion to time spent with the relational partner or family. A perception that more time is spent on one's job may lead to the belief that the job is more important than the partner or family.

Work also causes problems by clashing with expectations and values. Career-oriented females with children may be viewed as neglectful and uncaring, whereas career-focused males with children are seen as ambitious providers. Does quality time versus quantity of time come to mind? One question that is often raised about this issue is: How many professionals say on their death beds, "I wished I'd worked more!"?

Financial Problems

Money is a major issue in most relationships. DeVito notes that one-fourth to one-third of all couples rank it among their most troublesome problems. He also states that it is the close connection between money and power that makes it such a thorny issue. For example, the person who makes more money usually has the final say about the purchase of expen-

FIGURE 7.6

Why do you think financial problems are frequently a cause of relational decline?

sive items and about many other financial decisions. Also, money may cause problems in the sense that couples naturally argue about how it is to be spent in general. This problem affects most relationships in some form. Another reason why money may contribute to difficulties is that the partners often view money differently because of upbringing, spending habits, and gender.[19]

Relational Repair

The warning signs of a relationship in decline are often pretty obvious. An argument may get out of hand or a situation may cause misunderstandings that could have been corrected. One person may feel that not enough effort has been exerted; or the partners may simply "give up." Whatever the reason, people may feel a desire to repair the relationship. According to Duck, a relationship is in need of repair when one or more of the following four main factors emerge:

- A significant inconsistency occurs between the definition of the relationship as perceived by outsiders and the definition accepted by at least one partner.
- Obstacles emerge to block a mutually agreed upon shift from one relational stage to the next.
- Relational partners maintain significantly different definitions of the relationship along with different expectations of each other.
- A major difference exists between the definition of the relationship and the behaviors used to secure and maintain the desired definition.

Duck suggests the following repair tactics:

- Reduce turbulence in interactions.
- Improve communication.
- Bring out the partner's positive side.
- Focus on the positive aspects of the relationship.
- Reinterpret the behavior of the partner as positive and well intentioned.
- Reduce negativity toward the partner and adopt a more balanced view.
- Reevaluate the attractiveness and unattractiveness of alternative relationships and alternative partners.
- Enlist the support of others in order to hold the relationship together.
- Obtain help to correct matters or to end the relationship.

Relational partners have to decrease the amount of disagreement in their interactions. In order to repair their relationship, they must focus on the relationship itself and not the source of a particular argument. (For example, they should concentrate on the compatibility of the relationship instead of on the differences.) Next, the partners may need to improve the quality of their communication. Attending workshops on social skills training may help in this area. Inappropriately communicated messages can often be the source of the problems. Some relational partners need to work on their listening skills and strive to understand the other person's perspective. Like all communication, thinking about what you are about to say is also very important because words spoken harshly are not easily forgotten. Another element of repair is for the relational partners to display the attractive qualities that sparked the relationship in the first place. The partners also may consider increased intimacy in repairing their relationship, such as making more self-disclosures and spending quality time with one another.[20]

Repair tactics used during the final stages of termination will most likely involve one of three approaches: use of others outside the relationship to help hold the relationship together; social support from friends; and an accounting to others of why the relationship ended.

If you know that your relationship is in trouble but want to salvage it, you can take the additional actions that are discussed next. None of these is a cure-all, but one or more of them may help your situation.

Tell your partner how you feel. It is important to let your partner know that you see a problem in the relationship; this is essential to begin reversing the deterioration. It provides a starting place to work through the difficulties in your relationship. It also shows that you care about the relationship and that you trust your partner enough to express how you feel.

Have empathy. When your partner has communicated his or her feelings, be sure to demonstrate that you are interested in the way your partner feels about the relationship. There are no unimportant feelings. After all, if your partner also perceives something to be a problem in the relationship, it is a problem. Moreover, the partner's actions will be influenced by that perception until it is either worked through or dispelled.

Tell the truth. If any effort to save the relationship is to be effective, it must be based on an understanding of the problem or problems that the relationship is experiencing. For this understanding to occur, you and your partner must give each other accurate impressions of what you believe to be the problems. Honesty is the foundation stone for real progress.

Show you care. When you are trying to reverse deterioration it is important to say, "I care." This does not have to be stated verbally, and, more often than not, it will be communicated by other means. You might send a card or do a favor your partner has been requesting. In this way you let your relational partner know that you care not just in words but also in deeds. Such acts demonstrate your commitment to your partner and to your relationship.

Relational Disengagement

Duck identifies four phases in the process leading to disengagement
from and termination of relationships.[21]

The Intrapsychic Phase

In the *intrapsychic phase,* the partners watch each other's actions very
closely to try to determine why the other person is ending the relationship.
In this phase, people try to understand the motivations behind the partner's
actions, and they contemplate the quality of the relationship; they may
compare it to other relationships, and they may compare their partner to
other potential partners. Conflict occurs in this phase when an internal
struggle is caused by the partner's weighing of many issues. The relational
partner who is unhappy with the relationship analyzes the relationship, determines the reasons or causes of unhappiness, and decides which course of
action to take, either to work out the problems or to terminate the relationship.

The Dyadic Phase

In the *dyadic phase,* the partners discuss the problems with the relationship and work toward an agreement about whether the relationship should
be continued. According to Duck, the dissatisfied partner may go through
the following steps in this phase:

- Confront the partner with the dissatisfaction.
- Assess the costs of the relationship (as perceived by him- or herself) and
  how to deal with the dissatisfaction.
- Evaluate the partner's view of the relationship.

- Deal with the partner's excuses or apologies.
- Analyze the relationship together.
- Consider alternative forms of the relationship.
- Decide on the proper course of action.

The Social Phase

In the *social phase,* the partners acknowledge the demise of the relationship through their respective social networks. They can agree on postrelational status to the point that they mutually decide how each will treat the other. They can also create acceptable postrelational definitions for the partners.

"Even though we broke up, we're still friends."
"Oh, well, we were just acquaintances in the first place."
"He's a creep and I'll never speak to him again."

By formalizing this process, former relational partners come to terms with the new labels they have for one another. They must also consider implied status changes in terms of roles. (For example, will both continue to work for the same company or in the same department?) As part of the postmortem process, they can also evaluate the consequences of disengagement, try to place blame, attempt to save face, and seek to acquire public acceptance from others for the termination. Through this step former partners try to move the relationship into the social world in which they must live or work.

The Grave-Dressing Phase

In the final phase, *grave dressing,* the partners seek a final ending to the relationship on all levels, physically, psychologically, and socially. This is an important phase for both, allowing them to try to "make sense" of the relationship as a whole. Specifically, they seek to understand why the relationship ended and the reasons for each partner's actions, and to find some way to lay the issue to rest in their minds. This phase is important to each person's self-image and beliefs about his or her role in relationships in general.

Ending a Relationship

Every relationship is influenced by unique situations and circumstances; all the same, some generalizations are possible here. Davis identifies two general reasons for terminating relationships.[22]

The first reason he notes is *passing away.* This situation is characterized by a gradual fading of the relationship. The relationship loses its vitality perhaps because of another intimate or because of jealousy over the time one partner spends in activities not associated with the other partner. Also, the time available for interaction may have decreased, adding to the interaction distance. As a result, communication and intimacy may have declined, leading to a separation of attitudes between the partners. The relationship may also pass away because the partners simply do not continue making the effort needed to maintain an intimate relationship. This leads to a stagnant relationship and a decrease in communication between the partners.

Davis also identifies a situation of *sudden death.* This situation refers to an unexpected ending that comes suddenly. Here the partners may terminate a relationship that one or both of them have desired to end for some time. Feelings that were once present may have died. Nonetheless, the partners may have continued the relationship because of circumstances external to the relationship, such as the years invested together or the presence of children.

If only one partner wishes to terminate the relationship, he or she may suddenly act on this desire after a long period of uncertainty. The partner seeking an end to the relationship may previously have allowed it to drag on in response to alternating good and bad phases or to the efforts of the other partner to maintain the relationship. Whatever the reason, the dissatisfied partner, once resolved to terminate the relationship, will do so quickly and "move on."

Sudden relationship death may also occur when one partner, perceiving that the relationship is moving too fast, requests a slowdown. If this request is not met, the person may react by terminating the relationship altogether. A relationship may also be ended by isolated occurrences, such as a single argument that goes too far or a unique misunderstanding that ends an otherwise smoothly running relationship. Finally, a partner may violate some implicit or explicit rule of interaction that both had adopted earlier. For example, one partner may not attend an official holiday celebration with the partner's family, instead opting to visit a childhood friend in another state. This action may cause the other partner to be angry enough to end the relationship.

Strategies for Terminating a Relationship

As we mentioned earlier, the circumstances present in each relationship are different; accordingly, termination strategies vary with each person and each relationship. Several common methods of termination are listed in Table 7.1 (on p. 320). Which of these strategies have worked for you

TABLE 7.1 RELATIONAL TERMINATION STRATEGIES

STRATEGY	TACTICS	EXAMPLE
Positive-tone messages	Fairness	"It wouldn't be right to go on acting like we're in love when I know I am not!"
	Compromise	"I still care about you. We can still see each other occasionally."
	Fatalism	"Destiny would never let us go on for very long in this relationship."
Deescalation	Promise of friendship	"We can still be friends."
	Implied possible reconciliation	"We need time alone; maybe that will rekindle our feelings for each other."
	Blaming relationship	"It's not your fault, but this relationship is bogging us down."
	Appeal to independence	"We don't need to be tied down right now."
Withdrawal/avoidance	Same as strategy	Avoid contact with the person as much as possible.
Justification	Emphasize positive consequences of disengaging	"It's better for you and me to see other people, since we've changed so much."
	Emphasize negative consequences of not disengaging	"We will miss too many opportunities if we don't see other people."
Negative identity management	Emphasize enjoyment of life	"Life is too short to spend with just one person right now."
	Nonnegotiation	"I need to see other people—period!"

Source: Adapted from D. J. Canary & M. J. Cody (1994), *Interpersonal communication: A goals-based approach* (New York: St. Martin's Press), pp. 266–268.

in the past? What situational conditions would cause some of these tactics to work better?

Effects of Termination

The termination of serious or lengthy relationships can be both traumatic and stressful. A great deal of research has been done on the tactics individuals use to cope with a breakup. Harvey, Orbuch, and Weber, for example, have devised a model that focuses on psychological needs, communication, and post-termination mental health.[23] According to this model, after a traumatic experience, individuals experience a natural need to explain fully what happened. Months or even years may be needed to develop this accounting process fully because so much information, so many details, and so much potential for second-guessing have built up. The accounting process consists of forming a detailed, coherent story about the relationship, what happened, when, why, and with what consequences. In addition, emotional consequences must be dealt with when a relationship is terminated. Both partners will most likely experience some type of emotion in regard to the ending of their relationship. Feelings of distress, unhappiness, and disappointment are common. The relational partner who initiated the breakup may experience guilt, while the other partner may feel angry and depressed.

Reconciliation

Reconciliation is a repair strategy that goes the extra mile. It signals that one relational partner wants to rekindle an extinguished relationship. Reconciling a relationship entails a lot of risk because the receiver may have no interest in a "second chance." It takes a lot of guts and initiative for someone to risk another dose of rejection and humiliation. Nonetheless, some people will launch headfirst into a series of strategies designed to halt a deteriorating relationship. Other people may carefully consider the options available and construct a message that will appeal to an ex-partner.

Relationships that are begun anew may turn out in several different ways. The relationship may be strengthened by the termination and subsequent reconciliation. In this case, the partners are sure of their goals for the relationship and their feelings about each other. In another case, old issues may not be settled and may resurface, causing the same trouble or resulting in intensified disagreement and strife. There is no way to say with any certainty how a reconciliation attempt will turn out.

Types of Relationships

There are as many different types of relationships (e.g., collegial, peer, spiritual) as there are individuals who make up these relationships. Some common relationships are those between co-workers, between doctors and patients, and between salespeople and clients. However, this section will concern itself primarily with two main types that are considered important: friendship and family.

■ *Friendship*

Friendship is a relationship between two or more people that is perceived as mutually satisfying, productive, and beneficial. Everyone has a personal opinion as to what important characteristics a friend should have.

Characteristics of Friendship

In spite of individual differences as to what constitutes friendship, a near consensus seems to have been reached on seven characteristics.[24]

Availability

What good would a friend be who was never able to spend time with you? People want friends to make time for them and be accessible. If the parties in a relationship seldom interact with each other, the relationship often deteriorates or loses its closeness. Do your close friends make time for you even when they are busy? You may often make friends through your activities, classes, or work. You want to have common interests and activities with your friends. What would two people do together if they had absolutely nothing in common? Usually, these shared activities mean the difference between being acquaintances and being friends.

Caring

You want your friends to care about you. Even if something in your life appears to be of no great importance to them, you want and expect them to care about what happens because it's important to you. Your friends do not have to agree with the choices or events in your life, but they need to care about them. If an individual were to ignore you, have no regard for your feelings, and genuinely seem not to care about what happened to you, you would not identify that person as your friend.

Honesty

You want your friends to be open and honest with you. Honesty is a virtue that is vital in all relationships. When a relational partner deceives you, the deception tends to decrease the degree of closeness that the two of you shared. Along with being honest, sometimes your partners may have to be "brutally honest" and tell you things that you would rather not hear. You have to accept this honesty as constructive criticism and remember that, although you may not like what you are hearing, you may need to hear it, and that hearing it from a friend may actually be best.

Confidentiality

You want confidentiality from your friends, an assurance that what you disclose to your friends will not end up in the *National Inquirer* tomorrow. What you share with your friends may seem meaningless and trivial to them but may be extremely personal to you. You want to be able to trust your friends and know that they will not share your deepest, darkest secrets with others.

Loyalty

Have you ever had a friend who was extremely nice and supportive to your face, but the minute you left the room tore you and your reputation to shreds? A true friend is one who is loyal and would never allow others to degrade you without standing up for you or at least letting it be known that he or she did not agree with what was being said. A friend who can be loyal in even the worst of times is a lifelong friend.

Understanding

You want some understanding from your friends. If you have a deep fear of the water, a friend will understand why you don't enjoy spending a great deal of time around the pool or beach and why you don't like any type of horseplay near the water. Past experiences, history, and so on help your friends' level of understanding of why you act in certain ways in certain situations.

Empathy

You expect some degree of empathy from your friends. You like your friends to be able to see particular circumstances as you do and perhaps walk in your shoes. Even if they have never shared the same experience, you expect a friend to attempt to empathize with you.

In 1979, *Psychology Today* conducted a survey that confirmed this list of friendship qualities.[25] When the survey asked the respondents what they felt was the most important quality in a friend, the most often mentioned quality was that of keeping confidences. Trust seemed to be a major issue in all friendships. Along with trust came loyalty; people want to believe that their friends will stick by them come what may. The importance of warmth and affection rounded out the top three. The results of the survey are presented in Table 7.2.

Types of Friendship

Even though the list of qualities presented in Table 7.2 may seem to apply to all friendships, it is important to understand that there are different types of friendship. Reisman identifies three types: reciprocity, receptivity, and association.[26]

Reciprocity

Reciprocity is ideal in that it is composed of characteristics such as self-surrender, loyalty, mutual respect, affection, and support. Each individual in a reciprocal friendship equally gives and takes, and each person takes the responsibility of maintaining the relationship. Mike and Russell have been best friends as long as they can remember. The two met when they were in first grade and eventually ended up sharing an apartment together. They help one another in any way they can and they find spending time with one another to be enjoyable and beneficial. They feel they can trust one another, and they are always comfortable when they are together.

TABLE 7.2 QUALITIES MOST VALUED IN A FRIEND	
FRIENDSHIP QUALITIES	PERCENTAGE OF RESPONDENTS
1. Ability to keep confidences	89%
2. Loyalty	88
3. Warmth, affection	82
4. Supportiveness	76
5. Frankness	75
6. Sense of humor	74
7. Willingness to make time for me	62
8. Independence	61
9. Conversational skills	59
10. Intelligence	57

Source: Based on data from M. Parlee (1979), The friendship bond, *Psychology Today*, 13(10), 43–54, 113.

Receptivity

In **receptivity** there is a definite imbalance in the giving and taking, with one partner being the primary giver and the other the primary taker. However, this is not always a bad arrangement. The needs of each person can be met through the particular roles played. This type of friendship is often seen between individuals of different status. Dan is a teaching assistant for a class that Mark is taking. Mark is on the baseball team and traveling causes him to miss several classes. Mark must meet with Dan every time he misses class to get the information he needs, and through their frequent meetings the two have become friends. Mark is using Dan's access to information and Dan is not receiving anything from Mark in return, yet they still value each other's friendship.

Association

Association might be seen as a relationship with an acquaintance rather than as a true friendship. An associative friendship is most likely to develop between people who have frequent contact—for example, co-workers, classmates, and neighbors. Holly and Susan are in three classes together, and throughout the semester the two have become friends. Even though they do not do anything together outside class, they still consider each other friends.

Family

Whom do you consider your family? Whether it's your immediate family of father, mother, sisters, and brothers, or perhaps a more extended family including your grandparents, aunts, uncles, and cousins, you have relational and blood ties to other people whom you call family. Although families at times can be one of the biggest sources of stress and difficulty in your life, they can also be one of the greatest joys. Definitions of family range anywhere from all the people living in the same household to all those claiming descent from the same ancestor. For the purposes of this section, Nass and McDonald's definition is used.[27] They define a **family** as "a social group having specified roles and statuses (e.g., husband, wife, father, mother, son, daughter) with ties of blood, marriage, or adoption who usually share a common residence and cooperate economically."

Family members do a number of things that require competent communication. Since family provides much of the nurturing humans require in life, many of the family members' interactions are in support of one another. Healthy families strive for effective communication in ensuring mental, intellectual, and emotional growth, promoting family ties, and helping each other to succeed in their goals. It is through communication that families generate their strengths. The following section outlines the communication functions of family members.[28]

Functions of Families

Provision of Care

At the time of birth, a human infant is unable to care for him- or herself; a family is needed to ensure the infant's survival. The family fulfills needs such as food, shelter, clothing, and basic caretaking. Without the family, infants and most young children would be helpless. Older family members also require care. As more people live longer lives, their need for daily care increases. Whether older adults live within the household of an offspring, as in an extended family, or live elsewhere, their care usually falls to the family. Competent communication can be more difficult in the case of older adults but is still important at this stage of family development.

Socialization

Long before children enter school, they begin to learn important basic lessons. They learn about the behavioral differences between humans and animals, honesty and dishonesty, niceness and meanness, and so on. The family helps the child to discover what is appropriate behavior. Many of the beliefs and values you hold are shaped and influenced by your family through a process of observation and cultivation. Younger family members watch parents and older siblings as they interact with others in various contexts, learning how to handle themselves and other people in social situations. Family members also help to cultivate social skills in younger children through instructive and corrective communication practices.

Intellectual Development

The child's intellectual development is not stressed as much in some families as it is in others. As stated earlier, children begin learning before they ever enter a classroom. The family influences the child's opinions of learning and school in general. If the children perceive that their family sees education as extremely important, then they will understand the need or desire to study and make good grades. Children who believe that their family does not have a high opinion of education are not likely to exert much effort to further their knowledge. In addition, families can serve as a catalyst for learning by helping with homework, making applications to the real world, and attending school functions.

Recreation

Many families engage in activities that they enjoy doing together. Sports, working in the yard, or just lounging together on a lazy Sunday afternoon provide recreational opportunities for many family members.

FIGURE 7.7
*The family is the first
and most important
agent for developing a
person's values,
beliefs, and customs.*

Recreation also gives family members a chance to interact with one another in a unique context. Watching an otherwise quiet son become enthusiastic and cheer at a football game demonstrates a communication style seldom seen by his family members. Finally, recreational time can greatly influence the closeness of the family.

Transmission

The family is the medium through which family customs or basic cultural guidelines can be passed from one generation to the next. Children learn different ideas from a variety of sources: games, books, television, and the like, but the family can be helpful in explaining these ideas and introducing different concepts. Children tend to imitate their parents and other family members, so that many will arrange their homes like that of their parents, buy the same brands, or even vote for the same political candidate other members of their family vote for. When family members communicate stories about their parents, grandparents, and great grandparents, younger members get a sense of history and pride about the family lineage and want to help perpetuate family strength. In this way, transmission becomes an important communication function for many families.

Improving Family Relations

Just about every family could improve the relationships among its members. Today families face a host of communication challenges as they attempt to succeed in their busy lives. It takes a great deal of communication effort to ensure that family members use their relationships to maximum benefit. Here are several recommendations that will help enrich family relationships through competent communication.

Family Functions in the Media and Your Life

Watch a recent movie or an episode of a television program depicting a family. You can even select one of your favorite sitcom programs. List the various functions the "media family" demonstrates. How effective are the members' communication styles in serving these family functions? Now describe how your own family performs each item on the list of functions. Is the media family unrealistic in its portrayal of family life? Are there lessons to be learned from the media about communicating effectively within families?

EMPATHY
The understanding one has of another's experience.

Put yourself in their place. **Empathy** is the understanding you have of another's experience. To understand what a family member is feeling or experiencing, the others must show some degree of empathy, not just sympathy.

Let others know how you feel. Family members must be able to tell or show one another how they are feeling. If one member is hurt and angry about something that happened at school, the others will not know exactly what is wrong unless they are told. If the hurt individual keeps this feeling to him- or herself and just acts mad and upset, others may perceive that this anger is directed toward something they did. So allow others to know what is happening.

Be flexible. Relationships are constantly developing and moving from one stage to another, and relationships within a family are no exception. As each member grows and develops, so will the relationships with others. For example, a daughter in the family may be extremely close to her father at the age of 10, but at the age of 16 she may become significantly closer to her mother. The parents must recognize this change as normal and must not see it as a failing on their part.

Fight fairly. Conflict is present in all relationships and sometimes more so in families. Family members need to learn how to fight fairly without unnecessarily hurting the feelings of someone who does not deserve it. Fighting fairly means listening to the other person and at least attempting to understand the other person's point of view. You do not have to agree with that person's position, but it is only fair to know how the person feels. Fighting fairly also means that the family does not hit below the belt or gang up on one another. Families must recognize the importance of compromise and understand that there does not always have to be a definite winner and loser.

Give as much as you take. Each individual needs to try to recognize when he or she is demanding too much of the other members of the family. Everyone has times when they are allowed to take more than given, but then there are also times when people must give more than they take. Be reasonable in all that you do. Don't demand something from your family that is ridiculously out of the question. Remember, how would you like it if they expected or demanded that something from you?

Competent Relationships

Many of the experts on television and in self-help books seem to think that there is a simple formula that will produce a long and happy relationship. As any happy couple will tell you, however, their relationship took a lot of time and understanding to build. One analogy often made is that a relationship is like a house that you must build from the ground up. A solid foundation is required for a solid, secure house, just as a solid foundation is needed for a solid, lasting relationship. A competent relationship is based on three main components: the characteristics of each relational partner, the relationship itself, and each partner's own relational history.

According to the model of communicative competence, each relational partner brings a unique set of personal characteristics to the relationship, including behaviors, communication styles, values, cultural identity, perceptions, memories, and attributions. Although each partner must contribute to the relationship in these areas, each must also continue to develop these same areas in his or her own self-concept and perceptions of the world. It is also important that each relational partner cognitively understand how he or she fits into the relationship and into the world. These values and ideas that each partner brings to the relationship are used to develop perceptions of the relational partner and of self. From these perceptions, you can develop realistic expectations of your partner, your relationship, and yourself in the relationship. These perceptions and values, then, provide the tools that help you make the relationship work.

Two types of expectations are inherent in every relationship: current expectations and future expectations. *Current expectations* and goals are often developed through daily interactions and conversations with relational partners. In contrast, expectations for the future are not discussed on a daily basis. Often *future expectations* are expressed internally and are given a great deal of thought before they are actually expressed. The expression of expectations can give the relationship a clearer direction and set of goals, assuming both partners can agree on the direction to take.

Each individual also brings his or her own relational history into the relationship. This can be both a benefit and a hindrance. Although you should learn from your mistakes, you may often find yourself dwelling on the past and concentrating too much on not repeating the mistakes you made in a previous relationship in the present one instead of enjoying the current relationship as it develops. You may even become paranoid about making the same mistakes over and over again.

Every component that has been mentioned is greatly influenced by the culture in which it exists. A culture or society gives the "dos and don'ts" by which the relational partners may feel they should abide. The culture sets up the standards of what a "normal" relationship should be like, and often, if a relationship does not fit into society's mold, the partners may feel it is unsuccessful.

REVIEW

This chapter focused on developing, maintaining, repairing, and possibly ending relationships with other people. Relational knowledge, goals and motivations, and relational expectations constitute the preliminary processes that determine how and why people develop interpersonal relationships. The influences in forming relationships are interpersonal attraction, physical proximity, attitude similarity, alleviation of loneliness, stimulation, self-learning, and achievement of goals. Costs and rewards play an important role in the life of a relationship. Rewards are those aspects of the relationship that are valued, whereas costs are burdens to the relationship. Three categories of rewards are extrinsic, instrumental, and intrinsic. If costs exceed rewards, a relationship will not develop and be maintained as well as a relationship that enjoys a higher percentage of rewards. Uncertainty reduction is a process that helps relational partners to understand one another better. You can reduce uncertainty

through monitoring, proactive, and indirect strategies. As you reduce uncertainty, your ability to predict your relational partner is enhanced, facilitating the development of intimacy.

The model of interpersonal relationship development was proposed to explain the stages that relationships can go through. Relationships begin in the initiation stage, when acquaintances are formed. Uncertainty reduction occurs as relational partners attempt to determine whether this relationship is worth the effort (costs vs. rewards). If costs seem to exceed rewards, the relationship is likely to go into the decline stage and may eventually terminate (exit). If rewards exceed costs, the relationship has a much better chance of developing further. Subsequent stages of development are the exploratory, intensification, and stable phases, all of which are dependent on uncertainty reduction and assessments of rewards and costs. All the while a relationship develops, evaluations and modifications are made by relational partners in the areas of relational knowledge, motives and goals, and relational expectations. As these change with time and relational maturity, so too can costs and rewards change. If relationships do decline and cannot be repaired, termination strategies may be used to exit the relationship.

Friendship and families are specific types of relationships. Friendship is a special instance of relationships and includes a number of important qualities or characteristics that are meaningful to communicators, such as caring, honesty, loyalty, confidentiality, understanding, empathy, and availability. Families, like friendships, are important relationships. Families serve several important social and communication functions, including socialization and intellectual development, recreational needs, provision of care, and transmission.

SUGGESTED READINGS

Canary, D. J., & Cody, M. J. (1994). *Interpersonal communication: A goals-based approach.* New York: St. Martin's Press.

Duck, S. W. Issues in the series *Interpersonal relationships.* Beverly Hills, CA: Sage.

Knapp, M. L., & Miller, G. R. (1985). *Handbook of interpersonal communication.* Beverly Hills, CA: Sage.

Rawlins, W. (1992). *Friendship matters.* New York: Aldine de Gauthier.

Stewart, J. (1990). *Bridges, not walls.* New York: McGraw-Hill.

8

Managing Conflict in Interpersonal Relationships

Objectives

After reading this chapter, you should be able to

1. Identify four conditions that produce interpersonal conflict.

2. List four reasons why conflict is an inevitable and healthy communication strategy.

3. Describe the six stages of the model for conflict management.

4. Illustrate how you can develop a more competent conflict management style by using the model.

CHAPTER CONTENTS

YOU SHOULD PAY special attention to the title of this chapter. The goal of this chapter is to impress upon you the idea that competent interpersonal communicators *manage*, rather than minimize or eliminate, conflict in their relationships with others. You may think of managing conflict as bargaining, negotiating, debating, or arguing. When two people communicate while holding different positions on an issue, conflict occurs. This chapter emphasizes several strategies that help you manage conflict. Before presenting these strategies, however, we discuss how conflict is produced and why interpersonal relationships are stronger when they operate with productive conflict. First, however, conflict needs to be defined.

CONFLICT
A struggle between two or more interdependent parties who perceive incompatible goals, scarce rewards, and interference from the other party or parties in achieving their goals.

Conflict is defined by Hocker and Wilmot as "an expressed struggle between at least two interdependent parties who perceive incompatible goals, scarce rewards, and interference from the other party in achieving their goals."[1] There will be many instances in your life when you and another person or persons will have conflicting goals, or when you will face competition for scarce resources. You will even encounter people who will attempt to thwart your efforts to achieve important goals.

Conditions Producing Interpersonal Conflict

If you consider all the aspects of your relationships with other people, conflict is probably the issue that you have the least positive thoughts about. After all, you may think, "Who enjoys fighting and arguing?" Before assuming that conflict is necessarily negative, however, this section examines several reasons why conflict occurs in relationships in the first place. These include incompatible goals, unrealistic expectations, disparate relational growth, and inaccurate perceptions and attributions.

Incompatible Goals

When two people who must coordinate activities have different ideas about an outcome or end result, conflict is likely to arise. Here's a cultural conflict example. Blas Gomez and John Anders are social coordinators for their children's eighth grade Bar-Be-Que Bash. Blas, a native of Bogotá, Colombia, has one set of values about the function, and John, a native Californian, has another. Blas was raised to believe that 13-year-old students should be separated by gender, and John's North American culture encourages boys and girls of that age group to "mix and mingle."

These two very different outlooks require highly different strategies. Blas and John will likely conflict on many issues as they work together. Some of these issues include how to handle the segregation of genders and which group of children should enter the food line first. Whether Blas and John can manage their incompatible goals depends on the communication strategies they use.

Unrealistic Expectations

Conflict can also arise when one or both parties in a relationship have unrealistic expectations. You may know of an instance in which a head football coach, in his first year, expected to reach the playoffs. His main assistant coach, who had been on the staff more than ten years, considered the goal optimistic but unrealistic.

The assistant coach argued that the football team was young and inexperienced, that the players would need some time to adjust to a new strategic philosophy, and that the team had a difficult schedule. Numerous conflicts occurred all year between the two coaches because of their different expectations. While one coach would push fundamentals and mastery of basic skills, the other would push the execution of trick plays to ensure victory.

Differing Rates of Relational Growth

Conflict also occurs when two partners view their relationship as being at different levels of development. As an example, look at a romantic relationship. A couple has been dating for just under two years. Ricky views the relationship as very serious, having developed strong feelings of love and bonding, anticipating that this is the beginning of a long and happy future together. Shawna views the relationship as primarily "fun." She thinks the couple is just dating, without a long-term commitment or strong expectations for the future.

There can be little question that these partners have progressed in the relationship very differently. You can imagine the many conflicts that will surface between them. There are likely to be disagreements about sex, gifts, attendance at family outings, labels for each other, and even what to say to others about the nature of the relationship.

Relational growth may vary between relational partners because of external factors as well. If one person decides to earn a master's degree and develops an appreciation for a specialized area, say art, the relational partner may not know how to accommodate these new needs. Other examples of external factors affect relational growth differently. Maturity levels, new friends, and renewed friendships with old acquaintances can cause one partner to view the relationship in a new way.

Inaccurate Perceptions and Attributions

You have already seen the power of perception in Chapter 2. How and what you perceive frequently dictate your impressions, behaviors, and activities. If you are wrong, you are likely to invoke conflict. Consider this incident in which a supervisor, Terry, misperceived two of his newer employees, Bill and John. Terry had heard reports from various people in the company who knew Bill. These reports suggested that Bill was a very bright guy. John had worked in several different departments in the company before reporting to Terry and, unlike Bill, had the reputation of being slow. In actuality, these labels were not only inaccurate but also reversed. John was the bright one, and Bill was slow. Can you imagine the conflicts that occurred after Terry asked John a question? Rather than deliver a rapid-fire response to Terry, John paused and considered options or implications. Terry interpreted this delay as indicative of John's lack of intelligence. Incorrect perceptions about someone else's ability, personality, or behavior can produce serious conflict because people generally are quick to defend themselves in the face of inaccuracies.

Cultural Differences in Handling Conflict

Interpersonal conflict is not always viewed in the same way by everyone. Some cultural differences exist in defining and dealing with conflict. Ting-Toomey suggests that high- and low-context cultures manage conflict quite differently.[2] Recall that high-context cultures are those in which communication is indirect, relies heavily on nonverbal systems, and gives a great deal of meaning to the relationships between communicators. The Japanese, African American, and Latin American cultures are examples of high-context cultures. Low-context cultures use more explicit language, are more direct in their meanings, and stress goals and outcomes more than relationships. Examples include the German, Swedish, and English cultures. Conflict managers in high-context cultures are more likely to emphasize harmonious relations than personal goals. They will also attempt to maintain "face" for both themselves and the other people in the conflict. Their communication style is more likely to be nonconfrontational, indirect, and concealing. Communicators in low-context cultures manage conflict more directly by being more confrontational and more goal-oriented rather than being relationally focused, and they have less concern about "saving face." You can probably imagine that low-context conflict is more open, volatile, and threatening. Have you seen instances where people who live in a low-context culture manage conflict as if they lived in a high-context culture?

Conflict as Inevitable and Healthy Communication

Conflict is a common type of communication. You will encounter it often as you go through life. Regardless of how conflict arises, relationships are stronger when they are managed openly and productively. To begin the discussion of productive conflict, consider some of the assumptions people make about interpersonal conflict. List some of the words and phrases you usually associate with conflict. Does your list contain some of the following behaviors?

Heated emotions	Hot temper	Intolerance
Shouting	Red faces	Clenched fists
Uncontrolled arguing	Frustration	"In-your-face" behavior

If so, you are certainly not alone. These are the behaviors that most people commonly associate with conflict. Think of people who either get defensive quickly or who "cannot take a joke" or who take everything "too seriously." Those who act in these ways are prime candidates for unproductive conflict.

You may see many of these behaviors on a baseball field when a manager disputes an umpire's call. In many cases, these behaviors result in the ejection of the manager from the game. You probably see many of these behaviors in normal disputes between two or more people.

The point to stress here is that, although these behaviors may be associated with conflict in some relationships, they do not necessarily have to be present in all of them. You manage conflict by engaging in it productively. *Productive conflict* is based on issues rather than on the participants' personalities. It can and should be conducted without any of these behaviors. Furthermore, when behaviors such as those listed previously are present, the real purpose of conflict is weakened considerably. This is true because the focus of the conflict turns to individual variables and away from actual issues. A focus on issues is the key to competent conflict management.

If, like many people, you have a negative attitude toward conflict, try to keep an open mind as this subject is discussed. Be willing to believe that conflict can be productive rather than destructive. To do so, you need to consider the positive outcomes that can result when two people disagree and argue. Here are two advantages of conflict: decision making and enjoyment of conflict.

FIGURE 8.1
*To be productive,
conflict must focus
on issues rather than
personalities.*

Decision Making

The primary positive outcome of productive conflict is a better decision. When two people get together and fully debate an issue, the chance is far greater that a quality decision will be made. Why? Because conflict provides an arena in which ideas can be tested. Proposed solutions that are logical, workable, economical, and reasonable will stand up during the course of an argument; weaker solutions are likely to be exposed during debate as flawed.

Jack and Jennifer have been renting a duplex for the last five years of their seven-year marriage. Jack believes that it is now time for the couple to purchase a small home and begin to reap the rewards of that housing investment. If Jennifer wants to avoid conflict, she will respond simply "Sure" or "Let's do it." However, this may result in the couple's making a bad decision. In a discussion with Jack, Jennifer points out that they have only a limited amount of money in reserve, which the required down payment would significantly diminish; that interest rates are higher now than they are projected to be in the future; that at this time they could afford only a home that would be smaller than their current needs demand; and that the current housing market is to a seller's, not a buyer's, advantage. Through debate, argument, and conflict, Jack and Jennifer finally decide that they will wait two years to make a home purchase and that they will put $300 per month in a special savings account earmarked for that purchase. Only through conflict did the flaws in Jack's original proposal emerge. He certainly is glad Jennifer spoke up.

Conflict is the essence of decision-making meetings. Decisions are made primarily through conflict of issues arising out of competent communication. This is true whether the relationship is boss–employee, husband–wife, doctor–patient, or any other type of relationship. In fact, if two people who meet to make an important decision are unwilling to engage in conflict or at least consider opposing views, they should not be meeting in the first place. One person should simply have made the decision individually.

Strong relationships are those in which productive conflict is provoked rather than suppressed or avoided. Managing conflict, therefore, requires that the participants introduce and use conflict as a means of reaching satisfying decisions.

▨ Enjoyment of Conflict

In order to believe that conflict can be productive rather than destructive, you have to actively engage in, and even provoke conflict, rather than avoid it. Do you have a friend with whom you really enjoy sitting down and debating a topic? That's great. There is no greater intellectual exercise than exploring and testing ideas with another person. If you are interested in politics, discuss your party's philosophies with one of your friends who is a staunch supporter of the opposition. Through this exchange of conflict, you can have fun and learn a great deal. The key to success in doing this is to avoid taking your partner's arguments personally.

You might even think of conflict as a sport in which ideas, rather than a ball, are tossed between the participants. Healthy attitudes toward conflict are marked by a special kind of enjoyment that is created when two participants share ideas.

▨ Relational Growth

Conflict helps a relationship develop. As two people begin to explore issues together, trust and respect are fostered. For example, Jim didn't like the way Mary shopped for groceries. He always thought she spent too much. Mary had always believed that quality products simply cost more. When Jim confronted Mary on the issue and they discussed it, Mary's respect and attraction for Jim increased dramatically. Mary's desires to please herself and her partner were virtually equal, and Jim's concern helped build a communication style they had not previously explored. To discover that there were ways that both partners could be satisfied was attractive to them both. The relationship seemed to come alive in ways that would have never occurred without conflict. As a result, the couple began to talk about and work through more issues than they ever had before. Rather than have a relationship in which either partner suppressed feelings, anger, or resentment, the couple was much more open, which led to a stronger, healthier union.

■ Time

You may think that you save time when you reach a decision without questioning, arguing, or debating. That is certainly true. Meetings in which conflict is suppressed or avoided are shorter than those in which conflict is encouraged and allowed to run its course. Unfortunately, many decisions made in the absence of conflict are poor and require much more time later to correct. Had the time been taken at the outset to make a proper decision through productive conflict, less time would have been spent in the long term.

Several years ago, in a major company, a decision was reached to radically alter the way presentations were made to major customers and suppliers. For years, the accepted and practiced style was to present information on slides, using two screens, projecting one image to the left of the speaker and another separate image on the screen to the right. One day, a top executive made a unilateral decision that all presentations in the company would be given using only one screen and one projected image at a time.

After the order was implemented, problems cropped up immediately. Speakers who had used the old style for years had great difficulty adapting to the new technique. Standard presentations that were established for the two-screen method had to be reorganized to fit the new format. Even the seating arrangements for large meetings had to be altered so that everyone could see a single screen. After the new method had been in use for about eighteen months, a task force was created to review the decision. When the committee recommended a return to the old format, everyone accepted it. Permanent presentations that had been created in this interim period

---

SELF-CHECK

What Kinds of Conflict Have You Experienced?

- What was your best fighting experience? Your worst? Why?

- Have you ever experienced a conflict owing to different cultural ideas? How did you handle it? What would you do differently?

- Do you find yourself having more conflicts with people of the same or the opposite sex? Do you keep special concerns in mind during a conflict with a person of the opposite sex?

- How do you determine whether a fighting experience is a good or a bad one?

had to be reorganized. Managers who had joined the company in the last year and a half and were going to be giving presentations with the old two-screen format that *they* had never used had to undergo special training. Much time and effort could have been saved had the task force met at the outset to study the issue. Through productive conflict, debate, and argument, the group could have uncovered the flaws in the proposed one-screen design.

A Model of Competent Conflict Management

Competent, productive conflict can be divided into six distinct phases that adequately summarize how the competent communicator manages conflict. Approaching and engaging in conflict through this systematic manner will cause you to operate rationally rather than emotionally. Moreover, you are more likely to approach the topic proactively than reactively. Finally, and most important, you will focus the conflict on the issue and not on the other person. The remainder of this chapter examines these six phases: prelude, assessment, engagement, action, decision, and reflection.

Prelude

Conflict does not simply "happen." As you have seen, conflict has many sources. In addition, you and your conflict partners bring your own personality traits, tendencies, predispositions, and conflict styles to conflict episodes. You also cannot forget that conflict takes place within a relational context. The status of your relationship is a very important factor that can affect many of the conflict behaviors discussed in this chapter.

The first phase of conflict actually begins before any words are spoken. For example, traits, the relationship that provides the context and the predispositions, and tendencies you have in approaching your partner's style affect everything that occurs in a conflict situation.

Traits

Several traits (argumentativeness, verbal aggressiveness, and anxiety) play a key role in conflict situations. **Traits** refer to individual characteristics that typically do not vary from situation to situation; they are either physical

TRAITS
Individual physical and psychological characteristics that typically do not vary from situation to situation.

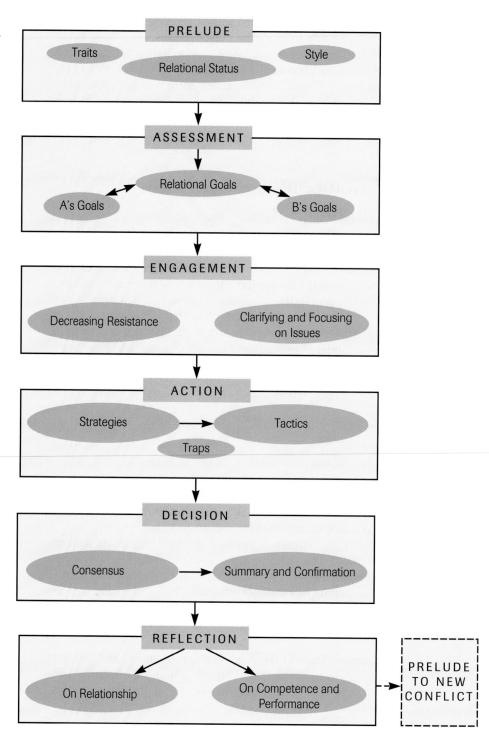

FIGURE 8.2
A model of competent conflict management.

PRELUDE

Traits

Relational Status

Style

ASSESSMENT

Relational Goals

A's Goals

B's Goals

ENGAGEMENT

Decreasing Resistance

Clarifying and Focusing on Issues

ACTION

Strategies

Tactics

Traps

DECISION

Consensus

Summary and Confirmation

REFLECTION

On Relationship

On Competence and Performance

PRELUDE TO NEW CONFLICT

(height, weight, eyesight) or psychological (open-mindedness, friendliness, intelligence).

Argumentativeness

In several studies, Infante and a number of his colleagues have linked personality and attempts to persuade others. One of the personality traits they have studied is **argumentativeness**. People who are highly argumentative typically do the following three things:

ARGUMENTATIVENESS
A conflict style that seeks out controversial issues and revels in debating them.

- Recognize issues that are "ripe" for controversy.
- Take positions on those issues and provide evidence and reasoning to support the positions.
- Refute others' positions if these are counter to the arguer's.

The more an individual uses these three behaviors, the more argumentative this person is. Conversely, the less someone engages in these behaviors, the less argumentative he or she is.

This trait is issue-focused, not person-focused. As a result, those individuals who enjoy arguing or debating with others on issues are likely also to be favorably disposed to productive conflict. They look for and engage in conflict on many issues. Argumentativeness is thus a positive trait for individuals to exhibit in conflict situations.

Verbal Aggressiveness

Verbal aggressiveness is a negative trait for individuals to exhibit in conflict situations. People who are verbally aggressive focus their arguments on individuals in addition to, or instead of, on issues.

VERBAL AGGRESSIVENESS
A conflict style that involves attacking the other party's self-concept.

When you are in a conflict situation with a person who is verbally aggressive, you typically encounter undesirable behaviors, especially name-calling, "mudslinging," or the reintroduction of downgrading examples from the relationship's past. One study by Infante and Wigely found that people who are deficient in argumentative skills often resort to verbal aggressiveness, for personal attacks may be the only way they can deal with another person in a conflict situation.[3]

People who are verbally aggressive typically shift the conflict away from issues and toward the participants as individuals. Demonstrating verbal aggressiveness toward your partner in a conflict situation is destructive, not productive. In fact, this trait is the *opposite* of a competency to be used in conflict situations.

To make sure that you see the difference between argumentativeness and verbal aggressiveness, suppose that two custodial supervisors are discussing whether or not only English should be spoken in the workplace. They have opposing views: Ms. Sanders believes that if people want to live and work in North America, they should speak English, whereas Ms. King believes that the mixture of ethnicities is what makes North America unique.

MS. SANDERS   If foreigners want to live in the United States, they should speak my language. I want to know if they're talking and laughing about me when I pass by them. It's like these people have their own code.

MS. KING   As far as I'm concerned, if they perform their work on time and we're able to communicate in a working situation, they can speak, sing, or whistle their native tongue while performing their tasks.

MS. SANDERS   Well, you must be an anti-American foreigner lover.

MS. KING   I believe that since we all originated from various continents, we're all foreigners, except for the Native Americans.

People in conflict must take the high road and use argumentativeness instead of aggressiveness. A focus on the issue and not the person is the key to productive conflict management. Issues can be left at the conflict table, and two people can carry on their relationships in a normal manner. Personality attacks are rarely forgotten and often become part of the relationship.

Anxiety

Another trait that affects conflict is the degree to which one or more of the partners possesses communication anxiety, or communication apprehension. McCroskey has defined **communication apprehension (CA)** as fear or anxiety about real or anticipated communication with another person or persons.[4] One or more of the partners may possess good arguments, rational data, exceptional reasoning, and strong stances, but may simply be too apprehensive to deliver them.

Still another type of anxiety that can affect conflict is the degree to which one partner believes that the relationship is too frail to withstand excessive argument. Typically, you will find this kind of person avoiding conflict rather than provoking or extending it. If the conflict is productive and issue-based as opposed to destructive and person-based, this anxiety is usually unfounded. As stated in Chapter 7, productive conflict actually strengthens relationships.

When you do experience anxiety about conflict, there are a few things you can do to minimize its effects. First, take some deep breaths and revive yourself with fresh oxygen. Next, alternately tense and relax those muscles that feel stiff from anxiety. Attempt to make your body as relaxed as possi-

COMMUNICATION APPREHENSION (CA)
Fear or anxiety associated with real or anticipated communication with another person or persons.

Hitting Above and Below the Belt

The concepts of argumentativeness and verbal aggressiveness are important to the study of conflict management because the first is more likely to produce positive consequences than the second. Examine the items below and mark each one according to how you feel about most conflicts (1 = true; 2 = undecided; 3 = false).

_____ 1. Arguing over controversial issues improves my intelligence.

_____ 2. I really come down hard on people if they don't see things my way.

_____ 3. I am good about not losing my temper during conflict situations.

_____ 4. Some people need to be insulted if they are to see reason.

_____ 5. I prefer being with people who disagree with me.

_____ 6. It is exhilarating to get into a good conflict.

_____ 7. I have the ability to do well in conflict situations.

_____ 8. It is not hard for me to go for the jugular if a person really deserves it.

_____ 9. I know how to construct effective arguments that can change people's minds.

_____ 10. I avoid getting into conflicts with people who know how to argue well.

_____ 11. I know how to find other people's personal weaknesses.

Scoring: Add your scores for items 1, 3, 5, 6, 7, and 9. Reverse your scores for the following items: 2, 4, 8, 10, 11 (1 = 3, 3 = 1). After converting the numbers, add all of these scores to your previous total. If you scored between 11 and 18, you are prone to argumentativeness. If you scored between 26 and 33, you are likely to be verbally aggressive when you are in conflict situations. If you scored between 19 and 25, you are probably neither very argumentative nor very aggressive.

Source: Adapted from D. Infante (1988), *Arguing constructively* (Prospect Heights, IL: Waveland Press).

ble. The next step is to view your conflict with another person as an opportunity, and not as a threat. Certainly, there are going to be some tough moments during a bona fide conflict, but handling these situations will develop your confidence for future conflicts. Recognizing conflict as a communication opportunity, rather than as a personal sacrifice, will go a long way toward minimizing your fears. Finally, understand that you are going to win some conflicts and that you are going to lose some. There is no disgrace in realizing that you can be wrong sometimes. As long as you view conflict productively, losing to a conflict partner may actually increase that person's opinion of you. Competent and gracious losers are some of the most admired people in the world.

Relational Status

A major factor that can produce profound differences in conflict is the status of the relationship. In the last chapter, we made a distinction between how relational partners perceive each other and how they perceive the "relationship." It is important to consider the relationship as a factor in viewing conflict, if for no other reason than the fact that relationships change as a result of how conflict is handled. As you refine your relational schemata about another person, you gain a greater understanding of the importance of three factors relating to conflict and relationships: valence, stability, and power.

Valence

As you recall from Chapter 3, *valence* refers to the feelings of satisfaction with the communication that takes place in the relationship. When the partners in a relationship are satisfied and pleased with their interaction, the communication has a positive valence. Conversely, if the interaction produces dissatisfaction and displeasure, communication has a negative valence.

Three different pairs of valences are possible in a relationship, and conflict is affected differently by each. One possibility is that both participants are dissatisfied with the communication that takes place in the relationship. In this kind of context, conflict is likely to fare very poorly. Because the partners do not even enjoy talking with each other under nonargumentative or nonconfrontive circumstances, the topics on which they have conflict are not likely to produce enjoyment either. How do you handle conflict with a person you do not particularly like? Think to yourself how much you have to lose by engaging in productive conflict with this person. Actually, if you already don't like one another, you probably have very little to lose through conflict, at least from a relational perspective. You might also examine what it is that you do not like about this relationship. You will probably be able to separate your relational feelings from the issues producing the conflict.

Second, when one participant is happy with the communication in the relationship and the other is not, any conflict that occurs is either going to help strengthen the bonds between the two (as in the case of Jim's dissatisfaction with Mary's shopping habits in the section "Relational Growth" earlier in this chapter) or weaken the ties between them. It is not always easy to know another person's attitude about his or her relationship with you. Sometimes you have to guess, but it is important to understand that varying relational views produce different conflict patterns. A conflict partner unconcerned about relational consequences will fight more aggressively than someone who cares about the relationship.

Third, when both partners are pleased with the communication between them, valence is at its highest and productive conflict has an excellent chance of succeeding. Liking someone helps to reduce the possibility of verbal aggressiveness and will promote instances of beneficial argumentation. You do have to be careful about these types of relationships. You should take one caution here, however. You do not want to be so overprotective of a particular relationship that you avoid conflict in order to preserve your relational status. Productive conflict management is an essential part of all relationships, even the good ones.

Stability

The degree to which the relationship experiences "peaks and valleys" is the measure of its *stability.* All relationships have good times and bad times as well as ups and downs. The more consistent a relationship is, the more stability it has. Over time, unstable relationships usually disintegrate. Usually one or both partners quickly tire of the unpredictability that accompanies unstable relationships. Of course, you hope that relationships stabilize on the positive side.

The implication for conflict is that stable relationships provide the best context for productive argument. When a relationship is typically consis-

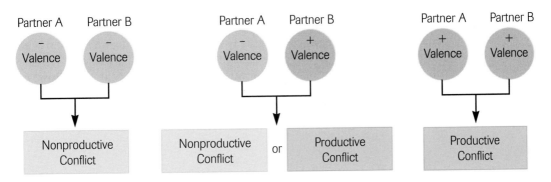

FIGURE 8.3
A positive valence in a communication partner's satisfaction with the relationship contributes to productive conflict, and a negative valence promotes nonproductive conflict.

tent in its experiences, and the partners are consistent in their reactions to each other's communication, productive conflict can thrive. When a relationship is virtually unpredictable, who knows what impact the conflict will have? On one day, conflict over spending money could result in the planning of a budget and a commitment by both partners to stick with it. Yet on another day, conflict on the same topic could result in an eruption of emotion and tension, including such remarks as "If you don't like the way I spend our money, then I'll just spend *my* money the way I want to." The best course of action is to determine what the relational status is at a particular time and then decide if conflict is the best communication strategy. Sometimes it is best to put off conflict until just the right moment.

Power

The last factor regarding relational status is *power*. When one partner has power over another, this kind of conflict is likely to be very different from conflict between equals. Consider, for example, the case of the boss and the employee in any company or business. Because the boss has the responsibility for hiring employees, setting salaries, determining schedules, and assigning tasks, he or she has considerable power over an employee. Invariably, you will find that the employees will initiate less conflict with the boss than the boss will with the employees. You will also find that the employees are likely to agree much more. To behave differently could produce undesirable outcomes for the employees.

Conversely, consider conflict between peers. Look at the example of two employees who work for the same boss. Because they have equal status, there is very little that one partner could "hold" over the other. As a result, both partners would likely initiate conflict at about the same rate. The refutation, argument, debate, and questioning that take place would be much more open and profound. Any consenting would occur because one partner was convinced of an argument, not because the other had power.

Power is not limited to simple hierarchical differences. Remember that people have power because you give it to them. Therefore, any person who controls resources that you desire has power over you. This is true whether the partner controls money you want, equipment you want to borrow, or even sex. Conflict with a person who holds power over you for these or any other reason will likely be very different from situations when the status is equal.

Style

Every individual who engages in conflict prefers certain behaviors over others. This preference in conflict behaviors defines your *style*. Hall has identified five different ways in which conflict styles operate:[5]

Win-lose, which emphasizes and protects the individual's personal goals to the exclusion of the relationship.

Yield-lose, which sacrifices personal goals and maintains those of the relationship, even at a high cost to the individual.

Lose-leave, which characterizes a hopeless attitude toward conflict and emphasizes neither personal nor relational goals.

Compromise, which seeks to soften the outcomes of losing by moderating the benefits of winning.

Synergistic, or cooperating, which places equal emphasis on relationship and personal goals.

You will notice that all these styles are attitudes; they are not the behaviors themselves. The assumption people make is that if they possess attitudes to act a certain way in a conflict situation, their behavior should follow accordingly. What are some of the behaviors that you would think would follow for each of the five styles noted above? There are probably no correct answers, but you can speculate about what most people would do in conflict situations with each of these tendencies. A person with *yield-lose* or *compromise* tendencies would probably not prolong any argument. This person would likely state a position but give in upon hearing a countering position. Someone with a *lose-leave* predisposition may place so little value on conflict that he or she may not even advance an initial position. What about a person with a *win-lose* style? You would certainly see much persistence and perhaps some irrationality as the individual continued to press for what he or she wanted out of the conflict. Most likely, an individual who operates from a *synergistic* or working-together predisposition will ask several questions of the other person in an attempt to assess the best possible outcome for both parties and the relationship in general.

SELF-CHECK

What Is Your Conflict Style?

Of the five conflict styles identified by Hall, which do you think best characterizes your own feelings toward conflict? How do you usually approach a conflict situation, and what behaviors do you usually enact from your perspective? Share your experiences with some of your classmates. Do you find that you share other traits with people who share your conflict style? Interview a trusted friend about his or her conflict style. Compare and contrast it with your own style. Are the five conflict styles used worldwide?

Another set of conflict styles is assessed by the Thomas-Kilmann Conflict Management of Differences (MODE) survey.6 The five styles vary according to the degree to which the individual is assertive or cooperative. **Assertiveness** is defined as emphasizing your own concerns and taking action to achieve your goals; **cooperativeness** is defined as emphasizing the other's concerns and working toward shared goals. The five styles are:

Collaborating (highly assertive and cooperative)

Compromising (moderately assertive and cooperative)

Competing (assertive and uncooperative)

Accommodating (unassertive and cooperative)

Avoiding (unassertive and uncooperative)

Although there are some people and some topics for which you may vary your conflict style, for the most part people are fairly consistent. The biggest factor that produces a change in style is probably the degree to which the topic or person is important to you. You may find, for example, that you behave differently in conflicts that arise over ideas about where you should live once you graduate versus what kind of movie you should attend. You may also find that you behave differently in conflicts with your

ASSERTIVENESS
A conflict style that emphasizes personal concerns.

COOPERATIVENESS
A conflict style that emphasizes the other's concerns.

FIGURE 8.4
The Thomas-Kilmann Conflict Management of Differences (MODE) Survey identifies five styles according to their degree of assertiveness and cooperativeness.

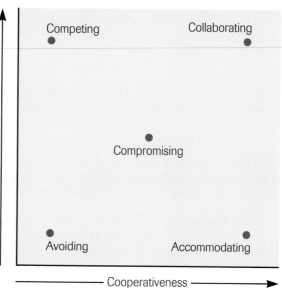

Assertiveness and Cooperativeness

How assertive and cooperative are you? Think for a moment about this set of styles in a different way than you did about the styles described earlier. List the names of five people you know and the topics about which you typically engage in conflict with them. Are the conflicts gender related, socioeconomically based, or focused on cultural differences? Does your style differ depending on the person or topic? How and why? Share your experiences with a few of your classmates.

significant other than you do with your boss. Nonetheless, most people have the same predispositions or tendencies toward conflict regardless of the topic or target person.

The Reality Check "How You See the Conflict Style of Others" (p. 352) asks about matching conflict styles. The idea is not necessarily that conflict styles should be identical, but that perhaps these styles match the people, issues, relationships, and goals involved. Is it possible to have a productive conflict if one participant uses a competing style and another seems to be avoiding conflict? Can conflict be managed if one person is accommodating and the other collaborates? The answers to these questions depend on many of the factors already discussed. Consider these issues of style when you confront conflict situations.

Assessment

In the second phase of conflict management, you must decide what you want out of the conflict. Is your own goal the more important of the two? Or is your partner's goal more important? Are the goals of the relationship more important than the personal goals of either participant? Questions such as these must be resolved before any communication can take place in a conflict situation.

Before engaging in communication during a conflict situation, competent participants conduct a thorough assessment of their own needs and those that they believe are important to their partner. In public speaking, speakers must analyze the audience and make certain adjustments based on whom they are addressing. Failure to do so may prove disastrous for the speakers. This same assessment must be performed prior to a conflict situation with a

How You See the Conflict Style of Others

Think about the conflict styles of some people you know. Do you carefully consider a person's style when he or she is having a conflict with you? When you engage in conflict with certain people, do they seem to use the same style each time? Does their style vary depending on whether they are in conflict with their mother or father? brothers or sisters? mate or best friend? Do particular issues incite them to use a particular conflict style? Which of the conflict styles you see in people really drive you up the wall? Is there any way to change their style to suit your own? Do styles have to match?

partner. Now look at some items (personal goals, the other's goals, relational goals, and "win-win" as the ultimate goal) that should be assessed.

Personal Goals

Your own goals and objectives are very important in any conflict situation; without them, you would not have any stake in the discussion. There are several questions that you will want to consider in advance. For example: When you enter into the conflict, what are you likely to gain? to lose? What do you desire as an outcome? How important is that desire? What positions do you plan to advance during the discussion? Can you substantiate the positions?

The Other's Goals

You are not the only one who has goals and objectives in a conflict situation; your partner has them too. Unless you consider what these goals and objectives are, you are likely to be unsuccessful in any influence attempt.

What is your partner's likely reaction to the conflict? How do your partner's interests differ from your own? What issue do you think is most important to your partner? What kind of experiences or background does the partner bring to this situation?

Relational Goals

Conflict does not take place in a vacuum. Whatever happens through conflict affects a relationship. As stated earlier, the relationship may grow stronger if the conflict is productive. If the conflict is personal instead of issue-based, the relationship may be adversely affected.

Before beginning a conversation that involves conflict, participants should ask what effect the argument or debate is likely to have on their relationship. Has this issue been discussed before? If so, what has been discussed and how? Is there any new information? If not, how much do you need to educate your partner prior to the discussion?

Is the topic one in which your partner's ego is heavily involved? Is your partner more knowledgeable about the issues than you are? What adjustments might you need to make in order to convince your partner that your position is the better one for the relationship?

"Win-Win" as the Ultimate Goal

The best reason to engage in conflict is to allow both participants to gain something from the discussion. If both parties can come away from conflict with more than they entered with, the conflict has been successful. This is called "win-win" and refers to the idea that *both* parties can meet their own goals and those for their relationship from the conflict situation.

The "win-win" philosophy of conflict means that you not only look out for yourself during an argument, but also monitor the role and status of the other party. This is not simply being fair; it means ensuring that both of you receive substantive outcomes from your efforts in the conversation. The idea is that productive conflict is not only issue-based but also conducive to both participants gaining from communicating in the situation.

Engagement

In the third phase of conflict, engagement, the partners create a context for conflict. The physical location for conflict as well as each participant's psychological readiness are very important. In many cases, one partner must actually entice the other into engaging in conflict. During engage-

---

REALITY CHECK

Major and Minor Conflicts

How do conflicts dealing with personal values and goals (attending religious services, raising children) differ from conflicts dealing with trivial matters (which television program to watch, what route to take home)?

ment both partners can clarify and focus on issues rather than on personalities. Decreasing resistance and clarifying and focusing on issues are discussed in this phase.

Decreasing Resistance

One of the greatest barriers to productive conflict occurs when one of the partners does not want to participate in a debate. Here are some reasons why people may be reluctant to engage in conflict:

- They do not see any alternatives or options to a solution that seems obvious to them.
- They do not see the issue as complex enough to merit argument.
- They are unaware of alternatives to their planned course of action.
- They do not enjoy arguing or debating issues.
- They are concerned that the relationship is not strong enough to endure argument.
- They do not believe that the time or place is right for conflict.

When your partner holds one or more of these beliefs, conflict cannot take place until you convince him or her to engage in it with you. You cannot *force* anyone to argue productively with you. To attempt to do so may result in your partner's leaving the scene by walking out on the decision. However, you can entice a partner to debate an issue with you—that is, you can make the differences seem significant, make the consequences seem important, promote different options, reassure your partner, and observe the physical environment.

Make the differences seem significant. When two or more options are possible and both parties recognize those options, one partner may believe the answer is "clear cut." In that case, that person may ask, "Why do we even need to talk about it?" We have already stated that any idea is worth testing. Testing an idea through debate, argument, questioning, and "devil's advocacy" is the best way to determine its real worth.

One of the best approaches you can use to convince your partner to argue is to make the differences seem real but very important. Now look at an example. Harry and Denise are planning their vacation from Des Moines, Iowa, to Providence, Rhode Island. Harry has found that there are actually two desirable routes. He tells Denise that one route would take six hours longer than the other. Upon hearing this, Denise proclaims, "That shorter one is what we want; no question about it." In order to entice Denise to debate the pros and cons of both routes, Harry must explain that the shorter route is all highway. They will miss much beautiful scenery and many cultural sites unless they take the longer route. "Speed or beauty? You can't have them both," Harry argues. Now that the differences between the options are clear to Denise, the debate can begin.

Make the consequences seem important. One reason why people are reluctant to engage in conflict is their attitude that "it doesn't matter" or "it doesn't make any difference." You may have felt exactly that way after just a few minutes in a conflict situation with another person.

Topics on which you dismiss the issues as unimportant are exactly those that come back to haunt you. Have you ever heard someone exclaim, "If only we had talked about it first." No matter what the topic, no matter how trivial it may seem to you or your partner, apply the tests of argument, debate, questioning, and devil's advocacy. A decision that seems unimportant at the moment may take on extremely important proportions later.

Promote different options. On any given topic, your partner may believe that there is only "one way" or, sometimes, "no way." In this case, you actually have to inform your partner about the possibilities *before* you can begin to argue. A few years ago, a school superintendent believed that one of the schools in the district had to be enlarged because of increasing enrollment and overcrowded classrooms. She was upset about all of the bids she had received from construction companies for the expansion. While sharing her tales of woe with a colleague, she learned that other options were available. Her friend informed her that many school districts have constructed portable buildings with classrooms and have placed them on school property at a fraction of the cost of expanding the size of a permanent building. Now she was ready to discuss the issue with the school board.

Reassure your partner. If your partner is reluctant to engage in a conflict situation because of a personal distaste for debate or a desire to protect what he or she regards as a fragile relationship with you, a straightforward explanation of your intentions might be in order. State your desire to resolve an issue involving differences between you. Present the issue as you see it. Reassure your partner that you want to focus on the point of disagreement and not on his or her personal weaknesses or traits that might be detrimental to the relationship. Emphasize your respect for your partner and his or her opinion and your desire to reach a solution that will be satisfactory for both of you. Making your case in a calm, quiet voice will demonstrate that conflict need not be hostile. Review some of the points we have discussed in this chapter so that you can convince your partner that debate can be an enjoyable experience and that positive conflict can strengthen your relationship.

Observe the physical environment. You may understand why some people are reluctant to engage in conflict because of where they are at the time. Public places, such as restaurants, bars, movie theaters, or lines at amusement parks, may call attention to the participants even if the conflict is productive and voices are kept low. In addition, some confidential or privileged information may be under discussion that cannot be shared or heard by outsiders. Both partners should be sensitive to the time and location of the conflict. If you have to move to another location in order to allow normal argument and debate, that movement should take place before the conflict.

Clarifying and Focusing on Issues

It has been said several times that competent communicators engage in productive conflict. This means that the conflict is based on issues and not on the personalities of the participants. One of the most important steps a communicator takes at the outset of conflict is to steer the conversation toward substantive issues. If this step does not take place, the conflict may get off to a very bad start and may never recover.

One of the best ways to safeguard the civilized tone of any encounter is to begin with lines that erase or minimize any link between the issue under discussion and the individual who is delivering a position on it. Here are some sample lines that you might use:

- "I don't want you to take this personally. We need to talk about . . ."
- "I know that you have put a lot of time and energy into this project and that it's very important to you. But I need to get you to step back a little and look at this a different way."
- "You have some strong views on this matter. I respect those views, and I want to listen to what you have to say. But there are some other pieces to the puzzle that I don't think you have considered."
- "I acknowledge that I work for you and whatever you decide will stand. However, I do want at least to have a chance to show you some flaws that I think we can correct now, before we get too deep into this project."

Lines such as these can also be used during the course of the conversation in which the conflict takes place. These can be very important in refo-

---

REALITY CHECK

Striking the Right Balance

You have recently begun a friendship with someone new, and the relationship is progressing, when you begin to experience a series of small conflicts. Your new friend tends to avoid confrontation and becomes passive in a conflict. You would like to discuss issues openly. What can you do to find a balance so that the blooming relationship does not suffer?

cusing the conflict on the issue being discussed. On some occasions you may need to be even more direct:

- "I'm sorry you are offended by what I said. I wasn't talking about you. I was talking about the position you've taken."
- "No, I would have said the same thing no matter *who* brought it up."

Competent communicators in conflict situations not only keep themselves focused on issues, but also are effective in keeping their partners focused on them.

Action

The action phase includes the "how" and "what" of conflict. The "how" involves the selection of *strategies* that a communicator uses in a conflict situation. The "what" involves the *tactics*, or messages, that the participant will use to enact the strategies. In addition, competent communicators in conflict remain aware of several traps that can move the conflict in unproductive directions.

Strategies

We cannot emphasize enough that productive conflict is a useful and positive enterprise for relationships. You may be thinking, "How do I engage in this kind of conflict?" This section discusses several strategies that you can use in order to engage in and manage productive conflict. One of the first determinations you need to make before engaging in conflict is to decide what is most important to you: your own goals, your partner's goals, or your relationship's goals. This decision is very important because without question you cannot have it all three ways. Here we focus on three options: cooperative, obstinate, and escapist.[7]

Cooperative strategies are those that promote the objectives of the relationship (see Table 8.1 on p. 358). The important factor is not whether you win or lose, but rather what is the best outcome for both partners in the relationship (similar to "win-win").

Obstinate or unyielding **strategies** promote the objectives of the individual's goals as opposed to those of a relational partner. These strategies operate with an outcome that is advantageous to the individual. The impact on the relationship is not considered very important (like "win-lose"). **Escapist strategies** attempt to prevent direct conflict. In some cases, this is simply avoidance. In other cases, you will find participants attempting to postpone conflict, change topics, and pass responsibility to other people. The objec-

COOPERATIVE STRATEGIES
In a conflict, strategies that promote the objectives of the relationship rather than those of one partner or the other.

OBSTINATE STRATEGIES
In a conflict, strategies that promote the objectives of an individual rather than those of the relational partner or both partners.

ESCAPIST STRATEGIES
In a conflict, strategies that attempt to prevent direct conflict.

TABLE 8.1 CONFLICT STRATEGIES

TYPE	DESCRIPTION	EXAMPLE
Cooperative	Conflict partners work together to maximize the goals of each person.	"Okay, since we both need time off, why don't I work today and you work tomorrow?"
Obstinate	Partners are self-centered and individualistic in their approach to attaining goals.	"I'm sorry, but I can't go along with any of your suggestions."
Escapist	Partners attempt to avoid conflict altogether.	"I don't want to talk about this anymore."

tive of this strategy is simply to ensure that conflict does not take place (corresponding to "yield-lose"). You will notice that these three general strategies take very different directions and are associated with different kinds of communication behaviors. Now look at a simple but common example.

Suppose that Lisa and Kathy ordered only one piece of lemon meringue pie at a restaurant to eat after their dinner. If you were to go inside their minds, both Lisa and Kathy would like to eat the pie. In discussing who gets the pie, if Lisa used a *cooperative strategy,* she would probably ask Kathy, "Which one of us do you think needs the extra calories the most?" This tactic would consider the feelings of both participants. Conversely, if Lisa used an *obstinate strategy,* she might argue, "I am not on a diet, so I deserve the pie." By using an *escapist strategy,* Lisa would simply say, "Kathy, go ahead and eat the lemon pie," even though she really wanted it.

What difference does it make whether you use one of these strategies instead of another? You get a clue from a study by Canary and Spitzberg, in which they discovered that cooperative-type strategies were more closely related to perceptions of *competence* than were the other two strategies.[8] They found that when the participants in a relationship demonstrate competence in using conflict, the quality of their relationship is higher. Furthermore, their results demonstrated that when compared with other strategies, cooperative-type strategies are associated with greater perceptions of satisfaction, trust, and intimacy in a relationship.

The cooperative strategy, in which the relationship is more important than the goals of either individual, may remind you of the "win-win" philosophy of negotiating. From a "win-win" perspective, both partners in a relationship can achieve greater outcomes than either could if the individual's own goals were more important ("win-lose") or if the other partner's goals were more important ("lose-win").

You may be wondering why and under what circumstances people use one of these strategies versus another. A study by Canary, Cunningham, and Cody revealed that obstinate-type strategies were used more when people were defending themselves.[9] Cooperative-type strategies were more frequently used by individuals to promote a change in a relationship. Why? Conflicts over the definition of a relationship are more likely to produce cooperative behaviors than would conflicts over the defense of a personal right.

For example, if one partner wants to define the relationship as "boyfriend and girlfriend" and the other partner prefers the relationship to be "just friends," there is likely to be conflict in reaching an acceptable and common conclusion. On the other hand, suppose conflict comes about because a friend has borrowed money from you, has not paid any of it back, and refuses to pay some higher interest rates that you believe are justified. This type of conflict is likely to produce obstinate or self-defending strategies.

Tactics

In the previous section, we discussed three general strategies that you can use in conflict situations. Next, we cover some specific message-based options that will help you place the strategy you select in motion. These options are called tactics. Tactics are the methods that conflict is made of: probing, debating/arguing, bargaining, making threats and promises, face-saving, summarizing, and compromising.

Probing

Press for clarifications and explanations from your partner. Don't be satisfied with general positions or vague and ambiguous answers. Ask **probing** questions that force the individual to be more specific and pointed. Try to find out your partner's motivations, goals, and attitudes toward you and the conflict issue. ("What do you mean?" "Can you give me an example?" "What's at risk for me? For you?")

PROBING
In a conflict, an attempt to make a partner provide clarifications, explanations, or further information.

If you suspect that your partner is not being truthful, probing may be an appropriate tactic. You will quickly notice that increased probing for specifics can cause your partner to be less deceitful. Why? You know that unrehearsed lies could produce generalities and inconsistencies. They are often delivered with disfluencies, hesitations, altered rates of speed, and other nonverbal behaviors that are simply not normal for the person when telling the truth.[10] In many cases, the more you probe, the less the person has to say and the more obvious these behaviors become.

Debating and Arguing

Throughout this chapter, we have mentioned that productive conflict depends on debate and argument between the parties involved in the relationship. Clearly, debate and argument do not mean yelling and shouting. Here are two ways you can argue and debate effectively.

First, take a *devil's advocate* position whenever possible. Before agreeing on an issue, ask what the worst-case scenario would be. Think of some issues that two people may discuss. Usually, they involve some tangible outcomes. Before an issue is decided, a devil's advocate may bring up questions such as

> What is the most money that could be lost?
> How much time could possibly be wasted?
> What is the longest distance we would have to travel?
> What is the biggest safety risk we are taking by engaging in this activity?

If the answer your partner gives to these types of questions is unsatisfying to you, certainly other alternatives must be generated and explored.

Second, argue against analogies that the other person offers to support this position. An analogy simply indicates that what is true in one instance or case will be true in another. This instance or case can be time, schools, years, countries, people—just about anything. When you hear people say, "It's just like ———" or "It's no different from ———," they are using analogies.

For productive conflict to take place, you need to demonstrate that the *differences* between the instances or cases that are being compared are so significant that the analogy is invalid. For example, say that two parents are arguing about whether their oldest daughter should attend a private school. The wife contends, "I went to a private school and my knowledge level became a grade ahead of most of my friends. If Betsy goes to this private school, she should accelerate the same way." The husband can argue against the analogy by suggesting the wide differences between his wife and daughter in terms of time periods of their schooling, types of friends, development levels, particular schools available, and so on.

The same logic can be used when someone tries to compare two presidents, two time periods, two brands of fertilizer, or two airlines. Your task as an advocate of productive conflict is to demonstrate that the analogy may not be valid. You may become persuaded that the similarities between the compared instances or cases are quite high. If that happens, then the argument succeeds, but it has been put to the test.

A word of caution is in order here. The message tactics just discussed (probing, playing devil's advocate, and resisting analogies) should be used for only one reason, and that is to facilitate productive conflict that will result in better decisions. Messages such as those described here should not be employed to harass or embarrass someone, to build ego strength, to play "one-up," or to focus on another person's personality or idiosyncrasies. Participants who do so are actually engaging in destructive, rather than productive, conflict.

When ideas and proposed solutions stand up to the tests just described and are adopted as decisions, you can't be guaranteed success, but you do know that they are decisions that were not arrived at hastily or without sound judgment. This is the real benefit of productive conflict.

Bargaining

Bargaining tactics constitute a special form of conflict in which the partners argue for their respective positions within mutually agreed upon guidelines.[11] You are probably most familiar with the bargaining tactics used in union and labor negotiations or courtroom bargaining pleas. Each side agrees to certain rules and procedures when arguing its case. Many conflict situations that you will face may resemble bargaining sessions, and it is a good idea to become competent in bargaining tactics. Briefly, bargaining tactics are very much like the conflict strategies discussed earlier (cooperative, obstinate, and escapist strategies). The key to **bargaining** is to develop a strategy that supports a favorable position for your side while promoting the value of your adversary's point of view. Based on research findings, the following steps make up a bargaining strategy that can lead to success.[12]

BARGAINING
In a conflict, arguing for one's own position while expressing understanding of and sensitivity to the other party's position.

- Begin with high but realistic offers. Starting high allows you to "give" some later.

- Present beginning offers in a cooperative manner so that adversaries know that you can be reasonable.

- Clear obstacles by compromising a little on your initial offer.

- Stand your ground when you feel the opposition is taking advantage of your good faith.

- Remain committed and enthusiastic about your goals throughout the bargaining session.

- Know what you are talking about. Be well informed about your own position and your adversary's position. Don't get caught off guard by something you ought to know about.

- Let the opposition know that you understand their position and are sensitive to their needs.

- Avoid obstinate and escapist tactics unless these are absolutely necessary. Seldom do these behaviors serve a useful purpose.

Making Threats and Promises

THREAT

An expressed intention to behave in a way that is detrimental to the other party in a conflict if that party does not comply with certain requests or terms.

PROMISE

In a conflict, an expressed intention to behave in a way that is beneficial to the other party provided that party complies with certain requests or terms.

Two interesting types of messages in interpersonal conflict are threats and promises.[13] **Threats** are expressed intentions to behave in ways that are detrimental to the other party if he or she does not comply with certain requests or terms. Conversely, **promises** are expressed intentions to behave in ways that are beneficial to the other party in return for compliance with certain requests or terms.

The effectiveness of threats and promises as strategies depends on five factors:

Specificity   The more specific the threat or promise, the more effective.
Credibility   The more trustworthy and believable the threat or promise, the more effective.
Immediacy   The more urgent the threat or promise, the more effective.
Equity   The fairer the threat or promise, the more effective.
Climate   The more cooperative the climate, the more effective the threat or promise.[14]

Threats and promises operate in conflict situations in two different ways: they provoke conflict and they resolve conflict. First, threats and promises can *provoke conflicts*. When threatened, many people retaliate rather than consent. A promise, especially from someone who has a bad history of keeping promises, can cause all kinds of problems. For instance, how many times have you heard a dialogue such as this?

MILTON   It's no problem. If I can have all the guys over to watch the game on Sunday, I'll clean up before they get here and after they leave.

LINDY   Right. Just like you said you would clean out the garage last month, fix the light in the kitchen last week, and pick up the dry cleaning this morning.

MILTON   Well, you're the one who never gets out of bed early on Sunday morning to get the kids ready for church. I've got to prepare breakfast and get the kids dressed and rounded up in the car. Where are you?

Second, threats and promises can *resolve conflicts*. In the heat of an argument between two people, a well-placed threat may put an end to a discussion. For example, a manager may tell an employee, "Well, if you *don't* finish this project by Wednesday, I'm putting somebody else on it." Promises can have the same effect. The employee may volunteer a line such as "We're arguing about nothing. I promise this will get finished by Wednesday."

Face Saving

Another concern is face-saving messages. How are people treated when they change their minds? First, Folger and Poole argue that the best solution is to create climates that avoid face saving altogether.[15] If one or more people get together in an atmosphere where the "best solution" wins, the victor is not the person but the solution. In this atmosphere, no one individual owns or is associated with a solution.

Second, the parties should try to minimize any defensiveness or retaliation that is associated with winning or losing an argument. These responses come about because someone is concerned about having an undesirable image or making an undesirable impression.

Finally, to save face, a party must be able to have a "way out" of a position. There is no real reason to devastate the other person even if you win the conflict. You can offer to help your partner out in other situations or even to act as a supporter during some other issue.

Summarizing

One of the most useful tactics that can be used in a conflict-based conversation is to offer periodic summaries of what has been discussed. Lines such as "Here's what I think we've said so far" or "What we have agreed to is" are extremely useful in keeping a discussion on track.

Offering summary lines gives your partner the chance to disagree, clarify a point, or amplify any part of the discussion before it moves on to another subtopic. The major advantage of summary lines is that the topic is still fresh on the participants' minds. If one partner has a different opinion, perception, or recollection of what was discussed, the best time to make a correction is right then, not ten minutes, one hour, one week, or six months later.

Compromising

As you read this chapter, you may have been thinking that there is a simple alternative to conflict, which is to compromise. A **compromise** can be obtained very easily through a number of tactics, including the following:

Averaging In conflicts over the cost of goods or services, the two parties may simply "split the difference"; for example, a compromise between $80 and $100 is $90.

Trading off Individuals may make concessions by taking the position "I'll give you this if I can get this in return."

Random selection Participants put two or more alternatives "in a hat"; each simply draws, and each has an equal chance of getting his or her way.

COMPROMISE
A conflict resolution tactic that involves agreeing on a method of deciding, rather than focusing on the quality of the decision.

FIGURE 8.5
*Majority rule is not
always the best way
to make a decision.*

THE FAR SIDE By GARY LARSON

"Okay, Williams, we'll vote . . . how many here say
the heart has four chambers?"

Voting Participants take a vote, and the majority wins. (This tactic is more often applied in groups than in dyads.)

Compromise tactics are used so often in relationships because they represent quick and simple methods of reaching a conclusion or a result. Notice that the focus of compromise is on reaching a quick decision by agreeing on the method of deciding, not on the quality of the decision. These methods do not provide for quality checks as to whether the outcome is desirable, fair, or correct.

You are aware that managing productive conflict requires much more than reaching an easy solution. It also calls for participants to explore the issues through debate, argument, and questioning in order to reach a proper conclusion.

Settling for a compromise rather than working through issues is not the most productive way to manage conflict in a relationship. However, it is helpful to resort to compromise under certain circumstances, such as when a decision must be made under severe time constraints. In that situation, there is no time to engage in active debate, argument, or questioning.

You should also resort to compromise when the outcomes are relatively unimportant to you and your partner. Is it really worth the mental and emotional effort to engage in conflict when the end result is not very important to you? Why not just split the difference when conflict is not worth the effort?

Traps

Competent communicators in conflict situations are those who avoid or minimize falling into traps. This section discusses several traps (sidetracking, deception, and hidden agendas) that are frequently part of conversations that involve conflict. Try as you might, you may not be able to prevent them altogether, but you can at least be prepared for them.

Sidetracking

Sidetracking occurs when a partner attempts to move the conversation to a peripheral topic that is often irrelevant. You will also encounter this trap when one of the participants makes a topic unnecessarily complex. Usually, a partner will revert to sidetracking when he or she is "losing" an issue and does not want to concede or modify the position. To avoid being caught in this trap, you must be firm about the focus of the conversation. Lines such as "We're not talking about that right now" can clearly signal your lack of desire to move away from the topic.

SIDETRACKING
In a conflict, an attempt to move the conversation to a peripheral, often irrelevant topic.

Deception

Conflict situations provide one of the "ripest" contexts for deception. When your partner feels that you are scrutinizing the presented ideas and feel "under fire," there is an increased chance you will hear a lie. The best opportunities for deception occur when a partner must produce data or substantiation for a general claim. Good examples include answers to questions such as "Have you ever seen that happen?" "About how much money would this take?" "Did you talk to her personally about it?"

Earlier in this book, in Chapter 5, we discussed the nonverbal indicator of deception. There we also discussed differences between spontaneous and prepared lies. This information is equally applicable to deception that takes place in conflict situations.

Intuitively, you may know that your partner is lying to you. One way you can get to the truth is to avoid directly confronting your partner with the fact that you know he or she is being deceitful. Lines such as "You liar" or "That's just B.S." could escalate the conflict and move it toward personalities instead of the issues. It is far better to use indirect confrontations. Hence, you might say, "If it did happen, just tell me; I really don't care, but I have to know the truth." Or you might say, "Can you think about that one more time, and let's be sure that's exactly the way it really does exist today." The important factor is to discover the truth, not to embarrass or confront your partner for deceiving you.

Hidden Agendas

You may find that your partner has not been truthful with you about why he or she has been arguing or debating with you. We call these deceptions **hidden agendas**; your partner is using the supposed goal of the argument to score a personal gain, to secure information from you, or to achieve some other secret purpose.

You should not become paranoid about it, but you should be "on guard" about hidden agendas. When Phil Rizzuto, a veteran shortstop for the New York Yankees, was in the twilight years of his career, he was called to the general manager's office. The general manager told Rizzuto that he had to release a player and wanted to discuss some of the options with him. At first, Rizzuto was flattered. As the debate continued and the strengths and weaknesses of various players were discussed, it became clear that the general manager wanted Rizzuto to identify *himself* as the player who needed to go. The general manager's hidden agenda for the conflict was to avoid having to fire Rizzuto directly by allowing him to do it himself.

The three traps described here have a number of ethical ramifications that you should consider. Experts on ethical communication differ in their recommendations for dealing with troublesome situations. Some ethicists believe that you should act or communicate only in the most moral and ethical ways regardless of the circumstances. They advise against all of these traps—sidetracking, deception, and hidden agendas. Other ethicists take a more situational approach, advising that communicators must decide on the ethics of each situation separately. They would view sidetracking, deception, and hidden agendas as poor choices for conflict management except in certain circumstances.

REALITY CHECK

Ethics and Traps

Can you think of situations, circumstances, or events during conflict in which the use of traps would be ethical? What ethical reasoning do you think people rely on when they use traps in conflict situations? Ask five people whom you respect to give their opinion about the ethical implications of traps discussed in the text. Be prepared to discuss your findings in class.

◢ Decision

The fifth phase of conflict involves agreeing on a consensus decision on the issues that the parties have argued and debated about. In this phase, the exact agreement must be clearly summarized, specified, and reiterated to avoid all disagreement about what the final conclusion is. In some cases, the participants actually sign a contract or other formal agreement.

Reaching a Consensus

Once all the positions have been advanced, data have been given, and reasoning has been proposed, the participants must reach a conclusion. Reaching this decision is what the conversation that involved conflict is all about. **Consensus**, defined as a mutually satisfying agreement reached by two or more parties, is very different from compromise (whose focus is on a quick decision).

CONSENSUS
A mutually satisfying agreement reached by two or more parties.

Before the parties to a conflict "sign on the dotted line," the following three factors should be considered:

Goals Do both parties meet their goals and objectives through this decision? If not, the decision will not be the "win-win" outcome discussed previously.

Partner Does each partner recognize the benefits gained from the conflict? If there are any concerns, these should be pointed out before the discussion is brought to a close.

Relationship How is the relationship different as a result of the conflict? Is it stronger? weaker? Are there topics that were alluded to but not discussed, that should be considered in a future conversation?

Summary and Confirmation

In many conflict situations, the parties must actually reach a formal agreement such as signing a contract or other legal document. In other situations, the outcome is far less formal.

Regardless of the situation, summarizing and confirming the outcome is an extremely important step. In all conversations involving conflict, at least one of the participants should summarize the conversation. Lines that are as simple as "So, our agreement is . . ." or "What we have decided to do is . . ." leave no room for confusion.

In some cases, one or both parties must engage in a series of followup steps. Even these behaviors must be agreed upon at the conclusion of a conflict-based conversation, or they may never be performed. One person may say, "So you have agreed to do these things by ———," or "We have six steps still to take. Let me read them to be sure we agree."

▥ Reflection

Resolution of the conflict does not mean it is over. Reflection, the sixth and final phase of productive conflict, is extremely important, for it calls for the participants to evaluate their behavior during the conflict situation and to assess the impact on their relationship. The participants must consider their strengths and weaknesses in the various communication skills they used in the conflict situation. Furthermore, they must decide what impact the conflict has on their feelings about the other person. In some cases the relation is stronger, and in other cases, some repair work needs to be done. The final phase of this model then is concerned with what happens afterward. You should look at two important factors: the relationship and the performance of communication.

Reevaluating the Relationship

Because conflict between two people takes place in a relational context, you can be assured that the relationship is different afterward. In many cases, the relationship is stronger, especially when the conflict is made productive by centering on the issues. The partners should capitalize on this advantage and find other topics or areas of concern that can be worked through together.

On some occasions conflict gets off course. Personalities may become involved, and the conflict may become destructive. If the relationship shows some "wear and tear" as a result of conflict, then several options are available to help you repair it.

- *Be open and frank with your partner about what happened.* Explain what you said and why. Ask your partner to do the same. Share your feelings and reactions about the experience with each other.

- *Agree to put the issue behind you.* Acknowledge that the topic was a difficult one for the two of you and now that it has been discussed, it is time to go on to other things. You need not give unrealistic promises such as "This won't ever happen again." If the relationship is to continue, conflict is inevitable.

- *Focus on the process.* Explain that, although one of you is not satisfied with the outcome, the opportunity to talk and work through a problem was very worthwhile. Encourage your partner to discuss other topics with you in the same way in the near future. Suggest that you believe the relationship is actually stronger because you took the time to talk. You may be sorry about the outcome but not dissatisfied with the process.

- *Use the relational repair strategies from Chapter 7.* Remember that relationships are often in need of repair and that conflict situations can bring relational difficulties to the surface. In repairing the relationships, do not hesitate to tell your partner how you feel, demonstrate empathy for his or her feelings, tell the truth about what you are experiencing, and show that you care. You will probably find that your conflict partner will return your repair strategies with some of his or her own.

Assessing Competence and Performance

Another factor to consider after your conflict with your partner has concluded is the degree to which you performed competently as a communicator. Assess your behavior and try to discover some skills that you need to focus on to be more effective in the future.

For example, how well did you really *listen* to your partner? Did you *ask* your partner clear and concise questions? How *strong* were your arguments? Did your data *support* the positions you took? Were you able to *substantiate* each of your claims? Were you able to focus on *issues* instead of your partner's personality or past behavior? Did you lose your *temper* at any time?

Exactly what is competence in conflict situations? Competence in communicating was defined earlier as effectively attaining goals in a manner appropriate to the context of the relationship. The context of a relationship can be defined in many different ways: maturity of the participants, length of the relationship, status differences or similarities of the participants, type of relationship (such as business or romantic), and many others.

Demonstrating competence in interpersonal conflict can be quite difficult. Conflict often exists because of the presence of incompatible goals. The participants must seek a successful outcome while considering each other's expectations for the relationship and the situation. Considering that most of these situations are emotion-laden, they are also ripe for inappropriate behavior.[16]

Focus now on one competency in productive conflict, *flexibility.* According to Folger and Poole, "In constructive conflicts, members engage in a wide variety of behaviors ranging from coercion and threat to negotiation, joking, and relaxation in order to reach a mutually acceptable solution. In contrast, parties in destructive conflicts are likely to be much less flexible because their goal is more narrowly defined; they are trying to defeat each other. . . . Neither avoidance nor hostile arguments are harmful in themselves—but rather the *inflexibility* of the parties which locks them" into escalating or avoiding conflict.[17]

Simply put, one tool that separates competent from incompetent participants in conflict is the *versatility* that each person brings to the situation. Versatile individuals, with a repertoire of all types of communication behaviors, can respond with greater flexibility than can those who typically behave in only one way.

The key to competence, however, is more than just possessing the ability to communicate in different ways. Competence requires the individual to communicate in the *appropriate* way, given situational demands. A person may be able to be sarcastic as well as serious, but how and under what circumstances these behaviors are used is the key to his or her competence. A flexible person who uses the wrong behaviors in certain circumstances is just as incompetent as an inflexible person who cannot use the behavior at all.

REVIEW

This chapter discusses effective strategies for managing conflict in interpersonal relationships and explores four conditions under which interpersonal conflict is produced—incompatible goals, unrealistic expectations, disparate relational growth, and inaccurate perceptions. Accepting the fact that conflict is inevitable and healthy is the foundation for conflict management. Conflict is usually seen as a negative aspect to any relationship, but it possesses some important advantages. Conflict can help a relationship grow, and it also helps people to make better decisions that in the long run will save time. In addition, debating a conflicting issue can be enjoyable.

The model for competent conflict management was developed to better manage conflict that exists in interpersonal relationships. Competent conflict can be divided into six distinct phases. Conflict begins in a prelude stage before any actual words are spoken. The participants' characteristics, the relationship that provides the context, and the predispositions and tendencies people have in approaching their partners affect everything that occurs in a conflict situation. In the second phase, the participants must decide what they want out of the conflict and how important it is to them. Their assessment of their own goals, their partner's goals, their relational goals, and the ultimate goal of winning greatly affects how they approach the conflict situation. In the engagement phase of conflict, the partners create a context for conflict. This phase also involves ways in which both partners can clarify and focus on issues rather than personalities. The action phase of conflict involves the "how" and "what" of conflict. The "how" involves the selection of strategies that a communicator uses in a conflict situation, and the "what" involves the tactics, or messages, that the participant uses to enact the strategies. The fifth phase of conflict involves reaching an agreement, or consensus, on the issues that have been debated. Just because the conflict has been resolved does not mean it is over. In the sixth phase, reflection, it is extremely important for the participants to evaluate their behavior during the conflict situation and assess the conflict's impact on their relationship.

The competent management of conflict involves many different aspects that the participants bring to the situation. The key to competence, however, is more than just possessing the ability to communicate in different ways. Competence requires the individual to communicate in the appropriate way given situational demands.

SUGGESTED READINGS

Bazerman, M. H., & Lewicki, R. J. (Eds.). (1983). *Negotiating in organizations*. Beverly Hills, CA: Sage.

Folger, J., & Poole, M. (1984). *Working through conflict*. Glenview, IL: Scott Foresman.

Hocker, J., & Wilmot, W. (1985). *Interpersonal conflict*. Dubuque, IA: W. C. Brown.

Kolb, D. M., & Bartunek, J. M. (Eds.). (1992). *Hidden conflict in organizations: Uncovering behind-the-scenes disputes*. Beverly Hills, CA: Sage.

Putnam, L. L., & Roloff, M. E. (Eds.). (1992). *Communication and negotiation*. Beverly Hills, CA: Sage

Sandole, D., & Sandole-Staroste, I. (Eds.). (1987). *Conflict management and problem solving: Interpersonal to international applications*. New York: New York University Press.

Stulberg, J. B. (1987). *Taking charge/managing conflict*. Lexington, MA: Lexington Books.

9

Principles of Competent Interviewing

Objectives

After reading this chapter, you should be able to

1. Identify examples of interpersonal communication as interviews or noninterviews and, for interviews, identify them as to type.

2. Describe the potential roles of interviewers and interviewees in various types of interviews.

3. Describe basic interviewing strategies, including developing clear goals, identifying potential barriers, and creating an effective structure.

4. Describe criteria for formulating questions in terms of type (open or closed, primary or secondary), potential impact, and sequence.

5. Specify and use an appropriate sequence of reacting moves.

6. Describe how to prepare for and participate in a screening employment interview.

CHAPTER CONTENTS

MARIBETH BERG is a college sophomore majoring in business administration. As a graded assignment for her introductory communication class, Maribeth has been asked to set up an interview with a person who (1) is engaged in business, industry, or professional work related to Maribeth's major and (2) has occasion to do a considerable amount of interviewing. Maribeth has made an appointment by telephone to interview Jim Walsh, an insurance agent. Her task is to learn about the interviewing training (What experiences have contributed to his knowledge of interviewing?) and interviewing practices (What methods does he use?) of Mr. Walsh. As you read through this chapter, think about the skills Maribeth Berg will need to have in order to conduct a successful interview with Jim Walsh. At the end of the chapter, we will return to this scenario and solicit your advice.

Defining the Interview

Chapter 7 identified multiple goals and motivations for initiating relationships with others: interpersonal attraction, physical proximity, attitude similarity, alleviation of loneliness, securing stimulation, learning about self, and achievement of goals. This chapter focuses on the last of these motivations—initiating relationships in order to achieve specific goals. Here you will gain an understanding of how the resources of knowledge and skills come together in a particular form of interpersonal communication known as the *interview* to produce the competency-based outcome of effective and appropriate communication.

Stewart and Cash describe a "situational schema" of seven goals that can be achieved by the interview.[1] Here are the goals, along with examples of each type of interview:

Information giving   Teaching a friend to use a new word-processing program; helping your sister improve her backhand for racquetball.

Information gathering   Conducting a public opinion survey concerning student attitudes toward campus parking availability and fees; asking your English professor about the career possibilities for an English major.

Selection   Interviewing for a part-time job at a store; meeting, as a candidate, with the selection committee charged with choosing the managing editor of the student newspaper.

Problem related to the interviewee's behavior   Talking with a counselor at the counseling center about your anxiety about giving speeches; being reprimanded by your French TA for missing the midterm examination.

Problem related to the interviewer's behavior   Returning a defective compact disc to the retailer; asking your English instructor to reconsider the grade she has assigned to your term project.

Problem solving   Working on a term project with a classmate in your American Government class; discussing with a friend problems you are having with your parents.

Persuasion   Convincing others to give blood during the campuswide Red Cross campaign; asking someone to go to a rock concert with you.

As these examples illustrate, every day you participate in numerous and varied interactions that can be labeled **interviews**. Each of them involves a process of planned, dyadic, interactive discourse.[2]

Interviews are planned discourse. Each of the above examples has a purpose that goes beyond the establishment and development of a relationship (e.g., affiliation, intimacy, self-fulfillment). Although the interpersonal relationship is often a necessary and important component of the interview, at least one of the two parties in the interview (and sometimes both) has an additional serious and predetermined reason for initiating the interview (e.g., to gather information, to inform, to persuade). Because this goal exists in advance of the interaction, it is possible (and beneficial) for at least one of the participants to plan a strategy for initiating, conducting, and concluding the interview. For example, if you intend to ask your English instructor to reconsider the grade assigned to your term project, you will have a better chance of achieving this goal if you consider the best way to adapt to the specific individual in the specific setting.

Interviews are dyadic discourse. Like most forms of interpersonal communication, the interview is dyadic; that is, it involves *two parties.* Although each of the two parties is typically a single person, that need not be the case. It is possible, for example, for survey researchers to conduct group interviews. It is also common for several representatives of an organization to interview job applicants in a group setting. In both cases, however, even though a number of individuals are involved, there are only two parties. Because there are only two parties, there is no one to act as a mediator or an arbiter should the two parties not agree.

Interviews are interactive discourse. Interviews involve two-way interactions in which both parties exchange speaking and listening roles. There is a heavy dependence on questions and answers, and both parties modify their verbal and nonverbal behaviors as they adapt to the ongoing process. Although most interviews occur face to face, interactions over the phone (or via computer) are also considered interviews.

INTERVIEW
A process of planned, dyadic, interactive discourse.

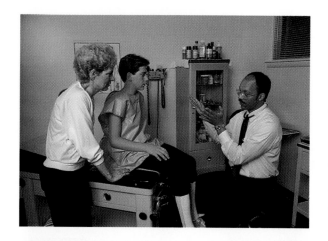

FIGURE 9.1
One feature of interviews that distinguishes them from other forms of interpersonal communication is that they have a planned purpose. How would you describe the purposes of these interviews?

Recognizing Interviews

List the dyadic encounters you participated in during the past week. What percentage of them were interviews? Of those that were interviews, which ones were concerned with information giving? information gathering? selection? a problem related to the interviewee's behavior? a problem related to the interviewer's behavior? problem solving? persuasion? From this exercise, what have you learned about the role of interviews in your life?

The Roles of Interviewer and Interviewee

Having examined the nature of interviews and some of the forms they can take, you should be ready to focus on general principles (concerning both knowledge and skills) that are applicable across all types of interviews and that can facilitate your development as a competent interviewer and interviewee. Before doing that, however, consider the role of the two parties in the interview.

For convenience, and as is common, the two parties in the interview can be designated as **interviewer** and **interviewee**. As a further convenience, in this chapter the last letter of each word (R = intervie*w*er and E = intervie*w*ee) is used to identify the two roles. Although this is a common and useful convention, other labels are sometimes more precise—for example, employer/applicant; survey researcher/subject; therapist/client.

Although both parties (R and E) to the interview have important roles to play that benefit from advance preparation, it is typically the R (interviewer) who assumes the major responsibility for the planning and success of the interview. Thus, to use some earlier examples, when teaching a friend how to use a new word-processing program, you would attempt to anticipate the best way to structure the lesson; when asking an English instructor to reconsider the grade assigned to your term project, you would try to anticipate how she would be likely to react and then develop your strategy accordingly; and when attempting to convince your friends to give blood during the campuswide Red Cross campaign, you would attempt to anticipate objections and think of ways of countering them. In general,

INTERVIEWER (R)
One of two parties in an interview; typically assumes the primary responsibility for the planning and success of the interview.

INTERVIEWEE (E)
One of two parties in an interview; typically follows the lead of the interviewer (R) during the interview.

then, the person who should and does accept the major responsibility for the success of the interview is the R. As with all general rules, however, there are exceptions. In some cases, the R may wish to ask the E to take over or share responsibility for taking the lead. For example, as the R, the counselor whom you are consulting about your anxiety about giving speeches may decide that the best approach to the interview is to allow you significant latitude concerning how the interview will proceed. In some situations, the R and the E ought to have equal responsibility for planning and conducting the interview. In problem-solving interviews, for example (as when you work on a term project with a classmate), the R and the E have equal responsibility for the outcome of the interview.

In short, then, there are always two parties in an interview: the R and the E. Although there are exceptions, in most situations the R has primary responsibility for setting the goals of the interview and, in advance of the interview, for devising a strategy to maximize the likelihood of achieving those goals. Thus, much of the advice in this chapter is targeted to the R. The E, however, also has much to gain from anticipating what will happen in the interview. Advice to the R, therefore, is relevant to both R and E.

Basic Interviewing Strategies

The general principles for developing competence as an interviewer can be summarized in the following five guidelines: (1) keep your goal clearly in mind; (2) identify potential barriers to the achievement of that goal; (3) create an appropriate structure for the development of the interview; (4) use effective questions to develop your structure; and (5) respond effectively during the interview.

Developing Clear Goals

By definition, an interview is planned discourse; that is, it has a purpose that goes beyond the establishment and development of a relationship. Using Stewart and Cash's taxonomy, you will find that the purpose might be information giving, information gathering, selection, resolving a problem related to the E's behavior, resolving a problem related to the R's behavior, problem solving, or persuasion. Thus, although the establishment and development of a relationship are important to the interview, they are secondary rather than primary goals. The primary goal is the task—and it is possible to focus so much or so little on the interpersonal relationship that the task doesn't get accomplished. Assume, for example, that you are the candidate meeting with the selection committee charged with choosing the managing editor of the student newspaper. Is it possible that you might focus so much on the task of getting selected that you are insensitive to the interpersonal needs of committee members? On the other hand, is it also possible that you might be so concerned about being perceived as a nice person that you don't do a thorough job of emphasizing your credentials for the position? The first guideline, then, is to develop a clear goal for the interview and remind yourself of that goal as you proceed through the interview. If you are trying to gather information, put the focus on that rather than on developing and maintaining the relationship.

Identifying Potential Barriers

With a clear vision of the goal in mind, the next guideline asks us to focus on potential pitfalls or barriers. What are the most likely issues that will prevent the accomplishment of the goal? In answering this question, it is useful to consider three major factors: the R, the E, and the setting.

The R Have you prepared carefully for the interview? Have you considered potential biases, misperceptions, or preconceived notions on your part that might interfere with the achievement of your goal? Have you done your homework in terms of the topic, the E, and the setting?

The E Is the E both able (e.g., is it reasonable to assume that the E has the information we need?) and willing (e.g., is it reasonable to assume that the E is motivated to share the information with us?) to con-

REALITY CHECK

Anticipating Barriers

Bill Smith is a production supervisor who oversees a crew of twelve workers. One new employee, Sara Heap-of-Birds, has been late three of her first five days on the job. Bill has scheduled a meeting with Sara but is not sure how to communicate to her that it is unacceptable to be late to work. He has no previous experience working with American Indians, but he once read that their attitude toward time is different from that of his Anglo-American co-culture. What potential pitfalls or barriers should Bill anticipate? Are they most likely to fall in the category of the R? the E? the setting? What positive and negative influences might Bill's belief that Sara's lateness is culture-based have on the interview? What can Bill do to overcome the anticipated barriers?

tribute to the R's goal? What are the likely attitudes of the E toward the R (independent of the goal)? Will these attitudes help or hinder the interview? What are the likely attitudes of the E toward the R's purpose for the interview? Will these attitudes facilitate or hurt the interview? What is known about the E (demographically, socially, psychologically) that can enhance or detract from the effectiveness of the interview?

The setting   Is there anything in the setting that will help or hinder the interview (e.g., the time of day or week, the location of the meeting, the seating pattern)? Can any of these features be changed to enhance the effectiveness of the interview?

Creating an Appropriate Interview Structure

Interviews are jointly created products. Although they should result from a plan, the fact that they are interactive means that the structure of the interview emerges from a dyadic process and cannot be completely specified in advance. Thus, it is useful and beneficial for you to plan and anticipate the likely structural development of each interview, but participating in the actual interview requires that you adapt that plan to the situation as it evolves.

In creating a plan for the structure of an interview, you should think of an interview as composed of three component parts: the opening, the body, and the closing.

The Opening

In thinking about the best way to start an interview, you should try to put yourself in the other person's shoes. If you were the E in an interview (e.g., a candidate interviewing for the position of managing editor of the student newspaper), what questions would be on your mind at the beginning of the interview? Although answers to this question will vary with the interview, in most interviewing situations three potential and interrelated issues emerge:

1. *Task:* What is the nature of this interview and how will it proceed?
2. *Relationship:* Will you like and can you trust this R?
3. *Motivation:* What can you hope to gain by participating in this interview?

Therefore, the R's responsibility is to anticipate which, if any, of these questions are important to the E and, then, to develop a strategy for dealing with them. Assume, for example, that you are doing a telephone survey on student attitudes toward parking on campus. Will issues of task, relationship, and motivation be important to the Es you intend to call? Will, for example, Es want to know about the nature of the interview and how long it will take? Will they want to know something about you and how you will be using the information you gather? Will they want to know how they will benefit from participating in the interview? Assuming an affirmative answer to one or more of these questions, what can you say or do at the start of the interview that is responsive to these needs of the Es?

As you consider the unique requirements of your interview, you may find one or more of the following common **opening techniques** responsive to the needs of the E for task, relationship, or motivational support:

1. A brief statement or rapid summary of a problem (need) facing the E and/or the R. (This technique is appropriate with an E who is *vaguely* aware of the problem but is not well informed about its details.)

2. A brief explanation of how the R happened to learn that a problem exists, coupled with the suggestion that the E will want to discuss it. (This technique avoids the appearance of lecturing or talking down to the E and encourages a spirit of cooperative, objective discussion of a *shared* problem.)

3. The statement of an incentive (goal or outcome) desired by the E and that may reasonably be expected *if* the proposal is accepted. (This opening is potentially the most powerful of all but is easily abused. Avoid a presentation that sounds like a high-pressure "sales pitch." Emphasize honesty and sincerity.)

4. A request for the E's advice or assistance with regard to a problem. (This approach is effective when it is sincere; don't use it as a slick gimmick.)

5. The statement of a striking, dramatic fact. (This is another potentially very powerful approach, but it can sound corny! The statement must be sincere, logically justified, and related to the motivations of the E; it can easily be tied in with No. 3—incentives. It is particularly appropriate when a real emergency exists and when the E is apathetic and must be aroused.)

6. A reference to the known position of the E regarding a situation. (This is the common-ground approach. It is an excellent one to use when the E has taken a public position or has already asked the R to bring in proposals, etc.)

7. A reference to the *background* (causes, origin, etc.) *leading up to* a problem (without stating the problem itself), when the E is fairly

OPENING TECHNIQUES
Strategies for the initial portion of an interview that deal with issues of task, relationship, and motivation.

familiar with this background. (This is another application of the common-ground principle. It may be useful if you expect the E to react in a hostile manner when you reveal the purpose of your proposal.)

8. Identification of the person who sent you to see the E. (This opening is appropriate when the E does not know you and may be wondering why you have sought out him or her. The opening can, of course, be used only when it is true—and when the third party is respected by the E.)

9. Identification of the company, organization, or group you represent. (This opening is appropriate when added prestige is needed or as an explanation of why the R is there.)

10. A request for a specified, brief period of time—for example, "ten minutes of your time." (Caution! Can be too apologetic! To be used only when necessary—e.g., when dealing with an impatient, irritable, or very busy E.)[3]

REALITY CHECK

Strategies for Opening an Interview

For each of the following situations, anticipate the need to deal with the task, relationship, and motivation concerns of potential Es. Which of the strategies discussed in the text (alone or in combination) would be a good opening for the interview?

1. *Information giving:* You are attempting to teach an E your company's policy concerning how to answer the telephone.
2. *Information gathering:* An E has just resigned as a waiter at your restaurant and you are conducting an exit interview.
3. *Selection:* You are a campus recruiter hiring people in your E's area of interest.
4. *Problem related to the E's behavior:* You are a counselor, and the E has come to you with a dating or relationship problem.
5. *Problem related to the R's behavior:* You received a C on an essay for an English class. You think the essay deserves an A. You've scheduled an appointment to talk about the grade.
6. *Problem solving:* You and another student are getting together for the first time to talk about a joint term paper you plan to write for your introductory sociology course.
7. *Persuasion:* The E has just walked onto your used car lot and is looking at a 1990 BMW.

The Body

Once the R has set the stage for the interview with an appropriate opening, he or she develops an overall strategy for the body of the interview that ranges on a continuum from nondirective to directive.

In a **nondirective interview**, the R deliberately grants the E control of the structure and pacing of the interview. The R may do this for a variety of reasons: The R may not have enough knowledge to be able to effectively structure the interview; the R may want to give the E greater freedom to generate relevant information; or the R may want to be able to better adapt to the unique characteristics of each E.

The following exchange illustrates a nondirective approach to a counseling interview between a student and an English instructor:

R: What goals would you like to set for yourself?

E: I'd like to be a better student.

R: What do you mean by that?

E: I'd like to learn how to write better and get better grades in my English class.

R: What do you think that would take?

E: I guess I would have to manage my time a little better than I have.

R: For example?

At the other end of the continuum is the **directive interview**. In such interviews, the R retains control of the purpose, structure, and pacing of the interview. The R may decide to retain control for a variety of reasons: The R may need to quantify the results obtained in the interview for purposes of comparison with other interviews, the R may not have the time required for conducting a nondirective interview, or the R may lack the training necessary to conduct a nondirective interview in a reliable and valid fashion. Whatever the reason, when choosing the directive interview option the R has four choices in terms of structure.

The nonscheduled interview. Here the R prepares an interview guide that lists potential topics and subtopics. The topics may or may not be covered in the actual interview, and they may or may not be covered in the listed order. What actually happens in the interview depends more on the responses of the E than on the R's interview guide. For example:

- What was your college major? (How did you choose it? If you were making the choice today, would you choose the same major? Did you con-

NONDIRECTIVE INTERVIEW

An interview in which the interviewer grants the interviewee control of the structure and pacing of the interview.

DIRECTIVE INTERVIEW

An interview in which the interviewer retains control of the purpose, structure, and pacing of the interview.

sider other majors? What do you like about your major? What do you dislike about your major?)

- What is your job experience? (Which of your jobs have you enjoyed the most? Why? Which have you enjoyed least? Why? Which of your supervisors would you consider a good role model? Why?)

The moderately scheduled interview. When using this option, the R prepares an interview guide that includes all the major questions, with possible probe questions under each major question. Although all of the major questions are asked, the order may be varied and the probes may or may not be used. For example, consider the following approach to a counseling interview:

- What is the problem? (What is unique about the problem right now? What part of the problem can we do something about right now? What part of it do you want to work on right now?)
- How have you handled similar problems or this problem in the past? (Can you do the same thing now? Who else have you talked to about this problem? What did they say? Did you do it? If not, why not? If it worked, can you do the same thing again now?)
- How can I help? (What do you want me to do?)
- Who else can be of help to you? (What about family? friends or neighbors? employers or teachers? spiritual leader, physician, or counselor? social agency, psychologist, or other specialist?)
- What do you plan to do about this problem? (When do you plan to do this? How about tomorrow?)

The highly scheduled interview. Here the R prepares an interview schedule that contains all the questions that will be asked (including all probe questions), using the exact wording that will be used with each E. Each E receives exactly the same questions in exactly the same order. There are, however, no precoded response options. For example:

- Did you vote in the last presidential election?
- Do you intend to vote in this election?
- Have you decided whom you will vote for?
- If "yes," whom are you likely to vote for?
- If "no," if the election were held today and you were voting, who would get your vote?

The highly scheduled, standardized interview. In this case the R prepares an interview schedule that includes all the questions to be asked in the order in which they are to be asked, with all the answer options. For example:

- Do you pay out-of-state or in-state tuition?
  _____out-of-state; _____in-state; _____don't know

- Is it fair to raise out-of-state tuition at a faster rate than in-state tuition?
  _____very fair; _____fair; _____not sure; _____unfair;
  _____very unfair

- How important is the issue of tuition increases to you?
  _____very important; _____important; _____uncertain;
  _____unimportant; _____very unimportant

The Closing

Once the purpose of the interview has been achieved, the R must consider how to bring the interview to a satisfying close. This phase of the interview, the **closing**, is especially important in that what occurs here is likely to determine E's impression of the interview as a whole. Knapp et al. studied the functions and norms involved when individuals take leave of each other.[4] Based on their review of the literature, they conclude that the termination phase of a conversation serves three functions: concluding, summarizing, and supporting. That is, in this part of the interview the R needs to utilize both verbal and nonverbal strategies (1) to signal the end of the interview, (2) to review the substantive conclusions produced by the in-

CLOSING
The termination phase of an interview.

terview, and (3) to express satisfaction with the interaction and project what will happen next. The following strategies may help you achieve these purposes.

1. *Offer to answer questions.* Be sincere in your desire to answer questions and give the interviewee adequate time to ask. Do not give a quick answer to one question and then end the interview.

2. *Use clearinghouse questions* (e.g., "Is there anything I've missed?"). The clearinghouse question allows you to determine whether you have covered all topics or answered all the interviewee's questions. It can be an effective closing if your request is perceived not as a formality or an attempt to be sociable, but as an honest effort to identify any questions, information, or areas of concern that have not been discussed adequately.

3. *Declare the completion of the purpose or task.* The four-letter word "well" probably brings more interviews to a close than any other phrase. When people hear it, they automatically assume the end is near and prepare for their leave-taking.

4. *Make personal inquiries.* Personal inquiries are pleasant ways to end interviews, but they must be sincere and show genuine interest in the interviewee. Interviewees judge sincerity by the way interviewers listen and react verbally and nonverbally.

5. *Signal that time is up.* This closing is most effective when a time limit has been announced or agreed upon in the opening. Be tactful in calling time, and try not to give the impression that you are moving the interviewee along an assembly line.

6. *Explain the reason for the closing.* Tell the person why you must close the interview and be sure the justifications are real. If an interviewee thinks you are giving phony excuses, any future interactions will be strained.

7. *Express appreciation or satisfaction.* A note of appreciation or satisfaction is a common closing because interviewers usually have received something—information, help, a sale, a story, and so on.

8. *Show concern.* Expressions of concern for the interviewee's health, welfare, or future are effective if they are sincere and not merely verbal habits.

9. *Plan for the next meeting.* It is often appropriate to arrange the next interview or reveal what will happen next, including date, time, place, topic, content, and purpose.

10. *Summarize the interview.* A summary is a common closing for informational, appraisal, counseling, and sales interviews. Summaries

may repeat important information, stages, and agreements, or verify accuracy or agreement.[5]

Using Effective Questions

In their book *The Language of the Classroom*, Bellack and colleagues describe classroom communication as a language game composed of four types of moves:

Structuring   Structuring moves serve the function of setting the context for subsequent behavior by either launching or halting-excluding interaction between students and teachers. For example, teachers frequently launch a class period with a structuring move in which they focus attention on the topic or problem to be discussed during that session.

Soliciting   Moves in this category are designed to elicit a verbal response, to encourage persons addressed to attend to something, or to elicit a physical response. All questions are solicitations, as are commands, imperatives, and requests.

Responding   These moves bear a reciprocal relationship to soliciting moves and occur only in relation to them. Their pedagogical function is to fulfill the expectation of soliciting moves; thus, students' answers to teachers' questions are classified as responding moves.

Reacting   These moves are occasioned by a structuring, soliciting, responding, or prior reacting move but are not directly elicited by them. Pedagogically, these moves serve to modify (by clarifying, synthesizing, or explaining) and/or to rate (positively or negatively) what has been said previously. Reacting moves differ from responding moves: Although a responding move is always directly elicited by a solicitation, preceding moves serve only as the occasion for reactions. A teacher's rating of a student's response, for example, is designated as a reacting move.[6]

It is easy to apply Bellack et al.'s analysis to the language game of the interview. The R starts an interview with a structuring move (perhaps by talking about the purpose of the interview) and then solicits a response from the E with a question. The E's response then serves as an opportunity for reactions by the R. In this section of this chapter, the focus is on the question or solicitation phase of this process. You can characterize a question in a wide variety of ways, including the latitude of response it provides an E, the antecedent of the question, the question-antecedent relationship, expectations and premises implicit in the question, the content or subject matter of the question, and the vocabulary used in wording the question. The primary concern in this chapter is with the type, impact, and sequence of questions in the interview.

Question Type

In evaluating question type, you should consider two characteristics: (1) the freedom the question grants the E in terms of possible response and (2) the antecedent of the question. As labels for these two characteristics of a question, the terms *open/closed* and *primary/secondary* are used.

In some situations you should give the E a great deal of flexibility in constructing a response to the question. Perhaps you are asking questions concerning a topic about which the E knows more than you do. Or perhaps you want to allow the E to become relaxed, and thus you ask a question for which there is no one correct answer. Or perhaps you are initiating questioning on a topic for which it is important not to bias or influence the attitudes of the E. In such situations, the R should ask a question that gives the E great freedom in terms of how to respond. That is, the R should ask an **open question**. For example: "Tell me about yourself." "How do you like being a student here?" "What issues will influence your decision to vote for one of the presidential candidates?"

In other situations, however, the R will want to give the E less freedom in responding. Perhaps, for example, the R is conducting a survey of student attitudes toward parking on campus and wants to compare the attitudes of such groups as commuters, dormitory residents, and sorority/fraternity members. Asking open questions in such a situation would make comparisons difficult. Thus, the R would be likely to ask questions at the **closed** end of the open/closed continuum.

The most closed form of a question is labeled a *bipolar* question, for which the R has two possible responses—"yes" and "no." Examples of bipolar questions are "Do you normally eat breakfast?" "Do you own a car?" and "Did you vote in the last election?" Closed questions can also take the multiple-choice form: "In which college are you currently enrolled—Arts and Sciences? Business? Education? Engineering? Fine Arts?" "What is your political party affiliation—Republican? Democrat? Independent? other? none?"

In terms of question type, then, interviewers need to consider the advantages and disadvantages of asking questions at a particular location on the open/closed continuum. That is, they need to ask themselves: "Given my particular interviewing situation, topic, and E, am I better off asking a question at the open or closed end of the continuum?"

A second consideration related to question form is that of question antecedent—that is, what is the relationship of this question to what has happened previously in the interview? The broad terms used to describe this re-

OPEN QUESTION
A question that gives the interviewee relative freedom in responding.

CLOSED QUESTION
A question that gives the interviewee little or no freedom in responding.

lationship are primary and secondary. **Primary questions** introduce new topics; **secondary questions** seek clarification or elaboration of responses to the primary question. Thus, an interviewer might start an area of questioning by asking "What are your beliefs about the topic of abortion?" This primary question might then be followed with a number of secondary questions such as: "Should there be parental notification for individuals of a certain age?" "Should the father be consulted?" "What restrictions, if any, should the state be allowed to impose on the decision?"

Secondary questions can take a variety of forms. Some of the more common forms of secondary questions are:

PRIMARY QUESTION
A question that initiates a new topic.

SECONDARY QUESTION
A question that develops a topic that has already been introduced.

Clarification   Directly requesting more information about a response (e.g., "Could you tell me a little more about the kind of person you would like to work for?").

Elaboration   Directly requesting an extension of a response (e.g., "Are there any other features of location that you would consider important?").

Paraphrasing   Putting the response in the questioner's language in an attempt to establish understanding (e.g., "Let's see if I've understood what you're saying: You consider the type of people you work with more important than salary and benefits?").

Silence   Waiting without speaking for the respondent to begin or resume speaking.

Encouragement   Using brief sounds and phrases that indicate attentiveness to, and interest in, what the respondent is saying (e.g., "Uh huh," "I see," "That's interesting," "Good," and "Yes, I understand").

Mirroring   Repeating the response using the language used by the respondent (e.g., "You say, then, that it is important to you to be located near a university?").

Summarizing   Summarizing several previous responses and seeking confirmation of the correctness of the summary (e.g., "Let's see if I've got it: Your ideal job involves an appreciative boss, supportive colleagues, interesting work, and living in a large metropolitan area?").

Clearinghouse   Asking if you have elicited all the important or available information (e.g., "Have I asked everything that I should have asked?").[7]

In terms of question type, then, a single question can be (1) identified in terms of its location on a continuum from open to closed and (2) labeled as either primary or secondary. If it is a secondary question, it can be further identified as a special type of secondary question (e.g., elaboration, encouragement, mirror). It is the R's responsibility to make wise decisions in selecting and using open/closed and primary/secondary questions.

Question Impact

In addition to considering question type, interviewers must also consider the likely impact of a question on the E; that is, is the E likely to find the question understandable, relevant, and unbiased?

First, will the E find the question understandable? Stanley Paine, in his book *The Art of Asking Questions*, makes a number of useful suggestions for enhancing the clarity of questions.[8] He suggests, first, that the questioner start by making sure that he or she understands the issue around which the question is organized. To achieve this understanding, the questioner should ask the stock journalistic questions of who, what, when, where, and how. Second, the questioner should use a dictionary and other resources to ensure that the wording of the question is as direct and simple as possible. Third, the questioner should keep the number of words in the question in the range of 20 or fewer. Longer questions create too much ambiguity. Fourth, the questioner should phrase questions positively because negative phrasing tends to be more confusing. Thus, instead of asking "You haven't ever voted in the campus student government elections, have you?" ask, "Have you ever voted in campus student government elections?"

Second, will the E find the question relevant? In addition to understanding the question, the E should also have an answer to the question and be willing to give it. Two strategies for ensuring this are pretests and the use of filter questions. When using a pretest, the R identifies a small number of individuals representative of Es who will eventually answer the question and asks them what they think the question means. Pretesting is also an excellent means to work on the clarity of the question wording. A second strategy for determining the relevance of the question can be made part of the interviewing process. This strategy involves asking a **filter question** before asking the question itself. With this strategy, the R asks respondents what they know about the topic before asking them a question about the topic. For example, an R might ask, "What, if anything, do you know about student government's position on the proposed new grading scale?" (a filter question) before asking, "Are you in favor of, against, or neutral toward the student government's position on the proposed new grading scale?" Both strategies, then, are ways of ensuring that the question is relevant to the E—that is, that the E is likely to have an answer to the question and be willing to provide it.

Third, is the question unbiased? The third test of the impact of a question on the E concerns the identification of unidentified assumptions or premises undergirding a question. The goal here is to avoid questions that unconsciously lead individuals to answer questions in a certain way. When a question suggests or implies the answer that is expected, it is called a **directed question**; that is, it directs the E to respond in a certain way. Some such questions, called **leading questions**, are subtle in the direction they

---

FILTER QUESTION
A question designed to find out what, if anything, an interviewee knows about a particular topic.

DIRECTED QUESTION
A question that clearly suggests or implies the answer that is expected.

LEADING QUESTION
A question that subtly suggests or implies the answer that is expected.

provide: for example, "You enjoy this class, don't you?" "Would you like to go get a cup of coffee with me?" Other questions are less subtle in their biasing effect: "Are you a bigot?" "When was the last time you cheated on an exam?" Both of these examples are **loaded questions**—the first is loaded with the use of an emotionally charged word ("bigot"), and the second is loaded because it asks two questions rather than one ("Have you ever cheated on an exam?" "When was the last time you cheated on an exam?"). Questions that provide no hint to the E concerning the expected response are labeled **neutral**—for example, "What, if anything, is your attitude toward the fraternities and sororities on this campus?" Although generally the R should ask neutral questions in an interview, there are exceptions. For example, when dealing with a topic that might threaten the ego of an E, you might get a more honest response by asking a directed question that reveals that you will not be shocked by the E's response. Thus, under some circumstances, a directed question such as "When was the last time you had too much to drink?" might produce a more honest response than the neutral question "Have you ever had too much to drink?" When Kinsey began to interview individuals about their sexual practices, for example, he

LOADED QUESTION
A question that implies or suggests the answer that is expected either by using emotional language or by asking two questions in the guise of one.

NEUTRAL QUESTION
A question that provides no clue as to the expected answer.

FIGURE 9.3
Sometimes the loaded question is really two questions in one.

"*If elected, would you try to fool some of the people all of the time, all of the people some of the time or go for the big one: All of the people all of the time!*"

used loaded questions such as "When was the last time you engaged in the following sexual practices?" His premise was that individuals who had not engaged in certain practices would be more than willing to tell him that fact, while individuals who had engaged in those practices would be more likely to say so when asked a loaded question that indicated he would not be shocked by their answer. The key point to be made, then, is that an R should know the difference between directed and neutral questions and should ask directed questions only when they are likely to serve the interviewer's purpose.

Question Sequence

Having considered the form (open/closed and primary/secondary) and the potential impact on an E (understandability, relevance, and bias) of a single question, we turn now to a consideration of options for sequencing questions. Although a variety of formats are possible, three of the main options have the visual labels of funnel, inverted funnel, and tunnel.

As the label **funnel sequence** implies, with this approach the interviewer starts with broad, open-ended questions and moves to narrower, more closed questions. Consider the case of a student interviewing another student concerning participation in sports:

What sports, if any, do you actually participate in?
What are your experiences with racquetball?
What are your experiences with golf?
What are your experiences with running?
Which of the three sports are you best at? Worst at?
Which of the three sports do you enjoy most? Least?

The **inverted funnel sequence** starts with narrow, closed questions and moves to more open-ended types of questions. An example of such an approach might involve an interviewer asking a student questions about computer usage:

Do you use a PC?
Do you own your own PC? If so, what brand is it?
What kinds of software do you use?
For what major functions do you use your computer?
How did you learn to use a computer?
Is there anything else you can tell me about your use of computers?

The **tunnel sequence** (to continue the visual metaphor) can be either large or small. A large tunnel would involve a series of broad, open-ended questions; a small tunnel (the more common form) would ask a series of

FUNNEL SEQUENCE
A question sequence that moves from broad, open-ended questions to narrower, closed ones.

INVERTED FUNNEL SEQUENCE
A question sequence that moves from narrow, closed questions to broad, open-ended ones.

TUNNEL SEQUENCE
A question sequence that utilizes questions at one level (i.e., either all of the questions are broad and open-ended or they are all narrow and closed).

narrow, closed questions. An interviewer might ask a student, for example, about participation in a variety of campus activities in the following way:

Using the following scale (VF = very frequently, F = frequently, O = occasionally, R = rarely, and N = never), indicate your participation in the following campus activities:

1. Attending sporting events (e.g., football, baseball)   VF F O R N
2. Attending cultural events (e.g., theater, art, music)   VF F O R N
3. Attending social events (e.g., parties)   VF F O R N
4. Attending academic events (e.g., lectures)   VF F O R N
5. Working for wages   VF F O R N
6. Working as a volunteer   VF F O R N

You can put together the three sequences that have been described in various combinations over the course of an interview. Say, for example, you are interviewing a political science professor concerning a research project she has recently completed on the role of hostages in international relations. You might start the interview with a funnel sequence, thus opening up avenues that you can explore with narrower secondary questions that probe for clarification. Later in the interview, you may find it useful to develop some topics with an inverted funnel sequence as a way of focusing the professor's memory—using a series of closed questions both to jog her memory on the topic and to enhance her motivation to respond to your more open-ended questions. As the interview proceeds, you may find uses for a tunnel sequence of either broad, open-ended questions or narrow, closed questions.

In addition to these three sequences, there are other options as well. Perhaps the best known of these is one developed by George Gallup for use when conducting public opinion polls aimed at determining intensity of opinions and attitudes. Labeled the **Quintamensional Plan,** it involves a five-step process:

1. Awareness of the topic is ascertained by a free-answer knowledge question (sometimes labeled a *filter question*): "What, if anything, do you know about bluegrass music?"
2. Uninfluenced attitudes on the subject are developed in a free-answer question: "What is your opinion of bluegrass music?"
3. Specific attitudes are elicited through a two-way or multiple-choice question: "How frequently do you purchase bluegrass music—often, occasionally, seldom, or never?"

QUINTAMENSIONAL PLAN
A five-step question sequence developed by George Gallup for use in conducting public opinion polls; involves examining awareness, uninfluenced attitudes, specific attitudes, reasoning, and intensity of feeling.

4. The reasoning behind the attitudes is examined via a free-answer, reason-why question: "Why do you feel this way?"

5. Intensity of feeling is examined via an intensity question: "How strongly do you feel about this—not very strongly, strongly, or very strongly?"[9]

Responding Effectively

In addition to asking good questions, Rs need to know how to react appropriately to the Es' responses to further the dialogue of the interview. In terms of our earlier description of the language game of the interview, Rs need to be able to use effective "reacting" moves—that is, develop an effective **response style.** Rogers conducted a number of research studies that are helpful in thinking about this process.[10]

RESPONSE STYLE
The pattern an individual develops for using Rogers's five reacting moves: evaluative, interpretive, supportive, probing, and understanding.

Rogers was interested in how people communicate with each other in face-to-face situations. One focus of his research was on the characteristic ways that one person responds to what another individual says (reacting moves). He found that 80 percent of all messages that people use can be summarized in five categories:

Evaluative   Indicates that the R has made a judgment of relative goodness, appropriateness, effectiveness, or rightness of the E's response. The R in some way implies what the E might or ought to do.

Interpretive   Indicates that the R's intent is to teach—to tell the E what the response means, how the E really feels. The R either obviously or subtly implies what the E might or ought to think.

Supportive   Indicates that the R's intent is to reassure, to pacify, and to reduce the E's intensity of feeling. The R implies that it is either appropriate or not necessary for the E to feel as he or she does.

Probing   Indicates that the R's intent is to seek further information and provoke further discussion.

Understanding   Indicates that the R's intent is only to make sure he or she correctly understands what the E is saying.[11]

To illustrate Rogers's categories, consider the following situation:

R: Now that you have your B.A., what do you intend to do with it?

E: I don't know. I got out of school last month and thought, "Now what?" I looked for a job, but the job market is the pits. I'm thinking about working on a graduate degree, but I'm not sure I want to be in school right now—or what I'd get my degree in if I did decide to go on.

Evaluative response   "The situation will improve with time. Why don't you go to the graduate school and talk with one of the advisers?"

Interpretive response   "You seem a little confused right now. Is there anyone you can talk to who might help to clarify your thinking?"

Supportive response   "Boy, do I know what you mean! The job market has done similar things to lots of us these days."

Probing response   "What graduate majors have you considered?"

Understanding response   "You're worried about whether you should try to work or try to go to graduate school?"

In addition to identifying the five categories, Rogers discovered that most people have a natural tendency to use evaluative and interpretive responses more frequently than the other three. In fact, he found the following order of frequency for the five categories: evaluative, interpretive, supportive, probing, and understanding.

REALITY CHECK

Conducting an Interview

Conduct an in-depth information-gathering interview and produce a written report (of no more than five typed pages) in which you summarize the information you received and comment on what you learned about the interview process.

    The interview must last at least two hours; the interviewee must be a close acquaintance older than you and must have children (consider interviewing one of your parents); and the interview must cover at least two of the following topics:

- The person's philosophy of raising children (consider topics such as discipline; teaching at home and at school; sex; finances; making friends; respect for authority; patriotism; character formation)

- The person's political beliefs (ask about political affiliation and commitment; involvement in civic affairs; involvement in government)

- The person's religious beliefs, their effect on the person's life, and how these beliefs relate to family life

- The person's goals in life and how the person is working to achieve these goals

- The person's philosophy of leisure time (How should one spend this time? Ideally, how would the person like to spend this time? In reality, how does the person spend this time?)

In describing the implications of his research, Rogers suggests that our natural tendency to evaluate and interpret other people's remarks interferes with rather than enhances communication. If we were to understand, probe, and support their responses before evaluating and interpreting them, we would be more likely to comprehend what the other person was trying to say. The other person would also be more likely to find the interaction satisfying. Thus, the message of Rogers's research for the interviewer is twofold: (1) master the ability to use all five reacting moves and be prepared to use them and (2) when using these moves, start with understanding, probing, and support before moving to interpretation and evaluation.

The Employment Interview

Now that the general principles that apply to all interviews have been examined, the remaining pages of this chapter are devoted to a special form of the interview—the selection or employment interview. For most college students, the employment interview occurs in two stages: (1) a screening interview that typically takes place in the campus placement center and (2) a determinate interview that occurs on the premises of the hiring organization. The **screening interview**, from the employer's perspective, is used to screen out applicants who do not meet organizational requirements. The **determinant interview** is used to determine whether a qualified applicant should be hired. In this chapter, the primary focus is on the screening interview, although the principles discussed apply to both types of employment interviews. The employment interview is featured here for a variety of reasons: (1) it emphasizes the main functions of information giving, information gathering, and persuasion; (2) it is an interview type in which both R and E are responsible for prior planning and for the success of the interview; and (3) it is an important interview that most members of society go through multiple times.

When we discussed the general principles of interviewing, we took the point of view of the R and asked you to consider the role of the E. In this section we do the reverse. We start by analyzing how an interviewee ought to prepare for an employment interview, and then we explore various aspects of the interview itself.

SCREENING INTERVIEW
The first stage in an employment interview; during this stage the interviewer tries to find out whether the applicant can do the job.

DETERMINANT INTERVIEW
The second stage in an employment interview; during this stage the interviewer decides whether or not to offer the job to the applicant.

Preparing for the Interview

Prior planning for the interview from the E's perspective involves four interrelated tasks: (1) conducting an honest self-assessment; (2) preparing materials to be used in the process; (3) locating jobs and doing homework on the business environment and organizations; and (4) building realistic expectations about the interviewing process.

Conducting a Self-Assessment

The starting point for a job search is an honest self-assessment. Most college and university campuses have a career planning and placement center that can provide excellent assistance to students on this and the other tasks related to the employment interview in the form of people, films, and written materials. If you haven't already visited the facility on your cam-

---

SELF-CHECK

Self-Assessment for Career Preparation

Divide a sheet of paper into three columns: "Life Goals," "Skills," and "Career Goals." As quickly as possible, list as many entries under each heading as you can. Once you have run out of ideas to list, read the entries in each column and edit them by combining ideas and deleting redundant items. Rank order the resulting ideas in each column in perceived order of importance. What, for example, is your most important life goal? skill? career goal? Finally, using what you perceive to be the most important ideas in each column, create a checklist that you can use to compare job possibilities.

Here is a sample checklist:

	Company		
Life goals:	*A*	*B*	*C*
1. Get married and have a family	+	+	?
2. Retire at age 60	+	−	+
Skills:			
1. Good at oral communication	+	+	+
2. Good "people" person	+	+	+
Career goals:			
1. Live in the Dallas area	−	+	+
2. Work with interesting people	+	?	+

Note: + means that company is good for my skills/goals; − means that company is bad for my skills/goals; ? means that I am unsure whether that company is good or bad for my skills/goals.

---

pus, you ought to do so. You are likely to find friendly people there with good advice about what you can be doing now to prepare yourself for the job search. It is never too early to begin the process. Campus counseling centers and the library are additional resources. In addition, local bookstores typically have a section of books that provide help on such tasks as conducting self-assessment, locating jobs, preparing résumés, and conducting employment interviews.

As you engage in the process of self-assessment, you should consider three areas: (1) life goals: What do you want to accomplish before you die? What is your life mission? (2) skills: What things do you enjoy? What activities do you do well? (3) career goals: Where do you wish to live and work? What will your life-style include? What income level do you need and want? What kind of work environment do you want? What level of responsibility do you want? What credentials are necessary?

Preparing a Résumé

A résumé is a printed summary of your educational and work experiences and accomplishments. It is a selling document whose sole purpose is to persuade employers to grant you an interview. It is the vehicle for making a positive first impression on potential employers. An effective résumé tells just enough about you to make employers believe that their company may need your skills and experience.

In thinking about putting together an effective résumé, consider the task of those who will read it. During the initial screening process, employers look at large numbers of résumés and most of them (95 to 99 percent) end up in the inactive file or the wastebasket. The conventional wisdom is that the average résumé has 45 seconds to make either a positive or a negative impression on the employer.

So how do you make a positive impression? Before considering content, consider form. Although there are no hard and fast rules, there are certain biases that should only be violated for a good reason. For example, unless you are looking for a creative position in areas such as advertising or graphic design, use white, off-white, or light beige paper. If possible, limit the résumé to a single page. If you must use two pages, print it front and back to avoid the possibility of losing a page. With personal computers as widely accessible as they are, employers expect the professional look of word processing. Use a readable typeface—Palatino and Times are good choices among fonts that are readily available. Avoid any font that has a city name—for example, New York or Chicago—because they are not constructed for high-quality printing. Make the résumé attractive by using white space appropriately.

What about the content of the résumé? Once again, there are no hard and fast rules. There are some important general principles, however. First, be 100 percent honest. Mention your assets rather than your liabilities but don't falsify or embellish those assets. Second, provide focus for your résumé. Although it might seem that nonspecific résumés might open more doors, the opposite is true. To capture the attention of an employer, the résumé should be designed with a specific employment objective in mind and should use that objective to make decisions about what to include and exclude. Third, while listing employment history and activities, use reverse chronological order—that is, list the most recent activity first and then go back in time. Fourth, when listing activities and jobs, emphasize those that relate to your job objective using action words that show results. Most young recent grads seeking their first full-time job have limited work experience. Include volunteer work and part-time employment, emphasizing activities that helped prepare you for the kind of work you are seeking. For each entry, ask yourself, "Did I (action word) anyone or anything?" For (action word), substitute such words as administered, supervised, constructed, established, coordinated, produced, and the like. Fifth, as you list things, remember that the employer may not be familiar with abbreviations and organizations that are very familiar to you. When in doubt, spell everything out.

Given these five general principles, consider what information you will include in each of the following categories:

Name, address, etc.　What will be the best way to reach you in writing? by phone? by fax? Will you need to include two addresses—one for campus and one for home?

Employment objective　Be concise and specific. It is better to create multiple résumés than to have widely diversified objectives in the same résumé. Underneath this statement, you may wish to include information about your availability—for example, *Available July 1, 1995.*

Education　In reverse chronological order (i.e., starting with the most recent), list the institutions you attended, their locations, and the dates of attendance. Also list degrees received (or date to be received) and academic majors and areas of concentration. Awards and GPA can also be listed here if they will enhance your marketability.

Work experience　As you list work experience in reverse chronological order, focus on concrete examples of achievement. Emphasize job functions rather than job titles. Remember that prospective employers read this section carefully to discover an answer to the question, "How do this person's experience, abilities, and achievements relate to my organization's needs?"

Jane A. Doe

Current Address:	**Permanent Address:**
1007 Thistlewood, Apt. 67	339 Grant Street
Norman, OK 73072	Dallas, TX 75275
(405) 555-8884	(214) 555-3231

OBJECTIVE
To obtain an entry-level business/marketing position in an organization seeking an individual with demonstrated leadership, public speaking skills, and marketing experience

EDUCATION
University of Oklahoma, Norman, OK
Bachelor of Arts, Public Relations, May 1995, GPA 3.5/4.0

HONORS
Outstanding Young Women of America; Dean's List; Academic Scholarship; Alpha Lambda Delta (women's honorary)

ACTIVITIES
Journalism Club Secretary; Panhellenic Vice President; Varsity Debate; Delta Delta Delta Social Sorority President; Academic Programs Council

RELEVANT EXPERIENCE
June 1992–present
AT&T Marketing Division, Oklahoma City, OK
Marketing Support Assistant
*Responsible for customer support, telemarketing for new accounts, and trouble-shooting for installed firms when marketing representatives were out of the office
*Designed brochure to update client knowledge of AT&T equipment
*Presented demonstrations at executive conference in Houston, TX

Summers 1990 and 1991
Dillard's Department Store, Norman, OK
Department Supervisor
*Maintained inventory control and stock rotation
*Recognized as a member of Dillard's $100,000 club

ADDITIONAL INFORMATION
Coursework includes 16 hours of communication studies
Knowledge of Macintosh and IBM computers
Willing to travel and relocate
Hobbies include running and racquetball

REFERENCES
Available upon request

FIGURE 9.4

A well-prepared résumé is a form of competent written communication. Like speech communication, it presents its author through verbal and nonverbal means.

Student activities   For employers, participation in a variety of academic, extracurricular, or social activities indicates that you are motivated and get involved. Thus, it can be beneficial to include several activities, especially if they are relevant to your career objective. Be selective in what you list and emphasize accomplishment.

Hobbies   You may want to indicate some of your hobbies and extracurricular activities that reveal what you do apart from your professional life. Employers usually react positively to the opportunity to learn more about you as a "total person."

Other possibilities

    Personal data   It is best not to include data such as marital status, age, race, religion, and the like. Employers know that they are liable for unlawful use of such information, even if you supply it, and some of them use gatekeepers to block out information such as the above that might be used to discriminate.

    Military status   If the information is relevant, include branch of the military, dates of active duty, discharge rank, and brief description of your duties.

    Publications   If the information is relevant, use a standard reference form to list articles, books, convention presentations, and so on.

    Professional memberships   If the information is relevant, include membership, offices held, and professional certifications and/or licenses.

    References   Because references are almost always glowingly positive, many employers don't value them a great deal. At most, therefore, include the statement "References available upon request."

Locating Jobs

The third element of preinterview preparation involves identifying potential jobs and doing homework on your field, the organizations to whom you are applying, and potential job positions.

Although there are almost an infinite variety of strategies for locating jobs, your three best sources are likely to be people you know, placement centers, and classified advertisements. The place to start is with family, friends, professors, former employers, and individuals working in your field. Let these individuals know the kind of job you are looking for and ask for suggestions. You might also make appointments with individuals who work in your field as a way of learning more about possible career opportunities and of establishing important contacts.

Placement centers are a second source of jobs. Most college campuses have a centralized placement center where recruiters from major companies come to interview potential employees. Some departments and colleges within the university provide additional services. In addition, many professional organizations provide resources for locating jobs. If you are unsure about the resources for your field of study, ask a faculty member who works in the area. The third source to consider is classified advertisements. In addition to your local newspaper, head over to the reading room of the library and look at the classified section of some of the national newspapers and periodicals that emphasize your field of study.

Once you begin getting leads on possible jobs, learn everything you can about the potential position and the organization in which it is located. Your best source for this information is likely to be your campus placement center. In addition to general reference works (e.g., *Occupational Outlook Handbook, Moody's Industrial Manual, Dictionary of Occupational Titles*), it is likely to have the company's annual report, recruiting literature, and perhaps even a public relations videotape. If your placement center doesn't have these resources, call the company directly and ask for a copy of its annual report and other descriptive literature. You can also talk to current or former employees and other individuals who have relevant information. The more information you have about the company and your possible position within it, the better able you will be to answer the questions you will be asked in the interviewing process. You will also be able to ask the interviewer intelligent questions.

Building Realistic Expectations

The final component of preinterview preparation involves developing realistic expectations about the interviewing process and preparing for "rejection shock."[12] In preparing for interviews, it is important to remember (1) that the interviewer is interviewing many individuals for each position and (2) that his or her decisions will often be influenced more by subjective factors such as intuition, attitudes, and stereotypes of a good employee than by objective factors such as job qualifications. Thus, a job applicant is very likely to face rejection numerous times during the course of a job search—because there was a better qualified applicant, because the interviewer made a mistake, or because an equally qualified candidate had an advantage (e.g., a personal contact in the company). A job candidate, therefore, needs to constantly remember that rejection is not uncommon—and that rejection is not personal, but is the inevitable result of a tight job market and a less than perfect selection tool. The attitude that the applicant needs to take, then, is that of the door-to-door salesperson who, knowing that she or he makes a sale at only one out of every ten homes, says: "If I get turned down at this door, it just makes it more likely that I'll make a sale at the next house." The applicant should also remember that persistence pays. If one approaches the job search intelligently and persistently, one will get a job.

◼ *Participating in the Interview*

Successful preparation for participation in the employment interview requires that you know the purpose of the interview and the likely structure; anticipate the questions the R is likely to ask; and prepare questions to ask the R.

Knowing the Purpose and Structure

From the perspective of the R, the screening interview has three major purposes: (1) to discover if there is a potential match between the applicant and the position; (2) to build goodwill for the company and the organization; and (3) to ensure that the applicant has enough information about the company and position to make an informed decision. From the perspective of the E, the employment interview involves convincing the R that the applicant possesses the qualifications to do an excellent job and obtaining enough information to make an informed decision, should a job be offered.

To discover whether there is a potential match between the applicant and the position, the R typically explores five areas of information as they relate to the specific job: ability, desire, personality, character, and health. First, based on the résumé and the interview, the R needs to discover if the E has the experience, education, training, intelligence, and ability to do what the job requires. Second, the R needs to discover if the E has the desire or motivation to use those abilities to do a good job. To gather this information, the R is likely to explore such things as the E's record of changes in jobs, schools, majors; the E's reasons for wanting this job; the E's knowledge of the company; and concrete examples of prior success that indicate desire to achieve. The third area involves an assessment of the E's personality and how well the E is likely to fit into the position and the company or organization. Depending on the job, this will likely involve an attempt to discover the E's personal goals, independence and self-reliance, imagination and creativity, and ability to manage or lead. A fourth area of judgment is that of character. What can be learned of the E's personal behavior, honesty, financial responsibility, and accuracy and objectivity in reports? The final area is that of health. Is there any physical barrier that might limit the E's successful performance of the job?

In order to achieve the multiple purposes of the screening interview, interviewers typically use between 20 and 35 minutes to accomplish the following five functions: opening, asking questions, giving information, answering questions, and closing.

Although there are many possible approaches to the structure of an interview, the following is typical: (1) A brief opening is used to put the E at ease and provide an overview of the structure of the interview. (2) This is followed by either a description of the company and the position or a series of questions that seek to gather information about the E's ability, desire, personality, character, and health. A major portion of the time will focus on the R's asking of questions. (3) The R then asks the E whether the E has any questions. (4) The R closes the interview by telling the E what will happen next.

Preparing Answers to the Interviewer's Questions

An important part of preparing for an employment interview is anticipating the kinds of questions you will be asked and thinking about strategies for responding to those questions in ways that best convey your ability and desire to succeed at the job. Knowing what the interviewer is looking for (ability, desire, personality, character, and health) should allow you to anticipate many of the questions you will be asked. Listed below are frequently asked questions generated from conversations with employment interviewers and from a search of the literature.[13]

- What led you to choose your particular field (or your academic major)? What do you like about it? What don't you like about it?
- In which kinds of positions are you most interested?
- Have you had summer or other previous employment in this or a related field?
- What have you learned from your previous work experience?
- What are the most important considerations for you in choosing a job?
- What kinds of courses have you taken that you think prepared you for this occupation?
- How did you do in courses related to this job? How did you do overall in high school? in college?
- Why did you interview with our company?
- Do you have any geographical preferences about where you work?
- What do you see yourself doing five years from now? ten years from now? What are your long-range goals?
- What percentage of your college expenses did you earn? How?
- How important is your personal life as compared with your work?

- What have you done that shows initiative and willingness to work?

- How do you spend your leisure time? What are your hobbies?

- What would you say is your strongest attribute? What is your weakest point?

- Have you ever had any problems interacting with fellow workers?

- What are your salary expectations? How much money do you want to be earning ten years from now?

- What can you contribute to our company that would make us want to hire you?

- Were you ever fired from a job? Did you ever quit a job? Why?

- Are there any questions that you want to ask?

It is a good idea to rehearse possible answers to questions like these before going into the employment interview. Ask a friend to randomly ask you the questions and then have him or her comment on your answers. Strive for answers that demonstrate your marketable skills in a direct and positive way. Interviewers are looking for results, so use stories and vignettes that show hard, tangible evidence that things you have done have produced bottom-line results. Although it is often uncomfortable to talk about accomplishments, in the screening interview there is no one but you who can tell the interviewer that you are able and willing to do the job well.

Several types of questions can pose special difficulties for the interviewee: illegal questions, surprise questions, and questions about weaknesses. Illegal questions are those that have no direct bearing on job performance and have the potential to lead to discrimination on the basis of race, creed, national origin, sex, handicap, and the like (e.g., "Do you have children, and if you do, what kind of child-care arrangements do you have?" "Do you have any disabilities?" "Are you married?" "This is a hectic office—can you keep up with the young people here?"). Although an organization whose employees ask illegal questions during employment interviews can be subject to a variety of legal penalties by the Equal Employment Opportunity Commission (EEOC) of the federal government, illegal questions continue to be asked and an applicant needs to consider how to answer them. Stewart and Cash suggest five tactics you can use to respond to illegal questions: (1) answer directly but briefly ("Do you attend church regularly?" "Yes, I do"); (2) pose a tactful inquiry ("What does your husband do?" "Why do you ask?"); (3) tactful refusal ("Do you have children?" "My plans to have a family will not interfere with my ability to perform the requirements of this position"); (4) neutralizing ("What happens if your husband gets transferred or needs to relocate?" "My husband and I would discuss locational moves that either of us might have to consider in the future"); and (5) take advantage of the question ("Where were you born?" "I am quite proud that my background is Egyptian because it has helped me to deal effectively with people of various ethnic backgrounds").14

A second category of difficult question is the completely unanticipated "surprise" question (e.g., "Tell me a story"; "If you were an animal, what animal would it be and why?"). If this happens, don't just start talking in a rambling fashion. Instead, either ask the R for additional information ("Did you have a particular kind of story in mind?") or ask for a moment or so to collect your thoughts ("That's a great question, and I've never thought about it. Can I have a minute or so to collect my thoughts?").

A third question type that can pose special difficulty is "Tell me about your weaknesses." One standard response is to talk about weaknesses that really aren't weaknesses (e.g., "I tend to be very picky when it comes to details and I have difficulty letting go of a job until I'm sure it's right"). Another strategy is to think about areas that you would like to develop and

 REALITY CHECK

Questionable Questions

How should a job applicant respond to the following questions from an interviewer? Some of these questions may be illegal, unethical, or both; others, though not obviously illegal, may seem to pry unnecessarily into the applicant's personal business. Is it worth risking a job opportunity to express unwillingness to answer a question? Is there a nonconfrontational way of responding without providing information that should be withheld? Is it ethical to provide the answer?

For each question, write an appropriate response for the interviewee or role-play the situation with a classmate. Be prepared to explain why your suggested response is effective and appropriate.

1. *Male employer to female applicant:* "Would you be willing to stay at the office late? It wouldn't necessarily be all work and no play."
2. *Employer to applicant who currently works for a competitor:* "What were your current employer's profits on widgets this past year?" [The information is confidential.]
3. *Employer to applicant who has a foreign name:* "You have an unusual name. Where does it come from?"
4. *Employer to applicant:* "I see from your résumé that you're new in town. Have you found a church to join yet?"
5. *Employer to applicant:* "Would you be willing to take a drug test? How about a test for HIV?"

talk about your plans for doing so (e.g., "It's kind of hard for most of us to talk about weaknesses. I do know, though, that there are some areas that I'd like to work on. For example, I've just purchased a time management utility for my computer, and I'm now working on strategies for using my time more effectively").

Preparing Questions to Ask the Interviewer

In addition to anticipating questions they might be asked, interviewees also need to prepare questions to ask the interviewer. These questions should indicate that the E has done solid homework and is able and willing to do a good job for the company. Instead of saying "I really don't have any questions right now" or "How much vacation will I get?" the interviewee should be prepared to ask questions such as: "I noticed in the *Wall Street Journal* that you're opening a new plant in Memphis. Do you have additional plans for expansion?" "I noticed in your annual report that you are developing a new training program. If I were hired, would I be in it?" "If you were sitting on my side of this desk, what would you say are the most attractive features of the job?"

Recognizing Inappropriate Tactics

We hope that this chapter has helped you begin to think about the knowledge and skills required in order to be a competent communicator in an employment interview. In closing, we would like to emphasize that, just as there are a number of tactics you can and should use to ensure that an employment interview works in your favor, there are also tactics and behaviors you should avoid. The following instances of actual interviewee behavior, as reported by the personnel executives who conducted the interviews, are examples of behavior that is almost guaranteed to work against you.

- "Said if he was hired, he'd teach me ballroom dancing at no charge, and started demonstrating."
- "She returned that afternoon asking if we could redo the entire interview."
- "Apologized for being late; said he accidentally locked his clothes in his closet."
- "Took three cellular phone calls. Said she had a similar business on the side."
- "Applicant walked in and inquired why he was here."

- "After a difficult question, she wanted to leave the room for a moment to meditate."
- "Candidate was told to take his time answering, so he began writing down each of his answers before speaking."
- "Shortly after sitting down, she brought out a line of cosmetics and started a strong sales pitch."
- "Man brought in his five children and cat."
- "Said if I hired him, I'd soon learn to regret it."
- "Wanted to borrow the fax machine to send out some personal letters."
- "Arrived with a snake around her neck. Said she took her pet everywhere."

REALITY CHECK

The Case of Maribeth

At the beginning of this chapter you met Maribeth Berg, a college sophomore who was preparing to interview Jim Walsh, an insurance agent, concerning his interviewing training and practices. What have you learned in this chapter that might help her prepare for this task?

- What characteristics of the anticipated interaction would allow you to label it an interview? What kind of interview is it?
- What should Maribeth consider as she thinks about the goals of her interview?
- How should Maribeth begin the interview?
- Where on the directive–nondirective continuum should this interview be conducted?
- What type of closing would work best for the interview?
- What can Maribeth do to be sure her questions are clear, relevant, and unbiased? What mixture of open/closed and primary/secondary questions should she anticipate? What combination of funnel, inverted funnel, and tunnel sequences should she plan? Is the Quintamensional Plan relevant for this interview?
- As Maribeth anticipates reacting to the responding moves of Jim Walsh, what combination of evaluative, interpretive, supportive, probing, and understanding responses is likely to be most appropriate?

- "Brought a mini tape recorder and said he always taped his job interviews."
- "Left his dry cleaner tag on his jacket and said he wanted to show he was a clean individual."
- "Applicant handed me an employment contract and said I'd have to sign it if he was going to be hired."
- "She sat in my chair and insisted that I sit in the interviewee's chair."
- "When asked about loyalty, showed a tattoo of his girlfriend's name."
- "Woman brought a large shopping bag of canceled checks and thumbed through them during the interview."
- "After a very long interview, he casually said he had already accepted another position."[15]

REVIEW

This chapter concentrates on the most common goal-oriented form of communication—the interview. It is difficult to imagine going through a day without engaging in some type of interview, whether it involves information gathering, information giving, selection, a problem related to the interviewee's behavior, a problem related to the interviewer's behavior, problem solving, or persuasion. The key to competence in interviewing is proper preparation, and five guidelines for preparing all types of interviews are: (1) Formulate a clear goal and keep it clearly in mind; (2) identify any potential barriers to achieving that goal that may reside in you, the other participant, or the setting; (3) create an appropriate structure for the interview on a continuum that ranges from nondirective to directive and add to that structure an effective opening and closing; (4) select questions that are appropriate in terms of type (open/closed; primary/secondary),

impact (understandable, relevant, unbiased), and sequence (funnel, inverted funnel, and tunnel); and (5) use reacting moves in the interview that will further your purpose (evaluative, interpretive, supportive, probing, and understanding).

In addition to general principles, the chapter explores a special type of interview—the selection type of employment interview. For this interview, the applicant's preparation is very important—first to get the interview and second to succeed at it. In terms of getting the interview, you engage in a self-assessment, prepare a résumé, locate appropriate jobs and do homework on them, and develop realistic expectations for the interview process. For actual participation in the interview, you should know the purpose and structure of the interview, think through appropriate responses to the interviewer's questions, and generate questions of your own for the interviewer.

SUGGESTED READINGS

Barbour, K., Berg, F., Eannace, M., Greene, J. R., Hessig, M. J., Papworth, M., Radin, C., Rezny, E., & Suarez, J. (1991). *The quest: A guide to the job interview.* Dubuque, IA: Kendall/Hunt Publishing Co.

Gorden, R. (1992). *Basic interviewing skills.* Itasca, IL: F. E. Peacock.

Hunt, G. T., & Eadie, W. F. (1987). *Interviewing: A communication approach.* New York: Holt, Rinehart & Winston.

Stewart, C. J., & Cash, W. B., Jr. (1991). *Interviewing: Principles and practices* (6th ed.). Dubuque, IA: Wm. C. Brown.

Wilson, G. L., & Goodall, H. L., Jr. (1991). *Interviewing in context.* New York: McGraw-Hill.

Competence in Interpersonal Communication

In this part of the book we discussed the nature of interpersonal relationships and how the way you communicate in these relationships makes them more or less satisfying and productive. We can't repeat too often that relationships are created by our communication with each other. When you begin a relationship, you make an investment of time, energy, and—most importantly—self-esteem. As relationships continue, that investment can grow or shrink, depending on (1) your commitment to the other person, (2) how much you depend on your partner for important rewards, and (3) the degree to which the relationship is voluntary.

Mutual Influence in Interpersonal Relationships

In regard to this last point, completely voluntary relationships are those that you enter into willingly—with your eyes open, so to speak—and that you can walk away from. Friendships are voluntary. Parent–child relationships are not; you are someone's child, for example, no matter what happens between you and that parent. As you make formal commitments to another, your relationship with your partner becomes more constrained and, therefore, less voluntary (as we are using the word). Co-signing a lease with a roommate constrains your relationship. Getting married constrains your relationship, making it less voluntary than when you and your partner were just dating.

This point is important because it captures the essence of relationships. When you begin them (or become active participants in them as in the case of parent–child and sibling relationships), you expose yourself to the influence of another; the expectation is that you will be changed by the relationship. Recall the model of communicative competence introduced in Chapter 1. People enter relationships as individuals, but as they work to negotiate control, affiliation, and goals, they are influencing and being influenced by their partners. Each person changes, possibly in important ways. The more meaningful the relationship is, the more the self-concept will be affected.

The goals discussed in Chapter 7 may begin as individual motivations, but they soon become joint goals that are agreed upon (either explicitly or implicitly) by both partners. In your relationships, you find your partners rewarding if they generally share your goals. That is, the less you have to modify your personal goals to accommodate those of your partner, the more rewarding you will think the relationship is. If one partner has to give up too much, the relationship will be costly for that person. Although the costs may be tolerated for a while, that person will eventually either try to change the relationship or leave it.

The growth and possible decline of relationships are directly dependent on the way you communicate with your partner. In growth stages, especially in exploratory and intensifying stages, you and your partner are frequently engaged in negotiations about the definition of the relationship. This is true for all types of relationships, whether they be romantic, supervisor–employee, or social friendships. These negotiations are about how much influence each will assert over the other and which communication behaviors are acceptable for influence attempts (control); how much liking each can show for the other and how that might be done; and on which goals or tasks the relationship should be focused. For example, a parent may teach his or her young child that it is OK to attempt to influence the parent to do something for the child, but only by saying "please" as part of the attempt. You may not think of this as a negotiation process unless you have attempted to do it yourself or have observed someone trying to get that "please" said!

Conflict in Interpersonal Relationships

Because negotiations are usually conducted in subtle ways (recall Chapter 1), it is not unusual for you and your partner to experience doubt, insecurity, frustration—and even anger. These feelings can produce conflict. It is important to remember that conflict is a normal part of competent relationships, a point made in Chapter 8. Skilled communicators get in arguments with each other for good reasons (and sometimes not-so-good reasons). The *manner* in which the conflict is conducted (the process

of having an argument) distinguishes between competent and incompetent relationships.

Why do people in competent relationships experience conflict? As was discussed in Chapter 8, clarifying issues and relational growth are two important reasons. As you work to define your relationship with another person, you are likely to find yourself giving up some things that you like to do or ways you like to act. That is the nature of negotiations. These are costs that your partner is exacting from you—and you don't like it. For example, you think of yourself as a spontaneous, carefree person (this is part of your self-concept), but your boss expects you to dress conservatively and be unassuming with customers. Or your prospective boyfriend or girlfriend indicates that you should spend a certain amount of time with him or her if the two of you are going to "get serious." The working out of these relational details can lead to open conflict, which can be healthy for the relationship. In the course of the conflict, aspects of the relationship can get "worked out." The temporary costs associated with the conflict can lead to long-term rewards if the conflict is managed effectively and stays focused on issues.

Interestingly, conflicts become part of your relational history and can influence the course your relationships take. In a relationship that has few conflicts, which are productive, you probably won't be afraid to confront your partner openly about issues that arise in the relationship. Although you probably will not look forward to conflict, you won't be afraid of it or especially threatened by it either. But if your conflicts in a relationship are unproductive and marked by personal hostility—name-calling, personal insults, and the like—you will be less likely to confront or be confronted by your partner until the frustration level is unbearable. In such a case, it is more difficult to make the conflict productive. Based on previous negative experiences, one or both of you may begin the conflict at a personal level and have a difficult time getting to the *issues* that promoted the conflict in the first place.

Not all conflict is about specific external issues (e.g., forgetting to take the trash out or "always" being late). Rather, the conflict can center on uncertainties about the status of the relationship. For example, people in the exploratory stage of a social relationship that has romantic potential may be led to quarrel because they are frustrated by the fact that they really don't know how their partner feels about them. Remember, people usually don't talk about the status of their relationships until they are at a "crisis point." Conflict may be a strategy for bringing the difficult topic of "where this relationship is going" to the surface. The argument about you "always" being late might really be about what your occasional lateness says about "how you feel about me."

Of course, conflict can lead to the termination of a relationship. That may be the competent thing to do. Competent communicators get themselves out of undesirable relationships with minimal harm to their partners and themselves.

Interviewing

The final chapter of Part 2 is about interviewing. It may have seemed odd to you that interviewing was grouped with chapters about interpersonal relationships and conflict. Our reason for this organization is to underscore the point that our model of competent communication and competent relationships applies to every kind of relationship. An interview is a relationship with the same characteristics as social and family relationships. It is composed of (usually) two people who want their self-concept confirmed, who have individual goals and hope to establish mutually desirable relational goals, who have a set of communication skills, and who want to use those skills to create a satisfying relationship.

There are some important differences between interviews and social relationships, as you might have guessed. Interviews are structured; the roles each individual plays are more or less predetermined. Because there is usually a clear status difference, there are fewer control issues to negotiate. Interviews are generally associated with "business" and are conducted by people we don't know very well, so an expression of affiliation is usually mildly positive and polite. The primary goal of the interview is almost always defined at the beginning of the meeting (if not before), but some secondary goals may need to be worked out.

It would be a mistake, however, to think that, because of the structure, there are no relational issues in interviews. Control, affiliation, and goal negotiation are as much a part of interviews as they are in any conversation between relational partners. In a highly structured situation—a job interview or a police interrogation, for example—the interviewee may decide to accept the relational definition imposed by the interviewer and the situation, but this is not necessarily the case.

Because of the structure of interviews, the interviewer (R) usually takes most of the responsibility for offering an initial definition of the relationship. This definition, for example, formal or casual, can be accepted by the interviewee (E), or E can attempt to modify the nature of the interaction. E can respond in a formal or tense manner, even though the R is communicating in a casual manner. E's behavior will eventually influence how R conducts the interview.

Another aspect of the structure of interviews is that the future of the relationship is usually predictable. Remember that one characteristic of a competent relationship is an anticipated future, but that future can take many forms. An interview conducted by a corporate recruiter, whose job it is to do initial screening interviews on campus, has only a limited antici-pated future with his or her interviewees. A final interview for an anticipated actual hire would be conducted quite differently and would have a clearer anticipated future. The definitional characteristics of the relationship should be more open to negotiation.

We don't want to give you the impression that interviewing is just like chatting with one of your classmates. That is certainly not the case. But the same principles that apply in social conversation and social relationships also apply in the more formal interviewing situation. If you have competent social relationships, you are well on your way to knowing how to establish competent relationships with people in interview contexts.

As you read the following case study, consider how relationships are negotiated in subtle ways and the confusion and discomfort that can result when issues are not resolved.

CASE STUDY 2

The Case of Jennifer's Problem at Work

Jennifer had been agonizing all week about whether or not to talk about her "real" communication problem in class discussion on Friday. Her communication class had a "real-life application" discussion once a week; three students were assigned a topic from the text and were asked to engage the class in meaningful discussion about relevant issues. Jennifer had been assigned the topic of communicating in work settings.

Jennifer could have talked about all sorts of issues, like interviewing for a new job, communicating with managers or peers, or communicating effectively with clients. But whenever she started thinking about how she would present any of those topics, the one thing bothering her at her own workplace plunged her into confusion and anger.

During the six months that Jennifer had been working at Flowers by Francis, she had become increasingly uncomfortable. The shop owner had always been very friendly to her; in fact, that had been one of the reasons why she took the job in the first place. Though the salary was not high, the work schedule allowed Jennifer to continue her classes at the university, and Francis had seemed so warm and open that she felt right at home the first day.

But Francis and his "friendliness" had come to be more than Jennifer expected. He asked her a lot of questions about her friends, especially the people she dated, and he had started touching her on the shoulder or the arm. Those touches seemed to last longer and longer until Jennifer became really uncomfortable. She hadn't said anything because Francis had seemed so nice at first, but she was beginning to conclude that the touches were more than just "friendly." Now Francis had started brushing against her behind the counter many times a day, when he could have asked her to move, excused himself, or gone around another way to get by her. He also made little comments about what she wore to work every day, saying things like how her skirt really showed off her great legs. Still, Jennifer said nothing, and now she was angry at Francis and at herself for letting the situation go on so long without saying anything.

Jennifer was worried about what might happen if she brought up the situation in class. Lots of people knew about Flowers by Francis; it was only a few blocks from the university. What if Francis really meant nothing and she had blown this situation out of proportion? Was she responsible for what she perceived as his sexual harassment, since she had let the "little things" pass for so long? Would the class deride her or help her? Would the professor think she was silly and was not taking the assignment seriously? Perhaps she should just talk about effective interviewing, after all.

DISCUSSION QUESTIONS

1. What do you think Jennifer should do about her class discussion?
2. What is the nature or definition of the relationship from both Francis's and Jennifer's perspectives? Use the model of communicative competence to identify places where their perspectives may differ.
3. What do you think Jennifer could do, verbally and nonverbally, to help correct the problem she is experiencing at work?
4. What advice would you give Francis and Jennifer to help them communicate more effectively?
5. How might Jennifer manage the conflict that is likely to result if she confronts Francis?
6. How widespread is the problem Jennifer has experienced? Does it affect only women?

Part *Three*

Group and Organizational Communication

10

Communicating in Small Groups

Objectives

After reading this chapter, you should be able to

1. Explain some features that distinguish groups from dyads.

2. Describe the ways in which cohesiveness and interdependence affect group competence.

3. Enact ways in which groupthink can be minimized through productive conflict.

4. Explain the four steps in effective goal setting for a group.

5. List the characteristics of personal growth groups.

CHAPTER CONTENTS

MAKE A LIST of all the groups in which you currently interact. List both formal groups (e.g., fraternities or sororities, classes, political societies, family, student groups, athletic teams, religious school classes, bowling leagues) and informal groups (e.g., lunch groups, "breakout" groups within a class, project teams, committees, friends you socialize with regularly, students studying at a table in the library, "user groups" learning how to master the campus computer). What your list will probably reveal is that right now you spend very little time by yourself or with only one other person.

Groups occupy a large amount of your time and energy while you are a student and occupy even more of your time afterward. You may participate in as many as 20 conferences or meetings a week if you decide to take a job in a large, complex organization. One estimate has suggested that 82 percent of all U.S. companies use problem-solving and decision-making groups or teams as an integral part of their operations and structure.[1]

Learning how to communicate effectively in groups is one of the most worthwhile investments you can make. Groups are critical to your success, regardless of what kinds of activities you are involved with now and what types of endeavors you may undertake in the future. Groups are so important in modern organizations that they are described as the building blocks for improving effectiveness.[2] As a manager or owner of a smaller business, you will hold frequent staff meetings with your employees. You may be asked to serve on a committee in your place of worship. You may participate in a group designed to prevent crime or improve safety in your neighborhood. Undoubtedly, you will meet some new friends with whom you may go out to eat on a regular basis, thus forming a new informal group.

In short, groups are everywhere. You are part of many groups now, and your involvement in groups is likely to increase rather than diminish in the future. Yet, being part of these groups and working well in them are two different matters. This chapter will help you become an effective and competent communicator as a participant in groups.

How Groups Differ from Dyads

As we mentioned in Chapter 1, *dyadic* communication occurs between *two* individuals. You might suspect, then, that some fundamental differences exist between communication within a group and within a dyad. These differences include number of interactants and complexity of relationships.

FIGURE 10.1
Much of human activity occurs in groups.

Number of Interactants

Communication between dyads and groups differs simply because the *number* of communicators differs. As the number of participants in an interaction increases:

- *The interaction is more formal.* Participants may feel the need to obtain permission to speak; they may limit the length and frequency of their contributions so that other members will not perceive them as dominant; they may be reluctant to interrupt a speaker.

- *Each member has fewer opportunities to contribute.* Participants may perceive the desire or be required by a leader to share "floor time" with other group members; time constraints can inhibit the quality and quantity of their contributions.

- *The communication becomes less intimate.* The greater the number of participants, the less comfortable participants feel self-disclosing or voicing controversial opinions.

- *The interaction consumes more time.* As more participants are invited to give input or to debate an idea, the interaction takes longer to complete.

Complexity of Relationships

Another factor that separates dyads from groups concerns the complexity of the relationships that are present and must be maintained. As more participants are added, the relationships become more complex. In the dyad, of course, there is only one relationship—that between person 1 and person 2.

As you can tell by examining Figure 10.2, when you add just one person to that dyad you now have to deal with four potential relationships—between persons 1 and 2; persons 1 and 3; persons 2 and 3; and persons 1, 2, and 3. In a group of four, there are 11 potential relationships; in a group of five, there are 90; and in a six-member group, there are 301 potential relationships!

Think about one of your relationships that you have right now with just one other person. In your relationship, you probably experience ups and downs, good times and bad times, harmony and discord. You may have often wondered whether investing the time and effort in your relationship with the other person was worth it. Before you become too hard on yourself, however, consider the complexity that working with a group adds to a relationship. Let's look at this complexity a bit deeper.

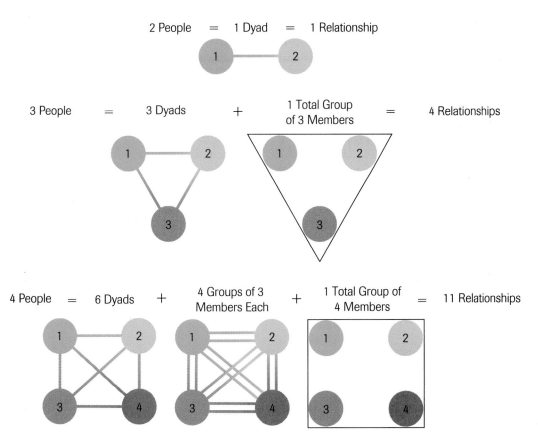

FIGURE 10.2
Each time a person is added to a group, the number of potential relationships increases substantially.

As you join a group, a couple of points immediately become clear. First, you will not be able to maintain satisfactory relationships with every other member of a group at all times. Over time, you will find evidence of misunderstanding, envy, jealousy, hatred, or possessiveness between any two or more members in a group. Group members do not voice many of these feelings in meetings; instead, they keep them inside in the hope that they will "blow over" with time. Many of these feelings also result from quick judgments that are not well founded, and, when people see them contradicted by evidence, they find themselves feeling guilty.

Second, most groups that function over a period of time develop cliques or coalitions. **Cliques** or **coalitions** are formed by individuals who have

CLIQUE (COALITION)
An exclusive group held together by common interests and activities.

bonded together in a group.[3] They typically sit next to each other in meetings, take breaks from meetings together, maintain contact with each other outside of meetings, act and think in similar ways, vote together, and support one another's position.

When cliques or coalitions are present in a group, relationships become more complex because now you are not dealing with individuals. Rather, you must maintain relationships with bonded subgroups. **Countercoalitions**, in which persons 1 and 2 position themselves against persons 3 and 4 on an issue, can leave a fifth, "unaffiliated" participant in a very awkward position. You may be able to think of occasions when you were undecided on how to vote on a problem because you did not want to align yourself with one coalition or the other and thereby cause hurt feelings or broken relationships.

COUNTERCOALITION
A relationship in which two or more people position themselves against two or more others with regard to an issue.

Factors Affecting Individual Competence

Groups are only as good as the individuals who participate in them. Although many groups are usually more effective as a collectivity working together than individuals working alone, the quality of a group's product is often determined by the competence that each person brings to a task. This section discusses several factors that affect individual competence in group activities, notably (1) individual identification, (2) critical thinking skills, (3) attributions, (4) perceptions, and (5) communication apprehension.

Individual Identification

Think of groups that you are proud to be a member of. How do you show your pride? You may wear a lapel pin, ring, sweatshirt, or jacket containing your group's logo or insignia. You may write the group's name on every job application or résumé you complete. You may make sure everyone knows when you are going to the group's meeting or function.

Groups that you are active with are typically those with which you hold the greatest identification. By **identification**, the goals, objectives, and mission of the group are closely aligned with your own beliefs, attitudes, and values.

If you proudly do volunteer work for a group in a nursing home on weekends, your pride stems from the fact that you believe the work offered by

IDENTIFICATION
Alignment of one's own beliefs, attitudes, and values with the goals, objectives, and mission of a group.

the group is worthwhile. Local, regional, and national officers for professional associations often travel on their own time and at their own expense. They are happy to be representatives of their group.

The Organization Man (1956), a book that received negative attention for a number of years, tells the story of how an employee adopted the values, goals, and perspective of the larger organization for which he worked.[4] In essence, this story demonstrated that a person can lose his or her individual identity and become a reflection of the organization. This kind of identification is not necessarily bad, however. Many individuals become better people and live more satisfying lives because of their group affiliations. Often, groups stand for values and principles that are superior to those held by the individual. This is one reason why many people take great pride in belonging to a group such as a junior league, a Rotary Club, or a local chapter of the National Organization for Women (NOW) or the National Association for the Advancement of Colored People (NAACP).

Critical Thinking

Critical thinking helps you view the world from a reasoned and proactive perspective. Thinking critically requires that you remain open-minded about what you perceive, while at the same time injecting a healthy dose of inquiry and skepticism into your perceptual awareness. It therefore means that you have to consider several different viewpoints before you are satisfied with the information you receive. Critical thinkers are always on the lookout for opinions, evidence, or facts that will lead them to accurate and responsible conclusions. This is an extremely important individual competency that you will want to develop as a group member.

CRITICAL THINKING
A method of viewing the world from a reasoned and proactive perspective.

Avoiding Traps

Critical thinkers are less likely to fall into some common traps that plague group communication. As an individual group member, you will want to be wary of certain obstacles to effective communication that are more likely to arise in group communication than in dyadic interactions.[5] Among the common traps to avoid are accepting communication at face value, oversimplifying issues, and making ad hominem attacks, overgeneralizations, and false assumptions.

During the course of group deliberation, group members come to rely on and trust one another. In situations where time is short, the tendency is to *accept communication at face value.* This is a serious flaw of group communicators inasmuch as a critical analysis of issues cannot be pursued when all communication is accepted without question. Competent communicators evaluate the worth of everything that is said based on previous discussion and information that the group knows is true. This strategy is designed not to attack others, but to provide a reasoned and logical approach to analyzing what other group members say. Sometimes a simple question is enough to begin an evaluation of someone's comment or argument ("Carol, are you saying that we should just accept these preliminary figures as our data?").

When groups deal with complex problems, they tend to *oversimplify the issues* involved. Think about the last time you and a couple of other people had to solve a problem that seemed overwhelming (e.g., travel plans, college costs, a wedding, family problems). Did you notice how some of your partners were willing to make claims that apparently oversimplified the issue? Consider the example below of a group attempting to make recommendations about increasing cultural diversity on a college campus.

BUD   This is simply a matter of time. Once people are around other folks from different cultural groups they will be more sensitive and less racially biased.

JAVIER   Hold it, Bud! Numerous cultural groups have been mingling in the United States for hundreds of years, yet we still see racial discrimination. To say that exposure to different cultural groups will solve the problem is a gross oversimplification of the issue.

Ad hominem attacks are statements that attack an individual's characteristics or traits instead of the person's argument. These statements can be explicit ("He's from Arkansas—what does *he* know?") or implied ("What makes you think he knows anything?"). Ad hominem attacks question an individual's credibility based on irrelevant characteristics rather than on opinions reached through relevant facts or evidence. One source of these attacks is rigid, inflexible stereotyping. When you form biased schemata about particular cultural groups, you often fall into the trap of evaluating others' opinions based on cultural stereotyping. Critical thinkers make judgments based on facts and accuracy of information and not on stereotypes.

A conclusion that is taken too far is known as an *overgeneralization*. This trap occurs when one piece of data is assumed to represent all comparable data. For example, if you assume that all teenagers experiment with drugs and alcohol, you are overgeneralizing. Critical thinkers test the validity of a generalization by determining whether the basis of support is biased in any way. A valid generalization is supported by different types of evidence and does not make claims beyond a reasonable point.

Another trap that prevents effective communication is *false assumptions*—conclusions drawn from faulty reasoning. False assumptions come primarily from (1) inappropriate causal relationships and (2) false dilemmas. Inappropriate causal relationships are incorrect conclusions based on cause and effect. Sometimes people assume that because two events occurred together or are related, then one must have caused the other. For example, if all males in a class received an "A" for the course, you might conclude that being male "caused" the grade. However, as is true of most events, numerous factors influenced the grades, such as individual achievement, study habits, related courses, or extra credit assignments. In other words, most events are too complex to establish a single causal-effect relationship. Although it is possible that all males in the class received an "A" based on gender, it is more likely that individual ability and work "caused" the grades. Thinking critically in a group means looking for alternative connections or explanations when a causal connection has been suggested.

The second source of false assumptions, a false dilemma, occurs when only two choices are offered as an either-or choice for a situation. For example, if you were in a group working on a presentation and one of the members concluded that a visual aid must include either a flip-chart or a video, that person would be posing a false dilemma by indicating that the choice must be one or the other. A visual aid could include posters, photographs, a performed skit, or three-dimensional objects. Making either-or statements creates false dilemmas. Critical thinkers recognize that verbalized choices are not the only alternatives and explore other possible options. The choices we have to make in this world are rarely black or white. *Think gray!*

Becoming a More Critical Thinker

Improving the way you think requires that you develop specific strategies to broaden your abilities in reasoning. The following strategies develop your skills in critical thinking:

- *Consider multiple perspectives.* As there is always more than one way to look at things, consider different perspectives and realize that your own perspective is subject to error.

- *Clarify values.* Determine the values that influence your judgment. Understand what your standards are and why you use them.

- *Clarify issues.* Clarify the question you must answer or the issue with which you must deal. Formulate the issue in a clearly stated sentence.

- *Evaluate information.* Recognize the source of the information. Is it opinion, or is it based on evidence and reasoning? Examine the credibility and relevance of the information.

- *Probe.* Ask searching questions about the issue. Look for underlying subjects, ideas, and specific details. Probe for reasons, causes, and alternative views.

- *Identify contradictions.* Recognize significant similarities and differences in opposing views, pinpointing contradictions between opposing arguments.

- *Consider the big picture.* Make plausible inferences and interpretations based on valid information. Explore the implications of statements and develop a fuller, more complete understanding of their meaning.

- *Pursue valid assumptions.* Avoid faulty assumptions based on inappropriate causal relationships, false dilemmas, and false analogies.

- *Summarize.* Summarize relevant facts and evidence in clear, understandable statements.

- *Draw appropriate conclusions.* Generate multiple solutions and analyze the feasibility of those solutions.[6]

Attributions

When you make *attributions,* you assign reasons or causes for another's behavior. Making attributions is one of the key features of the model of communicative competence. Whenever you attempt to explain why someone acts in a certain way or says certain things, you make attributions. Recall from Chapter 2 that you make attributions to understand the causes of behavior. Many of your attributions are based on observations of previous behaviors and predispositions, and these can affect your ability as a competent communicator.

Many people believe that making attributions is a normal part of getting to know people better. As you become more familiar with someone, you begin to think that you are privy to why the person behaves the way he or she does. For example, you see a friend drinking iced tea rather than a cocktail at a party. You may reason that this person is abstaining from alcohol to ensure he will feel fresh for a major presentation you know he is giving very early the next morning. You hear another friend criticize someone's lavish spending. Knowing that your friend grew up in a family with a limited income, you attribute this view to her upbringing. Note that in these two examples, more than a superficial knowledge of the individual is required.

Three variables are important in making attributions about others.[7] These variables are what you think about the other person's

Intent or motivation (internal force)
Ability (mediating force)
Environment (external force)

Now imagine that during a sorority's fund-raising committee meeting Rachel is trying to determine why someone cast a vote to approve a 25 percent increase in expenditures for promotional flyers. Rachel might reason that the individual enjoyed designing the flyers and wanted more money to increase their quality (*intent*), that this person had a good contact for printing the flyers (*ability*), and that an alumna's contributions provided the funds for their printing (*environment*).

In the small-group context, your attributions are often reactions to individual performance. People are usually interested in discovering why someone's behavior was exceptionally strong or very weak. For instance, someone may have given an outstanding report to the group, when in the past, mediocrity was a blessing. Another person may have failed to research an issue thoroughly before speaking on it. In the first case, you may attribute the quality report to the fact that the presenter was an expert on the topic. In the second case, family illness or time pressures may have presented major obstacles to proper research. Again, as your familiarity with another person increases, you believe you are more knowledgeable as to what made the individual behave the way he or she did.

Kelley suggests that, consciously or unconsciously, people arrive at a meaningful attribution for another person's behavior through three sources: *consistency, distinctiveness,* and *consensus.* These sources influence whether people attribute the behavior to an internal or external cause. An *internal cause* is something related to the individual (e.g., personality, ability, effort); an *external cause* is due to factors beyond the individual's control (e.g., the difficulty of the task, a lack of support, insufficient information). Imagine that you are attributing an unsatisfactory performance by a fellow group member. The impact of the three sources on your attributions would be as follows:

Consistency How the other person has behaved under similar circumstances in the past. High consistency (i.e., the person's behavior is typical of past performances) leads to an internal attribution; low consistency (i.e., the person's performance is worse than past performances) leads to an external attribution.

Distinctiveness How the other person has behaved under different circumstances in the past. High distinctiveness (i.e., the person performed well on other tasks but performs poorly on the one in question) leads to an external attribution; low distinctiveness (i.e., the person performs equally poorly on just about every task) leads to an internal attribution.

Consensus How *other* individuals have behaved in similar circumstances in the past. High consensus (i.e., other group members seemed to do equally poorly) leads to an external attribution; low consensus (i.e., other group members did well while the individual in question does poorly) leads to an internal attribution.

To see how this model of attributions is applied to the group context, pretend that you are part of a panel interviewing applicants for chairperson of a community golf tournament designed to raise thousands of dollars for local projects. During an interview, you note that one of the panel members, David, is unable to continue his line of questioning after three minutes. He stutters, stammers, and remarks that he's "forgotten all his questions." David promptly turns the floor over to Gary along with all of his remaining time. David had been a leader in all other interviews and all other tasks for the panel. Practically all of the group members, it might be added, have had at least one type of performance like this since the panel was formed.

In analyzing this example, note that this instance has low consistency (David did poorly here but has done very well in the past), high distinctiveness (on other tasks, David's performance was quite good), and high consensus (everyone on the panel has had some kind of a problem). Based on this evidence, you would probably attribute an *external* cause for David's unsatisfactory performance. Perhaps he performed badly during this interview because he was preoccupied with work or family issues.

Attributions influence your communication behavior in a group, demonstrating the adage "What you see is what you speak." If you perceive your committee chairperson as competent and intelligent, yet fiercely irritated during a meeting, you are likely to edit your comments and not antagonize this person further. If you attribute the leader's failure to stay organized and follow an agenda for a meeting to the fact that this person has flu symptoms, you may not say the negative things about the leader that you would otherwise say.

REALITY CHECK

Attributions and Groups

Divide into small groups during a class period and make a list of the various effects that attributions have had on groups that you have belonged to in the past. Report the findings to the class.

Perceptions

Group members continually form perceptions of one another. Recall from the model of communicative competence (in Chapter 1) and from Chapter 2 that perception is the process of making sense of your world. You receive input in the form of specific bits of information, such as someone's tone of voice, facial expression, or eye contact. Your existing schema and your immediate perceptions influence your perception of group members and group interaction. In reference to your interactions with other people, *perceptions* are your observations of other people's traits, or qualities that you consider part of their being.

Perception begins with information you receive from another person. This information can be practically anything, whether it be the way people greet you, their clothing, their tone of voice, or even the way they sit in a chair. You can either observe this information yourself or hear about it from other people. For instance, when you see a man walking across campus wearing a National Wildlife Federation T-shirt, you assume he supports that organization. Using that as information, you can begin to form certain perceptions about his personality or attitudes about certain topics.

Your perceptions are profoundly affected by the *vividness* of the information. That is, the more striking or conspicuous the information, the more likely you are to use it as the basis of perceiving others.

Take a closer look at our example. If the man in the T-shirt is whistling, you probably would not select that as information on which to base a perception of him because lots of people whistle as they walk across campus and his behavior is no different from anyone else's. Yet, if you view this same behavior in a small-group context, the outcome is very different. You are much more likely to select whistling to form a perception of him. Is he happy? Is the whistling a response to another person? Is he whistling his favorite tune?

Having noted another's distinctive behavior, you organize the information you have received. Consciously, you make sense of the information. To do so, you classify and assemble it in an effort to "size" someone up. Recall from our discussion of schemata in Chapter 2 that the pieces of information you assemble work together to create meaning and understanding. You continually discover new bits of information that combine with existing schemata to help you structure and understand different situations. This structuring develops a schema that helps you understand how things work or anticipate how they should proceed. Your schema develops perceptions and expectations about group members and the actions of the group.

To illustrate this step, use the following information about the man in the T-shirt, some of which you might have observed directly and some of which you might have learned from others:

mid-forties
male
slender
braided shoulder-length hair
frequently wears jeans and Army fatigues
friendly smile

Do the pieces of information seem to come together to give you a total impression? Hold your answer for just a moment.

In the next step, you decide what kind of person this is or what the person thinks about certain topics. Sometimes you sum up this person with one or two words such as "well dressed," "conceited," "airhead," or "humanitarian."

You see the T-shirt. You watch this person socialize and talk primarily with students whom you know to be biology majors. At one point he seems to be talking with them about their textbook. You perceive this person to be a member of the faculty in the biology department. As a result, you would probably perceive him to act and think the same way as most biologists act and think.

Did you also perceive the man to be an aged hippie, when you noted his age, clothing, and hair style? You may have made up your mind about this man very quickly; if so, don't be alarmed. Most people often form perceptions of others in a matter of seconds. For example, you drive past a twenty-something-year-old male driving a shiny new BMW and think, "spoiled brat." You see a woman sitting in a corner during a talkative party and think, "shy."

Furthermore, people think they're pretty accurate in the process—yet, how easy it is to be wrong. How do you know that the BMW is his? And maybe the woman in the corner is upset or attempting to draw attention to herself. Maybe the man in the T-shirt is a student rather than a professor. In short, you can make any number of interpretations of another person's be-

---

REALITY CHECK

What Do They Think of You?

How many wrong attributions do you think people make of you? For what reasons? Describe an incident in which you discovered that someone had made an incorrect attribution of your behavior. How is your opinion of people affected when they make erroneous attributions of your actions and behaviors?

havior, and not all of them are accurate. Although people are probably not as perceptive as they think they are, in a group context, they rarely have a chance to have their perceptions confirmed or denied.

Communication Apprehension

A final factor that affects an individual's competence in communicating within small groups is communication apprehension. As we mentioned in Chapter 8, *communication apprehension* may be defined as "fear or anxiety associated with real or anticipated communication with another person or group of persons."[8] Estimates suggest that about 20 percent of the population is highly apprehensive about communicating.[9]

Think about the times that you have been with a group and felt hesitant or apprehensive about contributing. Can you remember why? Perhaps you had some of the same reasons as are listed in the following section. Can you remember how you felt? Many people even experience physiological reactions such as increased heart rate, sweaty palms, quivering lips, locked knees, or an upset stomach!

Causes

Individuals experience communication apprehension in a group setting for several reasons. First, a person may be apprehensive in *every* context of communication. When an individual's apprehension is not unique to one particular setting or does not vary from context to context, that person is "trait" apprehensive. For this person, apprehension is as stable a characteristic as shoe size, height, or intelligence.

A second reason has to do with tenure in the group. New members are likely to be more hesitant about contributing until they "know the ropes."

Third, individuals who are less experienced on some topics will typically be more apprehensive about commenting about them, as opposed to subjects in which they are experienced and knowledgeable.

Fourth, individuals may have been repressed or even ridiculed during a previous meeting with the group and, therefore, may experience anxiety about contributing in the future.

Results

Simply put, participants in groups who are apprehensive about communicating are less likely to be effective than those who are not. Research into communication apprehension is quite extensive. Generally, highly apprehensive individuals report that this apprehension has a negative effect on many aspects of their lives.[10] Compared to those who are not apprehensive, individuals who report high communication apprehension are perceived to be less socially attractive, less competent, less sociable, less composed, and less able to lead. In addition, they are less likely to have high grades in college, to be offered interviews and jobs, and to be satisfied with their subsequent employment. However, there is no indication that they are any less intelligent.

McCroskey and Richmond discuss several results of communication apprehension that are specific to the small-group setting.[11] Compared to individuals who are not apprehensive, persons high in communication apprehension

- Are perceived by other group members as being more nervous and less dominant.
- Are perceived as being less task oriented and less socially attractive (because participants are biased in favor of individuals who contribute more frequently in meetings).
- Are seldom perceived as leaders.
- Are perceived as making less valuable contributions to the group.

Assessment

As you know by now, you can become a more competent communicator by assessing your current abilities and finding out where you stand. You can then move to higher levels of competence. Because apprehension can affect competence, respond to the Self-Check "How Well Do You Interact in a Group Setting?" to assess your group apprehension level.

Control

If you scored high on the Self-Check to test communication apprehension, don't worry! Remember, you are in good company; as much as 20 percent of the general population reports the same level of apprehension as you do. You can *manage* your apprehension in a group in three ways.

First, use relaxation techniques such as breathing and muscular control. Taking a deep breath is one of the simplest relaxation tools available to you. You can take several good deep breaths during meetings, and no one will even notice. You will find yourself much less rushed, aroused, or heightened about speaking if you do this.

Second, recognize that part of your apprehension is psychological. You feel anxiety or fear because of what you *think* about the situation you are

How Well Do You Interact in a Group Setting?

In order to test how apprehensive you might be in a group setting, complete the following six items, which are based on the Personal Report of Communication Apprehension (PRCA-24). Use the following scale: 1 = strongly agree; 2 = agree; 3 = undecided; 4 = disagree; and 5 = strongly disagree.

_____ 1. I do not like to participate in group discussions.

_____ 2. Generally, I feel comfortable participating in group discussions.

_____ 3. I am tense and nervous while participating in group discussions.

_____ 4. I like to get involved in group discussions.

_____ 5. I get tense and nervous when I engage in a group discussion with new people.

_____ 6. I am calm and relaxed while participating in group discussions.

Scoring: Use the following formula, in which the numbers in parentheses represent your answers to the six items. (For example, if you answered "4" for item 1, then replace the "(1)" in the formula with a 4.)

$$18 - (1) + (2) - (3) + (4) - (5) + (6)$$

A score of 24 or above indicates a high level of communication apprehension for participation in group discussions; a score of 12 or below indicates a low level of communication apprehension for this situation.

Source: Adapted from J. C. McCroskey (1982), *An introduction to rhetorical communication* (4th ed.) (Englewood Cliffs, NJ: Prentice-Hall).

about to communicate in. Often, telling yourself something like "I'll make a fool of myself if I bring up my view" produces a great deal of anxiety. Such statements are both negative and unfounded, for you have no evidence concerning whether you will or won't make a fool of yourself if you contribute to the group. If you can replace these types of statements with more realistic ones such as "Someone here will understand and appreciate my contribution," you will find yourself with a more positive attitude and considerably less apprehension.

Third, prepare carefully for the group meetings. Organize your thoughts into notes, bring any materials needed, such as paper and pens, and summarize any data you want to share with your group. You might want to practice stating your views before the group meeting, so that you can provide your ideas in clear, understandable statements.

Remember to *manage* apprehension, not *eliminate* it, because a small amount of apprehension will actually help you as a communicator. If you are totally confident of abilities and the anticipated outcome, you are likely to sound boring or even fail because of a lack of adrenaline. Normal levels of apprehension are actually quite beneficial to communicators in group settings.

Individual competence in group communication consists of individual identification with the goals of the group and development of critical thinking skills. Both pride and critical analysis give you a greater stake in the group and motivate you to excel in your group communication. Individual attributions, perceptions, and apprehension also affect the individual's contribution to group communication. You can use these internal processing components competently if you maintain objectivity and pursue a healthy sense of reality.

Factors Affecting Group Communication

The previous section examined factors that affect how well an *individual* contributes to the group. Now let's examine the *group's* communication by discussing factors that occur only when the group behaves as a collective unit. This section discusses (1) interdependence, (2) cohesion, (3) groupthink and productive conflict, (4) norms, and (5) group image.

Interdependence

INTERDEPENDENCE
In group relationships, how the behavior of each member affects and is affected by other members.

A key characteristic of most groups is **interdependence**. Simply put, the behavior of each member affects the behavior of every other member. In most groups today, no member exists in isolation. Many groups are organized with the goal of having their members share tasks.

In firms that emphasize production, employees frequently rotate tasks from time to time during the day. Later, this section discusses self-managing work teams, employed by all types of companies, in which two or more members typically work on the same task simultaneously. Members give feedback to each other and share responsibility for their performances.

Products, services, and results from groups with high degrees of interdependence truly belong to the "group" and not to an individual. Terms such as *we, us,* and *our* are frequently heard in meetings and conversations. Managers who would ordinarily be able to blame a particular person for a problem with a product have difficulty doing so when tasks are completed interdependently. The fault and responsibility, like the credit for successes, are shared among several group members.

A good example of interdependence in groups can be found in most office units. Consider an office with one manager, one secretary, and three staff employees. If the secretary does not distribute mail to the manager and the employees, neither the customers' nor other departmental needs within the organization will be met. If the manager does not work with each employee on scheduling, the work may be distributed unevenly, overburdening one person while causing another person to slack off. If the employees do not submit progress status reports, the manager will not adequately represent the department in meetings with upper management. In other words, the effectiveness and efficiency of each individual in the work group depend on the effectiveness and efficiency of each of the others.

Cohesion

The "togetherness" of a group is called its **cohesion**. A cohesive group is a tight unit that is able to hang together in the face of opposition. Rosenfeld argues that without cohesion, "Individual members are unlikely to commit themselves to the group, the task, or each other, and it is common for undesirable tasks . . . not to get done."[12]

You can determine group cohesion in two ways. First, how do the participants feel about their own membership in the group? The more that members are enthusiastic, identify with the purposes of the group, and tell outsiders about its activities, the more cohesive the group will be.

Second, how well does the group retain its members? The more that members receive satisfaction and fulfill their needs through their group participation that cannot be met through other sources, the more cohesive the group. Shaw provides numerous ideas about cohesiveness:

- Member satisfaction is greater in high-cohesive groups than in low-cohesive groups.
- High-cohesive groups exert greater influence over their members than do low-cohesive groups.
- Communication is more extensive and more positive in high-cohesive groups than in low-cohesive groups.
- High-cohesive groups are more effective than low-cohesive groups in achieving goals.[13]

COHESION
A group's ability to work as an integrated unit.

Even the language a group uses can increase its cohesion. Baird and Weinbert argue that as groups succeed and grow, they tend to develop a unique vocabulary.[14] Over time, the words become a code that is practically impossible for an outsider to understand.

Think about how a dentist may use a unique vocabulary in her office. Rather than frightening patients by specifying the names of instruments or drugs used in her procedures, Dr. Hanna communicates to her office staff in code. An assistant may be asked to bring in a "brown 2," standing for Novocaine to deaden the mouth. Similarly, "charcoal" is a term used for extraction forceps. The language used in the office among her staff, then, helps to solidify its cohesion.

Groupthink and Productive Conflict

Several years ago, Janis coined a term to describe situations in which groups strive to reach a consensus and minimize conflict by failing to critically examine ideas, analyze proposals, or test solutions, or experience too much cohesion.[15] He argued that **groupthink** results from strong feelings of loyalty and unity within a group. When these feelings are more motivating than the desire to evaluate alternative courses of action, a group's decision may be adversely affected.

GROUPTHINK
The tendency of group members to accept information and ideas without critical analysis.

Groups that are prone to groupthink typically exhibit these behaviors:

- Participants reach outward consensus and avoid conflict so as not to hurt others' feelings, even though they may not genuinely be in agreement.
- Members who do not agree with the majority of the group are pressured to conform.
- Disagreement, tough questions, and counterproposals are discouraged.
- More effort is spent rationalizing or justifying the decision than testing it.

The best way to avoid situations of groupthink is to encourage conflict in a group and use it productively. In Chapter 8, you learned that conflict is a healthy form of communication when managed properly. Competent conflict managers seize the opportunity for productive conflict by using the model for competent conflict management (prelude, assessment, engagement, action, and decision). In addition, you will also want to engage your critical thinking skills to ensure that you have an accurate understanding of the issue involved.

You must also learn to separate issue-based conflict from personal-based conflict. Groups that maximize issue-based conflict and minimize personal-based conflict are the most successful. Leaders and group members should maintain and encourage issue-based conflict, and remain watchful for instances of personal attacks.

The same advantages that issue-based conflict affords dyads (see Chapter 8) also apply to groups. Issue-based conflict allows a group to test and debate ideas and potential solutions. Issue-based conflict depends on each member asking tough questions, pressing for clarification, and presenting alternative views. Groups should have a "devil's advocate" for each issue. This is a person who "plays the other side," often bringing up the worst possible case or the wildest exception. If a proposal can stand the test of issue-based conflict in a group, you can have great confidence that the idea is a good one.

Conflict based on personalities detracts a group from its mission. When the members argue about each other instead of with each other, time is wasted and the motivation to work together is impaired. The tasks that the group works on remain incomplete and issues remain unresolved.

The best of all worlds occurs when group members "agree to disagree." This means that they accept the responsibilities that accompany issue-based conflict. Members know that they will be questioned, second-guessed, and required to defend their positions. They also know that they should not let any issue "slide by" without questioning, pressing another member for clarification and details, or presenting alternative ideas.

The issue of groupthink can generate several ethical considerations.[16] When groupthink causes the ideas, inquiries, and solutions of minority members to be ignored, the group may be acting in an unethical manner. All ideas are important, and the ethical group is one that searches for the best possible set of ideas. When the decision-making moment comes, only those solutions that have met the tests of critical examination and inquiry will be held as most ethical. In many cases, groupthink prevents critical inquiry. In a way, groupthink is a form of censorship because it squelches some members and their ideas. Striving for full participation by all members is a basic tenet of ethical communication.

Norms

All kinds of groups develop "sets of expectations held by group members concerning what kind of behavior or opinion is acceptable or unacceptable, good or bad, right or wrong, appropriate or inappropriate."[17] These are

NORMS
*Expectations held by
group members con-
cerning what behav-
iors and opinions are
acceptable in the
group.*

called group **norms**. Norms are determined by the group itself and are imposed by members on themselves and each other. Norms can be developed for just about anything a group does, and it is during the first few meetings of a group that they are developed.

Norms direct the behavior of the group as a whole and affect the conduct of individual members. For example, it may be a norm for members to arrive on time (group norm), and it may be a norm for the leader to begin discussion (individual member norm). Concerning communication behavior specifically, group norms can exist for (1) the kinds of topics that can be expressed in a meeting (Should nontask-related conversation be interjected? Are jokes appropriate?), (2) how long someone speaks, (3) who should speak first (Should the group sit quietly until the leader opens the meeting?), or (4) negative comments (Is it acceptable to criticize others publicly?). Group norms such as these can affect the communication behavior of the group. The quality (what is said) and quantity (how much is said) of contributions in the group are often determined by norms.

Two issues are important to note. First, new members learn which norms operate in a group through socialization; they cannot possibly know the norms until they observe them in group interaction. Often, this is a process of trial and error. A norm is frequently brought to the member's attention only after it has been violated, and he or she is alerted to the norm in some way. You may not know that your manager *detests* talk about weekend plans until you bring them up in a meeting and see how negatively the boss receives such talk. Actions that elicit negative responses, such as "Maybe you'll be prepared next time" or "Why haven't you finished that yet?" indicate that a norm has been violated. Other signs indicating a norm violation are head shaking, frowns, and disapproving glances passing between other members.[18]

Second, failure to follow the norms can lead to disastrous consequences. Publicly criticizing a manager who is not open to such criticism during a group meeting could result in your dismissal. Talking too much and too often in meetings could alienate you from your fellow group members.

As a group member, you should be aware of the norms, and you should also be prepared to change them if they appear to be detrimental. For example, groups that expect one member to dominate the conversation, criticize ideas before they are analyzed and discussed, or discourage disagreement have norms that are detrimental to communication and goals. Changing the group's norms can be managed diplomatically.[19] First, you should establish yourself as a loyal member dedicated to the group. In this way, you will demonstrate that you have the group's best interest at heart. Second, you should cite specific examples of the behavior you find harmful to the group's interactions. You cannot maintain credibility with those you are persuading unless you can back up your claims with specific instances of the norm. Third, you should confront the other members with open, honest communication about your concerns, calmly stating how the norm detracts from the goals of the group and asking for the opinions of the other members about the problem area. If the group feels that the norm is warranted, members may offer explanations, thus changing your perception, or the group may decide a change is needed. Whatever the consensus of the group members, they will appreciate your concern, and the group will not suffer undue tension.

Consider the following example. Joe was assigned to a group in his political science class that had been asked to make a class presentation on current environmental policies. The group met twice a week, at which time the members discussed the facts each had collected. The group then determined which data would be included for the presentation. At the end of each meeting, the members decided what needed to be done further and assigned specific jobs to each member. At the last meeting, Joe arrived late, handed copies of his research to the other members, and announced, "This needs to go in the report. I have to go." He then left, offering no explanation to the other members. When Joe arrived for the next meeting, the group members did not give him a chance to speak, nor did they assign him another job. He had neglected the group norms, and the group was sanctioning Joe for his behavior. What norms did Joe violate?

REALITY CHECK

A Cross-Cultural View of Group Norms

Not all cultures and subcultures view group norms in the same way. For example, political groups in the United States stress open participation by all members but adhere to strict parliamentary procedures when conducting official business. Japanese businesses have adopted norms whereby work groups do not recognize formal lines of authority and status during group meetings. What about gender norms? Can you think of specific norms that apply to males and females as they work in groups? What about people who belong to an older generation? Do you think they prefer group norms different from those of younger people? As part of a group exercise, generate sets of norms that you believe various cultural groups prefer. Interview members of these groups to confirm your expectations. Your group should be prepared to discuss its findings in class.

Group Image

When the Chicago Bulls captured their third straight NBA championship, their players believed they were members of the greatest team in NBA history. When a high school drill team received a perfect "1,000" score on its tactics competition, its members could have danced all night. These groups clearly had strong positive self-images.

A positive group image may yield several positive outcomes. First, success generates success. Having achieved one goal can motivate a group to "go for more."

Second, the group can be optimistic when facing obstacles. A group that has confidence in itself tends to minimize problems, eliminate barriers, and cope well with crises. In these cases, the members believe they cannot be defeated.

The third and final outcome is that membership in the group holds special significance. In fact, outsiders who are not part of the group frequently aspire to membership or even envy those who have it. People want to be part of groups that are doing well and that are perceived as "on the go." Many groups that achieve momentum after several successful activities may find that more people want to join and participate.

Groups can be just as motivated when they are pulling themselves back up on their feet. You can probably think of a number of groups whose very survival was uncertain. If its members perceived the group's existence as worthwhile, you probably saw them "pull together" with hard work to save the group. Teamwork and cooperation are almost always at their highest when group members are in a weak position, set a high performance objective, and work feverishly to achieve that objective.

Here's one example to illustrate this notion. One very small religious organization was about to fold several years ago. The membership had dwindled, and those who remained were elderly and inactive. Even paying

---

REALITY CHECK

Maintaining a Group Image

Think of some groups that maintain a positive image. How do these groups get a good image? What motivates group members to preserve the group's image? What are some specific things you can think of that can damage a group's image?

bills was a month-to-month proposition. One month there were simply no funds to spend. Yet, because of the members' perseverance, fund-raising projects and solicited contributions helped raise the money the organization needed to meet its obligations and keep the organization afloat. No one was going to shut down *their group;* the will to survive and the members' image as a "religious organization" became important motivators.

Improving Group Communication

Although communication is one of the most important functions for a group, not all of it is effective, efficient, or productive. On many occasions group communication is of poor quality and undesirable. Consistent with the theme of this book, we now turn to a discussion of how you can enhance communication competence in a group through (1) goal setting, (2) agenda setting, (3) deliberation and participation, (4) roles, and (5) networks.

Goal Setting

Think of the worst group meeting you have ever attended. How would you describe that meeting? Would you use words such as "unorganized," "waste of time," and "unproductive"? Do you wonder why you even spent the time that you did in meeting with the group? Did you leave the meeting with a bad attitude about working with the group again in the future?

One problem underlies most of these feelings: the lack of a clear goal. For any organized group, you should know the answer to these questions:

For what purpose(s) does your group exist?
Do all group members understand and accept the goals? Are they committed to them?
How close is your group to achieving its goals?
How well are your group's activities or functions aligned with the goals?

Goals vary considerably depending on the type of group involved. For example, a group in one of your classes may have the simple goal of completing a fifteen-minute, in-class exercise and reporting the results to the rest of the class. Your volunteer group at a rape crisis center may have the goal of providing quality assistance to rape survivors. An urban beautification fund-raising committee for underprivileged families you belong to may have a goal of collecting $4,000 for neighborhood housing improvements by auctioning off a donated entertainment system.

If you have a leadership role in the group, you should be a catalyst in setting group goals. You may either set the goals yourself or work with the group in establishing goals. The second option is preferable because group members are likely to be more committed and excited about a goal that they have helped create.

How can you do this?

1. *Identify the problem.* Specify what is to be accomplished or completed.

2. *Map out a strategy.* Determine the desired performance level and a means to evaluate whether the level has been attained.

3. *Set a performance goal.* Recognize the group's capabilities and limitations and establish a realistic target to achieve.

4. *Identify the resources necessary to achieve the goal.* Needed time, equipment, and money are among the important issues to consider before beginning.

5. *Recognize contingencies that may arise.* Think about the kinds of obstacles that are likely to prevent the group from achieving its goal and consider how to circumvent those obstacles.

 SELF-CHECK

Balancing Group Goals with Personal Goals

How do you balance group goals with personal goals? Think of a situation in which your personal goals were in conflict with a group's goals. Did group members try to convince you to adjust your own goals for the sake of the group? Did you attempt to change the group's goals to accommodate your own? Is it always right to subordinate personal goals to group goals or vice versa? Does it depend on the situation? As you read the following scenario, imagine yourself in the situation and consider the ethical issues involved.

At the advertising agency where you are a copy writer, you are assigned to a tobacco account. You are opposed to the advertising and promotion of smoking. The only way you can resign from the account is to resign from your job. If you stay on, how can you make a professional, conscientious effort to create effective advertising copy and still stay true to your beliefs about smoking?

6. *Obtain feedback.* Prepare to adjust directions or methods if necessary so that the group is doing its best.[20]

Your major responsibility as a leader is to keep the group "on course," assuring that its work is aligned with its goal. The more that you keep the group's goal as a benchmark from which to monitor your own activities, the better organized and the more efficient you will be.

As a group member, you should evaluate proposals, decisions, or other activities in light of your group's goal. You will frequently find it easy to go along with the majority or to become overly excited or emotional during a meeting. The more you use the group's goal to guide you, the more satisfied you are likely to be as a participant.

▨ *Agenda Setting*

An agenda is to a group what a city map is to a tourist or a compass is to a traveler. Without these aids, the group is likely to flounder aimlessly, waste time, and solve problems inefficiently.

What is an agenda? **Agendas** are more than simple outlines that a group leader follows while presiding over a meeting. Typically, at the top of the agenda is a list of the name of the group, meeting place, and time span. Then the agenda will list topics and subtopics that will be covered during the meeting. Many agendas include the name of the person who is primarily responsible for the topic and a time frame for the presentation. An agenda usually looks like the model shown in Figure 10.3.

AGENDA
A sequential plan of action, usually for organizing a group meeting.

A group leader should always prepare an agenda before a meeting. Even if the entire meeting will be devoted to brainstorming on a particular issue, an agenda should be prepared and presented to the group before the meeting. Participants of many committee and board meetings held in American corporations receive agendas a week in advance. Members of other groups may get copies of the agenda only at the beginning of a meeting. For others, the agenda is listed on a blackboard, a flip-chart, or an overhead transparency. For still others, the agenda is not listed on a hard copy at all but rather is simply read aloud to the participants.

Preparing an agenda in advance of a meeting does not mean that the group must adhere to it rigidly. Many group leaders distribute an agenda to participants and then ask if anyone has an item to add. During the course of a meeting, if the leader feels that a topic that is scheduled for discussion later on the agenda should be dealt with at the present time, he or she can make those adjustments.

The key advantage of using an agenda is that the leader and all participants can know where the group has been and where it is going. With an

> **Cleveland Engineering Society**
> Petroleum Club, Room 224
> Thursday, November 10, 1994
> 4:30—6:30 P.M.

   I. Call to Order (1 min.)   Jane Winer, President

  II. Roll Call (1 min.)   Jane Winer, President

 III. Reading of Minutes (3 min.)   Ralph Sikewa, Secretary

 IV. Financial Report   Barry Jefferson, Treasurer

  V. Old Business

         October meeting (5 min.)

         Volunteer update (10 min.)   Viola Florez-Cantu, Volunteer Chair

 VI. New Business

         December meeting (10 min.)   Randy Sato, Program Chair

         Scholarship progress (10 min.)

         Christmas party (10 min.)

         Guidelines for ethics document
         (30 min.)

 VII. Announcements

VIII. Adjournment

FIGURE 10.3
A printed agenda typically follows the format of the model shown here.

agenda, it is only minimally possible that a group will omit a key discussion point. An agenda helps ensure that a meeting is orderly, efficient, and organized.

Deliberation and Participation

Certainly, not all members of a group are equal; they have different backgrounds, ethnicity, experiences, education, biases, skills, competence, and interests. Therefore, to say that all members of a group should participate equally on all topics is nonsense and detrimental to its effectiveness.

Yet sometimes group members do not participate when their contributions would be beneficial. Even participants who are highly qualified in a particular area sometimes choose not to do so. Why? Let's look at a few reasons for nonparticipation:

Apprehension Members may experience fear or anxiety about expressing themselves in the group.

Lack of self-esteem Members may doubt the worth of their contributions.

Dominance Other group members may control the "floor."

Status differences Group members who are lower in their political or hierarchical position may choose not to comment on stances taken by superiors in a group.

Research indicates that an imbalance of participation in a group will present problems. A study by Hoffman and Maier found that the solution adopted in a group is the one that receives the largest number of favorable comments.[21] Furthermore, most of those comments come from a single member! If the "dominating" group member has inaccurate or incomplete information or less than an optimal solution to contribute, the group may make a faulty decision.

Groups can use several techniques to encourage participation:

• *Ask "gatekeeping" questions.* By asking a member to contribute ("Carolyn, we haven't heard from you yet"; "Doug, what do you think about this?"), a leader can directly influence involvement.

• *Divide participants into smaller groups for a collective response.* Group members who are reluctant to participate in the larger group can be encouraged or even obligated to provide input in a subgroup containing one or two other members. The leader may want to have each subgroup report the results of its discussion.

• *Remove personal identification.* By asking everyone to write one idea on a sheet of paper and turn it in anonymously, a leader can circumvent members' fear of bringing up a controversial topic publicly. The leader should read each idea aloud to the group and then initiate a productive discussion.

• *Confront the nonparticipants privately.* A leader may discover why an individual is not participating by simply remarking "You haven't said much today. Is something wrong?" This method allows the leader to identify and eliminate any obstacles to the quiet member's participation.

Roles

ROLE

In a group, the function a member performs.

Group members can have clearly identifiable roles. **Role** means the function that each member performs in the group. Roles are usually described with "-er" or "-or" suffixes. Words like "leader," "dominator," "gatekeeper," "joker," and "analyzer" are excellent examples of roles in a group.

Evolution of Group Roles

Roles can evolve in two ways. The first is to consider a position in a group and think of the behaviors you expect the person filling that position to perform. For instance, if there is an elected secretary of your group, you will expect that person to attend meetings, read and take minutes, distribute correspondence, write letters, and make phone calls. You may expect a chairperson of a committee to call meetings to order, set an agenda, introduce visitors, facilitate interaction among the members, summarize the proceedings, and so forth.

Second, a role can evolve by observing someone's behavior and then placing a label on that behavior. For example, if a group member is always the first to speak on every topic, cuts others off, and uses an exorbitant amount of "floor time," you might label that person a "dominator." Another member who is always prepared with statistics, facts, and evidence might be the "information giver."

Types of Roles

In most groups, each member performs or contributes to two basic functions: task and personal roles.

Task roles are concerned with the accomplishment of the goals, objectives, or mission of the group. They are based on the content and substance

---

REALITY CHECK

Roles in Your Group

Consider a formal or informal group in which you are active. List the members and try to identify the role of each person. You will probably find yourself using both of the methods described in the text.

---

of the group's interaction, apart from the members' personalities or personal characteristics. Elective offices in organizations and job titles in business firms indicate task roles. Some other examples of task roles are

Information giver   Offers facts, beliefs, personal experience, or other input.

Information seeker   Asks for additional input or clarification of ideas or opinions that have been presented.

Elaborator   Offers further clarification of points, often providing information about what others have said.

Initiator   Helps the group get moving by proposing a solution, giving new ideas, providing a new organizational scheme to solve a problem, or giving new definitions of an issue.

Administrator   Keeps people on track and aware of the time.

Personal roles are concerned with the relationships among the members of groups. Some people call these roles socio-emotional because they are not task related. Individuals who fill these roles help maintain the group as an operating whole. Some examples of this type of role are

Harmonizer   Seeks to smooth over tension in the group by settling differences among members.

Gatekeeper   Works to keep each member involved in a discussion by keeping communication channels open; may restrict information during periods of overload.

Sensor   Expresses group feelings, moods, or relationships in an effort to recognize the climate and capitalize on it.

Every member in a group plays both kinds of roles. Often the behaviors that accompany the role are prescribed or assigned. You probably expect people who assume certain roles to use particular behaviors. In other cases, you know the roles people play only by observing their behaviors.

Problems with Roles

Two kinds of problems exist in groups concerning roles. The first, *role conflict,* exists whenever competing expectations for your behavior are incompatible. The best example would be a leader of a group whose role is "friend" with many members but who must also be an "evaluator" of their performance. The friendship role would require you to be subjective and kind and to give the other person the benefit of the doubt. The evaluator role would require you to be objective, impartial, and governed by rule or policy. Experiencing role conflict is one of the most uncomfortable feelings you can have as a group member.

Antigroup Roles

Why do you think some people insist on playing the more destructive roles in a group? What personal communicative competencies are lacking in members who assume these roles? What is the best method for handling blockers, distractors, avoiders, and recognition seekers?

The second problem is the existence of *antigroup roles.* These roles consist of behaviors that attempt to satisfy individual rather than group needs, which are often irrelevant to the task at hand and are clearly not oriented toward maintaining the group as a team.

Think about how many times you have seen evidence of these roles in the groups you are members of.

Blocker   Indulges in negative and stubbornly resistant behavior, including disagreements and groundless opposition to ideas. Frequently, blockers will reintroduce an issue after the group has rejected or bypassed it.

Avoider   Displays noninvolvement in the group's proceedings by such behaviors as pouting, cynicism, nonchalance, or "horseplay."

Recognition seeker   Calls attention to himself or herself by behavior such as boasting, providing information to the group about his or her qualifications or experience, or reporting personal achievements.

Distractor   Goes off on tangents, tells stupid, irrelevant stories, and so on.

▓ Networks

NETWORKS
Communication patterns used within groups.

CENTRALITY
The degree to which a member of a group sends and receives messages from others in the group.

Still another factor that has a profound effect on group interaction is its networks. **Networks** are defined as the communication patterns used within the group. In essence, you are asking questions such as "Who speaks to whom?," "how often?," and "about what?"

Two key positions typically are important in describing networks in a group. The first is centrality. **Centrality** refers to the degree to which an individual sends and receives messages from others in the group. The most central person in the group receives and sends the highest number of messages in a given time period. You probably believe that leaders of discussion groups or managers of employee teams occupy highly centralized positions because of their status or power. If a leader calls on you to speak in a group, all communication will flow directly through that person. Therefore, that person occupies a highly centralized position in the group's network.

Another key position is **isolation**. Relative to others in the group, isolates receive and send fewer messages. You may believe that these are "thinkers" who keep their thoughts to themselves and in organizations do not give a great deal of importance to socializing or interacting with others during a given day. In some groups, members are isolates because they are not liked or perceived as competent by the other participants. In other groups, isolates choose to comment very selectively. You should note that these positions are highly dependent on the content that is being communicated.

Several different types of content-based networks are possible. One type is an *innovation* network whereby participants communicate about new ideas and directions. Another type is a *social* network in which participants discuss nonwork issues, including gossip. Still another type is a *task* network, which is defined by the job or work at hand or giving technical advice to another person.

One person can be very centralized in one network and yet be practically isolated in another. You may find many examples of this situation. Think for a moment about a group or committee of which you have been a member. Is the individual in your group who contributes and is asked the most about *task* functions the same person who also contributes the most and is asked the most about *social* activities? Probably not. You will likely find that the people who are particularly centralized in social networks are popular, outgoing, likable, and so forth. Highly centralized individuals in task networks are likely to be experienced, educated, and competent. In innovation networks, highly centralized persons are usually "insiders" with access to resources, information, and influential people.[22]

In the last few years most network research has focused on the effects of holding certain positions in network groups. In a study conducted with groups of Navy officers and enlisted personnel, Roberts and O'Reilly found that, compared to isolates, people in positions of greater centrality were more satisfied with their jobs, more committed to their organizations, and higher performers.[23] McLaughlin and Cheatham studied differences in job satisfaction between isolated bank tellers in outside drive-through windows and more centralized tellers who worked inside the bank.[24] Despite identical salary and promotion policies, the centralized inside tellers were significantly more satisfied with pay, supervision, work, and co-workers. Brass discovered that females who were not well centralized in male-dominated networks in their organizations were perceived to have less influence

FIGURE 10.4

In a group's communication network, a position of centrality is often occupied by a manager. Isolates, on the fringe of the network, send and receive fewer messages than do other members of the group.

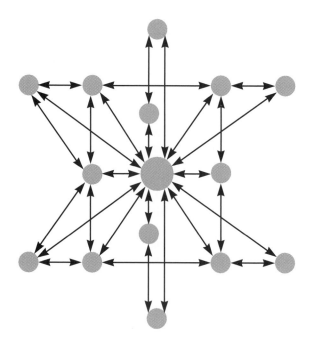

and were promoted to supervisory positions less often.[25] In a study of innovation networks, Albrecht and Hall discovered that less centralized participants perceived more centralized individuals as more supportive, trustworthy, influential, and receptive to new ideas than the other less centralized participants.[26]

These research studies have demonstrated substantial differences in the perceptions and behaviors of individuals in different network positions. Undoubtedly, you can think of groups where you have seen people occupying similar positions. The way to be more centralized in a group is to be more visible. Prepare some relevant and thought-provoking comments ahead of time. Speak up. Challenge members' ideas. Ask questions. If you will first increase the number of contributions you make in a group, people will direct comments to you as well. Depending on the quality of your contributions, you may move from an isolate to a central position rather swiftly.

The *group communication process* is a critical element in ensuring that a group's meetings will produce the desired outcomes. *Goal setting* is essential for charting the direction the group needs to take to be effective and efficient. *Setting an agenda* makes each of the group's meetings run smoothly by providing a structure for events and issues that are to be discussed by the group. Every group member is "on the same page," so to speak. It is also important that all group members contribute to the group through *deliberation and participation.* The whole idea behind groups is to bring different viewpoints together to reach a conclusion that is better than just one person's opinion. A competent group process is dependent on the effective use of roles within a group. The key is having group members assume roles that directly contribute to group competence, while minimizing roles that distract from the group's effectiveness. Members also need to be aware of the networks that exist in the group so that centrality is encouraged for all members. Preventing isolation is an important process of encouraging member participation.

Special Groups

This section discusses groups that meet in ways that deviate from the norm and with purposes that are different from those discussed in the earlier parts of the chapter. The characteristics of each group and the procedures it uses are discussed.

The Nominal Group Technique

Ironically, the nominal group technique is not a group process at all. Rather, the **nominal group technique** is a process used by individuals working alone in a group context (interaction among participants is not allowed) in order to produce a *basis* for discussion that reflects the views of all the group members.

The nominal group technique can be best explained by using an example. Say that you are chairperson of a special student committee in the School of Arts and Sciences designed to recruit majors for the various departments in the school. At an earlier discussion, an idea was proposed to conduct a three-hour "open house," with all faculty and majors available to visit with prospective students. You and several group members are not certain this is the best course of action; therefore, as chairperson, you have decided to put the idea to the test.

To use this technique, you first ask each member to make a separate listing of the advantages and disadvantages of the proposal. After about fifteen minutes, you call time and then by round-robin, you ask each member to contribute one of his or her advantages or disadvantages. You write each advantage and disadvantage on a flip-chart or transparency as it is mentioned. Each one, however, should be listed only once. When the content of everyone's list is exhausted, you proceed to the next step.

You ask the participants to copy the master list on a sheet of paper. You then announce that, as individuals, they are to rank order each advan-

NOMINAL GROUP TECHNIQUE
A process in which individuals work alone in a group context to produce a basis for discussion that reflects all group members' viewpoints.

tage and disadvantage from highest to lowest in priority. The lists are submitted to you. You might ask the group to take a break for a few minutes while you tabulate the priorities for the entire group. When the group reconvenes, you can select the top advantages and disadvantages of the issue to discuss.

Of course, "advantages/disadvantages" is only one of many possible topics for the nominal group technique. You may wish to pose a question and use the technique to brainstorm in a group. For example, you might ask, "What criteria should we use to distribute our scholarship money next year?" If this is the purpose, ideas are brainstormed, listed on a chart, prioritized, and then discussed.

Moore recommends that the nominal group technique conclude with a vote rather than a discussion.[27] He proposes that ideas be posted and then discussed or clarified among the members. After the discussion, participants select *five* ideas that are attractive to them, write them on a 3 × 5 card, and then assign a priority ranking to them. The cards are collected, rank ordered in front of the participants, and a final vote is taken for the best idea.

This technique is recommended when feelings of intimidation, domination, hesitancy, or apprehension surface in the group. Because each participant submits information simultaneously and anonymously, all input is weighted equally prior to the discussion. The technique is also useful when the group does not have a history from which to work. One study even indicated that four-person nominal groups outperformed four-person actual groups and individual groups on anagram tasks.[28]

The Delphi Method

The Delphi method is very similar to the nominal group technique in that communication among group members does not occur. In addition, groups that do not meet face to face use this method. For example, questions of national or international concern, requiring input from participants in diverse locations, could be decided by this method.

In most cases, the **Delphi method** is used to receive input from *experts* on a particular issue. After participants are selected, each completes a survey or questionnaire to voice their opinions, ideas, or recommendations about a particular topic. In most cases, the entire process is conducted by mail. Each contribution is anonymous.

These contributions are collected at a central location. After a period of time has passed, they are then listed and distributed to each participant. Each member is given a questionnaire and asked to react to the ideas received, using some preset criterion. Later, a third survey or questionnaire is sent, which provides the results from the second questionnaire and asks the participants either to revise their ratings in order to approach a consensus or to provide a rationale for their decision that dissents from the group.

After these instruments are collected, one final survey or questionnaire is distributed to all participants. This report includes the ratings, consensus trends, and deviant opinions. The participants are then given one final chance to revise their positions.

After these data have been analyzed, the participants may be called together for a face-to-face discussion in an attempt to achieve consensus. Alternatively, the results may be tabulated and presented as a recommendation to a panel or board that is not involved in the process.

Two characteristics of the Delphi method must be stressed. First, the results from one round of questions determine the questions for the following round. The questions cannot be determined in advance. Second, the method is time consuming. One study estimated that 44.5 days were needed to complete each round.[29] This technique is best used when time permits the work to be done before an actual face-to-face meeting (e.g., a group that meets only once or twice a year).

Personal Growth

A variety of small groups fall under the heading **personal growth groups**. These groups are designed for personal fulfillment and improvement and are variously known as encounter groups, therapy groups, T-groups, sensitivity groups, confrontation groups, and training groups. Some of these groups are national in scope and have chapters in many locales throughout the country. Among the more famous groups are Tough Love, Alcoholics Anonymous, Parents and Friends of Lesbians and Gays, Overeaters Anonymous, and Gamblers Anonymous.

One major distinction among some of these groups concerns the nature of the individual participants. Typically, participants in traditional T-groups are well-adjusted individuals who believe that group interaction will enable them to experience and enjoy life more fully. T-group participants are concerned mostly with internal conflicts such as setting priorities. Conversely, in therapeutic groups, the conflict is typically external to the individual participant; it is either among participants or in other relationships in a participant's life. Participants in therapeutic groups believe that a group experience will help them cope with the pressures of life.[30]

The one common thread that runs through all the groups referred to so far is that each individual participant has the *option* to participate or not participate. In many of these groups, the individual alone defines the total motivation to participate and the rewards that result from interaction. The groups discussed here are not made up of participants who have been coerced into participating or are committed to membership by an external source.

PERSONAL GROWTH GROUP
A group that people join in search of personal fulfillment or improvement.

Consistent with this idea of voluntary participation, Killilea suggests several important characteristics of these groups. He argues that

- Each participant tends to look to others for confirmation of his or her feelings.
- Each participant, because of common experience, is simultaneously a giver and receiver.
- The purpose of the group is to provide mutual aid and support.
- A person who *helps* another with a problem may receive greater benefit than the person who has the problem.
- The group is action-based in that participants learn by doing and change their behavior by doing, as opposed to simply talking.[31]

Here is one final point to stress about these groups. Thousands of individuals avoid participating because of their perception that membership would bring them social stigma. However, they are the only losers. In many cases the risk of social stigma is totally false, and in others, it is grossly exaggerated. Asking for help from others who gladly give it is not a sign of weakness or cowardice. If people fail to take advantage of the help that some of these groups can provide when they are faced with a problem, they are truly cheating themselves.

Self-Managing Teams

SELF-MANAGING
TEAM
*A group of highly
skilled workers
within a larger orga-
nization who are
completely responsi-
ble for producing
high-quality finished
work.*

One of the newest trends concerning small groups in modern organizations is the development of **self-managing teams**—teams consisting of highly skilled workers who are completely responsible for producing high-quality, finished work. Whether the work is manufacturing, such as a mahogany china cabinet, or a service, such as a financial statement, the result is always the product of a fully integrated team. Members of the team share responsibility for each step of the process, as opposed to a single, narrow individual function, such as would be found on an assembly line.[32] According to Dumaine, one-half of surveyed Fortune 500 companies plan to implement these teams in the near future.[33]

Self-managing work teams are actually an outgrowth of two major lines of thought. In the 1960s and early 1970s, *participative management* became very popular. In this style of management, supervisors would involve themselves with their subordinates in making decisions that were properly labeled group efforts. Supervisors would guide and facilitate discussions and problem-solving sessions but would not impose their decisions on the group. Rather, supervisors worked *with* their group to jointly address a problem.

In the late 1970s and early 1980s, participative management gave way to *quality circles* in many organizations. Quality circles were groups of employees from the same work area who met on a voluntary basis on company time to analyze and solve work-related problems. They were led by an experienced manager in meetings conducted with participative decision making. Quality circles were popular because organizations were able to save large amounts of time and money by allowing employees, who were closest to and most knowledgeable about their jobs, to make recommendations on how to improve the effectiveness and efficiency of work processes. The circles would present their findings to management, who would often enthusiastically consider, endorse, and implement the ideas.

Note that in both models the supervisor is still the focus. In participative management, a supervisor guides and facilitates the meetings; and in quality circles, a supervisor leads the meetings. In self-managing work teams, many of the typical management functions are completely controlled by the team members. Employees who are part of these teams arrange their own schedules, buy their own equipment, and set their own standards for productivity, quality, costs, and performance. They conduct their own peer evaluations, hire new members, and coordinate future plans with management. Members are committed to the group with positive attitudes.

While self-managing teams don't "work as they please," the organizational structure of self-managing teams allows them

- A clear sense of their own separate identity.
- Alignment of their activities with corporate objectives.
- Accountability for their activities.
- Conformity to fiscal, legal, and other critical guidelines.[34]

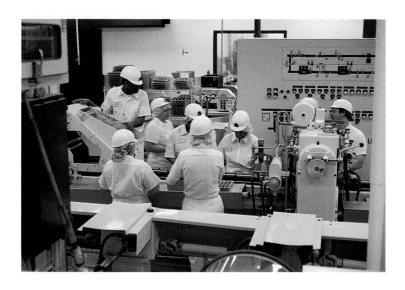

FIGURE 10.5
A self-managing work team within a larger organization is responsible for meeting the organization's objectives, but how the team accomplishes this is up to its members. By communicating with one another, team members determine what works best for the whole group.

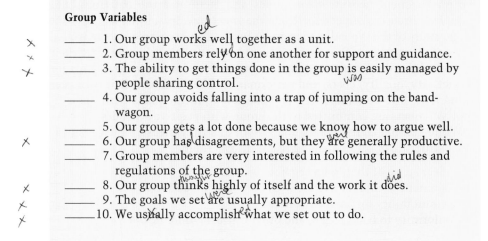

Group Competence Evaluation Form

Use the following evaluation form to assess a group you belong to in terms of the factors that are important for competent group communication. Your group may want to add other appropriate items to the list.

Assess how you and your group perform in the indicated areas, using the following scoring: E = excellent performance; A = average performance; and P = poor performance.

Group Variables

_____ 1. Our group works well together as a unit.

_____ 2. Group members rely on one another for support and guidance.

_____ 3. The ability to get things done in the group is easily managed by people sharing control.

_____ 4. Our group avoids falling into a trap of jumping on the bandwagon.

_____ 5. Our group gets a lot done because we know how to argue well.

_____ 6. Our group has disagreements, but they are generally productive.

_____ 7. Group members are very interested in following the rules and regulations of the group.

_____ 8. Our group thinks highly of itself and the work it does.

_____ 9. The goals we set are usually appropriate.

_____10. We usually accomplish what we set out to do.

An organization's move from other organizational structures toward self-managing work teams cannot be accomplished overnight. Most organizations need approximately 24 to 42 months to fully implement self-managing teams.[35]

Perhaps the most dramatic effect of self-managing teams is on the attitudes and skills of the workers. A competitive work environment changes to one of cooperation. Work in isolation changes to work with others. Managers training employees change to employees training their peers.

Evaluation: Competence in Group Communication

Determining the competence level of small-group communication can be made simpler by applying the model of communicative competence pre-

Individual Variables

_____11. Each member of the group has a special role that suits the group's needs.

_____12. The roles I play in the group are appropriate and effective.

_____13. Although I may experience anxiety or stress at times, I can usually handle it with no trouble.

_____14. All the members of the group participate effectively.

_____15. My own participation is timely, relevant, and informative.

_____16. Over time, group members have developed very accurate perceptions of other group members.

_____17. My perceptions of other people and important issues are usually correct.

_____18. When members attribute behavior to others, they are usually accurate.

_____19. I avoid making attributions to others when I do not have all the facts.

_____20. The individuals in my group are very capable members.

Look at your responses. How many responses were E? A? P? A large number of A's and P's indicates areas that could use improvement. Examining strengths and weaknesses of your group and your participation in it allows you to improve your overall group communication competence.

sented in Chapter 1. Two methods can be used to accomplish such an evaluation. First, individual member competence is evaluated by how well members accomplish their *roles*, how well they control their *apprehension* levels, and how well they *participate*, and by assessing the accuracy of their *perceptions* and *attributions*.

Second, group factors can be examined. *Affiliation* is an important component of communication competence and, in the case of groups, is best assessed by determining the interdependence and cohesiveness of group members. Another factor important in group competence is *control*. In groups, control is determined by assessing power levels, the extent of groupthink, the level of productive conflict, adherence to group norms, and the group's view of itself (image). Finally, *goal assessment* must be considered in assessing competence.

REVIEW

Groups are pervasive in each individual's environment. Small groups differ from dyads in two basic ways. First, because the number of interactants is larger in a group than in a dyad, the basic qualities and characteristics of communication are affected. Second, more relationships must be maintained in a group than in a dyad.

Several factors affect individual competence in group contexts: individual identification, critical thinking skills, attributions, perceptions, and communication apprehension. How well an individual identifies with the purposes and goals of the group is important. Because "what you see is what you say," the kinds of perceptions and attributions you make in a group affect your communication. The causes of communication apprehension in small groups include lack of experience in some areas and a person's newness to a group. As a result of communication apprehension, those who are anxious are liable to be less effective, more nervous, less task oriented, and less able to lead. Individuals can mitigate their communication anxiety by using relaxation techniques, developing a positive attitude, and preparing carefully for group meetings.

Several factors affect a group's communication as a unit. Key qualities include cohesion and interdependence among members. Groupthink can be a deterrent to effective decision making, but encouraging productive conflict can counteract the influence of groupthink. Norms also play a role in the small-group communication process. The three positive effects that a favorable group image can produce are success begetting success, optimism in the face of obstacles, and prestige of membership.

When groups interact, several processes occur simultaneously—namely, goal setting, agenda setting, deliberation and participation, role enactment, and network use. A multistep method for setting goals includes identifying the problem and mapping out a strategy. Participation among group members may be increased by asking "gatekeeping" questions and removing personal identification. Individuals exhibit task roles, personal roles, and antigroup roles in a group. The two characteristics of communication networks in small groups are centrality and isolation.

Special groups discussed in this chapter include those using nontraditional decision-making techniques, such as the nominal group technique and the Delphi method, as well as personal growth groups and self-managing teams.

SUGGESTED READINGS

Cathcart, R. S., & Samovar, L. A. (1988). *Small group communication: A reader* (5th ed.). Dubuque, IA: Wm. C. Brown.

Moore, C. M. (1987). *Group techniques for idea building.* Newbury Park, CA: Sage.

11

Leadership and Decision Making in Groups

*O*bjectives

After reading this chapter, you should be able to

1. Recall the three types of leadership.

2. Demonstrate the importance of shared leadership in groups.

3. Describe the four styles of situational leadership.

4. Define competent leadership.

5. Give examples of factors that affect the decision-making process.

6. List the eight steps to effective decision making.

7. Describe the three types of groups frequently used in the business world.

8. Effectively evaluate individual and group performance in decision-making groups.

CHAPTER CONTENTS

HAVE YOU EVER thought about the designs of conference tables? What types of interactive decisions are made at a meeting using an oval table? Think for a moment—What kind of leader of his "knights of the round table" was King Arthur? Why are most Japanese and corporate America's conference tables rectangular?

The previous chapter concentrated on communication processes that would affect any type of group. In this chapter, we continue the discussion of groups by examining two dimensions of communication essential for competent group work. The first is group leadership. Leadership is a much-researched area of communication, and using that information to develop effective leadership in groups is very important. The second dimension is decision making. All groups must reach decisions on one type or another, and making the right decision depends on the factors discussed in the previous chapter and on the decision-making skills described here. Leadership and group decision making are two interrelated processes that work together to produce valuable group outcomes. It is difficult to discuss one of these processes without discussing the other.

Group Leadership

Think of the last group you were in. What was the leader like? Was he or she effective? How would you define the effective traits of this leader? Was this leader you? Over the years, countless attempts have been made to define leadership in scholarly and academic literature. In this section, we will review some of the basic characteristics of leadership and discuss how different styles work in different groups.

Leadership Defined

LEADERSHIP
The exercise of interpersonal influence toward the attainment of goals.

Two key terms appear in many definitions of **leadership**—*direction* and *influence*. Many people believe that a leader's primary function is to provide direction. For example, Hemphill and Coons note that leadership is the "behavior of an individual when he [or she] is directing the activities of a group toward a shared goal."[1] Stogdill suggests that leadership is the "initiation and maintenance of structure in expectation and interaction."[2] Viewed in this way, leaders structure, guide, and facilitate a group's activities and interaction in ways that will lead to a desired outcome.

Still another popular component of definitions of leadership is influence, and scholars recognize the role of communication in influence. For example, consider these definitions of leadership:

- "Interpersonal influence, exercised in a situation, and directed, through the communication process, toward the attainment of a specified goal or goals."[3]
- "An interaction between persons in which one presents information of a sort and in such a manner that the other becomes convinced that his [or her] outcomes . . . will be improved if he [or she] behaves in the manner suggested or desired."[4]

These definitions highlight the notions that leaders have an impact on other group members and that people who can influence others become leaders. Frequently, group members are influenced by the leader's status or power. In other cases, the influence comes from the group members' admiration of or respect for the leader.

▨ Types of Leadership

Leaders of groups typically exhibit one of four decision-making styles: authoritarian, consultative, participative, and laissez-faire. Each of these styles has its own unique advantages and disadvantages.

Authoritarian Leaders

Authoritarian leadership involves control by the leader without input from other group members. In most instances, the leader makes a decision and simply communicates it to the group. Although this style produces faster decisions, it has been shown to result in lower group member satisfaction and commitment to the task.

Authoritarian leaders (1) provide opinions and input but do not actively solicit them from members, (2) announce decisions rather than open them for discussion, (3) maximize upward and downward interaction (leader to member; member to leader) while minimizing lateral interaction (member to member), (4) resolve conflicts when they arise, and (5) specialize assignments and tasks for group members. A group led by this style would also have shorter meetings.

AUTHORITARIAN LEADERSHIP
Control by a leader without input from group members.

Consultative Leaders

The consultative leader asks others for their opinions or ideas and then makes the decision alone after considering this input. Leaders use this style when they lack the necessary information to make an effective decision.

Many subordinates find **consultative leadership** to be a frustrating style because they see it as simply a facade the leader uses to make them *believe*

CONSULTATIVE LEADERSHIP
Leadership that bases decisions on the opinions or ideas of group members.

FIGURE 11.1
Why is authoritarian leadership appropriate for military forces?

that they are involved. In fact, they claim, very little that they suggest is ever achieved or implemented. Many subordinates wish the leader would not ask them for input in the first place! Nonetheless, leaders often use this style quite constructively to gather information and to test the waters before making a decision. This approach permits a more reasoned and educated outcome.

Participative Leaders

PARTICIPATIVE LEADERSHIP
A leadership style that involves a leader working with other group members to achieve a desired goal.

The **participative leadership** style of decision making is used by leaders who work together with a group in solving a problem or performing a task. The leader typically guides and facilitates but has no more influence over the outcome than does any other group member. Although the decisions made take longer to reach, they typically are of higher quality, result in greater satisfaction, and elicit greater commitment than do decisions made by any other leadership style.

Participative leaders (1) ask "gatekeeping" questions to involve nonparticipating members, (2) summarize discussions for group clarity, (3) give their own input and ask members for more, (4) "harmonize" discussions that may involve personal conflict, (5) announce a problem and open it for discussion rather than announce a solution, and (6) encourage all-channel participation, where communication flows laterally, upward and downward.

FIGURE 11.2
The chief justice of the U.S. Supreme Court, as a "leader among equals," is an example of a participative leader.

Laissez-Faire Leaders

The **laissez-faire leadership** style involves little or no leadership per se. The group simply proceeds with the task. According to Bass, "The satisfaction of followers will be lower under laissez-faire leadership than under autocratic leadership if the latter is nonpunitive, appropriate for the followers' levels of competence, or in keeping with the requirements of the situation. Most often, laissez-faire leadership has been consistently found to be the least satisfying and effective management style."[5]

A laissez-faire leader is one who, according to subordinates, stays out of the way, is difficult to find when there is a problem, communicates the absolute minimum for members to do their job, and, if not bothered, won't bother the group.

Most textbooks on leadership usually downgrade this style, although recently Altier has defended it.[6] Altier argues that poor problem-solving meetings are due not to a lack of leadership skills but to the person who called the meeting. As he suggests, "If the person who calls the meeting actively contributes and presents personal ideas and solutions (influenced by personal agendas and experiences), the leader's perspectives are frequently in opposition to those of other participants. The cold, hard fact is that such a leader is often no more objective than the condemned man at a hanging."[7] Notice that *both* authoritarian and participative leaders present personal

LAISSEZ-FAIRE LEADERSHIP
A leadership style that involves little or no leadership per se.

ideas and solutions. Altier argues that "a meeting leader who also partici-pates in the content discussion fails to recognize that these two roles are contradictory and conflicting."[8]

In essence, Altier contends that a leader should not switch back and forth between the roles of participant and leader. "The leader should pos-sess excellent process and facilitating skills; the participants should possess excellent knowledge about the problem. But the twain [two] should never meet in the leader."[9] Finally, Altier argues, "The more distant the meeting leader is, the more effective he or she can be. Only when the meeting leader possesses distance or 'stranger value' can this person hope to keep the group from falling into the 'they cannot see the forest for the trees' trap."[10] In essence, a case can be made for staying out of the way.

The authoritarian, participative, and laissez-faire leadership styles are the most famous and were the first to be identified. (The consultative style was recognized later.) The classification according to three styles came about through an early (1939) study using four groups of 10-year-old boys.[11] These boys met after school for three six-week periods, during which time they made paper masks and engaged in other hobbies. During each six-week period, they had a different adult leader, using a different leadership style. The three styles that were used were the authoritarian, participative, and laissez-faire. The authoritarian leader *told* the boys what to do, the partici-pative leader *facilitated* the work by involving the boys in making deci-sions, and the laissez-faire leader let the group "run itself." Records were kept of the group's behavior, including observations, member contribu-tions, movies of interaction, and records of the kinds of comments made.

The results were interesting. Hostility was 30 times as great and aggres-sion was 8 times as great in authoritarian-led as in participative-led groups. More scapegoating (meaning a boy was made the target of hostility) was present in the authoritarian-led groups. Ninety-five percent of the boys liked the participative leader, and 70 percent liked the laissez-faire leader better than the authoritarian leader.

The number of products issued did not differ, but the *quality* of products produced was judged superior in participatively led groups. The boys' be-havior toward the leader was as follows: Under the authoritarian leader, they were more submissive, critically discontent, aggressive, and demand-ing of attention. Under the participative leader, they were more friendly, confiding, group-minded in giving suggestions, open in "nontask" conver-sation, and "work-minded" when involved in the task. Under the laissez-faire leader, they asked for much more information.

Here is another illustration of the differences in leadership styles. One week, the veteran manager in a large corporation attended a three-day semi-nar on participative leadership during which this style was described. At the end of the seminar, he decided to give it a try. At the next week's staff meet-ing, he called everyone together, sat down, and described a problem. Instead

Choosing the Right Leader

During your class session, divide into groups. Select four well-known characters from books, television, or the movies who accurately depict authoritarian, participative, consultative, and laissez-faire leaders. For each leadership style, list some types of groups (or people) for which that particular style of leadership would be appropriate. What about your own group? What leadership styles were operating in your group as you worked through this exercise? Would a different style have worked better? At the end of the session, compare your answers with those of other groups.

of dictating a decision, he asked what everyone believed should be done. They sat there in silence. He asked again. Still they sat there without a word. He asked specific staff members. They were speechless. In their minds, they were thinking, "Has he been drinking?" "What's happened to him?"

So what do you think he did? He went back to his authoritarian behaviors. And why? Because the group forced him to! When he tried to be participative, and the group failed to participate, he had to use authoritarian behaviors to get the job done. Thus, just because your mind is set on a particular way to behave does not always mean you will be able to do so. Circumstances may require you to employ behaviors that you have no intent or desire to use.

Shared Leadership

Competent groups share leadership among their members. Many groups, as is well known, elect their leaders. For instance, in one large corporation, the safety board meets monthly. Each year, the board elects a chairperson, a vice-chairperson, and a secretary. In another corporation, the board leaders are appointed by an external source. If you consider your instructor to be the leader of your class, you are aware that administration told the instructor to "be in room 326 of University Hall from 1:00 to 2:00 P.M., Mondays, Wednesdays, and Fridays for Communication 211." All of these cases actually illustrate "headship" rather than "leadership." The person is in charge of the group because that person was formally placed in that position.

How many times have you seen that genuine leadership actually comes from someone other than the person who is the "head" of the group? Does "figurehead" come to mind when elected officials wait out the end of their terms after being defeated in their last elections? The organized manager with well-set agendas may not be nearly as useful to a group as the well-informed subordinate.

Leadership encompasses many different functions. As illustrated earlier, leaders inspire, organize, and inform. They also regulate interaction, plan, direct, control, offer opinions, empathize, question, and perform many other functions.

A variety of situations permit shared leadership. Consider a city council group faced with making a difficult decision about where to build a new park and how much money to spend. The group is flooded with data; among other things, the members may already have bids from contractors, maps, and expert testimonies. At some point, the members may "wave a white flag." They do not need any more information. Fortunately, a group member may emerge as a leader because that person can *organize* the group's information. This leader may have an uncanny knack of sorting, classifying, or discarding data, and will emerge as the leader because organization is what the group needs most at the present time.

Conversely, consider a task force at a department store whose responsibility is to recommend a security system to senior management. Although all members are enthusiastic about participating, only one person has insight into the store's past problems, types of systems, contact firms, and so forth. In all likelihood, this member will emerge as the group leader because he or she has the information the group needs at that time.

Heads of groups who encourage and facilitate shared leadership are more likely to be effective. When the talents of each individual in a group are brought out and applied, members are likely to be more motivated and the group's needs are more likely to have "all bases covered."

Cultural Influences on Leadership

SHARED LEADERSHIP
Leadership that may emerge from any interested and talented group member, depending on the context.

Many businesses and professional organizations in the United States are moving toward a **shared leadership** model. This means giving people who work at the lower levels of the organization decision-making and leadership responsibilities. Chapter 10 reinforced this idea with the discussion of self-managing teams. However, leadership styles can vary a great deal from one culture to another. In some parts of the Middle East, for example, leadership is reserved for those who hold power. There, organizations and groups tend to be run autocratically, with a few in charge giving directives and orders. This type of leadership style is natural for these Middle Eastern cultures because the families and social structures are based on the same philosophy: *Those with resources and power wield leadership.*

Culture and Shared Leadership

How receptive to shared leadership are the various cultural groups to which you belong? Examine a culture or co-culture with which you identify—for example, your ethnic group, your gender, your religious affiliation, or your age group. On a sheet of paper, draw a horizontal line representing a continuum from authoritarian leadership at one end to shared leadership at the other. Place the leadership style common to your culture on the continuum. Does the style change in either direction for groups in which all the members share your cultural identity? What about groups that also include other cultures? For example, is the leadership style of groups whose members are all about the same age as you different from that of groups in which some members are older or younger? Observing which leadership style seems most comfortable for your cultural group may help you to organize in ways that will facilitate reaching group goals.

Competent Leadership

The definition of leadership is consistent with the theme of this book, for it includes a component of competence. It is not enough to lead, whether one directs or influences followers. The major criterion should be *how well* the leader functions, performs, or behaves. **Competent leadership** may be authoritarian (although this is rarely the case), democratic, participative, or laissez-faire. Competent leaders may share leadership in the group and ensure that their style is a good match for the group. The important issue is that a leader exhibit competent communication in leading the group toward desirable results.

COMPETENT LEADERSHIP *Credible behavior by which an individual inspires and motivates group members to achieve desirable group outcomes through interaction.*

Based on the various definitions and descriptions of leadership proposed in this chapter, it is important to include three factors in a competency-based definition of leadership. First, the competent leader must behave in ways that bring about desirable *outcomes.* The outcomes need not necessarily be pre-planned or even consistent with previously established goals. The outcomes must, however, be successful, productive, or beneficial for the group. Because outcomes are heavily influenced by the group process, leaders must also possess competent communication skills that can move the process toward a successful conclusion.

Second, the competent leader must behave in ways that enhance *credibility* with the group. Credibility is typically assessed through reactions to

Seeing Yourself as a Leader

Examine again the definition of leadership. What could you do to increase your ability to demonstrate the characteristics of leadership? Can you recall examples in the past when you demonstrated these characteristics?

1. Credible behavior
2. Inspiration and motivation of group members
3. Desirable outcomes

What conditions would enable you to be more effective in demonstrating competent leadership?

questions such as "How knowledgeable is the leader?," "How experienced is the leader?" "How believable is the leader?" or "How much do I respect the leader?" Maybe the members do not like the leader personally, but they believe nonetheless that the person is an effective leader for the group. In that case, the leader certainly has credibility.

Finally, the competent leader must *inspire* and *motivate* the group members to participate as members. In some cases, the leader must be a "cheerleader" for the group. In other cases, an individual may "lead by example." In still others, the leader may offer tangible rewards that encourage group members to try to achieve.

Leadership has a quality component. There are standards or criteria by which to assess how well or what a leader does. The definition of leadership includes credible behavior by which an individual inspires and motivates group members to achieve desirable group outcomes through interaction.

The Complexity of Making Decisions in Groups

Making decisions with other people is a very complex process. In order to understand the process of group decision making, you need to become familiar with six concepts: (1) decision-making variables, (2) decision-making skills, (3) values and goals clarification, (4) expectations, (5) time pressures, and (6) conflict.

▨ Decision-Making Variables

Group decisions are never made in a vacuum. No matter what topic is under discussion, several factors can influence the attitudes and behaviors of individual group members and the climate of the group as a whole. These factors affect the final decision in significant ways. To illustrate how multiple decision-making factors (cognitive, psychological, and social) can interact with each other, consider this example.

One of the worst disasters of our time occurred as a result of poor group decision making. On January 28, 1986, the space shuttle *Challenger* exploded 92 seconds after takeoff, killing all seven of its crew members. NASA officials had decided to launch the shuttle even though they had received information that cast doubt on the safety of the mission.

In an analysis of the decision making that led to this tragedy, Hirokawa, Gouran, and Martz argue that three forces influenced the faulty decision.[12] These same forces operate in practically any type of group decision making. They are *cognitive, psychological,* and *social* forces.

Cognitive Forces

Cognitive processes are mental, referring to what someone thinks, believes, or feels. They specifically involve the beliefs individuals hold and the methods they use to make a decision. They influence "the manner in which group members attend to, make sense of, and utilize available information" to make a decision.[13]

Cognitive forces include the perception, interpretation, evaluation, storage, retrieval, and integration of information input to an individual. The outcome of any group decision can be greatly affected by the way group members interpret information.

A government commission's investigation of the *Challenger* disaster found that cognitive forces had been at work on the NASA officials who made the decision to launch the shuttle. The officials discounted the credibility of key negative information available to them at the time of the launch. The decision makers also used questionable reasoning by drawing incorrect conclusions from the data available to them. Finally, they held faulty beliefs about the shuttle system that led them to have unwarranted confidence in its ability to launch correctly.

Psychological Forces

Psychological forces refer to the personal motives, goals, attitudes, and values of group members. In the *Challenger* example, two psychological forces influenced the participants' decision making: perceived pressure and a criterion shift.

Lower-level NASA decision makers felt pressure to reverse an earlier recommendation to postpone the launch. Initially, the group had recommended that the launch be postponed until the temperature was higher. That decision was later reversed in the face of strong opposition from higher management officials.

The decision makers also shifted the criterion for postponing the launch. Ordinarily, NASA officials employ a rule that a launch should not take place if there is any doubt of its safety. With this rule, the burden of proof is on the *safety* of the launch. In this case, officials shifted to a rule suggesting that a launch should proceed unless there is conclusive evidence that it is unsafe to do so. With this rule, the burden of proof is on the *risk* of the launch. Because risk is always harder to prove than safety, the NASA officials used an incorrect decision criterion to proceed with the launch.

Social Forces

Social forces deal with communicative influences such as language use and persuasion. These forces are present whenever two or more people interact with each other. In the *Challenger* disaster, responsible engineers were unable to persuade their own management and higher NASA officials to postpone the launch. Their unsuccessful strategy was to prove that it was unsafe to launch rather than to take the tactic that no data were available to prove that it was safe to launch the *Challenger*. The government commission's investigation also revealed that much ambiguous and confusing language was communicated among various officials.

How often can these same forces operate in groups that people work with each day? Think about this point: Have your strongly held beliefs ever caused you to dismiss contrary information as unimportant or incorrect? Have you ever felt pressure to "go along with the crowd" as part of the decision-making process? Have you always insisted on understanding exactly what others meant when they expressed their views in a group before you would agree to a particular conclusion? Most people have been in groups where they could answer "yes" to all three of these questions. In the *Challenger* disaster, the loss was greater than seven lives. What will be the cost of your group's next decision?

Decision-Making Skills

Different people, of course, have different skills in decision making. Think for just a moment: What is involved when you make any of these decisions as an individual?

Ethics and O-Rings

Many experts have characterized the *Challenger* disaster as a "communication breakdown." Several communication problems contributed to the space shuttle explosion. Besides the psychological, cognitive, and social variables at work in this situation, it has been suggested that a number of ethical communication issues were involved.* In testimony during the hearings investigating the disaster, we learned that engineers for the O-ring manufacturer, Thiokol, were very vocal in their objections to the launch of the space shuttle in cold weather. After management overruled their objections and authorized the launch, the engineers were unhappy but silent. If they really believed that people's lives would be in danger, didn't they have a moral and ethical obligation to communicate their concerns to others in positions of authority? For example, would it have been ethical for the engineers to go over their bosses' heads to even higher authorities? Would it have been ethical for the engineers to talk to the media about their fears? On the other hand, don't decision makers such as the Thiokol engineers have a moral duty to support their superiors' decisions? Going over a boss's head or leaking information to the press is a good way to get fired. Didn't the engineers have an ethical obligation to themselves and their families to keep their jobs?

*See J. A. Jaksa & M. S. Pritchard (1994), *Communication ethics: Methods of analysis* (2nd ed.) (Belmont, CA: Wadsworth).

- Whether to drop or continue a course you are currently struggling in.
- Whether to sacrifice now by juggling school and work in order to benefit later with a better, more rewarding job.
- Whether to be frugal in your entertainment expenses (movies, eating out, concert tickets) for six months so that you can save the additional $300 you still need to attend a family reunion in Orlando, Florida.
- Whether to eat a light lunch today so that you can feast tonight without guilt at an all-you-can-eat seafood buffet.
- Whether to accept a job promotion and relocate to another city.

What processes do you engage in when you make these decisions or countless others like them? As an individual, you make decisions and solve problems many times every day. You may have even followed the same kind of problem-solving steps outlined earlier.

For any of these problems you probably (1) delineated the alternatives clearly, (2) decided how distinct the alternatives were, (3) analyzed the "state of affairs" for each alternative, (4) determined what criteria were the most important for you in making the decision, (5) using those criteria, conducted a cost/benefit or pro/con analysis for each alternative, (6) came to a conclusion and made the decision you thought was right, and (7) evaluated it later.

These same processes, and more, are present when individuals meet as a group to make a decision. Clearly, some people are better than others at these processes; consequently, some groups are better than other groups as well. Now look at some of these processes for a moment. This section refers specifically to group decision-making skills rather than the individual skills discussed in Chapter 10.

Analysis

Analysis refers to "taking apart" a problem and examining its components. When a group conducts an analysis, it probes for sources, causes, effects, and influences. Analysis mobilizes the individual skills (such as critical thinking) discussed in Chapter 10. (Analysis as a decision-making process is discussed later in this chapter.)

Perspective

The perspective a group brings to a problem influences its decision-making process in several different ways. How important is the problem? How many people does it affect? How much money might a particular decision save or cost? How much time should be spent on the issues? The answer to all of these questions is what perspective is all about. Groups that put the problem in proper perspective are better at decision making than those that do not.

Focus

Can the group keep its focus on its task? Or does it get lured and deeply involved in sub-issues or topics that are irrelevant to the problem at hand? It is easier than you think to become focused on issues that are not directly relevant to the problem under discussion, especially when some group members have partisan agendas they would like to pursue. Leaders and group members must be vigilant in identifying topics that can distract the group from its primary goal.

Summary

Summarizing is very important and should occur with regularity while a group makes decisions. Summary statements allow group members to assess "where they are" on a given decision. When these statements are voiced with clarity, participants have the opportunity to confirm, correct, or clarify what has occurred up to a certain point. Some textbooks call for the leaders to provide summary behaviors as part of their responsibilities. This may be true, but *any* participant can attempt to summarize the discussion at any point.

▒ *Values and Goals Clarification*

Before a group proceeds to make decisions, it should engage in values and goals clarification. Simply put, values help a group determine whether a decision is right or wrong; goals are the end-state for which the decision is made.

Values

A noted psychologist, Milton Rokeach, defined a **value** as "an enduring belief that a specific mode of conduct or end-state or existence is personally or socially preferable to an opposite or converse mode of conduct or end-state of existence."[14] When groups express the idea that certain behaviors are right or wrong or that certain end-states are desirable or undesirable, they are operating from their values. Values significantly affect a group's decision-making process.

For example, U.S. congressional committees hold the value that "democracy" is preferable to "dictatorship." Mothers Against Drunk Driving (MADD) has clearly sent the value-laden message that drinking alcoholic beverages before operating an automobile is very dangerous. Consumer advocacy groups suggest that "safety" in the manufacture of products is preferable to "risk." Raters for the Motion Picture Association of America (MPAA) determine that some material may not be suitable for pre-teenagers' viewing, while other material is not suitable for anyone under age 17 to witness. Any decision that groups such as these make is strongly driven by their values.

Many groups are defined by and exist because of their values. Their participants are together because they have a common concern or interest. For example, members of the Parents and Friends of Lesbians and Gays (PFLAG) all share heartfelt stories of guidance in understanding and accepting homosexual children and loved ones because they believe everyone deserves love,

VALUES
The enduring beliefs that individuals and groups hold about certain issues and behaviors.

respect, and dignity. Other groups develop their values as they continue to interact together. If you were asked to participate on a local Teenage Pregnancy Task Force, you would surely know that everyone on that task force believes in the general goal of "preventing kids from having kids is important." To find out what and how this value is applied to specific cases or problems would require that you obtain additional values clarification.

In summary, groups make decisions that are harmonious with their values. By the same token, the processes that groups engage in while making decisions are also value-driven. Most discussions on the kinds of alternatives available to a group, the quality of evidence, and the credibility of sources are likely to be highly controlled by a group's values. Even though a group may attempt to clarify its values in advance of its meetings or discussions, leaders may need to remind the members of these values as work continues on a task.

Goals

Effective groups are those whose members are working "on the same page." That is, all participants in a group envision, support, and devote their efforts to the same result or product. Goals are those results or products.

SELF-CHECK

Values Clarification

Rank the values in the left-hand column in their order of importance to you as an individual. Then rank the group values in the right-hand column in their order of importance to you.

INDIVIDUAL VALUES	GROUP VALUES
1. Spiritual fulfillment	1. Consensus building
2. World peace	2. Group productivity
3. Marital bliss	3. Conflict management
4. Honesty	4. Group cohesiveness
5. Career achievement	5. Cordial relations among members
6. Secure financial situation	6. Popularity among group members
7. Professional recognition	7. Group recognition

Look at your rankings. Do you find that your personal values match the group values?

FIGURE 11.3
Marches and civil disobedience have been the preferred modes of protest for groups that value nonviolence.

Recall from Chapter 10 the six steps you should follow in formulating and setting effective goals. That information is relevant to this discussion.

A group's failure to clarify its goals before beginning work on a project can prove disastrous. Here is a classic example of a group that was not goal directed. Several years ago, a university professor was working on an awards task force for a professional organization. All anyone knew about the task force was that it had been formed to make nominations and recommendations to the association's board of directors regarding individuals who should receive awards. Prior to the group's first meeting, no attempt was made to define any of the following: the kind of awards to be given, the number of people to be nominated for each award, the criteria for an award nominee, or even the date when the nominations had to be submitted for board approval. When the task force convened at the association's annual convention just two days before the award winners were to be announced, there was total chaos. After almost two hours of fruitless discussion, someone finally retrieved a copy of the association's bylaws and discovered that it contained exact titles for the awards and specific criteria for each.

You can probably think of other examples of groups in which individual members disagree or have misperceptions about the group's task. Refer back to the Teenage Pregnancy Task Force mentioned earlier. All members of the group agreed that preventing "children from having children" was an important and worthwhile goal. However, the members did not agree on preventive solutions. Several members believed that abstinence was the only direction to take. Others felt that birth control devices would help deter the unwanted and unplanned pregnancies. Still others encouraged the use of educational information explaining to female adolescents where, how, and when conception takes place. Not surprisingly, with individual members of the task force expressing their personal views, the group did not reach a consensus.

Many people confuse group goals with objectives and use these two terms interchangeably. Goals are the end-state or product that a group aspires to achieve, whereas objectives are the specific and measurable *means* that lead to the goals. A series of objectives usually relate to a single goal. For example, a hospital acquisitions task force has a goal of obtaining the newest X-ray equipment in all of its examination rooms by the end of the year. This group may have several objectives that lead to that goal: (1) to have six major community corporations make donations of $5,000 by June, (2) to persuade 65 percent of all employees to donate $1 from each paycheck for six months, (3) to make a 45 percent down payment on the equipment by September 1, and (4) to place six articles describing the project in community publications by March 3.

Expectations

Several factors determine whether a meeting is successful or unsuccessful. Without doubt, the expectations and goals that participants bring with them to a meeting play a major role. Recall from the model of communicative competence and previous chapters the importance of expectations in communication. Green and Lazarus conducted a survey of over 1,000 business leaders which revealed several of the expectations held by group members and leaders.[15]

- Approximately 85 percent of the respondents expected to spend as much or more time in meetings five years hence.
- One-third of the time spent in meetings is unproductive; therefore, although the time spent in meetings is increasing, time wasted is also growing, with an estimated loss to business in excess of $40 billion.
- Ninety-seven percent of respondents believed that participants should be prepared for meetings, but only 28 percent were prepared most of the time.
- Three out of four meetings fail to end on schedule.
- Two out of three meetings fail to achieve their goals.

- Eighty-one percent of all respondents believed that their perception of a person's ability was affected by the quality of his or her participation in meetings; 87 percent of those surveyed believed that a person's ability to lead meetings affected other individuals' perceptions of his or her management ability.

The many reasons for these opinions and observations are linked to individual expectations, which are so often violated, thus causing dissatisfaction with group processes.

Time Pressures

The amount of time a group has available can play a significant role in the way it makes decisions. **Time pressures** can influence two aspects of group decision making: planning and leadership styles.

TIME PRESSURES
The effects of a shortage of time on how a group makes decisions.

Planning

Planning and coordinating are essential activities for effective decision making. You've probably been with people in groups who would "build a bridge" before they knew what river or lake it was going to cover! Similarly, groups can make decisions without engaging in proper planning and coordinating activities. Although a group might have a variety of reasons to proceed without planning and coordinating, time pressures are usually the major reason why a group fails to do so.

Consider this example. A group from a professional corporation was working on team-building processes in an outdoor simulation. The group started the activity with its 12 members standing on a wooden platform. They had one long and one short wooden plank at their disposal to assist in moving to a second platform and then to a third. Neither the participants nor the wooden planks could touch the ground; if they did so, the group would have to start over.

The simulation had two trials. In the first trial the group was given only 5 minutes to complete the task. In the second, the group had unlimited time. Not surprisingly, in the first trial, very little advance planning or coordinating was possible. The group member with the loudest voice prevailed and announced the "plan" for the group to follow. The group did so, and it failed miserably. In the second trial, with plenty of time available to it, the group mapped out an elaborate strategy by which to complete the simulation. The participants debated and questioned each other, reevaluated ideas, and then finally reached a consensus agreement on how to proceed. The group completed the simulation successfully in only 12 minutes.

Leadership Styles

The style a group leader uses is also dependent on time. Remember the four different styles that vary in the degree to which the leader allows group members to be involved in making decisions for the group. Allowing participation takes more time. Think about some of the reasons why a group leader may choose not to involve subordinates in decision making. One of these reasons may be that the subordinates do not possess the knowledge or experience needed to assist in making the decision. Another may be that the subordinates do not desire to participate. Yet, of all the reasons you might suggest, time pressures appear to be the most important.

Participation takes time. For a group's leader to allow members to debate or question ideas, reassess or restructure its agenda, or test proposed solutions, time is a necessary element. Many leaders who believe in participative techniques are often forced to be authoritarian leaders simply because there is no time for the group to participate in making a particular decision. Without question, in crisis situations, participative techniques may yield a better decision, but time will not permit them to be used. Consider the example of a military unit in the field of battle, with grenades and enemy fire exploding around it. There is no time for the leader to say "What do you think we should do?" The leader must say, "Get your butt down in the ditch and don't move until I order you to!"

On the other hand, groups need not be at the mercy of time, even in the face of strong pressures. Here are three ways that groups can work around time and produce a quality decision. First, a group may begin a discussion by taking a nonbinding "straw poll." Suppose your focus is a city council discussing whether to join a regional mass transit association. The decision must be made by the end of the meeting. The leader may begin by asking how many of the members favor the union and how many are opposed to it. A straw poll can be taken on any issue and will save a group time discussing items on which all participants already agree. In addition, this vote gives the group an idea of how far apart the participants are on a topic.

Second, the leader may impose time limits on certain components of a discussion. For example, one rule that might be imposed is that no one speaker may have the floor for more than 5 minutes. Another might be that once a person has spoken on a topic, that person cannot contribute to the group without specific permission from the leader. Yet another might be that open discussion will take place for 60 minutes. At that time, the group will proceed to take a vote on the topic.

Third and most important, the group may not make any decision at all. No decision is often better than a bad decision. As Covey argues, "No deal basically means that if we can't find a solution that would benefit us both, we agree to disagree agreeably—No Deal. No expectations have been created, no performance contracts established."[16] Why make a bad decision that you will regret later because you have been forced into it because of time? Stop, table the discussion, or postpone reaching a conclusion.

◼ *Conflict*

In Chapters 8 and 10, as you will recall, we suggested that you should view conflict as a means by which group goals are achieved. When used properly, conflict is a productive, not a destructive, tool for groups.

The best decisions are usually those that have followed productive conflict. This means that clarification questions are asked, participants' ideas are challenged, counter-examples are presented, "worst-case" scenarios are considered, and proposals are reformulated. After such a process, the group can have confidence that its decision has been put to the test. If an idea survives the rigorous test of group participants, it has a fighting chance to be successful when it is applied in the environment.

The other advantage of conflict is that group members will have considerable ownership of the decision that is reached. Because they have had a part in analyzing, synthesizing, and constructing the decision, and because they have participated in its "shakedown," the decision is generally one they agree with, adhere to, and defend before others.

Ownership of the decision explains why people prefer *consensus* decision making to majority vote. When a group takes a split-decision vote, at least one person will be dissatisfied and believe that the decision was forced. Conversely, when the participants argue about the decision and have had a chance to question and test a proposal, they will have had their "ten cents' worth" put on the table and will have been logically persuaded in favor of the resulting decision. Unfortunately, time constraints may force a group not to use the consensus method. However, it should be employed whenever possible.

The Decision-Making Process

Effective groups do not make decisions arbitrarily or haphazardly.[17] Rather, they engage in very systematic processes that result in consensus decisions that all participants can understand and to which they can commit themselves. Here is an eight-step process that has worked for many groups. For clarity, one example is used throughout this section. Pretend that you are a member of a neighborhood group that is meeting to reduce crime in the area.

FIGURE 11.4
The decision-making process.

Evaluating the Results

Implementing the Solution

Selecting the Best Alternative

Evaluating Alternatives

Generating Alternatives

Establishing Guidelines and Criteria

Conducting Research

Identifying the Problem

▨ *Identifying the Problem*

As a first step, a group must make sure that all its members agree on the main problem to be solved. If the group's goal is to generate a solution, then all its members must understand the problem in the same way.

This step does not mean that the group simply announces the problem, then agrees on it and moves on. Thus, in the example, the simple statement, "We need to find a way to reduce crime in our neighborhood," would not be enough. Instead, this step involves gaining a thorough understanding of the problem the group is addressing.

It is recommended that the group begin by having each participant share his or her perception of the problem with the group. Each person should briefly state what the problem is all about. No debate or questions should be allowed until all members have had a chance to voice their perceptions. In this way, the leader will have an idea of how far apart the members are on their thinking about the problem. For example, one member might say, "We have inadequate street lighting," while another might suggest, "We do very little looking out for each other."

This step should be very interactive, allowing the group to engage in an extensive analysis of the problem. The members should question each other, debate ideas, and attempt to clarify positions. They should provide philosophies, statistics, case examples, incidents, or analogies in making their analysis. During this step, the group asks questions such as, What are the origins or causes of this problem? What are the possible ramifications if the problem is not solved? What is the philosophy behind the current state of affairs? Who is affected? to what extent?

Before moving on, the leader should make sure all the participants agree on the problem. The leader should summarize the discussion that has been held up to that point. If the members have not reached agreement, the leader should pinpoint the source of confusion and proceed to obtain a consensus.

Conducting Research

After the group has agreed on the exact problem to be solved, more information may be needed in some areas. Research may be required (1) to bridge gaps in information needed to analyze the problem properly, (2) to obtain clarification in order to resolve two or more inconsistent views or positions expressed by participants, or (3) to review the historical success of a proposed solution.

In the neighborhood example, the group may not know the exact number of burglaries or the approximate dollar figures lost because of crime in the area. Two sides may emerge in the group regarding the actual worth of motion detectors on each person's property. Someone in the group may oppose that view and propose investigating the cost of hiring a private security company to patrol the neighborhood on a regular basis.

Without research on these and other topics, the group operates out of ignorance or misperception. Better decisions are made when group members are armed with data and facts rather than with speculation.

Establishing Guidelines and Criteria

Once the group thoroughly understands and agrees on the nature of the problem, the participants should discuss the criteria by which any solution they propose will be judged. This is *not* the time to propose solutions; that comes later.

In this step, the group agrees on standards to be used to evaluate solutions. In the neighborhood crime example, the criteria may be requirements such as (1) a cost of under $500 per family, (2) the involvement of all families in the neighborhood, and (3) adherence to the guidelines of the city housing code.

This is an interactive step. As in step one, group members should question each other to obtain more information or clarification. The group's goal is to reach consensus on the criteria. Although several criteria may be selected, they must be independent of each other. Before proceeding, the leader should again verify that all members agree that these are the criteria they will use to judge the solutions. In the event of disagreements or problems, the leader should identify the point of confusion and open the discussion for clarification. In order to be able to use these criteria later, the leader should record each of them on a flip-chart or blackboard.

Generating Alternatives

Unlike the previous steps, this step is actually just brainstorming. Each group member should contribute as many desirable solutions as possible, and the leader should record them as they are expressed.

This step is not interactive; that is, the group members do not now debate the worth of the proposed solutions. Each step is simply stated and recorded.

In the neighborhood crime example, you may hear proposals such as (1) install professional security equipment in each home and negotiate the purchase with group buying power, (2) close off two access roads after 11:00 P.M., (3) have four to six residents patrol the area on foot in pairs each evening, (4) encourage each family to buy a guard dog, or (5) offer to house-sit for families who are out of town for extended periods of time.

Evaluating Alternatives

In this step, the group weighs each solution provided in the previous step against the criteria the members have agreed on earlier. The leader can direct the participants to look at the flip-charts, posters, or blackboards on which the criteria and solutions are displayed.

The leader can then announce the first proposed solution and ask the group whether the solution meets criterion number 1, and, if so, criterion number 2, and so forth, until the solution either meets *all* the criteria or is eliminated. This process should be continued until all of the solutions have been examined.

In the case of the neighborhood crime example, the leader may say, "Okay, let's look at the first proposal—that we install professional security equipment in each home and negotiate the price with our group buying power. Now, does that mesh well with our first criterion—that it cost under $500 per family?"

Selecting the Best Alternative

Once the group has arrived at a short list of alternatives, the members must select one alternative that can best fill their needs. Groups that are lucky may indeed find the perfect solution. That is, only *one* proposed solution successfully survives the evaluation. Frequently, however, one of two other things happens. Either more than one solution survives, or no solution survives. What should you do? In the first case, the group should determine whether the two or more viable solutions are mutually exclusive. Can you do them both? If so, there is no problem, for you have two (or more) solutions that you can implement immediately. If not, pick the solution that has met the criteria most completely. This is likely to be your best solution.

In the event that no solution survives, the group must choose at least one of the previously suggested solutions—that is, the proposed solution that meets the greatest number of criteria. Although that solution may not be optimal, it is superior to any of the others.

By following this example, you can probably see that the step that establishes criteria is just as important as, if not more than, the step that produces solutions. If the criteria are worthwhile standards, the group can feel comfortable with the solution it decides on.

Implementing Solutions

The last two steps in the decision-making process are implementing, and then evaluating, the solution reached by the group. Implementing a solution involves putting into action the ideas and decisions that the group has finalized. In some cases, this means submitting a report to a higher authority, with recommendations about how the solution can best be put into place. For example, a self-directed work team in business will go through the decision-making process to arrive at a recommendation for improving some aspect of the organization. The team's recommendation is forwarded to an executive committee, a task force, or an individual responsible for seeing that the solution is implemented in the organization.

In other cases, the group suggesting the solution is also expected to implement it and in order to do so is usually expected to convert general or abstract ideas into a practical plan of action. Because most group decisions affect more people than just the group members, directions and instructions for carrying out the decision must be clear, direct, and simple. In addition, many people will want to know why a particular decision was reached. Therefore, you will want to include some explanation of your decision and a justification for implementing it in the way you propose.

Evaluating the Results

Solutions resulting from the group decision-making process must stand the test of evaluation. Solutions are best evaluated by returning to the criteria that were established early in the process. The following questions can be helpful as you apply the group's criteria to your solution.

- Were the criteria useful and appropriate for the problem?
- How strictly were the criteria used in arriving at the decision?
- Does the solution resemble the criteria that were developed?
- What other criteria would have been helpful in reaching a better solution?
- Does the solution have any weaknesses or disadvantages?

Evaluating group decisions can make a good decision even better. A hard look at any result or outcome will uncover even minor shortcomings that can be improved on before full implementation takes place. Careful scrutiny can create opportunities for precision. In addition, evaluation can help groups to improve their decision making in the future. Learning from mistakes is rarely pleasant at the time, but it can be a valuable instructional experience that will help you prevent similar problems in subsequent group work.

The steps involved in the *decision-making process* are a proven method of producing competent group outcomes. The sequence of steps encourages group members to "think reflectively" about their task. In this way, all the relevant facts and opinions can be discussed and evaluated, thereby ensuring a better decision. You can even use this process for developing decisions in your personal and professional life.

Before we move to another topic, one other important point needs to be addressed. The leader who uses these steps cannot be shy and must keep control of the group. This does not mean that the leader must be authoritarian, but he or she should stay on top of the situation. For instance, if group members start to propose solutions when they are supposed to be listing criteria, the leader should tactfully steer them back to the topic at hand.

SELF-CHECK

Real-Life Problem Solving

Select a city, state, or campus problem that is relevant to the members of the class and that affects them directly. Divide into groups for the purpose of solving the problem. Using the eight-step process for decision making, develop the best solution you can for the problem. As a class, discuss the solutions proposed by the various groups. Mention any notable group dynamics (conflict, consensus building, shared leadership, etc.).

Similarly, if group members begin to debate or question a contribution someone makes when brainstorming is supposed to take place, the leader must restore order.

Working on Committees, Task Forces, and Boards

For those of you who are planning to enter the business world, be sure that you don't underestimate the importance of this section. Your professional life will be practically synonymous with meetings, especially those of committees, task forces, and boards. Your familiarity with these professional groups will enhance your competence as a group member or leader.

Committees

Organizations typically have two types of **committees**: temporary and permanent. Temporary committees are typically assigned to perform work on a particular project that is unique and nonrecurring. Good examples include committees that plan the company picnic or raise funds for charities.

Permanent committees usually have members who participate on a regular basis for a number of years. For example, a corporate finance committee may have six members, each appointed for a six-year term. One new member is appointed each year. In the sixth year, the member serves as chairperson. After the sixth year, this person rotates off and another member joins the board.

Good examples of permanent committees in a corporation include the compensation committee, the public relations committee, the community affairs committee, and the committee that reviews employee suggestions.

COMMITTEE
A special group that meets for specific purposes.

Task Forces

Task forces are also temporary groups. They differ from mere committees in that they typically perform an investigative or research function *before* discussions are held or decisions are made. For example, a university department chairperson may appoint faculty members to a task force to decide how the curriculum should be changed in the next five years. Another task force might be formed to investigate the rising teen pregnancy proportion, school dropout rate, and so on.

TASK FORCE
A group that researches an issue before discussions are held or decisions made.

Part *Four*

Public Communication

12

Preparing
and Delivering
Presentations

Objectives

After reading this chapter, you should be able to

1. Identify potential strategies for coping with both state and trait communication apprehension.
2. Identify the implicit assumptions that define public speaking.
3. Use a variety of techniques to select a topic for a speech.
4. Analyze audiences in terms of type of audience, relevant reference groups, and situational expectations.
5. Identify a specific purpose for a speech and use the topical system to generate thoughts supporting the specific purpose.
6. Choose among chronological, topical, spatial or geographical, cause–effect, and problem–solution patterns for organizing the main ideas of a speech.
7. Identify appropriate methods of supporting the main points and subpoints of a speaker's message.
8. Construct three types of speech outlines: a complete sentence outline, a topic outline, and a speaker's outline.
9. Compose effective introductions, transitions, and conclusions.
10. Describe four modes of delivery and the principles of effective delivery for them.

CHAPTER CONTENTS

S ANDRA RAGAN IS a college senior spending a portion of her final semester as an intern in the Human Resources Division of a local computer software firm. The firm is experiencing strained management–worker relations and a high attrition rate among employees. Mark Acker, vice president for Human Resources, believes that if the firm is to survive in the volatile computer software industry, it must foster a corporate environment that promotes employee loyalty and increased worker productivity. He believes that his company, operating in an industry characterized by severe growing pains, has an unsettled and ill-defined corporate culture. To help him set up an OD (Organizational Development) program aimed at changing this situation, he decides to conduct a company-wide needs assessment, and he involves Sandra Ragan. Sandra is given access to company records and to employees, and, using questionnaire surveys and individual and group interviews, she begins to develop a profile of the employees. As she begins to organize her findings, Mark asks Sandra to make a preliminary report within a week. The audience will consist of Mark himself; the company's CEO, Anne Nicoterra; and the chief financial officer, Akbar Javidi.

As you read through this chapter, you will learn to identify and develop the skills that Sandra Ragan must possess if she is to prepare and deliver an effective presentation. At the end of the chapter, we will return to this scene and solicit your advice.

This chapter makes two major points: First, the more successful you are in life, the more likely you will be asked to give speeches—be it at a church meeting, a presentation to upper management, or at a Rotary Club dinner. Second, although speechmaking is an art that can create much anxiety and that comes naturally to few, you can improve both your comfort and skill levels for giving speeches. Barbara Ehrenreich, author and political commentator, expresses these two points forcefully:

> There are people who are not afraid of public speaking. I have met some of them and they are not psychopaths. But for the rest of us, public speaking ranks just below snake-handling among the activities we would voluntarily choose to undertake. And this is unfortunate because, while very few occupations require snake-handling in the normal course of events, a great many of them require some form of speaking, if only to plead for an alternative assignment. Rather than speak in public, many otherwise brilliant and able people consider residence in a contemplative religious order. This is not entirely necessary. I have survived it, and so can you.[1]

Although this chapter focuses primarily on enhancing your skill at public speaking, we begin with a few words about that other barrier to effective presentations—communication apprehension.

Communication Apprehension

McCroskey defines *communication apprehension (CA)* as "an individual's level of fear or anxiety associated with either real or anticipated communication with another person or persons."[2] (Recall the discussion of CA in Chapter 8.)

Recognition of CA

If you are like most people, that means experiencing **state CA**—that is, a situational attack of anxiety that can be greater or lesser depending on such factors as the size of your audience, how well you know the people you are talking with, how well you know your subject, and the status of the individuals you are talking with. You might, for example, feel quite relaxed when talking with a friend about a movie you saw the previous evening, but feel a sudden surge of panic when asked to describe your reaction to that same movie for a professor and your classmates in an English class. For some people, CA operates as a trait; that is, they have an enduring tendency to be apprehensive about communication in all contexts. Persons with high levels of **trait CA** do everything they can to avoid communication situations and the fear or anxiety they have learned to associate with communication encounters. For such individuals, the level of fear or anxiety is high whether talking with friends or strangers, interacting in small groups, or giving a public speech.

STATE CA
Situational communication apprehension; can be greater or lesser depending on such features of the context as knowledge of the audience and topic.

TRAIT CA
A tendency to be apprehensive about communication in all contexts.

Consequences of CA

McCroskey and his colleagues have discovered that people with high levels of CA are perceived negatively by those with whom they interact. They are considered less attractive, less competent, less sociable, and less composed. In addition, academically, high levels of CA are associated with lower overall grade-point averages and lower achievement on standardized tests *despite* the absence of a meaningful relationship between level of CA and intelligence. High CA also has important effects on employment. Not only does it make it less likely that people will be interviewed and offered a job, but also the jobs such individuals do receive will likely be less pleasing to them.

Ways of Coping with CA

Whether you suffer from trait (enduring) CA or state (situational) CA, the good news is that you can control both forms. If you suspect that CA is a problem for you, ask your instructor or someone in your campus counseling center whether there are any programs on campus to help people reduce CA. Such programs are generally based on the two most common approaches for reducing high levels of CA—systematic desensitization and cognitive restructuring.

Treatments for Severe CA

SYSTEMATIC DESENSITIZATION
A method for reducing or treating communication apprehension that involves learning deep muscle relaxation, constructing hierarchies of anxiety-provoking stimuli, and pairing relaxation with anxiety-provoking stimuli.

Systematic desensitization was first used to reduce CA in 1966.[3] As a treatment package, it involves three components. The first is training in deep muscle relaxation. In this phase, the trainer may instruct the client to "tense your fist; now relax it." Second is the construction of hierarchies of CA-eliciting stimuli. The client thinks of a range of activities, from those that produce low anxiety (such as lying in bed just before going to sleep) to those that cause high anxiety (such as presenting a speech before an audience). The third component involves the graduated pairing, through imagery, of anxiety-eliciting stimuli with the relaxed state. Within each of these components many variations are possible. For example, wide variations exist in the timing of both the tension and relaxation phases of training in deep muscle relaxation. A great deal of research leaves little doubt that systematic desensitization is an effective approach to treating CA.

COGNITIVE RESTRUCTURING
A method for reducing or treating communication apprehension that teaches individuals how to identify anxiety-producing negative statements about communicating and replace them with coping statements.

A second common approach is **cognitive restructuring**.[4] With cognitive restructuring, communicatively anxious students are first taught to identify anxiety-producing negative statements (e.g., "I'll say something stupid") that create and enhance their CA. Once they have mastered this task, they are then taught to replace these negative statements with coping statements of three types: task statements ("Speak slowly, it helps"), context statements ("It's only a small group of students like me"), and self-evaluation statements ("This was easier than last time"). As with systematic desensitization, cognitive restructuring's effectiveness in reducing high levels of CA is demonstrated by much experimental research.

Guidelines for Controlling Mild CA

Although the professional use of systematic desensitization and cognitive restructuring does reduce high levels of trait CA, neither treatment is generally necessary for individuals suffering from milder versions of state

FIGURE 12.1
Knowing that you are prepared helps to control mild state communication apprehension. Rehearsing a public speech improves your self-confidence as well as your skill in delivering your presentation.

CA. Such individuals can often cope effectively with periodic bouts of elevated anxiety by remembering and applying the following advice:

1. Develop a constructive attitude toward fear and anxiety. Instead of wondering how you will get rid of these common emotions, ask yourself how you will use them. Individuals need tension—feelings of excitement and challenge—to increase their thinking ability and powers of concentration. You should therefore realize that everyone who speaks experiences some apprehension and fear before speaking and that some measure of anxiety is necessary for you to do your best.

2. Grab every opportunity to practice and experience. Whether you are skydiving, using a new computer program, or giving a speech, knowledge of the requirements of an activity is likely to increase your comfort level. For example, you will naturally be more comfortable the tenth time you've gone scuba diving than the first time. Thus, you should seek out opportunities to practice and gain experience.

3. Prepare thoroughly for each public presentation. If, when you get up to speak, you must worry about what you will say, how you will say it, and what the outcome will be, you will certainly be more anxious than if your only concern is about the outcome. Therefore, prepare your speech thoroughly and rehearse your delivery of it. Then, when

Personal Report of Public Speaking Anxiety

The following exercise consists of 34 statements concerning feelings about communicating with other people. Indicate the degree to which the statements apply to you by marking whether you strongly agree (SA), agree (A), are undecided (U), disagree (D), or strongly disagree (SD). Work quickly, recording just your first impressions. This exercise will be helpful to you only if you are completely honest.

1. While preparing to give a speech, I feel tense and nervous. SA A U D SD
2. I feel tense when I see the words "speech" and "public speech" on a course outline. SA A U D SD
3. My thoughts become confused and jumbled when I am giving a speech. SA A U D SD
4. Right after giving a speech I feel that I have had a pleasant experience. SA A U D SD
5. I get anxious when I think about a speech coming up. SA A U D SD
6. I have no fear of giving a speech. SA A U D SD
7. Although I am nervous just before starting a speech, after starting I soon settle down and feel calm and comfortable. SA A U D SD
8. I look forward to giving a speech. SA A U D SD
9. When the instructor announces a speaking assignment in class, I can feel myself getting tense. SA A U D SD
10. My hands tremble when I am giving a speech. SA A U D SD
11. I feel relaxed while giving a speech. SA A U D SD
12. I enjoy preparing for a speech. SA A U D SD
13. I am in constant fear of forgetting what I prepared to say. SA A U D SD
14. I get anxious if someone asks me something about my topic that I do not know. SA A U D SD
15. I face the prospect of giving a speech with confidence. SA A U D SD
16. I feel that I am in complete possession of myself while giving a speech. SA A U D SD
17. My mind is clear when I am giving a speech. SA A U D SD
18. I do not dread giving a speech. SA A U D SD
19. I perspire just before starting a speech. SA A U D SD
20. My heart beats very fast just as I start a speech. SA A U D SD

21. I experience considerable anxiety while sitting in the room just before my speech starts.   SA   A   U   D   SD

22. Certain parts of my body feel very tense and rigid while I am giving a speech.   SA   A   U   D   SD

23. Realizing that I have only a little time left to finish my speech makes me very tense and anxious.   SA   A   U   D   SD

24. While giving a speech, I know I can control my feelings of tension and stress.   SA   A   U   D   SD

25. I breathe faster just before starting a speech.   SA   A   U   D   SD

26. I feel comfortable and relaxed in the hour or so before giving a speech.   SA   A   U   D   SD

27. I do poorly on speeches because I am anxious.   SA   A   U   D   SD

28. I feel anxious when the teacher announces the date of a speaking assignment.   SA   A   U   D   SD

29. When I make a mistake while giving a speech, I find it hard to concentrate on the parts that follow.   SA   A   U   D   SD

30. During an important speech I experience a feeling of helplessness building up inside me.   SA   A   U   D   SD

31. I have trouble falling asleep the night before a speech.   SA   A   U   D   SD

32. My heart beats very fast while I present a speech.   SA   A   U   D   SD

33. I feel anxious while waiting to give my speech.   SA   A   U   D   SD

34. While giving a speech, I get so nervous I forget facts I really know.   SA   A   U   D   SD

Scoring: For items 1, 2, 3, 5, 9, 10, 13, 14, 19, 20, 21, 22, 23, 25, 27, 28, 29, 30, 31, 32, 33, and 34, use the following scores: SA = 5, A = 4, U = 3, D = 2, and SD = 5. For items 4, 6, 7, 8, 11, 12, 15, 16, 17, 18, 24, and 26, use the following scores: SA = 1, A = 2, U = 3, D = 4, and SD = 5. Add up the scores for all 34 items.

If you answered the questions honestly and your score is below 97, you probably feel comfortable in most public speaking situations; if your score is between 97 and 131, you need to remember and apply our five suggestions for coping with state communication anxiety; and if your score is above 131, you may want to ask your instructor or a counselor about the availability of systematic desensitization or cognitive restructuring to help you cope with your anxiety.

Source: J. C. McCroskey (1970), Measures of communication-bound anxiety, *Speech Monographs, 37,* 276–277. Used by permission of the Speech Communication Association.

you rise to speak, you will be able to concentrate on outcome rather than on content or delivery.

4. Concentrate on communicating with your audience. Once you get up to speak, focus on the question "How do I know that these individuals are hearing and understanding what I'm saying?" If you work hard at observing the reactions of your audience and attempt to adapt to them, you will be much too busy to worry about your anxiety or fear.

5. Remind yourself that your listeners want you to succeed. Your listeners are just like you—friendly people. Just as they want to succeed when they get up to speak, they want you to do well when you speak. Even if you do make a slip, they will understand and forgive you!

Having described communication apprehension and some ways of coping with it, we turn now to the heart of this chapter—the basic principles of public speaking. We cover eight tasks:

1. Understanding the nature of public speaking
2. Clarifying your purpose for speaking
3. Analyzing your audience
4. Identifying and organizing your main points
5. Providing support for ideas
6. Outlining the speech
7. Developing an introduction, signposts and transitions, and a conclusion for your speech
8. Selecting methods and following guidelines for speech delivery

The Nature of Public Speaking

What is a public speech and what are you conveying when you rise to give one? Hart, Friedrich, and Brummet answer these questions with eight implicit messages you send out when you address an audience:[5]

1. *You perceive that a problem exists.* Here "problem" means any set of conditions that the speaker feels requires change. You talk because you need to alter some portion of the environment in which you function. The "problem" can be as commonplace as the annual call to rededicate ourselves to the principles of America on the Fourth of July, or as controversial as a plea to nationalize the health care industry.

2. *You perceive that a problem exists that can be overcome by talk.* Not all problems can be resolved through communication. You cannot, in a single speech, change the eating habits of 200 million Americans. Still, when most sensible persons face a body of listeners, they must have some feeling that their message could at least begin to change a situation that they, the speakers, see as undesirable.

3. *You perceive that a problem exists that you cannot overcome by yourself.* Public communication is a pronounced social experience. It implies that collective effort is needed if you are to reorder the environment as desired. Although she could regale herself with laughter by "just thinking," comedienne Joan Rivers must realize that her need for self-fulfillment or her need to entertain others (or whatever else motivates a stand-up comic) can be achieved only by engaging some particular others in discourse.

4. *You perceive that a problem exists that cannot be overcome by convincing just one or two people.* By deciding to address a sizable audience, you apparently have reasoned ahead of time that speaking intimately to a friend is not sufficient for getting the job done. You apparently seek to influence a sizable portion of your social environment.

5. *You perceive that the topic is important enough for you to risk public exposure.* There are surely better ways of making a living than by standing in front of 60 pairs of eyes, 43 of which close two minutes after you have opened your mouth. A person who ventures to address a sizable public must somehow feel that the rewards to be garnered by the effective presentation of a message outweigh the possible "costs" of having self and ideas scrutinized in public.

6. *You perceive that the topic is important to a number of other people.* Many of the things that you feel or know need not (perhaps should not!) be visited upon unsuspecting others, but this does not seem to be part of the ground rules for public communication. When you presume to address a body of listeners, you must have some feeling that a significant number of people can find potential importance in what you have to say.

7. *You are willing to open yourself up to the possibilities of change.* Public speaking is not a one-way street. When addressing an audience, you implicitly realize that you, too, can be affected by the communicative surroundings. You may be shouted down, elected president of the organization, or encouraged to believe more strongly in the message being presented. Because communication outcomes are not predictable in any significant sense, change is always a possibility for the enterprising speaker.

8. *The audience is willing to open itself up to the possibility of change.* This proposition is perhaps so implicit that it is frequently over-

looked. As an auditor or observer of communication, you may forget that when people gather together for the purpose of hearing public discourse, each person is making an "implicit bargain" with the speaker that goes something like this: "I'm here, and you can try to change me—but you'd better make it good!" Furthermore, speaker and audience "agree" (except in especially turbulent times) beforehand that only symbols (as opposed to physical force) will act as an agent of change in public communication surroundings.

In summary, then, public speaking involves a situation in which you perceive that a problem exists that can be overcome and that overcoming it is worth the risk of talking simultaneously to many individuals. You also perceive that the topic is important enough to both you and your audience that you are all willing to be open to the possibilities of change.

Clarifying the Purpose for Speaking

In the "real world," choosing a topic and purpose for a speech is seldom a difficult task. You speak because you volunteered, or you were drafted to speak on a topic for which your expertise is relevant to the situation at hand. For example, your boss wants you to organize the Red Cross blood drive for your unit; the president of your club wants you, as chair of the fund-raising committee, to describe the status of the raffle ticket sales; your candidate for student government president wants you, as campaign manager, to make the nominating speech; or you are presenting a group gift at a farewell party for your classmate who has joined the Peace Corps. This class, then, will provide you with a challenge that you will seldom face after you leave it—namely, finding a speech topic and purpose that fit within the constraints of an instructor-generated assignment.

General Purposes for Speeches

The general purpose specified in your assignments will fit within one of three broad categories for speeches: to inform, to persuade, or to celebrate.

To Inform

Speeches to inform seek to provide an audience with information that it will find new, relevant, and useful. Such speeches can take a variety of forms. They might, for example, explain a process (e.g., how to play various styles of music on the five-string banjo, how to make a birdhouse for bats, or how a laser disc player works), describe objects or places (e.g., the Vietnam Memorial in Washington, D.C., the Black Hills of South Dakota, or roller blades), or provide definitions of things (e.g., classical music, philosophy, or communication). In the form of expository speeches, they might also answer questions that we would like to know about the world around us (e.g., what do we know about tornadoes, Lincoln's Gettysburg Address, or the differences between micro- and macroeconomics?). We discuss general principles for developing and presenting information presentations in Chapter 13.

To Persuade

Instead of describing what exists, persuasive speeches focus on building a case for what should be. Although they most frequently ask for a change in belief, attitude, or behavior (e.g., please vote no on state question 642, boycott this store to protest its unfair labor practices, or let's consider whether it is appropriate for our government to fund art that some people consider pornographic), they can also reaffirm existing attitudes and actions (e.g., we should continue to use the grading structure currently used at our university, our company should continue to sponsor a Little League team, or we should continue to ban public prayer in our nation's public schools). In Chapter 14 we elaborate on strategies that will help you build effective persuasive presentations.

To Celebrate

Ceremonial presentations utilize the principles of both informative and persuasive speaking to address the tasks posed by such special occasions as introducing a speaker, accepting an honor or award, making toasts, presenting a memorial or a eulogy, or celebrating the achievements of an individual or group. In the broadest sense, such presentations are used either

---

REALITY CHECK

To Inform? To Persuade? To Celebrate?

List public speeches that you have listened to, whether in the media or in person, in the past month. Which of them aimed to inform? to persuade? to celebrate?

FIGURE 12.2
In celebrating the achievements of an individual or group, a ceremonial presentation both informs the audience of the recipient's accomplishments and persuades the audience to feel appreciation or admiration.

to demonstrate the speaker's commitment to organizational ideals or to permit the speaker to articulate the organization's commitment to its value ideals. Although this text does not devote a separate chapter to speeches whose goal is to celebrate, the general principles we discuss are relevant to such occasions. In addition, the Suggested Readings section at the end of this chapter identifies texts that focus on such public speaking occasions.

Strategies for Choosing a Topic

The first filter for selecting a topic for a speech in this class is the instructor's assignment. What is it that you are asked to do? Inform? persuade? celebrate? To discover this general purpose, read the speech assignment carefully. If you are in doubt, ask your instructor for clarification. When you have a general purpose firmly in mind, the task becomes one of selecting a topic that will allow you to develop that purpose into an effective public presentation.

In searching for a good topic, you might try three excellent strategies for generating ideas: solo brainstorming, consultation with others, and research.

Solo Brainstorming

In order to give a good speech, you must be knowledgeable about and interested in the topic. Thus, the best place to start when exploring possible speech topics is your own knowledge and expertise. What experiences have you had? What do you know? What do you believe? For example, assume that the assignment requires you to give a two- to three-minute speech describing a place. When faced with this assignment, you might begin to think about the topic in terms of categories of personal experience and knowledge. What places do you know around your college or university? your local community? your state? adjacent states? the United States? other countries? You might also ask yourself what places, in each of these settings, you would like to know. As you engage in this process, avoid evaluation (e.g., "The class won't want to know about that!"). Just get as many ideas down as you can. Evaluation comes later, when you sort through the multiple possibilities for the one topic that will become the focus of your speech.

You might also consider using the technique called *clustering* as a way to free up your creative "right" brain in order to discover ideas in a judgment-free environment.[6] The process is somewhat similar to solo brainstorming; however, instead of resulting in a list of possibilities, clustering "spills" its ideas onto paper.

Clustering is a creative technique for identifying potential speech topics. It begins with a core idea, a nucleus word or phrase. Simply write a word in the center of a piece of paper and circle the word. The word can be whatever strikes you—for example, "baseball," as in Figure 12.3.

CLUSTERING
A creative technique for identifying potential speech topics.

From the nucleus word, create a web of associations. This web is a collection of ideas inspired by the nucleus word or phrase or by words spun off it. "Baseball" might make you think of Babe Ruth. "Babe Ruth" might bring to mind the Babe Ruth museum in Baltimore, which in turn might elicit thoughts of other tourist attractions in that city, and each of those thoughts might lead to other ideas. As the ideas come, write each one, circle it, and connect it to the word or phrase that inspired it.

As the process continues, you should eventually reach a point at which some concept strikes you as a good topic for a speech. To refine the topic, you can make *that* word or phrase the nucleus for a new web of associations.

One of the most important aspects of the clustering process may at first be hard to achieve: You must simply *do*, making no judgments about the suitability of a particular association or idea. If you reach a dead end while looking at a concept, ask yourself, "How does this make me feel?" or "What is the main thing that hits me here?"

Of course, judgment eventually has to come into play. You must bring your critical abilities to bear as you evaluate potential topics and adapt

FIGURE 12.3
An example of a web of associations produced by clustering.

Clustering

Now that you have learned about clustering, try to generate a cluster of speech topics suggested by the word "potato." Write the word in the center of a sheet of paper and circle it. In two minutes, spin off as many ideas as you can. Remember, do not evaluate the ideas until your time is up. Did you come up with a topic that might be appropriate for a speech?

those topics to your specific audience. The time for evaluation, however, is *after* clustering has indicated a topic, not during the clustering process.

After you have exhausted the power of your brain, it is time to turn to the second source of ideas—other people.

Consultation with Others

Friends, classmates, professors, family, and others can be an important source of topics for speeches. Not only can they help you generate speech topics that you may not have thought of ("two heads are better than one"), such individuals help you evaluate the potential interest and information value of these topics for your audience. Thus, as you talk to others about potential topics, you are not only acquiring new topics, you are also beginning the process of analyzing your topic's relevance for your audience.

Research

A third source of topics for speeches is the library—and its collection of books, journals, and other material. Sometimes browsing through the current newspapers and periodicals will remind you of or generate your interest in a particular topic. The reference librarian is also an excellent source of advice on the resources of the library—including general reference guides such as the *Readers' Guide to Periodical Literature*. Increasingly, general reference indexes are available for computer searching free of charge. For example, many libraries offer free access to CD-ROM indexes such as the following:

InfoTrac Access to about 1,000 popular magazines and journals.
ABI Inform Business articles from over 800 business and management journals.

Using CD-ROM Indexes

If you have not done so recently, go to your library and ask a reference librarian whether the library provides access to any CD-ROM indexes. If it does, learn how to use one of them.

Dissertation Abstracts   Ph.D. dissertations in all subject areas since 1861.

MLA Bibliography   Books and journal articles in literature, language, linguistics, and folklore since 1981.

SocioFile   Articles, books, convention papers, and so on in sociology since 1963.

PsycLit   Articles, books, convention papers, and the like in psychology since 1974.

ERIC   Educational Resources Information Center covering over 500 educational periodicals in addition to conference papers, speeches, monographs, research reports, bibliographies, and so on, on educational topics.

Making a Choice

Starting with an assignment from the instructor and a specified general purpose of informing, persuading, or celebrating, you search for potential topics that are relevant to this assignment by solo brainstorming, talking with others, and visiting the library. The next task is to select from among the potential topics the one that best meets the following three criteria:

1. It is a topic you are interested in and know something about.

2. It is a good topic for the general purpose specified in the assignment.

3. It is a topic that your audience will find worthwhile.

At this stage of your preparation, it is likely that most of the potential topics on your list will at least minimally satisfy the first two criteria. Thus, although you will certainly keep the first two criteria in mind, the third criterion will probably be the most significant in your final selection from among the potential topics you have generated. Which topic is most likely to be considered worthwhile by your audience? An answer to this question will require you to engage in audience analysis.

Audience Analysis

You will have multiple reasons for wanting to conduct an **audience analysis**—that is, a characterization of your audience and the situation in which members find themselves. Because you are asking them to change (e.g., to learn new information; to change their attitudes, beliefs, or actions; or to recommit themselves to an organization), it is important for you to know where they are starting from in terms of both your topic and perceptions of you as a speaker. It is also important that you know what kinds of reasons they are likely to find compelling as motivation for changing.

AUDIENCE ANALYSIS
A description of the individuals who will listen to a speech in terms of audience type (pedestrian, passive, selected, concerted, or organized), their relevant reference groups, and their situational expectations.

Types of Audiences

So how do you learn about the beliefs, attitudes and values, experiences, and needs of an audience? A good place for you to start is to classify the total audience in terms of its cohesiveness or togetherness. Hollingsworth uses this variable to group audiences into five types.[7]

The least cohesive group is the **pedestrian audience**—an audience of people who have come together for the moment but have no obvious connection with either the speaker or one another. On many college campuses, for example, a fundamentalist preacher will stand outside a busy classroom building and attempt to attract an audience by vividly describing people's sins and their need for salvation. The speaker's first task in this and similar situations is to capture the attention of individuals who are likely to have other things on their mind.

PEDESTRIAN AUDIENCE
An audience of people who have come together for the moment but have no obvious connection with either the speaker or one another.

The second type of audience is the one you are most likely to face in your communication class—the **passive audience**. Such audiences are already gathered to hear the speaker, but their motivation level is not necessarily high. When you speak in this class, for example, an attendance requirement is likely to guarantee you the physical presence of an audience; it will not, however, guarantee that your audience will be interested in everything you have to say. Because you are addressing a passive audience whose attention you have already claimed, your first task is to sustain and direct listeners' interest.

PASSIVE AUDIENCE
An audience that is gathered to hear the speaker but is not highly motivated to listen to or accept the message.

The **selected audience** is Hollingsworth's third type of audience. In this type, speaker and audience share a common and known purpose, but they do not necessarily agree on the best way to achieve their shared goals. As Democrats and Republicans gather at their respective conventions to put a party platform together, for example, they agree on a platform that will help get their party's candidates elected. Nevertheless, in the process many honest disagreements arise among them concerning the best approach to such

SELECTED AUDIENCE
An audience that shares the goal of the speaker but does not necessarily agree with the speaker's method for achieving the goal.

issues as the economy, defense, and various social issues in the party platform. Thus, your first task when addressing a selected audience is to channel common sources of motivation into some preconceived direction.

The **concerted audience** is quite similar to the selected audience. Its members share a strong need to achieve some end and are usually positively disposed to both the speaker and the speaker's topic. Although they are inclined to do what the speaker suggests, they still need to be convinced. To use our earlier example, when members of the Democratic party meet to put together a party platform, they are a selected audience—they have a common goal, but different wings of the party are likely to have different concerns about what should be included in the platform. A particular wing of the Democratic party, however, is likely to be a concerted audience. When New York Governor Mario Cuomo addresses the liberal wing of the party, for example, the audience is likely to be predisposed to do what he suggests. Thus, your task when addressing a concerted audience is to capitalize on the audience's predisposition to accept your ideas.

Hollingsworth's final audience type is the **organized audience**. Such audiences are completely devoted to the speaker and to the speaker's purpose. Extremist religious and political groups fall into this category, as do audiences who have committed themselves to a noncontroversial cause, such as honoring Julia Child on her eightieth birthday. Thus, informing and persuading organized audiences is typically less important than celebrating with them. Your main job in this instance is to specify the requested action and how it is to be taken.

Although identifying the type of audience you will face is an important component of audience analysis, it is only the first step. You will also need to discover (1) your audience's attitude and knowledge about you and about your topic and (2) what you will need to do to adapt your message to the audience. The most straightforward approach would seem to be to get a list of audience members and then learn everything you can about each member of the audience. Unfortunately, even if you had the time and resources to accomplish this task, you would end up with such an overwhelming mass of data that you would have difficulty figuring out how to use it in any productive way. As an alternative, then, it is useful to cluster your audience in terms of reference groups that help you anticipate how the audience is likely to respond to you and to your message.

Reference Groups

Reference groups are composed of persons who are like us or whom we aspire to be like. As a result, they exert significant influence on how their members are likely to respond to external stimuli such as a speaker and a speaker's message. Reference groups are of two types: demographic and vol-

CONCERTED AUDIENCE
An audience that shares the goal of the speaker and is disposed to accept the speaker's plan of action.

ORGANIZED AUDIENCE
An audience that is completely devoted to the speaker and to the speaker's purpose.

REFERENCE GROUP
A group of people who are like a particular individual or whom that individual aspires to be like.

Your Reference Groups

Jot down a list of reference groups of which you are a member—for example, college students, your political party, your gender, your ethnic background, your living arrangement, your religious affiliation. Which of these roles are demographic and which are voluntary? Which of your reference groups do you share with members of the class? Which do you not share? How will these similarities and differences influence your choice of topics to speak on? How will they influence how you speak about those topics?

untary. **Demographic reference groups** are defined by qualities over which they have little control: age, gender, sexual orientation, and ethnicity. **Voluntary reference groups** include chosen membership in, for example, religious, political, and social groups—or aspiration to membership in such groups.

When reference groups are salient for the situation (membership in a sorority is likely to be more salient in the sorority house than in the classroom), members of a reference group will use that group to establish "acceptable" and "unacceptable" behavior. By correctly identifying them, you can use salient reference groups to anticipate how an audience is likely to respond both to you and to your topic. Reference groups can also be used to identify a set of core values that you can invoke to further the adoption of your position.

Information about salient reference groups can often be obtained informally through casual conversation, observation, and inference. It is also possible to gather this information more systematically. In your communication class, for example, you might be able to use a questionnaire to generate an audience profile that focuses both on relevant reference groups and on attitudes, values, beliefs, experiences, and needs that will influence audience reaction to you, your topic, and your strategies for bringing about change.

Situational Expectations

In addition to analyzing audience cohesiveness and salient reference groups, audience analysis also involves consideration of **situational expectations**. Audiences come to public speaking situations with expectations that result from a variety of sources, including the time of day, month, or

DEMOGRAPHIC
REFERENCE GROUP
A group of people who share such traits as age, gender, and ethnicity.

VOLUNTARY
REFERENCE GROUP
A group of people who have chosen to belong to a specific religious, political, social, or other group.

SITUATIONAL
EXPECTATIONS
Expectations that audience members have about the speaker and the message.

week, events happening in the outside world, comfort and attractiveness of the room, and knowledge (or lack of knowledge) about the speaker or the topic. Thus, you need to know about these expectations in order to fulfill or deal with them. For every speaking situation, therefore, it is important to ask:

- Why are members of the audience here?
- What are they likely to expect to hear in this kind of situation?
- Do they have any expectations about me?
- What are they likely to expect to hear from me on this topic?
- Are there any features of the environment (both internal to the speaking room and external to it) that might affect audience expectations?

Identifying and Organizing Main Points

After a topic has been selected and filtered through the three lenses of assignment relevance, speaker expertise, and audience acceptability, the topic should be summarized in terms of a **statement of specific purpose**—a single declarative sentence that specifies what the audience is expected to know, do, believe, feel, and so on as a result of the speech.

STATEMENT OF SPECIFIC PURPOSE
A single declarative sentence that specifies what the audience is expected to know, do, believe, feel, and so on, after hearing a speech.

- "I want the audience to know about the history and current use of roller blades."
- "I want the audience to vote no on State Proposition 642."
- "I want the audience to understand the various meanings of the word 'communication.' "
- "I want the audience to understand what AIDS is and what we need to do to combat it."
- "I want the audience to appreciate the contributions of Dorothy Day to our society."

Identifying Main Points

With your statement of specific purpose in mind, you need to identify and organize the main points that will be used to lead the audience to accept what you tell them. When identifying main points, you are looking for those three to five key ideas which, if the audience understands and accepts them, will mean that you have successfully accomplished the specific purpose of the speech. If, for example, you want the audience to vote no on State Proposition 642, what are the three to five key points that, if the audience understands and accepts them, will cause it to vote no? If you want the audience to know about the history and current use of roller blades, what are the three to five main ideas that the audience must understand and accept before it will be knowledgeable about roller blades?

Generating Ideas through the Topical System

Although the generation of main ideas is an art rather than a science, a systematic approach is preferable to random reflection. Using the methods of such historical figures as Aristotle, Cicero, and Francis Bacon, authors Wilson, Arnold, and Wertheimer recommend a **Topical System for Generating Thoughts**[8] for this purpose. This approach involves using a small set of headings or topics that identify standard ways of thinking and talking about any subject. The basic premise of the approach is that, while people can and do talk about an infinite number of subjects, the themes used to discuss them are limited—a result of shared ways of thinking about human affairs. The authors of the system have narrowed the cues to 16 ideas that can be used to describe any subject that organizes a message. Empirical research using the system suggests that college students who use it to generate ideas for messages are able to generate significantly more ideas than unaided peers. The 16 topics are:

TOPICAL SYSTEM FOR GENERATING THOUGHTS
The use of 16 common themes for talking about any topic as a trigger for identifying ideas for inclusion in a speech.

A. Attributes commonly discussed
 1. Existence or nonexistence of things
 2. Degree or quantity of things, forces, and the like
 3. Spatial attributes, including adjacency, distribution, and place
 4. Attributes of time
 5. Motion or activity
 6. Form, either physical or abstract
 7. Substance—physical, abstract, or psychophysical
 8. Capacity to change, including predictability
 9. Potency—power or energy, including capacity to further or hinder anything
 10. Desirability in terms of rewards or punishments
 11. Feasibility—workability or practicability

Choosing a Main Topic from the Sixteen Themes

Assume that you have decided to give your informative speech on the history of modern art. Which of the 16 themes suggest possible main topics for such a speech?

B. Basic relationships commonly asserted or argued

    1. Causality—the relation of causes to effects, effects to causes, effects to effects, adequacy of causes, and so on

    2. Correlation—coexistence or coordination of things, forces, and so on

    3. Genus–species relationships

    4. Similarity or dissimilarity

    5. Possibility or impossibility

Selecting the Key Ideas

Assuming that you supplement the results of using the "topical system" with additional research, you are likely to generate dozens of potentially useful main ideas. Although it would be satisfying to be able to use all of them, doing so would not only test the audience's attention span and tolerance for fatigue, it would also require you to exceed the time normally made available to present a message. Thus, having generated dozens of potential ideas, you must next winnow them down to a smaller number that best supports audience acceptance of your specific purpose. Although there is no magic number of main points that works best for all occasions, for most messages it is wise to keep the number within the range of three to five.

Choosing an Organizational Pattern

At this point you have learned how to generate ideas and then process them through a series of three mental filters (your resources, your audience, and the occasion) that help you reduce them to the most telling ideas that provide support for your specific purpose (e.g., the three to five reasons that are likely to convince your audience to vote for your candidate for student body president). The next step involves arranging those ideas in some sequence. A natural starting place is to think in terms of the logical structure of the ideas themselves. Although you can organize ideas in many ways, students of public speaking have historically, with some variation in labels, identified the following five logical **organizational patterns**.

Chronological Pattern

When using this pattern, you organize the main points of the message in a time-related sequence. You might, for example, focus on the past, present, and future of calligraphy as an art form. When analyzing a process step by step, you are also using a chronological pattern. Thus, a message on how to use a new piece of equipment, say, a new fax machine, might be organized using a time pattern. The essence of a **chronological organizational pattern**, then, is that you describe the main points of the message forward (or backward) in a systematic fashion.

Topical Pattern

Also known as a categorical pattern, the **topical organizational pattern** organizes the main points of a message as parallel elements of the topic itself. Perhaps the most common pattern for organizing a presentation, it is useful when describing components of persons, places, things, or processes. Thus, for example, you might use it to describe the various departments within a college, the characteristics of a successful employment interview, or the reasons for giving a charitable contribution to the United Way. A secondary concern when selecting this approach is the sequencing of topics. Depending on the circumstances, this is often best handled in ascending or descending order—that is, according to the relative importance, familiarity, or complexity of the topics.

Spatial or Geographical Pattern

The **spatial or geographical organizational pattern** arranges main points in terms of physical proximity to or direction from each other (north to south, east to west, bottom to top, left to right, outside to inside, and so on). As an organizational pattern, it is most useful when explaining objects, places, or scenes in terms of component parts. Thus, you might describe a computer keyboard, the physical layout of a media-enhanced classroom, or the Mall in Washington, D.C., using a spatial pattern of organization.

ORGANIZATIONAL PATTERN
A method of arranging ideas in a logical sequence.

CHRONOLOGICAL ORGANIZATIONAL PATTERN
A pattern that presents the main points of a message in a time-related sequence.

TOPICAL ORGANIZATIONAL PATTERN
A pattern that presents the main points of a message as parallel elements of the topic itself.

SPATIAL OR GEOGRAPHICAL ORGANIZATIONAL PATTERN
A pattern that presents the main points of a message in terms of the discussed items' physical proximity to or direction from one another.

Cause–Effect Pattern

With the **cause–effect organizational pattern**, you attempt to organize the message around cause-to-effect or effect-to-cause relationships—that is, you either move from a discussion of the origins or causes of a phenomenon, say increases in the cost of fuel, to the eventual results or effects, such as increases in the cost of airplane tickets; or you move from a description of present conditions (effects) to an identification and description of apparent causes. The choice between these alternative strategies can often be productively grounded in the decision to start with that element—cause or effect—more familiar to the intended audience. The cause–effect pattern of organization is especially useful when the purpose of the message is to achieve understanding or agreement rather than action from the intended recipients of the message.

Problem–Solution Pattern

The **problem–solution organizational pattern** of involves dramatizing an obstacle and then narrowing alternative remedies to the one that you recommend. Thus, the main points of the message are organized to show that (1) there is a problem that requires a change in attitude, belief, or behavior, (2) a number of possible solutions might solve this problem, and (3) your solution is the one that will most effectively and efficiently provide a remedy. Topics that lend themselves to this pattern include a wide range of business, social, economic, and political problems for which you can propose a workable solution (e.g., proposing the implementation of a new course/faculty evaluation system for the college; choosing a method for conducting job performance interviews; or suggesting a plan for reducing the national deficit). The problem–solution pattern of organization is especially useful when the purpose of the message is to generate audience action.

Having identified five potential logical patterns for organizing main ideas, we are now ready to consider how you might best enhance the believability and credibility of these main points. What can you say or do that will help your audience understand and accept the points you wish to get across?

Providing Support for Main Ideas

Before exploring specific verbal and nonverbal devices that you can use to facilitate message retention and acceptance, it is helpful to conceptualize your task as that of facilitating learning. For everyone, learning is a life-long process in which experiences lead to changes within the individual. For many, change is uncomfortable and, therefore, resisted. Even more, individuals resist *being* changed.

Applying Principles of Learning

A speaker who wants to be a change agent should consider the best way to utilize what is known about principles of learning. Knowles provides a useful summary in the form of **andragogy**, which he uses as a label for the art and science of helping adults learn.[9] Andragogy makes five assumptions about adults:

ANDRAGOGY
The art and science of helping adults learn.

The need to know   Once an adult is sold on why learning is important, the motivation to learn follows.

The need to be self-directing   Adults have a strong need to take responsibility for their own lives.

Experience   Adults have more experience than do children and can help each other learn.

Readiness to learn   Adults must be ready, able, and willing to learn before teaching can occur.

Orientation to learning   Learning is most successful when its relevance to the actual task is apparent.

These principles suggest that as you select supporting material that helps your audience understand and accept your message—that is, learn it—you ought to consider that

- *Individuals have different motivations for learning.* Although "What's in it for me?" and "There might be something of value that I can use" may reflect the bottom-line motivators of audience members, each person can value a different motivator. Thus, it is important to build the message on the audience analysis.

- *Learning is an individual activity.* The accumulation of knowledge, skills, and attitudes is an experience that occurs within the learner and is activated by the learner. Although you can set the stage and do much to orchestrate a climate conducive to learning, learning is an internal process.

- *Audience members have prior experience.* The more you incorporate the audience's life experiences into the construction of the message, the more the audience can be expected to retain and use the information provided.

- *Learning results from stimulation to the senses.* An audience member will learn better when you appeal to multiple senses. Learners learn best by doing. As Confucius stated it: "I hear and I forget; I see and I remember; I do and I understand."

■ Using Verbal and Nonverbal Forms of Support

FORMS OF SUPPORT
Verbal and nonverbal devices such as language, explanations, examples, statistics, testimony, and visual aids that can focus audience interest on the speaker's message and help the audience to understand and accept the message.

Within a learning framework, then, what are the specific verbal and non-verbal **forms of support** that you can use to facilitate the retention and acceptance of a message? In the next few pages we highlight six.

Language

Words are only arbitrary collections of letters that serve as symbols for things we wish to think and talk about (e.g., people, things, events, ideas, beliefs, feelings). In addition to the fact that the letters "B-O-O-K" are an arbitrary label for what you are reading, as a vehicle for conveying meaning, these letters carry with them both denotative and connotative aspects (see Chapter 4). That is, the word "book" points to or denotes an object that the dictionary describes as "a volume made up of pages fastened along one side and encased between protective covers." It also carries a connotative meaning (i.e., an attitude toward such objects) that is likely to vary from person to person. Although everyone in our culture is likely to agree that "book" denotatively means the thing you are now reading, some readers will have had mostly negative experiences with books (especially textbooks), whereas others will have had more positive experiences.

Thus, even though an audience may share a relatively common denotative meaning for a word as concrete as "book," the wide range of connotations within an audience will make your task as a speaker quite challenging. As a result, when you begin to think through how best to convey the main ideas of a message, it is imperative that you consider word and language choices that have the potential to make the constructs of the message relevant, clear, and unbiased for audience members. Here are some guidelines that can help a public speaker achieve this goal:

- *Public language should be personal.* Don't borrow someone else's vocabulary. Use language that *you* can use easily. Never use a word in a speech that you haven't said *out loud* previously. Practice pronouncing a new word until you make it yours.

- *Public language should be fitting.* Listen carefully to the language patterns of your listeners before you speak to them. Adjust the formality of your language to fit the situation. Resist the temptation to use a pet phrase just because you like it. Don't be flip with a serious topic or melodramatic with a light one.

- *Public language should be strategic.* Ambiguity often has its advantages, especially when you're dealing with touchy topics or hostile listeners. Try out several different ways of phrasing a volatile idea. Don't depend on the inspiration of the moment to guide your language choice.

Think in advance about *what* you're going to say and *how* you're going to say it.

- *Public language should be oral.* Except in certain circumstances, manuscript speeches should be avoided. A speech is meant for the ear, not the eye. *Listen* to the words and phrases you intend to use. Put "catch phrases" in your outline rather than long, elaborate sentences. Use your voice and body to signal irony and rhetorical questions.

- *Public language should be consistent.* Be careful not to create a riotous collection of images for your listeners. Make them feel comfortable by using extended metaphors. Don't switch randomly from the active to the passive voice. Be sure that the referents for your personal pronouns are clear.

- *Public language should be precise.* If you're talking about bulldozers, don't call them earthmoving vehicles. Avoid jargon that is not necessary for comprehension. Define all technical terms for your listeners. Avoid vague generalities. Use concrete and specific language when providing descriptions.

- *Public language should be simple.* Use five-syllable words sparingly. Employ simple constructions (as opposed to compound or complex constructions) as often as possible. Avoid embedded clauses. Use your *voice* to emphasize a point, instead of repeating an idea several times.

- *Public language should be unaffected.* Don't seek to have your listeners remember your language. Don't get carried away with metaphors; a single simple image is always superior to several complex ones. Don't invent "cute" phrases. Euphemistic language often sounds ludicrous (e.g., referring to killing as "elimination").

- *Public language should be fresh.* It is doubtful that your listeners will be hearing your proposition for the first time. Examine how other speakers have phrased your proposition and find a new, audience-dependent way of wording it. Let your mind wander freely as you search for apt metaphors and similes. If your audience's eyes look glazed, you'll know you are not capturing their attention.

- *Public language should be "dickmottaish."* Dick Motta was a coach for the Philadelphia 76ers professional basketball team. A colorful and exciting coach, he was also verbally adroit. When being interviewed by the press, Motta almost always expressed his thoughts in simple, precise, fitting, and highly quotable terms. Motta's language was always personal and fresh as well, a welcome relief from the speech of the often pompous commentators who afflict our ears during sporting events. Motta's most famous phrase was delivered on the eve of certain disaster for his Philadelphia ballclub. When being prodded by sportscasters to throw in the emotional towel, Motta summoned up the very best sort of public language when he replied, "The opera isn't over until the fat lady sings." Now *there* is language worth listening to.[10]

Explanations

Explanation is the act or process of making something plain or comprehensible. It is often accomplished by a simple, concise exposition that sets forth the relation between a whole and its parts. For instance:

A state is one of the internally autonomous political units composing a federation under a sovereign government; for example, New York, Montana, and Alaska are states within the United States.

Explanation is also accomplished by providing a definition. This alternative can take a variety of forms:

- Providing a *dictionary definition* (which typically involves placing the construct to be defined in a category and then explaining the features that distinguish this construct from all other members of the category—e.g., "*Primary* means 'first in time, order, or importance'")
- Using *synonyms* (words with approximately the same meaning—e.g., "*Mawkish* as an adjective indicates that someone or something is sentimental, maudlin, or gushy") and/or *antonyms* (words that have opposite meanings)
- Using *comparisons* (showing listeners the similarities between something unfamiliar and something familiar) and *contrasts* (supporting an idea by emphasizing the differences between two constructs)
- Defining by *etymology* and *history* (e.g., "*Pedagogy,* a term used to describe the art and science of teaching children, is derived from the Greek *paid* meaning 'child,' and *agogus,* meaning 'leader of'")
- Providing an *operational definition* (defining a process by describing the steps involved in that process—e.g., "To create calligraphy, you begin with a wide-nibbed pen . . .")

To be effective, explanations must be framed within the experiences of members of the audience and cannot be too long or abstract.

Examples

Examples serve as an illustration, a model, or an instance of what is to be explained. They can either be developed in detail (an illustration) or presented in abbreviated, undeveloped fashion (a specific instance). An illustration—an extended example presented in narrative form—can be either hypothetical (a story that could but did not happen) or factual (a story that did happen). For example, a presenter might involve the listeners in a hypothetical illustration by suggesting, "Imagine yourself getting ready to get up to give a speech. You reach into your bag for the manuscript that you carefully prepared over the course of the past week. It isn't there! You madly search through everything in the bag." Whether hypothetical or factual, the illustration should be relevant and appropriate to the audience, typical rather than exceptional, and vivid and impressive in detail.

A specific instance is an undeveloped or condensed illustration or example. Therefore, it requires listeners to recognize the names, events, or situations in the instance. If a presenter, for example, uses "President Dewey" as a specific illustration of the dangers of poor sampling techniques when engaged in public opinion polling, and the audience has never heard of Thomas Dewey (Harry Truman's Republican opponent in the 1948 presidential election), this specific instance will not be an effective way of making the point clear and vivid.

Statistics

As a form of supporting material, **statistics** are used to describe the end result of collecting, organizing, and interpreting numerical data. They are especially useful when reducing large masses of information to general categories (e.g., in 1991–1992, 16.2 percent of the U.S. population had completed at least four years of college), when emphasizing the largeness or smallness of something (e.g., as of July 1992, Chrysler had orders for all 3,500 1993 Dodge Vipers—a twin-exhaust, 400-horsepower sports car with a list price of $53,300—it plans to build), or when describing indications of trends—where we've been and where we're going (e.g., in 1960, CBS paid $400,000 for U.S. television rights for the summer Olympic Games; in 1992, NBC paid $401 million for those same rights).

When using statistics, you should be aware of two basic concerns: (1) Are the statistics accurate and unbiased? (2) Are they clear and meaningful? Addressing the first issue involves responses to such questions as: Are the statistical techniques appropriate and are they appropriately used? Do the statistics cover enough cases and length of time? Although you may not have the expertise to answer such questions, you can ask about the credibility of the source of the statistics. Do you have any reason to believe that the person or group from whom you got the statistics might be biased? Are these statistics consistent with other things you know about the situation? Addressing the second issue involves more pragmatic considerations: Can you translate difficult-to-comprehend numbers into more immediately understandable terms? How, for example, might you make the difference between $400,000 and $401 million more vivid? How can you provide adequate context for the data? Is it fair, for example, to compare 1960 dollars with 1992 dollars? Could a graph or visual aid clarify the data and statistical trends? As we will see shortly, supplementing a verbal presentation with a visual aid can greatly increase comprehension and retention.

STATISTICS
In public speaking, a form of support that relies on collecting, organizing, and interpreting numerical data.

Testimony

TESTIMONY
In public speaking, a form of support that relies on using a credible person's statements to lend weight and authority to a message.

Testimony involves using a credible person's statement to lend weight and authority to aspects of your presentation. For this to happen, the person being cited must be qualified; that is, the testimony must come from a person who is perceived as an expert on *this* topic and free of bias and self-interest. Just as important as actual credentials is the perception the audience has of the source of the testimony. For example, is the individual known to the audience? If not, you will need to tell the audience why the individual is a good authority. If known, is the person accepted by the audience as both knowledgeable and unbiased on the topic ? In short, to lend support to a message, the testimony of a source must both *be* credible and *be perceived* as credible.

Visual Aids

VISUAL AIDS
In public speaking, a form of support that relies on using actual objects or models, pictorial reproductions, or pictorial symbols.

The primary purpose of **visual aids** is to enhance the clarity and credibility of the message. They can also help you control apprehension by providing a safety net in an uncertain situation.

Obtaining these advantages requires skill in selecting appropriate aids and using them well. Although many choices are available to you (e.g., actual objects, blackboard, cartoons, charts, demonstrations, drawings, flipcards, transparencies, graphs, maps, models, movies, people), they can be conveniently grouped into three categories:

1. The actual object or a model of it (a model airplane, a cooking demonstration)
2. Pictorial reproductions (photographs, slides, sketches, videotapes)
3. Pictorial symbols (graphs, charts, diagrams)

When selecting from among these choices, you should keep several criteria in mind:

- *Use visuals that are large enough to be seen.* When possible, this means taking the visual to the room where it will be used and pretesting for visibility from all positions the audience will occupy during the presentation. When this is not possible, you should solicit advice from people who know the setting and then make informed guesses about the potential number of listeners and average viewing distances.

- *Keep the content of visuals simple and focused.* The task here is to keep the pictorial content and the wording on the visual as uncrowded and simple as possible—avoiding all unnecessary details that might send audience thoughts in unrelated directions. Rather than cluttering an aid with too much information, use multiple visuals, each containing only those features and details essential to the clarity and vividness of the point being made.

- *Prepare visuals carefully and professionally.* The design and form of the visual will be interpreted by audience members as reflecting your attitude toward them and the message topic. The form of the visual enhances or detracts from your credibility as a presenter independent of the visuals' content. Software programs are available for preparing simple but polished looking visuals. If you lack the artistic skills or computer literacy to prepare professional looking visuals, hire a professional to prepare them, or do not use them at all.

Up to this point in the chapter, we have discussed guidelines for creating the "body" of a message. It is now time to solidify and organize these ideas in the form of a discussion of the principles of outlining.

Outlining the Speech

A speech **outline** visually displays the main and subpoints of a speech (as well as the support for those points) in a fashion that helps you develop the speech and helps the audience follow it. Consider the example in Figure 12.5. This outline is an abbreviated example of a **complete sentence outline** that contains five main points (I, II, III, IV, and V) and two subpoints (A and B) that develop each of the main points. Were it the actual outline for a speech, it would also include the actual supporting material (e.g., examples, testimony, statistics) that you would use to illustrate and support the main and subpoints. For example, for the first main point, the outline would show exactly how you intend to demonstrate that the effective leader is one who searches out challenging opportunities to change, grow, innovate, and improve through the use of such supporting material as examples, illustrations, and testimony.

Note that the outline alternates numbers and letters in clearly identifiable columns. This style is known as the "Harvard style " of labeling and can accommodate as many levels as you need:

I. Main point
   A. Subpoint
      1. Support
         a. Sub-support
            1) Sub-sub-support
            2) Sub-sub-support
         b. Sub-support
      2. Support
   B. Subpoint
II. Main point

Although Harvard-style labeling is the most common, another popular style is "legal-style" labeling:

1. First main point
   1.1. First subpoint
   1.2. Second subpoint
      1.2.1. First support
      1.2.2. Second support
2. Second main point

Thesis: Being an effective leader in any organization involves five behavioral commitments.

I. Being an effective leader involves searching for opportunities by confronting and changing the status quo.

    A. An effective leader searches out challenging opportunities to change, grow, innovate, and improve.

        1. Testimony from an acknowledged effective leader.

        2. An example of a leader who has done so.

    B. An effective leader experiments, takes risks, and learns from the accompanying mistakes.

II. Being an effective leader involves inspiring a shared vision.

    A. An effective leader envisions an uplifting and ennobling future.

    B. An effective leader enlists others in a common vision by appealing to their values, interests, hopes, and dreams.

III. Being an effective leader involves enabling others to act.

    A. An effective leader fosters collaboration by promoting cooperative goals and building trust.

    B. An effective leader strengthens people by sharing information and power and increasing followers' discretion and visibility.

IV. Being an effective leader involves modeling the way.

    A. An effective leader sets the example for others by behaving in ways that are consistent with the leader's stated values.

    B. An effective leader plans small wins that promote consistent progress and build commitment.

V. Being an effective leader involves encouraging the heart.

    A. An effective leader recognizes individual contributions to the success of every project.

    B. An effective leader celebrates team accomplishments regularly.

FIGURE 12.5
A sample outline.

Heads at a particular level of the outline, whether Harvard or legal style, are of equal importance. In a Harvard-style outline, the five main points (indicated by Roman numerals I, II, III, IV, and V) are the main divisions of the speech and are of equal importance. The subpoints (A and B) also designate equally important divisions of the main point to which they refer. The outline has two or more elements at any level; that is, there are two or more main points, two or more subpoints under any main point, and two or more levels of support. This is normally the case because a topic is not "divided" unless there are at least two parts. If you wish to make only one subpoint, do not show it on the outline.

Most speakers start their speech preparation with a full sentence outline. It is easy to share such outlines with other individuals and get their reactions to the logic and organization of the speech. For this reason, most instructors ask to see a full sentence outline. Once it has been developed, however, speakers find it useful to reduce the full sentence outline to a **topic outline**, one that reduces the sentences to brief phrases or single words, or a **speaker's outline**, key words and important phrases and statistics on a 3 × 5 index card, before they speak.

Developing Introductions, Transitions, and Conclusions

Having composed and outlined the message, you can now add the final ingredients—an introduction, transitions, and a conclusion.

The Introduction

In Chapter 9, we suggested that at the beginning of an interview, interviewees start with three interrelated questions for which they want answers: What is the nature of this interview and how will it proceed (a task issue)? Will I like and can I trust this interviewer (a relationship issue)? What can I hope to gain from my participation in this interview (a motivation issue)? An audience in a public speaking situation has similar questions: What will this speech be like? Will I like and can I trust this speaker? What can I hope to get out of listening to this speech? An **introduction** attempts to answer these questions. As you think through the issues of task, relationship, and motivation, it is important to consider which of them require attention and how best to attend to them. It may well be the case, for example, that the setting or the person introducing the speaker has already provided an overview of the speaker's message; or that the group is so fired

TOPIC OUTLINE
A visual, schematic summary of a speech that reduces a complete sentence outline to brief phrases or single words.

SPEAKER'S OUTLINE
A visual, schematic summary of a speech that includes only key ideas that a speaker needs to remember.

INTRODUCTION
The beginning portion of a speech; typically deals with issues of task, relationship, and motivation.

up about the topic that providing additional motivation is not necessary; or that the speaker's credibility is so high that it does not require additional development. In situations where this is not the case (in other words, for most of your presentations in this class), you will need to allocate about 5 to 10 percent of the speaking time to answering questions of task, relationship, and motivation.

Although there is no guaranteed approach, when thinking about strategies for dealing with task issues, you might consider explicitly stating the topic, thesis, title, or purpose; previewing the structure of the message ("The three points I will develop are . . ."); or explaining why you narrowed the topic. Strategies for motivating audiences include: linking topic and thesis to the listeners' lives; showing how the topic has, does, or will affect the audience's past, present, or future; or demonstrating how the topic is linked to a basic need or goal of the audience. Strategies for building credibility include (1) verbal strategies during the introduction (and throughout the speech) that demonstrate competence (e.g., citing highly credible individuals, placing the topic in historical context, describing your personal acquaintance with the topic) or trustworthiness (demonstrating that present behavior is consistent with past behavior, entertaining alternative points of view, making verbal and nonverbal behaviors consistent), (2) referring to the audience, setting, or occasion in complimentary fashion, and (3) using relevant humor that demonstrates that both you and your listeners laugh at the same things.

In considering these strategies and others, remember that not every situation requires attention to all three issues. Furthermore, many strategies can contribute to multiple functions. For example, a story or an analogy can address both task and motivation issues; humor can further both motivation and relationship issues. Thus, when you are developing a strategy for introducing a message, the best advice is to make the introduction as compact as possible while fulfilling the audience's expectations concerning task, relationship, and motivation issues.

▩ Transitions

Transitions are used to guide an audience through your speech. They serve as signs that tell an audience where you are going, where you are, and where you have been. Thus, they need to be overt, clear, and frequent.

The speaker might, for example, forecast the purpose and structure of the message toward the end of the introduction ("Today, I will talk about five behaviors that characterize effective leaders. They are . . ."). As the speech proceeds, the speaker might use internal previews and summaries to review a main point and anticipate the next one ("Having described why leaders need to challenge the process, let's turn now to the need to inspire a

TRANSITIONS
Verbal signs to an audience indicating where the speech is going, where it is, and where it has been.

The Rhetorical Jigsaw Puzzle

Each numbered paragraph below is a separate unit of a speech. When put together in the right order, the paragraphs make up a complete speech. Your task is to order the paragraphs so as to form the best possible speech. After you have done so, label each unit according to the type of rhetorical device it represents (statement of point, subject sentence, signpost transition, summary statement, example, etc.).

1. Finally, think of the ordinary door-to-door salesperson.

2. Have you ever noticed how easy it is to do something else when the TV announcer is droning out a commercial? But what happens when the golden tongue is still? You know that the set is on, but you don't hear the announcer's voice extolling the virtues of "lavish Camay soap." So what do you do? You look at the TV screen, of course, to see what is going on.

3. Well, one way is by a brief interval of silence before and after the name of a product or sponsor.

4. The next time someone says to you, "Silence is golden," just smile and think to yourself, "You don't know how right you are!"

5. Second, let us consider television.

6. Are you aware of the methods radio announcers use to call attention to their sponsor or product?

7. Such a salesperson is one who has learned that silence is golden.

8. So you see, people in the field of selling are indeed aware that silence is golden, for they know it can mean dollars and cents in radio, in TV, and even in door-to-door selling.

9. As you see, the announcer puts a parenthesis of *silence* around the name of the product in order to catch your attention.

10. Silence is golden. That's an old cliché that you've heard many times, especially when your parents wanted to impress upon you another cliché—namely, that children should be seen and not heard.

11. First of all, take radio selling.

12. Thus, you can see that the TV salesperson has also discovered that silence can be golden.

13. The announcer doesn't say: Women-all-over-the world-are-learning-that-delicious-Wrigley's-Spearmint-gum-is-a-grand-wholesome-family treat. Instead, the speaker says: Women—all over the world—are learning that delicious—Wrigley's Spearmint gum—is a grand—wholesome—family treat.

14. I contend, however, that silence really IS golden.

15. If salespeople are really good, they know better than to just reel off a "pitch"—they know how to listen to you.

16. And I would like to present three instances in the field of selling to prove my contention.

17. If you doubt the effectiveness of silence in TV, just try not looking at the picture and notice how irresistibly your eyes will be pulled to the screen by a few moments of silence.

18. Salespeople are willing, if necessary, to listen to all of your troubles. If you want to raise a question, they will be quiet while you do so. They will ask you a question, then be silent while you answer.

Solution to the Rhetorical Jigsaw Puzzle

10. Introduction: Attention material
14. Introduction: Subject sentence
16. Introduction: Purpose sentence
11. Signpost transition
 6. See next item
 3. This and preceding item state first main point
13. Comparison
 9. Restatement
 5. Signpost transition
17. Statement of second main point
 2. Comparison
12. Restatement
 1. Signpost transition
15. Statement of third main point
18. Examples
 7. Restatement
 8. Conclusion: Summary
 4. Conclusion: Punch line

Source: T. Clevenger, Jr. (1963), The rhetorical jigsaw puzzle: A device for teaching certain aspects of speech composition, *Speech Teacher, 12,* 139–146. Used by permission of the Speech Communication Association.

shared vision"). The conclusion of the speech might include a final summary ("I've talked today about five behaviors that characterize effective leaders. Effective leaders . . .").

The Conclusion

The **conclusion** is used to provide a sense of closure. Although it can be accomplished in a variety of ways, it typically involves a summary of the main points of the speech and an attempt to reinforce the importance of the message by demonstrating its potential impact. An effective way to accomplish this is by using the conclusion to elaborate on an example, illustration, or quotation that was used in the introduction.

Guidelines for Delivery

To this point in the chapter, the focus has been on generating something to say and putting that something in the most appropriate format. Having accomplished that difficult task, you need to think about effective approaches and strategies for presenting the message to listeners.

Students of speechmaking have long debated the relative emphasis a presenter ought to allocate to issues of content versus issues of delivery. In fourth-century B.C. Greece, for example, the philosopher Aristotle argued that speakers ought to place their major emphasis on the logic of their message. For him, issues of delivery, though necessary, were not an important subject of inquiry. His contemporary Demosthenes, an orator and political leader, reached exactly the opposite conclusion. The three rules of speaking he is reported to have sworn by are delivery, delivery, and—delivery.

Variations of this argument continue to the present day. Teachers in the Aristotelian tradition put little stress on delivery other than to commend students for good eye contact, appropriate posture, and conversational delivery. Their Demosthenian counterparts, however, place a major emphasis on the various components of voice and physical action that enhance or detract from a speaker's effectiveness.

Our position on this issue is that to be a competent speaker, you must emphasize both content and delivery. Although it is fundamental to have a clear and logical message to present, unless that message is presented effectively the only person who will understand and accept it is the speaker. Thus, having prepared an effective message, the speaker needs to devote considerable effort to developing effective strategies for the delivery of it. The first choice is that of *mode of delivery*. Will the speech be impromptu, extemporaneous, manuscript, or memorized?

Impromptu Speaking

Impromptu speaking is what people do all the time in informal conversations with others; that is, they speak on the spur of the moment without formal preparation. The only difference is that in a public setting the audience is larger, and often the stakes are higher. Thus, when entering into a situation where you might be called on to make an impromtu speech (e.g., attending a committee meeting where you have special expertise on the topic), do what you do for important *social* conversations (e.g., asking your parents for a special favor)—anticipate that contingency and prepare your message in advance. When advanced preparation is not possible (e.g., you are asked to answer a question or describe something on the spur of the moment), do the following:

IMPROMPTU SPEAKING
Speaking on the spur of the moment, without formal preparation.

1. Quickly think of a specific purpose (e.g., to supply needed information, to urge action, to clarify an issue, to provide humor).

2. Choose a simple organizational framework that will serve your purpose (e.g., cause–effect; problem–solution; past-present-future; what should we do first? second? third?; advantages/disadvantages).

3. Start with an introduction that captures attention and relates your message to the activities that preceded it.

4. Speak briefly. (If you ramble on, your message will be incoherent for your audience.)

5. When in doubt, summarize. (A quick review can often restore your perspective and get you back on track.)

6. Conclude with a brief summary of your speech and a projection of what accepting your message will produce.

Whatever you do, *don't apologize*—for your lack of preparation, your lack of information, or your lack of ability as a speaker.

Extemporaneous Speaking

Extemporaneous speaking is characterized by advance preparation of ideas and supporting material that are expressed in language whose precise wording is left to be composed at the moment of speaking. As a result, no matter how many times the speech is presented, the expression of the ideas is never exactly the same. Extemporaneous speaking has a number of important advantages: (1) It allows the speaker to adapt to unforeseen situations (e.g., adding a reference to something that occurred in the setting and adding or deleting an argument based on audience response); (2) it promotes

EXTEMPORANEOUS SPEAKING
Speaking characterized by advance preparation of ideas and supporting material, with the precise wording of the speech to be determined during the process of speaking.

FIGURE 12.6
Extemporaneous public speaking strengthens the relationship between the speaker and the audience.

a more personal relationship between speaker and audience; and (3) it leads, with experience, to a superior delivery—greater earnestness, greater sincerity, and greater power. As a result of such advantages, extemporaneous speaking is the preferred mode of speaking for most situations. When using it, the speaker starts by constructing a full sentence outline, which is then reduced to a speaker's outline. Using the speaker's outline, the speaker rehearses the presentation in front of a mirror, an audio- or video-recorder, and/or sympathetic friends. When the speech is finally delivered, the speaker watches the audience for clues about how it is being received and makes adaptations based on an interpretation of that feedback.

Speaking from a Manuscript

MANUSCRIPT SPEAKING
Speaking from a manuscript that contains the complete presentation word for word.

Although extemporaneous is the preferred mode of delivery for most situations, some occasions require you to write out the total presentation word for word and read the resulting speech to the audience. Situations that require or encourage **manuscript speaking** are those for which precision of expression is crucial. When President Clinton makes a major policy statement on an important issue, he is likely to want to be sure that the wording of the statement is such that it will not be misunderstood. Thus, he is likely to write out that statement and read it. Manuscript speaking is also encouraged in situations that require precise timing (e.g., a two-minute speech written for inclusion in a political commercial).

When preparing a manuscript speech, you go through the same process as when you prepare an extemporaneous speech. That is, you start with a full sentence outline, reduce it to a speaker's outline, and rehearse from this outline. Once you have experimented with an oral, conversational style for presenting the message, it is written down word for word and rehearsed and rewritten and rehearsed and rewritten. Once in final form, the manuscript speech is prepared for easy reading (e.g., put in a format and type size that make for easy reading and marked appropriately to indicate any special emphases). When presenting a manuscript speech, you attempt to establish a level of contact with the audience that approaches that of the extemporaneous speech, including good eye contact and a conversational style of delivery.

REALITY CHECK

Preparing a Presentation

At the beginning of this chapter we met Sandra Ragan, a college senior working as an intern at a computer software firm. As part of her internship, she has been poring over company records and talking with employees in an attempt to develop a profile of employee attitudes toward their work and the company. On Monday morning she will be presenting her findings to three individuals: her boss, the company's CEO, and the company's chief financial officer. What have we learned in this chapter that might help her to prepare for this task?

- What should be the general purpose of her presentation? To inform? to persuade? to celebrate? a combination of the three?

- Which of the three filters (her resources, her audience, the occasion) should be most influential in determining the specific purpose of her presentation?

- How might Sandra best go about generating and selecting main ideas for her presentation? Which patterns of organization are most likely to be useful?

- As Sandra thinks about ways of supporting her main points, will some forms of support be more important than others? What should be her concerns as she considers her alternatives?

- What should Sandra consider as she thinks about ways of introducing her presentation? What about the conclusion? Will there be any special requirements with regard to transitions?

- Which of the modes of delivery should Sandra use? Will any of the characteristics of effective delivery be especially crucial?

- Do you have any additional advice for Sandra?

◼ Speaking from Memory

Memorized speaking adds but one step to a manuscript speech: After writing out the manuscript, you memorize the speech and then deliver it from memory rather than reading it from a manuscript. In many situations, speakers will combine both approaches. That is, they will read parts of the manuscript and then deliver other parts of the message from memory in an apparently extemporaneous fashion. In some situations, however, speakers make the extra effort of memorizing the whole speech, especially for ceremonial speeches such as tributes and eulogies. When speakers make the special effort to memorize a speech, they also make a special effort to deliver it using a style of delivery that is as close to an extemporaneous style of delivery as possible.

Having chosen a mode of delivery, you next need to consider how to use delivery to focus attention on the message and not on you while helping the audience understand and accept the message. This means delivering the message in a conversational style that the audience can both hear and understand. Such a style is best developed by observing the skills of effective delivery in others, learning to recognize skills and deficiencies in your own delivery, and using guided practice to capitalize on existing skills and to remedy existing deficiencies.

REVIEW

This chapter has focused on the basic principles of public speaking. Now that you have read it, you should know what communication apprehension is and some methods for coping with it. You should also understand the eight tasks you face as a public speaker and some methods for completing them. The tasks are (1) understanding what public speaking is, (2) identifying and refining a specific reason for speaking, (3) analyzing your potential audience so as to successfully adapt the message to it, (4) identifying and organizing the major points that form the core of your message, (5) selecting methods of supporting your ideas in ways that clarify them and lead to their acceptance by the audience, (6) arranging your points and supporting material in the form of an outline, (7) providing your speech with an introduction, transitions, and a conclusion, and (8) choosing a mode of delivery that will allow you as the speaker to be responsive to the assignment, conversational, direct, intelligible, and unobtrusive. In the next two chapters we will apply these principles to two of the major tasks faced by speakers— sharing information and persuading.

SUGGESTED READINGS

Daly, J. A., & McCroskey, J. C. (1984). *Avoiding communication: Shyness, reticence, and communication apprehension.* Beverly Hills, CA: Sage.

Lucas, S. E. (1989). *The art of public speaking* (3rd ed.). New York: Random House.

Osborn, M., & Osborn, S. (1991). *Public speaking* (2nd ed.). Boston: Houghton Mifflin.

Sprague, J., & Stuart, D. (1992). *The speaker's handbook* (3rd ed.). Fort Worth, TX: Harcourt Brace Jovanovich.

Verderber, R. F. (1988). *The challenge of effective speaking* (7th ed.). Belmont, CA: Wadsworth Publishing Co.

13

Informative
Presentations

*O*bjectives

After reading this chapter, you should be able to

1. Define the concept *information society* and discuss its impact on the need for communication skills.

2. Use the eight categories of speech topics to identify potential subjects for informative speeches.

3. Define and distinguish among the four types of informative speeches: descrip-

tive, demonstration, definitional, and explanatory.

4. Describe strategies for coping with the eight most common barriers to the transmission of information.

5. Suggest guidelines for preparing and presenting effective informative speeches.

CHAPTER CONTENTS

as engineers and economists), process it (such as clerks and managers), distribute it (such as teachers and journalists), and run the technical system (such as machine operators and printers).

Our growing ability to store and retrieve information is amazing—and continues to expand. A CD-ROM less than five inches in diameter can contain the equivalent of 200,000 pages of book text. By using a combination of microchip and laser technology, everything in the Library of Congress can be stored on one wall of a large living room. This ability to store information—and to move it and use it regardless of distance and time—has transformed many of the previous ways of doing things. For example, investors can access information instantly on a video display terminal, enabling them to learn current stock prices anywhere in the world. When an investor calls up a particular stock, the computer can calculate its price/earnings ratio and yield, so that the investor can make a well-informed decision. In industrial plants, computer-to-computer communication provides the capability for machinery to manufacture products automatically, with little or no human intervention.

The ongoing transition from a postindustrial society, with an economy based largely on the creation and distribution of goods, to an economy based largely on the creation and use of information has made skillful communication the fundamental resource of our age. Individuals who know how to turn information into knowledge—by finding it, creating it, sorting it, organizing it, checking it for accuracy, and disseminating it—are and will continue to be hired, valued, and rewarded. Acquiring the key skills, however, is not an easy task. As Lindstrom observes:

> In a feeble effort to hold the information juggernaut at bay, you and I scan about 74 million words per year—double the volume of words in the *Encyclopedia Britannica*. We make lists, collect files, subscribe to data bases, but it's a losing battle.
>
> In his book "Information Anxiety," Richard Wurman explains that we are constantly in peril of falling into "the black hole between data and knowledge." At some point, like pinballs, we begin to collide with information and bounce away, without gaining anything but superficial knowledge.
>
> There is only one way to avoid falling into the black hole. We must develop systems for filtering, analyzing and communicating information that are as powerful as the systems we have for collecting it.[6]

In this chapter, then, we build on the fundamentals described in the last chapter as we focus on mastering the skills necessary for capturing and presenting information to an audience in ways that are interesting, understandable, and accurate and will be remembered by listeners. Our goal is to help you and your audience avoid the situation described in the next paragraph.

Information Overload

Have you ever felt overwhelmed by information when learning a new job, studying for a test, or learning a new skill? What did you do to cope with this situation?

In a study by the National Assessment of Educational Progress, a nationally representative sample of approximately 3,600 young adults (21- to 25-year-olds) were asked to complete eight speaking tasks. Their responses were tape recorded, and two trained raters listened to the tape and made judgments as to whether the response was off task, minimal, adequate, or superior. Several of the tasks asked respondents to provide information—for example, to imagine that the interviewer was new to the area and explain how to get from their present location to a nearby grocery. Do you think you could perform this task? Only 37.1 percent of the sample were rated as performing this task adequately or in a superior fashion.[7]

The task of an informative speaker is relatively straightforward: to present information that the audience will attend to, understand, and remember. Before explaining why this task is sometimes difficult and examining guidelines for making successful informative presentations, we will explore some of the types and forms of informative speaking.

Topics for Informative Presentations

Allen and McKerrow identify eight **categories of speech topics** appropriate for informative speeches.[8] As we go through them, ask yourself three questions: (1) Do I have knowledge of or experience with a subject suggested by the category? (2) Am I interested enough to do research on a subject suggested by the topic? (3) Would my audience find a subject suggested by this category interesting and worthy of attention?

CATEGORIES OF SPEECH TOPICS
Eight categories that can be used to generate topics for informative speeches— people, places, things, events, processes, concepts, problems, and plans and policies.

 People

Our fascination with the lives of others, past and present, is demonstrated in multiple ways: biographical shelves in local bookstores, sections devoted to people in newspapers and magazines, television programs about

Generating Speech Topics: People

For the category "people," jot down potential speech topics on a sheet of paper. Don't judge the topic; just list any idea that occurs to you. You can go back and sort through them later. What type of people are you most interested in? Athletes? politicians? artists? businesspeople? activists? As you read about the remaining seven categories of speech topics, repeat this activity for each of the categories.

the rich and famous (and the poor and not-so-famous), movies about politicians, athletes, movie stars, and other personalities, and a wide variety of tabloids at the checkout counter of grocery stores that "reveal" the details of the lives of celebrities. Speaking about people allows us to deepen our knowledge of individuals and their achievements and to share that knowledge with our listeners. The contributors can be past (Susan B. Anthony) or present (Patricia Ireland), and can perform in a wide variety of domains: work, religion, entertainment, sports, art, politics, and music. In thinking about potential subjects, don't restrict yourself to individuals who have made or are making contributions at the national or international level. Consider, for example, talking about past or present local personalities (businesspeople, professors, activists), people for whom buildings on your campus are named, or other individuals whom you admire.

Places

Places you have visited or would like to visit can also serve as a topic for an informative speech. Even if you have not traveled much, you have lived somewhere and thus have natural (lakes, historic sites) or created (monuments, cities) places to talk about. Thus, in addition to national or international historical, cultural, or recreational places (the Grand Canyon, the monuments and museums of Washington, D.C., Buckingham Palace, the Vatican), you might talk about a local museum, a nature park, or bicycle trails. You might even consider talking about fictitious places such as Lilliput, Brobdingnag, and Laputa in *Gulliver's Travels,* or the islands that served as home to Scylla and Charybdis in the *Odyssey.*

Repeat the Reality Check "Generating Speech Topics" for the category "places."

Things

A third source of ideas for informative speeches consists of objects or things. Like places, things can be either natural (spiders, plants, dinosaurs) or created (CDs, roller blades, glass art). They can also be imaginary (unicorns). As you consider objects as potential speech topics, think broadly in terms of both time and setting. Things are part of the past (spinning wheels) and the present (pacemakers), and they are present in a variety of settings (work, home, religion, art, entertainment).

Repeat the Reality Check "Generating Speech Topics" for the category "things."

Events

Events are occurrences or incidents of personal or historical significance. At a personal level, you might build an informative speech around important, funny, or instructive events in your personal life—the day you went skydiving, your visit with a tax auditor, the day your first child was born, or your bar mitzvah. Our understanding of history is also shaped by events—the Civil War, the assassination of Dr. Martin Luther King, Jr., the 1993 March on Washington for Lesbian, Gay, and Bi Equal Rights and Liberation, Operation Rescue blockades of abortion clinics. In addition to helping an audience understand the meaning of personal and historical *single* events, a speaker can also explore the social significance of *collections* of events. What, for example, is the role of dances for Native American tribes, Fourth of July celebrations, and weddings and funerals?

Repeat the Reality Check "Generating Speech Topics" for the category "events."

Processes

A process is a series of actions, changes, or functions that bring about a particular result. Thus, informative speeches about processes explain how something functions or is accomplished. Like places and things, processes can either be natural phenomena (photosynthesis—the process by which chlorophyll-containing cells in green plants use the energy of light to synthesize carbohydrates from carbon dioxide and water) or created phenomena (calligraphy—the art of fine handwriting). Process speeches help an audience understand the stages or steps through which a natural or created phenomenon is produced. Potential topics for process speeches can be identified by thinking about home life, hobbies, work experiences, and academic studies.

Repeat the Reality Check "Generating Speech Topics" for the category "processes."

Concepts

People, places, things, events, and processes tend to be concrete; that is, we can readily bring up specific images of them in our mind. Concepts, on the other hand, are abstractions drawn from the specific and are, therefore, more difficult for us to visualize. What image comes to mind, for example, when you encounter concepts like love, patriotism, and racism? The challenge of an informative speech, then, is to take a general idea, theory, or thought and make it concrete and meaningful for your audience. Although the challenge is great, many of the most worthwhile informative speeches we have listened to have focused on the elucidation of a concept.

Repeat the Reality Check "Generating Speech Topics" for the category "concepts."

Problems

As we go about living, we encounter personal and societal problems on a regular basis. Some of them relate to personal or psychological health (smoking, HIV/AIDS), and others to the quality of life at the level of campus, city, state, region, nation, or globe (pollution, energy shortages). Informative speeches that focus on problems help audiences to understand the symptoms, causes, and treatment of problems. Because problems frequently involve controversial issues, there is always the danger of moving from an informative purpose to a persuasive one. Thus, if you doubt your ability to describe a problem objectively, you probably ought to save the topic for a persuasive speech. If you have doubts, ask the advice of friends, fellow students, and/or your instructor.

Repeat the Reality Check "Generating Speech Topics" for the category "problems."

Plans and Policies

Our final category for informative speeches concerns plans and policies. In such speeches, the speaker seeks to help an audience understand the important dimensions of potential courses of action (e.g., passing the Equal Rights Amendment, changing the composition of the Electoral College). In such speeches, the speaker does not argue for a particular plan or policy. However, like speeches on problems, plan and policy speeches are easily turned into persuasive addresses. Thus, when in doubt, ask whether your proposed speech would be better saved for the persuasive speech assignment.

Repeat the Reality Check "Generating Speech Topics" for the category "plans and policies."

If you've followed our advice, at this point you will have filled a sheet of paper with a multitude of potentially good topics for an informative speech. If you need even more ideas, keep in mind the advice from Chapter 12—in searching for a good topic, use solo brainstorming or clustering, the ideas of others, and the library.

As potential topics occur to you, test each one using these criteria: (1) Is it a topic that interests you and that you have knowledge of? (2) Is it a good topic for the general purposes specified in the assignment? (3) Is it a topic that the audience will find worthwhile?

Types of Informative Speeches

Once you have selected a topic for an informative speech, you can develop it in a variety of ways. In this section, we briefly describe the four major types of informative speeches.

Descriptive Speeches

Description is one of the most basic categories for presenting information. When you use it, you put into words what you experience with your senses. You want your audience to feel, hear, and see what you felt, heard, and saw. Making **descriptive speeches** requires that you have a clear idea of what you want to describe and why, that you emphasize important details and eliminate unimportant ones, and, most of all, that you consider your audience as you think of ways to make details vivid enough that they call up an image in the listener's mind.

DESCRIPTIVE SPEECH
A speech that presents information so vividly that the audience can share the speaker's experiences.

Following is an excerpt from a descriptive speech by Major James N. Rowe delivered extemporaneously to students of the U.S. Army General Staff and Command College at Leavenworth, Kansas. Notice how he calls up details of his surroundings and his feelings as he describes his experience as an American prisoner of war in South Vietnam.

Now, in the camp, the physical conditions in South Vietnam with the Viet Cong are primitive. I was in the U Minh Forest; the camps were temporary at best. You had two to three feet of standing water during the rainy season; in the dry season it sank out, and you were hunting for drinking water. We had two meals of rice a day, and generally we got salt and nuoc mam with them. We did get infrequent fish from the guards, but always the castoff that the guards didn't want. If we got greens, it was maybe one meal's worth every two or three months. Immediately vitamin deficiency and malnutrition were a problem. This is a thing you are going to fight the whole way through. And you are fighting on two sides. You are fighting a physical survival, and you are fighting for mental survival. The physical survival is just staying alive. We found that we had to eat a quart pan of rice each meal, two meals a day, just to stay alive. We found that [we did better] if we could put down everything we had, and I think the most difficult thing initially was the nuoc mam. It is high in protein value, but the VC don't have that much money to spend on nuoc mam. You don't get Saigon nuoc mam. Theirs is called ten-meter nuoc mam. You can smell it within ten meters, and it is either repulsive or inedible, depending on how long you have been there. But this was the type of thing you are eating for nutritional value, and not for taste. So you are fighting on that side.[9]

Demonstration Speeches

Demonstration speeches use narration to answer "how" questions—how to use a communications program with a computer, how to line dance, or how to buy a used car. Giving demonstration speeches would seem to be a natural and easy task. After all, if we have figured out how things happen or work, we should be able to explain them to others! If we know how to get to the grocery store, we should be able to tell another person how to get there. Unfortunately, as you know, this is not always the case. Thus, consider the following advice as you prepare a demonstration speech. Start by identifying your audience and its level of knowledge about your topic. With a clear statement of purpose in mind, indicate the broad outline of the process and discuss the major steps in chronological order. Be sure your language is appropriate for your audience; where necessary define terms. Do not dwell on unimportant details, and relate each major step to the whole. Occasionally point out where you are in the process.

The following outline of the first steps in the printmaking process of producing woodcuts illustrates a demonstration speech. You can imagine the speaker showing each step.

A. To prepare the block

    1. Use a power sander to smooth rough, scratched, or dented boards.

    2. Lightly sandpaper the surface to ensure an even flatness.

3. To enhance the grain quality in prints, run a wire brush over the surface in the direction of the grain.

B. To transfer the design, use one of three methods:

1. Coat the block with white gouache, and draw directly on it.

2. Place carbon paper on the block, then your drawing, then tracing paper; press firmly with a pencil to draw in the main elements.

3. Paste the drawing onto the surface of the block and cut away the white areas.

C. To cut the block

1. Hold the knife with your forefinger along the top of the blade to apply downward pressure, and use your other fingers as guides.

2. Use a gouge by gently tapping it with a mallet; always direct the point of the tool away from your body.[10]

Definitional Speeches

With **definitional speeches**, speakers provide answers to "what" questions. Formal definitions—those found in dictionaries—have three parts:

DEFINITIONAL SPEECH
A speech that explains what words and/or concepts mean.

FIGURE 13.2
Demonstrating a process can convey information to your audience that is practical, interesting, or both.

the name of the thing to be defined, the class to which it belongs, and the quality that distinguishes it from other members of its class. Thus, notation is "a system of figures or symbols used to represent numbers, quantities, etc." Simple definitions like these, however, are often inadequate for describing complex ideas. To help listeners understand complex constructs requires that speakers use multiple strategies. Figures of speech—metaphors, similes, analogies, and the like—can be helpful. The speaker can compare and contrast a term with similar ones. Illustrations are also useful. The task is to establish a meaning the audience will understand and accept. Thus, the speaker needs to be as specific and concrete as possible.

Robert M. White, president of the National Academy of Engineering, defines "invention" in the following excerpt from his speech "Inventors, Invention, and Innovation":

> Invention is more than the development of useful and productive devices, although these are vital for material progress. Instead, it is a manifestation of the creativity in all human activities. The invention of the Gothic arch permitted the soaring cathedrals of the Middle Ages and the Renaissance. The paintings of Monet and Pissarro brought us the glories of impressionism. Our daily lives are uplifted by the songs of Irving Berlin and the symphonies of Beethoven.
>
> In short, invention is where you find it. And so it is in industry. Whatever the function, whether in research and development, design, production, or distribution of goods and services, inventions are at the root of new products and processes and also the source of the economic success of companies. Inventions are the lifeblood coursing through the heart of industrial competitiveness.[11]

Explanatory Speeches

The basic purpose of most informative speeches is to create awareness or understanding; explanatory speeches chiefly create understanding. For example, a speech demonstrating how to fax a document creates awareness, whereas a speech explaining how fax machines work deepens understanding. **Explanatory speeches** answer the question "Why?" or "What does that mean?" In terms of the eight categories of speech topics discussed earlier, they typically deal with problems and with plans and policies. Thus, they are usually more abstract than descriptive and demonstration speeches. The challenge to the speaker is to inform the audience and to explain the problem, action, or decision in question without persuading them.

There are at least three ways in which answers to "why" questions may be difficult for lay audiences to understand: (1) difficulty in understanding

EXPLANATORY SPEECH
A speech that explains the reasons underlying a problem, plan, or policy.

the meaning and use of a term, (2) difficulty abstracting the main points from complex information, and (3) hesitancy in grasping an implausible or counterintuitive proposition (such as Einstein's notion that we are accelerating toward the center of the earth). The challenge for explanatory speakers is diagnosing the principal difficulty facing their audience and shaping their speech to overcome that difficulty. The solution to these three difficulties comes in the form of elucidating, quasi-scientific, and transformative explanations.

Elucidating Explanations

If the audience's chief difficulty rests with understanding the meaning and use of a certain term, then speakers should develop speeches providing **elucidating explanations**. These explanations illuminate a concept's meaning and use. For example, speakers concerned principally with explaining concepts such as "evolution" and "municipal bond" should use elucidating explanations.

Good elucidating explanations (1) define a concept by listing each of its critical features, (2) contrast examples and nonexamples (nonexamples are instances that audiences often think are examples but are not) of the concept, and (3) present opportunities for audiences to distinguish examples from nonexamples by looking for the concept's critical features.

One effective elucidating speech explained what "science" means. The student began:

> We all know what science is. It's what Carl Sagan and Mr. Wizard do, right? Since we know, we should agree on some basic ideas. How many people think biology is a science? (Nearly all hands rise.) How many think psychology is? (A few hands rise.) How about astrology? (A few hands rise.)

This speech was effective because, after establishing that "science" is hard to explain, the speaker offered a definitional listing of the concept's critical features, gave an array of examples and nonexamples of science (e.g., psychology vs. astrology), and offered the audience opportunities to distinguish examples from nonexamples with a short oral quiz.

Quasi-Scientific Explanations

If an idea is difficult chiefly because its complexity obscures its main points or the "big picture," then speakers should present a quasi-scientific explanation. Just as scientists try to develop models of the world, **quasi-scientific explanations** model or picture the key dimensions of some phe-

ELUCIDATING EXPLANATION
An explanation that illuminates a concept's meaning and use.

QUASI-SCIENTIFIC EXPLANATION
An explanation that models or pictures the key dimensions of a phenomenon for a lay audience.

nomenon for a lay audience. Speakers presenting complex topics to laypeople—topics such as how microchips work, the similarities and differences between Buddhism and Christianity, or how DNA molecules pass along genetic information—should use quasi-scientific explanations.

Effective quasi-scientific explanations highlight the main points with features such as titles, organizing analogies, visual aids, and signaling phrases ("The first key point is"). Good quasi-scientific explanations also connect key points by using transitional phrases such as "for example," connectives ("because"), and diagrams depicting relationships among parts.

For example, a particularly good quasi-scientific speech explained how radar works. Using an organizing analogy, the speaker said that radar works essentially the way an echo does, except that radio waves, rather than sound waves, are sent and received. The presentation was effective because consistent references to this analogy highlighted its main points.

Transformative Explanations

If the chief source of difficulty is not a particular term, or a complex mass of information, but rather the counterintuitivity of the idea itself, then speakers should design their talks as **transformative explanations**. For example, the idea that when one pushes a concrete wall, that wall exerts an equal and opposite force on the pusher (Newton's Third Law of Motion) contains no difficult terms and little detail, but, from a lay perspective, it just seems hard to believe. Transformative explanations are designed to present such counterintuitive ideas by helping lay audiences transform their everyday "theories" about phenomena into more accepted notions.

"Why" questions frequently address controversial topics about which the audience is predisposed to skepticism or even hostility. Thus, an important function of transformative explanations is to calm the audience by telling why a condition exists or why an action is being taken. If, for example, members of a city's board of education are fully informed about the factors that led the mayor to reduce the school budget, they are likely to be more disposed to work with the new budget than if they had not been told about the conditions that led to the cuts.

Transformative explanations are most effective when they (1) state the audience's "implicit" or "lay" theory about a phenomenon, (2) acknowledge that this theory is plausible or reasonable, (3) demonstrate its inadequacy, (4) state the speaker's explanation, and (5) demonstrate that this explanation is in some way better than the other one.[12]

Topics for informative speeches, then, can be located in eight categories: people, places, things, events, processes, concepts, problems, and plans and policies. Once a topic has been identified, it can be developed via four types of speeches: descriptive, demonstration, definitional, or explanatory.

Types and Topics

To what degree are the eight categories of speech topics and the four types of speeches related? That is, are speeches about people most likely to fit into one of the four types of informative speeches? How about the other seven categories?

Barriers to Communicating Information

Having explored the nature of informative speaking and ways of generating topics for such speeches, we turn next to an identification of the potential difficulties an informative speaker will face. Hart identifies eight of the most common **communication barriers**, or barriers to the transmission of information, that speakers encounter as they begin to think about developing an informative message.[13]

COMMUNICATION BARRIERS
Eight dilemmas speakers face when they attempt to transmit information.

Content Can Raise Barriers

The first four barriers identified by Hart have to do with the choice of information to include.

There is too much or not enough information. "Information overload" produces frustration as an audience feels buried by an avalanche of information and stops listening. As we stated earlier in this chapter, information must be analyzed and communicated if it is to become useful knowledge. Erring in the other direction ("information underload"), however, can produce an equally undesirable result—audience boredom. The informative speaker must be aware of the audience's level of expertise and present enough information to challenge but not overwhelm the average member.

Information is too factual or too inferential. "Ideal" informative speakers are neither fact-spewing computers nor rambling philosophers. Rather, they know how to extend their listeners' knowledge by blending hard data and intelligent speculation. Most audiences want enough facts to support the inferences and enough inferences to answer the question "So what?" about the facts.

Information is too concrete or too abstract. Curious, searching audiences demand that a speaker satisfy their needs for both concrete and ab-

How Much Information Is the "Right" Amount?

In deciding how much information to present, does a speaker have an ethical responsibility to present all sides of an issue? For example, does a district attorney have a responsibility to tell the grand jury about all known facts of a case? Should a sales representative for a drug manufacturer tell doctors about the side effects of a drug? Should an Army recruiter tell potential recruits about both the advantages and the disadvantages of military life? What criteria did you use to arrive at answers to these questions?

stract information. Speakers who carefully mix and match material should be able to satisfy both demands of audiences.

Information is too general or too specific. By carefully and consciously moving from the general, to the specific, and back again, the speaker can both introduce variety and improve the audiences' chances of seeing both the forest and the trees.

Presentation Can Raise Barriers

The circumstances of the presentation and the speaker's style in organizing and delivering the informative speech can block effective communication.

Communication is feedback-poor or feedback-rich. Because public speaking is primarily a one-way transmission of information, the speaker must often be quite creative in finding ways to assess whether the audience is mastering the content of the presentation. Speakers can use a variety of techniques to obtain relevant feedback from an audience—for example, monitoring the reactions of one or two representative members of an audience or reminding the audience, "Ask questions if you don't understand something." Of course, the speaker can focus so much on the behaviors of one or two members of an audience that the focus on the dissemination of the message is lost. One listener may interrupt with questions that are of no interest to the rest of the audience. Delayed feedback can be obtained for future use from a friend who attended the presentation or from an audio- or videotape of the presentation (focusing on the speaker and/or on the audience).

Overcoming the Barriers

As you reflect on your experience as a listener, which of the eight communication barriers do you think is (or are) the most difficult for speakers to overcome? Explain your reasoning.

Information is presented too rapidly or too slowly. Research suggests that "normal conversational delivery" is best suited to covering material with clarity and efficiency. The important thing to remember is that both excessively rapid and inordinately slow delivery of a speech will decrease audience retention.

Information is presented too soon or too late. Fortunately, with careful preparation of the presentation and the knowledge of a few elementary principles of organization, the "too soon/too late" problem is easily solved. For example, by remembering that listeners find it easier to move from the simple to the complex, from the concrete to the abstract, and from the immediate to the anticipated, you can often avoid moving into material too quickly. Similarly, by knowing that listeners have a need for pattern, chronology, and completeness, you will be reminded that information must be "packaged" for an audience to be able to absorb and retain it.

Information is presented with too much or too little intensity. Speakers can get so involved in the material being presented that the audience comes to feel they are more concerned about preaching than they are about sharing information. On the other hand, an audience will probably share the lack of enthusiasm of the speaker who merely goes through the motions.

Guidelines for Informative Presentations

Once the topic has been selected, as you may recall from Chapter 12, the speaker has a number of tasks to perform in preparing and delivering a speech:

1. Analyzing the audience
2. Identifying and organizing main points

3. Providing support for ideas
4. Outlining the speech
5. Developing an introduction, transitions, and conclusion
6. Selecting a type of delivery and rehearsing and delivering the speech

In this chapter, we focus on elaborations and adaptations of the general principles to the tasks of an informative speaker.

Adapting Your Presentation to Your Audience

In Chapter 12, we suggested an analysis of audience type, reference groups, and situational expectations as a prerequisite to developing a message that will be understood and accepted by members of an audience. For your informative speech, ask yourself how you have adapted (or can adapt) your presentation to the knowledge and interest levels of your audience. As you work through this task, consider that there are three fairly easy ways to adapt a speech to a particular audience: (1) Establish the *relevance* of the

SELF-CHECK

Adjusting to Your Audience

To practice adapting an informative speech to a particular audience, consider how you would present a topic to a group for whom it seems to have no interest or relevance. From the lists below, select a topic and an audience. Create a preliminary outline of the speech that includes the speech topic, a thesis statement, general and specific purposes, main points, and a list of visual aids. Show in your thesis statement, purpose statements, and main points how you will make your speech significant, meaningful, personally beneficial, useful, practical, and/or comprehensible for your audience.

Speech Topic	Audience
Manicuring one's nails	Auto mechanics
French cuisine	Recent immigrants from India
Writing poetry	Inner-city youth gangs
The dynamics of hang gliding	Senior citizens at a weekly meeting

Source: Based on S. D. Downey (1988), Audience analysis exercise, *The Speech Communication Teacher,* 2(2), 1–2.

topic in the *introduction* and reiterate it in the *conclusion* of the speech. (2) Adjust the *language* of the speech to fit the age, education level, and comprehension of the audience. (3) Use *examples* or *analogies* that match the interests or hobbies of the audience.

Choosing Main Points, Organizational Patterns, and Forms of Support

In Chapter 12, we identified the main points that support a specific purpose using the "topical system," placed these main points into a pattern of organization (e.g., chronological, topical), provided support for the main points (e.g., language, explanation), and visually displayed the speech in the form of an outline. An alternative to the outline is Phillips's "structuring" approach, a visual presentation of the organization.[14] **Structuring** is a method of organizing messages by means of residual messages (ideas to be retained by the audience) and common patterns of message organization. After thinking about both approaches, you can decide which one works better for your purposes.

People have orderly minds. Structuring helps you organize ideas into patterns your audience can easily identify and understand. After formulating the residual message ("When I am done with my speech, I want my audience to know or believe that . . ."), choose one of seven structures by which to organize the speech. In addition to the five patterns discussed

FIGURE 13.3
Analogies to subjects or ideas that are familiar to an audience can help the listeners understand information about an unfamiliar topic.

in Chapter 12 (chronological, topical, spatial or geographical, cause–effect, and problem–solution), Phillips suggests structuring by *comparison* and by *contrast*.

The following examples using the general topic "cakes" are deliberately simplified to show how structuring works.

Chronological structure   The speaker outlines a series of events or steps in a process; the events or steps must follow a specific order.
Residual message   "When I am done with my speech, I want my audience to know that baking a cake is a simple process."
Buy ingredients
Mix ingredients
Bake mixture

Topical structure   Information giving is the speaker's primary goal; categories must be comprised of relatively equal, nonoverlapping main points.
Residual message   "When I am done with my speech, I want my audience to know that there are three superior cake mixes."
Betty Crocker
Pillsbury
Duncan Hines

Spatial structure   The speaker describes parts of something and how they form the whole, either literally or figuratively.
Residual message   "When I am done with my speech, I want my audience to know that a layer cake has four parts."
Icing
Layer
Filling
Layer

Comparison   The speaker compares things by showing their similarities.
Residual message   "When I am done with my speech, I want my audience to know that cake and pie are similar in three ways."

| Cake | Dessert; rich; baked |
| Pie | Dessert; rich; baked |

Contrast   The speaker compares things by showing their differences.
Residual message   "When I am done with my speech, I want my audience to know that cakes and poles are different in two ways."

| Cakes | Eat; batter |
| Poles | Build; wood |

Cause–effect The speaker establishes that a relationship exists between two events or that a certain result is the product of a certain event.

Residual message "When I am done with my speech, I want my audience to know that a person who celebrates a birthday usually receives a cake."

Cause   Birthday celebration
Effect   Cake

Problem–solution The speaker outlines a problem, offers a feasible solution, and illustrates the advantages of the solution or how the solution solves the problem.

Residual message "When I am done with my speech, I want my audience to know that the problem associated with eating too much cake is weight gain, and that the problem can be solved through decreased cake consumption."

Problem   Weight gain
Solution   Decreased consumption of cake
Advantage   Decreased weight

To further develop each main point, you can use *substructuring*. Examine each main point and, on the basis of that point, choose one of the seven structures to develop these ideas, as illustrated in the following example.

Residual message "When I am done with my speech, I want my audience to know that baking a cake is a simple process."

Chronological structure:
Buy ingredients
    Solids
    Liquids
Mix ingredients
    First do this
    Then do this
    Next do this
Bake mixture
    Baking times
    Doneness test

Substructures used:
Main point 1   Topical structure
Main point 2   Chronological structure
Main point 3   Topical structure

Preparing Contingency Plans for Public Speaking Situations

As a final step in the speech preparation process, consider how you would cope with a variety of unusual events that can confront the public speaker. Professional speakers routinely encounter situations that you, as a novice, are not likely to envision. If you are lucky, you will never be in any of the situations described here. However, if you do find yourself in such a situation, you cannot ignore it without endangering the effectiveness of your communication.

How would you address the following situations?

- Pillars in the room prevent some audience members from seeing the transparencies you are projecting.
- You arrive to give your speech and are asked to speak for an hour instead of 30 minutes because a second speaker has canceled.
- You take out your speaking notes but, just as you are being introduced to the audience, discover that some of the notes are missing.
- The bulb in the projector suddenly burns out, preventing you from showing your transparencies.
- Someone in the audience interrupts you to say that you are not speaking on the subject the audience has come to hear about.
- The preceding speaker covers all of your material.
- You are heckled.
- Your introducer undermines your credibility with some caustic remarks.
- Someone in your audience begins laughing uncontrollably.
- Nonverbal cues from your audience suggest that most members don't understand your supporting examples.
- An audience member challenges the statistics you have just cited.
- You can't tell whether the audience is accepting or rejecting your ideas.
- No one laughs at the joke you've just told to support a key idea.
- The movements and facial expressions of the audience signal boredom, even though you've just begun to speak.
- At the end of your speech the audience begins chanting, "Keep going!"
- Handouts are accidentally distributed ahead of schedule and the audience stops paying attention to your speech.
- A couple of audience questions can be interpreted as hints that your idea development is not sophisticated enough.

Source: Adapted from J. A. Jones (1981), Preparing contingency plans for public speaking situations, *Communication Education, 30,* 423–425.

▨ Polishing the Speech

Having developed a speech, you next polish it through rehearsal. This requires that the speech be ready about a week in advance to allow time to practice several times in front of the mirror or your friends. Assuming that you intend to speak extemporaneously, use the first couple of times to try out various phrasings of your ideas. As you start to feel comfortable with the flow of your speech, begin to work on time. Most classroom assignments will give you a range (say five to seven minutes). Most often, it is wise to develop your speech with the low end of the range in mind. That is, if the range is three to five minutes, develop a speech that requires three minutes to deliver during practice. When you make the actual presentation, you will find that because of audience reaction, impromptu remarks, and so on, the speech will go longer than it did during rehearsal. As you reach the end of the rehearsal process, try to schedule one session in the actual room where the speech will be delivered. This will add to your comfort level and

---

REALITY CHECK

Putting It All Together for an Informative Speech

At the beginning of this chapter we encountered Tommy Gomez, a member of the Dorothy Day Catholic Worker, whom Professor Kennedy has asked to speak to his social work class at Georgetown University. Tommy's presentation will focus on the nature of the Dorothy Day Catholic Worker Movement and its view of the societal problem of homelessness. What have you learned in this chapter that might help Tommy to prepare for his presentation?

- From which of the eight categories of speech topics should he draw his topic?

- Will his presentation best be described as descriptive, demonstration, definitional, or explanatory?

- Which of the barriers to communicating information will pose the greatest difficulty?

- What should Tommy do to analyze and adapt to his audience?

- What organizational patterns and forms of support should he use?

- What advice would you give him for practicing his presentation?

- Are there any contingency plans that he ought to formulate?

allow you to anticipate unforeseen contingencies. This is especially important if you are speaking in an unfamiliar setting or are using unfamiliar equipment such as a microphone, an overhead projector, or a liquid crystal display (LCD) panel.

REVIEW

Living in an "information age" means having vast quantities of data at our disposal. To take advantage of this array of facts and figures requires communication skills such as interpreting, analyzing, and transmitting information, as well as collecting it. The eight categories of informative speech topics—people, places, things, events, processes, concepts, problems, and plans and policies—can be developed within four types of informative speeches: descriptive, demonstration, definitional, and explanatory. Common barriers to the presentation of information include the following: too much or too little information; information that is too factual or inferential, too concrete or too abstract, too general or too specific; and information that is feedback-poor or feedback-rich or is presented too rapidly or too slowly, too soon or too late, or with too much or too little intensity. To develop and present effective speeches, you should gear your presentation to the knowledge and interest levels of your audience; select the main points, organizational pattern, and forms of support; polish the speech; prepare contingency plans; and then put it all together.

SUGGESTED READINGS

Baird, J. E., Jr. (1974). The effects of speech summaries upon audience comprehension of expository speeches of varying quality and complexity. *Central States Speech Journal, 25,* 119–127.

Hackman, M. Z. (1988). Reactions to the use of self-disparaging humor by informative public speakers. *The Southern Speech Communication Journal, 53,* 175–183.

Petrie, C. R., Jr. (1963). Informative speaking: A summary and bibliography of related research. *Communication Monographs, 30,* 79–91.

Rowan, K. E. (1988). A contemporary theory of explanatory writing. *Written Communication, 5,* 23–56.

Spicer, C., & Bassett, R. E. (1976). The effect of organization on learning from an informative message. *The Southern Speech Communication Journal, 41,* 290–299.

14

Persuasive
Presentations

Objectives

After reading this chapter, you should be able to

1. Explain what persuasion is and why it is important, and differentiate it from other communication purposes.

2. Give examples of four types of persuasive speeches.

3. Describe how to use the Toulmin model for displaying arguments visually.

4. Compare and contrast motivational, ethical, and logical proof.

5. Use Maslow's hierarchy to analyze an audience.

6. Identify and describe strategies for utilizing the dimensions of source credibility.

7. Discuss the impact of evidence on persuasion.

8. Describe how the Elaboration Likelihood Model can be used to plan strategies for a persuasive speech.

CHAPTER CONTENTS

STEVE IS A STUDENT in a communication class much like this one. He is a religious peace activist and practices veganism, a strict form of vegetarianism. As a vegan, he avoids eating all meat and dairy products because he believes that (1) a vegetarian diet is healthier than a carnivore diet, (2) eating meat wastes God-given resources, and (3) eating meat entails violence against animals. For a persuasive speech assignment, Steve has decided to talk about veganism.

As you read this chapter, you will learn the skills that Steve will need to make a successful persuasive presentation to his class. At the end of the chapter, we will return to this scenario and solicit your advice.

Persuasive Speaking, Past and Present

Speculation on how to persuade effectively was first recorded in the writings of an Egyptian sage, Ptahhotpe (pronounced "ta-ho-ta-pe"), some 4,500 years ago.[1] In his Maxims, Ptahhotpe tells us that he is 110 years old, has lived through seven kings in the fifth dynasty of Egypt, and is now advising King Isesi, ruler of Upper and Lower Egypt. His counsel to the king involves five principles of effective persuasion that remain applicable today: (1) When in doubt about what to say, keep silent; (2) wait for the right moment to speak; (3) restrain passionate words; (4) speak fluently but with great deliberation; and (5) above all, keep your tongue at one with your heart so that you speak the truth.

Although the Egyptians were the first to write about persuasion, it was the Greeks (and later the Romans) who produced the first systematic accounts of the art of persuasion. Starting in the fifth century B.C., Greek philosophers/teachers began to record their observations and recommendations about how to speak effectively as a participant in the government of the city-state, in the law courts, and on ceremonial occasions. Their advice was frequently summarized within the context of five canons: *invention*—discovering the content of the message (both issues and supporting material); *arrangement*—organizing the content into introduction, narration, proof, and conclusion; *style*—putting the content into words in a way that meets such criteria as correctness, clarity, ornamentation, and propriety; *memory*—developing and using techniques that allow the speaker to remember the presentation after it has been prepared; and *delivery*—using voice and gestures to present a message effectively.

Greek and Roman citizens considered it important to be able to speak persuasively. When they went to the law court (as either defendant or prosecutor), they served as their own lawyer. Because anyone could prosecute and, by winning the case, receive a percentage of the fine, lawsuits were fairly common. Although they could and often did hire someone to help them prepare the case, in the courtroom these Greek and Roman citizens were on their own. The situation was similar for the assembly, the legislative branch of government. When the assembly considered such issues as war, taxes, ostracism, or the granting of citizenship, all members of the assembly were invited to participate. In addition, Greek and Roman citizens were frequently asked to speak at ceremonial occasions—funerals, births, holidays, and the like. In short, early Greece—and to a lesser extent Rome—were oral societies that expected all citizens to master the skills of persuasive speaking.

The circumstances have changed, but the ability to speak clearly, eloquently, and persuasively remains the hallmark of an educated member of our society. Although proportionately fewer of us argue our case in court, speak in a legislative assembly, or make ceremonial remarks, all of us find many occasions to practice the important art of persuasion—at home, at church, at school, at work, with friends, in the market, or in any of the nu-

FIGURE 14.1
In ancient Greece and Rome, the skills of persuasive speaking were needed to perform the duties of citizenship. In Shakespeare's play Julius Caesar, *Mark Antony's persuasive funeral oration turns his listeners against the plotters of Caesar's assassination. (This dramatic moment is shown here in a still from the 1953 movie, in which the part of Mark Antony was played by Marlon Brando.)*

merous contexts in which we live our lives. Among the many reasons for the continuing importance of persuasion, the most central one results from two clashing features of our world: the continuing and ever escalating pace of change, concurrent with the general preference for a stable environment—one where people know what to do. For example, it is often easier to forgo the advanced features of a new VCR or computer program for the comfort of continuing to work with older equipment or familiar materials. Individuals unable to adapt to changes in their world may, for example, find themselves ill (e.g., because they have not taken precautions against a new disease), without work (caught in an environment of downsizing), or otherwise at a disadvantage. Competent persuasive speakers can convince their listeners to share their goals. Success in persuasion may actually affect the nature of change. If you can convince your audience to share your goals, you and your listeners can work together to cope with the rapidly changing environment in ways that benefit all of you.

In this chapter, therefore, we build on the previous two chapters as we focus on the special challenges of persuading an audience to accept our point of view. This chapter supplements the general principles of public speaking with more targeted advice for persuasive speaking situations. Before we proceed, however, we explore what it means to present a persuasive message. What is persuasion?

Defining Persuasion

Persuasive discourse is not a pure form of discourse. It is a complex mixture of factors found in other forms of discourse and applied to uniquely persuasive ends. In other words, a persuasive speech follows the general rules of informative speaking, but it organizes arguments and information in a way that elicits a desired response from the receiver of the message.[2] At a minimum, to be labeled persuasive, a communication situation must involve a conscious attempt by one individual to change the attitudes, beliefs, or behavior of another individual or group of individuals through the transmission of some message.[3]

PERSUASION

A conscious attempt by a persuader, using verbal and nonverbal messages, to change the beliefs, attitudes, or behaviors of one or more persuadees by engaging the persuadee(s) in an interactive process during which the persuadee(s) can accept or reject the persuader's message.

For our purposes, **persuasion** refers to the act of manipulating symbols in order to produce change in others.[4] For example, the desired effect of a speech on safe sex may be to encourage the audience to avoid dangerous sexual situations. In order to accomplish this outcome, an effective persuasive speaker should use examples and ideas (symbols) that convince (manipulate) the audience to alter or reevaluate its behavior.

Although many formal definitions of persuasion exist (focusing on some combination of intent, ability, methods, or effects—and including terms such as "modify," "influence," and "shaping" to describe the act of persuasion), the key to understanding persuasion is knowing the characteristics that identify persuasion as a communication event:

1. One individual (the persuader) must make a conscious, intended attempt to influence one or more other individuals.
2. The persuader generates and uses a variety of messages (both verbal and nonverbal) to accomplish this intended purpose.
3. The activity of persuasion is a process in which both persuader and persuadee are active participants.
4. The goal of persuasion is to change the beliefs, attitudes, or behavior of persuadees.
5. At some level, the persuadees must have a choice—that is, they must perceive that they have an option to accept or reject the persuader's message.

Consider the following 11 premises, which evolve from and elaborate on definitions of persuasion.[5]

Premise 1 Persuasion is built on common values that persuader and persuadees share, and on a search for common ground.

Premise 2 Persuaders must have (or develop) sufficient credibility to receive a hearing from persuadees. (Various sources of credibility are discussed later in this chapter.)

Premise 3 Freedom of choice underlies persuasion. If persuadees have no choice, the persuader has no reason to attempt to persuade them.

Premise 4 Persuasion presupposes a condition of inequality, with "superiority" residing with the persuader. (If you, as a persuader, don't believe that your idea, opinion, or solution to a problem is better than that of the persuadees, why are you talking to them?)

Premise 5 Before persuasion can be accomplished, the persuadee must be convinced of the need to change. The persuader does this by revealing to the persuadee that the latter is somehow dissatisfied with his or her present position. As a persuader you must identify this need for change in the persuadee's mind and develop a persuasive strategy that will present your position as the best way to satisfy the need.

Premise 6 Persuaders must see persuadees as ready to change when properly approached on an issue. Respect for the audience and a degree of confidence in its readiness to change enable persuaders to resist the temptation to resort to deceit or manipulative tactics.

Premise 7 Most people can be reached through a persuasive effort, and those who cannot generally deserve a chance to explain why such ef-

Do unto Others . . .

Is the Golden Rule ("Do unto others as you would have them do unto you") consistent with the 11 premises of persuasion outlined in the text? Why or why not?

forts will be wasted on them. A persuader should always start with the assumption that persuasion is possible.

Premise 8   A presentation based on the truth takes longer to prepare than a poorly researched or hurriedly planned persuasive message, but its effects are more potent and more lasting.

Premise 9   Any perceived threat to the stability of the persuadee's environment will tend to produce resistance. The persuader needs a strategy to address this problem. Although a persuader *must* temporarily disrupt the status quo in order to produce changes in positions, preparing persuadees for necessary disruption will help to reduce resistance.

Premise 10   Ends and means must be weighed together. To accomplish an ethical, worthwhile goal a persuader must use ethical means. While you may be able to rationalize the use of unethical means to achieve a good goal, a thoughtful analysis of means and ends will generally reveal the pitfalls of yielding to the temptations of expediency.

Premise 11   Persuasion is not always possible, but it is possible much more often than it is attempted. Respect for the persuadee implies a recognition of the persuadee's right to make a decision about whether or not to be persuaded.

Forms of Persuasive Speaking

The task of an informative speaker is to present information in such a fashion that an audience will focus on, understand, and remember it. The persuasive speaker has yet one more task. The speaker has chosen to present a message that, if accepted, requires the audience to change beliefs, attitudes, values, or behaviors. Historically, these changes have been categorized based on speeches that advance four types of propositions or arguments.[6]

Propositions of Fact

In **speeches that affirm propositions of fact**, you make and support designative claims. That is, you pose and answer the question "Was it/is it/will it be true?" The alleged fact that you want the audience to accept as true can concern an individual, an event, a process, a condition, a concept, or a policy. The following are examples of propositions that allege the existence of a fact: "The federal government has evidence that flying saucers are real." "Workers in smoky bars and restaurants face a great risk of lung cancer." "Your dealership will lose money on its sales of compact cars because your inventory is too small."

SPEECH THAT AFFIRMS A PROPOSITION OF FACT
A speech that answers the question "Was it/is it/will it be true?" by making designative claims.

Propositions of Value

Speeches that affirm propositions of value make evaluative claims. That is, they answer the question "Of what worth is it?" In speeches of this type, you seek to convince an audience that something meets or does not meet a specific value standard of goodness or quality. The value standard can be applied to an individual, an event, an object, a way of life, a process, a condition, or another value. You can urge the adoption of a new value, the adoption of a new perspective through redefining an old value, or a renewal of commitment to an already held value. Consider the following examples: "Lee Jones is the best professor in our communication department." "Nuclear weapons are immoral." "Organized religion has produced more harm than good."

SPEECH THAT AFFIRMS A PROPOSITION OF VALUE
A speech that answers the question "Of what worth is it?" by making evaluative claims.

Concern about a Problem

In **speeches that create concern about a problem**, you advance definitive claims. That is, you answer the question "What is it?" Although propositions of fact assert that something is true or false and propositions of value allege that something is or is not worthwhile, the speech designed to create concern about a problem asks an audience to agree that specific conditions should be perceived as a problem requiring solution. In addition to making a compelling presentation concerning the nature of the problem, in such speeches your attempt to create concern about problems should also show the impact of the problem on the audience. The following are examples of propositions asserting problems: "The United States' sale of arms to other countries is a cause for concern." "Sexual harassment is a continuing problem on college and university campuses." "We should be concerned about the depiction of violence on children's television."

SPEECH THAT CREATES CONCERN ABOUT A PROBLEM
A speech that answers the question "What is it?" by making definitive claims.

Propositions of Policy

SPEECH THAT
AFFIRMS A
PROPOSITION
OF POLICY

*A speech that
answers the question
"What course of
action should be pur-
sued?" by making
advocative claims.*

In **speeches that affirm propositions of policy**, you make advocative claims. That is, you answer the question "What course of action should be pursued?" In addition to urging adoption of a new policy or course of action, you can recommend either continuing or discontinuing an existing policy, or rejecting a proposed policy. Your task as the speaker is to recommend a course of action or policy as necessary and desirable (or unnecessary and undesirable). Examples of such propositions include: "Federal regulation of the airline industry should be reinstituted." "Gays and lesbians should have the same rights as all Americans." "Colleges and universities should not adopt speech codes."

Our fourfold category scheme is, of course, less mutually exclusive than it would at first appear. With slight modifications, a topic in one category could easily be made to fit another. It is how you shape the message that leads the speech to be categorized as one that affirms a fact, a value, a problem, or a policy.

Basic Resources for Persuasion

Chapter 12 identifies the basic principles of public speaking: selecting a topic; analyzing the audience; identifying and organizing main points; providing support for ideas; outlining the speech; developing an introduction, transitions, and a conclusion; and selecting a type of delivery and rehearsing and delivering the speech. In this chapter, we focus on elaborations of these principles and their adaptation to the tasks of a persuasive speaker.

Toulmin's Model

When you ask an audience to accept a proposition of fact, value, problem, or policy, you do so by offering good reasons—reasons that the audience will judge as either acceptable or unacceptable and hence persuasive or nonpersuasive. The analysis and terminology of English logician Stephen Toulmin provide a useful approach to generating and evaluating "good reasons."[7] As Toulmin describes it, when we give good reasons (an argument), we move from data, through a warrant, to a claim.

Claim (C) is the term Toulmin uses to describe the conclusion that you want the audience to accept. The claim might be a fact, a value, a problem, or a policy, or it might be an intermediate claim that supports your purpose. The claim is always potentially controversial and hence requires support that the audience will accept.

Data (D) answer the question "What is the support/grounding for the claim?" Data include the forms of support we described in Chapter 12: language, explanations, examples, statistics, testimony, and visuals. They can also include the credibility of the speaker or the values, motives, and beliefs of the audience.

Warrant (W) is the name Toulmin gives to the part of an argument that justifies the "jump" involved in advancing from accepting data to accepting a controversial claim. Whereas data answer the question "What have you got to support your claim?", the warrant answers the question "How do you get from the data to the claim?" The function of the warrant is to show that the data do in fact support the claim as true or acceptable.

Toulmin diagrammed the relationship among the three foundational components of an argument as shown in Figure 14.2.

In addition to the basic triad of **Toulmin's model** (data, claim, and warrant), there is a second triad of components, any or all of which may be part of an argument. Toulmin calls these backing, rebuttal, and qualifier.

Backing (B) provides support for a warrant when listeners are not willing to accept a warrant at its face value. Support for the warrant (backing) can consist of a single item or of an entire argument in itself complete with data and claim. In the sample argument given in Figure 14.3, it might be necessary to provide backing in the form of statistics that demonstrate the historical relationship between consumer confidence and consumer spending.

The *rebuttal* (R) is appended to the claim and recognizes conditions under which the claim will be true or not true only in a qualified or restricted way. The rebuttal anticipates objections that an audience might advance against the claim. In the argument on consumer confidence, for example, a potential rebuttal might be: "Unless other features of the economy, such as

TOULMIN'S MODEL
A method of generating, evaluating, and displaying "good reasons" for accepting a fact, value, problem, or policy in terms of a primary triad (data, warrant, claim) and a secondary triad (backing, rebuttal, qualifier).

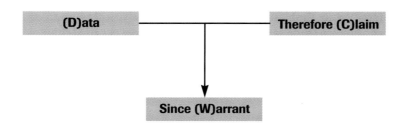

FIGURE 14.2
The three foundational components of an argument, as diagrammed by Toulmin.

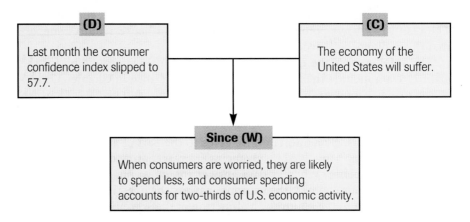

(D)

Last month the consumer confidence index slipped to 57.7.

(C)

The economy of the United States will suffer.

Since (W)

When consumers are worried, they are likely to spend less, and consumer spending accounts for two-thirds of U.S. economic activity.

FIGURE 14.3

An example of the use of Toulmin's model.

low interest rates combined with low housing prices, lead consumers to spend in spite of their fears."

The *qualifier* (Q) expresses the degree of force that you as the speaker believe the claim to possess. When you believe the claim to be incontrovertible, no qualifier is necessary. When you do not possess this conviction, you can qualify the claim with words such as "probably," "usually," and "possibly." The qualifier might also make specific reference to an anticipated rebuttal.

Figure 14.4 shows the model with all six elements.

Forms of Proof

Using Toulmin's model, you can think through and visually display the "good reasons" why you think your audience ought to accept your claim about a fact, value, problem, or policy. Traditionally, forms of proof have been organized into three categories. The ancient Greeks called them *pathos* (**motivational proof** based on the inner drives, values, or aspirations of the audience), *ethos* (**ethical proof** based on the credibility of the source of the message), and *logos* (**logical proof** based on evidence, such as statistics and examples). Using the Toulmin model, you can diagram any argument whether it is based on logical, ethical, or motivational proof. You can also use the model to anticipate objections your audience may raise (in the form of rebuttals) and think about means of dealing with those objections (qualifiers).

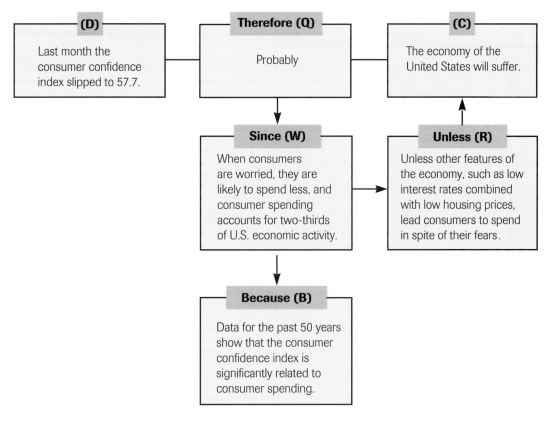

FIGURE 14.4
An example of Toulmin's model using all six elements.

Motivational Proof

At the heart of persuasion is the ability to adapt a message to the feelings, needs, and values of an audience. Helpful in this process is the work of psychologist Abraham Maslow.[8] Maslow argues that an individual's motivations, priorities, and behavior are influenced primarily by the needs that person is experiencing. A need is a deficit that creates tension. Maslow identifies these needs in a hierarchical structure of five categories. From low (immature) to high (mature), they are:

1. *Physiological/survival needs:* Things you need for basic survival—air, water, food, shelter, sleep, clothing, sex, and so on.

2. *Safety needs:* Need for security, orderliness, protective rules, and avoidance of risk. They include not only actual physical safety, but safety from emotional injury as well.

3. *Belongingness/social needs:* Needs that move beyond personal needs (basic and safety) to interpersonal needs centered around your interactions with others. They include the desire to be accepted and liked by other people and the need for love, affection, and affiliation. These needs are normally met by family ties, friendships, and membership in work and social groups.

4. *Esteem/ego-status needs:* The need to be accepted by some group and to be recognized for achievement, mastery, competence, and so on. The need to be perceived as worthy by self and others is satisfied by special recognition, social and professional rewards, promotions, awards, power, and achievement. Unlike the previous three categories of needs, esteem needs are not satisfied internally; they require outside feedback—that is, others must acknowledge the superior performance.

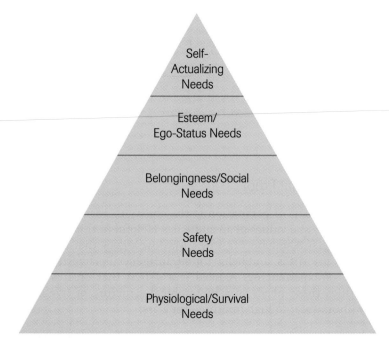

FIGURE 14.5
Maslow's hierarchy of needs.

Motivation and Culture

To what degree, in your opinion, does Maslow's hierarchy transcend cultural boundaries? For example, would Americans and Asians generally rank Maslow's needs in the same order?

5. *Self-actualizing needs:* The highest level of needs, focusing on the need for personal development and self-fulfillment—becoming what you can become. Instead of looking for recognition of your worth from others, you seek to measure up to your own criteria for personal success. Thus, self-actualizing behaviors are growth-motivated, not deficiency-motivated. Self-actualized people accept their own and others' frailties and become what they are capable of becoming.

In Maslow's view, people have an internal need that pushes them toward self-actualization and fulfillment. However, needs are arranged in a hierarchy of importance, and behavior is always determined by the lowest-order category or level of need remaining unsatisfied. Thus, when you are truly hungry and thirsty, it is difficult to be motivated by higher-level needs. The need that is motivating, then, depends on what you already have. Needs that are not satisfied influence behavior; satisfied needs do not.

The implications of Maslow's hierarchy for persuasive speaking are straightforward. The persuasive speaker must consider the level of the hierarchy that characterizes the majority of the audience and adapt the message appropriately. For the majority of speeches in this class, the appropriate levels are likely to be those of belongingness and esteem. You should not attempt to identify the appropriate level in a hasty manner, however. Appealing to a level that is too low or too high for the majority of the audience will result in decreased audience interest and attention.

Ethical Proof

The persuasiveness of a message is commonly assumed to be influenced by the person who delivers it. Business organizations therefore spend vast amounts of money hiring people who are held in esteem by the general public to sell their products and represent their interests. For example, fund-raising campaigns and membership drives list important persons on their letterheads. In social conversations, you drop the names of respectable sources as you pass along rumors and gossip.

Using a variety of labels (ethos, charisma, leadership, image, source credibility), students of communication, from classical to contemporary times, have devoted considerable effort to understanding this phenomenon. Their work supports our commonsense observation that **source credibility**—an audience's perception of a message source independent of that source's intent or purpose—is an important factor in whether or not listeners accept the message.

SOURCE CREDIBILITY
An audience's perception of a message source independent of that source's intent or purpose.

For example, in an early study, Hovland and Weiss presented identical messages on four topics (antihistamine drugs, atomic submarines, the steel shortage, and the future of movie theaters) to two groups.[9] One group was told that the author of the message was highly credible (e.g., the *New England Journal of Biology and Medicine* on antihistamine drugs); the other group was told the source of the message was less credible (a mass-circulation monthly illustrated magazine). Opinion questionnaires were administered before, immediately after, and a month after the communication. The researchers discovered that the subjects did perceive differences in the credibility of the sources: the four high-credibility sources were judged to be trustworthy by 81 to 95 percent of the subjects, whereas the low-credibility sources were judged trustworthy by only 1 to 21 percent. The researchers also discovered that these differences in the perception of the source produced different perceptions of the message. Even though the messages being judged were identical as to content, the presentation was considered to be "less fair" and the conclusions were thought to be "less justified" when the source was of low rather than of high credibility. In addition, opinions changed more often in the desired direction when information originated from a more credible source.

In another early study, Miller and Hewgill examined how the delivery of a speech might change an audience's perception of source credibility. Specifically, two types of vocal nonfluencies, *repetition* ("For New—uh—Newman") and *vocalized pauses* ("uh"), were considered.[10] The researchers tape recorded nine versions of a speech given by a trained speaker and actor who was arguing that the practice of granting scholarships to college or university students on the basis of athletic ability should be abolished. Four of the messages contained varying numbers of vocalized pauses, and four contained similarly varied amounts of repetition. One version of the speech was delivered smoothly, without "uhs" or repetition. As the authors predicted, subjects who heard the professionally delivered speech rated the speaker as significantly more competent than did subjects who heard a stumbling delivery. The professional speech was also judged to be dynamic. Contrary to the authors' hypothesis, however, judgments of trustworthiness were less affected by speech errors. In fact, the most trusted versions of the speech were those containing modest levels of vocal pauses and repetitions.

FIGURE 14.6
Martin Luther King, Jr., was highly regarded by his large following on all the dimensions of credibility. He was one of the most persuasive speakers in U.S. history.

Thus, these two studies illustrate that, in part, an audience accepts or rejects what a speaker says on the basis of personal characteristics they perceive in the speaker; and that these perceptions are changeable—that is, credibility can be built or destroyed by what a speaker says or does.

Clearly, then, credibility is not an all or nothing proposition. In fact, numerous studies have demonstrated that individuals weigh a number of factors when they are deciding whether to believe a speaker. Although these dimensions have varied from study to study, the two factors that have most consistently emerged in this body of research are competence and trustworthiness. They are the first two in a list of seven potential dimensions of credibility compiled by Hart, Friedrich, and Brummett.[11]

Competence   The speaker is perceived as having knowledge and experience about a topic that others do not have.

Trustworthiness   The speaker's present behaviors are seen as being consistent with past behaviors; in other words, the speaker is perceived as reliable.

Dynamism   The speaker is perceived as being aggressive, emphatic, and forceful.

Power   The speaker is perceived as one who can provide significant rewards and punishments for listeners.

Goodwill   The speaker is perceived as having his or her audience's best interest in mind.

Idealism   The speaker is perceived as possessing qualities and values that the audience esteems and to which it aspires.

Similarity   The speaker is perceived as resembling the audience in significant ways.

Research has found these dimensions to be relatively independent; that is, an audience's perception of a speaker on one dimension does not influence its views on the others. Thus, a speaker who is perceived as competent (knowing the subject matter) can be either trusted or not. You might consider two people—for example, your senator and a lawyer—to be equally competent, but you might trust one more than the other.

Given what we have said about source credibility, you would do well to begin your search for credibility strategies by finding out what your audience currently believes about you. A good starting point is listing your assets and liabilities in relation to the seven dimensions of source credibility. As you complete the Self-Check "Are You a Credible Source?", remember that by the time you deliver your first speech in this class, you will have interacted with most of your classmates. As a result, they will have formed impressions of you. Even if they have not interacted directly with you, they have a variety of sources of information on which to base credibility judgments—personal appearance and actions, reference group membership, endorsements. What are they likely to conclude?

Now that you have analyzed your assets and liabilities, it is time to consider strategies for building on assets and reducing liabilities. As you consider your options for building your credibility, think in terms of the five factors that can influence your image as you speak: source characteristics (e.g., mode of dress and fluency of delivery); message characteristics (e.g., use of evidence and language intensity); channel characteristics (e.g., visual aids and oral delivery); audience characteristics (e.g., ego involvement and identification with the speaker); and occasion characteristics (e.g., attractiveness of the setting and temperature of the room). To guide your thinking, next we list a number of possibilities for each of the dimensions of credibility.[12]

SELF-CHECK

Are You a Credible Source?

Imagine you are going to give a speech on a particular topic to your class or another group that you belong to. List your assets and liabilities for each of the seven dimensions of source credibility as you think they would be perceived by the group. Rank the dimensions in terms of how ethical you think it would be for you to use them.

Competence

To present yourself as an authority on your topic, you should rely on the following strategies:

Demonstrate personal acquaintance with the topic. It is important to let the audience know why you chose to speak on this topic—how you got involved and why you care. If the topic is something with which you are personally involved (you've done it, it's part of your job, it's your hobby, etc.), an audience is likely to accept what you say about the topic.

Demonstrate familiarity with the topic's special vocabulary. An additional way to demonstrate competence is through the correct use of terminology related to your topic. However, don't use jargon for the sake of jargon—and be sure to define unfamiliar terms.

Demonstrate familiarity with experts in the field. Citing such authorities in support of a point is especially important if the audience perceives you as a moderate or low credible source. When quoting experts, the more reliable your source is, the more it will do for your own believability. Therefore, it is wise to analyze your audience carefully to discover whose opinions it values.

Be sure that your speech is well organized. A well-organized message may not increase credibility, but a disorganized speech will usually decrease it. Thus, it pays to spend time organizing your speech so that your audience will find it easy to follow.

Trustworthiness

Your audience is likely to consider you reliable if you do the following:

If at all possible, establish verbal interaction with the audience. This is difficult at times, but speakers who open themselves up to ongoing public scrutiny give the impression that they are sure of themselves and their positions. Listeners reason that a speaker who accepts such a challenge is one who will maintain his or her views in other communicative situations.

Demonstrate that your present behavior is consistent with your past behavior. It is often good to "remind" audience members of what you have done in the past on their behalf or on behalf of the proposition you advocate.

Show that you can be trusted by being as explicit as possible and by entertaining other points of view. Most listeners appreciate someone who does not waste their time. Also, it is often wise to treat both sides of an issue in order to build an image of fairmindedness.

Make sure that your verbal and nonverbal behaviors are consistent. Thousands of subtle, nonverbal cues can suggest that you do not really believe what you are saying. Because people believe that nonverbal cues are harder to fake, they tend to believe the nonverbal more than the verbal.

Dynamism

To appear forceful and empathic, you should do the following:

Indicate exactly what behavioral commitments you have made to your position. If you can show what you have done on behalf of your proposal, you are likely to be perceived as dynamic.

Learn to control delivery variables. Practice your speech so that you can deliver it smoothly. Avoid speech errors such as "uh" and "er," which can call into question a speaker's dynamism.

Power

If you are in a position of power, you need not flaunt it. Here are strategies for maintaining your authority without intimidating your audience:

Use overt power strategies sparingly and subtly. If you have the ability to reward and punish an audience, you will not need to mention this fact. The audience will be aware of it. When reminded of a power imbalance, an audience is likely to resent it and rebel in some fashion.

Indicate that the balance of power between speaker and audience will be maintained. By this we mean that you should, if possible, indicate that you and your audience will profit equally from the interaction. In most situations, you are wise to acknowledge both what you expect to derive from the interaction and what "power" the audience itself is likely to garner.

Goodwill

To reassure your listeners about your positive attitude toward them, you should:

Demonstrate that your proposal will benefit the audience. Show how the audience will gain important rewards by accepting your position or, at least, that it will not lose by doing so.

Show that other groups of similar individuals have accepted your proposal. If other groups have perceived your goodwill, this one should too.

Communicate genuine interest and affection. The key word here is *genuine.* False expressions of interest and affection are often easily detected by listeners who have reason to be wary.

Idealism

Present yourself as a model for your listeners by doing the following:

Depict yourself as being both similar to and different from your audience. This is only one of the many dilemmas associated with building credibility. Obviously, listeners admire those who share their values, attitudes, and goals. On the other hand, unless you are somehow different from them, your listeners will have little reason to look up to you. Thus, by demonstrating that you have certain knowledge that the audience needs or that

Culturally Dependent Strategies

Which of the strategies for building credibility are most likely to be useful to audiences from all cultures? Which are most likely to be effective to different degrees in different cultures?

you embody certain aspirations of the audience in dramatic ways, you may be able to build an alike-but-different image of yourself.

Indicate what you have risked (or are willing to risk) on behalf of your proposal. Most people, it seems, tend to believe those who have taken a stand on behalf of something they strongly believe in.

Similarity

To show that you identify with the audience, use the following strategies:

Provide an overt statement of agreement with the audience on at least a peripheral issue. If you cannot agree with the audience on major issues, at least take a positive, agreeing position on a minor point. No matter who your audience is, you should be able to find some minor issue of agreement.

Learn to control your nonverbal behavior. Personal appearance and demeanor, such as nuances of posture, body position, physical distance, eye contact, dress, grooming, and the like, all provide audience members with cues for seeing you as similar to or different from themselves. The challenge for you as a speaker is to discover those nonverbal cues that communicate similarity for the particular audience in question.

Demonstrate that you represent the greatest common denominator of the audience's beliefs and values. In public communication situations, you must be especially careful not to alienate a sizable portion of the audience. Because a group of listeners usually harbors diverse and sometimes opposing viewpoints, you are wise to emphasize those aspects that are likely to elicit the greatest amount of collective agreement.

Logical Proof

As you may recall, in Chapter 12 we described six verbal and nonverbal devices that you can use to help an audience understand and accept your message:

Language   The word and language choices you use to make your messages clear and acceptable.

Explanations   Clear ideas achieved through simple, concise exposition or definitions.

Examples   Detailed or abbreviated illustrations, models, or instances of what is to be explained.

Statistics   Descriptions of events, persons, places, or other phenomena in quantitative terms.

Testimony   Use of a credible person's statement to lend weight and authority to an aspect of the message.

Visual aids   Actual objects, models of those objects, pictorial reproductions, or pictorial symbols to illustrate phenomena.

Evidence

Three of these forms (examples, statistics, and testimony) are especially useful as *evidence*—that is, information used as logical proof by a speaker. Evidence, in whatever form it takes, increases the persuasiveness of a message.[13] As you might expect, highly credible evidence sources are more persuasive than less credible sources. The use of high-quality evidence is especially effective if the audience is unfamiliar with the subject and if the evidence is from multiple sources. Old evidence and evidence already quite familiar to the audience do not produce highly persuasive effects.

To be persuasive, you should use multiple types of evidence—especially high-quality evidence from multiple sources. Although the research does not suggest that one form of evidence is superior to the others, there is some indication that examples may have greater impact than statistical evidence, perhaps because they create vivid images in the minds of receivers. Reinard suggests, however, that "although receivers may be inordinately impressed by a powerful example, persuasion is enhanced when a report is followed by a statistic that shows the example to be typical."[14]

Not all sources of information are of equal value, but how can you decide which are more credible than others? In order to evaluate your sources, whether you are presenting or listening to a persuasive message, consider Andrews's criteria: Is the source reliable? recent? accurate? complete?[15]

The *reliability* test holds that sources should be objective and competent. Be skeptical of sources who might have something to gain from promoting a particular point of view. The source should also be in a position to know about the subject at hand. The source should be competent to judge or comment on the specific issue, item, or idea. The *recency* test holds that one should strive for the most up-to-date information possible. The two final tests are closely related to one another. To meet the *completeness* criterion, evidence should be based on as many sources as possible to provide a complete view (not that one can ever know everything there is to know about a topic). Having multiple sources lets you test the evidence for *accu-*

Collecting and Evaluating Evidence

Imagine that you are trying to persuade your employer to buy a car of a particular make and model for employees to use for business trips. You are to make a presentation to a management committee, and you want to give the members convincing evidence for your recommendation. What sources of information (for example, people, publications, and the like) about the car might you cite? Use solo brainstorming to generate as many ideas as possible without evaluating the sources.

When you have created a list of sources, use Andrews's criteria to evaluate them. Why are the sources you rate as best likely to be credible to your audience?

Repeat this exercise for a presentation to your classmates to convince them to have an end-of-semester social dinner at a new Thai restaurant. Do some types of evidence provide especially strong support for propositions of fact? value? problem? policy?

racy. Accurate information is *redundant* and *verifiable.* In other words, a variety of sources should present similar information. You should be skeptical of the aberrant figure or idea.

Effective Use of Message Variables

Considerable research has been conducted on the effective use of certain message variables in persuasion. In reviewing these studies, O'Keefe presents the collective response of the experts to questions about how to make a message persuasive:[16]

1. *Where should a persuader put the message's most important arguments—first, last, or in the middle?* Perhaps, on average, some extremely small benefit might be obtained from placing them last, but this benefit is so small as to be negligible.

2. *Should the persuader state the point explicitly or let the receivers figure out the conclusion themselves?* Messages that include explicit conclusions or recommendations are more persuasive than messages that do not.

3. *Should a persuader ignore or answer opposing arguments?* Persuaders are well advised to employ two-sided messages, even on issues unfamiliar to the audience.

4. *Should the speaker ask for much or for little change?* The most plausible general image of the relationship between discrepancy and effectiveness is that of an inverted U-shaped curve, such that relatively little change is obtained by asking for too little or too much. The nature of this U-shaped curve will, however, vary with communicator credibility and with receiver involvement with the issue.

5. *Are stronger fear appeals more effective than weaker ones?* Material that induces greater fear or anxiety will enhance the effectiveness of the message.

A Theoretical Approach to Persuasive Effects

Having explored three forms of proof (motivational, ethical, and logical), it is time to think about blending them into a persuasive message. The **Elaboration Likelihood Model (ELM)** developed by Petty, Cacioppo, and their associates is especially helpful for this process.[17]

As the name suggests, ELM addresses the probability (likelihood) that a target of persuasion will engage in elaboration—that is, give careful thought to the message being received. ELM begins with the observation that people are constantly bombarded with more messages than they can possibly process. As a result, it is necessary to develop strategies for coping—strategies that allow people to process thoroughly and systematically those messages considered important and relevant, while paying less attention to messages considered insignificant.

According to ELM, messages are processed in one of two ways: the **central route**, whereby important messages are processed carefully, or the **peripheral route**, whereby less important messages receive less attention. An audience is most likely to follow the central route to persuasion (i.e., carefully examine the information in the persuader's message, scrutinize the arguments rigorously, and think about issues not raised by the persuader) under the following circumstances:

- The issue is one that the audience has encountered before.
- The audience is not distracted by other stimuli or tasks.
- The audience is interested and involved in the issue.
- The persuader develops a persuasive message that uses multiple sources and multiple arguments.
- Most members of the audience enjoy thinking about issues.

ELABORATION LIKELIHOOD MODEL (ELM)
A theory of persuasion that specifies the conditions under which an audience will process a message based on features of the message or features surrounding the message.

CENTRAL ROUTE TO PERSUASION
An ideal form of persuasion in which the audience carefully considers and analyzes the content of the message in deciding whether to accept or reject it.

PERIPHERAL ROUTE TO PERSUASION
An ideal form of persuasion in which the audience bases its decision about the message on characteristics external to the message—for example, source credibility or the reactions of other individuals.

ELM research provides both good news and bad news about the outcome when an audience is motivated and able to engage in elaboration. The potentially bad news is that an audience's initial disposition is difficult to overcome. That is, if listeners are already inclined to oppose the persuader's position, they will be less receptive to the message than if they are initially in favor. The good news is that if the message contains good evidence, powerful arguments, sound reasoning, and other persuasive features, it can overcome negative predispositions.

At the other end of the persuasion continuum, where an audience is less motivated and less able to elaborate on the persuasive message, lies the peripheral route to persuasion. Because the message is considered less central to an audience's concerns, the audience is less willing to take the time to do a careful analysis of the message. Instead, it is likely to employ some simple decision rules (a heuristic principle) to decide whether or not to accept

---

REALITY CHECK

Putting It All Together for a Persuasive Speech

At the beginning of this chapter we met Steve, a student in a communication class much like yours who is thinking about giving a persuasive speech on veganism. What have you learned in this chapter that might help Steve prepare for his presentation?

- Is veganism a good topic for his speech? Why or why not?

- Which of the four types of persuasive speeches (fact, value, problem, policy) would you advise him to develop? Why?

- How might he use Toulmin's model in preparing for this presentation?

- Which of the audience's needs and values might Steve find most useful for his purpose? Which ones might be the most detrimental?

- Which of the dimensions of source credibility will be assets for Steve? Which will be liabilities? Do you have any concrete suggestions for credibility-enhancing strategies?

- Which of the forms of evidence are likely to be most useful? least useful? Are there any message strategies that Steve should be especially concerned about?

- Would you advise Steve to adopt a persuasive strategy based primarily on a central or a peripheral route to persuasion? Why? How should he develop his strategy?

your message. Three signposts on the peripheral route are *credibility*—a belief that the message can be trusted if the source is credible, *liking*—a belief that the message can be trusted if the source is liked, and *consensus*—a belief that the message can be accepted if others accept it.

Two additional points need to be made about the two routes to persuasion. First, note that they are two ends on a continuum and, thus, if you are making a persuasive speech, you are not faced with an either/or choice. Instead of developing a message based solely on logical arguments for the central route to persuasion or ethical and motivational arguments for the peripheral route, analyze the situation carefully and decide on an appropriate balance of argumentative types. A second point is that the end result of the persuasive effort is different for the two ends of the continuum—that is, attitudes shaped through the central route last longer, are more predictive of subsequent behavior, and are more resistant to counterpersuasion than are attitudes shaped through peripheral route processes.

REVIEW

Five features define persuasion: a conscious attempt by one person to influence another; generation of a variety of messages; active participation by both persuader and persuadee; changes in the persuadee's attitudes, beliefs, and behaviors; and a perception of choice by the persuadee. Persuasive speeches advance four types of propositions: propositions of fact, value, concern about a problem, and policy. Toulmin's model can be used to generate "good reasons" for an audience to accept a speaker's proposition. In giving these reasons, the speaker moves from data to warrant to claim (sometimes adding backing, rebuttals, or qualifiers). Types of good reasons that serve as warrants are motivational, ethical, and logical

proof. Credibility (ethical proof) is perhaps the most important factor in persuading listeners. It can be built in terms of seven dimensions: competence, trustworthiness, dynamism, power, goodwill, idealism, and similarity. Finally, a speaker can use the Elaboration Likelihood Model to blend motivational, ethical, and logical proof into a persuasive message. The model will help the speaker determine whether the audience is likely to follow the central route to persuasion (i.e., devote considerable attention to the persuader's message because the audience considers the topic important) or the peripheral route (i.e., pay less attention to a message because the audience considers the topic less important).

SUGGESTED READINGS

Larson, C. U. (1992). *Persuasion: Reception and responsibility* (6th ed.). Belmont, CA: Wadsworth Publishing Co.

O'Keefe, D. J. (1990). *Persuasion: Theory and research.* Newbury Park, CA: Sage.

Perloff, R. M. (1993). *The dynamics of persuasion.* Hillsdale, NJ: Lawrence Erlbaum.

Pfau, M., & Parrott, R. (1993). *Persuasive communication campaigns.* Boston: Allyn & Bacon.

Reinard, J. C. (1988). The empirical study of the persuasive effects of evidence: The status after fifty years of research. *Human Communication Research, 15,* 3–59.

Trenholm, S. (1989). *Persuasion and social influence.* Englewood Cliffs, NJ: Prentice-Hall.

15

Understanding and Using Mass Communication

Objectives

After reading this chapter, you should be able to

1. Define *mass communication* and identify the different perspectives on the media's construction of reality.

2. Identify the types of controls placed on the media and define *gatekeeping, prior restraint,* and *FCC.*

3. Describe the characteristics of a critical consumer and use the guidelines for consuming mediated messages critically.

4. Compare and contrast five theoretical positions on media effects.

CHAPTER CONTENTS

HATICE GECOL IS a Turkish student attending college in the United States. For the past few weeks she has heard and seen news reports about the government elections soon to be held in Turkey. Many of the reports suggest that the election campaign has provoked unrest and protests, an issue of major concern for Hatice because her mother is a government official in her hometown of Izmir. Although she has also received several letters from her parents, they have mentioned nothing about the upcoming elections. Hatice is experiencing dissonance because she does not know whether the reports are accurate and her parents are trying to protect her, or whether the media have sensationalized the political events in Turkey.

As you read this chapter, you will learn to evaluate mediated messages and will be exposed to guidelines that will help Hatice assess the messages the media have produced about her native country. At the end of the chapter, we will return to this scenario and solicit your advice.

The Mediated Society

Most of you are daily consumers of numerous forms of mass communication. Your opinions on political issues are often based on information you have received through television and radio broadcasts or through stories printed in newspapers. You feel sympathy for the homeless and a greater respect for people with AIDS because you have been exposed to their plight through movies and newspaper coverage. Even the clothes you choose to wear, your knowledge of the latest medical breakthroughs, or your preferred brand of toothpaste are often results of information provided through mass communication.

Mass communication, a term used to describe the production or transmission of messages that are received and consumed by large audiences, is a dominant force in our society. It appears in many different forms, including books like the one you are reading now, magazines and newspapers, radio and television, and other mediums (vehicles for transmitting messages) intended for large audiences, such as movies and videos. Mass communication is used by the **media**—organizations that create and transmit messages to the general public—to provide information about culture and society, to entertain, to persuade us to buy products or accept new ideas, and to perpetuate what McLuhan coined the "global village"—that is, a world where millions of people feel connected to any place on the globe because of access to instant information.[1]

Currently, 98 percent of all U.S. homes are equipped with televisions and 99 percent have radios. These households access electronic information and entertainment from over 9,000 radio stations and 1,400 television sta-

MASS COMMUNICATION
The production and transmission of messages that are received and consumed by large audiences, including various forms of printed material and messages dispersed via the airwaves or through cable networks.

MEDIA
Organizations that create and transmit informative, entertaining, or persuasive messages designed for large audiences.

tions. In addition, despite the pervasiveness of the electronic age, 84 percent of Americans 18 years of age and older still receive some information via newspaper readership.[2] Thus, it is no wonder that Ruch suggests that, because of our access to information, the human knowledge base currently doubles every year,[3] or that McLuhan claimed our world had become a "global village."

As you read through this chapter, you will be exposed to ideas about various communication mediums that are the foundation of our information-oriented society. You will learn the purposes mass communication serves for members of society, how mass communication affects your everyday activities, and some regulations that control its development. You will also be provided with explanations concerning media effects and suggestions for ways to better process mass mediated messages. This chapter, then, seeks to increase your awareness of mass communication and to develop your skills as a critical consumer of it.

Functions of Mass Communication

The information you receive from mediums such as news broadcasts or magazine articles allows you to feel connected to the fast-paced world in which you live. Mediated information serves as a barometer to measure the successes and failures of society and as a resource for making decisions. Can you imagine a presidential election without media coverage? Would you buy a car without consulting consumer reports? Thus, although critics of the mass media suggest that the information the media provide to the general public is often distorted or inadequate, the fact remains that information is a desired commodity.[4]

FIGURE 15.1
How representative of U.S. culture do you think the subjects and guests on morning and afternoon talk shows are?

Even forms of media designed to entertain, such as television shows like *Home Improvement* or your favorite soap opera, offer insight into the culture in which you live. In recent years, movies such as *Splash* and *Encino Man* have depicted characters who learn English and the American way of life—however distorted their interpretations—by viewing U.S. society on television. Although these movies use unrealistic, humorous examples to portray traditional American culture, they are reminders that mediated messages can describe culture and reinforce or shape the perceptions people have about society. Thus, mass communication, though designed to inform and entertain, also functions as an avenue of instant information and persuasion.

Persuading

Some forms of persuasion that are prevalent in mass communication are obvious to even the most unsuspecting media consumer. Few people would question that the purpose of commercials for cars or fast food is to persuade. Public service announcements that discourage the use of illegal drugs or drinking and driving are also examples of obvious persuasive appeals. However, Gozzi and Haynes suggest that the mass media also use more subtle forms of persuasion because they provide the *receiver*—those of you who consume and use the media—with a unique and sometimes distorted definition of reality.[5] In other words, although you know that commercials were designed to sell you certain products and thus give you information that makes one product appear superior to another, you are not always aware that this same type of persuasion is used in other types of mediated messages.

For example, imagine that you are the news manager for a local television station. You have been notified that a demonstration is going on in

---

REALITY CHECK

The Persuasive Appeals of Advertising

Select two magazine advertisements for similar products. Based on what you learned about proof in Chapter 14, evaluate the persuasive appeals used in each ad. How do the ads differ? Watch television or listen to radio commercials for the same two products. Compare and contrast the broadcast and print advertising for each product. Do certain types of persuasive arguments work particularly well for selling certain products? Are the arguments valid? credible?

front of an area abortion clinic. You dispatch a news crew to cover the protest and interview both the protesters against the clinic and the doctors who run it. When the time comes to prepare the news story, decisions will have to be made concerning how the protest should be presented to the community. How much coverage—air time—will the story be given? Which excerpts from the interviews will be shown? Although you are providing the public with the news, the way in which the story is presented has the potential to affect people's understanding of the event. In effect, as the station manager you would have the ability to persuade people, or at least to provide a persuasive account of the local news. For those who watch your news broadcast, you would be creating reality.

Information Gatekeeping

Television, particularly television news, can take any given event and attempt to convey a story about it using words or pictures.[6] Because of time constraints, however, news events are rarely shown without editing. News coverage is, by default, a reconstruction or constructed reality of an event. Although factors such as government and consumer regulations and integrity and ethics play a role in how information is produced and transmitted, the fact remains that in our information-based society—where more information exists than the general public can possibly know—the media serve as regulators, or **gatekeepers**, of information.

GATEKEEPING
The process of regulating or determining what information will be carried over mass communication channels and what will not.

The media's gatekeeper function is not limited to television. The media determine what information will become front-page news and what articles are worthy of attention in magazines. Although movies are generally produced for entertainment, some recent films such as *Philadelphia* and *The Firm* have had a clear political message. The media decide what will become mass communication, and through their choices they can provide a persuasive or biased view of what is important to society.

Meeting Consumer Demand

Another perspective on how mass communication messages are created and interpreted—one that is often supported by the media—suggests that the messages presented to the public are not a result of media bias or attempts of persuasion, but simply of supply and demand. Every year television programs are canceled because of their limited viewing audience, and it is certainly not uncommon to hear a radio announcer play listeners' requests or to find that a book you had hoped to read is no longer in print. Simply said, the media only produce the kinds of messages requested by the public.

Media organizations spend thousands of dollars annually conducting public opinion polls and use the resulting data to determine the interests and concerns of their audiences.[7] The media must provide the information

Comparing Media Coverage

Compare and contrast how you believe CNN and MTV would cover a story about a piece of rap music that denigrates police officers. What factors would produce similarities in the stories? What factors would produce differences?

and entertainment desired by their consumers in order to maintain high ratings for their programs and publications, or they will ultimately lose their audiences, advertisers, and their profits. Thus, when interviews are edited or news stories are omitted, aren't the media simply doing their job?

Providing Facts

A variation on this perspective suggests that the media present information and that consumers create reality. Graber contends that the media do not attempt to distort or bias events.[8] Instead, she proposes that it is the public's perception of information that creates bias. Individuals working in the media provide information; they compile facts and present these facts as evidence of truth. The interpretation and meaning of that information are dependent on the consumer's view of reality. For example, in the 1992 presidential campaign, the media frequently discussed the fact that Bill Clinton had smoked marijuana as a young man. The media would argue that they did not suggest that this was bad or good, but simply provided information that the public could interpret as it wished.

Thus, when evaluating how information becomes mass communication, the critical question is: Who controls information? Do the media create reality? Do the media simply respond to public opinion? Or, do media interpretations depend on media consumers? Perhaps the answer lies partly in each function. Whatever your opinion, by answering this question for yourself, you will be taking the initial step in becoming a critical consumer of mass communication.

CRITICAL CONSUMER
An individual who, as the user of a product, carefully evaluates the product for its quality, worth, and usefulness. A critical consumer of the media assesses the content of mediated messages for their accuracy and reliability.

▨ Critical Evaluation of Mass Communication

Being a **critical consumer** means that as the user of a product—in this case mass mediated messages—you carefully evaluate the product for its quality, worth, and usefulness. To become a critical consumer of mass com-

There Are Two Sides to Every Story

Based on the following information, create two news reports, each telling one side of the story.

On Thursday at 7:00 P.M., two women, Irma Lupe and Maria Ortega, were followed from the University Library to a nearby parking lot. When they arrived at their car, they immediately jumped in the car, locked the doors, and drove to the campus police station to report the incident. Police later visited the parking lot in question and interrogated a college senior, William Fernandez. Fernandez claimed that the women had left a notebook in the library and he was trying to return it when they quickly drove away. Neither Ms. Lupe nor Ms. Ortega recognized the notebook in question.

If you were reporting this incident in the campus newspaper, would you report it as a "good Samaritan" case or as a notice—especially for women—to be cautious when leaving the library? What pieces of information would affect your decision? Would your opinion be different if two men leaving the library had been followed by a woman? If so, why?

munication, you must understand the dominance of mediated messages and how the media work, and have an understanding of the different perspectives used to evaluate mass media effects. Now that you are familiar with the purposes of mass communication—to inform, entertain, provide instant information, and persuade—and have been exposed to several perspectives on the role of the media in creating mass communication, the remaining pages of this chapter will be dedicated to your development as a critical consumer.

Understanding the Mass Communication Environment

Before you began reading this chapter, you probably had some occasion to consider the effects of mass communication on your life. Perhaps you grew up in a home where your parents or caretakers controlled the types of movies you were allowed to see or monitored the number of hours you watched television. Perhaps your thoughts about mass communication occurred because you were involved in a project in which mass communication was used as a resource to attract support or exposure. It is likely, however, that you were most aware of the mass media when they were absent from your life. For instance, consider the feelings of isolation you began to experience after a few days on a camping trip or when your television or radio was broken for an extended period of time.

Because everyone is constantly exposed to various forms of mass communication—from the time they are able to walk and talk and throughout adolescence and adulthood—the mass media have become a major presence in the culture, bringing their view of the world into virtually every American home. Research suggests that television viewing has dominated the family's use of leisure time for the past three decades and, with the fine tuning of cable television through the use of fiber optics, programming alternatives, and ultimately television viewing, will continue to increase.[9]

The Expanding Use of Mediated Messages

The expanding uses of mass communication seem to ensure its importance in the future. For example, C-SPAN (Cable-Satellite Public Affairs Network), a nonprofit cable television network created to provide unedited coverage of the U.S. political system, is being used in some college classrooms to generate discussion of political issues and ideas. Nickerson predicts that by the year 2020 our current educational system will be transformed through technological advances and extended uses of mass communication.[10] Not only will closed circuit television—offering multiple specialized classes—be an ordinary educational resource, but also textbooks will be available on computer disks and computer networks will allow students to access large databases such as the Library of Congress by the touch of a button. Thus, the amount of media exposure we receive is, and will continue to be, a dominant issue in the mass communication environment.

SELF-CHECK

You and the Media

Create a list of all the forms of media that you have been exposed to in the last 24 hours. Which of these information sources do you consider most credible? least credible? Why?

Distinctive Characteristics
of Mass Communication

In addition to understanding the functions of mass communication, a second factor that extends our understanding of the mass communication environment is recognizing the differences between mass communication and communication in other contexts. Unlike face-to-face communication (such as talking to a friend or participating in a meeting at work), mass communication is best characterized as delayed communication to large groups of individuals. If you think about mass communication in terms of the model of communicative competence, the two partners are the media organization and the individuals and groups that comprise the audience. They are connected to each other and to their relationship by separate arrows because they do not interact simultaneously. Instead, the interaction occurs as the media organization and the audience take turns sending and receiving messages.

The media create and send messages via the airwaves, or through cable networks and printed forms; messages are received without the opportunity to immediately question or paraphrase their content; and, in most instances, the ability to discern how the message was intended or interpreted is based on chance or probability. Thus, mass mediated messages differ from communication in other contexts in four primary ways: (1) the channels used, (2) the types and forms of feedback available, (3) the format of the messages, and (4) the message content.

Channels

During interpersonal, group, and organizational communication events, the sender of a message generally uses a direct, person-to-person channel to communicate. Messages are interpreted and feedback is given simultaneously. Furthermore, people use perceptions to assess the appropriateness and effectiveness of a message, and they usually have the opportunity to clarify or adjust their message or message response based on the verbal and nonverbal cues received from the other participant(s) in the communication. In mass communication, however, the channels for messages are more broadly diffused and are characterized by indirect, delayed, or limited feedback.[11]

Feedback

Because mass mediated messages have different objectives than the words of face-to-face interactions, feedback also serves different purposes. For instance, consider the uses of public opinion polls or market reports such as the Nielsen ratings of television programs. Although these types of feedback tell television networks whether they are receiving their share of the television viewing audience, the information received by the networks is quite different from the feedback you would provide to a friend in day-to-day conversation. Unless opinions are collected systematically using appropriate research methods and sampling techniques, the results of public opinion polls and surveys to assess consumer viewpoints may be unreliable or invalid.[12] A classic example of inaccurate surveying occurred in the 1936 presidential election when a survey administered by the *Literary Digest* predicted that Republican Alf Landon would defeat Democratic incumbent Franklin D. Roosevelt in the upcoming presidential election. Ultimately, in that election, Landon received only 8 electoral votes to Roosevelt's 523. How did such an error in prediction occur? Although the survey contacted a large number of people, their names were drawn from telephone directories and automobile registrations, so that the group sampled contained a disproportionate number of wealthy people—and Republicans.[13]

Today, public opinion pollsters generally use scientific methods to obtain and collect feedback. They cannot, however, totally eliminate the communication difficulties associated with indirect, delayed, and limited feedback. Feedback that occurs after the fact or provides a partial representation of the public's ideas and opinions will continue to be a challenge to effective mass communication.

Format and Content

Mediated messages are created for large audiences and cannot rely on familiarity or history to clarify meaning. Consequently, mediated messages do not possess the spontaneity of everyday conversations; are usually scripted in order to maintain accuracy and precision; and, when carefully evaluated, may appear ambiguous in content. Communication for the masses must provide a middle ground—that is, a message that appeals to large numbers of different individuals.

In order to become a more critical consumer of mass communication, you must increase your understanding of the mass communication environ-

 REALITY CHECK

Ethical Responsibilities

Should the media's ethical responsibility (for example, to tell the truth; to present both sides of an issue) vary more with mass media functions (for example, entertainment vs. news) or with mass media type (for example, television vs. newspapers)? Why?

ment. By acknowledging the exposure you receive to mediated messages and by recognizing the differences and constraints that exist when comparing mass communication to person-to-person interaction, it will be easier for you to recognize and evaluate the benefits and limitations of mass mediated messages. However, your development as a critical consumer also includes understanding the controls placed on the media, which ultimately determine the mediated messages that you see, read, and hear.

Regulators of Mass Media

Because the U.S. society is dedicated to the ideal of freedom, the American mass media have a tremendous amount of discretion in handling and producing information. Nonetheless, there are constraining factors on the media. Some of these are official or legal regulations, whereas others have evolved because, as private businesses, the media have to operate within a capitalistic framework.

Formal Controls

One of the most basic legal considerations involving media control concerns the meaning of the phrase "Congress shall make no law . . . abridging the freedom of speech, or of the press," which appears in the First Amendment to the Constitution. Nelson, Teeter, and Le Duc note that, despite the noble intentions often ascribed to the First Amendment and the rest of the Bill of Rights, they were the result of political deal-making necessary to ratify the rest of the document.[14]

One of the main purposes of the "freedom of press" guarantee is to protect the people against prior restraint.[15] **Prior restraint** is the practice of banning certain publications before they have even been produced. It amounts to telling a publisher beforehand what it can publish rather than questioning the legality of a work after the fact. Along with any legal wranglings concerning what freedom of the press means, the electronic media are constrained by more specific governmental regulation. These media face the unique obstacle of sending their messages out over crowded airwaves. The airwaves are regulated by the Federal Communications Commission.

The **Federal Communications Commission (FCC)** was established in 1934. This regulatory agency oversees the physical resources of the media such as radio, television, wire, satellite, and cable communications. Beyond managing the physical resources, the FCC has two additional objectives: (1) to ensure that broadcasters use the airwaves in the public interest, and (2) to make sure the public has access to the airwaves.

Although censorship by the FCC is illegal, and although recent changes in government regulations provide broadcasters with a substantial amount of

PRIOR RESTRAINT
The practice of banning certain publications before they have been produced.

FEDERAL COMMUNICATIONS COMMISSION (FCC)
A regulatory agency that oversees the physical resources of the media to ensure that broadcasters use the airwaves in the public interest and that the public has access to the airwaves.

freedom to broadcast information at their discretion (e.g., the Cable Communication Act of 1984 freed cable television from FCC regulation), the FCC does attempt to balance the type of programming produced by electronic media. It also supports the inclusion of controversial issues by the media and encourages diversity in the viewpoints presented via the airwaves. For instance, the FCC suggests that news stations that use editorials to present controversial issues might be well advised to present both sides of an issue.

Thus, the mere existence of the FCC represents a strong government control of broadcasting that the print media do not have to concern themselves with. Broadcasters may not have to worry about official censorship by the FCC, but they do have to rely on the commission for licensing and renewal. Broadcasters have to take this type of power into consideration as they make decisions concerning station operations. Along with the pressure felt by individual stations, the industry as a whole must respond to any broad mandates handed down by the commission.

Informal Controls

The informal controls placed on the mass media in a free society are probably more constraining than any legal regulation of these industries. As in other industries, the media must deal with structural limitations that affect the carrying out of their given functions. And like any other business venture, the media in the United States also have the burden of turning a profit.

Hiebert, Ungurait, and Bohn point out that much media regulation is self-imposed in order not to offend audiences or provide the government with any reason to impose restrictions.[16] A key component of self-regulation is gatekeeping (as we saw earlier in this chapter). Because gatekeepers determine what information will be carried over mass communication channels and, conversely, what will not, they "keep the gate" on the huge amount of mass communication information available.

Although the media employ gatekeeping so as not to offend, some of the gatekeeping function has more to do with practical constraints of time and space. No newspaper, no matter how large, has enough space to print all the possible stories of the day. Editors have to make choices as to which stories are the most important and/or entertaining. Similarly, television news directors have remarkably little time in which to provide the day's top stories. Consider how many choices must be made and how many potential stories must be eliminated in order to produce a 22-minute national news broadcast titled "World News Tonight." Obviously, from a news standpoint it can be a very small world indeed. In the same way, entertainment programming directors must choose programs based on availability, entertainment value, and affordability to their particular station.

To a certain extent, each mass medium is also constrained by unique characteristics. As Hiebert, Ungurait, and Bohn note, the newspaper cannot compete with radio and television in terms of speed, but its format permits better display of the news, letting the reader see on one page the most important stories. Newspapers also provide greater depth in their stories and more detailed local information. Radio is unique in that it serves a highly fragmented audience, with most stations trying to serve the needs of a homogeneous group.[17] Similar to newspapers, radio is a local medium. People listen to it to fulfill very individual needs, such as finding out what the weather will be like on a particular day. Radio listening is a secondary activity that people engage in while they are doing something else, such as driving. Television has the unique ability to combine audio, text, and moving pictures. Television news producers understandably want to highlight the visual elements in their presentations. Focus on the visual also helps offset the inability to go into as much depth in stories as a newspaper owing to time limitations.

The advent of cable, with its multitude of channel possibilities, has enabled television to serve more specific audiences. Because they rely on advertisers for revenue, however, broadcasters have to establish as wide an audience as possible. The need to make a profit in order to stay in business and subsequent reliance on advertisers to do so point to a disturbing constraint on all the media.

Bagdikian argues that corporate ownership of the media and the media's reliance on mass advertising have negatively affected the information society receives.[18] Bagdikian believes that, despite corporate complaints about the media's antibusiness bias, the industry has always been biased in favor of corporate America. He suggests that because of the reliance on large corporate advertisers, media content attempts to be neutral and avoids controversy so as not to offend advertisers.

Because of corporate ownership of the media and its reliance on corporate advertising, the media, once the watchdogs of big business, have become partners in the big business enterprise. Consequently, although the American media operate in a relatively free environment, and although many people believe that the media serve as protector or watchdog for the American public, the media's needs and objectives must be considered when evaluating the messages presented to the public and the method of presentation. In other words, in order to be a critical consumer, you cannot ignore the goals of the media as you listen to their messages.

Effects of Mass Communication

The pervasiveness of the mass media in twentieth-century America has sparked academic researchers to study the phenomenon, often with the aim of discovering how mass communication affects society. Beginning with

FIGURE 15.2
By deciding what stories to cover, newscasters necessarily interpret their audiences' interests and help to shape the issues that will receive public attention. Here, a television news crew reports on efforts to repair a highway damaged by the earthquake that shook southern California in 1993.

the study of propaganda during World War I, theorists and researchers have provided many speculations and explanations concerning the consequences of mass media.

DIRECT EFFECTS
MODEL
An early theory of mass communication which states that all individual members of society receive messages in the same way and that direct and uniform outcomes result.

Direct Effects

Initially, it was believed that the media had direct effects on their audiences. Often called the hypodermic needle perspective, the **direct effects model** states that all individual members of society will receive mass communication messages in the same manner. The result will be direct and uniform for all members of a given audience. From the direct effects' point of view, if everyone in your communication class were to watch the local news, each of you would be affected by the broadcast in the same way and the effect would be immediate.

TWO-STEP FLOW
MODEL
An early view of media effects which proposes that the mass media are used by "opinion leaders" to disseminate information to individuals through social networks.

Two-Step Flow

Later work on mass media effects dispelled the notion of uniform direct effects. McQuail and Windahl have traced this research, which produced an indirect effect or **two-step flow model** of communication.[19] According to this model, the mass media are utilized by "opinion leaders," who then disseminate information to individuals through social networks. The model recognizes the idea that the "mass media do not operate in a social vacuum but have an input into a very complex web of social relationships and compete with other sources of idea, knowledge and power."[20]

The direct effects and two-step flow theories of mass communication were relatively early and broad attempts to explain the effects of mass communication. In the past twenty years, theories such as agenda setting, cultivation, and uses and gratifications have emerged as more probable explanations of mass communication.

Agenda Setting

Agenda setting refers to the media's ability to determine through the content of their presentations which issues or topics will be important to individual members of society. For example, if the news media highlight stories about the crime rate, then the theory of agenda setting predicts that crime will be an issue of importance to viewers. It is important to note that agenda setting is concerned primarily with the notion that the media have the power to help determine which issues are important.

AGENDA SETTING
The media's ability to determine, through the content of media presentations, which issues or topics will be important to individual members of society.

Cultivation

Cultivation theory investigates the cultural outcomes of television exposure. As Gerbner et al. (1986) suggest, "Television is a centralized system of storytelling . . . its drama, commercials, news, and other programs bring a relatively coherent world of common images and messages into every

CULTIVATION THEORY
A perspective on media effects which suggests that television is a socializing agent of culture that provides its viewers with a common world view.

REALITY CHECK

Agenda Setting in Local News Reports

While watching the evening news on one of the major television networks, create a chart of all the topics that are discussed and how many minutes/seconds are spent covering each topic. Based on your chart, what do you believe is the news agenda for the evening? In your opinion, which topics did not receive as much coverage as was required in order to understand the issue, problem, or information?

As a follow-up exercise, search for each of the news topics in the next day's newspaper. Were all the topics covered? How did coverage of the stories differ between the television and the newspaper medium? What information, if any, is still missing from the coverage? What resources could you use to "fill in the gaps" left by media coverage?

home. Television cultivates from infancy the very predispositions and preferences that used to be acquired from other primary sources."[21] Based on cultivation theory, then, television may be regarded as a socializing agent of culture that provides its viewers with a common understanding of how to view the world.[22]

■ *Uses and Gratifications*

The **uses and gratifications theory** emphasizes the idea that the consumer is key to understanding media effects. Consumers—those who use the media—have certain expectations concerning what mass communication is supposed to do. For example, if you believe that the evening news should provide a sports report and it does provide one, then you will evaluate the news as a positive event that meets your expectations. Thus, uses and gratifications theory suggests that you have an expectation (use) and evaluate (or are gratified by media) if this expectation is met.[23]

The five theories discussed here, though not an exhaustive list of explanations for mass media effects, do provide different perspectives for understanding mass communication. In addition, by considering theories such as direct effects or uses and gratifications, it becomes possible to view and evaluate the effects of media in a critical way based on the research of experts. Including expert opinions in the knowledge base used to understand mass communication gives everyone the opportunity to become more critical and more competent consumers of the media.

Calvin and Hobbes
by Bill Watterson

FIGURE 15.3
Do you believe that the role of mass media should be to respond to consumer demand?

The Historical Record

Most records and stories pertaining to the past contain at least some discrepancies. Consider the following scenario: It is the year 2200, and a college professor is trying to produce an account of an epidemic disease known as AIDS that swept the earth in the late 1900s. What do you think will be said about AIDS? How will the information about AIDS differ from what you have been taught about the bubonic plague, or Black Death, that swept Europe and parts of Asia in the 1300s? What role do the media play in the creation of history?

Being a Critical Consumer

Now that you are familiar with some of the basic views and explanations of mass communication and its effects, consider some guidelines that will help you become a critical consumer of the ever present mass media. These guidelines include evaluating message content, being mindful, being aware of the media, and doing your homework.

Evaluating Message Content

The first and perhaps most important guideline for evaluating mass communication messages is the need to *evaluate the content of the message.* Message content quite simply refers to what is being said or communicated. In order to effectively evaluate content, you must consider what information has been given about a topic and what information may have been omitted from a mediated message.

For example, people in the United States have been bombarded with information indicating that homosexual males are the group at the highest risk for AIDS. This information is true for U.S. residents but not for the world population.[24] In this country, the implication that AIDS is a "gay disease" has been very damaging to that segment of the population. By questioning the facts provided in mass mediated messages and by seeking out information independently in order to fill in the gaps left by media coverage, you can make clearer judgments about messages and their meanings.

Are You a Critical Consumer of Advertising?

Create a list of five products that you buy regularly. How are these products sold through the media? Are you a critical consumer when buying these products? Why or why not? In what ways do you act as a critical consumer of mediated messages about these products? Is it necessary to be mindful when purchasing such everyday, relatively inexpensive items as laundry soap or pretzels?

Being Mindful

A second guideline for becoming a critical consumer is related to the concept of mindfulness. *Mindfulness* refers to the withholding of immediate judgment on a message and the search for new categories, that is, new ways to interpret and assign meaning to the message. For example, a newscaster on a local television station presented a news update that went something like this: "Are children's jackets that bear the logos and names of professional football teams dangerous to your child? Tune in at 10:00 P.M. to find out more." Consider all the possible explanations of such an announcement. Is there something in the clothing dye that irritates children's skin? Are the coats a new symbol for the gangs that dominate urban schools? There are endless possibilities. However, the basis of the news story was none of these. It actually referred to a child whose coat was stolen because it was so expensive. Being mindful will allow you to consider multiple possibilities about the relationship between such issues as a popular item of clothing and danger. It will also allow you to recognize that the theft of one child's coat does not necessarily augur a crime wave or a need to panic. Using mindful communication is a technique that will allow you to listen to mass communication while reserving judgment and to avoid stereotyping messages that present common themes or ideas.

Increasing Awareness of the Media

A third guideline influencing your development as a critical consumer relates to your *awareness of the media.* Because you constantly use electronic media, you may be less sensitive to the messages you are receiving

FIGURE 15.4
Broadcasting of this amateur videotape of the beating of Rodney King by Los Angeles
police officers led to the officers' arrest. The tape became the primary piece of evidence
at their trial, and portions of the tape were minutely and repeatedly examined. The
interpretation by the jury that the officers were not guilty of using excessive force
ignited the Los Angeles riot of 1992. Live news coverage of the riot then became the
subject of differing interpretations.

from it. Lack of sensitivity can affect your evaluation of mass communication messages. Often you turn on the television or radio or pick up a magazine and thumb through it, giving very little thought to the effect of the information you are receiving. Your cognitive processes allow you to absorb the numerous messages that bombard you and to believe they provide credible information.

The source credibility of Walter Cronkite, dubbed "the most trusted man in America" while a news anchor for CBS, is an excellent example of how cognitive processes lead to acceptance of messages sent by the media. The popular perception was that, if Walter Cronkite said something, it was true. As Jamieson suggests, you use your belief that the media are credible sources of information to draw conclusions from mediated messages.[25] In other words, you can absorb vast amounts of information without being sensitive to it and then accept it because you assume that the source of the information is credible.

The Complete Critical Consumer of Mass Communication

At the beginning of this chapter, you were introduced to Hatice Gecol, a Turkish student studying in the United States. Hatice was concerned about the safety of her family because of news reports about political activities occurring in Turkey. Based on your new knowledge of mass communication, what advice would you offer Hatice? How is the gate-keeping function affecting her perceptions?

If, in a phone call to her parents, Hatice learned that protests had occurred near her home but that they had involved only small groups of picketers who wanted to register additional candidates for the elections, what theoretical perspective do you believe would best describe the media coverage? Why? How would this change in information reinforce your position as a critical consumer of mediated messages? Is it possible for you to be a competent communicator when dealing with the media?

Doing Your Homework

The final guideline for improving your critical thinking skills requires you to *"do your homework."* Frequently you hear or read information that could drastically affect your life, and yet far too often you do not question the reliability of this information. You would probably not have a heart transplant or even minor surgery without a second opinion, and you would think nothing of asking two or three people at work their opinion about a change in company policy. Mass communication must be used with the same discretion. When an issue is important to you, take the time to investigate it. Watch or listen to multiple accounts of it from different people. Compare newspaper and magazine reports to those of television and radio. When necessary, seek out less popular forms of media such as journals and government documents. The options are endless, and the key is to do your homework and thereby become a more critical consumer.

REVIEW

The purposes of mass communication are to inform, entertain, provide instant information, and persuade.

Many theories have been proposed to explain mass communication. Early attempts were the direct effects and two-step flow theories. More recent theories have been agenda setting, cultivation, and uses and gratifications.

Finally, you may use several overlapping guidelines to improve your consumption of the media: evaluating the content of mediated messages by being mindful and aware of them. You should also conduct your own research when topics presented by the media will affect you personally. In other words, a critical consumer of messages evaluates those same messages for their appropriateness and effectiveness. Thus, as a critical consumer you will utilize the skills associated with competent communication.

The media will always be a dominant force in U.S. society. Everyone needs the media for information and entertainment, and yet no one wants to rely on misinformation. In order to combat the possible negative effects of mass communication, you must develop critical thinking skills about the media and their messages, thereby becoming a more critical consumer of information.

SUGGESTED READINGS

Alexander, A. (1993). Exploring media in everyday life. *Communication Monographs, 60*, 55–61.

Altheide, D. (1976). *Creating reality: How T.V. news distorts events.* Beverly Hills, CA: Sage.

Cantor, M., & Cantor, J. (1994). *Prime-time television.* Thousand Oaks, CA: Sage.

Fowles, J. (1994). *Why viewers watch.* Thousand Oaks, CA: Sage.

Gurvetch, M., & Kavoori, A. (1992). Television spectacles as politics. *Communication Monographs, 59,* 415–420.

Competence in Public Communication

In Part 4 we move into the public arena. Although the basic characteristics of communication and the manner in which the communication process works are the same here as they are in intimate dyads, communication in the public arena differs in several important ways from interpersonal and small-group communication.

The primary difference is that one partner takes sole responsibility for constructing the message. For convenience, we will refer to this person as "the speaker." In the case of mass media messages, this responsible partner may be a small group of people. Two other characteristics of public communication are that audiences are typically large and frequently anonymous. (That is, the person designing the message doesn't know the audience members personally.) Neither of these characteristics is as important as the nearly complete shift of responsibility (and therefore control) to one participant.

This is not to say that there is no negotiation of communication relationships in public communication. Competent communication relationships are negotiated and maintained in much the same way as are friendships, work relationships, and the like, but the negotiation is usually indirect, with any one audience member having a difficult time influencing the speaker. The speaker, however, designs his or her message with the intent of influencing as many audience members as possible. Influence here, as in other communication contexts, refers to the ability to get your

partners to do what you want them to do or feel the way you want them to feel. Thus, trying to entertain your audience is as much an influence attempt as is trying to get the audience to vote for you or buy your product.

Two Control Strategies: Staying Calm and Establishing Credibility

Before we talk explicitly about how relational negotiations take place in public communication episodes, we want to mention that individuals bring the same characteristics to these episodes as they do to social and business relationships. Your cognitive and behavioral predispositions are the same no matter what sort of episode you're involved in. You will plan your messages and process information in the same way, although you may be more conscious in your planning. For example, you will probably write a speech and practice it before making a public presentation. You also will probably monitor yourself more carefully in public situations than in social ones because you have less experience with public situations. But careful preparation and practice are also common when you are about to engage in *any* new, important communication episode. For example, before a job interview you will probably mentally rehearse how you will answer possible questions.

Two aspects of an individual's communication predispositions highlighted in this part of the book are communication apprehension and communicator credibility. These are characteristics of individuals, and they come into play in all communication episodes. Because they take on special importance in public episodes, they are dealt with in detail in this part, but *both* a low amount of apprehension and a reasonable amount of credibility are important in any competent relationship, be it intimate, social, or public.

Overly apprehensive people are unpredictable; you can't be sure what they will do. Specifically, you can't be sure that they can hold up their end of the interaction or that they will be able to get through their speech. Thus, they tend to make those around them apprehensive, too. You probably avoid people who are overly apprehensive when you can—and you don't enjoy being with them when you can't avoid them. It is difficult to have a competent relationship with a speaker who is overly apprehensive. Because the speaker appears to be focused on just getting his or her message out, you can't be sure he or she is paying appropriate attention to the audience—which means you as an audience member have little or no chance of influencing the speaker. This type of situation doesn't provide a very good basis for reciprocity, and it leads to an unsatisfying—and not very competent—relationship.

Similarly, credibility is an issue in all types of relationships. In those relationships in which you have first-hand knowledge of a person, you know how believable or trustworthy your partner is. Even interpersonal interactions with a stranger provide you with a direct opportunity to "feel out the other person" and decide how much you can trust him or her. But that sort of firsthand experience with another is not possible in public communication, especially when the messages are mediated. If you are an audience member, you are responsible for searching for and evaluating cues of the speaker's credibility. People in the public eye, such as politicians, spend a great deal of time, effort, and money cultivating an air of credibility. The press frequently sees itself as the public audience's agent in checking on the credibility of public figures.

When you are the speaker, you must take steps to encourage your audience to see you as a person who should be listened to (see Chapter 14). Typically, this means constructing your messages in such a way that your trustworthiness, dynamism, similarity to target others, and so on, are obvious to your audience. Your own ethical standards play a big role here. If your past public messages have conveyed that you can be trusted, that you check your facts, and that you respect other people, your audiences are more likely to see you as a credible communicator.

In terms of building a competent public relationship, this means that as a speaker communicating to your audience, you see audience members as credible, too. You do this by being realistic in your influence attempts, presenting yourself and your message in such a way that it does not compromise listeners' self-concepts (as you perceive them, at least), and structuring your message so that it is in tune with your audience's expectations and comprehension level. Audience analysis procedures discussed in Chapter 12 are designed to help you construct your messages appropriately and effectively.

It is difficult to think about a relationship with a speaker or audience you see once or only a few times, and then usually only at a distance. This is especially the case in mass communication, where there is very little contact—if any at all—between speaker and audience. But, as a speaker, you do develop at least a limited relationship with audience members. You attempt to exercise control in the relationship by influencing them in some way. You attempt to develop at least a moderately positive affiliation with your audience. You want them to like you. And you want them to adopt your definition of a collective goal and the tasks necessary to meet that goal.

Affiliation at a Distance

Affiliation is typically developed by being responsive to your audience, especially by being enthusiastic about your topic and expressing concern for your audience's needs and expectations. In other words, you express affiliation by showing an interest in audience members, just as you hope they do to you. (You will like your audience more if members communicate that they are interested in your message.) Speakers who are mildly apprehensive may be liked by some audience members who perceive the apprehensive speaker as similar to themselves, but overly apprehensive speakers make audience members uncomfortable with the speaker and with themselves. For example, they might feel powerless to help the speaker. Under these conditions, affiliation decreases.

Negotiation between speaker and audience is usually indirect and often spread out over a period of time. However, in public speaking situations where the audience is small or the speaker and audience are well known to each other, the negotiation can be very direct. In a competent speaker–audience relationship, the speaker is responsive to the audience's behaviors, both before the public communication event takes place (e.g., by learning what the audience already knows about a topic or what sort of entertainment it will like) and during the event (e.g., by changing the pace of the speech if audience members get restless or by responding to questions). If the speaker expects to talk before the same audience on more than one occasion, this sort of negotiation can take place over time and can include responses from the audience after the communication event is finished. For example, during a political campaign, after hearing a candidate's speech, audience members may call the candidate's campaign office to express their feelings about the issues raised, or they might write a letter to the editor of the local newspaper—thus attempting to influence both the candidate and other audience members.

Negotiation: Time and Space Constraints

Because people in public relationships frequently are separated by time and space, the negotiation of the relationship lacks the precision possible in face-to-face relationships. It is difficult for a speaker to know how representative an individual response is or how much adaptation the speaker should make. These difficulties are exaggerated when the messages are mediated. If you don't like a television program, how can you influence the program's producers? You could write a letter to your local television station or to the network that distributed the program; you could stop buying the products of the sponsors; or—the most common response—you could simply turn off the program. It takes some time for any of these negotiation attempts to have an impact on the "speaker," if they have any impact at all. And because there is the perception (usually real) of large physical distances between speaker and audience, there is less inclination to communicate directly with the speaker or for the speaker to respond.

Responsibility in the Public Relationship

Just as the speaker takes on most of the control in public communication episodes, so should the speaker take on most of the responsibility for en-suring that his or her relational partners—the audience members—are satisfied and feel the relationship is appropriate and effective. If the speaker fails to make the extra effort necessary to relate to the audience, the relationship will not be marked by competent communication. It will fail, like any other relationship characterized by an inappropriate distribution of control, an unsatisfactory level of affiliation, or a lack of agreement on the goals of the relationship.

In the following case study, consider how the speaker relates to his audience. Pay particular attention to the assumptions he makes about his audience's beliefs, expectations, and knowledge of his topic. Because the audience is small and knows the speaker relatively well, the matter of credibility is more complex than when the speaker and audience are more distant.

CASE STUDY 4

The Case of Scott's Speech

Scott Sterling had prepared his deliberative speech for weeks. He had researched the topic of undocumented workers in southern California by reading newspapers, magazines, and books in the library. He had interviewed a local landscaper and a local farmer who reportedly had each occasionally hired undocumented workers. Scott had also prepared visual aids appropriate to his speech and had outlined and rehearsed his points.

Scott used a number of quotations in his speech, using the words of others to show the class how different people felt about the workers. He thought he did a good job of representing all aspects of the issue.

After his speech, the professor conducted the usual discussion. One student, Rosalinda Flores, started yelling at Scott for saying there was a "Mexican problem" in the county. The professor and others in the class pointed out that Scott had been quoting the mayor of an adjacent city when he said that. "I don't care who said it," Rosalinda replied. "It's racist for anyone to

continued on next page

say that kind of thing, and it's irresponsible to perpetuate that kind of misinformation. Scott's a racist or he wouldn't have slipped it in so smoothly. That plants a seed of suspicion about all of us with Mexican ancestry. It's degrading."

Scott's friend Miguel Ortega came to his defense. "Scott's not racist," Miguel said. "I've played baseball with him for years, and many different ethnic groups have been represented on our teams. Scott's always been a friend to everyone, and I've never heard him utter a bigoted word. He's never acted racist in any way."

"I think we have a number of issues going on here," the professor intervened. "One is the content and quality of this speech, including Scott's word choice. Another is the integrity of the speaker. And yet another is interpretations by different audience members. Of course, what counts as racism is also an important issue. Let's discuss each of these issues in turn."

DISCUSSION QUESTIONS

1. Does Scott have a credibility problem? If so, on which dimension(s) of credibility? If a problem exists now, how might Scott have avoided it?
2. Is it unethical (racist, in this case) to quote someone else in the interest of giving a well-balanced presentation if the speaker believes that some audience members might consider the quotation negative? Should the speaker censor remarks or change the original words of a source so as not to offend anyone in the audience? Is it unethical to omit a potentially offensive or controversial opinion that would provide a balanced view of an issue?
3. Given an audience that is divided on a topic, is it possible for the speaker to have a competent relationship with the audience? How might such a relationship be described in terms of control, affiliation, and goals?
4. Can you, as a public speaker, reasonably expect your audience members to interpret your message the same way you do? If not, why not? What strategies can you use to help them understand your interpretation? If your speech is presented as informative rather than persuasive, is it appropriate to express your opinion?
5. What does count as racist communication? Is racism in the interpretations of the audience members or in the intentions or words of the speaker?
6. How can the speaker's desire to express a position on an issue be balanced with an audience member's desire not to have an offensive position expressed at all?

Notes

CHAPTER 1
COMMUNICATING COMPETENTLY

[1]F. E. X. Dance & C. Larson, (1976), *Functions of human communication: A theoretical approach*, New York: Holt, Rinehart & Winston.

[2]See M. von Cranach & I. Vine (1973), Introduction, *Social Communication and Movement*, New York: Academic Press, pp. 1–25.

[3]N. Coupland, J. M. Wiemann, & H. Giles (1991), Talk as "problem" and communication as "miscommunication." In N. Coupland, H. Giles, & J. M. Wiemann (Eds.), *"Miscommunication" and problematic talk*, Newbury Park, CA: Sage, pp. 1–17.

[4]J. K. Burgoon, D. B. Buller, & W. G. Woodall (1988), *Nonverbal communication: The unspoken dialogue*, New York: Harper & Row, p. 18. Also see R. P. Harrison (1974), *Beyond words: An introduction to nonverbal communication*, Englewood Cliffs, NJ: Prentice-Hall, pp. 65–67.

[5]A. Kendon (1983), Gesture and speech: How they interact. In J. M. Wiemann & R. P. Harrison (Eds.), *Nonverbal interaction*, Beverly Hills, CA: Sage, pp. 13–45.

[6]P. Ekman & W. V. Friesen (1975), *Unmasking the face*, Englewood Cliffs, NJ: Prentice-Hall.

[7]See J. M. Wiemann & J. J. Bradac (1989), Metatheoretical issues in the study of communication competence: Structural and functional approaches, *Progress in Communication Sciences*, 9, 261–284. The combination of several characteristics—symbolicity, intentionality, and shared code—was seen as a necessary condition for a behavior to be communicative.

[8]Ekman & Friesen (1975).

[9]R. Buck (1988), Emotional education and mass media: A new view of the global village. In R. P. Hawkins, J. M. Wiemann, & S. Pingree (Eds.), *Advancing communication science: Merging mass and interpersonal processes*, Beverly Hills, CA: Sage, pp. 44–76; G. Cronkhite (1986), On the focus, scope, and coherence of the study of human symbolic activity, *Quarterly Journal of Speech*, 3, 231–243; M. T. Motley (1990), On whether one can(not) communicate: An examination via traditional communication postulates, *Western Journal of Speech Communication*, 56, 1–20.

[10]E. Goffman (1967), *Interaction ritual: Essays on face-to-face behavior*, Garden City, NY: Doubleday.

[11]S. J. Ball-Rokeach & K. Reardon (1988), Monologue, dialogue, and telelog: Comparing an emergent form of communication with traditional forms. In Hawkins et al., *Advancing communication science*, pp. 135–161.

[12]S. Planalp, & J. M. Honeycutt (1985), Events that increase uncertainty in personal relationships, *Human Communication Research*, 11, 593–604.

[13]B. Whorf (1956), *Language, thought, and reality*, New York: Wiley.

[14]E. T. Hall (1959), *The silent language*, Greenwich, CT: Fawcett Publications; and E. T. Hall (1966), *The hidden dimension*, Garden City, NY: Doubleday.

[15]G. Philipsen (1975), Speaking like a man in Teamsterville: Cultural patterns of role enactment in an urban neighborhood, *Quarterly Journal of Speech*, 61, 13–22.

[16]Buck (1988). Also see Ekman & Friesen (1975).

[17]Ekman & Friesen (1975).

[18]P. Watzlawick, J. H. Beavin, & D. D. Jackson (1967), *Pragmatics of human communication*, New York: Norton.

[19]See R. P. Hart & D. M. Burks (1972), Rhetorical sensitivity and social interaction, *Communication Monographs*, 39, 75–91. Also see J. M. Wiemann & J. A. Daly (1994), On getting your own way. In J. A. Daly & J. M. Wiemann (Eds.), *Strategic interpersonal communication*, Hillsdale, NJ: Lawrence Erlbaum, pp. vii–xiv.

[20]See J. M. Wiemann & D. L. Krueger (1980), The language of relationships. In H. Giles, W. P. Robinson, & P. M. Smith (Eds.), *Language: Social psychological perspectives*, Oxford, England: Pergamon, pp. 55–62.

[21]Dance and Larson (1976) used the term *ubiquitous* to refer to a slightly different set of functions. Their thinking about how every message inevitably accomplishes specific things—for example, control—has greatly influenced our analysis of communication from a functional perspective. Similarly, Watzlawick et al.'s (1967) discussion of meta-communication implies that messages have ubiquitous relational-level functions that communicators cannot ignore.

[22]L. E. Rogers & R. V. Farace (1975), An analysis of relational communication in dyads: New measurement procedures, *Human Communication Research*, 1, 222–239.

[23]J. A. Daly & J. C. McCroskey (Eds.) (1984), *Avoiding communication: Shyness, reticence, and communication apprehension*, Newbury Park, CA: Sage.

[24]D. J. Cegala (1981), Interaction involvement: A cognitive dimension of communicative competence, *Communication Education*, 30, 109–121.

[25]There is more to empathy than this. The concept can be broken down in several ways. For example, you can *know* how the other person feels (cognitive role taking), which can be differentiated from *feeling* as the other person feels. See G. R. Miller & M. Steinberg (1975), *Between people: A new analysis of interpersonal communication*, Chicago: Science Research Associates. For our purposes, the more general definition of empathy is the most useful.

[26]A widely accepted definition of communication apprehension is "an individual's level of fear or anxiety associated with either real or anticipated communication with another person or persons." See J. C. McCroskey (1984), A communication apprehension perspective, in Daly & McCroskey (Eds.), *Avoiding communication*, p. 13.

27Miller & Steinberg's (1975) discussion of interpersonal communication has influenced our thinking about these levels of analysis.

28J. J. Lynch (1985), *The language of the heart: The body's response to human dialogue*, New York: Basic Books.

29J. M. Wiemann (1977), Explication and test of a model of communicative competence, *Human Communication Research*, 3, 195–213. Also see B. Spitzberg & W. Cupach (1984), *Interpersonal communication competence*, Newbury Park, CA: Sage.

30B. O'Keefe & S. A. McCormack (1987), Message design logic and message goal structure: Effects on perceptions of message quality in regulative communication situations, *Human Communication Research*, 14, 68–85. Also see D. J. Canary, M. J. Cody, & S. Smith (1994), Compliance-gaining goals: An inductive analysis of actors' goal types, strategies, and successes. In Daly & Wiemann, *Strategic interpersonal communication*, Hillsdale, NJ: Lawrence Erlbaum, pp. 33–90.

31Spitzberg & Cupach (1984).

32H. Blumer (1969), *Symbolic interactionism: Perspective and method*, Englewood Cliffs, NJ: Prentice-Hall.

33W. B. Gudykunst & Y. Y. Kim (1984), *Communicating with strangers*, Reading, MA: Addison-Wesley; S. P. Banks, G. Ge, & J. Baker (1991), Intercultural encounters and miscommunication. In Coupland, Giles, & Wiemann (Eds.), "*Miscommunication*" *and problematic talk*, pp. 103–120.

34See D. Cushman & D. Cahn (1984), *Communication in interpersonal relationships*, Albany, NY: SUNY Press.

35Ibid.

36R. Anderson & V. Ross (1994), *Questions of communication: A practical introduction to theory*, New York: St. Martin's Press, Chapter 10.

37J. G. Delia, B. J. O'Keefe, & D. J. O'Keefe (1982), The constructivist approach to communication. In F. E. X. Dance (Ed.), *Human communication theory*, New York: Harper & Row, pp. 147–191.

38R. Norton (1983), *Communicator style: Theory applications and measures*, Newbury Park, CA: Sage.

CHAPTER 2
PROCESSING COMMUNICATION

1C. E. Cohen (1981), Goals and schemata in person perception: Making sense from the stream of behavior. In N. Cantor & J. F. Kihlstrom (Eds.), *Personality, cognition, and social interaction*, Hillsdale, NJ: Lawrence Erlbaum.

2S. E. Taylor & J. Crocker (1981), Schematic basis of social information processing. In E. T. Higgins, C. Herman, & M. Zanna (Eds.), *Social cognition: The Ontario Symposium on Personality and Social Psychology*, Hillsdale, NJ: Lawrence Erlbaum.

3U. Neisser (1976), *Cognition and reality: Principles and implications of cognitive psychology*, San Francisco: W. H. Freeman.

4M. J. Smith (1982), Cognitive schema theory and the perseverance and attenuation of unwarranted empirical beliefs, *Communication Monographs*, 49, 115–126.

5M. E. Roloff (1980), Self-awareness and the persuasion process: Do we really know what we are doing? In M. Roloff & G. Miller (Eds.), *Persuasion: New directions in theory and research*, Newbury Park, CA: Sage.

6J. H. Hilton & J. D. Darley (1991), The effects of interaction goals on person perception. In M. P. Zanna (1991), *Advances in experimental social psychology*, Vol. 24, San Diego: Academic Press; Harcourt Brace Jovanovich, pp. 236–262.

7J. Burgoon & J. Walther (1990), Nonverbal expectations and the evaluative consequences of violations, *Human Communication Research*, 17, 232–265.

8K. Kellerman (1986), Anticipation of future interaction and information exchange in initial interactions, *Human Communication Research*, 13, 41–75.

9Burgoon & Walther (1990).

10E. E. Jones (1990), *Interpersonal perception*, New York: W. H. Freeman.

11E. Loftus (1980), *Memory*, Reading, MA: Addison-Wesley.

12H. M. Schroder, M. J. Driver, & S. Streufert (1969), *Human information processing: Individuals and groups functioning in complex social situations*, New York: Holt, Rinehart & Winston.

13R. Farace, P. Monge, & H. Russell (1977), *Communication and organizing*, New York: Random House, p. 100.

14R. L. Daft & R. H. Lengel (1986), Organizational information requirements, media richness, and structural design, *Management Science*, 32, 554–571.

15R. L. Daft & R. H. Lengel (1984), Information richness: A new approach to managerial behavior and organization design, *Research in Organizational Behavior*, 6, 191–233.

16L. K. Trevino, R. L. Daft, & R. H. Lengel (1990), Understanding managers' media choices: A symbolic interactionist perspective. In J. Fulk & C. Steinfield (Eds.), *Organizations and Communication Technology*, Newbury Park, CA: Sage, pp. 71–94.

17M. Cassady (1992), An international perspective of the United States, *Bulletin of the Association for Business Communication*, 55, 20–26.

18Y. Y. Kim (1988), *Communication and cross-cultural adaptation*, Philadelphia: Multilingual Matters Ltd.

19M. Loden & J. B. Rosener (1991), *Workforce America! Managing employee diversity as a vital resource*, Chicago: Business One Irwin, pp. 196–197.

20Ibid.

21R. Wiseman, M. Hammer, & H. Nishida (1989), Predictors of intercultural communication competence, *International Journal of International Relations*, 13, 349–370.

22R. K. Merton (1957), *Social theory and social structure*, New York: Free Press.

23Adapted from M. Brewer & N. Miller (1988), Contact and cooperation. In P. Katz & D. Taylor (Eds.), *Eliminating racism*, New York: Plenum.

24C. R. Berger & J. J. Jordan (1992), Planning sources, planning difficulty and verbal fluency, *Communication Monographs*, 59, 130–149.

CHAPTER 3
THE SELF AND COMMUNICATION

1M. Snyder (1979), Self monitoring processes. In L. Berkowitz (Ed.), *Advances in social psychology*, Vol. 12, New York: Academic Press, pp. 86–128.

2S. E. Cross & H. R. Markus (1990), The willful self, *Personality and Social Psychology Bulletin*, 16, 726–742; H. Markus (1983), Self-knowledge: An expanded view, *Journal of Personality*, 51, 543–565.

[3]J. C. McCroskey (1984), The communication apprehension perspective. In J. A. Daly & J. C. McCroskey (Eds.), *Avoiding communication: Shyness, reticence, and communication apprehension*, Beverly Hills, CA: Sage, pp. 13–38.

[4]D. Cegala (1981), Interaction involvement: A cognitive dimension of communicative competence, *Communication Education, 30*, 109–121.

[5]R. Edwards (1990), Sensitivity to feedback and the development of self, *Communication Quarterly, 38*, 101–111.

[6]Studies summarized by ibid.

[7]Ibid.

[8]H. Markus (1977), Self-schemata and processing information about the self, *Journal of Personality and Social Psychology, 35*, 64.

[9]C. Berger (1987), Self-conception and social information processing. In J. McCroskey & J. Daly (Eds.), *Personality and interpersonal communication*, Beverly Hills, CA: Sage, pp. 275–304.

[10]Markus (1983).

[11]Berger (1987).

[12]Ibid.

[13]Markus (1983), p. 554.

[14]H. Markus & P. Nurius (1986), Possible selves, *American Psychologist, 41*, 954–969.

[15]Ibid.

[16]J. D. Campbell (1990), Self-esteem and clarity of the self-concept, *Journal of Personality and Social Psychology, 59*, 538–549.

[17]Ibid.

[18]B. R. Schlenker, M. F. Weigold & J. R. Hallam (1990), Self-serving attributions in social context: Effects of self-esteem and social pressure, *Journal of Personality and Social Psychology, 58*, 855–863.

[19]Research summarized by ibid.

[20]Baumgardner (1990), To know oneself is to like oneself, *Journal of Personality and Social Psychology, 58*, 1062–1072.

[21]Ibid.

[22]Ibid.

[23]A. Bandura (1982), Self-efficacy mechanism in human agency, *American Psychologist, 37*, 122.

[24]D. J. Canary & M. J. Cody (1993), *Interpersonal communication: A goals-based approach*, New York: St. Martin's Press.

[25]E. J. Langer (1989), Minding matters: The consequences of mindlessness/mindfulness. In L. Berkowitz (Ed.), *Advances in experimental social psychology*, New York: Academic Press.

[26]E. E. Jones, F. Rhodewalt, S. Berglas, & J. A. Skelton (1981), Effects of strategic self-presentation on subsequent self-esteem, *Journal of Personality and Social Psychology, 41*, 407–421.

[27]Schlenker et al. (1990).

[28]Snyder (1979), p. 89.

[29]Ibid., p. 94.

[30]L. R. Wheeless & J. Grotz (1976), Conceptualization and measurement of reported self-disclosure, *Human Communication Research, 2*, 338–346.

[31]L. R. Wheeless (1978), A follow-up study of the relationships among trust, disclosure, and interpersonal solidarity, *Human Communication Research, 4*, 143–157.

[32]S. M. Jourard & M. J. Landsman (1960), Cognition, cathexis, and the dyadic effect in men's self-disclosing behavior, *Merrill-Palmer Quarterly, 6*, 178–186.

[33]S. M. Jourard (1959), Self-disclosure and other-cathexis, *Journal of Abnormal and Social Psychology, 59*, 428–431.

[34]A. L. Chaikin & V. J. Derlega (1974), Liking for the norm-breaker in self-discloser, *Journal of Personality, 42*, 117–129; D. I. Slobin, S. H. Miller, & L. W. Porter (1968), Forms of address and social relations in a business organization, *Journal of Personality and Social Psychology, 8*, 289–293.

[35]W. B. Pearce & S. M. Sharp (1973), Self-disclosing communication, *Journal of Communication, 23*, 409–425.

[36]L. D. Steinberg (1989), Pubertal maturation and family relations: Evidence for the distancing hypothesis. In G. R. Adams, R. Montemayor, & T. Gullotta (Eds.), *Advances in adolescent development*, Vol. 1, Beverly Hills, CA: Sage, pp. 71–97.

[37]D. R. Papini, F. F. Farmer, S. M. Clark, J. C. Micka, & J. K. Barnett (1990), Early adolescent age and gender differences in patterns of emotional self-disclosure to parents and friends, *Adolescence, 25*, 959–976.

[38]Ibid.

[39]Ibid.

[40]Wheeless (1978).

[41]M. Zuckerman (1979), *Sensation seeking: Beyond the optimal level of arousal*, Hillsdale, NJ: Lawrence Erlbaum.

[42]R. E. Franken, K. J. Gibson, & P. Mohan (1990), Sensation seeking and disclosure to close and casual friends, *Personal Individual Differences, 11*, 829–832.

[43]L. C. Miller, L. L. Cooke, J. Tsang, & F. Morgan (1992), Should I brag? Nature and impact of positive boastful disclosures for women and men, *Human Communication Research, 18*, 364–399.

[44]S. J. Gilbert & D. Horstein (1975), The communication of self-disclosure: Level versus valence, *Human Communication Research, 1*, 316–322.

[45]Miller et al. (1992).

[46]E. M. O'Connor & C. M. Simms (1990), Self-revelation as manipulation: The effects of sex and Machiavellianism on self-disclosure, *Social Behavior and Personality, 18*, 95–100.

[47]Papini et al. (1990).

[48]A. Howell & M. Conway (1990), Perceived intimacy of expressed emotion, *The Journal of Social Psychology, 130*, 467–476.

[49]S. Sommers (1984), Reported emotions and conventions of emotionality among college students, *Journal of Personality and Social Psychology, 46*, 207–215.

[50]Howell & Conway (1990).

[51]P. Himelstein & B. Lubin (1965), Attempted validation of the self-disclosure inventory by the peer nomination technique, *Journal of Psychology, 61*, 13–16; E. LeVina & J. N. Franco (1981), A reassessment of self-disclosure patterns among Anglo-Americans and Hispanics, *Journal of Counseling Psychology, 28*, 522–524; S. Petronio, J. Martin, & R. Littlefield (1984), Prerequisite conditions for self-disclosing: A gender issue, *Human Communication Research, 51*, 268–273.

[52]P. R. McCarthy & N. E. Betz (1978), Differential effects of self-disclosing versus self-involving counselor statements, *Journal of Counseling Psychology, 25*, 251–256; J. D. Balswick & J. W. Blakwell (1977), Self-disclosure to same- and opposite-sex parents: An empirical test of insights from role theory, *Sociometery, 40*, 282–286; F. W. Vondracek & M. K. Marshall (1971), Self-disclosure

and interpersonal trust: An exploratory study, *Psychological Reports*, 28, 235–240.

53Jourard & Landsman (1960).

54L. B. Rosenfeld (1979), Self-disclosure avoidance: Why am I afraid to tell you who I am? *Communication Monographs*, 46, 63–74.

55W. E. Snell, Jr., R. S. Miller, S. S. Belk, R. Garcia-Falconi, & J. E. Hernandez-Sanchez (1989), Men's and women's emotional disclosures: The impact of disclosure recipient, culture, and the masculine role, *Sex Roles*, 21, 467–486.

56H. M. Hacker (1981), Blabbermouth and claims: Sex differences in disclosure in same-sex and cross-sex friendship dyads, *Psychology of Women Quarterly*, 5, 385–401.

57Summarized by Schlenker et al. (1990).

58Ibid.

59E. E. Jones (1989), The framing of competence, *Personality and Social Psychology Bulletin*, 15, 477–492.

60J. T. Tedeschi & N. Norman (1985), Social power, self-presentation, and the self. In B. Schlenker (Ed.), *The self and social life*, New York: McGraw-Hill, pp. 293–322.

61D. G. Larson & R. L. Chastain (1990), Self-concealment: Conceptualization, measurement, and health implications, *Journal of Social and Clinical Psychology*, 9, 440.

62J. W. Pennebaker (1985), Traumatic experience and psychosomatic disease: Exploring the roles of behavioral inhibition, obsession, and confiding, *Canadian Psychology*, 26, 82.

63Larson & Chastain (1990).

64Edwards (1990).

65Ibid.

66Ibid.

67P. D. Sweeny & L. E. Wells (1990), Reactions to feedback about performance: A test of three competing models, *Journal of Applied Social Psychology*, 20, 818–834.

68Ibid.

69J. S. Shrauger (1975), Responses to evaluation as a function of initial self-perceptions, *Psychological Bulletin*, 82, 581–596.

10K. Nelson (1978), *Early speech in its communicative context*. In F. Minific & L. Lloyd (Eds.), *Communicative and cognitive abilities: Early behavioral assessment*, Baltimore: University Park Press.

11C. K. Ogden & I. A. Richards (1923), *The message of meaning*, New York: Harcourt Brace Jovanovich, p. 11.

12S. I. Hayakawa (1964), *Language in thought and action*, New York: Harcourt Brace Jovanovich.

13From E. Sapir and B. Whorf (1956), The relation of habitual thought and behavior to language. In J. B. Carrol (Ed.), *Language, thought and reality*, Cambridge, MA: MIT Press.

14W. B. Gudykunst (1991), *Bridging differences: Effective intergroup communication*, Newbury Park, CA: Sage.

15A. Haas & M. A. Sherman (1982), Reported topics of conversation among same-sex adults, *Communication Quarterly*, 30, 332–342.

16H. Giles & R. L. Street, Jr. (1985), Communication characteristics and behavior. In M. L. Knapp & G. R. Miller (Eds.), *Handbook of interpersonal communication*, Beverly Hills, CA: Sage, pp. 205–261.

17A. J. Mulac, J. M. Wiemann, S. J. Widenmann, & T. W. Gibson (1988), Male-female language differences and effects in same-sex and mixed-sex dyads: The gender-linked language effect, *Communication Monographs*, 55, 315–335.

18K. Fiedler, G. Semin, & C. Finkenauer (1993), The battle of words between gender groups: A language-based approach to intergroup processes, *Human Communication Research*, 19(3), 409–441.

19J. Harwood, H. Giles, S. Fox, E. B. Ryan, & G. Williams (1993), Patronizing young and elderly adults: Response strategies in a community setting, *Journal of Applied Communication Research*, 21(3), 211–226.

20J. J. Bradac (1983), The language of lovers, flovers and friends: Communicating in social and personal relationships. In W. P. Robinson (Ed.), *Journal of Language and Social Psychology*, 2(2, 3, 4).

21M. L. Knapp (1978), *Social intercourse: From greeting to goodbye*, Boston: Allyn & Bacon.

CHAPTER 4
LANGUAGE AND COMMUNICATION

1J. Piaget (1962), *Play, dreams and imitation in childhood*, New York: W. W. Norton.

2B. Wood (1982), *Children and communication: Verbal and nonverbal language development* (2nd ed.), Englewood Cliffs, NJ: Prentice-Hall.

3For an excellent summary of animal language studies and language-deprived children, see the Verbal Communication chapter (pp. 32–64) of M. L. DeFleur, P. Kearney, & T. G. Plax (1993), *Fundamentals of human communication*, Mountain View, CA: Mayfield Publishing Co.

4N. Chomsky (1957), *Syntactic structures*, The Hague: Mouton, p. 17.

5B. F. Skinner (1953), *Science and human behavior*, New York: Macmillan.

6E. Bates (1979), *The emergence of symbols: Cognition and communication in infancy*, New York: Academic Press.

7Ibid., p. 6.

8Ibid., p. 103.

9Wood (1982), p. 288.

CHAPTER 5
NONVERBAL COMMUNICATION

1M. L. Knapp & A. L. Vangelisti (1992), *Interpersonal communication and human relationships*, Boston: Allyn & Bacon.

2J. K. Burgoon, D. A. Newton, J. B. Walther, & E. J. Baesler (1989), Nonverbal expectancy violations and conversational involvement, *Journal of Nonverbal Behavior*, 13(2), 97–119.

3G. H. Graham, J. Unrah, & P. Jennings (1991), The impact of nonverbal communication in organizations: A survey of perceptions, *Journal of Business Communication*, 28, 45–62.

4I. Eibl-Eibesfeldt (1973), *Social communication and movement*, New York: Academic Press.

5P. Ekman & W. V. Friesen (1971), Constants across cultures in the face and emotion, *Journal of Personality and Social Psychology*, 17, 124–129.

6G. Michael & F. N. Willis (1968), The development of gestures as a function of social class, education, and sex, *Psychological Record*, 18, 515–519.

[7]L. Kumin & M. Lazar (1974), Gestural communication in preschool children, *Perceptual and Motor Skills, 38,* 708–710.

[8]C. Golomb (1972), Evolution of the human figure in a three-dimensional medium, *Journal of Educational Psychology, 6,* 385–391.

[9]R. M. Lerner & C. Schroeder (1971), Physique identification, preference, and aversion in kindergarten children, *Developmental Psychology, 11,* 538.

[10]S. Jones & J. Aiello (1973), Proxemic behavior of black and white first-, third-, and fifth-grade children, *Journal of Personality and Social Psychology, 25,* 21–27.

[11]D. K. Fromme, W. E. Jaynes, D. K. Taylor, E. G. Hanold, J. Daniell, J. R. Rountree, & M. L. Fromme (1989), Nonverbal behavior and attitudes toward touch, *Journal of Nonverbal Behavior, 13(1),* 3–14.

[12]V. P. Richmond, J. C. McCroskey, & S. K. Payne (1991), *Nonverbal behavior in interpersonal relations,* Englewood Cliffs, NJ: Prentice-Hall.

[13]M. G. Efran (1974), The effect of physical appearance on the judgement of guilt, interpersonal attraction, and severity of recommended punishment in a simulated jury task, *Journal of Research in Personality, 8,* 45–54.

[14]J. T. Molloy (1983), *Molloy's live for success,* New York: Bantam Books.

[15]E. H. Walster, E. Aronson, D. Abrahams, & L. Rohmann (1966), Importance of physical attractiveness in dating behavior, *Journal of Personality and Social Psychology, 4,* 508–516.

[16]D. Morris (1985), *Bodywatching,* New York: Crown.

[17]R. Sybers & M. E. Roach (1962), Clothing and human behavior, *Journal of Home Economics, 54,* 184–187.

[18]J. P. Davidson (1988), Shaping an image that boosts your career, *Marketing Communication, 13,* 55–56.

[19]Richmond et al. (1991), pp. 44–45.

[20]Sybers & Roach (1962).

[21]L. R. Aiken (1963), The relationship of dress to selected measures of personality in undergraduate women, *Journal of Social Psychology, 59,* 119–128.

[22]L. B. Rosenfeld & T. G. Plax (1977), Clothing as communication, *Journal of Communication, 27,* 24–31.

[23]P. Ekman & W. Friesen (1969), The repertoire of nonverbal behavior: Categories, origins, usage, and coding, *Semiotica, 1,* 49–98.

[24]B. Goss & D. O'Hair (1988), *Communicating in interpersonal relationships,* New York: Macmillan.

[25]A. Mehrabian (1981), *Silent messages: Implicit communication of emotions and attitudes,* Belmont, CA: Wadsworth.

[26]A. E. Scheflen (1964), The significance of posture in communication systems, *Psychiatry, 27,* 316–331.

[27]Richmond et al. (1991), pp. 64–65.

[28]R. Norton (1983), *Communicator style: Theory, applications, and measures,* Beverly Hills, CA: Sage.

[29]P. Ekman, W. Friesen, & R. Ellsworth (1972), *Emotion in the human face: Guidelines for research and an integration of findings,* New York: Pergamon.

[30]J. Boucher & P. Ekman (1975), Facial areas of emotional information, *Journal of Communication, 25,* 21–29.

[31]Ekman & Friesen (1971).

[32]Richmond et al. (1991), p. 81.

[33]P. Ekman & W. V. Friesen (1975), *Unmasking the face: A guide to recognizing emotions from facial cues,* Englewood Cliffs, NJ: Prentice-Hall.

[34]Gallagher (Performer), M. Fowlkes, & J. Simon (Producers) (1983), *Gallagher: The maddest* [Videotape], Hollywood: Wizard of Odd & Paramount Home Videos.

[35]Ekman & Friesen (1975).

[36]D. Leathers (1986), *Successful nonverbal communication: Principles and applications,* New York: Macmillan.

[37]M. L. Knapp & J. A. Hall (1992), *Nonverbal communication in human interaction,* Fort Worth, TX: Holt, Rinehart & Winston; D. W. Addington (1968), The relationship of selected vocal characteristics to personality perception, *Speech Monographs, 35,* 492–503.

[38]G. L. Trager (1958), Paralanguage: A first approximation, *Studies in Linguistics, 13,* 1–12.

[39]Goss & O'Hair (1988).

[40]H. Giles & R. L. Street, Jr. (1985), *Handbook of interpersonal communication,* Beverly Hills, CA: Sage; W. B. Putman & R. L. Street (1984), Implications for speech accommodation theory, *International Journal of the Sociology of Language, 46,* 97–114; and J. Jaffe & S. Feldstein (1970), *Rhythms of dialogue,* New York: Academic Press.

[41]R. Heslin (1974), Steps toward a taxonomy of touching. Paper presented at the Western Psychological Association Convention, Chicago.

[42]D. Morris (1977), *Manwatching,* New York: Abrams.

[43]Knapp & Hall (1992), p. 234.

[44]J. F. Anderson, P. A. Anderson, & M. W. Lustig (1987), Opposite sex touch avoidance: A national replication and extension, *Journal of Nonverbal Behavior, 11,* 89–109; J. F. Deethardt & D. G. Hines (1983), Tactile communication and personality differences, *Journal of Nonverbal Behavior, 8,* 143–156.

[45]E. Hall (1959), *The silent language,* New York: Doubleday.

[46]R. G. Harper, A. N. Wiens, & J. D. Matarazzo (1978), *Nonverbal communication: The state of the art,* New York: Wiley.

[47]L. A. Malandro & L. Barker (1983), *Nonverbal communication,* New York: Random House.

[48]Goss & O'Hair (1988).

[49]M. Riess & P. Rosenfeld (1980), Seating preferences as nonverbal communication: A self-presentational analysis, *Journal of Applied Communications Research, 8,* 22–28.

[50]Richmond et al. (1991), pp. 190–191.

[51]J. K. Burgoon, D. B. Buller, & W. G. Woodall (1989), *Nonverbal communication: The unspoken dialogue,* New York: Harper & Row.

[52]Richmond et al. (1991), p. 195.

[53]Hall (1959).

[54]Ibid.

[55]Richmond et al. (1991), pp. 184–185.

[56]Ibid.

[57]P. Ekman (1965), Communication through nonverbal behavior: A source of information about an interpersonal relationship. In S. S. Tomkins & C. E. Izard (Eds.), *Affect, cognition, and personality,* New York: Springer.

[58]R. E. Axtell (1991), *Gestures: The do's and taboos of body language around the world,* New York: Wiley.

[59]Richmond et al. (1991), pp. 202–203.

[60]Burgoon et al. (1989).

[61]A. Mehrabian (1972), *Nonverbal communication,* Chicago: Aldine-Atherton.

[62]Burgoon et al. (1989).

[63]Goss & O'Hair (1988).

64J. C. Pearson, L. H. Turner, & W. Todd-Mancillas (1985), *Gender and communication*, Dubuque, IA: Wm. C. Brown.

65E. Goffman (1971), *Relations in public: Microstudies of the public order*, New York: Basic Books.

66A. Kendon & A. Ferber (1971), A description of some human greetings. In R.P.M. Michael & J. H. Crook (Eds.), *Comparative ecology and behavior of primates*, New York: Academic Press.

67Burgoon et al. (1989).

68Ibid.

69Ibid.

70V. O'Donnell & J. Kable (1982), *Persuasion: An interactive dependency approach*, New York: Random House.

71Burgoon et al. (1989).

72J. Burgoon, T. Birk, & M. Pfau (1994), Nonverbal behaviors, persuasion, and credibility, *Human Communication Research, 17*, 140–169.

73See D. O'Hair & M. Cody, Interpersonal deception, *The dark side of interpersonal communication*, Hillsdale, NJ: Lawrence Erlbaum.

74Ibid.

75Goss & O'Hair (1988).

76Burgoon et al. (1989).

77Goss & O'Hair (1988).

78D. O'Hair, M. Cody, & M. McLaughlin (1981), Prepared lies, spontaneous lies, Machiavellianism, and nonverbal communication, *Human Communication Research, 7*, 325–339.

79Burgoon et al. (1989).

80C. R. Berger & J. J. Bradac (1982), *Language and social knowledge: Uncertainty in interpersonal relations*, London: Arnold.

81Richmond et al. (1991), pp. 34–35.

82Knapp & Hall (1992), pp. 456–458.

CHAPTER 6
DEVELOPING LISTENING SKILLS

1J. E. Goldman, in L. K. Steil, J. Summerfield, & G. de Mare (1983), *Listening: It can change your life*, New York: Wiley, pp. 148–149.

2M. T. Perras & A. R. Weitzel (1981), Measuring daily communication activities, *The Florida Speech Communication Journal, 9*, 19–23; C. G. Coakley & A. D. Wolvin (1990), Listening pedagogy and andragogy: The state of the art, *Journal of the International Listening Association, 4*, 33–61.

3J. Brownell (1987), Perceptions of good listeners: A management study, in *Proceedings of the Association for Business Communication International Convention*, Atlanta.

4Steil et al. (1983), p. 177.

5J. Stewart (1986), *Bridges, not walls* (4th ed.), New York: Random House, p. 181.

6A. Wolvin & C. G. Coakley (1988), *Listening* (3rd ed.), Dubuque, IA: W. C. Brown.

7Steil et al. (1983), p. 22.

8Wolvin & Coakley (1988); L. K. Steil, L. L. Barker, & K. W. Watson (1983), *Effective listening: Key to success*, Reading, MA: Addison-Wesley; F. I. Wolff, N. C. Marsnik, W. S. Tacey, & R. G. Nichols (1983), *Perceptive listening*, New York: Holt, Rinehart, & Winston.

9R. Norton (1983), *Communicator style*, Beverly Hills, CA: Sage.

10L. Gambrell & R. Bales (1987), Visual imagery: A strategy for enhancing listening, reading, and writing, *Australian Journal of Reading, 10*, 146–153.

CHAPTER 7
DEVELOPING AND MAINTAINING RELATIONSHIPS

1S. Planalp (1985), Relational schemata: A test of alternative forms of relational knowledge as guides to communication, *Human Communication Research, 12*(1), 3–29.

2R. A. Bell (1985), Conversational involvement and loneliness, *Communication Monographs, 52*, 218–235.

3I. Altman & D. Taylor (1973), *Social penetration theory*, New York: Holt, Rinehart & Winston.

4J. Rempel, J. Holmes, & M. Zanna (1985), Trust in close relationships, *Journal of Personality and Social Psychology, 49*, 95–112.

5C. Berger & R. Calabrese (1975), Some explorations in initial interaction and beyond: Toward a developmental theory of interpersonal communication, *Human Communication Research, 1*, 100.

6W. Douglas (1987), Affinity-testing in initial interactions, *Journal of Social and Personal Relationships, 4*, 3–15.

7L. Baxter & W. Wilmot (1984), Secret tests: Social strategies for acquiring information about the state of the relationship, *Human Communication Research, 11*, 171–201.

8This model is based on the following research: G. Miller & M. Steinberg (1975), *Between people*, Palo Alto, CA: Science Research Associates; Altman & Taylor (1973); M. L. Knapp & A. L. Vangelisti (1992), *Interpersonal communication and human relationships* (2nd ed.), Boston: Allyn & Bacon.

9W. Wilmot (1981), Relationship stages: Initiation and stabilization. In J. Civikly (Ed.), *Contexts of communication*, New York: Holt, Rinehart & Winston.

10Knapp & Vangelisti (1992).

11E. Goffman (1971), *Relations in public*, New York: Harper & Row.

12Knapp & Vangelisti (1992).

13R. J. Sternberg (1986), A triangular theory of love, *Psychological Review, 93*, 119–135.

14J. A. Lee (1973), *The colors of love: An exploration of the ways of loving*, Don Mills, Ontario: New Press; S. S. Hendrick & C. Hendrick (1992), *Liking, loving, and relating*, Pacific Grove, CA: Brooks/Cole Publishing Co.

15B. Goss & D. O'Hair (1988), *Communicating in interpersonal relationships*, New York: Macmillan.

16S. Planalp & J. Honeycutt (1985), Events that increase uncertainty in personal relationships, *Human Communication Research, 11*, 593–604.

17DeVito, J. A. (1992), *The interpersonal communication book* (6th ed.), New York: HarperCollins.

18C. Hill, Z. Rubion, & L. A. Peplau (1976), Breakups before marriage: The end of 103 affairs, *Journal of Social Issues, 32*, 147–168.

19P. Blumstein & P. Schwartz (1983), *American couples: Money, work, sex*, New York: Morrow.

20Ibid.

21S. W. Duck (1984), A perspective on the repair of personal relationships: Repair of what, when? In S. W. Duck (Ed.), *Personal relationships 5: Repairing personal relationships*, New York: Macmillan.

[22]M. S. Davis (1973), *Intimate relations*, New York: Free Press, pp. 245–283.

[23]J. H. Harvey, T. L. Orbuch, & A. L. Weber (1990), A social psychological model of account-making in response to severe stress, *Journal of Language and Social Psychology*, 9, 191–207; J. H. Harvey, G. Agostinelli, & A. L. Weber (1989), Account-making and the formation of expectations about close relationships, in C. Hendrick (Ed.), *Close relationships*, Newbury Park, CA: Sage; J. H. Harvey, A. L. Weber, K. S. Galvin, H. C. Huszti, & N. N. Garnick (1986), Attribution in the termination of close relationships: A special focus on the account, in R. Gilmour & S. W. Duck (Eds.), *The emerging field of personal relationships*, Hillsdale, NJ: Lawrence Erlbaum; J. H. Harvey, A. L. Weber, & T. L. Orbuch (1990), *Interpersonal accounts: A social psychological perspective*, Cambridge, MA: Basil Blackwell.

[24]J. C. Pearson & B. H. Spitzberg (1990), *Interpersonal communication: Concepts, components, and contexts* (2nd ed.), Dubuque, IA: Wm. C. Brown.

[25]M. Parlee (1979), The friendship bond, *Psychology Today*, 13(10), 43–54, 113.

[26]J. Reisman (1979), *Anatomy of friendship*, Lexington, MA: Lewis Publishers.

[27]G. D. Nass & G. W. McDonald (1982), *Marriage and the family*, New York: Random House.

[28]S. Trenholm & A. Jensen (1988), *Interpersonal communication*, Belmont, CA: Wadsworth Publishing Co.

CHAPTER 8
MANAGING CONFLICT IN INTERPERSONAL RELATIONSHIPS

[1]J. L. Hocker & W. Wilmot (1985), *Interpersonal conflict* (2nd ed.), Dubuque, IA: Wm. C. Brown.

[2]S. Ting-Toomey (1985), Toward a theory of conflict and culture. In W. B. Gudykunst, L. Stewart, & S. Ting-Toomey (Eds.), *Communication, culture, and organizational processes*, Beverly Hills, CA: Sage.

[3]D. Infante & C. Wigely (1986), Verbal aggressiveness: An interpersonal model and measure, *Communication Monographs*, 53, 61–69.

[4]J. C. McCroskey (1977), Oral communication apprehension: A summary of recent theory and research, *Human Communication Research*, 4, 78–96.

[5]J. Hall (1986), *Conflict management survey: A survey of one's characteristic reaction to and handling of conflicts between himself and others*, Conroe, TX: Teleometrics.

[6]K. W. Thomas & R. H. Kilmann (1974), *Thomas-Kilmann Conflict MODE Instrument*, Tuxedo, NY: Xiacom.

[7]These strategies summarize and categorize the many conflict strategies and tactics reported by others.

[8]D. J. Canary & B. H. Spitzberg (1989), A model of the perceived competence of conflict strategies, *Human Communication Research*, 15(4), 630–649.

[9]D. J. Canary, E. M. Cunningham, & M. J. Cody (1988), Goal types, gender and locus of control in managing interpersonal conflict, *Communication Research*, 15(4), 426–446.

[10]D. Buller & J. Burgoon (1994), Deception: Strategic and nonstrategic communication. In J. Daly & J. Wiemann (Eds.), *Strategic interpersonal communication*, Hillsdale, NJ: Lawrence Erlbaum.

[11]L. Putnam & M. Poole (1987), Conflict and negotiation. In F. Jablin et al. (Eds.), *Handbook of organizational communication*, Beverly Hills, CA: Sage.

[12]W. Donahue, M. Deiz, & M. Hamilton (1984), Coding naturalistic negotiation interaction, *Human Communication Research*, 10, 403–426.

[13]J. P. Folger & M. S. Poole (1984), *Working through conflict: A communication perspective*, Glenview, IL: Scott, Foresman & Co.

[14]Ibid.

[15]Ibid.

[16]Canary & Spitzberg (1989).

[17]Folger & Poole (1984).

CHAPTER 9
PRINCIPLES OF COMPETENT INTERVIEWING

[1]C. J. Stewart & W. B. Cash, Jr. (1991), *Interviewing: Principles and practices* (6th ed.), Dubuque, IA: Wm. C. Brown, p. 6.

[2]D. O'Hair & G. W. Friedrich (1992), *Strategic communication in business and the professions*, Boston: Houghton Mifflin, p. 205.

[3]Slightly modified version of R. S. Goyer & J. T. Rickey (1968), *Interviewing principles and techniques: A project text* (rev. ed.), Dubuque, IA: Wm. C. Brown, p. 10.

[4]M. L. Knapp, R. P. Hart, G. W. Friedrich, & G. M. Shulman (1973), The rhetoric of goodbye: Verbal and nonverbal correlates of human leave-taking, *Communication Monographs*, 40, 182–198.

[5]Stewart & Cash (1991), pp. 48–49.

[6]A. A. Bellack, H. M. Kleibard, R. T. Hyman, & F. L. Smith, Jr. (1967), *The language of the classroom*, New York: Teachers College Press, Columbia University, p. 4.

[7]The labels and definitions are from O'Hair & Friedrich (1992), pp. 220–221.

[8]S. L. Payne (1951), *The art of asking questions*, Princeton, NJ: Princeton University Press.

[9]G. Gallup (1947), The quintamensional plan of question design, *Public Opinion Quarterly*, 11, 385.

[10]C. R. Rogers (1951), *Client-centered therapy*, Boston: Houghton Mifflin.

[11]Paraphrased from D. W. Johnson (1972), *Reaching out: Interpersonal effectiveness and self-actualization*, Englewood Cliffs, NJ: Prentice-Hall, p. 125.

[12]J. P. Galassi & M. Galassi (1978), Preparing individuals for job interviews: Suggestions from more than 60 years of research, *Personnel and Guidance Journal*, 57, 188–192.

[13]B. Greco (1977), Recruiting and retaining high achievers, *Journal of College Placement*, 37(2), 34–40.

[14]Stewart & Cash (1991), pp. 155–156.

[15]R. Miller (1991), Personnel execs reveal the truth about job applicants, *Dallas Morning News*, January 31, p. 2D.

CHAPTER 10
COMMUNICATING IN SMALL GROUPS

[1]J. Gordon (1992), Work teams: How far have they come? *Training*, 29, 59–65.

[2]R. Y. Hirokawa & D. Gouran (1989), Facilitation of group communication: A critique of prior research and an agenda for future research, *Management Communication Quarterly*, 3, 71–92.

[3]W. W. Wilmot (1987), *Dyadic communication* (3rd ed.), New York: Random House.

4W. H. Whyte (1956), *The organization man*, New York: Simon & Schuster.

5J. K. Brilhart & G. J. Galanes (1992), *Effective group discussion* (7th ed.), Dubuque, IA: Wm. C. Brown.

6D. O'Hair, J. S. O'Rourke, & M. J. O'Hair (in press), *HarperCollins' business communication book*, New York: HarperCollins.

7H. H. Kelley (1971), The process of causal attributions, *American Psychologist, 28,* 107–128.

8J. C. McCroskey (1977), Oral communication apprehension: A summary of recent theory and research, *Human Communication Research, 4,* 78–96.

9J. C. McCroskey (1982), *An introduction to rhetorical communication* (4th ed.), Englewood Cliffs, NJ: Prentice-Hall.

10McCroskey (1977).

11J. C. McCroskey & V. P. Richmond (1988), Communication apprehension and small group communication. In R. S. Cathcart & L. A. Samovar (Eds.), *Small group communication: A reader* (5th ed.), Dubuque, IA: Wm. C. Brown.

12L. B. Rosenfeld (1988), Self-disclosure and small group interaction. In Cathcart & Samovar (Eds.), *Small group communication,* 288–305.

13M. E. Shaw (1988), Group composition and group cohesiveness. In Cathcart & Samovar (Eds.), *Small group communication,* 42–49.

14J. E. Baird, Jr., & S. Weinert (1977), *Communication: The essence of a group synergy,* Dubuque, IA: Wm. C. Brown.

15I. L. Janis (1972), *Victims of groupthink,* Boston: Houghton Mifflin.

16J. A. Jaksa & M. S. Pritchard (1994), *Communication ethics: Methods of analysis* (2nd ed.), Belmont, CA: Wadsworth.

17P. H. Andrews (1988), Group conformity. In Cathcart & Samovar (Eds.), *Small group communication: A reader,* Dubuque, IA: Wm. C. Brown.

18Brilhart & Galanes (1992).

19Ibid.

20D. O'Hair & G. Friedrich (1992), *Strategic communication in business and the professions,* Boston: Houghton Mifflin.

21L. R. Hoffman & N. R. F. Maier (1964), Valence in the adoption of solutions by problem-solving groups: Concept, method, and results, *Journal of Abnormal and Social Psychology, 69,* 264–271.

22T. L. Albrecht & B. Hall (1991), Relational and content differences between elites and outsiders in innovation networks, *Human Communication Research, 17,* 535–561.

23K. H. Roberts & C. A. O'Reilly (1979), *Academy of Management Review, 22,* 42–57.

24M. L. McLaughlin & T. R. Cheatham (1977), Effects of communication isolation on job satisfaction of bank tellers: A research note, *Human Communication Research, 3,* 171–175.

25D. J. Brass, (1985), Men's and women's networks: A study of interaction patterns influence in an organization, *Academy of Management Journal, 28,* 327–323.

26Albrecht & Hall (1991).

27C. M. Moore (1987), *Group techniques for idea building,* Newbury Park, CA: Sage.

28S. Kanekar & M. E. Rosenbaum (1972), Group performance on a multiple-solution task as a function of available time, *Psychometric Science, 27,* 331–332.

29A. L. Delbecq, A. H. Van de Ven, & D. H. Gustafson (1975), *Group techniques for program planning: A guide to nominal group and Delphi processes,* Glenview, IL: Scott Foresman.

30J. R. Bittner (1985), *Fundamentals of communication,* Englewood Cliffs, NJ: Prentice-Hall.

31M. Killilea (1976), Mutual help organizations: Interpretations in the literature. In G. Caplan & M. Killilea (Eds.), *Support systems and mutual help: Multidisciplinary explorations,* New York: Grune & Stratton.

32J. D. Orsburn, L. Moran, E. Musselwhite, & J. H. Zenger (1990), *Self-directed work teams: The new American challenge,* Homewood, IL: Business One Irwin.

33B. Dumaine (1990), Who needs a boss? *Fortune, 121* (10): pp. 52–60.

34Orsburn et al. (1990).

35A. B. Cheney (1991), Self-managed work teams, *Executive Excellence, 8,* 11–12.

CHAPTER 11
LEADERSHIP AND DECISION MAKING IN GROUPS

1J. K. Hemphill & A. E. Coons (1957), Development of the leader behavior description questionnaire. In R. M. Stogdill & A. E. Coons (Eds.), *Leader behavior: Its description and measurement,* Columbus, OH: Bureau of Business Research, Ohio State University, p. 7.

2R. M. Stogdill (1974), *Handbook of leadership: A survey of the literature,* New York: Free Press, p. 411.

3R. Tannenbaum, I. R. Weschler, & F. Massarik (1961), *Leadership and organization,* New York: McGraw-Hill, p. 24.

4T. O. Jacobs (1970), *Leadership and exchange in formal organizations,* Alexandria, VA: Human Resources Research Organization, p. 232.

5B. M. Bass (1990), *Bass and Stogdill's handbook of leadership,* New York: Free Press, p. 546.

6W. J. Altier (1990), Problem-solving meetings, *Executive Excellence, 10,* 10.

7Ibid.

8Ibid.

9Ibid.

10Ibid.

11K. Lewin, R. Lippitt, & R. K. White (1939), Patterns of aggressive behavior in experimentally created "social climates," *Journal of Social Psychology, 10,* 271–299.

12R. Y. Hirokawa, D. S. Gouran, & A. E. Martz (1988), Understanding the sources of faulty group decision-making: A lesson from the Challenger disaster, *Small Group Behavior, 19,* 411–433.

13Ibid., p. 416.

14M. Rokeach (1973), *The nature of human values,* New York: Free Press, p. 6.

15W. A. Green & H. Lazarus (1990), Are you meeting with success? *Executive Excellence, 7,* 11–12.

16S. R. Covey (1989), *The seven habits of highly effective people,* New York: Simon & Schuster, p. 213.

17J. Dewey (1933), *How we think,* Lexington, MA: Heath.

18A. C. Kowitz & T. J. Knutson (1980), *Decision making in small groups: The search for alternatives,* New York: Allyn & Bacon.

[19]L. A. Samovar & S. W. King (1981), *Communication and discussion in small groups*, New York: Gorsuch Scarisbrick Publishers.

CHAPTER 12
PREPARING AND DELIVERING PRESENTATIONS

[1]B. Ehrenreich (1989), Public freaking, *Ms.*, September, p. 40.
[2]J. C. McCroskey (1977), Oral communication apprehension: A summary of recent theory and research, *Human Communication Research*, 4, 78.
[3]G. W. Friedrich & B. Goss (1984), Systematic desensitization. In J. A. Daly & J. C. McCroskey (Eds.), *Avoiding communication: Shyness, reticence and communication apprehension*, Beverly Hills, CA: Sage, pp. 173–188.
[4]W. J. Fremouw & M. D. Scott (1979), Cognitive restructuring: An alternative method for the treatment of communication apprehension, *Communication Education*, 28, 129–133.
[5]R. P. Hart, G. W. Friedrich, & B. Brummet (1983), *Public Communication* (2nd ed.), New York: Harper & Row, pp. 13–15.
[6]R. E. Smith (1993), Clustering: A way to discover speech topics, *The Speech Teacher*, 7(2), 6–7.
[7]H. L. Hollingsworth (1935), *The psychology of the audience*, New York: American Book.
[8]J. F. Wilson, C. C. Arnold, & M. M. Wertheimer (1990), *Public speaking as a liberal art* (6th ed.), Boston: Allyn & Bacon, pp. 112–113.
[9]M. S. Knowles (1975), *Self-directed learning: A guide for learners and teachers*, New York: Cambridge Book Co.
[10]Hart, Friedrich, & Brummet (1983), pp. 170–171.

CHAPTER 13
INFORMATIVE PRESENTATIONS

[1]F. Machlup (1962), *The production and distribution of knowledge in the United States*, Princeton, NJ: Princeton University Press.
[2]N. Postman & C. Weingarten (1969), *Teaching as a subversive activity*, New York: Dell, p. 10.
[3]Staff (1985, March/April), The information society, *The Royal Bank letter*, p. 1.
[4]As cited in J. Fiala (1987), Citation analysis controls the information flood, *Thermochimica Acta*, 110, 11–22.
[5]F. Wallin (1983, March), Universities for a small planet—a time to reconceptualize our role, *Change*, pp. 7–8.
[6]R. Lindstrom (1992, February), Facing facts, *Presentation Products*, p. 6.
[7]A. L. Vangelisti & J. A. Daly (1989), Correlates of speaking skills in the United States: A national assessment, *Communication Education*, 38, 132–143.
[8]R. R. Allen & R. E. McKerrow (1981), *The pragmatics of public communication* (2nd ed.), Dubuque, IA: Kendall/Hunt Publishing Co., pp. 106–107.
[9]R. L. Johannesen, R. R. Allen, & W. L. Linkugel (1992), *Contemporary American speeches* (7th ed.), Dubuque, IA: Kendall/Hunt Publishing Co., p. 52.
[10]Adapted from B. Robertson & D. Gormley (1987), *Step-by-step printing*, London: Diagram Visual Information Ltd., p. 71.
[11]Johannesen, Allen, & Linkugel (1992), p. 66.

[12]K. Rowan (1990), The speech to explain difficult ideas, *The Speech Communication Teacher*, 4(4), 2–3.
[13]R. P. Hart (1975), *Lecturing as communication*, unpublished manuscript, Purdue University, Purdue Research Foundation, 1975.
[14]M. Mino (1991), Structuring: An alternative approach for developing clear organization, *The Speech Communication Teacher*, 5(2), 14–15.

CHAPTER 14
PERSUASIVE PRESENTATIONS

[1]M. V. Fox (1983), Ancient Egyptian rhetoric, *Rhetorica*, 1, 9–22.
[2]K. E. Andersen (1971), *Persuasion: Theory and practice*, Boston: Allyn & Bacon.
[3]E. P. Bettinghaus & M. J. Cody (1987), *Persuasive communication* (4th ed.), New York: Holt, Rinehart and Winston.
[4]G. Cronkhite (1969), *Persuasion: Speech and behavioral change*, Indianapolis, IN: Bobbs-Merrill.
[5]R. L. Garrett (1991), The premises of persuasion, *The Speech Communication Teacher*, 5(3), 13.
[6]R. L. Johannesen, R. R. Allen, & W. A. Linkugel (1992), *Contemporary American speeches* (7th ed.), Dubuque, IA: Kendall/Hunt Publishing Co.
[7]S. Toulmin (1958), *The uses of argument*, Cambridge: Cambridge University Press. The treatment in this chapter draws from W. Brockriede & D. Ehninger (1960), Toulmin on argument: An interpretation and application, *Quarterly Journal of Speech*, 46, 44–53.
[8]See A. H. Maslow (1943), A theory of human motivation, *Psychological Review*, 50, 370–396; A. H. Maslow (1970), *Motivation and personality* (2nd ed.), New York: Harper & Row.
[9]C. I. Hovland & W. Weiss (1951), The influence of source credibility on communication effectiveness, *Public Opinion Quarterly*, 15, 635–650.
[10]G. R. Miller & M. A. Hewgill (1964), The effect of variations in nonfluency on audience ratings of source credibility, *Quarterly Journal of Speech*, 50, 36–44.
[11]R. P. Hart, G. W. Friedrich, & B. Brummett (1983), *Public Communication* (2nd ed.), New York: Harper & Row, pp. 208–209.
[12]Ibid., pp. 213–217.
[13]J. C. Reinard (1988), The empirical study of the persuasive effects of evidence: The status after fifty years of research, *Human Communication Research*, 15, 3–59.
[14]Ibid., p. 25.
[15]P. B. Andrews (1985), *Basic public speaking*, New York: Harper & Row.
[16]D. J. O'Keefe (1990), *Persuasion: Theory and research*, Newbury Park, CA: Sage.
[17]R. E. Petty & J. T. Cacioppo (1986), *Communication and persuasion: Central and peripheral routes to attitudes change*, New York: Springer-Verlag.

CHAPTER 15
UNDERSTANDING AND USING MASS COMMUNICATION

[1]M. McLuhan (1964), *Understanding media*, New York: McGraw-Hill.
[2]U.S. Bureau of the Census (1993), *Statistical Abstract of*

the United States 1993 (113th ed.), Washington, DC: Author.

³W. V. Ruch (1989), *International handbook of corporate communication*, Jefferson, NC: McFarland.

⁴S. J. Baran & D. K. Davis (1981), *Mass communication and everyday life: A perspective on theory and effects*, Belmont, CA: Wadsworth Publishing Co.

⁵R. Gozzi, Jr., & W. L. Haynes (1992), Electric media and electric epistemology: Empathy at a distance, *Critical Studies in Mass Communication, 9,* 217–228.

⁶D. Altheide (1976), *Creating reality: How T.V. news distorts events*, Beverly Hills, CA: Sage.

⁷E. Babbie (1990), *Survey research methods* (2nd ed.), Belmont, CA: Wadsworth Publishing Co.

⁸D. Graber (1989), *Mass media and American politics* (3rd ed.), Washington, DC: Congressional Quarterly Press.

⁹A. Alexander (1993), Exploring media in everyday life, *Communication Monographs, 60,* 55–61.

¹⁰R. S. Nickerson (1988), Technology in education in 2020: Thinking about the not-distant future. In R. Nickerson & P. Zodhiates (Eds.), *Technology in education: Looking toward 2020* (pp. 1–10), Hillsdale, NJ: Lawrence Erlbaum.

¹¹This information is not intended to include messages generated through computer networks, for mediated messages are a type of interpersonal communication exchange.

¹²E. Singer & S. Presser (1989), *Survey research: A reader*, Chicago: University of Chicago Press.

¹³E. Babbie (1989), *The practice of social research* (5th ed.), Belmont, CA: Wadsworth Publishing Co.

¹⁴H. Nelson, D. Teeter, & D. Le Duc (1989), *Law of mass communications: Freedom and control of print and broadcast media* (6th ed.), Westbury, NY: The Foundation Press.

¹⁵Ibid.

¹⁶R. Hiebert, D. Ungurait, & T. Bohn (1988), *Mass media V: An introduction to modern communication*, New York: Longman.

¹⁷Ibid.

¹⁸B. Bagdikian (1990), *The media monopoly* (3rd ed.), Boston: Beacon.

¹⁹D. McQuail & S. Windahl (1981), *Communication models for the study of mass communications*, New York: Longman.

²⁰Ibid., p. 50.

²¹G. Gerbner, L. Gross, M. Morgan, & N. Signorielli (1986), Living with television: The dynamics of the cultivation process. In J. Bryant & D. Zillmann (Eds.), *Perspectives on media effects* (pp. 17–40), Hillsdale, NJ: Lawrence Erlbaum, p. 18.

²²S. Littlejohn (1989), *Theories of human communication* (3rd ed.), Belmont, CA: Wadsworth Publishing Co.

²³Ibid.

²⁴S. Francisco (Ed.) (1990), *AIDS: Education and prevention*, Official publication of the International Society for AIDS Education, San Francisco.

²⁵K. Jamieson (1992), *Dirty politics: Deception, distraction, and democracy*, New York: Oxford University Press.

Glossary

ABSTRACTION LADDER An illustration of how words can be used to describe topics ranging from the specific to the general.

ACCENTING Nonverbal behavior that emphasizes the accompanying verbal message.

ADAPTER A movement or gesture that satisfies some physical or psychological need.

AFFECT DISPLAY An unintentional movement or expression that conveys a mood or emotional state.

AFFILIATION The function of communication that is concerned with how feelings for another, ranging from love (high positive affiliation) to hate (high negative affiliation), are communicated; one of the three primary functions of communication.

AGENDA A sequential plan of action, usually for organizing a group meeting.

AGENDA SETTING The media's ability to determine, through the content of media presentations, which issues or topics will be important to individual members of society.

ANDRAGOGY The art and science of helping adults learn.

APPRECIATIVE LISTENING Listening in order to appreciate the sounds received by one's listening mechanism.

APPROACHING The use of actions that imply a desire for greater intimacy.

ARGUMENTATIVENESS A conflict style that seeks out controversial issues and revels in debating them.

ARTIFACT An accessory used for decoration or identification.

ASSERTIVENESS A conflict style that emphasizes personal concerns.

ASSOCIATION A type of friendship that develops through frequent contact; more an acquaintance than a true friendship.

ATTRIBUTION A generalization that uses personal characteristics to explain communication behavior.

AUDIENCE One or more people who are listening to what a person is saying and/or watching what that person is doing.

AUDIENCE ANALYSIS A description of the individuals who will listen to a speech in terms of audience type (pedestrian, passive, selected, concerted, or organized), their relevant reference groups, and their situational expectations.

AUTHORITARIAN LEADERSHIP Control by a leader without input from group members.

BARGAINING In a conflict, arguing for one's own position while expressing understanding of and sensitivity to the other party's position.

BOARD An elected or appointed group that makes important decisions regarding the functioning of an organization.

CATEGORIES OF SPEECH TOPICS Eight categories that can be used to generate topics for informative speeches—people, places, things, events, processes, concepts, problems, and plans and policies.

CAUSE–EFFECT ORGANIZATIONAL PATTERN A pattern that presents the main points of a message in terms of cause-to-effect or effect-to-cause relationships.

CENTRAL ROUTE TO PERSUASION   An ideal form of persuasion in which the audience carefully considers and analyzes the content of the message in deciding whether to accept or reject it.

CENTRALITY   The degree to which a member of a group sends and receives messages from others in the group.

CHANNEL   A vehicle or mechanism that transmits a message from sender to receiver.

CHANNEL CAPACITY   The ability to process information competently via a particular communication channel or channels (e.g., face to face or over the telephone).

CHANNEL DISCREPANCY   The use of two or more channels to send contradictory messages.

CHANNEL PREFERENCE   The preference of a communicator for one type of communication channel over others.

CHRONEMICS   The communicative ability of the use of time.

CHRONOLOGICAL ORGANIZATIONAL PATTERN   A pattern that presents the main points of a message in a time-related sequence.

CLIQUE   An exclusive group held together by common interests and activities.

CLOSED QUESTION   A question that gives the interviewee little or no freedom in responding.

CLOSING   The termination phase of an interview.

CLOTHING ORIENTATION   Clothing preferences.

CLUSTERING   A creative technique for identifying potential speech topics.

COALITION   See *clique*.

CO-CULTURE   One of two or more subcultures within a culture.

CODE   The symbols, signals, or signs used to construct messages.

COGNITIVE COMPLEXITY   The degree to which one can perceive information in more complicated and intricate ways.

COGNITIVE LOAD   The amount of information a person has to process at one time.

COGNITIVE RESTRUCTURING   A method for reducing or treating communication apprehension that teaches individuals how to identify anxiety-producing negative statements about communicating and replace them with coping statements.

COGNITIVE SKILLS   Mental capacities including the ability to think, reason, remember, and make sense of one's world.

COHESION   A group's ability to work as an integrated unit.

COMMITTEE   A special group that meets for specific purposes. Committees may be temporary (formed to solve a particular problem) or permanent (meeting to address issues on a regular basis).

COMMUNICATION ANXIETY   See *communication apprehension*.

COMMUNICATION APPREHENSION (CA)   Fear or anxiety associated with real or anticipated communication with another person or persons. See also *state CA; trait CA*.

COMMUNICATION BARRIERS   Eight dilemmas speakers face when they attempt to transmit information.

COMMUNICATION COMPETENCIES   Skills and understandings that enable communication partners to exchange messages appropriately and effectively.

COMMUNICATION CONTEXT   See *context*.

COMMUNICATION GOAL   A desired outcome that can affect how communication takes place.

COMMUNICATION PROCESSING   The means by which one gathers, organizes, and evaluates received information.

COMMUNICATION SKILLS   Behavioral routines based on social understandings and used by communicators to achieve their goals.

COMMUNICATION STYLE   An overall characterization consisting of a communicator's nonverbal cues, word choice, and impression formation.

COMMUNICATIVE COMPETENCE   The ability of two or more people jointly to create and maintain a mutually satisfying relationship through the construction of appropriate and effective messages.

COMPETENCY   See *communication competencies; communicative competence.*

COMPETENT LEADERSHIP   Credible behavior by which an individual inspires and motivates group members to achieve desirable group outcomes through interaction.

COMPLEMENTING   Nonverbal behavior that clarifies the meaning of a verbal message.

COMPLETE SENTENCE OUTLINE   A visual, schematic summary of a speech that allows others to understand the speaker's plan for the speech.

COMPREHENSIVE LISTENING   Listening in order to understand the message of another person.

COMPROMISE   A conflict resolution tactic that involves agreeing on a method of deciding, rather than focusing on the quality of the decision.

CONCERTED AUDIENCE   An audience that shares the goal of the speaker and is disposed to accept the speaker's plan of action.

CONCLUSION   The final portion of a speech; typically brings closure in the form of a summary and a statement of impact.

CONFLICT   A struggle between two or more interdependent parties who perceive incompatible goals, scarce rewards, and interference from the other party or parties in achieving their goals.

CONFRONTING   The use of direct questions to a relational partner to ascertain the partner's feelings.

CONSENSUS   A mutually satisfying agreement reached by two or more parties.

CONSTRUCTS   Mental structures that enable a person to make differentiations in judgments.

CONSULTATIVE LEADERSHIP   Leadership that bases decisions on the opinions or ideas of group members.

CONTEXT   The physical and psychological setting of an interaction.

CONTRADICTING   Nonverbal behavior that conveys a meaning opposite to that of the sender's verbal message.

CONTROL   The function of communication that is concerned with the ability of one person to influence another person or persons and the manner in which their relationship is conducted; one of the three primary functions of communication.

COOPERATIVE STRATEGIES   In a conflict, strategies that promote the objectives of the relationship rather than those of one partner or the other.

COOPERATIVENESS   A conflict style that emphasizes the other's concerns. See also *cooperative strategies.*

CORRESPONDENCE BIAS   The belief, excluding other possible factors, that another individual is the sole cause of an action or actions.

COUNTERCOALITION   A relationship in which two or more people position themselves against two or more others with regard to an issue.

CRITICAL CONSUMER   An individual who, as the user of a product, carefully evaluates the product for its quality, worth, and usefulness. A critical consumer of the media assesses the content of mediated messages for their accuracy and reliability.

CRITICAL LISTENING   Listening in order to evaluate or analyze information, evidence, ideas, or opinions.

CRITICAL THINKING   A method of viewing the world from a reasoned and proactive perspective.

CULTIVATION THEORY   A perspective on media effects which suggests that television is a socializing agent of culture that provides its viewers with a common world view.

CULTURAL FACTORS   Ways in which different cultural backgrounds can affect communication processing.

CULTURE   The shared beliefs, values, and practices of a group of people.

DEFINITIONAL SPEECH   A speech that explains what words and/or concepts mean.

DEINTENSIFICATION   The facial management technique of downplaying what is felt.

DELPHI METHOD   A method used to gather input from a group of experts on a particular issue.

DEMOGRAPHIC REFERENCE GROUP   A group of people who share such traits as age, gender, and ethnicity.

DEMONSTRATION SPEECH   A speech that uses narration and examples to describe how things happen.

DESCRIPTIVE SPEECH   A speech that presents information so vividly that the audience can share the speaker's experiences.

DETERMINANT INTERVIEW   The second stage in an employment interview; during this stage the interviewer decides whether or not to offer the job to the applicant.

DIRECT EFFECTS MODEL   An early theory of mass communication which states that all individual members of society receive messages in the same way and that direct and uniform outcomes result.

DIRECTED QUESTION   A question that clearly suggests or implies the answer that is expected.

DIRECTIVE INTERVIEW   An interview in which the interviewer retains control of the purpose, structure, and pacing of the interview.

DISTRACTIONS   Various factors that compete for one's attention, such as environmental, emotional, and psychological circumstances.

DYAD   A pair of individuals maintaining a relationship.

DYADIC RELATIONSHIP   See *dyad.*

ECTOMORPH   A person with a thin, angular body.

ELABORATION LIKELIHOOD MODEL (ELM)   A theory of persuasion that specifies the conditions under which an audience will process a message based on features of the message or features surrounding the message.

ELUCIDATING EXPLANATION   An explanation that illuminates a concept's meaning and use.

EMBLEM   A movement or gesture that has a direct verbal translation.

EMPATHIC LISTENING   Listening to people with an open, sensitive, and caring ear.

EMPATHY   The understanding one has of another's experience.

ENDOMORPH   A person with a rounded, oval, or pear-shaped and often heavy body.

ESCAPIST STRATEGIES   In a conflict, strategies that attempt to prevent direct conflict.

ETHICAL PROOF   Proof that asks an audience to accept a claim concerning a fact, value, problem, or policy because of the speaker's competence, trustworthiness, dynamism, power, goodwill, idealism, or similarity to the audience. See also *source credibility.*

EXAMPLE   In public speaking, a form of support that relies on illustration, models, or instances of what is to be explained.

EXPECTATION An intuitive thought or conscious desire in regard to an upcoming encounter.

EXPLANATION The act or process of making something plain or comprehensible; in public speaking, a form of support that relies on exposition and definition.

EXPLANATORY SPEECH A speech that explains the reasons underlying a problem, plan, or policy.

EXTEMPORANEOUS SPEAKING Speaking characterized by advance preparation of ideas and supporting material, with the precise wording of the speech to be determined during the process of speaking.

EXTRINSIC REWARDS Benefits gained from association with another person, including new opportunities and contacts.

FAMILY A social group whose members are related by blood, marriage, or adoption; have specified roles (e.g., husband, wife, son, mother) and statuses; and usually share a common residence and cooperate economically.

FEDERAL COMMUNICATIONS COMMISSION (FCC) A regulatory agency that oversees the physical resources of the media to ensure that broadcasters use the airwaves in the public interest and that the public has access to the airwaves.

FEEDBACK Information learned about the self that is used by the self to learn and mature.

FILTER QUESTION A question designed to find out what, if anything, an interviewee knows about a particular topic.

FORMS OF SUPPORT Verbal and nonverbal devices such as language, explanations, examples, statistics, testimony, and visual aids that can focus audience interest on the speaker's message and help the audience to understand and accept the message.

FRIENDSHIP A relationship between two or more people that is perceived as mutually satisfying, productive, and beneficial.

FUNCTIONAL PERSPECTIVE A focus on what kinds of communication behaviors work for people, and why they work, in various situations.

FUNNEL SEQUENCE A question sequence that moves from broad, open-ended questions to narrower, closed ones.

GATEKEEPING In mass communication, the process of regulating or determining what information will be carried over mass communication channels and what will not. Gatekeeping helps to regulate messages that might otherwise offend large audiences and to manage constraints of time and space encountered by the media. (In group communication, gatekeeping refers to keeping lines of communication open among group members.)

GEOGRAPHICAL ORGANIZATIONAL PATTERN See *spatial or geographical organizational pattern.*

GOAL ACHIEVEMENT The function of communication that is concerned with the focusing of attention on the task at hand in order to achieve a goal; one of the three primary functions of communication. Also called *task orientation.*

GROUP EVALUATION An evaluation of how competently a group performs as a whole.

GROUPTHINK The tendency of group members to accept information and ideas without critical analysis.

HAPTICS Touching behavior.

HAZING The use of negative actions to discover whether one's partner feels the relationship is worthwhile.

HIDDEN AGENDA A secret goal that one partner in a conflict is pursuing under the guise of another, expressed goal.

HIGH LANGUAGE   The language used in the more formal contexts of a person's life, such as work.

HIGH-CONTEXT CULTURE   A culture that avoids the use of direct language, relying more on context to convey meaning.

HOMOLOGY MODEL   A model of language acquisition which holds that thinking, coordination, and language capabilities develop simultaneously.

IDENTIFICATION   Alignment of one's own beliefs, attitudes, and values with the goals, objectives, and mission of a group.

ILLUSTRATOR   A movement or gesture that accompanies and illustrates a verbal message.

IMMEDIACY   The dimension of nonverbal communication that reflects the degree of closeness felt toward another.

IMPRESSION FORMATION   The general effect that a communicator has on a listener.

IMPROMPTU SPEAKING   Speaking on the spur of the moment, without formal preparation.

INDIVIDUAL EVALUATION   An evaluation of how competently an individual performs as a member of a group.

INFORMATION SOCIETY   Our current society, in which individuals working with information are the largest segment of the work force.

INSTRUMENTAL REWARDS   Rewards that relational partners give to each other, including material benefits.

INTEGRATIVE CAPACITY   The ability to make connections between different concepts; an aspect of cognitive complexity.

INTENSIFICATION   The facial management technique of exaggerating what is felt.

INTENTIONALITY   The level of consciousness or purposefulness of a communicator in the encoding of messages.

INTERDEPENDENCE   In group relationships, how the behavior of each member affects and is affected by other members.

INTERVIEW   A process of planned, dyadic, interactive discourse.

INTERVIEWEE (E)   One of two parties in an interview; typically follows the lead of the interviewer (R) during the interview.

INTERVIEWER (R)   One of two parties in an interview; typically assumes the primary responsibility for the planning and success of the interview.

INTIMACY   A relationship in which the relational partners share a deep understanding of each other.

INTRINSIC REWARDS   Benefits that result from an exchange of intimacy.

INTRODUCTION   The beginning portion of a speech; typically deals with issues of task, relationship, and motivation.

INVERTED FUNNEL SEQUENCE   A question sequence that moves from narrow, closed questions to broad, open-ended ones.

ISOLATION   A position within a group in which the member receives and sends fewer messages than do other members.

KINESICS   The communicative ability of gestures and body movements.

LAISSEZ-FAIRE LEADERSHIP   A leadership style that involves little or no leadership per se.

LANGUAGE   A symbol system used to think about and communicate experiences and feelings.

LEADERSHIP   The exercise of interpersonal influence toward the attainment of goals. See also *authoritarian leadership; competent leadership; consultative leadership; laissez-faire leadership; participative leadership; shared leadership.*

LEADING QUESTION A question that subtly suggests or implies the answer that is expected.

LISTENING The process of recognizing, understanding, and accurately interpreting the messages communicated by others.

LISTENING APPREHENSION A state of uneasiness, anxiety, fear, or dread associated with a listening opportunity.

LISTENING ATTITUDES One's view of one's own listening competence and the listening abilities of others.

LISTENING BARRIERS Factors that interfere with competent listening (e.g., laziness, insincerity, boredom, and closed-mindedness).

LISTENING COSTS Direct and indirect penalties associated with poor listening; can be economic, physical, emotional, or psychological.

LISTENING FUNCTIONS Different types of listening that satisfy different needs. See *appreciative listening; comprehensive listening; critical listening; empathic listening.*

LISTENING GOAL A specific plan or objective for listening.

LISTENING HABITS Routine listening behaviors such as neglect, apathy, overconfidence, and defensiveness.

LISTENING REWARDS Benefits of competent listening, such as time saving, enhanced relationships, and professional advancement.

LISTENING SELF-ASSESSMENT Evaluation of one's own listening abilities and skills.

LISTENING SELF-CONCEPT The image one has of oneself as a listener.

LOADED QUESTION A question that implies or suggests the answer that is expected either by using emotional language or by asking two questions in the guise of one.

LOGICAL PROOF Proof that asks an audience to accept a claim concerning a fact, value, problem, or policy because objective evidence supports the claim.

LOVE A relationship that is more exclusive than friendship; a deep affection for and attraction to another person.

LOW LANGUAGE The relaxed language usually used in the home or with close friends.

LOW-CONTEXT CULTURE A culture that relies more on the use of direct language than on the nuances of context to impart meaning.

MAIN POINT The thesis of a speaker's message; a key to understanding and remembering the message.

MANUSCRIPT SPEAKING Speaking from a manuscript that contains the complete presentation word for word.

MASKING The facial management technique of replacing an expression that shows true feeling with one that is deemed appropriate for a particular situation.

MASS COMMUNICATION The production and transmission of messages that are received and consumed by large audiences, including various forms of printed material and messages dispersed via the airwaves or through cable networks.

MEDIA (*pl. of* medium) Organizations that create and transmit informative, entertaining, or persuasive messages designed for large audiences. (*Mediums,* in contrast, are the channels—for example, newspapers and television—that the media use to transmit messages. Sometimes the plural form *media* is used to refer to mediums.) See also *channel.*

MEMORIZED SPEAKING Delivering from memory a speech that has first been written out.

MESOMORPH A person with a triangular and athletic body.

MINDFULNESS The process of focusing one's mind on the task at hand. (*Expressed mind-*

fulness is a state of mind in which one's knowledge and skills are summoned to consciousness in order to attend to the needs of a particular situation. *Latent mindfulness* is a state of mind in which self-presentation has become so routine and automatic that one is not aware of one's efforts. Self-presentational goals and associated behaviors can then be stored deep in consciousness so that one can concentrate on more immediate matters. See also *mindlessness*.)

MINDLESSNESS   The process of performing behaviors or actions without being conscious of what one is doing.

MOTIVATIONAL PROOF   Proof that asks an audience to accept a claim concerning a fact, value, problem, or policy on the grounds that the claim is consistent with listeners' needs and values.

NATURE APPROACH   An approach to language acquisition which holds that language acquisition is an innate human developmental process and does not depend on environmental factors.

NETWORKING   Learning about a relational partner by asking questions of others who know that person.

NETWORKS   Communication patterns used within groups.

NEUTRAL QUESTION   A question that provides no clue as to the expected answer.

NEUTRALIZATION   The facial management technique of eliminating all expression of emotion.

NOMINAL GROUP TECHNIQUE   A process in which individuals work alone in a group context to produce a basis for discussion that reflects all group members' viewpoints.

NONDIRECTIVE INTERVIEW   An interview in which the interviewer grants the interviewee control of the structure and pacing of the interview.

NONVERBAL COMMUNICATION   The process of signaling meaning through behavior that does not involve the content of spoken words.

NONVERBAL CUES   Nonverbal behaviors that allow listeners to better understand a verbal message; also, behaviors that listeners use to show the speaker that they understand the message.

NORMS   Expectations held by group members concerning what behaviors and opinions are acceptable in the group.

NURTURE APPROACH   An approach to language acquisition which holds that language is acquired because of the language environment surrounding a person.

OBSTINATE STRATEGIES   In a conflict, strategies that promote the objectives of an individual rather than those of the relational partner or both partners.

OCULESICS   Eye behavior.

OFFERING   Increasing opportunities for frequent interaction with someone by setting up situations that will promote interaction.

OLFACTICS   The communicative characteristics of smells.

ONTOGENY   The course of development of an individual organism (as distinguished from the development of a species over time).

OPEN QUESTION   A question that gives the interviewee relative freedom in responding.

OPENING TECHNIQUES   Strategies for the initial portion of an interview that deal with issues of task, relationship, and motivation.

ORGANIZATIONAL PATTERN   A method of arranging ideas in a logical sequence. See also *cause–effect organizational pattern; chronological organizational pattern; problem–solution organizational pattern; spatial or geographical organizational pattern; topical organizational pattern.*

ORGANIZED AUDIENCE An audience that is completely devoted to the speaker and to the speaker's purpose.

OUTCOME The product or end state of a communication encounter or series of encounters.

OUTLINE A visual, schematic summary of a speech that shows the order of ideas and the general relationships among them. See also *complete sentence outline; speaker's outline; topic outline.*

PARALANGUAGE The communicative value of vocal behavior; the meaning of how something is said.

PARTICIPATIVE LEADERSHIP A leadership style that involves a leader working with other group members to achieve a desired goal.

PASSIVE AUDIENCE An audience that is gathered to hear the speaker but is not highly motivated to listen to or accept the message.

PEDESTRIAN AUDIENCE An audience of people who have come together for the moment but have no obvious connection with either the speaker or one another.

PERCEPTION CYCLE A continual process of receiving information, enacting a schema, and exploring for more information based on the schema.

PERIPHERAL ROUTE TO PERSUASION An ideal form of persuasion in which the audience bases its decision about the message on characteristics external to the message—for example, source credibility or the reactions of other individuals.

PERSONAL GROWTH GROUP A group that people join in search of personal fulfillment or improvement.

PERSONAL SPACE The space around one's body to which one attaches ownership.

PERSUASION A conscious attempt by a persuader, using verbal and nonverbal messages, to change the beliefs, attitudes, or behaviors of one or more persuadees by engaging the persuadee(s) in an interactive process during which the persuadee(s) can accept or reject the persuader's message.

PHYLOGENY The evolutionary development of a species over time (as distinguished from the development of individual members of that species).

POSSIBLE SELVES A view of self-concept as composed of different possible selves, each with its own values, viewpoints, knowledge base, feelings, and the like.

POSTURE The way one stands, sits, or walks.

PRAGMATICS The appropriate use of language in context; requires mastery of communication rules, not merely language rules.

PRIMARY QUESTION A question that initiates a new topic.

PRIOR RESTRAINT The practice of banning certain publications before they have been produced.

PROBING In a conflict, an attempt to make a partner provide clarifications, explanations, or further information.

PROBLEM–SOLUTION ORGANIZATIONAL PATTERN A pattern that presents the main points of a message in terms of problems and solutions to those problems.

PROCESS The manner in which a communication encounter is conducted.

PROMISE In a conflict, an expressed intention to behave in a way that is beneficial to the other party provided that party complies with certain requests or terms.

PROXEMICS The communicative aspects of the use of space.

QUASI-SCIENTIFIC EXPLANATION An explanation that models or pictures the key dimensions of a phenomenon for a lay audience.

QUESTIONING TECHNIQUES   Inquiries that a listener can make to coordinate what the speaker is saying with what the listener is hearing.

QUINTAMENSIONAL PLAN   A five-step question sequence developed by George Gallup for use in conducting public opinion polls; involves examining awareness, uninfluenced attitudes, specific attitudes, reasoning, and intensity of feeling.

RECEPTIVITY   A characteristic of a friendship in which one partner is the primary giver and the other is the primary taker.

RECIPROCITY   A characteristic of a friendship that involves self-surrender, loyalty, mutual respect, affection, and support, and in which the partners give and take equally and share responsibility for maintaining the relationship.

REFERENCE   The thoughts that occur in a person when symbols are used or referents encountered.

REFERENCE GROUP   A group of people who are like a particular individual or whom that individual aspires to be like. See also *demographic reference group; voluntary reference group.*

REFERENT   The actual person or thing that a symbol or symbols represent.

REGULATING   Nonverbal behavior that is used to coordinate verbal interaction. See also *regulator.*

REGULATOR   A movement or gesture that regulates conversation. See also *regulating.*

REHEARSAL   A temporary storage area that processes information directed from short-term memory to long-term memory.

RELATIONAL HISTORY   The sum of the "objective" events in a relationship and the shared experiences of relational partners; also, a set of thoughts, perceptions, and impressions that one has formed about one's previous relational partners.

RELATIONAL SCHEMATA   Information used to interpret messages received in a relationship.

RELATIONSHIP   The interdependence of two or more people.

RELAXATION   The dimension of posture that, combined with immediacy, can reflect openness or willingness to communicate.

REPEATING   Nonverbal behavior that mirrors the accompanying verbal message.

RESPONSE STYLE   The pattern an individual develops for using Carl Rogers's five reacting moves: evaluative, interpretive, supportive, probing, and understanding.

ROLE   In a group, the function a member performs.

SCHEMA   See *schemata.*

SCHEMA THEORY   See *schemata.*

SCHEMATA (*pl. of* schema)   Mental structures that assemble chunks of remembered information, which in turn work together to create meaning and understanding.

SCREENING INTERVIEW   The first stage in an employment interview; during this stage the interviewer tries to find out whether the applicant can do the job.

SECONDARY QUESTION   A question that develops a topic that has already been introduced.

SELECTED AUDIENCE   An audience that shares the goal of the speaker but does not necessarily agree with the speaker's method for achieving the goal.

SELECTIVE PERCEPTION   Biased or filtered processing of information based on strongly held attitudes, timing, or other phenomena.

SELF-ACTUALIZATION   The most positive evaluation one can make about one's competence level.

SELF-ADEQUACY   Assessment of one's communication competence as suffcient or acceptable.

SELF-CERTAINTY   A strong sense of identity; composed of strong self-attributes or ideas about self that are unaffected by adverse or competing information.

SELF-CONCEALMENT   Conscious concealment of negative aspects of the self from others.

SELF-CONCEPT   Awareness and understanding of who one is as interpreted and influenced by one's thoughts, actions, abilities, values, goals, and ideals.

SELF-CONTENTMENT   A person's reaction to knowing that he or she is very competent at something.

SELF-DENIGRATION   The most negative assessment one can make about one's communication performance.

SELF-DISCLOSURE   Revealing parts of the self to others.

SELF-DOUBT   A feeling that one's communication performance was probably below average, coupled with uncertainty about assessing one's overall skill level.

SELF-EFFICACY   The ability to predict actual success from one's self-certainty; viewing oneself and predicting how competent one can be in anticipated situations.

SELF-ESTEEM   A set of attitudes that one holds about one's feelings, thoughts, abilities, skills, behavior, and beliefs.

SELF-IMPROVEMENT   Recognition, based on one's assessment of one's communicative competence in a particular situation, that one could communicate even better the next time around.

SELF-MANAGING TEAM   A group of highly skilled workers within a larger organization who are completely responsible for producing high-quality finished work.

SELF-MONITORING   The process of viewing communication as portraying "the right person in the right place at the right time."

SELF-PRESENTATION   An intentional communication tactic intended to unveil elements of self for strategic purposes.

SELF-PROMOTION   Presentation of the self in a way that will create a favorable impression in others.

SELF-PROTECTION   The self's use of communication as a device for warding off the harmful effects of negative evaluation (by both self and others) owing to failure.

SELF-SCHEMA   A structure or framework, composed of the various pieces of information that a person attributes to self, that helps that person develop a sense of self, guides the person's actions, and facilitates the acquisition and storage of new information as it pertains to self.

SEMANTICS   The meaning created between communicators by language and thought.

SHARED LEADERSHIP   Leadership that may emerge from any interested and talented group member, depending on the context.

SIDETRACKING   In a conflict, an attempt to move the conversation to a peripheral, often irrelevant topic.

SITUATION   A sequence of events that has a unifying goal.

SITUATIONAL EXPECTATIONS   Expectations that audience members have about the speaker and the message.

SOCIAL INFLUENCE   A process in which one person's actions cause changes in another's thoughts and behavior.

SOURCE CREDIBILITY   An audience's perception of a message source independent of that source's intent or purpose. See also *ethical proof.*

SPATIAL OR GEOGRAPHICAL ORGANIZATIONAL PATTERN   A pattern that presents the main points of a message in terms of the discussed items' physical proximity to or direction from one another.

Speaker's Outline   A visual, schematic summary of a speech that includes only key ideas that a speaker needs to remember.

Speech Repertoires   The possibilities communicators have for language use in any given situation, based on their experiences, cognitions, and acquired skills.

Speech That Affirms a Proposition of Fact   A speech that answers the question "Was it/is it/will it be true?" by making designative claims.

Speech That Affirms a Proposition of Policy   A speech that answers the question "What course of action should be pursued?" by making advocative claims.

Speech That Affirms a Proposition of Value   A speech that answers the question "Of what worth is it?" by making evaluative claims.

Speech That Creates Concern about a Problem   A speech that answers the question "What is it?" by making definitive claims.

Speech Topics   See *categories of speech topics.*

State CA   Situational communication apprehension; can be greater or lesser depending on such features of the context as knowledge of the audience and topic.

Statement of Specific Purpose   A single declarative sentence that specifies what the audience is expected to know, do, believe, feel, and so on, after hearing a speech.

Statistics   In public speaking, a form of support that relies on collecting, organizing, and interpreting numerical data.

Structuring   A method of organizing messages by means of residual messages (ideas to be retained by the audience) and common patterns of message organization.

Subculture   A group that is part of a larger culture but distinguished from it by various characteristics.

Substituting   Nonverbal behavior that replaces the use of words.

Sustaining   Keeping an interaction going; continuing a conversation with a particular individual.

Symbol   A sign (usually a word) used to describe a person, idea, or thing (a referent).

Symbolic Behavior   Behavior that uses a shared symbol system.

Systematic Desensitization   A method for reducing or treating communication apprehension that involves learning deep muscle relaxation, constructing hierarchies of anxiety-provoking stimuli, and pairing relaxation with anxiety-provoking stimuli.

Task Force   A group that researches an issue before discussions are held or decisions made.

Territoriality   The claiming of an area, with or without a legal basis.

Testimony   In public speaking, a form of support that relies on using a credible person's statements to lend weight and authority to a message.

Threat   An expressed intention to behave in a way that is detrimental to the other party in a conflict if that party does not comply with certain requests or terms.

Time Organizational Pattern   See *chronological organizational pattern.*

Time Orientation   Time preferences.

Time Pressures   The effects of a shortage of time on how a group makes decisions.

Topic Outline   A visual, schematic summary of a speech that reduces a complete sentence outline to brief phrases or single words.

Topical Organizational Pattern   A pattern that presents the main points of a message as parallel elements of the topic itself.

Topical System for Generating Thoughts   The use of 16 common themes for talking about any topic as a trigger for identifying ideas for inclusion in a speech.

TOULMIN'S MODEL   A method of generating, evaluating, and displaying "good reasons" for accepting a fact, value, problem, or policy in terms of a primary triad (data, warrant, claim) and a secondary triad (backing, rebuttal, qualifier).

TRAIT CA   A tendency to be apprehensive about communication in all contexts.

TRAITS   Individual physical and psychological characteristics that typically do not vary from situation to situation.

TRANSACTIONAL PROCESS   A process in which two or more people exchange speaker and listener roles, and in which the behavior of each person is dependent on and influenced by the behavior of the other.

TRANSFORMATIVE EXPLANATION   An explanation that helps a lay audience to understand counterintuitive ideas.

TRANSITIONS   Verbal signs to an audience indicating where the speech is going, where it is, and where it has been.

TUNNEL SEQUENCE   A question sequence that utilizes questions at one level (i.e., either all of the questions are broad and open-ended or they are all narrow and closed).

TURN-TAKING BEHAVIORS   Cues used by a listener to signal to a speaker that the listener is attentive to the speaker, to encourage the speaker to continue to talk, or to indicate that the listener would like to speak; also, cues used by a speaker to signal to his or her partner that the speaker role is (or is not) available at that moment in the conversation.

TWO-STEP FLOW MODEL   An early view of media effects which proposes that the mass media are used by "opinion leaders" to disseminate information to individuals through social networks.

UNCERTAINTY EVENT   An event that causes uncertainty in a relationship (e.g., a compet-

ing relationship, unexplained loss of closeness, deception, or an unexplained change in the personality of one partner).

USES AND GRATIFICATIONS THEORY   A theory of media effects that emphasizes the consumer's role and expectations when evaluating the outcomes of media exposure. Consumers use the media based on their needs and consider the media effective when those needs are met.

VALUES   The enduring beliefs that individuals and groups hold about certain issues and behaviors.

VERBAL AGGRESSIVENESS   A conflict style that involves attacking the other party's self-concept.

VERBAL REINFORCERS   Short verbal cues used by listeners to coordinate speaker–listener communication.

VISUAL AIDS   In public speaking, a form of support that relies on using actual objects or models, pictorial reproductions, or pictorial symbols.

VOCAL CHARACTERIZER   A sound that conveys the emotional or physical state of the speaker.

VOCAL QUALIFIER   A vocal cue that qualifies or regulates verbal messages.

VOCAL SEGREGATE   A sound with a connotative meaning.

VOCALIZATION   A vocal cue that does not have the structure of language. See *vocal characterizer; vocal qualifier; vocal segregate*.

VOICE QUALITIES   The vocal cues of tempo, resonance, rhythm, articulation, pitch and glottis control, and pitch range.

VOLUNTARY REFERENCE GROUP   A group of people who have chosen to belong to a specific religious, political, social, or other group.

WITHDRAWING   The use of silence or distance in order to see how a relational partner will act.

Index

Numbers in boldface type refer to pages on which terms are defined.

message structure and, 17
primary, 16–21
secondary, 21–23
funnel sequence, **392**
future talk, 180

gatekeeper, group leadership
and, 449
gatekeeping (in group communication), 447, 492
gatekeeping (in mass communication), **605,** 612
gaze aversion, 203
gaze omission, 203
gender differences
nonverbal communication
and, 217
relationships and, 314, 315
self-disclosure and, 126–27
in speech repertoires, 172–73
geographical organizational
pattern, **527**
gestures, autonomous, 7
gesturing, 252–53
goals (goal achievement), **21,**
33, 34, 43–44. *See also*
intentionality
as function of communi-
cation, 14–16, 21
conflict and, 334–35, 352–53
decision making and, 478–80
as function of communi-
cation, 14–16, 21
general vs. specific, 15
group communication and,
443–45
of interviews, 374–75,
378–79, 403–4
processing communication
and, 91–92
relationship between
stimulus and, 15–16
relationship between
strategies and, 15–16
goodwill, 589, 592
graphic representations, 7
grave-dressing phase of
relational disengagement,
318
greetings, 196, 217–19
group evaluation, **491,** 491–92
group identity, codes and, 9–10

group image, 442–43
groups (group communication),
420–60. *See also specific
topics*
agendas and, 445–46
attributions and, 428–30
boards, 490
cohesion and, 437–38
committees, 489
communication apprehen-
sion (CA) and, 433–36
complexity of relationships
in, 422–24
critical thinking and, 425–28
cultural factors and, 441
decision making in, 472–89
deliberation and, 446–47,
453
Delphi method and, 454–55
dyads compared to, 420,
422–24
evaluating competence in,
458–60
evaluating performance of,
490–93
goal setting and, 443–45,
452
group image and, 442–43
groupthink and, 438–39
identification and, 424–25
interdependence and, 436–37
leadership of, 464–72
networks and, 450–53
nominal group technique,
453–54
nonparticipation and, 447
norms and, 439–41
number of interactants in,
422
participation and, 446–47,
453
perceptions and, 431–33
personal growth, 455–56
productive conflict and,
438–39
roles in, 448–50
self-managing teams, 456–58
task forces, 489
groupthink, **438,** 438–39

Hall's zones of personal space,
209

haptics (touching behavior),
204, 204–8
harmonizer, 449
hazing, **300**
hearing, listening and, 237,
244–45
hidden agendas, **366**
high language, **172,** 176
high-context cultures, **169,**
169–70
highly scheduled interview,
384–85
high-self-monitoring
individuals, 111–12
homology, language acquisition
and, 150
homology model, **150**
honesty
friendships and, 323
of self-disclosure, 116, 128
host culture, responsibilities
of, 83

idealism, 589, 592–93
identification, **424,** 424–25
identity, 107. *See also headings
starting with* self-
illegal questions, 405–6
illustrators, **197**
imagining, as functional
competency, 154
immediacy, **197**
impression formation, 222–23,
254
listening and, 254–55
self-disclosure and, 122
impromptu speaking, **543**
inclusion, 179–80
individual, in communication
relationships, 24–25, 38
individual evaluation, **492,**
492–93
individualized trust scale, 117
influence, self-disclosure and,
123. *See also* control
informal–formal dimension, of
interpersonal communi-
cation, 215–16
information giver, 449
information seeker, 449
information society, **550,**
550–52

Figure 4.3: C. K. Ogden and I. A. Richards (1923), *The Meaning of Meaning* (New York: Harcourt Brace Jovanovich), p. 11.

Figure 4.5: Copyright © 1986 by Nicole Hollander. From the book THE WHOLE ENCHILADA. Reprinted with permission from St. Martin's Press, Inc., New York, NY.

Figure 4.6: Will & Deni McIntyre/Photo Researchers, Inc.

Figure 5.1: (left) Photofest; (right) Randy Brooke/Sygma.

Figure 5.2: (top left) Tomas D. W. Friedmann/Photo Researchers, Inc.; (center left) Fujifotos/The Image Works; (bottom left) Stephanie Maze/Woodfin Camp & Associates; (top right) Bettina Cirone/Photo Researchers, Inc.; (bottom right) Hermine Dreyfuss/Monkmeyer Press.

Figure 5.3: (top left) Art Glauberman/Photo Researchers, Inc.; (center left) Topham/OB/The Image Bank; (bottom left) Catherine Karnow/Woodfin Camp & Associates; (top right) Harriet Gans/The Image Works; (center right) Renee Lynn/Photo Researchers, Inc.; (bottom right) Jeff Greenberg/Photo Researchers, Inc.

Figure 5.5: CLOSE TO HOME copyright 1992 John McPherson. Reprinted with permission of UNIVERSAL PRESS SYNDICATE. All rights reserved.

Figure 6.3: Cynthia Johnson/Liaison.

Figure 6.5: Rhoda Sidney/Monkmeyer Press.

Part 2 opener: Richard Hutchings/Photo Researchers, Inc.

Figure 7.1: Richard Hutchings/Photo Researchers, Inc.

Figure 7.4: CATHY copyright 1988 Cathy Guisewite. Reprinted with permission of UNIVERSAL PRESS SYNDICATE. All rights reserved.

Figure 7.5: Michael L. Abramson/Woodfin Camp & Associates.

Figure 7.6: Esbin-Anderson/The Image Works.

Figure 7.7: Michal Heron/Woodfin Camp & Associates.

Figure 8.1: Alan Carey/The Image Works.

Figure 8.5: *The Far Side* cartoon by Gary Larson is reprinted by permission of Chronicle Features, San Francisco, CA. All rights reserved.

Figure 9.1: (top left) Blair Seitz/Photo Researchers, Inc.; (center left) Bob Daemmrich/The Image Works; (bottom left) Michal Heron/Woodfin Camp & Associates; (right) Mark Reinstein/The Image Works.

Figure 9.2: Rhoda Sidney/The Image Works.

Figure 9.3: © 1980 Henry R. Martin. Reprinted by permission.

Part 3 opener: John Waterman/Tony Stone Images.

Figure 10.1: (top left) John Waterman/Tony Stone Images; (middle left) Spencer Grant/Monkmeyer Press; (bottom left) Robert E. Daemmrich/Tony Stone Images, Inc.; (top right) Thomas Ives/The Stock Market; (bottom right) John V. A. F. Neal/Photo Researchers, Inc.

Figure 10.5: Michael Siluk/The Image Works.

Figure 11.1: John Chiasson/Liaison.

Figure 11.2: Ken Heinen/AP/Wide World Photos.

Figure 11.3: Ruben Perez/Sygma.

Part 4 opener: Bob Daemmrich/The Image Works.

Figure 12.1: Mike Kagan/Monkmeyer Press.

Figure 12.2: Arlene Collins/Monkmeyer Press.

Figure 12.4: Chuck Savage/The Stock Market.

Figure 12.5: Based on J. M. Kouzes and B. Z. Posner (1988), *The Leadership Challenge: How to Get Extraordinary Things Done in Organizations* (San Francisco: Jossey-Bass).

Figure 12.6: Mark Reinstein/FPG.

Figure 13.1: Burt Glinn/Magnum.

Figure 13.2: J. P. Laffont/Sygma.

Figure 14.1: Culver Pictures.

Figure 14.6: Bob Adelman/Magnum.

Figure 15.1: Andy Uzzle/Sygma.

Figure 15.2: Gilles Mingasson/Liaison.

Figure 15.3: CALVIN AND HOBBES copyright 1990 Watterson. Dist. by UNIVERSAL PRESS SYNDICATE. Reprinted with permission. All rights reserved.

Figure 15.4: KTLA/Sygma.